A Companion to California History

BLACKWELL COMPANIONS TO AMERICAN HISTORY

This series provides essential and authoritative overviews of the scholarship that has shaped our present understanding of the American past. Edited by eminent historians, each volume tackles one of the major periods or themes of American history, with individual topics authored by key scholars who have spent considerable time in research on the questions and controversies that have sparked debate in their field of interest. The volumes are accessible for the non-specialist, while also engaging scholars seeking a reference to the historiography or future concerns.

Published

In preparation

A COMPANION TO CALIFORNIA HISTORY

Edited by

William Deverell and David Igler

A John Wiley & Sons, Ltd., Publication

This edition first published 2008

Blackwell Publishing was acquired by John Wiley & Sons in February 2007. Blackwell's publishing program has been merged with Wiley's global Scientific, Technical, and Medical business to form Wiley-Blackwell.

Registered Office
John Wiley & Sons Ltd, The Atrium, Southern Gate, Chichester, West Sussex, PO19 8SQ, United Kingdom

Editorial Offices
350 Main Street, Malden, MA 02148-5020, USA
9600 Garsington Road, Oxford, OX4 2DQ, UK
The Atrium, Southern Gate, Chichester, West Sussex, PO19 8SQ, UK

For details of our global editorial offices, for customer services, and for information about how to apply for permission to reuse the copyright material in this book please see our website at www.wiley.com/wiley-blackwell.

The right of William Deverell and David Igler to be identified as the authors of the editorial material in this work has been asserted in accordance with the Copyright, Designs and Patents Act 1988.

Wiley also publishes its books in a variety of electronic formats. Some content that appears in print may not be available in electronic books.

Designations used by companies to distinguish their products are often claimed as trademarks. All brand names and product names used in this book are trade names, service marks, trademarks or registered trademarks of their respective owners. The publisher is not associated with any product or vendor mentioned in this book. This publication is designed to provide accurate and authoritative information in regard to the subject matter covered. It is sold on the understanding that the publisher is not engaged in rendering professional services. If professional advice or other expert assistance is required, the services of a competent professional should be sought.

Library of Congress Cataloging-in-Publication Data

A companion to California history / edited by William Deverell and David Igler.
    p. cm. – (Blackwell companions to American history; 17)
    Includes bibliographical references and index.
    ISBN 978-1-4051-6183-1 (hardcover : alk. paper) 1. California–History. 2. California–Social conditions. 3. California–Politics and government. I. Deverell, William Francis. II. Igler, David, 1964–

F861.C76 2008
979.4–dc22
                   2008018465

ISBN: 978-1-4051-6183-1 (hardback)

A catalogue record for this book is available from the British Library.

Set in 11 on 13 pt Galliard by SNP Best-set Typesetter Ltd., Hong Kong
Printed in Singapore by Fabulous Printers Pte Ltd

01 2008

Contents

Figures

Contributors

William Bauer, Jr. is Assistant Professor of American Indian Ethnohistory at the University of Wyoming. He is an enrolled member of Round Valley Indian Tribes. Professor Bauer's research examines labor and economic change on the Round Valley Reservation.

Shana Bernstein is Assistant Professor of History at Southwestern University, California. She received her PhD from Stanford University in 2003, after which she spent a year as a Mellon Postdoctoral Fellow in Latino Studies at Northwestern University. Her book on civil rights coalitions in World War II and Cold War Los Angeles will be published by Oxford University Press.

Jon Christensen is a full-time environmental reporter and science writer. He returned to Stanford University to work on a PhD in history after visiting for a year on a Knight Fellowship, a mid-career sabbatical for journalists. His work has appeared in *The New York Times, Science Times, High Country News*, and other newspapers, magazines, and journals, including *Nature, Conservation in Practice*, and *Environmental History*.

William Deverell is Director of the Huntington-USC Institute on California and the West and Professor of History at the University of Southern California. He is the author of *Whitewashed Adobe: The Rise of Los Angeles and the Remaking of Its Mexican Past*. He edited *The Blackwell Companion to the American West* and, with Greg Hise, is co-editor of *The Blackwell Companion to the History of Los Angeles*.

Darren Dochuk is Assistant Professor of History at Purdue University. He has published widely on the history of religion, politics, and culture in twentieth-century Canada and the United States. His book *From Bible Belt to Sunbelt: Plain Folk Religion and Grassroots Politics in California's Southland* is forthcoming.

Catherine Gudis is Associate Professor of History at the University of California, Riverside. She is the author of *Buyways: Billboards, Automobiles, and the American Landscape* (2004) and co-editor with Elspeth Brown and Marina Moskowitz of *Cultures of Commerce: Representation and American Business Culture, 1877–1960* (2006). Among the art books she has edited are *Ray Johnson: Correspondences* (with Donna DeSalvo, 1999), *Helter Skelter: LA Art in the 1990s* (1992), and *A Forest of Signs: Art in the Crisis of Representation* (1989).

Steven W. Hackel is Associate Professor of History at the University of California, Riverside, where he specializes in the Spanish Borderlands, the colonial West, and California Indians. He is the author of *Children of Coyote, Missionaries of Saint Francis: Indian–Spanish Relations in Colonial California, 1769–1850*. He is currently writing a biography of Junípero Serra, and is the general editor of the Early California Population Project.

Bill Ong Hing is a Professor of Law at the University of California, Davis, where he teaches Immigration Policy, Judicial Process, and Negotiations. His books include *Deporting Our Souls: Morality, Values, and Immigration Policy* (2006) and *Defining America through Immigration Policy* (2004). He was also co-counsel in the precedent-setting Supreme Court asylum case, *INS vs. Cardoza-Fonseca* (1987), and he is the founder of the Immigrant Legal Resource Center in San Francisco.

John Horn is a staff writer at the *Los Angeles Times*, where he covers the film business for the Calendar section. Before joining the *Times* in 2002, Horn was a senior writer for *Newsweek* magazine, a senior editor for *Premiere* magazine, and served as the entertainment writer for The Associated Press and as a staff writer for *The Orange County Register*. He was a recipient of a fellowship under the National Arts Journalism Program, and is a member of its board.

Daniel Hurewitz teaches in the history department at Hunter College in New York City. His latest book, *Bohemian Los Angeles and the Making of Modern Politics* (2007), examines the cultural milieu that gave birth to the American gay political movement. He has also written a book about New York's gay history.

David Igler is Associate Professor of History at the University of California, Irvine. He is the author of *Industrial Cowboys: Miller & Lux and the Transformation of the Far West, 1850–1920* (2001) and co-editor of *The Human Tradition in California* (2002). His current research focuses on the Pacific Basin and western Americas prior to 1850.

Benjamin Heber Johnson is Associate Professor of History at Southern Methodist University, where he teaches classes on environmental history, the US–Mexico Borderlands, and race in the modern US South and Southwest. Author of *Revolution in Texas: How a Forgotten Rebellion and Its Bloody Suppression Turned Mexicans into Americans* (2003), Johnson is writing a synthetic history of environmental politics and culture in the Progressive Era United States.

Lon Kurashige is Associate Professor of History and American Studies and Ethnicity at the University of Southern California. He is author of the award-winning *Japanese American Celebration and Conflict: A History of Ethnic Identity and Festival in Los Angeles, 1934–1990* (2002) and co-editor of *Major Problems in Asian American History* (2003). He is currently researching the history of Asian immigration exclusion in the United States, as well as working on a new US history college textbook.

Kevin Allen Leonard studied at Pomona College and the University of California, Davis, where he earned his PhD in history in 1992. Since 1997 he has taught in the history department at Western Washington University. He is the author of *The Battle for Los Angeles: Racial Ideology and World War II*, which was published by the University of New Mexico Press in 2006.

Kirse Granat May received her PhD in history from the University of Utah. She is the author of *Golden State, Golden Youth: California Youth Images in Popular Culture, 1955–1966* (2002). She has taught at the University of Utah, the Massachusetts College of Art, and Clark College in Vancouver, Washington, where she currently resides.

Miriam Pawel is a 2007 Alicia Patterson Foundation fellow researching the history of efforts to organize farm workers in the United States. She worked for more than two decades as a journalist at *Newsday* and the *Los Angeles Times*, where she authored a groundbreaking four-part series on the United Farm Workers. She is currently writing a book about the history of the UFW and the farm worker movement in California.

James Quay has served as executive director of the California Council for the Humanities (CCH) since 1983. A native of Pennsylvania, he earned a BA in English literature from Lafayette College. He and his wife moved in 1970 to California, where he earned an MA and PhD in English literature from the University of California, Berkeley. Prior to joining CCH, he was a lecturer at the University of California, Santa Cruz and an associate producer with California Public Radio. He is co-editor of *California Uncovered: Stories for the Twenty-First Century* (2005).

Robert Chao Romero is Assistant Professor in the Cesar E. Chavez Department of Chicana/o Studies at the University of California, Los Angeles. His current book project, *The Dragon in Big Lusong: Chinese Immigration and Settlement in Mexico, 1882–1940*, is a social history of the Chinese in Mexico.

Nicolas G. Rosenthal is Assistant Professor of History at Loyola Marymount University, Los Angeles. He is working on a book-length history of American Indians and cities in modern America.

Douglas Cazaux Sackman is Associate Professor of History at the University of Puget Sound. He is the author of *Orange Empire: California and the Fruits of Eden*, a cultural and environmental history of California focusing on the citrus industry. It received the Martin Ridge Award from the Historical Society of Southern California. His next book *Wild Men: Ishi and Kroeber in the Wilderness of Modern America* will be part of the New Narratives in American History series.

Josh Sides is the Whitsett Professor of California History and the Director of the Center for Southern California Studies at California State University, Northridge. He is the author of *LA City Limits: African American Los Angeles from the Great Depression to the Present* (2004), as well as a forthcoming book about the history of the sexual revolution in San Francisco.

Douglas Smith teaches history at Occidental College and is the past recipient of fellowships from the American Council of Learned Societies and the National Endowment for the Humanities. He is the author of *Managing White Supremacy: Race, Politics, and Citizenship in Jim Crow Virginia* (2002), and is currently writing a national study of reapportionment politics in the postwar period.

Raphael J. Sonenshein, Professor of Political Science at California State University, Fullerton, received his BA in public policy from Princeton, and his PhD in political science from Yale. His book *Politics in Black and White: Race and Power in Los Angeles* (1993) received the 1994 Ralph J. Bunche Award from the American Political Science Association. He served as Executive Director of the Los Angeles (Appointed) Charter Reform Commission, described in his book *The City at Stake: Secession, Reform, and the Battle for Los Angeles* (2004). In 2006, the League of Women Voters published his book *Los Angeles: Structure of a City Government*. He is co-writing a book on urban coalitions in an age of immigration.

Rosamaría Toruño Tanghetti focuses her scholarship on California and the US Southwest, conquest narratives, gender, family, and identity. She is currently completing a book entitled *Intimate Unions: Conquest and Marriage in California, 1769–1880*. She published "Maria Amparo Ruiz Burton and *The Squatter and the Don*" in *The Human Tradition in the American West* (2002).

Omar Valerio-Jiménez, an assistant professor of history at the University of Iowa, teaches courses on borderlands, Latinas/os, and immigration history. He is currently finishing his first book, *Rio Grande Borderlands: Identity and Nation along the Mexico–Texas Border, 1749–1900*, and his next project will examine the history and memory of the US conquest of Mexico's Far North.

David Vaught is Professor of History at Texas A&M University. He is the author of *Cultivating California: Growers, Specialty Crops, and Labor, 1875–1920* (1999) and *After the Gold Rush: Tarnished Dreams in the Sacra-* mento Valley (2007). He is currently working on a history of baseball in rural America.

Arthur Verge is a Professor of History at El Camino College in Torrance, California. He is the author of *Paradise Transformed: Los Angeles during the Second World War* (1993), and, with Andrew Rolle, co-author of *California: A History* (7th edition).

D. J. Waldie is the author of *Holy Land: A Suburban Memoir* (1996) and other books that deal with the history of Southern California.

Richard A. Walker is Professor and past Chair of Geography at the University of California, Berkeley. He holds a BA from Stanford and a doctorate from Johns Hopkins, and is a past recipient of Fulbright and Guggenheim Fellowships. He is author of two books on California, *The Conquest of Bread* (2004) and *The Country in the City* (2007), as well as essays on the state's economy, cities, natural resources, race relations, and politics. He is co-author of two books on economic geography, *The Capitalist Imperative* (1989) and *The New Social Economy* (1992).

Rick Wartzman is the director of the Drucker Institute at Claremont Graduate University and an Irvine senior fellow at the New America Foundation. He is the co-author (with Mark Arax) of *The King of California: J. G. Boswell and the Making of a Secret American Empire* (2003) and the author of the forthcoming *Obscene in the Extreme: The Burning and Banning of John Steinbeck's "The Grapes of Wrath."*

Introduction

California holds a more prominent place in national and international affairs than any other state in the Union. Whether measured by familiar yardsticks of population, electoral weight, global economic power, and cultural production, or the less common meters of political eccentricity, environmental innovation, social heterogeneity, and immigrant nexus – California's influence is impossible to ignore around the globe.

California has played this role for a very long time. Place-named by the feverish imagination of a sixteenth-century Spaniard who dreamed of Queen Califia's gold-laden island paradise, California was simultaneously conceived in very different ways by its indigenous inhabitants who could not have imagined the future of their ancestral homeland. Between then and now, California has been endlessly re-envisioned and reinvented as an imaginary island, as Alta California, as the thirty-first state of the Union, as *Gam Saan*, as a critical Pacific entrepôt, as Tomorrowland, and as Turtle Island. Each of these designations, and countless others in turn, expressed ambitions and realities that reached well beyond the physical terra of the place.

Coming to terms with the history of California has occupied writers for centuries. In recent decades such writings have grown to a cottage industry of the historical profession through the combined output of academic presses, mass-market publishers, and independent houses. *A Companion to California History* reflects this growing interest in, and serious engagement with, the state's remarkable past. But more than mere interest, this volume reflects the way that the study of California intersects with and influences historical scholarship and contemporary issues well beyond its boundaries.

What does this mean? Most directly, it means that many if not most of the essays in this volume attempt to reconceptualize key California events, social groups, and issues in broader and interconnected ways. It means that much of California history has regional, national, and international dimensions in addition to local roots. And it also means that many key characteristics of California – such as the ever-growing population, the technological innovations, even much of the flora and fauna – are transplants or reconfigurations with origins outside or beyond the state's borders. Rather than an exercise in historical exceptionalism, this volume traces California history as part and parcel of related geographies, different historical scales, and critical scholarly currents.

The 30 chapters in this volume are organized into five parts. Four introductory essays in Part I offer broad syntheses and analyses of California as a whole. We asked James Quay, D. J. Waldie, Catherine Gudis, and Richard A. Walker to do something exceedingly difficult: to *define* California through distinct prisms of culture, history, visual culture, and the global economy. The resulting essays thoughtfully propose innovative and exciting ways to understand the state's past and present. Designed as overarching statements about their respective topics and disciplines, each essay also suggests a myriad of subjects for future research and analysis. Similarly, the three "prospects" essays in Part V are designed to forecast developments for the twenty-first century in the realms of immigration and race, politics, and the environment. While historically minded scholars usually shy away from forecasting the future, essayists Bill Ong Hing, Raphael J. Sonenshein, and Jon Christensen have embraced their respective challenges; their fascinating prognostications demonstrate the need to understand the past in order to grapple with the future. These two bookends – the introductory "defining" and closing "prospects" essays – showcase the promise and vitality of California studies today.

The middle three parts of this volume periodize California history into "Early California," "Conquest and Statehood," and "Modern California." We have deliberately tweaked conventional periodization with these three temporal assignments, in that we have stretched out the conquest and statehood period well into the twentieth century and, in consequence, narrowed the era in which California has been "modern." And, while the greatest number of essays delve into twentieth-century topics (certainly a reflection of recent scholarly interest and emphasis), we have made every effort to cover nineteenth-century California with inventive approaches to a wide range of issues. We both believe that many, if not all, of the momentous developments in twentieth-century California are deeply rooted in the history of the previous century, if not earlier. The volume also links the nineteenth and twentieth centuries through a number of paired essays on the topics of race and immigration, Native Californians, the 1850s/1950s, and environmental transformations.

A Companion to California History highlights numerous arenas of innovative scholarly focus on American and global issues in recent years. We believe that a focus on California and its historical trajectories can serve to further illuminate these themes. Transnational and global history is certainly one such trend, reflected in this volume with essays by Richard A. Walker, David Igler, Robert Chao Romero, Lon Kurashige, and Kevin Allen Leonard. The critical study of gender and sexuality represents a second area of tremendous scholarly growth, as illustrated by essayists Rosamaría Toruño Tanghetti, Daniel Hurewitz, and Josh Sides. Environmental history, an already well-established field by any measure, has matured alongside the study of California during the past three decades. In testament to this overlapping scholarly maturity, this volume includes creative approaches to the environment for the nineteenth century (Douglas Cazaux Sackman), twentieth century (Benjamin Heber Johnson), and twenty-first century (Jon Christensen). Finally, some of these essays examine vitally important topics that have simply not gained the attention they merit: Catherine Gudis's essay on visual culture, William Deverell's work on the "lost" 1850s, David Vaught's attention to rural California, or Miriam Pawel's re-examination of Cesar Chavez's legacy, among others.

The study of California is no longer *just* the study of California. Critical scholarship on California has shed its vestiges of parochialism and now represents one of the most innovative arenas for studying the past beyond regional or national boundaries. California history speaks to the region, the nation, and the world on some of today's most pertinent topics – including the struggles of a pluralist society, immigration debates, political reform, religion, and globalization. *A Companion to California History* attempts to reflect that engagement within and beyond the state by showcasing the work of 30 scholars who are deeply invested in the question of what compels them about California. We hope you appreciate and learn from their answers.

William Deverell and David Igler

Part I

Introductory Essays

Chapter One

BEYOND DREAMS AND DISAPPOINTMENTS: DEFINING CALIFORNIA THROUGH CULTURE

James Quay

Anyone who knows enough to define California through culture knows better than to try. California is too large, too diverse, and too dynamic to be defined. Transposed to the east coast of the United States, California would stretch from Charleston to Boston, encompassing all or part of 11 states from the Atlantic Coast to the Appalachian Trail. It contains a greater range of landforms and more species of plants and animals than any area of comparable size in North America, with a human population equally as diverse. Santa Clara County, now better known as Silicon Valley, by itself has residents from 177 of the 194 nations of the world (Moriarty 2004: 8). California is home to *sizable* immigrant communities from 60 different countries.

As someone who has spent more than two decades supporting public programs in which Californians describe and analyze life as it's lived in California, I have experienced this cultural diversity firsthand. In groups large and small Californians have shared how and why they or their ancestors came to be here, discussed issues both historical and contemporary, and shared their hopes and fears for communities both ethnic and geographic. Listen to California Native Americans collecting stories of their ancestors' encounters with Europeans in the nineteenth century, residents of the Sierra Nevada foothills discussing the population boom they face, Japanese Americans recalling their internment during World War II, Afghan artists recently displaced by war to the San Francisco Bay Area, and you can't help but recognize that California doesn't have *a* culture, it has many cultures.

The state is also too dynamic to define. As the California economy cycles through boom and bust, today's confident definition becomes tomorrow's embarrassment. In November 1991, *Time* magazine dedicated an entire issue to examining "California: The Endangered Dream," observing how drought, traffic, sprawl, and economic downturn were driving people out of the state. Four years later, the California economy was ascending up the side of the dot-com bubble and by the decade's end the state's population had grown by more than four million people and California boasted the fifth highest gross domestic product in the world. Five years after that, the dot-com bubble burst and the state plunged into fiscal crisis once again. "California defies efforts to characterize it as a single state," complains Peter Schrag, who has been studying California for three decades, "even as you describe it, it seems to obey some geographic uncertainty principle, and changes" (2006: 40).

Then there's the problem of "culture." If we take culture in its anthropological sense, as the totality of socially transmitted behavior patterns, arts, beliefs, institutions, and all of the products of human work and thought, the task of defining California expands well beyond the limits of my expertise and space. Nearly 50 years ago, two dozen scholars, writers, and critics assembled in Carmel, California to discuss the question, "Has the West Coast an Identifiable Culture?" One of the group, the novelist Wallace Stegner, summarized the group's findings:

> Two days at Carmel convinced most of us that we felt pretty much like the rest of the United States, only more so. Our language is a representative amalgam almost undistinguished by local dialectal peculiarities; ethnically we are more mixed even than the eastern seaboard cities; in a prosperous country, we are more prosperous than most; in an urban country, more urban than most; in a gadget-happy country, more addicted to gadgets; in a mobile country, more mobile; in a tasteless country, more tasteless; in a creative country, more energetically creative; in an optimistic society, more optimistic; in an anxious society, more anxious. (1982: 106)

If you're looking for a shorthand definition of California by culture, "America only more so" is as good as any.

But the most striking thing about defining California by culture is that despite the impossibility of the task, commentators both glib and serious persist in trying to do so. Why? No one seems to think it important to define the culture of my home state of Pennsylvania, or Iowa, or Arizona. Why California? Of the many places in the world blessed with natural wonders, favorable climates, energetic economies, and dynamic populations, why should California hold such a distinctive place in the national and global imagination?

The question leads us to California's defining cultural feature: its persistence as a location where the deepest human yearnings can be realized. "California" has sometimes been a blank screen onto which people have projected their desires, sometimes a real place that promises opportunity never before imagined, and sometimes a bitter example of disillusion and disappointment. But a definition of California always refers not just to the real place called California, but to an imagined place of the same name.

When commentators attempt to define California, they use powerful human metaphors such as Paradise, Eden, El Dorado – all places that exist in the imagination, places challenging people to find them, to lose them, to regain them. As a consequence, defining California by culture means encountering a perpetual tension that exists between California the imagined and California the real. In other states, serious culture can be created without reference to the images promoters concoct to attract new business, tourists, and investments. In California these images are always there, to be dismissed, qualified, ridiculed, or embraced, perhaps, but always there and demanding attention. I know of no other place whose culture is created by such a tension. But as a result, California affords observers here and abroad an opportunity to think upon human possibility and its limits.

Tension between the imagined and the real begins the same instant California is named. Other American states derive their names from their indigenous inhabitants, from descriptions of tangible natural features, or from people to be honored. California alone is named for a completely imaginary place. No one has found a convincing etymology for the name, but "California" first appears in a popular romance, *Las Sergas de Esplandian*, written by Garci Rodriguez Ordonez de Montalvo and first published in Madrid in 1510:

> Know, then, that, on the right hand of the Indies, there is an island called California, very close to the side of the Terrestrial Paradise, and it was peopled by black women, without any man among them, for they lived in the fashion of Amazons. They were of strong and hardy bodies, of ardent courage and great force. Their island was the strongest in all the world, with its steep cliffs and rocky shores. Their arms were all of gold, and so was the harness of the wild beasts which they tamed and rode. For, in the whole island, there was no metal but gold. (Hicks et al. 2000: 76)

Edward Everett Hale, best known as the author of "The Man without a Country," offered a plausible explanation in 1862 for how this imaginary name came to be fixed to a portion of the Pacific coast. Montalvo's romance, which went through several editions, was popular enough to remain in the memory of some unknown member of a naval expedition sent by Cortés to explore the northwest coast of Mexico in 1533, and when he saw what he thought was an island with steep cliffs and rocky shores, the name stuck (Hart 1978: 398).

No less than two defining metaphors for California make their appearance in this single passage: California as paradise and California as El

Dorado. Also making its immediate appearance is the disjuncture between the imagined destination and the real place. The land the unknown explorer called California had "steep cliffs and rocky shores," to be sure, but it turned out to be the peninsula of Baja California, not an island, and it fostered no black Amazons and contained no gold. In a pattern that would be repeated by many individuals looking for "California," disappointment came soon after discovery. Spanish explorers found nothing that resembled a terrestrial paradise in California and, after a few sixteenth-century expeditions, Spain sent no more for nearly two centuries.

If there were ever a people who experienced California as paradise, it was the indigenous people who had been living there ten thousand years before their encounter with Europeans. They were hunter-gatherer cultures who had no metal tools and left no written records. Social classes hardly existed and communities were small. Except for tribes along the Colorado River, they appear to have been a peaceable people, though conflict was not unknown. We need not place them into an alien mythic place to acknowledge that conditions in what became California must have favored them, for at the time when European colonization began in 1769, they are estimated to have numbered 300,000, the densest concentration of Indians north of Mexico.

California's indigenous people spoke over a hundred different mutually unintelligible languages and Rawls notes that "elements of culture occurring only in part of California, most of them only in a small part, greatly outnumbered those that were universal" (Rawls & Bean 2003: 15–16). The only feature common to both indigenous and contemporary California culture is its diversity. Unfortunately, much of this cultural richness has been lost. Disease and confinement brought by Europeans halved their numbers to about 150,000 by the mid-nineteenth century. Then came the catastrophe that decimated California Indians, the event that fixed California forever in the world's imagination: the Gold Rush.

The Gold Rush was a defining moment for California, one that turned a sleepy province on the far edge of the continent into a true El Dorado. The search for gold had motivated Spanish explorers since the sixteenth century, but no one could seriously identify California as El Dorado until James Marshall's discovery of gold in January 1848. As news and evidence overcame initial skepticism, men poured into California, first from Oregon and Hawaii, then Mexico and Chile, and finally from the east coast, Europe, and Asia. In 1847 San Francisco had a population of 800 and California's non-indigenous population was perhaps 13,000. Eighty thousand men arrived in 1849 alone and by 1854 there were upwards of 300,000 in California. It was the greatest mass migration in American history and vaulted the state into national and world attention (Rohrbough 1997: 8).

For sheer drama the Gold Rush is hard to beat. Hundreds of thousands of men, and a much smaller number of women, crossed oceans or a continent to test their individual wills against nature and fortune. It was "the adventure of a lifetime and the journey of the century," and the experiences of the Argonauts filled personal diaries and letters and made newspaper copy for years, but the reality was that the discoveries of successful claims that inspired gold fever lasted less than three years. Most miners eventually returned to their homes without realizing the fantasies of wealth that had once motivated them. In their diaries and letters, California became an archetype for possibility and for disappointment (Rohrbough 1997).

The California Gold Rush also became an archetype for California's pattern of development as it was succeeded by a series of speculative booms that brought more attention and more migrants to California. "Elsewhere the tempo of development was slow at first, and gradually accelerated as energy accumulated," wrote Carey McWilliams a century later, "but in California the lights went on all at once, in a blaze, and they have never been dimmed" (1949: 25).

The most recent assessment of the Gold Rush came during California's Sesquicentennial which began, appropriately enough, in 1998 when California was enjoying yet another boom – the dot-com boom of internet technology companies – and ended in 2000 as that boom went bust. The new social history made it impossible to ignore the dark side of the Gold Rush – its racial violence, its catastrophic effect on Native Americans and the environment, the dislocation of families throughout the nation – and historian Kevin Starr, then chair of the Sesquicentennial Commission, accepted such revaluations as a necessary acknowledgment of California's "sin." Yet he insisted that in the Gold Rush lay the genes of California's cultural DNA: exploitation of technology, a pattern of booms, a multicultural population, intense entrepreneurial energy, liberation of women, and an opening to Asian influence (1998: 61).

One Gold Rush feature that has persisted throughout California's subsequent history is immigration. Immigration rates have waxed and waned with fluctuation in the economy and legal restrictions, but it has *averaged* 1,000 people a day since 1920 and, since the turn of the new century, the daily average increase is 1,670. The year my wife and I moved here, 1970, there were 20 million people living in California. In 2010 that number is expected to be 40 million. Since 1980, California has been receiving an average of 300,000 immigrants per year.

Underlying the diversity of immigrants to California is one feature universal to all: the decision to leave one's home and the decision that California is where one wants to be. One of the few common threads of California identity is this exercise of choice: at some point everyone in California is – or is related to – someone who left his or her home and

came to California looking for something better. Immigrants have come
to California to pursue many versions of "gold": opportunities, artistic or
economic; freedoms, political or sexual; or openness, geographical or intellectual. These diverse motivations get lumped into a single term, "the
California Dream" – a term often invoked and seldom defined.

Kevin Starr is the great chronicler of the California Dream. The title he
chose for the first volume of his magisterial history of California, *Americans
and the California Dream: 1850–1915*, announces the trope that has carried
his history through six volumes and a century of California's history. In succeeding volumes Starr has chronicled the dream invented, endangered, embattled and enduring. "While yet barely a name on the map, it entered American
awareness as a symbol of renewal," he writes in his preface. "Obscurely, at a
distance – then with rushes of clarity and delight – Americans glimpsed a California of beauty and justice, where on the land or in well-ordered cities they
might enter into prosperity and peace" (1973: vii–viii).

When the Santa Fe railroad arrived in Los Angeles in 1887, it broke the
monopoly of the Southern Pacific, briefly lowering the one-way fare from
Kansas City from $125 to $1 and creating the first land boom in Southern
California (Barron et al. 2000: 54). Almost immediately, California was
portrayed as a natural paradise, an image that prevailed into the first
decades of the twentieth century (ibid.: 100). The rise of Hollywood as
the center of motion pictures added images of urban glamour to the definition of California, while the Great Depression of the 1930s added images
of rural misery and labor struggle. In the aftermath of World War II, California was no longer seen as a pre-industrial Garden of Eden. Driven by
scientific and technological advances during and after the war, California
was the place where the future begins.

This was not the claim of promoters and boosters. As that group of
scholars that assembled in Carmel discussed West Coast culture – its architecture, its opera and jazz, its painters and theaters and museums – their
confidence grew. Never mind, Stegner reports, that "half of the people
cited as signs of great creative growth were in-migrants, as were half of
ourselves." That was simply the defining feature of West Coast culture.
They have come to prepare the coast "as a launching platform for the
future" (Stegner 1982: 108). When Stegner's article appeared in late 1959,
the idea of California as the future may have looked attractive. The state's
freeway system was not yet clogged with traffic, its master plan of education was widely admired, and its legislature was seen as a model. But the
Golden State's golden age could not last. Enter Joan Didion, the great
chronicler of California disappointment.

A California native whose parents arrived in California in the years just
before and after statehood in 1850, Didion and her husband, John Gregory
Dunne, began writing a column called "Points West" in 1967 for the

Saturday Evening Post. She published some of these columns in *Slouching towards Bethlehem* in 1968, the same year that California officially adopted "The Golden State" as its state motto. Didion's lead story, "Some Dreamers of the Golden Dream," announces itself as "a story about love and death in the golden land," but, typically, Didion is being ironic. It is a story of unhappy marriage, adultery, and murder in San Bernardino. In "Notes from a Native Daughter," she writes to those who have visited Los Angeles or San Francisco and believe they have been to California, whereas it is her hometown, Sacramento, that really *is* California and "California is a place in which a boom mentality and a sense of Chekhovian loss meet in uneasy suspension" (1968: 172). We are a long way from Starr's view of California as a symbol of renewal. If California be the future, Didion warns, the nation and the world were in trouble.

Joan Didion left California for good in 1988, but she returned to the subject of California again 15 years later with *Where I Was From.* When her husband protested that the title should properly be "Where I Am From," she insisted on "Where I Was From" as more accurate, more definitive in its separation. Yet even in this final work, she pays tribute to the compulsion to make something of the state, a compulsion that survives even the most severe disappointment. "California has remained in some way impenetrable to me, a wearying enigma, as it has to many of us who are from there," she writes. "We worry it, correct and revise it, try and fail to define our relationship to it and its relationship to the rest of the country" (2003: 38). Her critique of California is a serious contribution to California's literature of disappointment, but the California she writes about no longer exists, for in Didion's book you will find not a single person of color.

Didion's omission is the more astonishing given the dramatic impact of immigration: the most important definer of California in the last few decades has been the growing diversity of its population. In 1962, when Governor Edmund G. Brown proclaimed "California First Days" to celebrate California's passing New York as the nation's most populous state, the state had nearly 17 million people, of whom 14 million were non-Hispanic white. The primary language of foreign-born Californians was English, as most had come from either Canada or Great Britain. Now, one-fourth of California's schoolchildren come from homes where English is not the primary language (Schrag 2006: 22–4).

Late in 1999, California officially became a majority–minority state, a state in which no ethnic group was a majority. According to official estimates, California's current population is 45 percent Anglo, 35 percent Hispanic, 11 percent Asian, 6 percent black, 2 percent multi-race, and 1 percent Native American and Asian Pacific Islander (State of California, March 2006). As of 2000, nearly nine million California residents (26 percent) were born outside of the United States (compared with 12 percent nationally) and nearly 60 percent are from Latin America – 44 percent from Mexico alone – while 33 percent are from Asia. By 2011, Latinos are projected to surpass Anglos as the largest minority group.

Mexicans account for 44 percent of the foreign-born population in California, six times the percentage of the next highest group, Filipinos. The fact that two-thirds of foreign-born families are from Mexico and other Spanish-speaking countries has sparked concern, fear, and reaction. During the 1994 election, California Governor Pete Wilson's campaign ran a television advertisement that showed Mexicans running across the California border while a voiceover ominously repeated, "They keep coming." He endorsed a ballot initiative denying public education and other services to undocumented residents. Wilson was re-elected and Proposition 187 passed with nearly 60 percent of the vote. Four years later, California voters passed Proposition 227, which dismantled the state's existing bilingual education programs and decreed that public school children be taught in English only. Cultural conservatives warned that Hispanic immigrants were not learning English and were not assimilating to core American values and that California was in danger of becoming "Mexifornia" and the US a "bilingual, bicultural" society (Hanson 2003; Huntington 2004).

The debate rages on – about how many illegal immigrants are in California and their impact on local economies and services – but some studies suggest that such fears may be based on demographic trends which are temporary. The foreign-born presence in California was 15 percent in 1980 and 26 percent in 2000, much higher than in any other state, but immigrants are now increasingly migrating to states other than California. Even if the number of immigrant arrivals in California were to remain constant, the share of Californians who are foreign-born in 2030 will still be less than 30 percent. In addition, the immigrants' average *length* of residence is increasing. From 1970 to 1990, during the phase of accelerating immigration, half of all the foreign born each decade were recently arrived, but that fraction is receding to only one-third or one-quarter of the total foreign born. English proficiency increases significantly between first-generation immigrants and those in the second generation and the proportion speaking English exclusively rises from 10 percent in the first generation to 29 percent in the second generation to 94 percent in the third generation (Ramakrishnan & Johnson 2005: 11).

Meanwhile California's culture is becoming increasingly and unselfconsciously multicultural and no recent survey of California culture that I have seen ignores this. In late 2000, the Los Angeles County Museum of Art mounted "Made in California: Art, Image, and Identity, 1900–2000," a comprehensive exhibition that explored the diversity of California art in the twentieth century. Essays that accompanied the exhibition repeatedly acknowledged the importance of immigration in the creation of California's art, music, and literature. The University of California's definitive anthology of California literature to 1945 contains only a few non-Anglo voices – William Saroyan, Carlos Bulosan, Toshio Mori, or Jade Snow Wong – whereas a recent anthology contains native Californians like Maxine Hong Kingston, David Mas Masumoto, Yxta Maya Murray, Richard Rodriguez, and Gary Soto, not to mention immigrants like Khaled Hosseini, Chitra Divakaruni, or le thi diem thuy (Divakaruni et al. 2005).

The Next California Culture

In California, traditional cultural forms are transplants which adapt to local conditions, while modern cultural forms are often invented here. The list of items invented in California includes Barbie dolls and the hula hoops, the Frisbee and the freeway. California is the source of trend-setting environmental regulations and low emissivity windows; digital video recorders and computer-generated imagery; iPods and search engines; the discovery and treatment of AIDS and state-sponsored stem cell research; and venture capital and venture philanthropy (*California* 2007: 14–34). The three major entertainment media of the twentieth century – radio, television, and motion pictures – depended on technologies which developed in California, flourished here as industries, and changed the way America experienced culture.

Now the new media of the twenty-first century – the internet, search engines and web.2.0 – are again developing and flourishing as industries in California and changing patterns of cultural consumption once more. In a recent article, Bill Ivey and Steven Tepper argue that nineteenth-century inventions like the phonograph, the motion picture camera, and radio broadcasting made it possible for Americans who had no access to symphony halls or theaters to experience cultural performance, albeit performances packaged by others at a distance. "Local and vernacular art and entertainment were eclipsed by a culture that was increasingly defined by the tastes of a national elite at Columbia Records, or Universal Studios, or nonprofit arts organizations," they argue, "the amateurs at home were overshadowed by the new class of creative 'professionals,' and audiences were increasingly socialized to be passive consumers, awaiting their favorite radio broadcasts or sitting in darkened theaters and concert halls, applauding on cue" (Ivey & Tepper 2006).

The new technology is reducing the high costs of artistic production and the challenges of finding an audience. Computer software enables people to compose their own music, make their own films, compose their own books and then distribute them over the internet. At the same time, thanks to the iPod or TiVo (both invented in California), cultural experiences which could only be had from one source at a specific time can now be captured for consumption when and where the consumer wants. "The combination of the rise of serious amateur art making, the explosion of choice, and the sophistication of Internet-savvy consumers will create new micromarkets, challenging the dominance of 20th century mass markets" (Ivey & Tepper 2006).

The promises of this new cultural delivery system are many: decentralization of cultural authority and production, greater opportunities for people to express themselves culturally, more exposure to cultural products from others and especially from people in distant places, and more opportunities for direct connection between people. There are also concomitant dangers: a growing divide between people who have access to these resources and people who do not, a flattening out of cultural quality, and the demise of some of the cultural organizations that have provided much of the "live" culture in recent decades. This last development has already caught the attention of Californians.

There are an estimated 10,000 cultural organizations in California, ranging in size from the multi-billion-dollar endowment of the Getty Museum in Los Angeles to small non-profit cultural organizations living from performance to performance. As their name suggests, many of these organizations cannot support themselves on the strength of ticket sales alone, but they have proliferated because of support from private foundations and public cultural agencies. Such support was justified because the commercial market was widely viewed as unable to produce cultural products of sufficient quality, ethnic variety, and popular access. While their numbers have grown since the 1960s, a recent study shows they are now challenged by shrinking audiences and diminishing funding. "Audiences at nonprofit arts organizations are generally flat or shrinking," the report warns, "and it is generally assumed that the field of cultural institutions is overcrowded" (AEA 2006: 6).

Unlike their counterparts in Canada and Europe, California cultural organizations cannot look to government agencies for significant support. California has a population slightly larger than that of Canada, but while Canada spends $243 million on the arts at the federal level, more than $7 per capita, the state of California spends $2.1 million, about 6 cents per capita (California Arts Council 2006). State support for the California Arts Council, which averaged $21.5 million annually for the period 1997–2003, was slashed to $1 million in the wake of fiscal crisis following the dot-com bust. Only the personal intervention of the Chairman of the National Endowment for the Arts prevented California's Arts Council funding from being zeroed out, and though the state's economy has recovered, funding to the Arts Council has not. More than half of the agency's current $3 million budget comes from proceeds from the sale of a special arts license plate. Other statewide cultural organizations, such as the California Council for the Humanities, the California Association of Museums, and the California Historical Society receive no state funding and never have.

The future of California's cultural ecosystem is still unclear, as is the future of its education system, its highway system, its prison system, and its state government. More population growth is projected and polls indicate that most Californians believe the state's infrastructure is inadequate to future demand (Baldassare 2000). The newest metaphor to describe California is as a "high stakes experiment" (Schrag 2006), a significant departure from earlier descriptors. The state is still positioned in the old tension between the real and the imagined but gone is the old Edenic innocence. If California continues to offer a glimpse of the world's future, it is not because it has the solutions, but because it is encountering the challenges first.

The California Hope

I am not a disinterested observer of this experiment. I have a personal stake in how California's culture is defined. Several years ago, I interviewed Californians from different parts of the state and different walks of life – writers, artists, scientists, activists, educators, public officials – some prominent, some not, some natives, some not. I wanted to know what, if anything, it meant to be a Californian. The state's diversity showed itself in the answers I heard, of course, but after the first dozen or so, I found that one particular word kept surfacing: hope. These people or their parents or grandparents may have been drawn to California because of a dream – something as glorious as gold or as modest as a good job and good weather. They often encountered realities that tested or even destroyed those initial images or dreams. But those who stayed – and everyone I interviewed had obviously stayed – spoke about the persistence of hope which they identified with California.

As a result of the answers I heard, I can no longer think of California as a culture defined by dreams. A dream is somehow too insubstantial, too subjective, to propel and sustain a living culture. A dream is what people project on to the state before they arrive here, and the only thing that makes it a California dream is their chosen destination, their belief that California is a place where one can change one's place, one's neighbors, and make a new start. This has proven to be true often enough to encourage many to come here, but disappointment is what they feel when those dreams are not confirmed by their experience here. Those who try to impose their dreams on the landscape, who meet neighbors they do not like or who do not like them, who never make California home, find the California dream turns into the California disappointment. This too has proven to be true often enough to drive people from the state. But dream and disappointment do not and cannot define California culture. Something more durable defines the culture that people who live here are creating, and hope is as good a word for this as any.

California has no special claim to being a culture of hope, of course. Every culture is necessarily a culture of hope, for every culture offers its people stories about what is worth living for, exemplary lives, resources for explaining and living through misfortune. But because people from so many parts of the world have come to California, because it remains at the forefront of so many technological innovations that will shape the culture of the future, and because it has a long history as a showcase for individual and social possibility, the contours of California hope continue to interest and influence the world.

In order to see all of California, you have to rise more than 1,000 miles above its surface. I have spent most of this essay defining California from a great distance in order not to be overwhelmed by the diversity of its surface features. In order to see examples of hope, however, we need to meet a few real Californians. These people are not particularly powerful or influential people, but the lives they are living accurately reflect the fundamental hope that is defining contemporary California's culture.

Pai Yang doesn't know the exact year of her birth; it was either 1969 or 1970, when what Americans call the Vietnam War spilled into Cambodia and Laos as well and her people, the Hmong, were fighting a secret war for the United States. When the Americans withdrew, her family fled to a refugee camp in Thailand, from where they were flown to Oregon under the sponsorship of a church. After five months as the only refugee family there, they moved to Iowa where there was a large Hmong community. When she was 10, the family came to Fresno to participate in the first Hmong New Year celebration there. They decided to stay in California because for Hmong elders, used to a warm climate year round, Fresno's midwinter sunshine was far preferable to the snows of Iowa.

The Hmong had not left their homeland voluntarily, but fled the aftermath of the war in 1975 as refugees. They came not intending to stay and talked always about returning, a thought that sustained them through the prejudice and discrimination they had encountered in Fresno. By the 1990s, though, their children had begun calling America home and the elders began to realize they were not going to return. Like other immigrant communities before them, the Hmong community began to organize itself to obtain the economic and social services it needed in this new land, and they began to make a home in California.

The Hmong are a mountain people, and Fresno sits in a very wide valley, flanked by the Sierra Nevada range to the east. Pai occasionally takes community elders to the mountains of Yosemite National Park, for a taste of the freedom, the freshness of the air they once knew in Laos. She takes them to Glacier Point, which overlooks Yosemite Valley and the granite peaks of the Yosemite back country, one of the most spectacular views on the face of the earth. But for the Hmong elders, the view is a painful reminder of the home they have left and will never see again. "Some of them start crying," Pai told me, "not just crying, but howling, you know? And loud, because they miss the old home so much." For the first generation, the costs of immigration are high.

The New Year's festival in Fresno that first brought Pai Yang and her family to the city is the largest festival of its kind, attracting thousands of Hmong from around the country and the world. This week-long celebration of their traditional music, food, and dance not only brings the Hmong community together, it serves as an occasion for strengthening connections with the rest of Fresno. Pai Yang is here to stay, working as a community organizer to create a place for her people. When I spoke with her, she was pregnant with her second child. On her desk was a picture of the first, a four-year-old daughter with a big smile. "Right now, you ask her, 'where are you from?' she says 'I'm from California.' And she'll point towards California." What's her name, I asked. "Sunshine," said Pai Yang. "Sunshine."

Malcolm Margolin was born in Boston and his first impression of California came from three wild men on motorcycles who pulled up in front of a local bar and told him they were from San Bernardino. The name conjured up the usual images of beaches and palm trees and beautiful women in skimpy bathing suits (San Bernardino, far from the ocean, sits on the edge of the Mojave Desert). Malcolm and his wife drove to California in 1967 and were captivated by the beauty of Yosemite Valley and the vibrancy of street life in the Haight-Ashbury district of San Francisco. The next year they moved to California.

In 1974 Margolin launched the publishing company that became Heyday Books by single-handedly writing, typesetting, designing, and distributing a natural history guidebook of the hills and shoreline of the eastern San Francisco Bay. He then wrote and published *The Ohlone Way*, a reconstruction of the life of the original inhabitants of the San Francisco Bay Area that became a California classic. At a time when most Californians were unaware that any Indians still lived in California, Margolin began publishing books by and about California Indians. His newsletter, *News from Native California*, created a network among indigenous people and their advocates that has helped create and sustain a cultural renaissance among California Indians.

Now Heyday Books is one of the state's most important regional publishers, with a booklist essential to anyone who cares about California's cultural and natural history. A migrant from the Atlantic coast, he came to California and found deep wisdom in indigenous cultures few Californians knew. "These are people that have been around for ten or twelve thousand years, and they have in their bone, in their tissue, in their tonality, something that echoes a kind of California that those of us who are guests never see," he told me. "It's a sadder California, a deeper California, a California that moves along more slow-moving currents. These for me are the true Californians."

Alice Waters was a teenager when her family moved to Southern California. She opened Chez Panisse restaurant in Berkeley in 1971 and began featuring meals made with locally grown, seasonal produce. As she and other chefs experimented with traditional recipes, a recognizable "California cuisine" emerged, more as a set of practices than a set of recipes. It doesn't matter if a combination of ingredients is traditional or not. What matters is whether the ingredients are fresh and tasty. California cuisine uses dishes from other cuisines and fills them with local content.

Waters herself does not care for the term "California cuisine." "Cuisine," she believes, implies methods of food selection and preparation that have stood the test of centuries, while what she calls California cooking is still a work in progress. California cooking is "very influenced by Mediterranean cooking, but with some dishes that feel more unique because of the ways that we have integrated influences, whether they're Asian influences or Native American or whatever influences into what we are doing right here." In the same way, California's own culture is a work in progress, built originally on a European base but increasingly influenced by cultures from around the world, a culture old enough to have birthed some recognizable trends, but too young to merit a distinct definition.

Waters' insistence on using local seasonable produce led her inevitably to concern for the sources of that produce, the land it grows on, the way it is grown, and the people who grow it. Her restaurant has developed a network of local farmers and ranchers dedicated to sustainable agricultural practices. She is a strong advocate for farmers' markets, whose numbers have grown in California from a handful in the 1970s to over 500 today. She founded the Edible Schoolyard at a local middle school, a project in which students grow and prepare their own food and which integrates that experience into the school's curriculum. Waters insists that the everyday act of eating a meal can make us mindful of our connections to the farmer and the land.

David Mas Masumoto is the kind of peach farmer Alice Waters adores. Born and raised in Selma in the southern San Joaquin Valley, his Japanese grandfathers were both second sons, which meant they would not inherit land in Japan, and when they landed in California looking for a better life, they naturally gravitated toward the Central Valley, the agricultural heartland of California. Mas's family chose California not once, but twice: first, when they came to California, and again after they were released from the relocation camp in Arizona where the American government confined them during World War II. They returned to Selma and eventually were able to buy the small farm on which Mas was later born.

Mas's farm is an anomaly of California agriculture. It is small (80 acres) and farmed by his family and seasonal agricultural workers. He left the Valley to attend the University of California, Berkeley, never intending to return, but decided to do so both to make a living and to give voice to the people that lived there. His book, *Epitaph for a Peach*, chronicles a season trying to grow and market a peach that, while delicious, is shunned by supermarkets because it is "ugly" and doesn't ship well.

Much of California produce is grown on huge mechanized farms – "factories in the field," as Carey McWilliams called them. Mas and other family farmers in California have to struggle to survive, and Mas has found ingenious ways to connect his produce with the people who consume it. For the past several years, he has offered some of his peach trees for "adoption." The people who are approved as "parents" receive e-mail reports on their peach tree's progress throughout the growing season and then come to his farm on two summer weekends to harvest the fruit from their tree. The whole experience puts city dwellers in touch with the vagaries of weather that make farming so risky and makes them understand that produce does not come from supermarkets, it comes from a particular place inhabited by particular people.

Mas lives in multicultural California. His daughter's high school classroom held Latinos, Japanese Americans, Southeast Asian, German Mennonites, and Portuguese, all reading John Steinbeck's *The Grapes of Wrath* and discussing what it means to come to a place and call it home. That diversity is what makes him feel like a Californian; that, and the ability to invent a life. We normally think immigrants come to California to remake themselves, but Mas believes native Californians can and do. "I actually think that, as a native Californian, there's this constant ability to renew yourself," he told me as we talked on his front porch. "Traditions have helped us make connections but hasn't prevent us from doing things, whereas in rural America, the Midwest, traditions sometimes stop change." Mas Masumoto, roots deep in California soil, is one face of California culture.

Whether refugee, immigrant, or native Californian, these four people illustrate what is happening in contemporary California culture at ground level. Pai Yang, born abroad, brings her talents and her Hmong heritage to the culture. Malcolm Margolin makes available the wisdom of

California's first cultures, so that the state's future can learn from its past. Alice Waters plants a French restaurant in California soil and seeds a movement based on the most basic cultural activity. Mas Masumoto connects his family farm to the people who eat his produce and gives a voice to small, sustainable agriculture in the midst of industrial agriculture.

The dreams that bring people to California are various, but when people make the choice to come here, an unexpected consequence has been to find they are among very diverse people who all have made the same choice. The California hope that has emerged in the last generation embraces this consequence, hoping that people from different cultures might find a way to live and thrive together, taking risks and working hard to enrich themselves economically, and helping and enriching one another culturally and spiritually as well. Both dreams and hopes are imaginary things, but hopes are seasoned by experience where dreams are not. Peter Schrag ends his recent book by describing the challenge facing California in stark terms: "In trying to forge a modern postindustrial democratic society not only from its cultural diversity but also from a population consisting in considerable part of Third World immigrants, California was undertaking something that had never been done in human history" (Schrag 2006: 262).

Here again we find the old tension between the real and the imagined. California is no longer Eden, no longer a dream and therefore no longer a disappointment, but a place where the future is being invented. California didn't intend to become a multicultural population, but it is one. As California goes, so goes the world, not because California has cornered the market on solutions, but because California is encountering the challenges early and intensely. If the culture of hope is to survive and prevail, California will need the kind of cultural hope that my four examples embody. A happy outcome is far from assured, but the culture being forged in California will continue to be the focus of world attention – for California, once America only more so, has become the world, only more so.

REFERENCES

AEA Consulting. 2006. "Critical Issues Facing the Arts in California: A Working Paper from the James Irvine Foundation." September 2006. Available at: http://www.irvine.org/assets/pdf/pubs/arts/Critical_Issues_Arts.pdf

Baldassare, Mark. 2000. *California in the New Millennium: The Changing Social and Political Landscape*. Berkeley: University of California Press.

Barron, Stephanie et al., eds. 2000. *Made in California: Art, Image, and Identity, 1900–2000*. Los Angeles: University of California Press.

California. 2007. "Eureka! Inventing California," *California* (January/February), 118 (1): 14–34.

California Arts Council. 2006. *California Arts Council's 10-Year State Appropria-tions History*. Available at: http://www.cac.ca.gov/files/10yearstateappropria tions.pdf

Davis, Erik. 2006. *The Visionary State: A Journey Through California's Spiritual Landscape*. San Francisco: Chronicle Books.

Didion, Joan. 1968. *Slouching Toward Bethlehem*. New York: Farrar, Straus, & Giroux.

Didion, Joan. 2003. *Where I Was From*. New York: Alfred A. Knopf.

Divakaruni, Chitra Banerjee et al., eds. 2005. *California Uncovered: Stories for the 21st Century*. Berkeley: Heyday Books.

Hanson, Victor Davis. 2003. *Mexifornia: A State of Becoming*. San Francisco: Encounter Books.

Hart, James D. 1978. *A Companion to California*. New York: Oxford University Press.

Hicks, Jack et al., eds. 2000. *The Literature of California: Writings from the Golden State*. Berkeley: University of California Press.

Huntington, Samuel P. 2004. *Who are We? The Challenge to America's National Identity*. New York: Simon & Schuster.

Ivey, Bill and Tepper, Steven J. 2006. "Cultural Renaissance or Cultural Divide?" *The Chronicle of Higher Education*, May 19, 2006. Available at: http:// chronicle.com/weekly/v52/i37/37b00601.htm

McWilliams, Carey. 1949. *California: The Great Exception*. Berkeley: University of California Press.

McWilliams, Carey. 2001. "Mecca of the Miraculous," in *Fool's Paradise: A Carey McWilliams Reader*. Berkeley: Heyday Books.

Moriarty, Pia. 2004. *Immigrant Participatory Arts: An Insight into Community-Building in Silicon Valley*. San José: Cultural Initiatives Silicon Valley.

Ramakrishnan, Karthick and Johnson, Hans P. 2005. "Second-Generation Immi-grants in California," *California Counts* 6 (4), Public Policy Institute of California.

Rawls, James J. and Bean, Walton. 2003. *California: An Interpretive History*, 8th edn. San Francisco: McGraw-Hill.

Rodriguez, Richard Rodriguez. 2006. "Disappointment," *California Magazine* (January/February), 117 (1): 15.

Rohrbough, Malcolm J. 1997. *Days of Gold: The California Gold Rush and the American Nation*. Berkeley: University of California Press.

Schrag, Peter. 1998. *Paradise Lost: California's Experience, America's Future*. Berkeley: University of California Press.

Schrag, Peter. 2006. *California: America's High-Stakes Experiment*. Berkeley: University of California Press.

Starr, Kevin. 1973. *Americans and the California Dream, 1850–1915*. London: Oxford University Press.

Starr, Kevin. 1998. "The Gold Rush and the California Dream," *California History* 77 (1): 57–67.

Starr, Kevin. 2004. *Coast of Dreams: California on the Edge, 1990–2003*. New York: Alfred A. Knopf.

State of California. 2006. *California County Race/Ethnic Population Estimates and Components of Change by Year, July 1, 2000–2004.* Department of Finance, Demographic Research Unit, Sacramento, California, March 2006.

Stegner, Wallace. 1982. "The West Coast: Region with a View," in *One Way to Spell Man.* Garden City, NY: Doubleday. Originally published in *The Saturday Evening Post*, 1959.

Time. 1991. November 18.

FURTHER READING

Austin, Mary. 1903. *Land of Little Rain.* New York: Penguin.

Callenbach, Ernest. 1977 *Ecotopia.* New York: Bantam Books. (First self-published in 1975, recently republished by Heyday Books with a new Afterword by the author.)

Didion, Joan. 1979. *The White Album.* New York: Simon & Schuster.

Haslam, Gerry. 2005. *Haslam's Valley.* Berkeley: Heyday Books.

Holliday, James S. 1999. *The Rush for Riches: Gold Fever and the Making of California.* Berkeley: University of California Press.

Houston, James D. 1985. *Californians: Searching for the Golden State.* Berkeley: Creative Arts Book Co. (First published in hardback by Alfred A. Knopf in 1982.)

Houston, Jeanne Wakatsuki and Houston, James D. 1973. *Farewell to Manzanar.* Boston, MA: Houghton Mifflin.

Isenberg, Barbara. 2000. *State of the Arts: California Artists Talk about Their Work.* New York: William W. Morrow.

Jimenez, Francisco. 1997. *The Circuit: Stories from the Life of a Migrant Child.* Albuquerque: University of New Mexico Press.

Jimenez, Francisco. 2001. *Breaking Through.* Boston, MA: Houghton Mifflin.

Kroeber, Theodora. 1962. *Ishi in Two Worlds: A Biography of the Last Wild Indian in North America.* Berkeley: University of California Press.

Margolin, Malcolm. 1978. *The Ohlone Way: Indian Life in the San Francisco – Monterey Bay Area.* Berkeley: Heyday Books.

Masumoto, David Mas. 1995. *Epitaph for a Peach: Four Seasons on My Family Farm.* San Francisco: HarperCollins.

Rodriguez, Richard. 1983. *Hunger of Memory.* New York: Bantam.

Shavelson, Lonny and Setterberg, Fred. 2007. *Under the Dragon: California's New Culture.* Berkeley: Heyday Books.

Starr, Kevin. *Americans and the California Dream* series (6 volumes):

Starr, Kevin. 1973. *Americans and the California Dream, 1850–1915.* New York: Oxford University Press.

Starr, Kevin. 1985. *Inventing the Dream: California through the Progressive Era.* New York: Oxford University Press.

Starr, Kevin. 1990. *Material Dreams: Southern California through the 1920s.* New York: Oxford University Press.

Starr, Kevin. 1996. *Endangered Dreams: The Great Depression in California.* New York: Oxford University Press.

Starr, Kevin. 1997. *The Dream Endures: California Enters the 1940s.* New York: Oxford University Press.

Starr, Kevin. 2002. *Embattled Dreams: California in War and Peace, 1940–1950.* New York: Oxford University Press.

Starr, Kevin. 2004. *Coast of Dreams: California on the Edge, 1990–2003.* New York: Vintage.

Stewart, George R. 1936. *Ordeal by Hunger: The Story of the Donner Party.* Lincoln: University of Nebraska Press.

Stewart, George R. 1962. *The California Trail: An Epic with Many Heroes.* Lincoln: University of Nebraska Press.

Waldie, D. J. 1996. *Holy Land: A Suburban Memoir.* New York: W. W. Norton.

Wyatt, David. 1997. *Five Fires: Race, Catastrophe, and the Shaping of California.* Menlo Park, CA: Addison-Wesley.

Chapter Two

REREADING, MISREADING, AND REDEEMING THE GOLDEN STATE: DEFINING CALIFORNIA THROUGH HISTORY

D. J. Waldie

The only true paradise is a paradise we have lost.
Marcel Proust, *Finding Time Again*

Misreading Ramona

Because of its Catholic past, its capture in war and fears of Mexican irre-dentism, and its persistent cycles of speculative boom and bust framed on every extravagant human desire from gold dust to movie stardom, Califor-nia has always seemed uniquely poised between its bright metaphors and its many tragedies. California is a place, above all, that was imagined before it was any place: as the fictive island of Queen Califia, who was said to be rich, buxom, and dangerous and with many fierce daughters; but they all might be tamed by romance and a certain amount of violence. California would resist its conquistadors, Garcí Ordóñez de Montalvo asserted with the bluff confidence of a Pizzaro or Cortés in *Las Sergas de Esplandian*, but California would ultimately yield to the occupiers' desires out of Cali-fornia's longing for what it lacked. Falling in love, after a sometimes brutal wooing, and love's often-disillusioned aftermath is the briefest and truest history of California. The waves of the amorous were gallant readers of romances (mocked by Miguel de Cervantes in *Don Quixote*) and pitying readers of Helen Hunt Jackson's *Ramona* (who willfully misunderstood Jackson's plea for California's Native American and mestizo communities); small-town beauty queens reading breathless filmland gossip in Hollywood magazines and mid-twentieth-century middle-class aspirants with smaller, more realizable longings for a small house on a small lot in Sacramento,

Richmond, the San Fernando Valley, or San Diego – a California that would end their seeking for a place to satisfy their modest desires.

California's suitors assumed that whatever indigenous resistance they initially encountered, they would prevail against native ignorance, because they also assumed that California (in order to be California) required their presence. That lack defines the essential deficiency in what was otherwise an earthly paradise. *Et in Arcadia, Ego* might be the ironic motto of Californians, unfamiliar with the many interpretations of who or what would eventually tinge Arcadian perfection with enough melancholic regret to make dystopian histories a substantial subset of California's historiography. When the innocent shepherds point to the stone on which those words are engraved in Nicholas Poussin's *The Shepherds of Arcadia* (painted about 1650 but referring to versions by earlier artists), the naïve incomprehension of the shepherds is meant to be both heartbreaking and intellectually fortifying, just as Neapolitan humanist Jacopo Sannazaro intended when in 1480 he gave fictional Arcadia a template of earthly virtues and its poetic gloss as a vanished place of idyllic bliss and, in retrospect, fit only for sophisticated nostalgia. To assert *I am in Arcadia, too* presumes much about both the occupier and what is occupied and about the inevitability and mutuality of their relationship. Poussin's shepherds and shepherdess, standing in for the Chumash of the California coast, may wonder what so fraught an emblem can mean to them (because they presumably lack the knowledge to render all of its implications) but we can see from our perspective outside the frame that they are powerless to change it. Their fate is carved in stone.

Not much of the Americas matched Sannazaro's bucolic pre-conquest imagining of Arcadia, either in Protestant New England or in Catholic New Spain, although the Arcadian model was, as a form of aggressive marketing, applied again and again to the great emptiness of eighteenth- and nineteenth-century North America. But large parts of coastwise California, from below the state's present southern border to the rain forests of its northern frontier, did approximate temperate perfection, and there, in the aftermath of the American occupation of 1847, new emblems of California would expand on new occupiers' inherited longing and reverie.

William Alexander McClung in *Landscapes of Desire: Anglo Mythologies of Los Angeles* parses a lemon crate label rendered by an anonymous commercial artist as a tableau of pre-World War I Southern California and as a series of "idealized juxtapositions" in the landscape. The brightly colored label only incidentally sold lemons. It shows "four approximately equal zones, starting at the mountains, which are wilderness (the land as it was and can, without damage to profits, be allowed to remain), and progressing to the citrus groves, an orderly and proper exploitation of nature. A boulevard next announces a modern city and its technological panache, displaying the imagery not of mass (i.e., rail) but of leisured transportation," including a modern touring car and a soon-to-be-antique pony cart. "Finally a lady appears on foot, hatted and handbagged, as if going to pay a call." None of these distinct categories of place contradicts the others, the label and its satisfied lemon-dealer patron assert. Wilderness, feminine high fashion, the classic order of citrus culture, virile technology, and implied speed – in effect, all of nature and all of civilization – "are perfectly in scale" (McClung 2000: 27). The unstable synthesis of these places – unresolved in space as well as in time – is one factor that has produced in some observers a much remarked-on unease, despite assertions about the palliative and ordered pace of California's imagined life. Comparable images flowed into the markets and kitchens of millions of American homes at the end of the eighteenth and the start of the nineteenth century, long before the same jump cuts in time and space flickered onto the screens of East Coast nickelodeons in the form of one-reel comedies and melodramas (also made in California). California, before most of its occupiers in the twentieth century arrived, already possessed a highly mediated narrative marked by inevitability, triumph, anxiety, and loss.

Although her purpose was to reveal the injustice done to the remnants of California's Native American population and the insults endured by Mexican Americans, Helen Hunt Jackson in *Ramona* (1884) failed to arouse for California's indigenous communities the level of political passion she believed *Uncle Tom's Cabin* had ignited for the condition of slaves. Jackson had wished to speak to the hearts of an educated, sympathetic, and Christian middle class largely outside California for whom, she thought, the wrenching melodrama of the doomed marriage of Ramona (a mestiza) and a Native American shepherd, Alessandro, would be read as the next, post-Civil War chapter in the redemption of America's marginalized citizens. Gathering California's mestizos and Native Americans into an enlarged American narrative, she believed, could right historic wrongs and invest the American experience with a native romance she found profoundly lacking in a rapidly industrializing and urbanizing nation. Readers (however they felt about the injustice) predictably fell in love with the romance. Jackson's strategy of identifying the qualities of the pastoral landscape of mid-nineteenth-century Southern California with the character of Californians was her undoing. Environmental essentialism – a complicated inheritance from both Darwinism and the English Romantics – framed the astonishing success of *Ramona* as a enduring work of popular literature, going through dozens of editions, and *Ramona*'s long afterlife as the guarantor of meaning for the Californian experience.

Ramona was understood to be about the landscape of California (but less so about the actors in the landscape), and very soon it was in the landscape in the form of towns named for the suffering heroine and housing tracts, schools, hotels, and unashamed tourist traps: a vast "Ramon-aland" of consoling and profitable fictions. Dydia DeLyser in *Ramona Memories: Tourism and the Shaping of Southern California* makes the argument that "elements from a work of fiction became factual through the landscape and came to influence the way residents and visitors in Southern California thought about their past – which is to say, they became part of Southern California social memory" (2005: xvi). Jackson's reward was the internalization, not of her social values, but of her literary strategy of equating place with character, a trope that continues to cling to California and Californians in fiction and social criticism and comedy.

The Anglo inheritors of California, who were completing the erasure of the mixed-race culture Jackson had defended and were uneasy about backsliding into a "mongrel" society, asked metaphorically: "How do we become 'indigenous' to this place?" In Los Angeles at the turn of the twentieth century, they supplied what they lacked with a pageant, a history lesson on wheels drawn on wagons though the few big streets of the still raw American city. As William Deverell describes it in *Whitewashed Adobe: The Rise of Los Angeles and the Remaking of Its Mexican Past*, the communal narrative of Los Angeles was going to be a parade with floats: *La Fiesta de Los Angeles*. The lead floats in the 1895 parade illustrated "Aztec" daily life, followed by Native Americans imported from Yuma, Arizona enacting a raiding party, then a float of mission padres bringing Western civilization, and then – in further slow procession – floats showing a typical scene of the "sleepy" Mexican town of the 1820s, a scene from the era of the ranchos, and Sutter's discovery of gold in 1849. Interspersed among the floats were the "other" Angeleños; among them was a team of Chinese dragon dancers whose presence in the parade was both fascinatingly exotic and deeply troubling to Anglo spectators. The parade they witnessed was a story of replacement. In each era, one people inevitably supplanted another, until both the parade and history ended with a final float: an allegory of the triumphant Anglo city situated in a timeless countryside (a version on wheels of the lithographed citrus crate label). The final float promised that the Anglo city would be the culmination of Caucasian civilization in a land of sunshine where nature and enlightened industry coexisted in harmony. The harmony shattered almost at once, and the bickering over the point of the story began. The mission padres were found to be Catholic and agents of Roman superstition, at least according to the sterner elements of the city's dominant Protestant community. Were the dancing Chinese and sullen Indians officially part of the story (even if the pageant clearly demonstrated their subordinate status)? And the dashing caballeros on parade day – didn't they become just Mexicans the day after? In 1898, the Spanish-American War made it impossible to script a useable past that included a place for Spanish conquistadors. In 1902, the descendants of the haciendado Lugo and Yorba families threatened to pull out – not for the first time – and leave the parade without living proof of how the principle of succession in California worked. As a theory of history, the fiesta parade came with the presumption that the past was not safely "in the past," but could rumble into the present and make claims that most Anglo Californians refused to understand. Perhaps the fiesta's organizing principle implied that the final float in the parade might not always end the story with "Caucasian triumph" and that the Anglo supplanters standing on the sidewalk might themselves be made to ride one day in a slow-moving tableau for the education of newer inheritors of the landscape. The fiesta sputtered out in these unresolved conflicts, wrecked on the impossible problem of giving Ramonaland a history that could be located somewhere else than in reverie. The contemporaneous Tournament of Roses in Pasadena flourished, perhaps because the Pasadena parade wasn't a narrative but only an opportunity for looking at pretty flowers and pretty girls.

The quest for timelessness in the landscape of the southern half of California is counterpoised by the north's heedless consumption of tens of thousands of acres of it. Gold from the north made California, propelled it from annexed backwater to international desire, drove it Minerva-like (just as the state seal emblemizes) into full statehood without the normal progression through territorial status, obliterated the native societies of the gold fields, settled the state's commerce and industry in the north well into the second half of the twentieth century, made San Francisco the anomalous metropolis it remains, and nearly severed California into free state and secessionist through the Civil War. Just between 1849 and 1855, at least $400 million in gold was wrested from the gullies, streams, and arroyos of the Sierras by a polyglot army of filthy, lonely, and violent young men (to see a woman or an old man was astonishingly rare) who were as likely to have come from Hilo or Paris as from Philadelphia or Charleston. In 1848, the non-Indian population of California was roughly 13,000; by 1854, the number was 300,000. But many more anxious thousands "back home in the States" participated vicariously in the possibility of sudden riches brought on by the gold fever. Rightly called a shared national experience by Malcolm Rohrbough, the Gold Rush was translated eastward to waiting wives and parents as a marvel of economic democracy (despite its feral aspects) and westward, into the spirit of California, as an eagerness for anything quickly earned. It was, as Rohrbough notes, "the most significant event in the first half of the nineteenth century, from Thomas Jefferson's purchase of Louisiana in the autumn of 1803 to South Carolina's secession from the Union in the winter of 1860" (1998: 2; see also William Deverell's essay in this volume). Although one in five of the "forty-niners" would die within six months of reaching the gold fields from disease, accident, or suicide, and hardly more than a handful of the thousands who arrived would take out more than the cost of their getting there and their upkeep, the self-styled Argonauts arrived in the foothills of the Sierras filled with the fierce belief that California would yield to them. Their counterparts in later migrations in the 1930s, 1940s, and 1950s claimed to feel that same visceral rush as they passed the unmarked border between the first portion of their life and their new life in California. Henry David Thoreau, on the other hand, compared an expedition to California as getting three thousand miles closer to hell, a not uncommon view of the state in the late twentieth century as well.

Far more than in Southern California in the period between the Mexican War and World War I, Northern California's story is personal, often breathlessly epistolary, and of extraordinary volume, in part because so many gold-feverish doctors, lawyers, sea captains, shopkeepers, and tradesmen joined in the stampede into the Sierras. Prussian-born Harris Newmark, who was 19 when he came to somnambulant Los Angeles in 1853 and who learned Spanish before he learned English in order to run his store, almost alone recorded the city's commonplaces in the pre- and post-Civil War period. (Deverell has noted elsewhere that a mostly untapped record of the everyday experiences of Southern California immigrants, largely from the post-Depression period but not exclusively, lies in the personal memoirs self-published by their authors, which are found in city libraries and on sale at historical society bookshops.) By contrast, scores of energetic letter writers and journal keepers give the historian an almost cinematic view of life and manners in the diggings, making the Gold Rush one of the most written-about episodes (save for the Civil War) in American history. And yet the rush and its aftermath seem strangely absent from the ways in which Californians read their story of themselves today. As Czeslaw Milosz ruefully notes:

> The truth of that bygone California, of all America, is elusive, ambiguous, and it would be pointless to seek in it myths devised to keep us from being overly troubled by the disorder of the world. . . . I have often been inclined to predict that someday a completely different sort of Western will appear in America, a Western able to extract from the documents and annals the unrelieved terror and strangeness of those days. But I cannot be sure, because the truth will still be opposed by the age-old tastes of the listeners, readers, viewers, who long to identify with heroes. Besides, let's be fair, those annals are full of heroism, for the most part the heroism of nameless people. (Kowalewski 1997: 445)

Thoughtful and lively historical research has brought the gunpowder stink and hallucinatory suddenness of the Gold Rush to life, but it has not made Californians the willing inheritors of its effects on both the landscape and ourselves. Hardly anyone bothers to remember how the events of 1849 set the arc of our story, but Californians continue to live in the remains of the Gold Rush – to their wonder and dismay. We inherited the poisoned tailings of New Alamaden, once one of the world's largest mercury mines. The mercury now leeching to city water systems was once used to amalgamate the flecks of gold dredged from riverbeds or sluiced from foothills by hydraulic mining. We also inherited the badlands that hydraulic mining produced. More than a hundred years after hydraulic mining was outlawed for its environmental impacts, these badlands still choke the state's streams and silt up its dams. And we inherited the seepage from literally uncounted numbers of abandoned hardrock mines. The mines are uncounted because the state Water Quality Control Board was given no funding to count them. Far worse, we inherited habits of seeing and using the land that began with the first claim staked on the American River and which continue each time a house lot in California changes hands. A miner named Thomas Swain wrote in 1851: "Large cities have sprung into existence almost in a day . . . The people have been to each other as strangers in a strange land . . . Their hearts have been left at home" (Brechin & Dawson 1999: xiv). Fifty years later, the speculators in Frank Norris's *The Octopus* still had no heart for their home in California. "They had no love for the land," Norris wrote,

> They were not attached to the soil. They worked their ranches as . . . they had worked their mines. To get all there was out of the land, to squeeze it dry, to exhaust it, seemed their policy. When at last the land worn out would refuse to yield, they would invest their money in something else; by then, they would all have made fortunes. They did not care. (2007: 257)

Nearly a hundred years after Norris, many who control the land still do not care. As Gray Brechin and Robert Dawson point out in *Farewell, Promised Land: Waking from the California Dream*, not just the Gold Rush but the broader environmental history of California has been an epic bender, engineered and financed largely through San Francisco (to the discomfort of Los Angeles provincials). That 150-year spree was fueled by gold, timber, cattle, wheat, oil, subsidized water, subsidized agriculture, subsidized suburban housing, and a marketing campaign of seductive power that substituted desire and reverie to replace a harsher story in which clear-cut forests made pasture for cattle until the forage was gone, then the pasture was sold for wheat until the soil was exhausted, and then it was sold for irrigated farms to smallholders until the last crop was killed by the salt that irrigation deposits in arid ground. Finally, the land was subdivided for house lots. At every stage, the tailings of previous boom are dressed as El Dorado for the next wave of the hopelessly infatuated until the newcomers are persuaded to buy what's left of whatever had lately gone bust. This shell game is the California Dream, and in its service, memory, people, and places are continually being erased. Lured to the state's archipelago of exploitable and often unforgiving ecologies, and without the experience to temper them fully into domesticity, ordinary Californians still cling to all the possibilities that a culture of endless erasure offers.

California was a promised land – promised to be a land of "health, wealth, and happiness in the sunshine" – but it was also a place on the periphery, very far from where many hearts might feel at home, and the merchandise of grandeur filled some of their hollowness. For almost as long as its landscape has been exploited, from William Henry Jackson in the 1870s through Ansel Adams in the 1950s to the latest Sierra Club calendar, California has produced sublime and misleading landscape photography. Beautifully composed photographs of the Yosemite Valley hang over California like a glowing billboard, promoting the view that wildness is permanently out there, unmarred by our labor, and ready for contemplation. The photographs make the rapturous assumption that none of us was ever here. But we were. A few photographs picked up from the detritus of history show us at work. We're sluicing mountains into rivers to get at the gold, taking down forests to built a wood and iron technology gone before our parents were born, erecting groves of derricks over oil fields, and taking harvests from the compliant ground. There is almost no memory of this for Californians, save in these snapshots. A few faces of men, dirty and hard, stare out from a quarry, along a railroad cut, or during a grape harvest from that remote era when most men actually worked and before views of a gorgeously depopulated nature supplanted men and their black-and-white labor.

The choice for Californians north and south after the cataclysm of 1849 was not between the wild and the despoiled, but the further terms on which our encounter with nature would be framed. John Muir, a founder of the Sierra Club, gave nature a privileged autonomy, a kind of green divinity for acolytes with backpacks. Frederick Law Olmsted, the builder of New York's Central Park, concluded that nature in California would never be sublimely alone, despite what the photographs said, and that nature must inevitably be enmeshed in the community of people living here. Olmsted struggled for a word to describe the tie that might bind a place and its people and settled on "communitiveness." It is an awkward word for something that tries to define both civility to one's neighbors and trusteeship of the land. Olmsted, as Muir and Jackson did, sought to read a redemptive narrative – and something of the wider American experience – into the landscape of California. Those who were led into the California landscape by their longing for the redeeming qualities Jackson, Muir, and Olmsted imagined there – qualities variously ennobling, consoling, and

romantic – unalterably changed the landscape and must struggle now to
extract new meanings from their home ground.

Historiography – in the broadest sense of communal stories – necessarily
evolves from the time-obscured record to the problematic interpretations
of that record and to equally problematic and soon-to-be-contested beliefs
and behaviors based on those interpretations. The histories we tell about
the places in which we live have a shaping power over those places. If you
had stood on a levee overlooking the Los Angeles River on any summer
day in the last 30 years, anywhere below the sharp loop the river makes at
the industrial city of Vernon, when the only thing stirring on the flat waste
of riverbed concrete is the reclaimed waste water running in the "low flow"
slot down the middle of the channel, skepticism surely would have triumphed over any hope that meaning still clings to so many miles of glaring
whiteness. Los Angeles had made this river, over a hundred years and for
more than a billion dollars, for the purpose of flood protection but also to
make suburban real estate more profitable and Los Angeles harbor industrialization possible and to put Latino immigrant families just a little further
from the Anglo west of the city. What else Los Angeles might have made
of the river eluded us, bereft of history, until that lack was made up by a
weighty handful of new interpretations – *City of Quartz: Excavating the
Future in Los Angeles* (Davis 1990), *The Los Angeles River: Its Life, Death,
and Possible Rebirth* (Gumprecht 1999), *Eden by Design: the 1930 Olmsted–
Bartholomew Plan for the Los Angeles Region* (Deverell & Hise 2000),
Hazardous Metropolis: Flooding and Urban Ecology in Los Angeles (Orsi
2004), and *Land of Sunshine: An Environmental History of Metropolitan
Los Angeles* (Deverell & Hise 2005) – and in the journalism and popular
writing about the Los Angeles River that flowed into and out of these
histories and into the decisions of city, county, and state officials. Today,
the once empty and trespass-forbidden riverside is imaginatively crowded
with planners from public agencies and environmental organizations, volunteers, county workers, schoolchildren, and politicians who are working
to thread the city with a 51-mile-long Los Angeles River Parkway, a name
that deliberately recalls the monumental park plan proposed in 1930 by
the famed landscape firms of Olmsted Brothers and Bartholomew Associates. Jennifer Price experienced this sudden joining of history and place as
a kind of epiphany in the bed of the Los Angeles River:

> I lead informal tours of the river – for friends and friends of their friends,
> who like to think about LA and who have heard that LA has a river and
> want to see it. We stop at the new park sites, but also . . . visit the wasteland
> of the confluence, which I finally found on my own third try. We wander
> through the trash and skirt the homeless tents and lean on the massive pylons
> of the freeway overpasses. Here, we say, is the most hopeless as well as the

most hopeful spot on the LA River. The confluence is perhaps the most extreme testament to LA's erasure of nature, community and the past. . . . Here, we say, is one of the best places to think about LA – and LA historically has been one of the best places to think about America. You are standing, we allow, at an American narrative vortex. (Deverell & Hise 2005: 244)

A great and subtle work is underway in the landscape of California, something not any less a collision with nature than the original transformation of Gold Rush California into a place to live for its present and still growing millions. Ordinary men and women – and state bureaucrats, Native American councils, farmers, scientists, federal regulators, and calculating men in boardrooms a continent away – have collided with the natural limits of California. Knowledge of limits makes everything inside them precious, not just the exemplary parts in photographs. The collisions that Californians have had with limits have struck off hundreds of efforts to husband all the landscape within them. Some are as charismatic as preservation of the Headwaters Forest on California's North Coast. Some are as difficult to grasp as changing the flow of billions of gallons of Sierra runoff in the Sacramento–San Joaquin Delta. Most of these remediation and preservation efforts are as parochial as the Natural Communities Conservation Planning programs on the fringes of suburban housing tracts in Carlsbad and Irvine. Californians, led by the exemplary stories they have managed to recover, are not preserving spectacular views, but natural communities and, in the imperfect way that we have, remaking human communities too. Economic downturns, the obstinacy of politics, and the frailty of public/ private conservation partnerships can derail this process. And ahead of California is the waning of an Anglo majority that had been taught to see the landscape as a commodity, a trophy of aesthetic privilege, or a place of aching regret. That California is passing away.

Near the end of Brechin & Dawson's *Farewell, Promised Land* is a two-page panorama of the Gerbode Valley near San Francisco. Its significance is in what's missing in the photograph – the rows of suburban houses that were to have been built there until the valley was preserved as part of the Golden Gate National Recreation Area. When I gaze at the undulating hills in the photograph, the short grass sweeping up to the hills' summits, and at the meander of the dirt road and the trees in the distance, I see ground every foot of which has been shaped by human intention. For the houses to remain absent, the valley will forever require the presence of people on its periphery. In another photograph, a backhoe is raking through the muck of a streambed while an overseer looks on. This is where the California spree began at Sutter's mill, if you look past the new machinery. Without a caption, however, you cannot tell if this is rape or redemption.

It happens to be a picture of redemption, but not being able to know for sure is the moral burden of being in California's history. California's conflicted history and pervasive illusions have made me more aware of the costs of putting all kinds of people in this landscape – working people, immigrant people, undocumented people, and people who will never read any history at all. But at least enough of them must have a feeling for the stories in our landscape and aspire to complicity with their place.

But complicity with place and history in California does not always inspire wonder or even hope. Joan Didion's *Where I Was From* (2003) is a meditation on California brokenheartedness in the form of a memoir of flinty realism. *Where I Was From* will not accept anything from history except, aiming at the few who can bear it, a measure of endurance after disillusionment. Anglo Californians, Didion suggests, had expected something more than this as they transformed California around them.

This question of "changes," involving as it does some reflexive suggestion of a birthright squandered, a paradise lost, is a vexed issue. I was many times told as a child that the grass in the Sacramento Valley had at the time the American settlers arrived in the 1840s grown so high that it could be tied over a saddle, the point being that it did no more. California, in this telling, had then been "spoiled." The logical extension of this thought, that we were the people who had spoiled it, remained unexplored (Didion 2003: 170).

Didion questions the instructional value of California's narratives (surely the most serious question that can be asked of a people's history) and finds no moral value in the eccentric substitutions and evasions that replace California history. For Didion, the attempt to create a narrative unencumbered by irony had failed at its beginning, even as the wagon trains of the mid-1840s set out west with narratives of suffering, providential escape, and future redemption already packed into the baggage of the immigrant families. Ironies seem to be the point in Marc Reisner's dystopian histories *Cadillac Desert: The American West and Its Disappearing Water* (1993 [1986]) and *A Dangerous Place: California's Unsettling Fate* (2003), which exactly mirror American anxiety about the double meaning of California (and the West generally) as simultaneously El Dorado and the Donner Pass, as an unearned gift of fortune and the curse of being reduced to cannibalism. Reisner and Mike Davis in *Ecology of Fear: Los Angeles and the Imagination of Disaster* (1998) mean to seriously trouble readers' assumptions about California, but there is another intoxicating library of popular accounts from the turn of the twentieth century forward in which – as satire, parody, or fable – California is rendered as a place without a usable past, a livable present, or any future anyone would want. The story may be both glamorous and sordid, but it is just another burlesque best witnessed while slightly sedated. Low and high, the "exceptionalist" literature of California – the stories that maroon their tellers somewhere off the edge of the continent – are glossed by Reyner Banham's evocative claim in *Los Angeles: The Architecture of Four Ecologies* (which could as easily be applied to the whole of California) that, "[T]he splendors and miseries of Los Angeles, the graces of [its] grotesqueries, appear to me as unrepeatable as they are unprecedented" (1971: 24). Kevin Starr, observing the state from the eminence of his scenic panorama of the state's history and civilization in his California Dream series, asked himself in *Coast of Dreams: California on the Edge, 1990–2003*, "Was California an aberration, a sideshow, or, worse, a case study in how things could go wrong for the United States? . . . I had invested most of my professional energies in California in the belief that the history of California was mainstream American history. . . . Had I made a terrible mistake?" (2004: xi).

Acquiring a "Sense of Place"

Where I live is where most Californians live – in a tract house on a block of more tract houses hardly distinguishable from the next and all of them extending as far as the street grid allows. My exact place on the grid is at the extreme southeast corner of Los Angeles County, but that's mostly by accident. Although I reside in Lakewood my home might as well be almost anywhere in this most suburban of states. I've lived my whole life in the 957-square-foot house my parents bought in 1946 when the idea of that kind of house and that kind of neighborhood were new, and no one knew what would happen as tens of thousands of working-class husbands and wives – so young and so inexperienced – were thrown together and expected to make a fit place to live. What happened after was the usual redemptive mix of joy and everyday tragedy, for which the "white blues" of Hank Williams and the country music coming out of Bakersfield was consolation. There are Californians who cannot regard their tract house as a place of pilgrimage, but my parents and their friends did. They were grateful for the comforts of their not-quite-middle-class life. Despite every-thing that was ignored or squandered in its making, I believe a kind of dignity was gained. More men than just my father have said to me that living here gave them habits that did not make them feel ashamed. They knew what they found and lost. My neighbors are not ironists.

My neighborhood was a place where California stories were mass-produced by the tens of thousands for the hopeful millions of the mid-twentieth century in flight from the agricultural depression of the 1920s, the industrial depression of the 1930s, the years of World War II, and the bitter months of the Korean Conflict. They were stories then for displaced Okies and Arkies, Jews who knew the pain of exclusion, Catholics who thought they did, and anyone white with a steady job. Left out until quite recently were many tens of thousands of others: people of color whose exclusion was not just a Californian transgression. And today, suburban stories still begin where I live, except the anxious, hopeful people who tell them now are as mixed in their colors and ethnicities as our whole, mongrel California. (The Public Policy Institute of California reported in 2001 that Lakewood had one of the highest rates of ethnic diversification of any California city.)

When I walk out the door of my home, I see the human-scale and specific landscape into which was poured the commonplaces that have shaped my work, my convictions, and my aspirations. I live here with continued anticipation because I want to find out what happens next in stories I already know. My loyalty is the last habit that anyone would impute to those of us who live here; we're supposed to be so dissatisfied here (or numbed at least). I live here because Lakewood is adequate to my desire, although I know there's been a price to pay. Lakewood, in *Where I Was From*, is the summation of all that is unearned in California.

I live in a place of presumed exile, and the "hunger of memory" (to use Richard Rodriguez's troubling phrase) is acute here, but it is only a localization of the larger hunger of California, which itself is only a portion of the immigrant's experience of the West; and the problem of California and the West is only an especially perplexing subset of the everlasting problem of America, which is: *How do we make a home here?* We long for a home in California, but doubt its worth when we have it. We depend on our place, but dislike its claims on us. Californians are certain about our own preferences for a home, but we're ready to question our neighbor's choice. And no home is immune from the peculiarly American certainty that something better is just beyond the next bend in the road. California, as a representation of America's divided heart, poses large questions about the uses of history in the making of a fit place to live, and this bears on the historian's hope: *Can any part of our past be of any value to us, except as nostalgia or irony?* For philosopher George Santayana, California was "beauty without permanence, harmony without intention." And these disorders, for his contemporary Josiah Royce, made Californians "sojourners with a dwelling place, but with no home." Home, Royce thought, was located in an "intentional community" – a community of shared memory leading outward to a community of hope, neither of which he thought impossible in the suddenness of mid-nineteenth-century California or (to expand the problem for which California is an example) even in the suddenness of our now suburban and soon to be mestizo nation, a place of many lesser Californias everywhere. Royce's raw material for the making of "genuine communities" or "communities of grace" was even less appealing than my suburbia; in his letters he remembers his boyhood Grass Valley as "a community of irresponsible strangers" and "a blind and stupid and homeless generation of selfish wanderers." Yet he saw the possibility of localized loyalties arising among these men and even the greater possibility of their loyalty to the idea of loyalty, from which a genuine community – bounded by personal interests and individual biography but greater than they – might intentionally be made. Royce's recollection of his experiences of California (see Glendenning 1970) propelled him to believe that the virtue of "loyalty to the idea of loyalty" is possible, even if the objects of loyalty are uncertain, our application of this virtue is conflicted, and the outcomes of our shared efforts are distant (if not unknown). There can be no perfect places, Royce argued, but there can be places where memories and longings will persist.

Californians often find it difficult to talk coherently about issues of place because of our willful amnesia, which inevitably leads to confusion about the best means to make a home here (which is not homeowner determinism, which reads mostly as loyalty to property values, as if the only conversation Californians can have about place is the negotiation between seller and buyer). There will soon be nearly 45 million of us in California, and very few of them north or south will know how our landscapes were made or what are the true sources of our water or who sustains the infrastructure of our daily life. Lacking a usable rhetoric of place, burdened by narratives of regret, and unencumbered by history, California's official makers of public policy have lately failed to give Californians what they critically need.

The environmentalist Barry Lopez (author of *Arctic Dreams: Imagination and Desire in a Northern Landscape*) asked a question some years ago about the San Fernando Valley, his boyhood home and like Lakewood once a sudden place on terms comparable to Royce's Grass Valley. For Lopez, becoming Californian does not begin with any of the conventional markers of community building: its social institutions, political processes, or the assertions of a tradition (all of which were Royce's concern). Lopez, as a good storyteller will, asked a different but parallel question: *How can we become vulnerable to a place?* and answered that vulnerability comes with the deepening and widening of the imagination. History (in its capacity to frame a moral imagination) is where Royce and Lopez meet, at the confluence of recollection and the projection of sympathy into the future. Because of history and historians, I actually imagine the place in which I live is, in Royce's striking term, a "beloved community." By enlarging my moral imagination, history has shown me how to acquire a sense of place (I almost said, how to fall in love).

California's history is riven – north and south, costal and inland, urban and rural, Anglo and indigenous, American and Mexican American, temperate and desert, valley and foothill, Los Angeles and San Francisco – but what cuts through these many "islands on the land" is the question of what had been gained by the dreams or desperation that brought Californians here. Do our stories record what had been hard won or do they merely dress up unbounded longings, ethnic and sectarian grievances, or lucky accidents – the gifts of nature and later the federal government – from which California's illusions are made? Falling in love, although true to the California experience, is not very hard. Are, Didion asks, all the stories of California unearned?

Becoming Mestizo

California: Just the name conjures up visions – wealth, escape, creative futures, El Dorado, Hollywood, the Sierra Nevada Mountains, Big Sur, the Pacific Ocean, San Francisco, the Golden Gate Bridge, Disneyland, the red-woods, and maybe Death Valley. California's landscapes, its land uses, its physicality are intimately bound up with its mythology (Pincetl 1999: vii).

For at least some observers, these are the elements of California, to which fire, Compton, Calexico, Route 99 from Fresno to Bakersfield, earthquakes, San Diego-Tijuana, the Russian River, gated and guarded suburban enclaves, Sacramento, the Silicon Valley, the San Fernando Valley, the Central Valley, and the whole of "la frontera" from the Colorado River to the Pacific might be added. California, with speed as the state's ecstatic solvent, dissolves so easily into its constituent elements, the simplest of which are sun, earth, water, and mythology (as de Montalvo imagined five hundred years before).

At the end of *The King of California: J. G. Boswell and the Making of a Secret American Empire*, Mark Arax and Rick Wartzman allow J. G. Boswell to tell another old story of the Central Valley: Water was topping a key levee; Boswell's cotton land would be reclaimed by the flood; the crop would be lost. He learns that an "old colored guy on the other side of town" has 40 or 50 junk cars. Boswell buys them and dumps them into the breech, but the water will not stop. He buys, at $15 each, all the junk cars from Dinuba to Los Angeles and dumps them onto the levee, too. "By the time we finished, we had six miles of cars stashed in and we saved some of the crop" (2003: 430). Boswell's story could be about a pioneer's indomitable tenacity, or it could be about the catastrophe of sustaining a federally subsidized agricultural empire in the bed of a sometimes dry lake. It could be about preserving a fit place to live or about the cost of preserv-ing one of California's many extractive industries. It could be about all of California, where we periodically and heroically dump the junked and unwanted parts of our past into the gaps that open in illusion's threatened levee.

Then what does California mean? That question is first asked in this state when you are 10 years old. If you are a fourth grade student, California means a tabletop model of an eighteenth-century Franciscan mission constructed with the help of a tired parent. Assembling one of these mission models makes California seem mostly about building materials. If you are the painter David Hockney, California is a specific quality of light. "As a child, growing up in . . . the north of England," Hockney remembers in *Hand Eye Heart: Watercolors of the East Yorkshire Landscape* (a catalog of his recent work), "I remember how my father used to take me along with him to the Laurel and Hardy movies. And one of the things I noticed right away . . . was how Stan and Ollie, bundled in their winter coats, were casting these wonderfully strong, crisp shadows. We never got shadows of any sort in winter. And already I knew that someday I wanted to settle in a place with winter shadows like that" (Weschler & Goulds 2005: 17). For Hockney, California means "shadows in winter" and a place longed for because of a parade of moving shadows in a movie theater. Hockney's desire after seeing Californian shadows was transforming. And so for Hockney, California means becoming Californian before coming to California.

But if you were among the two million middle-aged and older Anglos since 1990 who have migrated to "greater California" – located in Idaho, Nevada, Montana, and Arizona – California means some measure of inadequacy to the desire that propelled them west. Their departure might be the inevitable backwash at the end of one of the greatest migrations in human history or symptomatic of something else that characterizes California and Californians, something in our history or in our character as a people. If you are Joan Didion, California is the prize for leaving the past behind. If you are the novelist and playwright William Saroyan, California is "my native land."

If you are Richard Rodriguez, California means being brown, that is, being mixed, mingled, hybrid, heterogeneous . . . to be mestizo, to be impure. California means orienting yourself, but not east to west with California as the beautiful but melancholy terrain on the edge of the sundown sea, but reorienting yourself so that the axis of meaning goes north and south.

And California also means to be increasingly ordinary (and I am grateful for it). But if California isn't a "great exception," isn't the best or worst of places where the wilderness is no longer wild and the desert no longer deserted, then how do historians describe California when it is not exactly "Californian" anymore, not as lurid or alluring as the clichés of the dystopian and utopian accounts said it was?

Sitting on the patio of a perfectly ordinary tract house in Buena Park in Orange County not long ago, I listened to my two Mexican American goddaughters playing in their backyard pool while an elderly Algerian immigrant told a Taiwanese businessman and an Alsatian insurance executive stories about his new home in Temecula in Riverside County. He spoke of its elemental sun, air, and its wine, rather than its water. He could not find the right words in English, apologized, and continued in the French he knew better. He said that he thought his new place has a soul.

REFERENCES

Arax, Mark and Wartzman, Rick. 2003. *The King of California: J. G. Boswell and the Making of a Secret American Empire.* New York: PublicAffairs.

Banham, Reyner. 2001. *Los Angeles: The Architecture of Four Ecologies.* Berkeley: University of California Press.

Brechin, Gray and Dawson, Robert. 1999. *Farewell, Promised Land: Waking from the California Dream.* Berkeley: University of California Press.

Davis, Mike. 1990. *City of Quartz: Excavating the Future in Los Angeles.* London: Verso.

DeLyser, Dydia. 2005. *Ramona Memories: Tourism and the Shaping of Southern California.* Minneapolis: University of Minnesota Press.

Deverell, William. 2004. *Whitewashed Adobe: The Rise of Los Angeles and the Remaking of Its Mexican Past.* Berkeley: University of California Press.

Deverell, William and Hise, Greg, eds. 2000. *Eden by Design: The 1930 Olmsted–Bartholomew Plan for the Los Angeles Region.* Berkeley: University of California Press.

Deverell, William and Hise, Greg, eds. 2005. *Land of Sunshine: An Environmental History of Metropolitan Los Angeles.* Pittsburgh: University of Pittsburgh Press.

Didion, Joan. 2003. *Where I Was From.* New York: Alfred A. Knopf.

Glendenning, John, ed. 1970. *The Letters of Josiah Royce.* Chicago: University of Chicago Press.

Gumprecht, Blake. 1999. *The Los Angeles River: Its Life, Death, and Possible Rebirth.* Baltimore, MD: Johns Hopkins University Press.

Kowalewski, Michael, ed. 1997. *Gold Rush: A Literary Exploration.* Berkeley: Heyday Books.

La Chapelle, Peter. 2007. *Proud to Be an Okie: Cultural Politics, Country Music, and Migration to Southern California.* Berkeley: University of California Press.

McClung, William Alexander. 2000. *Landscapes of Desire: Anglo Mythologies of Los Angeles.* Berkeley: University of California Press.

Norris, Frank. 2007. *The Octopus.* BiblioBazaar.

Pincetl, Stephanie S. 1999. *Transforming California: A Political History of Land Use and Development.* Baltimore, MD: Johns Hopkins University Press.

Proust, Marcel. 2003. *Finding Time Again.* London: Penguin.

Reisner, Marc. 1993. *Cadillac Desert: The American West and Its Disappearing Water*, 2nd ed. New York: Penguin.

Reisner, Marc. 2003. *A Dangerous Place: California's Unsettling Fate.* New York: Pantheon.

Rohrbough, Malcolm. 1998. *Days of Gold: The California Gold Rush and the American Nation.* Berkeley: University of California Press.

Starr, Kevin. 2004. *Coast of Dreams: California on the Edge, 1990–2003.* New York: Alfred A. Knopf.

Weschler, Lawrence and Goulds, Peter. 2005. *Hand Eye Heart: Watercolors of the East Yorkshire Landscape.* Venice, CA: L. A. Louver.

FURTHER READING

Davis, Mike. 1998. *Ecology of Fear: Los Angeles and the Imagination of Disaster.* New York: Metropolitan Books.

Orsi, Jared. 2004. *Hazardous Metropolis: Flooding the Urban Ecology in Los Angeles.* Berkeley: University of California Press.

Rodriguez, Richard. 1982. *Hunger of Memory: The Education of Richard Rodriguez.* Boston, MA: David R. Godine.

Rodriguez, Richard. 2002. *Brown: The Last Discovery of America.* New York: Viking.

Starr, Kevin. 1973. *Americans and the California Dream: 1850–1915.* New York: Oxford University Press.

Chapter Three

I THOUGHT CALIFORNIA WOULD BE DIFFERENT: DEFINING CALIFORNIA THROUGH VISUAL CULTURE

Catherine Gudis

The title of this essay is drawn from a work by Los Angeles artist Raymond Pettibon entitled *I Thought California Would Be Different* (1989) (Figure 1). A tall, haunted-looking man in a broad-shouldered suit walks away dejectedly, infusing the piece with a sense of loss and disillusionment. As if taking long strides down mean streets, he conjures up the dark, unnamed symptoms of a postwar *noir* sensibility. Pettibon's slanted handwriting at the top underscores this, the comic-book nature of the work calling forth a milieu of shady, criminal characters and acts. As a cell from a comic strip shorn from its larger context, the work asks us, the viewers, to fill in the storyline, to be complicit in the act of making meaning. It also begs a series of questions. What did he – the man depicted, the artist, the viewer put in the position of narrator – expect from California? How have his expectations been defied? And if the place from which he walks is not *different*, then what is the *sameness* to which it has succumbed?

Imagine for a moment that the title of Pettibon's drawing were instead *I Thought Iowa Would Be Different*. Substitute "Texas," or even "New York" and the piece would not be so powerful. By this thought experiment the viewer will realize that "California," the word and the place, is a symbol. Its symbolic meanings are of course constructed by many people in various ways, through different media, and with assorted agendas and interests. Some are privately held, and others are publicly circulated with great repetition and at great expense. Though any construction necessarily flattens the complexity of life, and certainly cannot capture every political and economic tension, the sum total of these cultural fabrications does comprise the range of meanings one intends when one speaks of California.

The meaning of California has been framed, sometimes literally, by its visual culture. In visual culture lie the roots of many of the most commonly

Figure 1   Raymond Pettibon, *I Thought California Would Be Different*, 1989. Serigraph, 40 × 30 in. Laguna Art Museum Collection, gift of Ed Boswell. Courtesy Regen Projects, Los Angeles.

constructed tropes about California: as land of sunshine and *noir*, hope and doom, opportunity and failed promise. Though this master dichotomy is often mentioned, it is not sufficiently noted just how particular it is to the cultural construction of California as opposed to the fabrication of other places. By the end of this essay I hope the reader will at least acknowledge that a tenet of California's historical construction, held widely by all kinds of diverse peoples in radically different social and economic situations, is of a unique promise of California: the promise of mobility, a fresh start, access. Some tout the promise, some lament its shortcomings, but most constructions presume as if axiomatic that California is *supposed* to be different, a place where everyone *should* get a fair shake. As such, California has acted, more than any other place, as a symbol of American hopes, accomplishments, and failures.

The idea of California as a land of promise began with the arrival of those who chose to see the place as a tabula rasa, ignoring all cultures that had fabricated its meaning before. A frontier ideology of individualism, unlimited opportunity, and democracy fed this construction in the nineteenth century, while speculation (first gold then real estate) reinforced the ideas of the quick fix, fast money, and transience as hallmarks of California opportunity. The social, economic, and physical mobility at the heart of American views of liberal democracy and capitalism thus had even greater saliency in California, a place construed as vacant until populated by migrants and immigrants, and whose biggest growth came with mobile technologies of the train and car, and with visual media that compressed time and space, such as photography and film. In the twentieth century those same technologies propagated the image of California, and not just Hollywood, as a dream factory, a place of self-invention and mobility of all sorts.

The promise associated with California is the promise of the American Way put into a Petri dish and tested with microscopic intensity. California has stood in the twentieth and twenty-first centuries as the place where liberalism and capitalism's promise of egalitarian access to the pursuit of happiness glitters in the sunshine. Perhaps it glitters like fool's gold, but a perusal of California's visual culture over the last century reveals that people really do imagine California will somehow "be different" – and their disappointments are even more substantial for having so believed. It is the aim of this essay to describe the historical development of the meaning of California as it has been constructed within visual culture. In it I look at some dominant examples of twentieth-century California visual and material culture in their relationships to the fabrication of place identity, including Mission and Spanish Colonial architecture, Farm Security Administration photography, *noir* film, and contemporary art. Perhaps these few examples will illuminate at least the contour of a pattern of place *construction*, *critique*, and *reconfiguration* that has occurred in the visual culture of California, and that, despite all human failures, has succeeded in turning these 150,000 square miles into a symbol of American potential and hope.

Erasure and Construction

The construction of California through visual culture in the twentieth century was made possible by the displacement of previous California cultures. The erasure often worked implicitly and is what William Deverell has called the "whitewashing" of California. Creation in this vein invented an alternate historical narrative of California's past in which native and excluded populations were not so much overtly vanquished, but rather their participation in California history was rendered picturesque and ultimately insignificant. The Mission Revival movement in architecture embodied this kind of erasure/creation, in which California's surrender came by the persuasions of noble conquistadors and men of the cloth. Later, the larger Spanish Colonial movement continued the same kind of implicit erasure, making California into a tablet scraped bare and ready for writing, a tabula rasa.

The Mission Revival craze of the 1890s to the 1910s comprised the origin and core of the more generalized style of Spanish Colonial architecture that eventually superseded it. The origins of the Mission style itself lay partially in the *Ramona*-mania that followed publication in 1884 of Helen Hunt Jackson's sentimentalist novel of the star-crossed life and loves of an orphaned half-Indian beauty named Ramona. Although intended by Jackson to galvanize public support for the plight of Indians and Mexicans in California, the book's runaway success sprang more from its romantic images of a fading rancho lifestyle set in a pre-industrial picturesque landscape. Jackson's descriptions of an enchanted Arcadia of fragrant orange groves, vibrant sunsets over verdant mesas, and white adobe haciendas with red-tiled roofs were immensely reproducible, and jibed well with the imagery and rhetoric already employed by railroad companies, tourist hotels, and land speculators advertising southern California as a "land of sunshine" with year-round curative powers and agricultural bounties (Starr 1985: 45–9, 54). The book also put California's 21 crumbling missions from Sonoma to San Diego onto tourist maps and into popular culture through commemorative items, from postcards and paintings to products and plays (McWilliams 1973: 72–5; DeLyser 2005). Boosters' search for a usable past by which to sell California to tourists and settlers was complete: missions served as "authentic" references to a past that began with Europeans, was unique to California, and was exceptionally well suited to being reproduced in two and three dimensions (Gebhard 1980: 138) (Figure 2).

Frank Miller, a mover and shaker regionally and in Riverside, birthplace of the citrus industry and by 1895 the wealthiest city per capita in California, also recognized the sales potential of the Mission Revival. He played a role in city planning, owned a local trolley line, and championed the use of Mission Revival as central to the city's identity. At first he may have taken his cues from the railroads, which described the actual missions in their tourist guidebooks, then advertised them further through the architecture of their train depots, which were among the first buildings in California to self-consciously employ the limited repertoire of elements associated with

Figure 2   Promotional brochure, California Parlor Car Tours Company, *c.*1930.
Tom Zimmerman Collection.

the Mission style – stucco surfaces, tiled roofs, scalloped gables, quatrefoil
windows, arched loggia (Weitze 1978: 194, 5–6; Gebhard 1980: 139, 141).
With the depots setting the stage, a tourist to Riverside would disembark
from the train, guidebook in hand, looking for the ghosts of the Franciscan
padres and Ramona. Miller first advocated the style for Riverside's Sherman
Indian Institute, a boarding school for Native Americans, located on land
next to his train station, and later for the city's public library, cultural institutions, and municipal buildings (Patterson 1971: 240). Conveniently, Miller's
trolley went from Sherman Indian Institute to his hotel downtown, a logical
fit for tourists wanting to see the whole gamut of regional history, from
"actual" Indians (in the process of being assimilated) to orange groves to
symbols of Spanish-California history found throughout the city's graceful
Mission and Spanish Colonial architecture.

The *pièce de résistance* for the tour, and any sojourn to the area, was the
Mission Inn, which Miller opened in 1903 after extensive alterations and

additions by architect Arthur Benton to the Glenwood Tavern, an adobe structure that had been Miller's family home, boarding house, and modest hotel in the previous decades. The Mission Inn was Miller's obsession through the 1930s, and he added to it incessantly with arcades, bell towers, red tile roofs, Mexican mosaics, patios, courtyards, a cathedral, and, in the Cloister Wing, a warren of underground galleries called the Catacombs that housed a small portion of his vast art collection. Though the hotel was neither an actual mission nor even near one, Miller built its identity and that of the city around a polyglot of Mexican, Indian, and Spanish references with a fair number of Moorish and Byzantine details thrown in for good measure, funneled through the symbolic use of Mission and Spanish Colonial architecture. Non-discriminating tourists often failed to realize this, willingly embracing the mission drama as historically connected to the city.

The Mission Revival style reached its apotheosis by the time of the 1915 Panama–California Exposition held in San Diego, when it became subsumed by the more lavish architectural umbrella of "Spanish Colonial." Visitors to the San Diego fair at Balboa Park entered a carefully constructed *tableau vivant* that enacted a romanticized Spanish Colonial history of California (Kropp 2006: 126). Richly ornamented buildings were bedecked in a resplendent revival of Spanish baroque, Plateresque, and Moorish details (Figure 3). While a previous generation of fairs had employed monumental, classical motifs, contemporary observers praised the Panama–California Exposition for its adherence to architectural styles of "native significance" "peculiarly belonging to California and reaching back to the glorious period of its inception" (Neuhaus 1916: 11). One guidebook claimed: "Here was something which was at one with the land and its people – a visible expression of the collective soul of the Southwest" (Brinton 1916). President of the Panama–California Exposition Company, Gilbert Aubrey Davidson, described the fair as such: "Here is pictured in this happy combination of splendid temples, the story of the friars, the thrilling tale of the pioneers, the orderly conquest of commerce, coupled with the hopes of an El Dorado where life can expand in this fragrant land of opportunity" (Amero 1990). Selective and deracinated, Davidson's historical progression employed the past to invoke a golden future. The idea of conquest is shorn from its violent context and from social strife, and includes Spanish missionaries, white pioneers, and capitalist developers on an innocent quest to bring order and civilization to ultimate ends: an El Dorado get-rich-quick scheme.

Within 10 years of the San Diego fair, over 15 cities would appropriate the Spanish style, including Ojai, Palos Verdes, Rancho Santa Fe (north of San Diego), Montecito, and San Clemente. Scores of individual contractors and tract developers built Spanish-styled houses, while homeowners were

Figure 3   Cover of *The Official Guide and Descriptive Book of the Panama California International Exposition, San Diego, 1916.* Reproduced by permission of the San Diego Public Library.

sold pattern books and kits to build their own (McMillian 2002: 32–5; Kropp 2006: 159–206). When Santa Barbara was devastated by an earthquake in 1925, it was rebuilt in the Spanish theme, with the courthouse and mission centerpieces of the city; comprehensive zoning laws and, later, architectural review boards safeguarded elements of the comprehensive design to be followed on every level, down to mailboxes and trash cans (Sagarena 2002) (Figure 4).

Figure 4   Santa Barbara County Courthouse, built 1926–9. Photo by Herman Schultheis. Security Pacific Collection/Los Angeles Public Library.

As California developed in the 1920s and 1930s with the rise of the automobile, its linear expansion outward from the old central business districts most often was marked by residential, commercial, and public buildings boasting Spanish Colonial elements, especially in southern California. The first drive-in markets in the country, the most fanciful gasoline stations, and commercial centers of the new car culture, such as Westwood Village in Los Angeles, employed the style as a means of creating buildings as advertisements for civic identity, the automobile lifestyle, and the strip itself. In Westwood, the red-tiled roofs and mosaic domes of offices and retail spaces were augmented by drive-in restaurants and gas stations with rooftop pylons and blade signs that could attract motorists from the main thoroughfare in the area, Wilshire Boulevard. All along Wilshire, Spanish-styled buildings sprang up, as if to invest mobile audiences with a sense of history that staked a claim to the regional past of land grants and ranchos. But could the faux Spanish-Moorish gas station whose female attendants were clad in Turkish costume really be construed as providing meaningful connections to place identity?

While it may have developed in order to forge place-specific historical connections to the past, over the century Spanish Colonialism became an emblem of large-scale suburbanization and strip development. As in the 1920s, when the style became a means of cleaning up highways and byways marred by ad hoc and hastily constructed gas stations and eateries, by the end of the century it was a marker of upper-crust tract developments such as Mission Viejo (which has no historical connection to an old mission) that sought to distinguish themselves from a previous generation of postwar "ticky tacky" box houses, and strip malls that forge a cohesive look through a repetition of vaguely Spanish-Mediterranean motifs.

But where does this lead us when we think about the role of invented traditions, fabricated identities, and the ceaseless repetition of visual tropes? Though these are inventions of marketers, they function as more than just marketing tools. They create meaning for the place symbol "California." The deeply circumscribed historical narrative evoked by the mission and the California colonial past was of course critical to the centralization of power in the hands of mostly white civic leaders, boosters, and real-estate developers. But equally critical to those ends was the repetition of visual styles. If the life of a Spanish grandee was the life to which a Californian was asked to aspire, then the availability of nearly identical Spanish Colonial homes and townships was critical to the success of that California dream. This repetition of visual cues helped Californians forge connections between past and present, people and places, and widely divergent racial and ethnic groups. Carey McWilliams's statement in the 1940s thus still holds fast, that the Mission–Spanish style was an "evocation of a mythology which could give people a sense of continuity in a region long characterized by rapid social dislocations" (McWilliams 1973: 71).

Critique: Failed Promises

Even as California was being fashioned by boosters, their image of California as a "land of sunshine" and white Arcadia was being offset by more pessimistic paroxysms. From writers and artists to photographers and filmmakers bent on capturing the social tensions and failed promises of the California dream, regional representations were seen through a lens more darkly hued, creating a chiaroscuro where rosy optimism dissolved into despair, mobility stalled, and faith – in human nature, government largess, commercial enterprise, and the American Way – doubted. Historian Mike Davis most famously labeled the contrasting depictions as a "master dialectic of sunshine and *noir*," ushering in a revisionist history that gained resonance in the years following his publication of *City of Quartz* (1990), as riots, fires, floods, and earthquakes ravaged the region. Davis viewed the Depression and its shattering of a "broad strata of the dream-addicted Los

Angeles middle classes" as a turning point for *noir* sensibilities. Indeed, the failure of both Progressive politics and Depression-era New Deal policies fueled an extensive body of work that depicted California as anything but a peaceful, verdant utopia. Rather, it was the site of unfulfilled promises.

Perhaps the most iconic and widely reproduced of the Depression era's documentary works was Dorothea Lange's *Migrant Mother* (1936), which was part of a larger series of photographs of rural agricultural workers she took for the Farm Security Administration (FSA). Based in her home city of San Francisco throughout her tenure with the FSA, Lange became best known for Dust Bowl photographs, though the greater proportion of her photographs were of California, featuring the results of Okie migration and that of other workers (Gordon 2006a: 704, 701). The unnamed 32-year-old mother of seven who was featured in *Migrant Mother* was among the "destitute pea pickers" Lange met in Nipomo, California, where families huddled together in makeshift tents and lean-tos in frozen, desiccated fields that yielded few crops, awaiting aid or a climatic shift that never came.

Lange's other images of jalopies overstuffed with the life possessions of families encamped at the side of seemingly endless highways west similarly suggested unyielding landscapes and bleak prospects. They provided stark contrast to previous decades of promotional literature featuring smiling tourists, truckloads of oversized oranges, and lush landscaping. And though chambers of commerce continued to pitch the climate and good life of California, their ads included a caveat in fine print: good views were more easily had than good jobs – don't come if you expect the latter. More aggressive in asserting the same message were citizens' groups organized to curb the "invasion" of indigent hordes (Lange & Taylor 2000: 143) and policemen (Gordon 2006a: 714) from Los Angeles who formed "bum blockades" at the Arizona border hundreds of miles away to turn back migrants (see also Rick Wartzman's chapter in this volume).

Lange's images refuted the myth of California as the land of opportunity and redefined its role in the new west. She and her husband Paul Taylor, an agricultural economist from the University of California at Berkeley, documented the bleak state of agricultural affairs in California and its impact on workers as an index for what was happening nationwide. In their 1939 book *American Exodus*, the title an ironic reference to California as the Promised Land, Taylor and Lange explained that "[I]ndustrialized agriculture has its fullest development in California," where more than one-third of the nation's large-scale farms could be found. This was their pithy caption for a photograph featuring row upon row of mechanically tilled fields, whose furrows reveal the marked remains of the tractors' tread. Nearby were other images in which crouched and stooped workers do the handwork behind the machines, their bent bodies more malleable, expendable, and transient, in service and secondary to a primarily industrial enterprise. This was the

Figure 5   Dorothea Lange, "Billboard along US 99, behind which three destitute families of migrants are camped, Kern County, California," 1938. Library of Congress (LC-USF34-018619-C).

fate of the new pioneer on the new frontier, a "large, landless, and mobile proletariat" (Lange & Taylor 2000: 135), for whom settling the land was less an option than seasonally squatting on it.

A third category of Lange's photographs in *American Exodus* as well as her larger body of work for the FSA featured the highway, especially California's US 101 and 99. A paved expanse of concrete extends into the horizon as a visual analogue to the industrially tilled fields and its overwhelmed denizens, some of whom are on foot, are slow or stalled in their efforts to make it in America. Though her sober sociological portraits aimed to reveal economic injustices, Lange was not above employing sharp-edged irony to do so. Against Southern Pacific's billboard "Next Time Take the Train–Relax," with its image of a reclining, suited businessman, she juxtaposes two migrant workers in jeans and jackets, laden with suitcases, walking the dusty road. Underneath another billboard for the Southern Pacific, "Travel while you sleep," she shows migrant families setting up their impromptu housing, their swatch of canvas tenting strung to the back of the billboard, the litter-strewn roadside now their domicile (Figure 5). In these photographs, the migrants are on the road but their mobility marks the antithesis of that which is represented in the advertisement, their poverty a rejoinder to capitalism's vacant promises of social and economic traction.

Lange posed rootlessness and mobility as a threat to the ability of migrant workers to exercise their rights as citizens, and used photography as both an investigative and activist tool. How could the dislocated forge communities, build unions, lobby for their rights? How could the displaced garner state and local aid when they were not in residence? Many of Lange's photos were widely reproduced and therefore had the potential to galvanize political action or at least stir audiences. The same could not be said for the series of nearly 800 photographs that Lange was commissioned to take by the War Relocation Authority beginning in 1942. Her assignment was to document the round-up and relocation of California residents of Japanese heritage, who, by the authority of Executive Order 9066, were declared a threat to national security following the bombing of Pearl Harbor. Yet her photos never saw the light of day during the war, squirreled away by the army and quietly deposited in the National Archives for undisclosed reasons (Gordon 2006b: 5–6).

Lange's internment photos speak of failed California promises in even more poignant terms than her FSA photographs, perhaps because the indignities appear to be directed against comfortably middle-class people, well integrated into urbane society, and suffering only the adversities that have been federally imposed. Signs and symbols of mobility and its antithesis dominate the series, which begins with Lange's pre-internment photographs of everyday Japanese American San Franciscans who have embraced the American Way. They are patriotic, hard-working, and upwardly mobile; there are no images of the down and out, and a middle-class gentility infuses many of the domestic scenes (Gordon 2006b: 28–9) (Figure 6). They've done everything right, making it in America against the odds. Yet here they stand in subsequent photos, young and old, US citizens and residents alike, dressed in their best traveling clothes, but collected and tagged like the suitcases and bundles that surround them as they await relocation. Trains and buses taking them to distant "camps" here indicate enclosure and removal rather than carefree tourism, as Lange sarcastically illustrates in one photo of internees' bundles stacked on a sidewalk in front of a Bekins Storage ad bearing a picture of a cruise ship and a smiling woman, who claims, "Such a load off my mind, Bekins stored my things."

Lange's photographs indicate that race trumps class, and point to the illusory nature of the good life for those of color, no matter their citizenship. Although some eventually returned, the removal of Japanese Americans from California's cities and agricultural areas was just one means by which white political, economic, and social dominance asserted itself. Lange's photos and their focus on middle-class Japanese Americans

Figure 6   Dorothea Lange, "Mountain View, California. Scene at Santa Clara home of the Shibuya family who raised select chrysanthemums for eastern markets. Madoka Shibuya (right), 25, was a student at Stanford Medical School when the picture was taken on April 18, 1942. Evacuees of Japanese ancestry will be housed in War Relocation Authority centers for the duration." National Archives (NWDNS-210-g-c121).

dramatically illustrate this assertion, while the removal of the photographs from public view demonstrates yet another whitewashing and historical erasure.

Suspicion about the veracity of working- and middle-class dreams was even more significant in the domain of film. Although Depression and wartime Hollywood fare was prone to frothy escapism, in the 1940s and 1950s a collection of loosely related movies retrospectively labeled "film noir" used California as a significant setting for the demise of liberal/capitalist ideology. Frequently filmed on location in black and white, *noir*'s California context was where individual and societal corruption, greed, criminality, and obsession festered in the long shadows cast by the bright sun. From the craggy cliffs at ocean's edge, *noir* protagonists could either watch the sunset or be catapulted over the precipice, their comeuppance for believing in America's dream and Hollywood's illusory promises of easy money and social mobility. Trying to make it in the land of sunshine, in other words, came with a high moral, social, and physical price tag.

It's not just that *noir*'s tales of murderous relationships between strong-women-gone-bad and the similarly bad-men-who-love-them ruined the reputation of the places where the stories were most often set – Los Angeles, in particular, the "dystopianization" of which, as Mike Davis says, did more to undermine the early boosters' view of the region than anything before it (1990: 21). Rather, *noir* served as a means of spatial representation and memorialization, mapping social anxieties and urban transformations of wartime and postwar culture (Dimendberg 2004: 10–13). Film historian Norman Klein explains that *noir* at once created a "white male social imaginary" in which "the crime on dark streets stands in for the fears about foreigners, jobs, speculation, and cheap hype" and, by extension, urged "white flight" from such despair (1997: 80). Fragments of the changing urban landscape populate *noir*, the heyday of which was simultaneous with the growth of suburbs and urban renewal schemes. For instance, the downtown Los Angeles neighborhood of Bunker Hill, featured in the film *Kiss Me Deadly* (1955), among others, was mostly depicted as down at the heels, populated by elderly immigrants, criminals, and the ne'er-do-well. It is a portrayal of spaces left behind by the car, the road, and the suburb, its dark decay a de facto endorsement of the redevelopment plans that would soon raze the buildings and level the site, even as the film commemorated those spaces by capturing them forever (Dimendberg 2004: 162–3). This is the *noir* promotional, a marketing of the flip side of the boosters' promises of sunshine, Eden, and white Protestantism (Klein 1997: 55). Fictional film became the real evidence of an urban environment more safely experienced by suburbanized audiences from the plush seats of a movie theater, and these became visual souvenirs of buildings and a built environment "bulldozed out of existence" in the 1960s (Dimendberg 2004: 121, 152).

Suburban spaces suffer equally in the world of *noir*. The story of *Double Indemnity* (1944), based on the novel by James Cain, begins on the sunny streets of suburban Los Angeles, where off-the-rack Spanish Colonial houses line the block as children play outside. The image of domestic tranquility is quickly revealed to be inauthentic, as ersatz as the historical style in which the houses are constructed. Façade is soon shattered by adultery, greed, and murder. Sick of her soused, dull husband and his tight grip on her spending, Phyllis Dietrichson in *Double Indemnity* lies in wait for someone to come along to help her plot another murder (she has done it before); easily corruptible insurance salesman Walter Neff is that someone, himself in wait for something to revivify a life of small claims. Is *this* the

California Dream or American Way? So much for the safety and stability of the suburbs, now the stomping ground of white middle-class anomie and worse.

Indeed, the urban–suburban condition and the social and moral vacuity of mid-twentieth-century commercial life were frequently conjoined themes for California *noir*. We first meet Walter Neff as he careens down the dark streets of nighttime LA's central business district. He gets to his office at the Pacific All-Risk Insurance Company and the camera pans over repeating rows of identical desks, identically equipped in the best spirit of Taylorized managerial efficiency (Naremore 1998: 88; Dimendberg 2004: 174). Rationalization is a hallmark of Neff's profession, in which human risks are reduced to equations and lives are financially quantified. Bureaucracy and technology in modern society have replaced human interaction; even Neff's life confession is made to his Dictaphone. Beating this system becomes Neff's central motivation. His quest is a desperate attempt to feel something and get somewhere. It offers him a kind of repersonalization or reinvigoration of selfhood lost in the commercial and business culture of mid-twentieth-century life.

Indeed, Walter's daily life treks him through a southern California landscape of consumption. He assesses with considerable detail the Dietrichson home's canned Spanish Colonial décor, putting its class value down to a style "everyone was nuts about ten or fifteen years ago" and its price at about $30,000. He takes a drive when he doesn't know what to do with himself; to kill time he sometimes bowls, or drinks beer at drive-in restaurants, itself an invention of Southern California car culture. Even his clandestine meetings with Phyllis are at another California landmark of consumption, Jerry's Market, the supermarket being another Los Angeles front runner, where towers of mass-produced and packaged goods offer the ultimate anonymity for the conspirators (Figure 7). Both the private and the public spaces through which Walter circulates, as well as the car that carries him, are standardized and mass-produced. In order to be marketed and made available to the widest possible set of California dream chasers, they have to be. Accordingly, these are the spaces in which social and moral alienation fester and through which Los Angeles is portrayed, as critic James Naremore has written, as a "dangerously seductive El Dorado – a center of advanced capitalism, instrumental reason, and death" (1998: 83, 88–9).

Reconstruction through Art and Activism

Despite all the criticism, the postwar commercial landscape and consumer culture provided the subject and source material for art as far-ranging as

Figure 7   Still from *Double Indemnity* (1944). Paramount Pictures/Photofest.
© Paramount Pictures.

beat and assemblage works in San Francisco and "finish fetish," pop, and
conceptual works in Los Angeles, all of which drew international media
attention to the West Coast. Critics scratched their heads at what was
unseating the hegemony of the East Coast art establishment. How had
California – the "home of nuts," "the palm-studded land of Disney and
DayGlo . . . and movieland Babylon," "an intellectual desert" – become
the "second city" and wellspring for new art (Schrank 2004: 663; Fox
2000: 274; Plagens 1999: 155)? It was isolated from New York and
Europe, barren of history much less an art historical legacy, and lacked a
discernible center to serve as a crucible for artistic creation.

   In trying to explain the new California art, critics trotted out virtually
every fabrication that had been used by earlier boosters to characterize the
identity of the region. Peter Plagens, summarizing the postwar scene in
1974, identified sunshine as the muse for West Coast artists, and claimed
that the high-gloss, hard-edged geometric abstractions and works using
Plexiglas and aluminum reflected the "desert air, youthful cleanliness," and
"optimism" of the coast, not to mention its superficial lifestyles. The
California good life was why, Plagens and other critics suggested, works

Figuer 8   Von Dutch (Kenneth Howard) custom-painted car for Barris Kustom
Industries, 1960s. Courtesy Greg Sharp.

by Bay Area abstractionists and Southern California minimalists were said
to be less intellectual and angst-ridden than their New York counterparts.
How could weighty art be created in such good weather, big studios, and
attractive locales (Plagens 1999: 119–20, 41–2)? And how deep could art
be that shared its methods and materials (resins, plastics, and fiberglass)
with surfers and "Kalifornia kustom kar kulture," as Tom Wolfe (1963)
called the work of hot rodders Ed "Big Daddy" Roth, who used fiberglass
bodywork, and Von Dutch, whose airbrushed pin stripes, flames, and flying
eyeballs inspired generations of graphic artists and customizers (Figure 8)?
Indeed, the categories coined to describe much of this new work, such as
"finish fetish" and the "LA Look," accentuated the supposed superficiality
of West Coast artists, who were thus set off from their more aesthetically
profound East Coast brethren.
      Instead of refuting these characterizations, California artists embraced
and enhanced them. Ceramicist Kenneth Price, who used auto lacquer to

Figure 9   Announcement for exhibition "Kenneth Price," Ferus Gallery, Los Angeles, 1961. © Kenneth Price.

finish his non-functional "pottery," advertised his 1961 exhibition at Ferus (the LA gallery open from 1957 to 1966 that helped put California art on the map) with a poster of himself on a surfboard (Figure 9). That same year, painter Billy Al Bengston, whose "canvases" were sprayed polymer plastics on hard industrial materials such as Masonite, aluminum, and Formica, used a photo of himself straddling a motorcycle on the cover of his Ferus exhibition catalogue. Judy Chicago also thumbed her nose at traditional sources for weighty art: she attended auto body school to learn to spray paint, then hung on the gallery wall the hood of a 1964 Corvair that she had decorated with acrylic lacquer, a projection of both literal heft and gender bending (Plagens 1999: 146; Whiting 2006: 83–4) (Figure 10). All of these artists took function and decoration as serious artistic

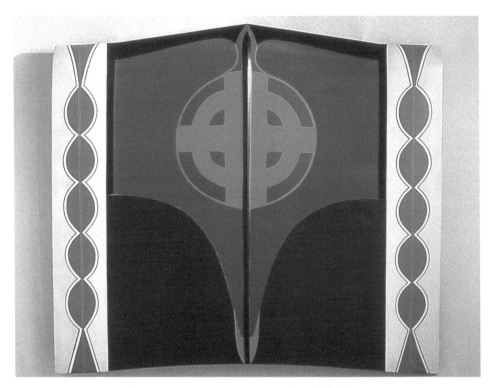

Figure 10 Judy Chicago, *Car Hood*, 1964. Sprayed acrylic on car hood. Collection of Rad and Elaine Sutnar, Los Angeles. © Judy Chicago. Photo © Through the Flower Archives.

strategies, and played with the tensions between handcraft, space-age technology, and traditional fine arts. Perhaps most importantly, they knew from advertising, the Hollywood dream factory, and even the architecture they saw all around them, the importance of mining the repetitious and mass-produced tropes of popular visual culture for their own ends.

Despite the critics' claims and artists' promotionals, the Los Angeles scene was not all artifice nor did it spring up as a desert bloom just at the moment of critics' attention. Rather, as Sarah Schrank has argued, it "benefited from decades of struggle between diverse creative communities and Los Angeles's conservative authorities" (Schrank 2004: 664). Though from the turn of the century to the 1920s, boosters saw civic art as part of promoting LA as a fertile paradise, their visions were challenged in the 1930s by modernist murals and exhibitions by Mexican, Jewish, and African American artists that were met with diffidence or whitewashed out of existence – David Alfaro Siqueiros's 1932 *America Tropical*, a symbolic depiction of oppressive American imperialism, among them. Racism and red baiting then wracked public art programs in the 1950s. So it was only in the 1960s that artists gathering at Ferus Gallery and at Venice coffeehouses began operating successfully "on the margins of Los Angeles's civic art world," where they created their own centralized communities from which a robust art market eventually emerged (Schrank 2004: 665–73). Despite the urban sprawl and reputed isolation of Los Angeles, artists came together to form a scene that had a history, though itself somewhat whitewashed: most of the artists affiliated with Ferus, for instance, were white men (ibid.: 673–84).

Sprawl, decentralization, placelessness, and repetition of architectural visual cues were central to the work of Ed Ruscha, part of the same stable of Ferus artists as Bengston and Price. In *Twentysix Gasoline Stations* (1962), *Some Los Angeles Apartments* (1965), *Every Building on the Sunset Strip* (1966), and *Thirtyfour Parking Lots in Los Angeles* (1967), he takes ordinary and repetitive features of the commercial landscape and calls them art by framing them, but hardly treats them as such. Taken from the windows of moving cars and helicopters, the photographs seem cropped by the randomness of the camera's angle and are labeled typographically with their geographic location and nothing else (Wolf 2004: 139, 144). What becomes stressed in these photographs are the ways in which the urban environment is mediated and standardized by industrial technology (the car, the camera, mass production techniques). Geometry prevails, perhaps a jab at California modernist architecture and the ways its high art forms have filtered down to the masses in wildly different ways than the "masters" approved. Some photographs from *Los Angeles Apartments*, for instance, depict the antithesis of the internationally renowned California Case Study House program of the 1940s and 1950s. Instead of pristine steel-and-glass cubes, Ruscha gives us boxy beige stucco, dingbat apartments built right over their parking with exotic names which almost mock residents' tired dreams of mobility, leisure, and California's Mediterranean idyll life: the Capri, Algiers, St. Tropez, Fountain Blu (*sic*) (Figure 11).

In his version of documentary photography, Ruscha does not provide social commentary or a call to political action, as Dorothea Lange or other FSA photographers did in the 1930s. Gone, too, are film noir's moralistic associations of urban and suburban spatial diffusion, or LA as the setting for crime and despair. Ruscha has no bone to pick with the illusory promises of Hollywood and its glittery façade. This he accepts for what it is. "All I was after," explains Ruscha, speaking of *Every Building on the Sunset Strip*, "was that store-front plane. . . . A store-front plane of a Western town is just paper, and everything behind is just nothing" (Brougher 2000: 164). He is at once defining the Sunset Strip as a Hollywood back lot of stage sets, and analogizing the practice of photography as a fabrication of fiction, its own kind of façade of reality. In this way, he reflects on how

Figure 11   Ed Ruscha, *St. Tropez*, 1965/2003. Gelatin silver print, 7⅜ × 7⅜ in. Originally published in *Some Los Angeles Apartments* (1965). © Ed Ruscha, courtesy of Gagosian Gallery.

meaning and place identity are constructed – from surface glances and viewers' predilections or, as he puts it, from "a collage in your mind of what this place is all about" (Wolf 2004: 128).

Ruscha's mapping of LA was also simultaneous with the work of urban theorists Donald Appleyard, Kevin Lynch, and John Myers, whose book *A View from the Road* (1964) declared "road-watching" a delight and the highway a work of art, and sought to use motorists' cognitive experiences of driving in order to design way-finding systems. Like Ruscha and his cohort of artists, they legitimized a vehicular rather than pedestrian orientation to urban space and, as Lynch had found in his previous work, *Image of the City* (1960), understood that people construct "mental maps" of places that derive from their experiences and memories of commercial signage, landmarks, or other notable features. Lynch discovered that Los Angeles did not fare well in terms of its "imageability," or the ease with which residents could create a coherent sense of place. Rather, they talked about its sprawl and their disorientation: "It's as if you were going somewhere for a long time, and when you got there you discovered there was nothing there, after all." The same could be said for the experience of reading Ruscha's books, which document the ways in which standardized repeating forms render the city placeless (Whiting 2006: 102–5). Unlike Lynch (or even architects Robert Venturi, Denise Scott Brown, and Steven Izenour, whose 1968 study of the Las Vegas Strip was published as *Learning from Las Vegas*), Ruscha's appreciation of the aesthetic and communicative powers of commercial signage and vernacular architecture was not intended to advocate design solutions to urban problems nor to serve as a polemic for postmodern architecture and urbanism. In this sense, his work was disengaged from the social activism and urban theorizing of the era, his imagery sheared from its larger neighborhood and social context. Indeed, his works are for the most part bereft of people altogether, as if he means somehow to capture and reclaim the visual culture itself.

In the popular press of the 1960s and 1970s, social landscapes that had been hidden from public view suddenly made news, as ethnic and racial minorities, women, and pacifist activists attempted to reclaim representational and public space. Though in 1960s San Francisco, photographs and footage of Haight Street hippies and "love-ins" depicted a kooky countercultural California, these images were tempered by others featuring stick-wielding police poised to decimate campus and street agitation against the Vietnam War. In Southern California, the growth of the military-industrial complex during the war sharpened political and racial tensions, with defense jobs going disproportionately to whites and Asians while blacks and Mexican Americans were being drafted with equal disproportion into the military (Landauer 2006: 4–7). It was in this context that the Los Angeles neighborhood of Watts erupted into violence on August 11, 1965, after an incident between a white police officer and a black motorist suspected of drunk driving. Over six days, people across the nation watched from their living rooms an "unscheduled 'spectacular,'" according to Budd Schulberg: "the damnedest television show ever put on the tube." South Central Los Angeles was on fire, smoke billowing from blocks of commercial frontage (Figure 12). Rioters ran past burned-out cars down ravaged streets, looting "establishments that had been quietly looting the community on the installment plan over the years" (Grenier 2006: 142).

These broadcasts, the first urban rebellions to be documented on the small screen (Massood 1999: 21), finally brought to public attention the depth and despair of black discontent. Though African American migrants

Figure 12 Buildings burn during Watts riots, Los Angeles, 1965. Herald Examiner Collection/Los Angeles Public Library.

of the 1940s and 1950s had suffered similar hardships to white migrants of previous decades, the government had sent no photographers to document the black urban *Migrant Mother*. Only extraordinary amounts of violence and property damage could bring cameras to the devastated black communities of Los Angeles, and even this live coverage of the Watts riot reduced decades of poverty, employment and housing discrimination, and police brutality, as well as government and media indifference, to the ephemeral level of current events. The onscreen spectacle appeared suddenly, chaotically, without a past or future. The cameras and news helicopters, which had done their part in creating the sounds and sights of war, abandoned these devastated communities as quickly as they had come to exploit their destruction. The same would later characterize the televised 1992 Rodney King uprisings (Gooding-Williams 1993: 2).

   As the fires smoldered and died, artist Noah Purifoy and musician Judson Powell, Area residents and directors of the Watts Towers art center, "ventured into the rubble" and collected charred wood, melted neon signage,

Figure 13   Cover of the exhibition catalogue, *Junk Art: 66 Signs of Neon*, 1966. Collection of the California African American Museum, courtesy Noah Purifoy Foundation, c/o 354 So. Harvard Blvd., Los Angeles, CA 90020.

twisted metal, and other debris that they and six other artists used to create works of assemblage that toured internationally under the exhibition title "Junk Art: 66 Signs of Neon" (Whiting 2006: 159) (Figure 13). These were the detritus of commercial culture, including broken-down car parts, smashed television sets, office equipment, and store display mannequins. While the show implied that from the ashes Watts could rise phoenix-like, the "junk" scavenged and recast as art, nevertheless it also reminded viewers of frustrated desires and impeded access routes to American affluence (Schrank 2004: 686; Whiting 2006: 159–64).

By the 1970s, a group of independent African and African American filmmakers, referred to as the "LA School" or "LA Rebellion," began to use Watts as "an alternative site for cinematic production." Separate from the movie industry, these filmmakers sought representational space for recasting Hollywood's racial stereotypes of black culture and black urban space (Young

Figure 14   Still from Charles Burnett, *Killer of Sheep*, 1977.

2006: 220–2). Charles Burnett, in *Killer of Sheep* (1977), employed non-actors from the community, location shooting, and his experiences and observations growing up in Watts. Though a work of fiction, the film takes the appearance of documentary to show the contours of working-class life in post-Civil Rights, post-rebellion Watts. Burnett portrays the place as disconnected from the larger world, the other side of American apartheid (James 1998: 34; Massood 1999: 26–7). At its center is Stan, the counter and killer of sheep. He is an insomniac who works in a slaughterhouse to support his family of four. Stan suffers from an advanced state of existential crisis: he is immobilized by his stultifying job, his broken-down car and failed attempts to fix it, and his inability, despite hard work, to get ahead (Massood 1999: 35–6). In fact, the film's unifying tension (it lacks a traditional narrative arc) is how he will keep from sliding into crime and poverty. The film's only act of heroism is daily survival (Young 2006: 214). The physical landscape of Watts underscores Stan's alienation and emotional torpor; as David James describes, it is "flat, monotonous, dilapidated, of limited imageability, and with no conspicuous internal differentiation" (1998: 34). Burnett thus replaces Hollywood high drama with everyday reality, its heroes with working stiffs, its landmarks with vacant lots (Figure 14). Instead of an overt political message, he offers documentary images to be read. As he intercuts shots of Watts and the slaughterhouse, Stan

Figure 15 Protestors led by César Chávez (fourth from left), leader of the United Farm Workers, rally on behalf of striking grape workers, Delano, California, 1966. © 1976 George Ballis/Take Stock.

and the sheep, Burnett forces viewers to question just who is being brought to slaughter and how (Young 2006: 243). If, according to Dorothea Lange, the biblical Exodus story had characterized the hopes of Depression migrants, Burnett surmised that for residents of Watts, life in California had become a passion and sacrifice like that of Christ the lamb. This is not a sunny view of Los Angeles but neither is it simply *noir* or ironic. In the hands of Burnett, everyday reality is more historically complex, more humanizing, and yet in its own mythological way more transcendental.

The Chicano liberation movement, which came of age in the same year as the Watts riots with César Chávez's United Farm Workers (UFW) grape strike in the San Joaquin Valley, set out to expose the same forces of institutional racism, government indifference, and housing, education, and employment discrimination that operated in California's black communities (see, for context, Miriam Pawel's essay in this volume). Similarly, participants in the Chicano movement took to the streets as part of their reclamation of public space, memory, identity, and history. The poster and other graphics became a primary tool of communication to mobilize masses of people, first for UFW strikes, marches, and boycotts and then for student walkouts, anti-war rallies, and other political events (Goldman & Ybarro-Frausto 1991: 83–91) (Figure 15). Murals, too, emerged as a

Figure 16 Esteban Villa/RCAF Mujeres Muralistas, *Cosmic Woman/Mujer Cósmica and Female Intelligentsia* (*The Women Hold Up the Universe*) mural at Chicano Park, San Diego, 1985. Photo © James Prigoff, courtesy of California Ethnic and Multicultural Archives, Dept. of Special Collections, Donald Davidson Library, University of California, Santa Barbara.

means of publicly recording historical events and establishing a Chicano stake to the community and place identity. Judy Baca and the Social and Public Art Center produced *The Great Wall of Los Angeles* (1978–83) on the concrete wash of the Tujunga Wash Drainage Canal of the Los Angeles River. There was also the ongoing painting of murals in Chicano Park beneath the freeway interchange that in the mid-1960s cut through a Chicano neighborhood in San Diego (Brookman 1991: 185) (Figure 16). Taken together, the painted and printed graphics of the movement, whether plastered on walls and telephone poles, painted onto buildings, distributed as handouts, or presented in newly formed art collectives across the state, were a means of creating a public sphere where issues of politics and identity could be inscribed on the urban landscape and a collective ideology forged (Lipsitz 2001).

Early in the movement, Andrew Zermeño's posters and cartoons in the UFW paper, *El Malcriado: The Voice of the Farmworker*, developed an iconography that included easily recognizable emblems of Mexican culture, to which were added in the 1970s images expressing solidarity with other oppressed groups internationally. These also drew upon the shared history of Mexicans and Mexican Americans. Among them were the stylized black eagle with outstretched wings stepped like an Aztec pyramid which became part of the UFW logo, the Virgen de Guadalupe, calaveras (skeletons), revolutionary Mexican and Cuban figures (Zapato, Che Guevara), and pre-Columbian motifs (Romo 2001: 95–9). Such images carved out a space and a language of opposition, insurgency, and affirmation of a history predating European conquest (Goldman & Ybarro-Frausto 1991: 83–91). It marked the redemption from historical erasures.

Formative for many artists involved in the movement were two events in East Los Angeles: the high school student "blowouts" of 1968, in which students staged a walkout to protest substandard education in the barrio, and the 1970 National Chicano Moratorium, in which violence broke out between police and the 20,000–30,000 Vietnam War protestors, resulting in the death of Chicano *Los Angeles Times* journalist Ruben Salazar, who was killed by a tear gas projectile as he sat in the Silver Dollar Café. Salazar's murder was commemorated in posters by Leo Limon and Rupert Garcia, a painting by Frank Romero, and performances and exhibitions (Selz 2006: 168, 182). It also marked for many the requisite need for self-representation, especially in the face of media exclusion. As Harry Gamboa, Jr., who was an organizer of the blowouts, recounts, there was a huge disjunction between those events and the ways in which they were depicted in the mass media. "I saw cops acting like dogs, but the next day in the newspapers the cops were represented as the victims: all the photographs were images of the cops getting hit." Gamboa realized at that point that if he didn't represent the scenes he saw, then "they're going to get lost, and ultimately other people will define them for me" (Chavoya 1998: 69).

Gamboa went on to create photos, film, performance, and written pieces to document artistically what the media had made a "phantom culture" of Chicano influence on Los Angeles (Chavoya 1998: 55). In 1972, with artists Gronk, Willie Herrón, and Patssi Valdez, he founded ASCO, which simultaneously asserted a Chicano presence on the urban landscape, a rejection of modernist high art, and a critique of ethnic community-based art. Their name, which translates as disgust or nausea, was meant to capture the response they anticipated from audiences, their proclaimed response to their own practices, and the social environment of poverty, racism, sexism, and militarism in which they worked (Sanchez-Tranquilino & Tagg 1991). Their approach was conceptual and idea-based, rather than an object-based form of art; they utilized public space and the urban landscape rather than museums and galleries (to which they had no access); they engaged Chicano social protest rather than the art world (Noriega 2000: 362–3). For a series of "murals," they used their bodies, taped to the wall or walking down the street, to call attention to the cultural boundaries that had come to define

Figure 17 Rubén Ortiz-Torres, *California Taco, Santa Barbara, CA*, 1995.
Fuji, flex SG, 20 × 24 in. Courtesy of the artist.

Chicano art. In another 1972 work, in response to a Los Angeles County
Museum of Art (LACMA) curator rebuffing the idea of a Chicano art
exhibition by saying "Chicanos don't make art, they're in gangs," ASCO
members signed their *placas* on the walls of the museum itself, claiming
the museum and its contents as their art, thus mocking their status as
outsiders and achieving the first exhibition of Chicano art at LACMA
(Sanchez-Tranquilino & Tagg 1991). By marking the institutional spaces
of the city as their territory, they were writing themselves back into the
history of California and claiming ownership of its visual construction.

The project of critiquing ownership and the ways in which the fine arts,
mass media, and capitalist forces construct and erase identity through visual
culture remain central to the work of contemporary artists. In *California
Taco, Santa Barbara, CA* (1995), Mexican-born, LA-based artist Rubén
Ortiz-Torres photographed a small, overdressed blonde "senorita" riding
on a taco float in a Santa Barbara parade (Figure 17). By framing this bit
of Americana, he invites scrutiny of the cultural stereotype, as well as the
way that California's Mexican past continues to be whitewashed, much as
earlier boosters did by staging fiestas in Los Angeles or inventing the
Mission revival as an "authentic" representation of a Spanish Colonial past.
Here, the only authentic reference to Mexico is Ortiz-Torres' artistic

authorship, a bemused gesture at ownership of an unfortunate icon of Mexican identity that has had too much popular circulation to be reclaimed, though perhaps it can be rendered ridiculous by Ortiz-Torres' humor.

Less facetious are the visual spectacles documented in photographs and television news coverage of the May 1, 2006 "A Day without an Immigrant," in which the laborers upon whose backs the American Dream has been built demonstrated for "a fair deal," as many a handwritten placard expressed. By rescinding their labor for the day and taking to American streets, more than a million immigrants (Univision reported over two million) made visible their otherwise invisible role in the economy. With overwhelming numbers participating in Los Angeles where the boycott was organized, Los Angeles became the symbolic center of the protests, where 90 percent of commerce at the Port of LA and other businesses were stalled by workers' walkouts. Images of mobilized masses waving American flags (at the request of Mayor Antonio Villaraigosa) along Wilshire Boulevard and in MacArthur Park became the focus of media coverage. Perhaps more than any other set of images, these articulate California's promise to be a beacon of the American Way, where reaping the material benefits of one's labor is expected and demanded, if not provided.

Over the course of the twentieth century, the place identity of California has been constructed though booster visions, critical revisions, artist reclamations, activist redeployments, and myriad other ways in which visual cues are produced, distributed, and consumed. Because the wide circulation of images is critical to the success of any perspective as it makes its way through the public realm, it is no wonder that the market and its forces have played so central a role in California image making. It also may explain why liberal and capitalist views have been attached so successfully to the visual meaning of California. Repetitions inherent to capitalism, both via mass production of images and by the streamlining and dumbing down of their visual cues, are crucial to the conveyance of meaning in the public sphere. Herein lies a source of the "sameness" about which Raymond Pettibon's critique warned.

Despite the increasing "sameness" of California visual culture, most views of California, whether proclaimed by booster or critic, continue to rely on a common optimistic assumption: California ought to be a place where everyone has the opportunity to make it. Common to these visual constructions of California, in other words, is the belief that in this place egalitarian access to the pursuit of happiness, especially through access to material wealth, should be possible. Despite all experiences to the contrary, this California dream and the American Way it represents are still widely believed by thousands as they make their ways to California, legally and otherwise. As a final example of California visual culture, please consider the highway sign posted on Interstate 5 just north of the California border

Figure 18   Highway sign near California border with Mexico. Photo © Mark Allen Johnson/ZUMA/Corbis.

with Mexico, by which motorists are warned to watch out for illegal immigrants (Figure 18). The image is menacing, racist, and deeply indicative of the dark fantasies of those who have forgotten we are a nation of immigrants. Still, at least at some fundamental economic level, those who risk that dangerous border crossing actually believe, despite Raymond Pettibon's acute warning, that California will be different. At least in the visual idea of it, California remains a land of promise and a symbol of hope.

REFERENCES

Amero, R. 1990. The Southwest on Display at the Panama–California Exposition, 1915. *Journal of SD History* (online), 36 (4). Available from: http://www. sandiegohistory.org/journal/90fall/amero.htm (cited May 5, 2007).

Appleyard, D., Lynch, K., and Myer, J. R. 1964. *The View from the Road.* Cambridge, MA: MIT Press.

Brinton, Christian. 1916. *Impressions of the Art at the Panama Pacific Expositions.* New York: John Lane Company. (Online). Available from: http://www.books-about-california.com/Pages/Impressions_PPIE/Impressions_PPIE_Ch02. html (cited May 17, 2006).

Brookman, P. 1991. "Looking for Alternatives: Notes on Chicano Art, 1960–90." In R. Criswold Del Castillo et al., eds., *Chicano Art: Resistance and Affirmation, 1965–1985*. Los Angeles: Wight Art Gallery, University of California.

Brougher, K. 2000. "Words as Landscape." In K. Brougher and N. Benezra, *Ed Ruscha*. Washington, DC: Hirshhorn Museum and Sculpture Garden, Smithsonian Institution, and Oxford: Museum of Modern Art.

Chavoya, C. O. 1998. "Social Unwest: An Interview with Harry Gamboa, Jr.," *Wide Angle* 20 (3): 55–78.

Cohen, Lizabeth. 2003. *A Consumers' Republic: The Politics of Mass Consumption in Postwar America*. New York: Knopf.

Davis, M. 1990. *City of Quartz: Excavating the Future of Los Angeles*. London and New York: Verso.

DeLyser, D. 2005. *Ramona Memories: Tourism and the Shaping of Southern California*. Minneapolis and London: University of Minnesota Press.

Deverell, W. 2004. *Whitewashed Adobe: The Rise of Los Angeles and the Remaking of Its Mexican Past*. Berkeley and Los Angeles: University of California Press.

Dimendberg, E., 2004. *Film Noir and the Spaces of Modernity*. Cambridge, MA, and London: Harvard University Press.

Fox, H. N. 2000. "Dreamworks: A Concept of Concept Art in California." In S. Barron, S. Bernstein, and I. S. Fort, eds., *Reading California: Art, Image, and Identity, 1900–2000*. Berkeley and Los Angeles: University of California Press.

Gebhard, D. 1980. "Architectural Imagery, the Mission, and California," *Harvard Architecture Review* 1 (Spring): 136–45.

Goldman, S. and Ybarro-Frausto, T. 1991. In R. Criswold Del Castillo et al., eds., *Chicano Art: Resistance and Affirmation, 1965–1985*. Los Angeles: Wight Art Gallery, University of California.

Gooding-Williams, R., ed. 1993. *Reading Rodney King: Reading Urban Uprising*. New York and London: Routledge.

Gordon, L. 2006a. "Dorothea Lange: The Photographer as Agricultural Sociologist," *Journal of American History* 93 (3): 698–727.

Gordon, L. 2006b. "Dorothea Lange Photographs the Japanese American Internment." In L. Gordon and G. Okihiro, eds., *Impounded: Dorothea Lange and the Censored Images of Japanese American Internment*. New York and London: W. W. Norton.

Grenier, C. ed. 2006. *Los Angeles, 1955–1985: Birth of an Art Capital*. Paris: Centre Pompidou and Panama Musées.

James, D. E. 1998. "Toward a Geo-Cinematic Hermeneutics: Representations of Los Angeles in Non-Industrial Cinema – *Killer of Sheep* and *Water and Power*," *Wide Angle* 20 (3): 23–53.

Klein, N. 1997. *The History of Forgetting: Los Angeles and the Erasure of Memory*. London and New York: Verso.

Kropp, P. S. 2006. *California Vieja: Culture and Memory in a Modern American Place*. Berkeley and Los Angeles: University of California Press.

Landauer, S. 2006. "Countering Cultures: The California Context." In P. Selz, *Art of Engagement: Visual Politics in California and Beyond*. Berkeley and Los Angeles: University of California Press.

Lange, D. and Taylor, P. S. 2000. *An American Exodus: A Record of Human Erosion*. Facsimile of 1939 edition. Paris: Éditions Jean-Michel Place.

Lipsitz, G. 2001. "Not Just Another Social Movement: Poster Art and the *Movimiento Chicano*." In C. A. Noriega, ed., *Just Another Poster? Chicano Graphic Arts in California*. Santa Barbara: University Art Museum, University of California.

Lynch, K. 1960. *The Image of the City*. Cambridge, MA: MIT Press.

Massood, P. J. 1999. "An Aesthetic Appropriate to Conditions: *Killer of Sheep*, (Neo)Realism, and the Documentary Impulse," *Wide Angle* 21 (4): 20–41.

McMillian, E. 2002. *California Colonial: The Spanish and Rancho Revival Styles*. Atglen, PA: Schiffer Publishing.

McWilliams, C. 1973. *Southern California: An Island on the Land*. Salt Lake City: Peregrine Smith Books.

Naremore, J. 1998. *More than Night: Film Noir in Its Contexts*. Berkeley and Los Angeles: University of California Press.

Neuhaus, E. 1916. *The San Diego Garden Fair*. San Francisco: Paul Elder.

Noriega, C. A. 2000. "From Beats to Borders: An Alternative History of Chicano Art in California." In S. Barron, S. Bernstein, and I. S. Fort, eds., *Reading California: Art, Image, and Identity, 1900–2000*. Berkeley and Los Angeles: University of California Press.

Patterson, T. 1971. *A Colony for California: Riverside's First Hundred Years*. Riverside, CA: Press-Enterprise Company.

Plagens, P. 1999. *Sunshine Muse: Art on the West Coast, 1945–1970*, 2nd edn. Berkeley: University of California Press.

Romo, T. 2001. "Points of Convergence: The Iconography of the Chicano Poster." In C. A. Noriega, ed., *Just Another Poster? Chicano Graphic Arts in California*. Santa Barbara: University Art Museum, University of California.

Sagarena, R. L. 2002. "Building California's Past: Mission Revival Architecture and Regional Identity," *Journal of Urban History*, 28 (6): 429–44.

Sanchez-Tranquilino, M. and Tagg, J. 1991. "The Pachuco's Flayed Hide: The Museum, Identity, and Buenas Garras." In R. Criswold Del Castillo et al., eds., *Chicano Art: Resistance and Affirmation, 1965–1985*. Los Angeles: Wight Art Gallery, University of California.

Schrank, S. 2004. "The Art of the City: Modernism, Censorship, and the Emergence of Los Angeles's Postwar Art Scene," *American Quarterly* 56 (3): 663–91.

Selz, P. 2006. *Art of Engagement: Visual Politics in California and Beyond*. Berkeley: University of California Press.

Starr, K. 1985. *Inventing the Dream: California Through the Progressive Era*. New York and Oxford: Oxford University Press.

Weitze, K. J. 1978. "Origins and Early Development of the Mission Revival in California." PhD, Stanford University, California.

Whiting, C. 2006. *Pop L.A.: Art and the City in the 1960s*. Berkeley: University of California Press.

Wolf, S. 2004. *Ed Ruscha and Photography*. New York: Whitney Museum of American Art, and Göttingen; Germany: Steidl.

Wolfe, T. 1963. "There Goes (Varoom! Varoom!) That Kandy Kolored (Thphhhhhh!) . . . ," *Esquire* 42 (5).

Young, C. A. 2006. *Soul Power: Culture, Radicalism, and the Making of a U.S. Third World Left*. Durham and London: Duke University Press.

FURTHER READING

Barron, S., Bernstein, S., and Fort, I. S., eds. 2000. *Made in California: Art, Image, and Identity, 1900–2000*. Berkeley and Los Angeles: University of California Press.

Cockcroft, E. S. and Barnet-Sanchez, H., eds. 1993. *Signs from the Heart: California Chicano Murals*. Albuquerque: University of New Mexico Press, and Venice, CA: Social and Public Art Resource Center.

Dear, M. and Leclerc, G., eds. 2003. *Postborder City: Cultural Spaces of Bajalta California*. New York and London: Routledge.

Gudis, C., ed. 1992. *Helter Skelter: L.A. Art in the 1990s*. Los Angeles: Museum of Contemporary Art.

Higa, K. and Wride, T. 2001. "Manzanar Inside and Out: Photo Documentation of the Japanese Wartime Incarceration." In S. Barron, S. Bernstein, and I. S. Fort, eds., *Reading California: Art, Image, and Identity, 1900–2000*. Berkeley and Los Angeles: University of California Press.

Karlstrom, P. J., ed. 1996. *On the Edge of America: California Modernist Art, 1900–1950*. Berkeley and Los Angeles: University of California Press.

Lee, A. W. 1999. *Painting on the Left: Diego Rivera, Radical Politics, and San Francisco's Public Murals*. Berkeley and Los Angeles: University of California Press.

McClung, W. A. 2001. *Landscapes of Desire: Anglo Mythologies of Los Angeles*. Berkeley and Los Angeles: University of California Press.

Moure, N. D. W. 1998. *California Art: 450 Years of Painting and Other Media*. Los Angeles: Dustin Publications.

Nittve, L. and Crenzien, H., eds. 1997. *Sunshine and Noir: Art in Los Angeles, 1960–1977*. Humblebaek, Denmark: Louisiana Museum of Modern Art.

Noriega, C., ed. 1998. *Urban Exile: Collected Writings of Harry Gamboa, Jr*. Minneapolis: University of Minnesota Press.

Perry, C. 1999. *Pacific Arcadia: Images of California, 1600–1915*. Oxford: Oxford University Press.

Sandweiss, M. A. 2002. *Print the Legend: Photography and the American West*. New Haven and London: Yale University Press.

Smith, R. C. 1995. *Utopia and Dissent: Art, Poetry, and Politics in California*. Berkeley and Los Angeles: University of California Press.

Solnit, R. 1990. *Secret Exhibition: Six California Artists of the Cold War Era*. San Francisco: City Lights Books.

Thomas, D. H. 1991. "Harvesting Ramona's Garden: Life in California's Mythical Mission Past." In D. H. Thomas, ed., *Columbian Consequences*, vol. 3. Washington and London: Smithsonian Institution Press.

Watts, J. 2004. "Picture Taking in Paradise: Los Angeles and the Creation of Regional Identity, 1880–1920." In V. R. Schwartz and J. M. Przyblyski, eds., *The Nineteenth-Century Visual Culture Reader*. New York and London: Routledge, pp. 218–32.

Zimmerman, T. Forthcoming. *Paradise Promoted: The Selling of Los Angeles, 1870–1930*. Santa Monica: Angel City Press.

Chapter Four

AT THE CROSSROADS: DEFINING CALIFORNIA THROUGH THE GLOBAL ECONOMY

Richard A. Walker

California has been globalized from the moment the European empires cast covetous eyes on the west coast of North America, and the state's economy has been deeply engaged with global trade, production, and finance since before the Gold Rush. It is not possible to tell the story of California's economic development without connecting it to the rest of the world. At the same time, an exaggerated notion of contemporary globalization runs the risk of eliding certain realities of history and geography. Therefore, the narrator of the state's economic history must be cognizant of the following puzzles of handling time and place.

The first thing to be alert to is the multifaceted nature of globalization (Dicken 2007). While much beloved of economists, trade (commodity flows) is the barest measure. One must be attentive to finance (capital flows), migration (labor flows), and production linkages (complex divisions of labor), as well as business ties through multinational corporations and alliances, and, conversely, competition with foreign companies. One must also account for technological connections, such as the import of machinery and export of new ideas. In this sense, California is suspended from a global web made up of Asian food markets and computer assembly, British and Japanese investment, Asian and Latin immigration, Indonesian and Venezuelan oil, and technologies of nuclear power, microchips, and concrete dams.

A second difficulty is how to cope with multiple geographic scales. To accept national boundaries as the sole markers of territory is to miss much of significance about the way local economies relate to outside forces (Cox 1997; Gibson et al. 2000). Virtually everything that touches a small place, such as Luxembourg, can be categorized as incipient globalism; but with a country as large as the United States, most economic relations are domestic. California's economic history extends outward to the Pacific Coast,

New York and Washington, DC, as well as to Canada, across the Pacific, and south of the border. Indeed, California is so large that key long-distance ties have even been between its own cities.

A third puzzle is how to calibrate economic trajectories over time. Is California's economy more globalized than before? One cannot trace a simple rising line from regional to national to global economic integration, because all three have been operative from the beginning. No doubt the intensity of global reach has deepened in many ways, but there have been reversals. What about the losses of such key links as precious metals export, the wheat trade, or Bank of America? Moreover, the intensity of globalism has waxed and waned. World-shaking events, from American continental conquest to war in the Pacific, have triggered makeovers in California; yet the state also shared in the worldwide involution of the interwar period.

A fourth quandary is to determine the sources of growth in one place within a global economy. What is the leading factor in regional development: agriculture or industry, exports or the home market, local firms or branch plants? The local economy may prosper thanks to the opportunities created by global demand, foreign investment, or new technologies. Conversely, it may suffer from indebtedness to outside capitalists, declining terms of trade, and technical backwardness. California was a classic resource periphery that could have been bled of its wealth in the manner of Peru or West Virginia; yet it was able to turn gold and silver into capital; adventurers and plunderers into industrialists; Argonauts and immigrants into creative workers; and distance from global centers of capitalism into room to maneuver. Global connections are a necessary but insufficient explanation for California's success; internal social relations were the real crucibles of growth (Page & Walker 1991; Walker 2001).

The last warning for historians and economic geographers is to recognize that localities can change the world. The prevailing view has long been that global expansion from the European core merely added territory to the world system without shaking up the hierarchy of places, and without injecting anything particularly new into the system: Britain conquers India and subordinates it to European imperialism; America expands westward but New York remains on top; Japan industrializes but remains a secondary power in world capitalism. A different view of things has taken hold of late, in which peripheries can be hotbeds of innovation, and empires rise and fall (Storper & Walker 1989; Arrighi 1994). This is certainly the case for California, which has had any number of decisive impacts on the world economy, from quicksilver to filmmaking to microelectronics.

We must consider all these puzzles as we define and outline global California.

The Golden Globe

Alta California became part of the global system as soon as the Spanish moved northward in the 1770s to consolidate their claim to this piece of earth, in opposition to the other, fast-approaching European empires. The Missions established by the Spanish created little economic traffic with the outside world, but the native peoples no doubt felt that the globe had fallen on them. Trade began to quicken after Mexican independence in 1821, when a commercially minded *ranchero* class started shipping out hides and tallow, mostly to the eastern United States. Hudson's Bay Company set up office in San Francisco, and Boston merchants made it a regular port of call. Quicksilver was soon added to California's exports, after the discovery of New Almaden mine near San José (Francis 1976).

British, American, and other adventurers trickled in with the rivulets of commerce (often via Latin America), marrying Mexicans, setting up trading posts, and exporting beaver pelts. By 1840, California had become a prime target of the upstart United States as it consolidated its grip on the North American continent. Saber-rattling President Polk started a war with Mexico in 1844 in large part to gain access to Pacific ports and seize the mineral riches of the Far West; Mexico was forced to cede one-third of its territory to the great blond beast of the north (Harlow 1982). But nothing thus far could have prepared California for the deluge of globalization to come.

With the Gold Rush of 1848–55, California was propelled into the global spotlight. Miners poured in from all corners of the world, while gold flowed out in quantities not seen since the Spanish conquest of the Andes: $1 billion in the first 20 years (Walker 2001). The US economy, previously suffering from lack of specie, found itself awash in liquidity. California gold went on to lubricate the wheels of Victorian transatlantic commerce. In the 1860s, Nevada silver flooded the world, helping to finance the Civil War, and eventually driving the USA and Europe firmly onto the gold standard (Doti & Schweikart 1991).

Quicksilver was California's third leading metal export, and had a dramatic effect on the global production of precious metals. California mercury made up over half the world's production from 1850 to 1880 and broke the Rothschilds' Old World cartel. The New Almaden mine was itself international: developed by a Mexican, bought by an Anglo-Mexican company, then taken over by Boston capitalists (St. Clair 1994).

Mining fortunes created California's first large banks and led to San Francisco's emergence as a new pole of accumulation in the world system. San Francisco became the financial hub of the West. San Francisco also served as a regional sub-center in the nineteenth-century global financial network centered in London, with direct links to Paris, Berlin, Tokyo, Montreal, Bombay, Vancouver, and Hong Kong. The San Francisco Mining Exchange briefly surpassed New York as the largest stock market in the world during the Comstock bubble of the early 1870s (Carlson 1942).

San Francisco capitalists reigned over an extractive empire stretching from Alaska to Mexico. San Francisco used its mercantile network, transportation system, and financial clout to bring the western United States under its hegemony. Merchants sent agents from Seattle to Phoenix, while the Central (Southern) Pacific "Octopus" spread its tentacles throughout California and the Southwest. With 150,000 people by 1870, the city had become one of the 10 largest cities in the country (Pomeroy 1965; Issel & Cherny 1986).

San Francisco was by far the chief Pacific coast port in the nineteenth century, and dominated traffic to northeast Asia. Hawaii was the linchpin of San Francisco's empire in the Pacific, and its sugar kings held the islands in thrall by the 1880s (Adler 1966; Brechin 1999). Great steamship companies grew up to ply the Pacific routes, especially Pacific Mail (owned by Southern Pacific), Dollar Lines and Matson Lines (a spin-off from Spreckels' Sugar). The city was the nation's fourth largest foreign trade entrepôt by 1890 (Issel & Cherny 1986).

California mining technology fanned out across the globe. Mining equipment built by San Francisco machine shops was shipped around the world (Bailey 1996). Explosives fabricated in the East Bay were used in mines from Alaska to Spain. Mining engineers such as John Hays Hammond became major international consultants. After a brief period advising British investors in the western United States, Herbert Hoover became the key engineer in the West Australian fields, worked in China, founded the Zinc Corporation (Rio Tinto), and rose to prominence as a technical advisor to London's global mining investors before World War I.

By the 1880s, agriculture had become the leading edge of the California economy. It took root in the 1860s with the wheat trade, which made up two-thirds of non-mineral exports during the 1870s and 1880s (Paul 1973). Wheat also supported a vigorous farm machinery sector of considerable ingenuity, while cattle and meatpacking spawned the first agribusiness corporation in America (Igler 2001). Fruit surged ahead as the state's leading cash crop by 1890, because canning and drying made California produce saleable around the world. The North Bay became America's leading wine region, and city merchants shipped in bulk to Britain (Walker 2004a).

California's economy rapidly diversified from the Civil War onward (Issel & Cherny 1986). By 1870, San Francisco produced more manufactured goods than all other western cities combined and dominated the regional market. San Francisco industry was force-fed with locally accumulated capital (Trusk 1960) and benefited from a high level of skilled labor and innovation. Educated Americans and Europeans (chiefly British, Germans, Scandinavians, and northern Italians) poured into San Francisco to partake of its high wages and burgeoning labor demand. The city reached extraordinary proportions of foreign-born, highest in the United States in the post-Civil War era (Kahn 1979). California's wealth of capital and human talent unleashed the same process of technical change we still see today in Silicon Valley (Walker 2001).

Los Angeles Forges Ahead

As the US economy surpassed Britain's by the end of the nineteenth century, the country began to eye overseas trade and territory. San Francisco's leading burghers promoted the city as the American Gateway to the Pacific and Asia. Yet these lofty imperial ambitions were soon checked by global rivalry with Japan and revolution in China. Overall, California turned inward to concentrate on its deepening powers of production and consumption, with upstart Los Angeles leading the way in a period of rapid industrial ascent.

San Francisco capitalists especially coveted the Philippines, a ripe fruit among the dead branches of Spanish colonialism. William Randolph Hearst – who turned his father's mining fortune into a publishing empire – helped trump up war with Spain in 1898. Several of the warships that turned Manila to flame were built in San Francisco and the scorched-earth war against Philippine rebels was directed from the Presidio, while the commander in the field was Oakland's General Arthur MacArthur (Brechin 1999). The bloodletting took the gloss off the imperial adventure, however.

California capitalists also cast covetous eyes on Mexico, making major investments in railroads, mines, and farms during the *Porfiriato* (Coatsworth 1981). These incursions contributed to mass peasant displacement and disgruntlement which helped trigger the Revolution of 1910–17. Hearst once more turned up the volume on his media empire in a vain effort to have the United States take control of Mexico; but the national agenda was absorbed by recession and European conflagration (Brechin 1999).

San Francisco had climbed to the nation's seventh largest metropolis by 1900, with 350,000 plus 50,000 more in Oakland, but its reach was exceeding its grasp. To make matters worse, the city was destroyed by the earthquake and fire of 1906. It was rebuilt furiously in hopes of recovering lost business, but would never recover its primacy. San Francisco faced sharp competition from upstart cities such as Seattle and Portland (Kahn

1979). Locally, the city was losing industry and residents to Oakland, the second city of the metropolitan area (Scott 1983; Walker 2004b). But it did retain its primacy in finance, with the biggest banks, most international connections, and a stock exchange, as well as the Federal Reserve Bank for the Western District.

Above all, Los Angeles was awakening. The arrival of the Santa Fe and Southern Pacific railroads triggered a land rush in the 1880s, and LA built itself an artificial port. Eastern migrants began to arrive in large numbers and Southern California found an agricultural base shipping citrus east (Tobey & Wetherell 1995). But the springboard for Southern California's ascendance was black gold. Over the first 30 years of the twentieth century, California was the leading oil-producing region in the United States (which contributed two-thirds of world output between the world wars), peaking at about 20 percent of world production in the 1910s. Los Angeles leapfrogged over San Francisco-Oakland to become the largest metropolis in the west by 1910 with over 650,000 people.

California oil did not travel far; most was consumed within the state, with a small amount exported to China and the East Coast. Instead, California became a major site of experimentation in the uses of petroleum. Industry and transport learned to use fuel oil instead of coal, setting an example for the world (Johnson 1970). Asphaltic crude was put to good use paving the highway system and natural gas funneled into domestic use in the cities.

A most potent symbol of California's global reach at the time was the Panama Canal, celebrated in the twin Panama–Pacific International Exhibitions of 1915 in San Francisco and San Diego. The fairs were linked up by the longest paved highway of the day, the 500-mile El Camino Real. Panama's narrows had first come under San Francisco's suzerainty during the Gold Rush (Lewis 1949), yet Los Angeles benefited more from the canal because its port is a day's voyage closer. San Diego, meanwhile, wrested the Navy's new Pacific Fleet away from San Francisco Bay, and finally found a sustained economic base (Lotchin 1992). San Francisco's leadership in shipping and naval installations was blindsided by internal rivals.

Between the Wars

By the 1920s, California came to lead the nation, and the world, in agricultural productivity, agro-processing, farm organization, and marketing. The state developed the world's largest concentration of canneries, the most modern agro-corporations and cooperatives, the most advanced system of contracting, and the biggest supermarkets and most modern grocery chains. California agribusiness continued its conquest of national fresh fruit and vegetable markets, and grabbed cotton from the South in the 1920s. Raisins, canned asparagus, and other delicacies went to Europe. Two California agricultural innovations changed the world: the caterpillar tractor (1904), soon converted to tanks and earth-moving machines, and the submersible electric pump (1905), invented in Ohio but generalized and produced here (Walker 2004a).

Los Angeles continued its spectacular growth, and had doubled the Bay Area in population by the end of the "roaring twenties," with over 2.5 million people in the metropolitan area. With huge new oil discoveries at Signal Hill and Huntington Beach, the Southern California economy was fueled by $6 billion in oil wealth by 1930 – twice the total mineral riches dug up in Northern California (Walker 2001). Industrialization proceeded at a rapid clip in Los Angeles. The blockbuster industries were film, which moved west from New York in the 1910s; motor vehicles, which expanded rapidly after World War I; and aircraft, on the basis of the single-winged airplane invented by David Douglas in the early 1920s (Hise 2004). In these years, however, Hollywood movies did not yet circle the globe, cars and parts were for the western market, and airplanes were still made in modest numbers. Two-thirds of LA's manufacturing went to regional markets (Calkins & Hoadley 1941). Indeed, the striking thing about Los Angeles was the way local growth created its own market, absorbing the majority of output from local industry, whether for oil equipment, furnishings, foodstuffs, or vehicles (Hise 2004).

California led the nation's way in large-scale construction, from pipelines and bridges to highways and housing tracts, in the period between the two world wars. A ferocious rate of growth had much to do with the innovative stance of local firms, but so did a tradition of engineering achievement, skilled work, and bravado that accepted new challenges. The bulldozer was invented by Robert LeTourneau of Stockton in the 1920s, who then partnered with Henry Kaiser (Wilson & Taylor 1957; Fluor 1978; Atkinson 1985).

Oakland's Henry Kaiser and Warren Bechtel soared above the rest after leading the consortium of eight firms ("the Six Companies") that built the world's first high-arch concrete dam at Boulder Canyon on the Colorado River in the early 1930s. That success was followed by a stream of major projects, such as Bonneville and Grand Coulee dams on the Columbia and oil pipelines in Canada and Texas, mostly carried out by the innovative means of recombinant joint ventures (Tassava 2003). Most of the work was still domestic, although there were already forays internationally (Kaiser in Cuba in the 1920s and Bechtel in Venezuela in the 1930s). California also bred the first large-scale housing developers in the interwar period, such as Henry Dolger of San Francisco, Walter Leimert of Oakland and Los Angeles, and Arthur Burns Homes of Los Angeles.

The rise of A. P. Giannini and his Bank of Italy is the leading example of California's amazing accumulation of capital in the twentieth century. Bank of America (as it was renamed in 1929) grew along with the region, gathering in the savings of the state of California and lending to businesses and consumers to grease the wheels of development (Nash 1992). Giannini's empire rested on aggressive use of branch banking and a willingness to risk lending to small borrowers and large companies with big ideas. By 1940, Bank of America was the biggest bank in the world and San Francisco the second banking city in the United States (Borchert 1978).

External ownership in California never amounted to more than perhaps one-quarter of industrial holdings, and branch plants were not the basis of manufacturing growth (Trice 1955). San Francisco retained its key banks, including Wells Fargo, Crocker, and Anglo, and developed its own investment banks, led by Blyth and Witter (who underwrote the growth of PG&E). California petroleum was locally and widely owned (helped by the breakup of Standard Oil in 1911), and did not fall into the hands of the majors until the 1930s. When buyouts did occur, the argument can just as well be made that eastern capital was buying into California's strengths and its burgeoning markets; and many acquired companies kept their headquarters, purchasing, and decision making in the state.

California's oil industry had a decisive global impact as it moved offshore in the 1930s. Local engineers, such as Ralph Arnold, helped to open up oil fields around the world. Most significantly, Standard Oil of California opened up the Persian Gulf oil fields with discoveries at Bahrain and Saudi Arabia in 1932–3, revolutionizing the geography of global oil and politics. Lacking distributors in the eastern hemisphere, Standard joined with Texas Oil (Texaco) to form Cal-Tex and Aramco to exploit the enormous Gulf fields.

Wartime Powerhouse

The global calamity of World War II pushed California once again to the front of the world's stage. The crucial geographic fact was the global shift marked by the war in the Pacific. The West Coast was the staging area for the Pacific theater, with the Bay Area as its pivot. Like another gold rush, the war brought 10 percent of federal wartime expenditure to the state, including 38.5 percent of all continental US military construction (Brubaker 1955). It also channeled millions of people through California bases, ports, and war industries – many of whom came back to stay (Johnson 1993; Sides 2003). Conversely, it led to the dispersal of Japanese

Americans, who were ignominiously shunted into concentration camps all over the western United States (Daniels 1977).

California was ready to seize the new opportunities of wartime. Federal spending did not flow to an empty land, making an economic desert bloom (Rhode 1994). Instead, California had already reached a high level of industrialization, and its leading sectors would have attracted millions in Army and Navy contracts regardless of the transects of global warfare and federal spending. But California capitalists and politicians had learned very well the art of milking the Feds for government aid and contracts (Adams 1997; Brechin 1999). The key beneficiaries were aircraft and movies in the south, and electronics and construction in the north, but oil companies, garments, agribusiness, steel, vehicles, and machinery all sold well to the government.

The greatest of the war stories was the build-up of aircraft manufacture in Los Angeles. Douglas, Hughes, Northrop, and others operated enormous factories employing hundreds of thousands of workers (Scott 1993). Los Angeles's explosive growth knew no rival, with its metro population surging toward five million, and a huge crescent of development added to the west side (Hise 1997). After a brief pause, the Korean War and Cold War militarization kept feeding the fires of Southern California without letup, bringing close to one-quarter of all defense contracts to the state through the rest of the twentieth century.

The war was good for construction companies, who tackled everything from tunnels to dry docks, and grabbed contracts from Panama to Hawaii (Adams 1997). Kaiser and Bechtel-McCone won huge contracts for merchant ships, converting California into the biggest shipyard the world has ever seen (some 200,000 workers in the Bay Area, plus another 150,000 in Los Angeles and Portland). Knowing little about ship-building, they put into effect revolutionary mass-production systems of the Fordist type so as to be able to produce ships in record time (Tassava 2003). By the end of the war, Kaiser had become one of the biggest industrialists in the world (Foster 1989). Meanwhile, Bechtel-McCone was building a dozen refineries around the world, including in the Persian Gulf. California oilmen invented offshore drilling in the 1940s, which would prove essential to opening up new supplies from Louisiana to the North Sea.

World War II brought a new generation of West Coast whizkids into the limelight in electronics. Hewlett-Packard and Varian became major players overnight thanks to their advanced technology in tubes for radar and sonar. By the Korean War, Lockheed (which had started in the Bay Area before jumping to Los Angeles) had moved its enormous aircraft and missile electronics operations back to the South Bay (Schoenberger 1997). The Bay Area and Los Angeles were partners in crime in creating the technology for the military-industrial complex that ruled the Cold War world (Lowen 1997; Brechin 1999).

The Great Postwar Boom

Microelectronics became a significant engine of growth for California, especially the Bay Area, in the postwar era. Silicon Valley had seized hold of global leadership in the technology of micro-circuitry on a chip in the 1950s and 1960s, as semiconductor firms begat new semiconductor firms in ever-new rounds of spin-offs. Mainframe and mid-sized computers, and their key parts, became specialties of the Valley, along with medical and scientific instruments and aerospace guidance systems. The leading companies of the Valley, such as Fairchild, Intel, National, Amdahl, and Hewlett-Packard, clambered high in the Fortune 500. These, in turn, set up global operations, from assembly houses in Southeast Asia to computer and components plants in Silicon Glen, Scotland – pioneering the new global division of labor by the late 1960s (Rogers & Larsen 1984; O'Mara 2004).

After the war, California construction companies went international in a big way, building railroads, dams, smelters, refineries, and pipelines along lines laid down at home (Wilson & Taylor 1957). Guy Atkinson, Utah Construction, Kaiser Engineers, and Morrison-Knudson (their international office was in San Francisco) were active in a score of countries, chiefly in Latin America and the Middle East. Bechtel had become the world's largest engineering firm by the 1970s (Strassman & Wells 1982). In the 1980s, two Bechtel directors, George Schultz and Caspar Weinberger, garnered the most powerful positions in the Reagan cabinet, the better to oversee the global dominions of the American empire (McCartney 1989).

Henry Kaiser's attention had turned to heavy industry by war's end, when he decided to dive into the automobiles and household appliance sector. Kaiser Industries put the first auto plants in Brazil and Argentina in the mid-1950s. In keeping with the shift to industrialist, Kaiser shifted from the ad hoc and joint venture modes of organization to a more standard divisional corporation (Tassava 2003). But Kaiser-Fraser was defeated by the "Big 3" automakers, and shut down in 1954 (Hoffman 1992).

California agribusiness began a new wave of globalization after the war. Del Monte (CalPak) was the world's largest agro-processing firm and Safeway the world's fastest-growing supermarket chain, and the largest during the 1970s and 1980s. Del Monte set up its first canneries outside the Pacific basin in the 1950s, in South Africa and Italy, expanding into Britain, Kenya, Venezuela, and Mexico in the next decade. Safeway went to Europe and Latin America, while J. G. Boswell was growing cotton in Australia. More generally, the California agro-production system set the pattern for industrialized agriculture around the world (Walker 2004a).

The Bay Area was also pivotal in the Faustian pact with atomic energy, and E. O. Lawrence was the uncrowned emperor of Big Physics – leveraging millions of dollars out of local capitalists, the state of California, and the US government to build his cyclotrons – and the driving force behind the Manhattan Project (Brechin 1999). University of California scientists and Pacific Gas and Electric Company also pioneered the so-called "peaceful atom" campaign, but it was a bust and only four commercial nuclear power plants were ever built in California (Wellock 1998).

By the end of the war, Bank of America was moving aggressively into Asia and Europe, becoming the first international bank outside of New York. San Francisco joined the second tier of global financial centers by the 1950s even though its other big banks, Wells Fargo and Crocker-Anglo, had almost no overseas presence (Reed 1981). Los Angeles's banks, led by Security and National, were entirely domestic. Nonetheless, because California banks were the most concentrated in the United States, four of them could be counted among the top dozen in the country (Bank of America alone held 45 percent of California savings in 1959 (Doti & Schweikart 1991)), and San Francisco leapt to second place among US banking centers (Borchert 1978). Bank of America introduced the first universal credit card in 1959, which soon swept the nation and the world as the Visa system. Another group of California banks, led by Wells and Crocker, followed with the Master Charge (MasterCard), which became the second global standard in consumer credit (Doti & Schweikart 1991: 196).

The postwar boom drew in huge numbers of people to work in California, mostly from the eastern and southern United States. The state rode the wave to become the most populous state by the 1960s, and counted some 20 million people by 1970. In the same year, Greater Los Angeles had hit almost 10 million and the Bay Area was closing in on 5 million.

The Triumph of Electronics

By 1970, the United States was feeling the heat of global competition, coming first from Japan and Germany, later from East Asia (Brenner 2006). But California would prosper in the new era of globalism, even as the rest of the country felt the hammer blows of factory closures and disinvestment in the recessions of the early 1970s, 1980s, and 1990s. As overseas trade rose, California garnered more exports than any other state. As foreign direct investment flooded the United States in the 1980s, California grabbed over half of it (Ettlinger 1991). California companies moved aggressively into global construction, oil extraction, shipping, and other traditional strengths: Chevron secured concessions in Central Asia; Bechtel built Hong Kong's new airport and a technopolis outside Moscow; Matson became one of the world's largest container shippers.

The late twentieth century brought the age of electronics to fruition. Micro-circuitry moved beyond stand-alone computing and weaponry to revolutionize communications, processing, design, distribution, and retailing. Electronics became the world's largest industrial sector in output and employment. As the United States rebounded smartly from the profit and productivity doldrums of the 1970s and the deep recession of the early 1980s, the bounce came, above all, from high tech, representing 8 percent of GDP and no less than one-third of US economic growth in the 1990s (Brenner 2004: 94). California was both the greatest engine of this change and its greatest beneficiary. Globalization is a wonderful thing when you have what everyone else wants.

Success was by no means assured. In the 1980s, Asian and European competitors were breathing down the neck of Silicon Valley companies, as were Boston's Route 128 and Dallas and Austin, Texas. Japanese mastery of mass production, which had swept aside American producers of consumer electronic goods, was poised to do the same in semiconductors. Doomsayers seemed vindicated as the fire in Silicon Valley turned to ashes in 1984–6, leaving acres of speculative industrial buildings vacant (Kroll & Kimball 1986). But the Valley was already reinventing itself. Standardized semiconductors were shed as unprofitable, replaced by personal computers and pre-programmed specialty chips, as more circuitry was crammed on chips, disk drives became smaller, distributed networks were introduced, and semiconductors began to be designed by computers – led by new companies such as Apple, LSI Logic, Sun, and Silicon Graphics (Saxenian 1994). The Valley also developed the largest concentration of software firms in the world, including Oracle, Adobe, and PeopleSoft.

In the 1990s, Silicon Valley became the home of the internet revolution. Its companies designed more of the equipment for the internet, offered more of the software to run it, and was more densely wired than anywhere else in the world. A new generation of start-ups led the way, such as Netscape, Yahoo, Cisco Systems, and JDS Uniphase. Silicon Valley became the prime example of the new way of doing business in the global age, concentrating engineers, designers, and marketers, while shedding manufacturing offshore and plucking employees from the ranks of temp agencies like home-grown Adia Personnel Services. Upstart internet media like *The Industry Standard* shouted the news from the electronic rooftops: this was the New Economy, simultaneously an historic break with the past and the apotheosis of American entrepreneurialism (Miles 2001; Walker 2006).

Meanwhile, Southern California experienced phenomenal growth during the red-hot 1980s (Soja 1986; Davis 1990). Southern California generated two-thirds of California's trillion-dollar economy, with Greater Los Angeles employing over seven million people and housing nearly 15 million. LA manufacturing alone surpassed one million jobs – twice the number of the next biggest US industrial city (even as many old-line industries succumbed to international competition). Leading the charge was aerospace, fed by Reagan's unprecedented peacetime military build-up, which brought billions in new weapons contracts to Greater Los Angeles and San Diego (Markusen et al. 1992; Scott 1993).

Hollywood and the entertainment complex of Los Angeles shifted into a new gear after the studio system was broken up in the 1960s. It retooled as a more open web of interconnected firms, independent directors and actors, all subcontracting film by film, TV series by series, or musical project by project. By the 1980s, it was hitting on all cylinders, churning out hundreds of films a year and generating huge profits. The talent core became even more international, looking beyond Britain to Europe, Australia, and Hong Kong. European filmmaking suffered under the competition, particularly in Italy and Britain (Scott 2005).

With this rampant economic growth, the metropolis exploded outward. The population of Los Angeles County reached nearly nine million by 1990 and the five-county metropolitan area almost 15 million. Orange County filled in; the Inland Empire around Riverside and San Bernardino burgeoned; and even Ventura County and the Antelope Valley to the north suburbanized. San Diego passed one million people and the metro area surpassed two million by 1990. Construction during the boom was itself a major engine of urban growth, employing hundreds of thousands of people in building, finance, and sales.

The most striking effect of the new age of globalization was certainly the arrival of millions of immigrants, mostly from Mexico, Central America, and East Asia (Waldinger & Bozorgmehr 1996). Los Angeles served as the country's primary reception area, changing the face of the city forever (Valle & Torres 2000). By 1990, people of color had become a majority in Los Angeles and one-third of the city was foreign born. The Bay Area and San Diego were not far behind.

A new star was rising in the firmament of the 1980s – biotechnology. It grew up in the Bay Area, Los Angeles, and San Diego, thanks to their long traditions of medical research and infusions of federal money at the University of California, Stanford, and private institutes such as Salk. In addition, venture capital has funded start-ups, starting with Genentech in 1978, showing the usual California verve for entrepreneurism and ability to attract research talent. To this day, California boasts half the revenues and capitalization of US biotech companies, and the Bay Area remains the leading biotech node in the nation and the world (Zhang & Patel 2005).

Too Fast and Furious

An early sign of financial globalization in California was the influx of overseas bank branches. By 1980, foreign bank subsidiaries were making 35 percent of all business loans in California, compared to 20 percent nationally (Doti & Schweikart 1991: 194). Conversely, Bank of America made a dramatic move into international lending, when it joined in the global euphoria of Eurodollar lending in the 1970s – quadrupling in size and garnering 40 percent of its profits abroad. It syndicated loans from Brazil to Indonesia, laying the basis for the debt debacle of the 1980s. But as loans went sour by the billions, Bank of America nearly collapsed in 1985 (Johnston 1990). San Francisco's #3 bank, Crocker, also nearly failed after being bought out by Britain's Midland Bank, chiefly because of unsound local real-estate lending; it became part of Wells Fargo in 1986.

While the Bay Area sagged after the mid-1980s, the fires of fast finance raged across Southern California for the rest of the decade. The "capital of the twentieth century" was a fool's paradise of speculation. When the bubble burst in 1989, the wreckage produced the worst depression in California since the 1930s (wrongly blamed on the military cutback alone). Lofty predictions of Los Angeles as the new financial capital of the West were quickly belied by the implosion of its biggest banks. Bank of America recovered to buy LA's biggest bank, Security Pacific, in 1990 (Smith & Crowley 2000).

Another popular notion was that Japanese capital might take over the state (Davis 1990). By 1988, the Japanese held five of the 11 largest California banks, as well as a host of prime properties, such as Bank of America's downtown Los Angeles skyscraper, Pebble Beach golf course, and San Francisco's Palace Hotel. Nevertheless, the biggest international players in local property development were Canada's Cadillac Fairview and Olympia and York. In any case, the Japanese real-estate bubble imploded and Cadillac Fairview and O&Y went belly up in the early 1990s, proving once again that nothing is secure in the fast-moving world of capital (Stewart 1993).

California is still the second biggest center of financial operations in the United States. The Bay Area remains the state's premier financial center, despite losing Bank of America to North Carolina in 1999. Wells Fargo (merged with Minneapolis's Bank One) is the country's fifth largest bank. The region hosts the largest pool of venture capital in the world and attracts billions from around the globe (Kenney & Florida 2000). The key international players are no longer the commercial banks but boutique investment houses generating billions in high-stakes funds, led by the likes of Richard Blum, Warren Hellman, and George Roberts (Kohlberg, Kravis, and Roberts' 1988 purchase of Nabisco launched the era of big-time private equity buyouts).

The decade of the 1990s saw the Bay Area take its turn playing fool to fast money. In the years after the 1995 public offering of Netscape, the first popular internet search engine, Bay Area companies absorbed more venture capital and more speculative stock investment than any place on earth. They became the premier target of investors flush with cash from the meteoric rise of the NASDAQ and other exchanges, taking on nearly one-third of the $7 trillion rise of all US equities from 1995 to 2000 (Walker 2006). When that bubble collapsed, the Bay Area economy was clobbered. Los Angeles, in the meantime, had risen from the dead looking bigger, richer, and more cosmopolitan than ever by the end of the century.

At the Global Crossroads

By the end of the century, global outsourcing had become standard practice among American manufacturers, with subsidiaries and subcontractors in Mexico, East Asia, and from the new powerhouse, China (Walker & Buck 2007). California companies were again among the leaders in seeking cheaper supplies abroad, with The Gap riding the strategy to become the world's #1 fashion retailer (Levi's, which bucked the trend, fell on hard times). Of course, the US trade deficit shot up wildly and US manufacturing shrank. But California did very well from international trade, exporting more than $100 billion in goods, more than any other state, by 2000 – double the total of 1980.

The state also gained from the wave of imports. Traffic through the ports of Los Angeles-Long Beach doubled through the 1990s and was carrying over one-third of all US containers in the 2000s (LA ranks #1, Long Beach #2, and Oakland #7 in the country). LA-Long Beach ranks as the fifth largest container port in the world (after four Chinese cities). With the eclipse of San Francisco's port by Oakland, American President Lines (APL; formerly Dollar) and Matson moved across the bay; they also grew into two of the largest container shippers in the world (APL is now a subsidiary of a Singapore company and Matson is owned by Alexander and Baldwin of Hawaii).

By the end of the millennium, electronics was spinning new webs – not just the internet, but webs of worldwide production, innovation, and technology transfer. California remains deeply embedded in a largely transpacific network that dominates global high tech, with Silicon Valley still the chief nerve center. One major development was the vast improvement of production capabilities in East Asia beyond Japan: Korea, Taiwan, Singapore, and beyond. This meant that the finest producers for a range of components for computers and IT systems were now to be found outside the United States. American companies moved upstream to product design and systems engineering, while subcontracting parts and assembly to the Far East (Dedrick & Kraemer 1998; McKendrick et al. 2000).

Hollywood remained king of global entertainment in the new millennium, but faced new challenges (Scott 2005). One was external buyouts, such as Sony's purchase of Columbia, and Time, Inc.'s merger with Warner Brothers. Another was the growing popularity of Asian films produced in Hong Kong and Bombay, which turn out more films per year than American companies. Hollywood producers also faced rising costs, leading them to seek out cheaper locations, particularly in Canada, where acting talent is abundant, prices lower, and cities tidier. Southern California's entertainment industry faced a different challenge from Northern California's electronic gamers (now earning as much revenue as films) and the file-sharing revolution (MP3, iPod, YouTube). On the other hand, computer animation has injected new life into Hollywood fantasy films, starting with *Star Wars'* special effects, then with cartoons by Pixar. The new entertainment age is yet another marriage of Bay Area and Southern California industry and talent.

One of the largest employers in California today is tourism. Eighty percent of travelers come from within state, but that still leaves 50 million out-of-staters who visit every year and more than 14 million foreigners (one-fifth of all international travelers to the United States). The Bay Area and Los Angeles County each boast around 100,000 hotel rooms. Only Las Vegas and New York City have more, but Greater LA has more visitors annually than either. The Disney theme park has been cloned around the world – at Disney World in Florida, EuroDisney, Disney Japan, and most recently Disney Hong Kong (Watts 1997).

Agribusiness is no longer the leading edge of California development, but it remains a huge segment of the state's economy. California is still the world's largest producer of fresh vegetables, strawberries, raisins, and processing tomatoes, though its hegemony in fresh fruits has been broken by Florida and Texas and winter produce coming from as far away as Chile and New Zealand. A globalized agro-export system has increased competition from companies operating on principles first developed in California: high-input, high-intensity farming organized by contract system and huge agribusiness corporations. California growers have responded in two ways: by moving into higher-value crops and products, such as tropical fruits, exotic greens, and wine; and by exploiting overseas markets more intensively, such as shipping oranges and rice to Japan, table grapes to Hong Kong, wine to Canada, and almonds worldwide. Wine exports, for example, quadrupled from 1980 to 2000. Growth in this labor-intensive domain has been so formidable that demand has drawn in hundreds of thousands of immigrants from Mexico, over 90 percent of whom are undocumented (Walker 2004a).

With the economic boom of the second half of the 1990s, California's population continued to grow, hitting 33 million by 2000. Over one-quarter of Californians were foreign born; LA, San Francisco, and Santa Clara counties were all over one-third foreign born. While the state's economy was boosted by poor immigrants, skilled newcomers were just as important. For example, the new generation of electronic entrepreneurs was dominated by immigrants from Taiwan, Singapore, China, and India, who had their feet planted on both sides of the Pacific (Saxenian 2006).

Clearly, globalism has impinged repeatedly on California's economic prospects. Nonetheless, the central lesson one can draw is that globalization is a challenge from which a local economy can profit mightily, if it is well prepared by history and geography. Indeed, it can lead the way, making what was local into what becomes global, whether mining equipment, credit cards, or search engines. To do that, California has had to be extraordinarily good at what it does and to innovate its way to the head of the pack. In the global competitive race, the state's key advantages have been these: a fully capitalist society from the outset; rapid exploitation and capitalization of natural resources; accumulation of capital locally; reinvestment in production, research, and education; an agglomeration of complementary activities; and – most of all – an exceptional wealth of human labor, including the talents brought by in-migrants and those developed in the crucibles of dynamic industries (Walker 2001). Both labor and capital would have done less, of course, without the relatively egalitarian opportunity structure and the vigorous ideology of openness and possibility. None of this forgives the exploitation and conquest that went hand in hand with the success (so obviously tilted to white men), only to say that the opportunity of the few was relatively large, and not squandered. This fact fundamentally sets California apart from less fortunate places facing the global juggernaut of capital. To an amazing degree, California had become the world.

REFERENCES

Adams, Stephen. 1997. *Mr. Kaiser Goes to Washington: The Rise of a Government Entrepreneur*. Chapel Hill: University of North Carolina Press.
Adler, Jacob. 1966. *Claus Spreckels: The Sugar King in Hawaii*. Honolulu: University of Hawaii Press.

Arrighi, Giovanni. 1994. *The Long Twentieth Century: Money, Power and the Origins of Our Times*. London: Verso.

Atkinson, Ray. 1985. *The Guy F. Atkinson Company of California: A Free Enterprise Success Story*. New York: Newcomen Society of the United States.

Bailey, Lynn. 1996. *Supplying the Mining World: The Mining Equipment Manufacturers of San Francisco, 1850–1900*. Tucson: Westernlore Press.

Becker, Jules. 1991. *The Course of Exclusion, 1882–1924: San Francisco Newspaper Coverage of the Chinese and Japanese in the United States*. San Francisco: Mellen Research University Press.

Borchert, John. 1978. "Major Control Points in American Economic Geography," *Annals of the Association of American Geographers* 68 (2): 214–32.

Brechin, Gray. 1999. *Imperial San Francisco: Urban Power, Earthly Ruin*. Berkeley: University of California Press.

Brenner, Robert. 2004. "New Boom or New Bubble? The Trajectory of the US Economy," *New Left Review* 25: 57–99.

Brenner, Robert. 2006. *The Economics of Global Turbulence*. London and New York: Verso Press.

Brubaker, Sterling. 1955. *The Significance of Military Installations for California's Economic Growth, 1930–52*. San Francisco: Bank of America Economics Department.

Calkins, Robert and Hoadley, Walter. 1941. *An Economic and Industrial Survey of the San Francisco Bay Area*. Sacramento: California State Planning Board.

Carlson, Wallin. 1942. "A History of the San Francisco Mining Exchange." Unpublished Master's Thesis, Department of Economics, University of California, Berkeley.

Coatsworth, John. 1981. *Growth Against Development: The Economic Impact of Railroads in Porfirian Mexico*. DeKalb, IL: Northern Illinois University Press.

Cox, Kevin, ed. 1997. *Spaces of Globalization*. New York: Guilford.

Daniels, Roger. 1977. *The Politics of Prejudice: The Anti-Japanese Movement in California and the Struggle for Japanese Exclusion*, 2nd edn. Berkeley: University of California Press.

Davis, Mike. 1990. *City of Quartz: Excavating the Future in Los Angeles*. London: Verso.

Dedrick, Jason and Kraemer, Kenneth. 1998. *Asia's Computer Challenge*. New York: Oxford University Press.

Dicken, Peter. 2007. *Global Shift: The Changing Contours of the Global Economy*, 5th edn. London: Guilford Press.

Doti, Lynne and Schweikart, Lawrence. 1991. *Banking in the American West*. Norman: University of Oklahoma Press.

Erie, Steven. 2004. *Globalizing L.A.: Trade, Infrastructure and Regional Development*. Stanford, CA: Stanford University Press.

Ettlinger, Nancy. 1991. "The Roots of Competitive Advantage in California and Japan," *Annals of the Association of American Geographers* 81 (3): 391–407.

Fluor, J. Robert. 1978. *Fluor Corporation: A 65-Year History*. New York: Newcomen Society of North America.

Foster, Mark. 1989. *Henry Kaiser: Builder in the American West*. Austin: University of Texas Press.

Francis, Jesse. 1976 [1935]. *An Economic and Social History of Mexican California, 1822–1846*. New York: Arno Press.

Gibson, Clark, Ostrom, Elinor, and Ahn, T. K. 2000. "The Concept of Scale and the Human Dimensions of Global Change: A Survey," *Ecological Economics* 32: 217–39.

Harlow, Neil. 1982. *California Conquered: War and Peace in the Pacific, 1846–1850*. Berkeley: University of California Press.

Hirst, Paul and Thompson, Grahame. 1996. *Globalization in Question*. Cambridge: Polity Press.

Hise, Greg. 1997. *Magnetic Los Angeles: Planning the Twentieth-Century Metropolis*. Baltimore, MD: Johns Hopkins University Press.

Hise, Greg. 2004. "Nature's Workshop: Industry and Urban Expansion in Southern California, 1900–1950." In Robert Lewis, ed., *Manufacturing Suburbs*. Philadelphia: Temple University Press, pp. 178–99.

Hock, Dee and Senge, Peter. 2005. *One from Many: VISA and the Rise of Chaordic Organization*. San Francisco: Berrett-Koehler.

Hoffman, Elizabeth. 1992. *The Rich Neighbor Policy: Rockefeller and Kaiser in Brazil*. New Haven, CT: Yale University Press.

Igler, David. 2001. *Industrial Cowboys: Nature, Private Property and the Regional Expansion of Miller and Lux, 1850–1920*. Berkeley: University of California Press.

Issel, William and Cherny, Robert. 1986. *San Francisco, 1865–1932*. Berkeley: University of California Press.

Jackson, W. Turentine. 1968. *The Enterprising Scot: Investors in the West*. Edinburgh: University of Edinburgh Press.

Johnson, Arthur. 1970. "California and the National Oil Industry," *Pacific Historical Review* 39 (2): 155–71.

Johnson, Marilyn. 1993. *A Second Gold Rush: Oakland and the East Bay in World War II*. Berkeley: University of California Press.

Johnston, Moira. 1990. *Roller Coaster: The Bank of America and the Future of American Banking*. New York: Ticknor & Fields.

Kador, John. 2002. *Charles Schwab: How One Company Beat Wall Street and Reinvented the Brokerage Industry*. New York: John Wiley.

Kahn, Judd. 1979. *Imperial San Francisco: Politics and Planning in an American City, 1897–1906*. Lincoln: University of Nebraska Press.

Kenney, Martin and Florida, Richard. 2000. "Venture Capital in Silicon Valley: Fueling New Firm Formation." In Martin Kenney, ed., *Understanding Silicon Valley*. Stanford, CA: Stanford University Press, pp. 98–123.

Kroll, Cynthia and Kimball, Linda. 1986. *The R&D Dilemma: The Real Estate Industry and High Tech Growth*. Working Paper no. 86–116. Berkeley: Fisher Center for Real Estate and Urban Economics, University of California.

Lewis, Oscar. 1949. *Sea Routes to the Gold Fields: The Migration by Water to California, 1848–1852*. New York: Alfred A. Knopf.

Lotchin, Roger. 1992. *Fortress California, 1910–1961.* New York: Oxford University Press.

Lowen, Rebecca. 1997. *Creating the Cold War University: The Transformation of Stanford.* Berkeley: University of California Press.

Markusen, Ann, Hall, Peter, Deitrich, Sabina, and Campbell, Scott. 1992. *The Rise of the Gun Belt.* New York: Oxford University Press.

McCartney, Laton. 1989. *Friends in High Places: The Bechtel Story – the Most Secret Corporation and How It Engineered the World.* New York: Ballantine.

McKendrick, David, Doner, Richard, and Haggard, Stephan. 2000. *From Silicon Valley to Singapore: Location and Competitive Advantage in the Hard Disk Drive Industry.* Stanford, CA: Stanford University Press.

Meyer, David. 1983. "Emergence of the American Manufacturing Belt: An Interpretation," *Journal of Historical Geography* 9 (2): 145–74.

Miles, Sara. 2001. *How to Hack a Party Line: The Democrats and Silicon Valley,* rev. ed. Berkeley: University of California Press.

Nash, George. 1983. *The Life of Herbert Hoover,* vol. I. New York: W. W. Norton.

Nash, Gerald. 1985. *The American West Transformed: The Impact of the Second World War.* Bloomington: Indiana University Press.

Nash, Gerald. 1992. *A. P. Giannini and the Bank of America.* Norman: University of Oklahoma Press.

O'Mara, Margaret. 2004. *Cities of Knowledge: Cold War Science and the Search for the Next Silicon Valley.* Princeton, NJ: Princeton University Press.

Page, Brian and Walker, Richard. 1991. "From Settlement to Fordism: The Agro-industrial Revolution in the American Midwest," *Economic Geography* 67 (4): 281–315.

Paul, Rodman. 1973. "The Wheat Trade between California and the United Kingdom," *Mississippi Valley Historical Review* 45: 391–412.

Pomeroy, Earl. 1965. *The Pacific Slope.* New York: Alfred A. Knopf.

Reed, Howard. 1981. *The Preeminence of International Financial Centres.* New York: Praeger.

Rhode, Paul. 1994. "The Nash Thesis Revisited: An Economic Historian's View," *Pacific Historical Review* 63 (1): 363–92.

Rogers, Everett and Larsen, Judith. 1984. *Silicon Valley Fever.* New York: Basic Books.

Rosen, Kenneth and Jordan, Susan. 1988. *San Francisco Real Estate Market: The City, the Peninsula and the East Bay.* November. Working Paper 88–152, Fischer Center for Real Estate and Urban Economics, University of California, Berkeley.

Saxenian, Annalee. 1994. *Regional Advantage: Silicon Valley and Route 128 in Comparative Perspective.* Cambridge, MA: Harvard University Press.

Saxenian, Annalee. 2006. *The New Argonauts: Regional Advantage in a Global Economy.* Cambridge, MA: Harvard University Press.

Schoenberger, Erica. 1997. *The Cultural Crisis of the Firm.* Oxford: Blackwell.

Scott, Allen. 1988. *New Industrial Spaces.* London: Pion.

Scott, Allen. 1993. *Technopolis: High Technology Industry and Regional Development in Southern California*. Los Angeles: University of California Press.

Scott, Allen. 2002. *The Cultural Economy of Cities*. Thousand Oaks, CA: Sage Publications.

Scott, Allen. 2005. *On Hollywood*. Princeton, NJ: Princeton University Press.

Scott, Allen and Soja, Edward. 1986. "Los Angeles: The Capital of the Late Twentieth Century," *Society and Space* 4 (3): 249–54.

Scott, Allen and Soja, Edward, eds. 1996. *The City: Los Angeles and Urban Theory at the End of the Twentieth Century*. Los Angeles: University of California Press.

Scott, Mel. 1985 [1959]. *The San Francisco Bay Area: A Metropolis in Perspective*, 2nd edn. Berkeley: University of California Press.

Sides, Josh. 2003. *L.A. City Limits: African American Los Angeles from the Great Depression to the Present*. Berkeley: University of California Press.

Smith, Robert H. and Crowley, Michael. 2000. *Dead Bank Walking: One Gutsy Bank's Struggle for Survival and the Merger That Changed Banking Forever*. Winchester, VA: OakHill Press.

Soja, Edward. 1986. "Economic Restructuring and the Internationalization of Los Angeles." In Michael Smith and Joe Feagin, eds., *The Capitalist City*. Oxford: Basil Blackwell, pp. 178–98.

St. Clair, David. 1994/95. "New Almaden and California Quicksilver in the Pacific Rim Economy," *California History* 73 (4) (Winter): 278–96.

Stewart, Walter. 1993. *Too Big to Fail: Olympia & York, The Story Behind the Headlines*. Toronto: McClelland and Stewart.

Storper, Michael and Walker, Richard. 1989. *The Capitalist Imperative: Territory, Technology and Industrial Growth*. Oxford: Basil Blackwell.

Strassman, W. Paul and Wells, Jill, eds. 1988. *The Global Construction Industry*. London: Unwin Hyman.

Tassava, Christopher. 2003. "Multiples of Six: The Six Companies and West Coast Industrialization, 1930–1945," *Enterprise and Society* 4: 1–27.

Tobey, Ronald and Wetherell, Charles. 1995. "The Citrus Industry and the Revolution of Corporate Capitalism in Southern California, 1887–1944," *California History* 74: 6–22.

Trice, Andrew. 1955. "California Manufacturing Branches of National Firms, 1899–1948: Their Place in the Economic Development of the State." PhD dissertation, Department of Economics, University of California, Berkeley.

Trusk, Robert. 1960. "Sources of Capital of Early California Manufacturers, 1850–1880." Doctoral dissertation, University of Illinois, Urbana.

Valle, Victor and Torres, Rodolfo. 2000. *Latino Metropolis*. Minneapolis: University of Minnesota Press.

Waldinger, Roger and Bozorgmehr, Mehdi, eds. 1996. *Ethnic Los Angeles*. Newbury Park: Sage.

Walker, Richard. 2001. "California's Golden Road to Riches: Natural Resources and Regional Capitalism, 1848–1940," *Annals of the Association of American Geographers* 91 (1): 167–99.

Walker, Richard. 2004a. *The Conquest of Bread: 150 Years of Agribusiness in California*. New York: The New Press.

Walker, Richard. 2004b. "Industry Builds Out the City: Industrial Decentralization in the San Francisco Bay Area, 1850–1950." In Robert Lewis, ed., *Manufacturing Suburbs: Building Work and Home on the Metropolitan Fringe*. Philadelphia: Temple University Press, pp. 92–123.

Walker, Richard. 2006. "The Boom and the Bombshell: The New Economy Bubble and the San Francisco Bay Area." In Giovanna Vertova, ed., *The Changing Economic Geography of Globalization*. London: Routledge, pp. 121–47.

Walker, Richard and Buck, Daniel. 2007. "Engine of History? The Transition to Capitalism in China's Cities," *New Left Review* 46: 1–27.

Walker, Richard and the Bay Area Study Group. 1990. "The Playground of US Capitalism? The Political Economy of the San Francisco Bay Area in the 1980s." In Mike Davis, Steve Hiatt, M. Kennedy, Susan Ruddick, and Mike Sprinker, eds., *Fire in the Hearth: The Radical Politics of Place in America*. London: Verso, pp. 3–82.

Watts, Stephen. 1997. *The Magic Kingdom: Walt Disney and the American Way of Life*. Boston: Houghton-Mifflin.

Wellock, Thomas. 1998. *Critical Masses: Opposition to Nuclear Power in California, 1958–1978*. Madison: University of Wisconsin Press.

Wilson, Neill and Taylor, Frank. 1957. *The Earth Changers*. Garden City, NY: Doubleday.

Zhang, Junfu and Patel, Nikesh. 2005. *The Dynamics of California's Biotechnology Industry*. San Francisco: Public Policy Institute of California.

Part II

EARLY CALIFORNIA

Chapter Five

Junípero Serra across the Generations

Steven W. Hackel

Arguably the most famous and controversial person to have lived in California before 1850, Junípero Serra is also among the most remote. Born nearly three centuries ago, he self-consciously lived an ascetic life of Catholic devotion in defiance even of his own day and age. That life now stands in contrast to much of what Californians seem to embrace: diversity, hedonism, materialism, celebrity, economic advancement, and the here and now. Serra's fame does not rest on a contribution to Roman Catholic liturgy, practice, or thought. Nor does his fame rest in anything he wrote. Rather, his renown rests on the missions he helped establish in California and upon what he has come to represent and how various groups have understood him. Thus, this essay is not so much about the historical Serra but about how successive Franciscans, historians, Indians, and others have come to know Serra, how they have constructed memory of him, and how the various meanings of California's mission system have diverged. Serra has had no shortage of biographers, but few have written about Serra with anything approaching scholarly objectivity. Most of the writing on Serra has been hagiographical, and only recently have these treatments of Serra's life been called into question. Serra, therefore, remains a promising subject of inquiry – a man of surpassing historical significance who remains as controversial to some as he is inspirational to others.

The Life of Serra

Miguel José Serra was born on November 24, 1713, in Petra, a small rural community on Mallorca, an island in the Mediterranean Sea. He was the third child of Antonio Serra and Margarita Ferrer, whose first two children died in infancy. Two girls would follow, one of whom would also die as an infant. Miguel José's father and mother were Catholic, and they had the boy baptized the day of his birth. They were also peasants, and early in his youth the boy joined his father in the fields. Before long the Serras entrusted the education of Miguel José to the Franciscan Convento de San Bernardino, just down the street from their home. Miguel José must have shown promise; at the age of 15 he began studying for the priesthood at the Franciscan Convento de San Francisco in Palma, the capital city of the island. At this time, Palma had some 33,000 residents, roughly a quarter of the island's inhabitants. The city was a vibrant port with a wealthy merchant class, a strong Catholic tradition, and a long history of oppressing its Jewish inhabitants.

In January 1730, Miguel José attempted to join the Franciscan Order, but he was denied entry. His small size had led Church officials to conclude that he was too young. But that fall he gained acceptance to the Order. A year later he took vows to live in obedience, without property, and in chastity, and adopted for himself the name Junípero after one of the followers of Saint Francis.

Junípero Serra grew into a man of immense talents and enduring accomplishments. While it is not now known when he was ordained as a priest, he received his faculties to preach in 1737 and was granted authority to hear confessions two years later. During the 1730s he studied philosophy and theology in Palma, and in 1740 he began teaching a three-year course in philosophy at Lullian University in Palma. A gifted orator and a popular teacher, he won appointment to a chair in Scotistic theology at Lullian University in 1743 and preached in many towns and villages of Mallorca, and even from the pulpit of the great Cathedral of Palma. By the mid-1740s, Serra had risen from humble beginnings to a place of respect and honor on the island.

Serra left Mallorca in 1749 for a missionary life in New Spain. Apparently, for many years before his departure Serra had secretly prayed for permission to go to the New World. Mallorca had a long tradition of sending its sons out as missionaries. Among the most notable was Ramón Lull, who traveled to North Africa on three occasions between 1285 and 1308 seeking souls to convert. In the seventeenth and eighteenth centuries, Mallorca made its mark on Christian evangelism in the New World. Fray Antonio Llinás de Jesús María was instrumental in establishing one of the most important training centers for missionaries in New Spain, the Convento de Santa Cruz in Querétaro, founded in 1683. During Serra's lifetime seven Mallorcans became missionaries in Alta California, and another, Raphael Verger, became an administrator of missionaries and later a Bishop in New Spain.

From his youth Serra seems to have taken special inspiration from Saint Francis of Solano (1549–1610), a Spanish Franciscan who went to the New World in 1589, labored for over two decades among the Indians of Peru, and was canonized in 1726, only a few years before Serra entered the Franciscan Order. Serra was also inspired by María de Agreda de Jesús.

Born in 1602, she became a Poor Clare nun at the age of 17 and ardently desired to convert Indians to Catholicism. In 1631, it was reported that she had bilocated to the American Southwest on many occasions between 1620 and 1631 and had preached to various Indian groups. Serra was no doubt moved by her appeal that the lives of the Apostles were particularly praiseworthy and glorious in the eyes of the Lord, given that they had "suffered for the conversion of souls" (Geiger 1955: 304). By the late 1740s, Serra also might have grown weary of Mallorca. In 1744, plague claimed an estimated 10,000 Mallorcans. Three years later, all single men found on the streets of Palma, including those in the Orders, were rounded up and sent into military service in Italy. Drought gripped the island at mid-century and food had to be rationed. Finally, a measles outbreak compounded the island's great suffering in 1748.

In retrospect, it is not wholly surprising that Serra sought a mission in the New World. He went to New Spain with his companion and student, Francisco Palóu. After making landfall in Puerto Rico, the Franciscans sailed to Vera Cruz and walked to Mexico City, where they arrived before the end of 1749. At some point on the overland journey Serra developed a sore and ulcerated leg, possibly due to an insect bite. Whatever its origin, the wound would afflict him for the rest of his days and greatly contribute to the impression that he bravely struggled against physical infirmity and personal hardship in the service of Roman Catholicism and the Indians of New Spain.

Serra spent the first five months of 1750 in Mexico City at the College of San Fernando, the administrative headquarters and training center for many of the missionaries of northern Mexico. Before long he was sent as a missionary to the Pame Indians of the Sierra Gorda, a region situated some 150 miles north of Mexico City. He served with distinction and held the position of Father President of the five missions of the Sierra Gorda between 1751 and 1758. Serra and Palóu were recalled to Mexico City in anticipation of their transfer to Texas, but Comanche Indians destroyed the mission at San Sabá on the eve of their move. Serra's activities between 1758 and 1767 are a mystery, but apparently he and Palóu divided their time between the College of San Fernando in Mexico City and the countryside, where they traveled for months at a time preaching to both the converted and the unconverted.

When Charles III expelled the Jesuits from his empire in 1767, the Franciscans took their place in Baja California. At the age of 54 Serra became the president of these missions. The following year the Viceroy chose Serra to oversee the new missionary expansion into Alta California. Serra founded Mission San Diego in July 1769 and established Mission San Carlos Borromeo in Monterey in 1770. He soon relocated the latter mission a few miles south to the Carmel River; this would be his headquarters for the remaining years of his life. Serra established a total of nine missions in Alta California. During this period Franciscan missions were in decline and undergoing secularization nearly everywhere in New Spain. His tenure, perhaps predictably, was marked by disagreements with the region's governors over Indian policy, military personnel, relations between missions and presidios, and the prerogatives of the missionaries. He won nearly all these battles due to his administrative skill and tireless defense of the missions. In the process, he placed the California missions on a relatively secure foundation and garnered for himself a reputation as California's most important founding father. He died at San Carlos in 1784, in bed and clutching a large cross. Palóu, his fellow Mallorcan, administered the last rites at his side.

Palóu, Bancroft, Engelhardt, and the Catholic Tradition

Serra might have drifted into semi-obscurity had Palóu not written his hagiographical *Relación Histórica de la Vida y Apostólicas Tareas del Venerable Padre Fray Junípero Serra*, published in Mexico City in 1787 (Palóu 1787). Copies circulated in Mexico and Spain and were sent back to Mallorca to encourage a new generation of Franciscans to become New World missionaries. The *Relación Histórica* is a lengthy book, composed of 61 chapters and more than 300 pages. The frontispiece consists of a woodcut showing Serra surrounded by Indians. Serra clutches a rock, an allusion to his practice of pounding his chest, and at his feet rest burning tapers and a heavy chain, both of which he used to mortify his body. While the book did not launch a wave of volunteers for the mission enterprise, its publication shaped nearly everything subsequently written about Serra and the California missions. Palóu's other great historical work, his *Historical Memoirs of New California*, was not published until the twentieth century, yet it too sheds much light on Serra's life and times (Palóu 1926). Both studies depicted Serra's deep piety, religious orthodoxy, virtuous temperament, and exemplary commitment to the mission enterprise. It was Palóu who first suggested that California's Indians returned Serra's efforts with love. Palóu's *Relación Histórica* went through multiple editions during the subsequent 150 years. Largely because of Palóu's work, Serra has consistently been portrayed as a man of great strength and saintly virtue who brought civilization to California in the form of Christianity, agriculture, and civil settlements. The degree to which the Palóuian vision of Serra took hold in the literature on Serra and Alta California can be seen in the writing of Hubert Howe Bancroft, the first great secular historian of California. Bancroft maintained that Serra could be stubborn in his dealings with Alta California's governors, but he offered a glowing overall assessment: "No ardent churchman entertains a more exalted opinion of the virtues of Junípero Serra, his pure-mindedness, his self-sacrificing devotion, his industry and zeal than myself" (Bancroft 1884, vol. I: 327). Bancroft concluded that Serra was "kind-hearted and charitable to all" and that his faults – his strict and narrow belief that the Franciscan way was the only way – "were those of his cloth" (Bancroft 1884, vol. I: 415, 416).

Bancroft's contemporary and fellow historian, Theodore H. Hittell, had a similar view and even compared Serra to Saint Francis. Serra, Hittell wrote, "was in every respect as pure in his motives, as strong in his character, and as great in his actions." But Hittell also concluded that the mission system – Serra's great project – was not of enduring value, because "it looked only to the aggrandizement of a system and dominion that had long outlived their usefulness," and "did not contemplate or in any proper sense regard the progress of true civilization" (Hittell 1885, vol. I: 300, 508). The subsequent works of historians Irving B. Richman, Charles Edward Chapman, Agnes Repplier, and Theodore Maynard are all within the tradition established by Bancroft and Hittell – hugely respectful of the man but critical of the mission system as a whole. Maynard's conclusion deftly captures the tenor of much of this vein of Serra literature: "We have here [in Serra] an extraordinary man whose work seems to have failed but which still bears fruit though the missions he founded have long since gone" (Richman 1911; Chapman 1928; Repplier 1933; Maynard 1954: 291).

Although Bancroft's treatment of Serra was judicious, some in the Catholic Church, especially Franciscan Zephyrin Engelhardt, could tolerate no criticism of the man. Engelhardt considered Bancroft's statement that Serra could be stubborn a vicious and unprincipled attack. In *The Franciscans in California*, Engelhardt accused Bancroft of demonstrating "bigotry" and "ignorance of Catholic affairs" (Engelhardt 1897: i). Engelhardt went further in his monumental four-volume *Missions and Missionaries of California*, arguing that Bancroft's criticisms of Serra were part of an "agitation against the founder of Christianity and civilization in California" (Engelhardt 1908–15: 674). Putting his own mark on Serrana, Engelhardt added a strong dose of late nineteenth- and early twentieth-century racism to Palóu's hagiography: California Indians appear far more savage than in Serra's correspondence or Palóu's writings about Serra or Alta California.

Engelhardt was more than a reactionary seeking to burnish and protect Serra's reputation. His writing cast a long shadow over Serra studies and examinations of Alta California. He was the most important Franciscan scholar of his generation, and he served for many years as director of the important Santa Barbara Mission Archive-Library. His work, at least until the middle of the twentieth century and the publication of Geiger's edition of the *Relación Histórica*, remained by default the most important source for many historians of Serra, especially those who did not read Spanish or those who had no access to Serra's own correspondence.

The influence of both Palóu and Engelhardt on Serra studies is evident in the steady stream of books during the twentieth century that presented Serra as saintly and heroic. Charles J. G. Maximin Piette's *Évocation de Junípero Serra: Fondateur de la Californie* presents Serra's life and a chronological list of Serra's known correspondence (Piette 1946). Piette's other major work, the posthumously published two-volume *Le Secret de Junípero Serra: Fondateur de la Californie-Nouvelle, 1769–1784* (Piette 1949), was the first modern biography of Serra (complete with extended excerpts from much of Serra's correspondence). Franciscan Omer Englebert's *The Last of the Conquistadors: Junípero Serra (1713–1784)* was included in the Catholic Book of the Month Club, but it drew heavy criticism for what Father Eric O'Brien, O.F.M., believed were the book's many factual errors (Englebert 1956). Don DeNevi and Noel Francis Moholy broke little new ground in their *Junípero Serra: The Illustrated Story of the Franciscan Founder of California's Missions*, but the volume does contain numerous useful illustrations and photographs relating to Serra's life and work (DeNevi & Moholy 1985). Finally, M. N. L. Couve de Murville, Archbishop of Birmingham, England, has provided a clear, learned, and richly illustrated biography of Serra squarely within the Catholic tradition. To his credit Couve de Murville acknowledged a wide range of views of Serra, some of them critical (Couve de Murville 2000).

Secular Hagiographers

Palou's biography secured Serra's reputation within the Catholic Church. Serra's fame became widespread among non-Catholic Californians during the late nineteenth and early twentieth centuries. Alongside the Catholic tradition of Serra admiration has been a secular body of writing that usually – but not always – remained only a step short of hagiography. Perhaps the earliest and most important secular admirer of Serra was Charles F. Lummis, who arrived in Southern California in 1885. Lummis took a keen interest in the life and legacy of Serra (Gordon 1969) and founded the Landmarks Club, which he devoted in part to the preservation and conservation of the California missions. Lummis's early statements about Serra were nearly indistinguishable from those of Catholic historians like Engelhardt and were extremely influential in California and beyond.

Lummis wrote about Serra as part of his larger effort to rescue Spanish pioneers and missionaries from what he saw as America's blinding Anglo-Saxonism. Lummis believed that Americans had denied Spaniards –

especially men like Serra – their proper place in American history. Typical of his day, Lummis saw history as the story of manhood, and he passionately believed that "the Spanish pioneering of the Americas was the largest and most marvelous feat of manhood in all of history" (Lummis 1929: preface). Lummis further argued that the California missions had kept other European powers out of the Far West, allowing the United States to achieve its Manifest Destiny (ibid.: 297). Lummis broke with Bancroft and Hittell, and argued that the mission was a transcendent institution that "lives dominant in the ideals of mankind forever" (ibid.: 302). And perhaps most interestingly, Lummis compared the Pilgrims, who he believed had little use for Indians, and whose venture he considered "as purely selfish a venture as history records," with the Franciscans, whose attempts to save Indian souls he deemed "as clear a piece of devoted unselfishness as the annals of man can show" (ibid.: 304). To Lummis, first and foremost among those missionaries was Serra, "The Apostle of California – Founder of Civilization," who, he wrote, "made a deeper and more lasting dent on the history and the ideals and the future of California than any other man of any race who ever lived within these boundaries" (ibid.: 327).

With the help of Lummis and others, the celebration and commemoration of Serra occurred not just in print but in the public arena as well. The opening and inspection of Serra's tomb at Mission San Carlos in 1882 was the occasion for speeches by the Governor of California and the Mayor of San Francisco. In 1884, on the centennial of Serra's death, the California Legislature asked the governor to proclaim a holiday. In 1891, Jane Lathrop Stanford financed a monument of Serra to the Presidio of Monterey, marking the place where Serra is believed to have held Mass in 1770. In 1907 a statue in honor of Serra was dedicated in San Francisco's Golden Gate Park. And in 1913, on the bicentennial of Serra's birth, California Governor Hiram Johnson proclaimed a legal holiday. These commemorations reflected the consensus that Serra was a great man who embodied timeless virtues.

The culmination of these commemorations was Serra's selection as one of two historical figures to represent the State of California in the US Capitol's Statuary Hall. While it is not clear how many people have seen this statue, the fact that it resides in the US Capitol gives Serra a prominence and validity well beyond the Catholic Church. Serra was chosen for this honor by a commission of five Californians, one of whom was historian Herbert E. Bolton, a professor of history at the University of California at Berkeley from 1911 to 1944. On the day that Serra's statue was unveiled in 1932, he was lauded as "the torch bearer of civilization." In the words of Ray Lyman Wilbur, Secretary of the Department of Interior, Serra, "imbued with divine spirit, charged with an exalted mission and sustained by an unfaltering faith, faced with supreme courage, danger, privation, suffering, disease, to carry the message of salvation over unknown paths along the uncharted shores of the Pacific to the hostile, ignorant, lowly Indian dwellers in that wild empire of the West. He was the torch bearer of civilization" (Wilbur 1932: 29). A generation later, in 1959, on the 175th anniversary of Serra's death, a similar cast of luminaries gathered in Statuary Hall to offer glowing tribute to the Franciscan missionary (Conmy 1960).

The participation of historians in the adulation of Serra has caused concern in some academic circles. In an important article in the *American Historical Review*, James A. Sandos criticized Bolton for his unflagging and seemingly politically motivated support of Serra and urged historians to regain their independence and objectivity in their scholarship on church figures like Serra (Sandos 1988). And in his most recent book, *Converting California: Indians and Franciscans in the Missions* (Sandos 2004), Sandos situates Serra's life and work not in the realm of timeless Catholic virtues but in the ideas and writings of three figures who inspired Serra: Francis of Assisi, John Duns Scotus, and María de Jesús de Agreda.

Serra in Mexico and Spain

While Serra has cast a long shadow over the history and historiography of Spanish California and has been a figure of interest to American scholars of the Borderlands, by comparison, he is not a person of great interest or tremendous controversy in either Spain or Mexico. In Petra and Mallorca the memory of Serra was revived in the late nineteenth century by Francisco Torrens y Nicolau, who, while studying for the priesthood in Palma, came across Palóu's *Relación Histórica* in a bookshop. From that point forward he dedicated his life to the commemoration of Serra (Ramis n.d.). In 1913, on the bicentennial of Serra's birth, Torrens y Nicolau published his own hagiography of Serra, *Bosquejo Histórico del Insigne Franciscano, V.P.F. Junípero Serra, Fundador y Apóstol de la California Septentrional* (Torrens y Nicolau, 1913). Torrens y Nicolau's volume is largely an abbreviation of Palóu's, and it rekindled the memory of Serra on Mallorca. More enduring than the volume is the monument to Serra in Petra, unveiled in 1913 on the 200th anniversary of Serra's birth.

The most important Mallorcan Serra scholar since Torrens y Nicolau is the recently deceased Bartomeu Font Obrador, author of the richly illustrated *Fr. Junípero Serra: Mallorca–Mexico–Sierra Gorda–Californias*. Co-authored with art historian Norman Neuerburg, this volume captures the full arc of Serra's life and provides an illuminating discussion of various intellectual influences on Serra (Font Obrador & Neuerburg 1992). Font Obrador's essay "Mallorquines en California" (1978) is the most thorough discussion of the Mallorcans who came to California as missionaries. His last book, *Fray Junípero Serra: Doctor de Gentiles*, contains a transcription of various prayers purportedly authored by Serra and concludes with tributes and prayers on behalf of Serra's sainthood (Font Obrador 1998).

In Mexico today, Serra is all but unknown outside of academic circles and the Sierra Gorda. A small group of scholars have examined the missions of the Sierra Gorda as objects of local interest. Foremost among them is Monique Gustin, whose *El Barroco en la Sierra Gorda: Misiones Franciscanas en el Estado de Querétaro, Siglo XVIII*, is the best study of the religious iconography that enriches the missions of the Sierra Gorda (Gustin 1969). The late Franciscan historian Lino Gómez Canedo's *Sierra Gorda: Un Típico Enclave Misional en el Centro de México (Siglos XVII–XVIII)* is the best study of the history of the missions where Serra lived and worked during the 1750s (Canedo 1988). Canedo's magnum opus, *Evangelización, Cultura, y Promoción Social* contains two valuable essays on Serra's years in the Sierra Gorda, a time from which unfortunately there are no surviving letters from Serra (Canedo 1993).

The Serra Cause

In 1934 the Catholic Church formally initiated proceedings to investigate the worthiness of Serra for canonization and his recognition as a saint. The Church established a historical commission composed of Bolton, Father Maynard J. Geiger (archivist of the Santa Barbara Mission Archive-Library), and Monsignor James E. Culleton (chancellor of the diocese of Fresno-Monterey). The three testified before an ecclesiastical court convened to examine Serra's life. In 1949, the testimony given in the investigation and nearly 2,500 documents relating to Serra's life were sent to Rome for further scrutiny. Thirty-six years later, in 1985, Pope John Paul II declared Serra Venerable, and in 1988 he beatified the Mallorcan, leaving Serra one miracle short of qualifying for sainthood. This miracle may have already happened. In April 2007, the Denver Archdiocese concluded its investigation into whether or not an unborn girl was cured *in utero* of a grave illness through the intercession of Serra. Apparently, a team of medical doctors had detected fetal abnormalities during a woman's pregnancy, advised the parents to consider an abortion, and warned that the baby would be born disabled. The parents prayed to Serra for the baby's healthy delivery and she was born healthy, although prematurely. Should the Vatican declare that this was indeed a miracle, Serra will have met the canonical requirements for sainthood.

Beyond bolstering Serra's reputation in the Catholic Church, the promotion of Serra for sainthood has proven to be a watershed in Serra studies. As a result of what has become known as the "Serra Cause," all of Serra's known correspondence has been transcribed, translated, and published by the Academy of American Franciscan History. This project was first suggested by Piette, who proposed that all of Serra's letters be published in both Spanish and English. This massive project occupied Piette from 1939 until his sudden death in 1948. In gathering the letters together, Piette was aided by Maynard J. Geiger, who had been charged with compiling the correspondence for the official canonical investigation of Serra's virtues. After Piette's death, determination of the final shape of the project fell to the Franciscan historian Antonine Tibesar. Lino Gómez Canedo contributed greatly to the project by helping to write the informative notes that accompany the letters. The result was the landmark four-volume collection of 270 Serra letters, *The Writings of Junípero Serra* (Tibesar 1955–66).

In a related effort to make Serra's life and character more widely accessible, Geiger translated and edited Palóu's biography of Serra, making this seminal text available to a wide audience in 1955 (Geiger 1955). Geiger also wrote a monumental two-volume biography of Serra. A half-century after its publication, *The Life and Times of Junípero Serra, O.F.M.* remains the definitive cradle-to-grave biography of Serra and the starting point for all serious research on the missionary from Mallorca (Geiger 1959). Geiger's biography has found company recently in an array of kindred studies. Martin J. Morgado's two pictorial illustrations of Serra's life, *Junípero Serra's Legacy* and *Junípero Serra: A Pictorial Biography*, are predictably stilted but the spectacular photographs by Patrick Treganza, which cover everything from Serra's home in Petra to his grave in San Carlos Borromeo, bring an added dimension to the life and times of Junípero Serra (Morgado 1987 and 1991).

Beyond public proclamations, commemorative statues, hagiographic texts, and richly illustrated volumes, the celebration of Serra as a soon-to-be saint found its place during the second half of the twentieth century in an extensive children's literature. Nearly all children's books on Serra discuss Serra's slight build and provide the lesson that he overcame his size and his sore leg to accomplish great things. Typical of this genre is Leo Politi's *The Mission Bell*, which dwells on Serra's "lame leg," kindly nature, and love for Indians (Politi 1953). The same didactic prose – minus the lame leg – can be found in Donna Genet's *Father Junípero Serra: Founder of California Missions* (1996), which presents Serra just as Palóu had many generations earlier.

The Serra Controversy

If the Serra Cause cemented Serra's saintly reputation within the Catholic Church and among a good portion of the public, it also infuriated those who saw injustice in Spain's colonization of California and in Serra's missions. Just as the Serra Cause was gaining momentum in the decades after World War II, American society underwent dramatic transformations that led many to call into question rosy accounts of Spanish colonization of California, peaceful Franciscan missions, and the benign nature of Serra's life work – views which had dominated California history into the twentieth century. It had become increasingly clear to many observers that the pro-Serra scholarship (since the days of Palóu) willfully neglected to take into account Native life within the mission system. The glaring fact that some Indian cultures had been all but destroyed as a result of policies implemented by Serra and his followers lay at the heart of this critique.

The roots of such criticism can be traced to controversies in Serra's own day and to the earliest writings on the motivations and actions of the first Europeans who set foot in the New World. The early governors of California – Pedro Fages (1770–4, 1782–90), Fernando Rivera y Moncada (1774–6), and Felipe de Neve (1777–82) – often considered Serra arrogant, stubborn, and obstructionist. Moreover, the military in colonial California frequently charged that the padres' cruelty drove the Indians from the missions, a problem which in turn forced the military to occasionally lead dangerous expeditions to force Indians back into the padres' arms. Serra in turn considered the governors to be hostile to the mission enterprise and meddlesome in the affairs of the padres. In a sense the Spanish military, just like Serra and other Franciscan missionaries, personalized an intensifying debate in eighteenth-century New Spain between the Church and the State over who had ultimate control over Indians, and representatives of both crown and cross condemned the other to get the upper hand in this struggle.

The scholar Sherburne F. Cook brought to light these accusations of cruelty against the missionaries (Cook 1976). Cook did not explicitly criticize Serra, but he portrayed the missions and missionaries in a highly unfavorable light. Cook described a colonial order in which padres forced Indians into the missions, where they were routinely beaten, forced to labor, provided a bland and meager diet, and provoked to the point of rebellion. Cook also gave the first modern account of the devastating diseases that drastically reduced the mission Indian population. Cook's essays were influential in their day, but it was only after the Serra Cause had gained momentum that his work drew a sustained response from the pro-Serra camp. Francis F. Guest, O.F.M., who had taken over for Geiger as head of the Santa Barbara Mission Archive-Library, attempted to refute or defuse Cook's claims. Guest described the intellectual and religious worlds from which Serra had come, and he argued that Franciscan missionaries did not force Indians to convert to Catholicism (Guest 1979, 1983, 1985, 1988, 1989, 1990, 1994). Guest appropriately situated Serra in his own time, but his willingness to equate the padres' corporal punishment of Indians with gentle parental spanking revealed Guest's deep sympathies for Serra and his insensitivities to Indian understandings of these beatings. Guest's refutation may have played well with Serra's supporters, but it was of limited success elsewhere. In the tradition of Cook, scholars Robert H. Jackson and Edward Castillo called attention to the oppressiveness of the missionaries and the degree to which the padres' rule led neophytes to despair and demographic collapse (Jackson & Castillo 1995; Jackson 1994). The study of Indian population decline in the California missions has been discussed most recently in detail in *Children of Coyote, Missionaries of Saint Francis: Indian–Spanish Relations in Colonial California, 1769–1850* (Hackel 2005).

Cook's criticism of the missions and missionaries was a harbinger of things to come. While Cook and his followers directed their fire at the whole mission enterprise, a group of academics pointed their guns directly at Serra. California Indians, political activists, and academic scholars blasted the Church's declaration in 1985 that Serra was worthy of veneration. In response, the Bishop of Monterey published "The Serra Report," a defense of Serra that served only to fuel the controversy by pulling into the debate some of California's leading scholars on Spanish colonization and American Indian life. Then, on the eve of Pope John Paul II's visit to Monterey in 1988, Rupert Costo and Jeannette Henry Costo published a scathing and polemical attack on Serra and the missions. The Costos' *The Missions of California: A Legacy of Genocide* was largely written by Indians and it accused academic historians of falsifying California history and California missionaries of enslaving and killing California Indians. The Costos' argument was clear: Serra was no saint! (Costo & Costo 1987). While some dismissed this book out of hand soon after it was published, it unquestionably gave new prominence to the growing critique of Serra and the missionaries, and it added Native voice to the debate for the first time.

The Costos' *The Missions of California* did not constitute the most extreme criticism directed at Serra, as a small group of activist scholars vilified Serra in a manner that did gross violence to history (Tinker 1993). The most outrageous attack on Serra came from Ward Churchill, who described Serra as "a man whose personal brutality was noteworthy . . . he appears to have delighted in the direct torture of victims, had to be restrained from hanging Indians in lots, à la Columbus, and is quoted as asserting that 'the entire race' of Indians 'should be put to the knife'" (Churchill 1997: 143). A more sober critique on Serra can be found in Daniel Fogel's *Junípero Serra, the Vatican, and Enslavement Theology* (Fogel 1988). Fogel shifted the debate from the saintly qualities of Serra to the political motivations of the Catholic Church in promoting his canonization.

Serra Studies Today

While the Serra Cause and the controversy surrounding it have probably only reinforced peoples' opinions about Serra, there is no doubt that it has dramatically transformed the image of Serra. It is unlikely that Serra will ever be viewed again without some ambivalence, except by his most ardent admirers. Since the 1980s nearly everything written about Serra acknowledges that he and other missionaries ushered in a period of extreme hardship and great dislocation for California Indians, and that the methods missionaries used in eighteenth-century California are no longer consistent with a modern and civilized society. Moreover, recent scholarship recognizes that Indians in California and across the Americas are still struggling with the consequences of colonization by missionization, and that men like Serra played a significant role in the institutions and practices that brought extreme hardship and pain to native communities.

This sea change in the way missions and Serra are viewed can be seen in grade-school textbooks for California children. Almost a century ago, Herbert E. Bolton and Ephraim D. Adams collaborated on a short textbook for California children. The book, *California's Story*, gives Serra short and sympathetic treatment and says little about Indian life in the missions. But it does claim that "the missions founded by the great Serra and his noble companions and successors were the glory of Spanish California" and that "the friars treated the Indians kindly, as if they were children" (Bolton & Adams 1922: 78–81). Today, the leading textbook for California children has no such praise for Serra and starkly points out the hardships Indians faced in the missions:

> Many Indians suffered at the missions. They were unhappy with this new way of life. Indian women and young girls were forced to live in crowded, dirty rooms when they were not working. Indian men had to do the most difficult work. By living at the missions, the Indians gave up their own culture, the way of life they had known in their tribal villages. They could only leave the mission grounds with permission from the padres. (Armento et al. 1999: 78–9)

Serra continues to inspire countless individuals through his life of courage and discipline. The California missions are popular tourist destinations, and Serra International, a lay organization founded in 1933 to promote the priesthood and honor Serra, claims some 10,000 members. The missions of the Sierra Gorda, where Serra lived and worked and whose construction he largely oversaw, have been lovingly restored and were declared a World Heritage Site by UNESCO in 2003. Doubtless, Serra's fame will endure, ensuring that future generations of Californians learn of his contributions to California history and debate the legacy of his life and the mission system he helped to establish. It is to be hoped that future scholarship will take its cues from questions related to the life of the historical Serra as much as from debates emanating from within the Catholic Church.

REFERENCES

Armento, Beverly J. et al. 1999. *Oh, California*. Boston: Houghton Mifflin.

Bancroft, Hubert Howe. 1884. *History of California*, vol. I. San Francisco: The History Company.

Bolton, Herbert E. and Adams, Ephraim D. 1922. *California's Story*. Boston, MA: Allyn & Bacon.

Canedo, Lino Gómez. 1993. *Evangelización, Cultura, y Promoción Social: Ensayos y Estudios Críticos sobre la Contribución Franciscana a los Orígenes Cristianos de México (Siglos XVI–XVIII)*. Mexico: Editorial Porrúa, Mexico.

Canedo, Lino Gómez. 1994. *Sierra Gorda: Pasado y Presente, Coloquio en Homenaje a Lino Gómez Canedo, 1991*. Querétaro, Mexico: Fondo Editorial de Querétaro.

Chapman, Charles E. 1928. *A History of California: The Spanish Period*. New York: Macmillan.

Churchill, Ward. 1997. *A Little Matter of Genocide: Holocaust and Denial in the Americas, 1492 to the Present*. San Francisco: City Lights Books.

Conmy, Peter Thomas. 1960. *Miguel Jose Serra, Padre Junípero, O.F.M.* San Francisco: Dolores Press.

Cook, Sherburne F. 1976. *The Conflict between the California Indian and White Civilization*. Berkeley: University of California Press.

Costo, Rupert and Costo, Jeannette Henry, eds. 1987. *The Missions of California: A Legacy of Genocide*. San Francisco: The Indian Historian Press for the American Indian Historical Society.

Couve de Murville, M.N.L. 2000. *The Man Who Founded California: The Life of Blessed Junípero Serra*. San Francisco: Ignatius Press.

DeNevi, Don and Moholy, Noel Francis. 1985. *Junípero Serra: The Illustrated Story of the Franciscan Founder of California's Missions*. San Francisco: Harper & Row.

Engelhardt, Zephyrin. 1897. *The Franciscans in California*. Harbor Springs, MI: Holy Childhood Indian School.

Engelhardt, Zephyrin. 1908–15. *The Missions and Missionaries of California*, vol. II: *Upper California*. San Francisco: J. H. Barry.

Englebert, Omer. 1956. *The Last of the Conquistadors: Junípero Serra (1713–1784)*. New York: Harcourt, Brace.

Fogel, Daniel. 1988. *Junípero Serra, the Vatican, and Enslavement Theology*. San Francisco: Ism Press.

Font Obrador, Bartomeu. 1978. "Mallorquines en California." In J. Mascaró Pasarius, ed., *História de Mallorca*, vol. 1. Palma de Mallorca: Vicente Colom Rosellò, pp. 299–372.

Font Obrador, Bartomeu. 1998. *Fray Junípero Serra: Doctor de Gentiles.* Mallorca: Miquel Font.

Font Obrador, Bartomeu and Neuerburg, Norman. 1992. *Fr. Junípero Serra: Mallorca–Mexico–Sierra Gorda–Californias.* Comissió de Cultura, Consell Insular de Mallorca.

Geiger, Maynard J., trans. and ed. 1955. *Palóu's Life of Fray Junípero Serra,* 2 vols. Washington, DC: Academy of American Franciscan History.

Geiger, Maynard J. 1959. *The Life and Times of Fray Junípero Serra, O.F.M., or The Man Who Never Turned Back (1713–1784).* Washington, DC: Academy of American Franciscan History.

Geiger, Maynard J. 1976. "Beatification of Fray Junípero Serra." In Francis J. Weber, *Some California Catholic Reminiscences for the United States Bicentennial,* pp. 127–37. [New Haven, CT]: Published for the California Catholic Conference by the Knights of Columbus.

Genet, Donna. 1996. *Father Junípero Serra: Founder of California Missions.* Berkeley Heights, NJ: Enslow Publishers.

Gordon, Dudley. 1969. "Father Serra and Charles F. Lummis: Builder and Preserver of Missions." In Dudley Gordon, *Junípero Serra: California's First Citizen.* Los Angeles: Cultural Assets Press, pp. 23–38.

Guest, Francis F. 1979. "An Examination of the Thesis of S. F. Cook on the Forced Conversion of Indians in the California Missions," *Southern California Quarterly* 61 (1): 1–77.

Guest, Francis F. 1983. "Cultural Perspectives on California Mission Life," *Southern California Quarterly* 65 (1): 1–65.

Guest, Francis F. 1985. "Junípero Serra and His Approach to the Indians," *Southern California Quarterly* 67 (3): 223–61.

Guest, Francis F. 1988. "Principles for an Interpretation of the History of the California Missions (1769–1893)," *Hispania Sacra* 40 (July–December): 791–805.

Guest, Francis F. 1989. "An Inquiry into the Role of the Discipline in California Mission Life," *SCQ* 71 (1): 1–68.

Guest, Francis F. 1990. "Pedro Fages' Five Complaints against Junípero Serra," *Californians* 8 (2): 39–48.

Guest, Francis F. 1994. "The California Missions Were Far from Faultless," *Southern California Quarterly* 76 (3): 255–307.

Gustin, Monique. 1969. *El Barroco en la Sierra Gorda: Misiones Franciscanas en el Estado de Querétaro, Siglo XVIII.* Mexico: Instituto Nacional de Antropología e Historia.

Hackel, Steven W. 2005. *Children of Coyote, Missionaries of Saint Francis: Indian–Spanish Relations in Colonial California, 1769–1850.* Chapel Hill, NC: University of North Carolina Press for the Omohundro Institute of Early American History and Culture.

Hittell, Theodore H. 1885. *The History of California,* vol. I. San Francisco: Pacific Press Publishing House and Occidental Publishing.

Jackson, Robert H. 1994. *Indian Population Decline: The Missions of Northwestern New Spain, 1687–1840.* Albuquerque, NM: University of New Mexico Press.

Jackson, Robert H. and Castillo, Edward. 1995. *Indians, Franciscans, and Spanish Colonization: The Impact of the Mission System on California Indians.* Albuquerque, NM: University of New Mexico Press.

Lummis, Charles F. 1929. *The Spanish Pioneers and the California Missions.* Chicago: A. C. McClurg.

Maynard, Theodore. 1954. *The Long Road of Father Serra.* New York: Appleton-Century-Crofts.

Morgado, Martin J. 1987. *Junípero Serra's Legacy.* Pacific Grove, CA: Mount Carmel.

Morgado, Martin J. 1991. *Junípero Serra: A Pictorial Biography.* Monterey, CA: Siempre Adelante.

Palóu, Francisco. 1787. *Relación Histórica de la Vida y Apostólicas Tareas del Venerable Padre Fray Junípero Serra, y de las Misiones que Fundó en la California Septentrional, y Nuevos Establecimientos de Monterey.* Mexico: Don Felipe de Zúñiga y Ontiveros.

Palóu, Francisco. 1884. *Life of Ven. Padre Junípero Serra*, translated by Very Rev. J. Adam. San Francisco: P. E. Dougherty.

Palóu, Francisco. 1913. *Francisco Palóu's Life and Apostolic Labors of the Venerable Father Junípero Serra: Founder of the Franciscan Missions of California*, translated by C. Scott Williams. Pasadena, CA: George Wharton James.

Palóu, Francisco. 1926. *Historical Memoirs of New California*, translated and edited by Herbert E. Bolton. Berkeley: University of California Press.

Piette, Charles J. G. Maximin. 1946. *Évocation de Junípero Serra: Fondateur de la Californie.* Washington, DC: Academy of American Franciscan History.

Piette, Charles J. G. Maximin. 1949. *Le Secret de Junípero Serra: Fondateur de la Californie-Nouvelle, 1769–1784.* Washington, DC: Academy of American Franciscan History.

Politi, Leo. 1953. *The Mission Bell.* New York: Charles Scribner's Sons.

Ramis, Miguel. n.d. *Petra: Junípero Serra.* Palma: Politenica-Maura.

Repplier, Agnes. 1933. *Junípero Serra: Pioneer Colonist of California.* Garden City, NY: Doubleday Doran.

Richman, Irving B. 1911. *California under Spain and Mexico, 1535–1847: A Contribution Toward the History of the Pacific Coast of the United States, Based on Original Sources (Chiefly Manuscript) in the Spanish and Mexican Archives and Other Repositories.* Boston, MA: Houghton Mifflin.

Sandos, James A. 1988. "Junípero Serra's Canonization and the Historical Record," *The American Historical Review* 95 (5) (December): 1253–69.

Sandos, James A. 2004. *Converting California: Indians and Franciscans in the Missions.* New Haven, CT: Yale University Press.

Tibesar, Antonine, ed. 1955–66. *Writings of Junípero Serra*, 4 vols. Washington, DC: Academy of American Franciscan History.

Tinker, George E. 1993. *Missionary Conquest: The Gospel and Native American Cultural Genocide.* Minneapolis, MN: Fortress Press.

Torrens y Nicolau, Francisco. 1913. *Bosquejo Histórico del Insigne Franciscano, V.P.F. Junípero Serra, Fundador y Apóstol de la California Septentrional.* Felanitx: Establecimiento Tipográfico de B. Reus.

Wilbur, Ray Lyman. 1932. In "Acceptance and Unveiling of the Statues of Junípero Serra and Thomas Starr King; Presented by the State of California; Proceedings in the Congress and in Statuary Hall, United States Capitol" (United States Congress, 72nd Congress, 1st session, 1931–1932). Washington, DC: United States Government Printing Office.

FURTHER READING

Canedo, Lino Gómez. 1976. *Sierra Gorda: Un Típico Enclave Misional en el Centro de México (Siglos XVII–XVIII)*. Pachuca: Centro Hidalguense de Investigaciones Históricas.

Carrillo, Pablo Herrera. 1943. *Fray Junípero Serra: Civilizador de las Californias*. Mexico: Editorial Jus.

Demarest, Donald. 1963. *The First Californian: The Story of Fray Junípero Serra*. New York: Hawthorn Books.

Dominguez Paulin, Arturo. 1977. *Queretaro en la Conquista de las Californias*. México, s.n.

Duque, Sally. 1958. *California's Father Serra*. Portland, OR: Binfords & Mort.

Fitch, A. H. 1914. *Junípero Serra: The Man and His Work*. Chicago: A. C. McClurg.

Font Obrador, Bartomeu. 1989. *Fra Junípero Serra: Las Balears i el Nou Món*. Caixa de Balears.

Galmés Más, Lorenzo. 1988. *Fray Junípero Serra: Apostól de California*. Madrid: Biblioteca de Autores Cristianos.

Gleiter, Jan and Thompson, Kathleen. 1989. *Junípero Serra*. Milwaukee, WI: Raintree Publishers.

Habig, Marion A. and Steck, Francis Borgia. 1964. *Man of Greatness: Father Junípero Serra*. Chicago: Franciscan Herald Press.

King, Kenneth M. 1956. *Mission to Paradise: The Story of Junípero Serra and the Missions of California*. London: Burns & Oates.

Martini, Teri. 1959. *Sandals on the Golden Highway: A Life of Junípero Serra*. Paterson, NJ: St. Anthony Guild Press.

Meyer, Kathleen Allan. 1990. *Father Serra: Traveler on the Golden Chain*. Huntington, IN: Our Sunday Visitor.

Stanley, Jerry. 1997. *Digger: The Tragic Fate of the California Indians from the Missions to the Gold Rush*. New York: Crown Publishers.

White, Florence Meiman. 1987. *The Story of Junípero Serra: Brave Adventurer*. New York: Dell.

Woodgate, M. V. 1966. *Junípero Serra: Apostle of California, 1713–1784*. Westminster, MD: The Newman Press.

Chapter Six

ALTA CALIFORNIA, THE PACIFIC, AND INTERNATIONAL COMMERCE BEFORE THE GOLD RUSH

David Igler

In 1827 30 commercial vessels arrived on the coast of Alta California. Many of the ships' names leave little doubt as to their national origin: the *Baikal*, *Golovnin*, and *Okhotsk* (Russia), the *Massachusetts*, *Franklin*, and *Eagle* (United States), the *Comete* and *Heros* (France), the *Kamahalo* and *Karaimoku* (Hawaii), the *San Magdale* (Mexico), and the *Aurora*, *Cadboro*, and *Thomas Knowland* (England), among numerous others. While more than one-third of these commercial voyages hailed from the United States, the rest originated from nations and polities in the European Atlantic and Pacific oceans. Many of the vessels along the Alta California coast in 1827 exhibited a fusion of Pacific and Atlantic commercial parentage: a Peruvian-based partnership flew the British flag over the *Aurora*, the Alaska-based Russian American Company owned the *Baikal*, *Golovnin*, and *Okhotsk*, the two Hawaiian-owned ships were constructed in Atlantic shipyards, while the *Cadboro* carried out business for England's Hudson's Bay Company (and its forts in the Pacific Northwest). If an odd mixture of Atlantic and Pacific commercial interests characterized these vessels, an international cast also described the ships' crews, which were gathered or impressed from all parts and ports of the globe.

International commerce – rather than national or imperial motives – had drawn these vessels to Alta California's littoral zone. Once there, the ship captains acquired basic supplies and certain commodities, while offloading manufactured goods, specie, and sometimes personnel. A few of the vessels acquired items of special note: the British brig *Fulham* carried the Santa Cruz Mission bell (in dire need of recasting) to Callao, Peru, while the Boston-bound *Franklin* transported 1,600 pounds of beaver pelts recently skinned by the legendary American mountain man Jedediah Smith (whose group had trapped its way across the Rocky and Sierra Nevada mountains before descending the Pacific Slope). Commerce drew those 30 ships to many other places in the Pacific prior to and after their visit to Alta

California. Taken as a whole, they docked at every North and South American port on the Pacific; almost half dropped anchor in Hawaii, and some voyaged on to other Pacific islands or to Canton. The Pacific Ocean as a whole was the general destination, and vessels tacked back and forth across that ocean in pursuit of profitable exchange. The British writer Daniel Defoe captured the essence of this commerce decades earlier in *A Plan of the English Commerce*: "The Commerce of the World, especially as it is now carried on, is an unbounded Ocean of Business; Trackless and unknown, like the Seas it is managed upon" (Defoe 1728: vii).

Despite the vibrant trade carried on in this one year, pre-Gold Rush California is rarely thought of as a significant site of maritime commerce, much less a nexus of truly *international* trade. Similarly, Alta California's relationship with the Pacific Ocean – obviously its most proximate and important geographic connection – has been largely unexamined by historians of the period. Such omissions are all the more surprising given the recent trend of placing California in transnational and oceanic contexts: for instance, the "world rushed in" with the gravitational pull of the Gold Rush; successive waves of transpacific migrations from Asian nations marked the late nineteenth and early twentieth centuries; and global flows of technology, capital, and immigrants after World War II transformed California into the world's fifth largest economy and cultural trendsetter (Holliday 1981; Takaki 1989; Lee 2003; Starr 2006). These and many other now-common themes project a California history rich in international and Pacific influences. But this reading of the past portrays this internationalism as product of US conquest and twentieth-century global forces.

The traditional periodization of California history contributes to the problem. We tend to break California history into four, relatively neat and discrete, stages: Native California (before 1769), Spanish California (1769–1821), Mexican California (1821–46), and US rule after 1848. Such stages make a great deal of historical, conceptual, and pedagogical sense. Yet they also prioritize a boundaried and exclusive sense of the place and its peoples, essentially removing the region and its occupants from broader, outside influences. My concern lies with the middle two stages. The Spanish empire and subsequent Republic of Mexico held dominion over Alta California between 1769 and 1848 – that is, to the extent we consider their settlement of a coastal swath of territory from Sonoma to San Diego to represent California as a whole (Native Californians continued to control a much larger region). Spain and Mexico also sought to control a range of relationships between Alta California and the outside world through trade restrictions, naturalization laws, and land ownership requirements (Hackel 2005). For these and other reasons, historians tend to accept Alta California as a secure, inward-looking, self-contained province. The world did not "rush in" but kept its distance.

Commerce on the California coast tells a different story, one filled with contraband trade, international presences, and eventual acceptance (by Mexican authorities) of the reality that California bordered a vast ocean filled with opportunities for exchange. We might benefit by adopting a different point of view to understand this increasingly international pre-Gold Rush California – a point of view drawn chiefly from the ocean (Igler 2004). From this vantage point, California provided a primary destination for vessels that trafficked the Pacific Ocean in ever-expanding numbers after 1800. Those vessels originated in European, American, and some Pacific ports, and they represented a mounting awareness of the Pacific as a new commercial frontier. Long before California's gold, rich soils, and climate drew settlers from around the world, other commodities and prospects attracted trading vessels to Alta California's shoreline.

The origins of international trade in Alta California began with Spain. Spanish ships comprised the overwhelming majority of vessels entering Alta California waters prior to 1800 – these vessels carried supplies for the missions, soldiers, and some settlers for the Spanish garrisons and pueblos. Spanish trade policy sought to safeguard this province by restricting foreign ships from entering Alta California's ports. In general, Spain's imperial theory throughout the Americas sought security and internal economies over engagements with foreign interests (Weber 1992). But while trade *policy* in Spanish California was highly restrictive, commercial *practice* played out quite differently. We can almost date the advent and subsequent rise of foreign traders in California waters to 1800, when two American ships (the *Betsey* and *Eliza*) trafficked along the coastline. Within three years, however, foreign ships outnumbered Spanish vessels on the coastline, and that pattern only grew more pronounced in the next few years (Ogden 1979).

What enticed foreign traders to Alta California and how did they circumvent Spanish trade restrictions? The American ship captain William Shaler penned one of the best descriptions of California trade for this early period. Shaler's vessel, the *Lelia Byrd*, crisscrossed the Pacific four times between 1803 and 1805, primarily acquiring North American sea otter pelts and furs for resale in Canton's bustling marketplace. During this period he repeatedly visited the Alta and Baja California coastline, bartering on shipdeck and shore near San Luis Obispo, Santa Barbara, Santa Catalina Island, the Channel Islands, San Diego, Cedros Island, and what soon became the well-known contraband port at San Pedro (near Alta California's second pueblo, Los Angeles). Some Spanish officials discreetly welcomed the chance to trade with this American privateer. One group of Spanish officials dined on board the *Lelia Byrd* and "behaved with great civility, though rigid in their duty," Shaler noted with obvious sarcasm (Shaler 1808: 144). The padre of Mission San Luis Obispo reported to Spanish authorities that he received Shaler "with little amiability," though the meeting between these two men indicates that trade certainly took place (Ogden 1941: 42). Shaler bartered with members of Juan Ortega's family at Rancho Refugio (near Santa Barbara) and the Tongva people ("our Indian friends") on Catalina Island (Shaler 1808: 144). Many other commercial exchanges transpired between Shaler and Spanish or native individuals – all of it illegal under Spanish law.

Rather than a difficult trade environment, Shaler's account highlighted the ease with which commerce took place in Alta and Baja California. "At present," he observed, "a person acquainted with the coast may always procure abundant supplies and provisions" (Shaler 1808: 153). He specifically designated knowledge of "the coast" as crucial to a trader's success because Native Californians and Spaniards alike could safely trade most anywhere along the coast outside the main ports. California's littoral zone – from ship to beach to shoreline dwellings – became the active mart where all parties could pay little heed to Spain's trade restrictions. The "abundant supplies and provisions" procured by Shaler suggest a lively and enthusiastic trade with Franciscan missionaries, a fact he confirmed in an 1804 letter to another trader: "They take skins [hunted by California Indians] now at all the upper Missions" (Cleveland 1855: 406). Shaler concluded his account of trading on the coast with a remark subsequently echoed by numerous visitors to Alta California: "All these circumstances prove, that, under a good government, the Californias would soon rise to ease and affluence" (Shaler 1808: 153). Shaler here refers to "the Californias" as a place rather than its Spanish inhabitants – an odd phrasing, for sure, but one that displays his understanding of Alta California's potential within the Pacific's new commercial environment.

Though deemed illegal by Spanish law, trade on the California coast accelerated sharply during the next two decades. By 1827 – the year that opened this essay, also a representative year in terms of commerce – trade flourished throughout Alta California. Mexico, not Spain, now governed the province, and Mexican officials had curtailed most trade restrictions previously enacted by Spain. However, import and export taxes continued to make clandestine trade the most common form of commodity exchange for foreign traders, missionaries, settlers, Indians, and Mexican officials alike. Governor José Darío Argüello best summed up the trade environment of the 1820s: "Necessity makes licit what is not licit by law" (Hackel 2005: 371). California cattle hides and tallow constituted the largest export item, while sea otters were virtually extinct on the coastline due to overhunting. The primary labor force of mission Indians – and Native Californians as a whole – continued to decline in numbers through infertility, infant mortality, and introduced diseases. In 1827 – just a few years before William Shaler died in Cuba during a cholera epidemic – measles raged through the missions and killed more than 10 percent of the Indian population (Hackel 2005). Shaler could not have predicted these and the many other changes to the province, but his prophecy of California's prominent role in the Pacific's bustling marketplace proved correct. An energetic commerce carried on by maritime traders from around the world had connected California to the surrounding ocean basin.

To understand California's escalating trade we might benefit by taking a giant step back from any particular date to view the larger trends and wider connections of pre-Gold Rush commerce. In all, at least 953 vessels either docked in a California port or trafficked on the coast between 1786 and 1848, making it one of the most visited parts of the eastern Pacific.[1] These voyages, if studied individually, range from short coastal runs to voyages "round the world" (as an endless number of mariners titled their published accounts). Examined collectively, these voyages cast light on Alta California's place within the widening networks of Pacific and world trade.

The decadal growth of trade offers one important characteristic. Based on the 953 ships entering Alta California waters, 5.6 percent arrived in the 1790s, 5.7 percent in the decade after 1800, 7.6 percent in the 1810s, 24 percent in the 1820s, 22 percent in the 1830s, and 34 percent in the first eight years of the 1840s. In short, trade gradually increased each decade until the 1820s, when it swelled due to developments in California and throughout the Pacific, including Mexican independence, the termination of trade restrictions in many ports (especially Spanish-controlled ports), and the global spread of information about Pacific trading opportunities. This surge in trade also coincided with the entrance of the American whaling fleet into Pacific waters during the 1820s; Alta California became a key site for provisioning and refurbishing whaling vessels. The subsequent decline of whaling vessels in California accounts for the slight dip in traffic during the 1830s. California maritime commerce reached astonishing heights in the 1840s, with almost one-third of all pre-Gold Rush ships arriving and departing in the eight years between 1840 and 1848.

As the number of vessels increased each decade – especially in the 1820s and 1840s – so grew the international cast of participants. This point is significant for both California and Pacific commerce as a whole. The largest share of ships entering California waters came from five nations: the United States (45 percent), England (13 percent), Spain (12 percent), Mexico (12 percent), and Russia (7 percent). But trading vessels from at least 17 other Pacific and European nations also visited California in the first half of the nineteenth century. To borrow historian Karen Kupperman's characterization of *eastern* colonial America – California and the future American far West bordering the Pacific was "international before it became national" (Kupperman 2002: 105).

This overview of ship national origins raises two additional points. First, while Spanish supply ships from Mexico made up the largest share of Alta California traffic before 1800, United States vessels soon surpassed all other trading nations by a large margin. US *commercial* interests in the Pacific therefore anticipated and ultimately influenced its geopolitical and military interests of the mid-nineteenth century (Gibson 1993). Second, despite the strong position attained by US trading vessels in California and the Pacific, at least 527 ships sailing under more than 20 different flags also entered California waters. Thus, when the American "Pathfinder" John Charles Fremont surveyed the California coastline aboard the *Sterling* in 1844–5, he shared those waters with ships from England, France, Russia, Mexico, the United States, Germany, Sweden, Hamburg, Canada, and Alta California itself, not to mention the truly international cast of shipboard workers. The point here deserves emphasis: California's commercial activity was international prior to the worldwide convergence of gold seekers, and, perhaps more importantly, this internationalization of commerce mirrored developments elsewhere in the Pacific Basin.

A final point drawn from this overview of shipping is the way Alta California commerce intersected with Pacific trade as a whole. The voyage routes of the 953 vessels reveal these connections. Based on vessels entering California, the most frequently visited ports were Hawaii (42 percent of ships), Callao (22 percent), San Blas (19 percent), Acapulco (18 percent), the Russian port at Sitka (12 percent), and Canton (7 percent). In addition, 13 percent of ships stopped somewhere along the Northwest Coast of North America, trading at established forts and coastal native communities. The island Pacific – beyond Hawaii – also witnessed increased trade, with the Galapagos, Marquesas, Tahiti, and Philippine islands leading all others. Over 50 percent of ships visiting California had also docked on a Pacific island, which shows that islands played a prominent role in transoceanic commerce.

While the Gold Rush attracted people from around the world specifically to California, the previous six decades had witnessed the growth of California commerce as one part of wider trade patterns in the Pacific Ocean. Indeed, only Spanish ships from Mexico and some Russian ships from Alaska arrived in Alta California as their sole destination. This fact hardly lessens the significance of Alta California's trade; instead, it forces us to examine why international traders stopped there as one place on their oceanic voyages. For many traders, Hawaii was the Pacific's central market while California was a peripheral supplier of certain goods (Richards 2000).

Consider the activities of the English schooner *Columbia*, which ran a constant course between the North American coast, Hawaii, and Canton between June 1814 and Christmas Day 1817 (Corney 1965). The *Columbia* crossed the entire Pacific four times to sell North American furs and Hawaiian sandalwood in Canton: twice exchanging basic necessities for furs in New Archangel (Sitka), five times collecting furs and other goods near the Columbia River, and stopping three times in Alta California for beef, hides, and agricultural produce from the missions. The *Columbia* anchored in

Hawaii four times during its three years of Pacific crossings – for repairs, to gather new crew members, and to sell goods. The *Columbia*'s crisscrossing of the Pacific superimposed at least three common trade routes, all of which involved Hawaii: the "triangle" fur trade between the Pacific Northwest, Hawaii, and Canton; the Russian trade connecting Sitka and California to Hawaii; and the bilateral California–Hawaii trade. Each of these "trades" used Hawaii as a place of exchange for Pacific goods (furs, hides, sandalwood) and American luxury products (imported mostly on New England ships). California commerce blossomed as one contributing part of the Hawaiian trade. Ties between Hawaii and California only strengthened in the 1830s and grew more pronounced in subsequent decades (Whitehead 1992).

What commodities or exchanges did Alta California offer the maritime trader? Ships entering California arrived and departed with many different items. Spanish ships from Mexico (prior to 1821) primarily shuttled supplies to the California missions and returned with items produced by mission Indian laborers, such as hemp. Russian traders brought pelts and returned with the barest foodstuffs to their isolated settlement at Sitka. American whaling vessels arrived and left with whale oil plus provisions to sustain the crews. But California served as a trade depot for a variety of other resources, including sea otter pelts (before their extinction in the 1820s), skins from other animals, timber, giant tortoises, and crops (Ogden 1941; Gibson 1993; Hardee 2002). California Indians (inside or outside the influence of missions and secular authority) contributed to most of these productions and often gained trade items in exchange, though they also fell victim to diseases brought by traders and settlers. The biological impact on native birthrates and mortality was horrendous (Igler 2004).

California's legendary "hide and tallow" trade during the Mexican period has gained the most notice by historians. The "cattle on a thousand hills" – the cattle, once stripped of hides and fat reduced to tallow – allowed wealthy rancheros to barter with maritime traders for luxury goods, enriched numerous Yankee-California traders (such as Abel Stearns and Thomas O. Larkin), and filled many Boston-bound ships with salted hides (Cleland 1941; Pitt 1966; Hardee 2002). Indeed, hides and tallow contributed to cargos in almost one-third of vessels departing from Alta California. But the well-documented life of this trade has almost become the solitary symbol of pre-Gold Rush commerce and thereby reduces Alta California to a sun-crusted Pacific abattoir for the city of Boston. Alta California's commerce was more multifaceted and dynamic than suggested by that stereotype.

Far more interesting and revealing lessons about California's trade can be learned from those Boston ships that carried neither hides nor tallow. Take the *Eagle* and the *Clarion*: each ship left Boston in 1817 and arrived in California the following year. The *Clarion* sailed by way of the Cape of Good Hope to Tasmania, then across the Pacific to California after a stop in Hawaii. The *Eagle* entered the Pacific from the opposite direction: around the Horn to Hawaii, a short stop in Sitka for sea otter pelts, and back to Hawaii before arriving on the California coast. Both captains found eager trading partners in California. Captain Henry Gyzelaar of the *Clarion* was "able to purchase of the people on shore some furs very valuable in Canton, paying therefore everything they had on board, saving what was indispensable to the safe navigation of the vessel" (Ogden 1941: 79). Captain William Heath Davis of the *Eagle* traded with Juan Ortega and Ignacio Martinez, both of Santa Barbara, and "realized about $25,000 profit in Spanish doubloons and sea otter skins, from sales in California, aside from profits in the Russian settlements" (Davis 1889: 299). Both ships sailed for China by way of Sitka and Hawaii, arriving in Canton in 1820.

These ships reveal many important elements of California trade and its connection to a broader oceanic commerce: the willingness of Spanish Californians to covertly engage in contraband trade, the ease with which foreign captains circumvented Spanish law, the attraction of markets in Hawaii and Canton, and the commercial engagements throughout the Pacific between people of many nations (indigenous communities, American, Spanish, British, Russian, Chinese, and many others). The voyages of the *Eagle* and *Clarion* illustrate something else about international trade in California and the Pacific – the entrepreneurial nature and often circuitous routes taken by commercial vessels. Ships arrived in Alta California, tacked up and down the coast in search of profitable exchanges, left the region, and frequently returned for more trading within the same voyage. Such meandering routes marked Pacific commercial voyages as a whole, especially for American ship captains, noted the British trader Alexander M'Konochie. "Each American vessel," he wrote, "leaves its own port on general speculation[.] Wherever they unload, they are ready and willing to embark in any speculation." Rather than criticizing the "circuitous and desultory manner" of these American entrepreneurs, M'Konochie heralded them as "an active, busy band, sagacious to discover and eager to improve every promising opportunity" (M'Konochie 1818: 98). And those "sagacious" Americans increasingly set their sails for Alta California – over half the commercial vessels to visit its shores after 1800 flew the US flag.

From the 1770s to the mid-1840s, ships arriving in Alta California revealed one of the most elementary characteristics of the place: its proximity and relationship to the Pacific Ocean. California Indians had benefited by this proximity for thousands of years by harvesting the Pacific's natural resources and, in some cases, using Pacific waters for short-range exchanges with indigenous trade partners (Arnold 2001). The trade activity that developed alongside Spanish settlement was something new and developed gradually over time: commercial voyages originating from distant shores visiting Alta California as one stop on transoceanic ventures. By the early 1800s, Alta California was known to international traders who plied the Pacific in search of pelts, furs, and many other profitable goods.

The fact that Spain did not profit from this international trade – and, in fact, attempted to curtail its existence – was only one of many indications that the Spanish American empire would not survive the commercial trends of the early modern world. However, many Spanish officials and settlers in Alta California would benefit from the clandestine trade, in the process forging an identity more *Californio* than Spanish. With Mexican independence, those *Californios* jettisoned most previous trade restrictions and developed a pastoral economy dependent on maritime imports and exports. As a result, the number of commercial vessels visiting Alta California boomed in the 1820s, 1830s, and 1840s prior to the global maritime onslaught of the Gold Rush.

What should we know about the commercial voyages visiting Alta California during the half century before American conquest? First, voyages from ports in the Atlantic Ocean comprised the largest share of traffic – meaning that European and American traders viewed California as a place of new and profitable opportunities. Second, the vast majority of vessels entering California waters continued on to the Northwest Coast, Alaska, and/or Hawaii, illustrating the Pacific network of ports that united the future American Far West *long before* the United States annexed its Pacific territories. Commerce, in this way, paved the way for American territorial expansion, and Pacific-based trade predated the national association of California, Hawaii, the Northwest Coast, and Alaska. Finally, the nature of those voyages may best be described as *free* trade. Whether viewed from Alta California or some other shore in the ocean, the Pacific increasingly functioned as a free trade waterscape. Maritime traders and some *Californios* benefited from this situation, while California Indians decidedly did not benefit in the long run.

Most of us believe that California is a very international place. Californians have debated the merits of this internationalism since the 1850s, welcoming some groups and cultural characteristics while also practicing explicit forms of social and cultural exclusion. Today, most Californians value (or at the very least recognize) that international texture: its multi-cultured cosmopolitanism, varied regionalism, distinctive and hodge-podge cuisines, and vibrant global economy. But California's internationalism did not stem from twentieth-century developments nor did it result from American conquest and gold strikes. This phenomenon was also quite independent from American, or Mexican, or Spanish rule. California's internationalism originated not so much on the terra itself as in the coastal waters, with maritime traders searching for new markets, commodities, and trading partners. Californians – Indian, Spanish, and Mexican – met those traders and shared their desire for profitable exchange. International California was born in the process.

NOTE

1   The following statistics derive from a database I constructed with records from Adele Ogden's collection, "Trading Vessels on the California Coast, 1786–1848" (1979). Ogden's sources for each vessel include the original shipping logs, travel accounts, Mexican and Spanish archival collections, and an extensive survey of secondary literature. I entered each record into a spreadsheet with 44 possible entry fields (including ownership, flag, types of cargo, and destinations). While Ogden's records may not be entirely complete, they represent by far the most comprehensive (and unexamined) compilation of California shipping prior to the Gold Rush.

REFERENCES

Arnold, Jeanne E. (ed.) 2001. *The Origins of a Pacific Coast Chiefdom: The Chumash of the Channel Islands.* Salt Lake City: University of Utah Press.

Cleland, Robert Glass. 1941. *The Cattle of a Thousand Hills: Southern California, 1850–1870.* San Marino, CA: Huntington Library.

Cleveland, Richard J. 1855. *Voyages and Commercial Enterprises of the Sons of New England.* New York: Leavitt & Allen.

Corney, Peter. 1965. *Early Voyages in the North Pacific.* Fairfield, WA: Ye Galleon Press.

Davis, William Heath. 1889. *Sixty Years in California.* San Francisco: A. J. Leary.

Defoe, Daniel. 1728. *A Plan of the English Commerce: Being a Compleat Prospect of the Trade of this Nation.* London: Charles Rivington.

Gibson, Arrell Morgan. 1993. *Yankees in Paradise: The Pacific Basin Frontier.* Albuquerque: University of New Mexico Press.

Hackel, Steven W. 2005. *Children of Coyote, Missionaries of Saint Francis: Indian–Spanish Relations in Colonial California, 1769–1850.* Chapel Hill: University of North Carolina Press.

Hardee, Jim. 2002. "Soft Gold: Animal Skins and the Early Economy of California." In Dennis O. Flynn, Arturo Giraldez, and James Sobredo, eds., *Studies in Pacific History: Economics, Politics, and Migration.* London: Ashgate, pp. 23–39.

Holliday, J. S. 1981. *The World Rushed In: The California Gold Rush Experience.* New York: Simon & Schuster.

Igler, David. 2004. "Diseased Goods: Global Exchanges in the Eastern Pacific Basin, 1770–1850," *American Historical Review* 109 (June): 693–719.

Kupperman, Karen Ordahl. 2002. "International at the Creation: Early Modern American History." In Thomas Bender, *Rethinking American History in a Global Age.* Berkeley: University of California Press, pp. 103–22.

Lee, Erika. 2003. *At America's Gates: Chinese Immigration during the Exclusion Era, 1882–1943.* Chapel Hill: University of North Carolina Press.

M'Konochie, Alexander. 1818. *A Summary View of the Statistics and Existing Commerce of the Principal Shores of the Pacific Ocean.* London: J. M. Richardson.

Ogden, Adele. 1941. *The California Sea Otter Trade, 1784–1848.* Berkeley: University of California Press.

Ogden, Adele. 1979. "Trading Vessels on the California Coast, 1786–1848." Archival collection, Bancroft Library, University of California, Berkeley.

Pitt, Leonard. 1966. *The Decline of the Californios: A Social History of the Spanish-Speaking Californians, 1846–1890.* Berkeley: University of California Press.

Richards, Rhys. 2000. *Honolulu: Centre of Trans-Pacific Trade, Shipping Arrivals and Departures, 1820–1840.* Honolulu: Hawaiian Historical Society.

Shaler, William. 1808. *Journal of a Voyage between China and the North-Western Coast of America, Made in 1804.* Philadelphia.

Starr, Kevin. 2006. *Coast of Dreams: California on the Edge, 1990–2003.* New York: Vintage.

Takaki, Ronald T. 1989. *Strangers from a Different Shore: A History of Asian Americans.* Boston, MA: Little, Brown.

Weber, David J. 1992. *The Spanish Frontier in North America.* New Haven, CT: Yale University Press.

Whitehead, John. 1992. "Hawai'i: The First and Last Far West?" *Western Historical Quarterly* 23 (May): 153–77.

FURTHER READING

Cook, Warren. 1973. *Flood Tide of Empire: Spain and the Pacific Northwest, 1543–1848.* New Haven, CT: Yale University Press.

Heffer, Jean. 2002. *The United States and the Pacific: History of a Frontier.* Notre Dame: University of Notre Dame Press.

Layton, Thomas N. 1997. *The Voyage of the 'Frolic': New England Merchants and the Opium Trade.* Stanford, CA: Stanford University Press.

Ogden, Adele. 1941. *The California Sea Otter Trade, 1784–1848.* Berkeley: University of California Press.

Walton, John. 2001. *Storied Land: Community and Memory in Monterey.* Berkeley: University of California Press.

Chapter Seven

LICIT AND ILLICIT UNIONS: ENGENDERING MEXICAN SOCIETY

Rosamaría Toruño Tanghetti

Recent works on California's Spanish colonial and Mexican national periods reveal a healthy coming of age for California history. Once relegated to the margins of two distinct national histories, pre-Gold Rush California has earned a long-overdue place in the colonial and early national story of the United States and Mexico. This move away from an Atlantic-centered colonial and early national American history has been salutary. The once dominant narrative of the British experience in North America has given way to a richly nuanced multifocal story of the various colonial and national projects that unfolded here. Alan Taylor's *American Colonies*, a masterful synthesis of recent colonial North American scholarship, serves as one example of this transformation (2001). Scholars working in California's Spanish colonial and Mexican national periods have begun linking this state's Hispanic and indigenous past more firmly to this evolving narrative. *Children of Coyote, Missionaries of Saint Francis* by Steven Hackel signals these shifts in the temporal and regional boundaries of American history (2005). At the same time, scholars mining Spanish-language archival sources have reconnected pre-1850 California to colonial New Spain and early national Mexico (Pubols 2000; Chávez-García 2004; Tanghetti 2004; González 2005; Hackel 2005).

As the once Anglo-centric narrative of North American history has broadened to include the myriad encounters between native peoples, French, Spanish, and Russian colonists, so the dominant paradigm of California history has begun to unravel as scholars shed light on the Mexican era (1821–46) and on the two successive territorial conquests – the Spanish in 1769 and the American in 1846. A simple narrative of conquest characterized by a binary model that relegates the invaders and the invaded into two distinct and opposing camps no longer satisfies. While keeping sight of the catastrophic demographic collapse of California's Indians in the missions and of the profound economic and social consequences of Spanish colonialism, Mexican independence, and the American conquest, scholars have recently demonstrated the ways in which Indians, and later Mexicans, fashioned lives for themselves within these changing circumstances. For one, Hackel's work on Indian–Spanish relations reveals how Indians negotiated positions of authority for themselves and worked in concert with Franciscan friars to regulate discipline within California's missions. Using municipal records, Chávez-García demonstrates how women used courts to protect their rights within two patriarchal cultures – Mexican and American. She finds that Mexican women took advantage of new American laws after 1848 to challenge power relations within their families and communities. Historians working on inter-ethnic relations have begun focusing on how social and sexual relations bridged the seemingly stark divide between Indians, Spanish, Mexicans, and Americans. This new, finely grained social history has uncovered the complex interplay of status, gender, and ethnicity in Spanish and Mexican California to reveal contested power relations and a more nuanced understanding of conquest (Hurtado 1999; Pubols 2000; Chávez-García 2004; Sandos 2004; Tanghetti 2004; González 2005; Hackel 2005; Lightfoot 2005; Casas 2007).

This essay explores marriage and sexuality in Mexican California to understand how decisions about intimate matters had a hand in shaping local society. Public sacramental registers – in this case, baptismal records from San Carlos Borromeo Mission – provide access to the most private of places. In recording birth details, mission clerics unwittingly opened the doors for scholars to people's bedrooms, thus revealing the interstitial and less readily apparent personal connections between Mexican California's inhabitants – Indians, Mexicans, and Euro-Americans. Sex, both licit and illicit, bound people into legitimate and informal kinship networks that cut across social boundaries delineated by ethnicity, nationality, and status.

Soon after Mexico gained independence from Spain in 1821, foreign merchants, traders, and trappers began arriving in Alta California in search of lucrative commercial opportunities. In an effort to stimulate economic growth, lawmakers in faraway Mexico City lifted restrictive mercantilist trade policies promulgated earlier by crown officials throughout Spanish colonial America. The provincial capital of Monterey served as the main port of entry where the only customs house in California was located. Thus mariners and, less frequently, fur trappers traveling overland from New Mexico, made their way to that small coastal settlement if they chose to engage in legitimate commerce.

Travelers often described what they saw as they approached Monterey. If no fog or low-lying clouds shrouded the bay, mariners would spot Point Pinos – a pine-covered land mass that rose abruptly from water's edge – a landmark that reminded seafarers to continue sailing northwest a bit before turning sharply southeast into the head of the bay. Nearing land, observant sailors might focus on the presidio, a military fort comprised of one-story buildings arranged in a square. They might also discern 40 or so whitewashed houses situated mostly to the south of the garrison. Scanning their eyes to take in the entirety of this Mexican frontier settlement, they would see a smattering of thatched huts and other structures nestled near small, gently rounded hills. None could miss the towering pines and other assorted trees that framed this provincial capital (Duhaut-Cilly 1997: 72).

Visual impressions continued as merchants and ship captains disembarked and then waded through the crashing waves to reach the presidio or the customs house. During the 1820s, Monterey had no docks. But it did have plenty of people who congregated near shore, curious about the newcomers, their cargo, and eager to engage in commerce. Self-subsistent horticulturalists, many residents of Mexican California also traded cattle hides and tallow for luxury items – fancy beds, fine clothing, jewelry – and manufactured goods (Nunis, Jr. 1998: 310). As newcomers took note of Monterey's physical setting, they also noticed the social landscape of Mexican California.

An ethnically and linguistically diverse people inhabited California. The Hispanic residents, the majority of whom lived in settlements such as San Diego, Los Angeles, Santa Barbara, San José, Monterey, and their environs, comprised but a minuscule fraction of the territory's population. At the time of independence in 1821, they numbered approximately 3,500 – a handful when one considers they lived amidst nearly 22,000 coastal Indians (Hackel 1998: 122). By the end of the Mexican era in 1848, these settlers totaled approximately 7,500 (Weber 1982: 206). Descended from the 600 or so Spanish colonists who had migrated to Alta California from Sonora and Sinaloa between 1769 and 1781, these were a mixed-race people. Mostly they were mestizos – products of years of Spanish–Indian sexual intermingling – and mulattos – people of mixed Spanish and African ancestry. They called themselves *gente de razón*, which means "people of reason," to distinguish themselves from the Indians, whom, they believed possessed little or no reason. In addition, they used the term "californio" in self-reference, indicating their strong identification with the land in much the same way that Hispanic Texans and New Mexicans used the words "tejano" and "nuevomexicano."

California's Indian population comprised a veritable mosaic of human diversity. At the time of contact with the first Spanish colonizing expedition in 1769, aboriginal Californians spoke upwards of one hundred distinct languages, and lived by a combination of hunting, gathering, and proto-agriculture, depending on the natural resources of their localities. Whether Chumash, Rumsen, Esselen, or Miwok, California Indians organized themselves socially into villages and politically into semi-autonomous tribelets (Bean 1974, 1992). However, Mexican Californians, as their colonial forebears, viewed Indians as *neófitos* if they were or had been attached to one of the Franciscan missions or *gentiles* if they were not. The collapse of

California's diverse Indian population into a simple dualistic scheme – *neófito/gentil* – reflected Franciscan missionaries' views of Indians as converts or heathens and, at the very least, masked the dense web of kin relations that belied the distinctiveness of these categories.

Foreigners, primarily from the United States but also from England and other parts of northern Europe such as France, Belgium, and Germany, trickled into California beginning in 1821, adding additional ethnic and linguistic diversity to the territory. Despite these national differences, Mexican Californians called foreigners *ingleses*, which means "English," because of the language most of them spoke (Dana 2001: 91).

Newcomers invariably noticed California's diverse inhabitants, even when the terms they used did not adequately describe them, capture their diversity, or allude to the family and social ties that bound them to one another. Foreigners referred to Hispanics as "Spaniards," "Mexicans," or "Californians," and indigenous peoples as "Indians." But Mexican society was not organized around these categories. Rather, as John Walton aptly observed, family and kinship networks "mapped local society" (Walton 2001: 69). Marriage formally united individuals into conjugal pairs and linked families into broader kin networks. Personal decisions about whom one married and with whom one had sex – not always the same person – shaped the broad contours of Mexican society. Licit and illicit sex had much to do with the ordering of Mexican society into hierarchies of social difference; indeed, these most intimate of decisions were informed by concerns of social status. Moreover, sex within and out of marriage created family and kinship networks that cut across and belied the seemingly fixed boundaries between *gente de razón*, *indios*, and *ingleses*.

At first glance, the newly arrived could not readily see the personal intimate relations that linked Californians of different ethnicities into family networks. Categories often mask the connections between people. To see the connections, foreigners had to tarry awhile, acquaint themselves with the locals, integrate themselves into local families through marriage, and perhaps overhear snippets of hushed rumors in order to perceive how the most intimate of private decisions and actions shaped the public face of Mexican society. Of course, we cannot physically travel back to nineteenth-century Monterey to gain such insights. Nevertheless, the assiduous record keeping by California's Franciscan missionaries of important life events – baptisms and marriages – offers ample evidence of the intimate relations that ordered local society.

The story of one-time Monterey resident and prominent Californian Mariano Guadalupe Vallejo provides a useful portal into Mexican society. In particular, his marriage to Francisca Benicia Carrillo and his illicit sexual relations with other women illustrate how marriage and sexuality mediated the formation of Mexican society. Specifically, his story reveals the importance of social status in marriage decisions, the social repercussions of illicit sexual relations, the patriarchal nature of Mexican society, and the role of honor in shaping people's sexual conduct. Moreover, it demonstrates that kinship networks, legitimate and otherwise, cut across social boundaries defined by status, ethnicity, and nationality. Focusing on women, gender, conquest, inter-ethnic encounters, and power, recent scholars have mined rich archival sources to reveal a previously hidden world of intimate social relations (Hurtado 1999; Pubols 2000; Chávez-García 2004; Sandos 2004; Tanghetti 2004; Hackel 2005; Lightfoot 2005; Casas 2007). Indeed, the new scholarship on Mexican California foregrounds this world.

For the 23-year-old Mariano Guadalupe Vallejo, a military mission to San Diego in January of 1830 proved fortuitous. There the 15-year-old Francisca Benicia Carrillo caught his eye, and he became smitten. With her parents' approval, Mariano began courting the young Francisca. And while considering her as a marriage partner, Mariano counted on his parents' sanction. A longstanding relationship dating from 1774 when the Vallejos and Carrillos lived at the San Diego presidio facilitated parental consent for this potential match. With an affirmative nod from both sets of parents, Mariano requested permission to marry from his military superiors. A colonial legacy, Mexican soldiers could not marry without official authorization from their commanding officers (Weber 1992: 330). Noting her legitimate birth and honorable ancestry in his petition, Mariano hoped to persuade his superiors that Francisca was indeed a worthy marriage partner. In the meantime, the couple also underwent lengthy ecclesiastical prenuptial investigations called *diligencias matrimoniales*. In the presence of notaries, Franciscan clerics verified the couple had parental permission and determined if impediments such as consanguinity existed. When official endorsement finally arrived, Mariano and Francisca wed on March 6, 1832, a little over two years after they had met (Emparan Brown 1968: 5).

Their age at marriage, the length of courtship, the steps they took in reaching the altar typify the experiences of their *gente de razón* contemporaries, especially those whose families had achieved a modicum of material comfort and social status. On average, *gente de razón* men married in their mid-20s and women at 17, although women ranged in age from 15 to 19 years at first marriage (Lockhart 1986: 104; Mason 1998: 76). In this regard, California's *gente de razón* resembled their contemporaries in other parts of northern Mexico, namely frontier territories such as New Mexico (Gutíerrez 1991: 274). However, Alta California women differed markedly from their contemporaries in central Mexico and Western Europe, where women typically wed in their early and late 20s, respectively (Arrom 1978: 379). For further comparison, the age at marriage for white women of the United States in the Early Republic varied depending on whether they lived in the commercial, urban centers of the northern Atlantic seaboard or in the rural hinterlands. Those living in the urban, commercial coastal settlements typically married in their mid-20s, and their rural counterparts wed at the young age of 19 or 20 (Clinton 1982: 60; Faragher 1986: 88–9).

Marrying at or near the age when they reached sexual maturity, *gente de razón* women were less apt to conceive before exchanging vows. For this reason, high rates of legitimacy characterized Mexican society. In Monterey alone, for example, legitimate births represented 93 percent of all *gente de razón* births recorded at the San Carlos Borromeo Mission church between 1774 and 1833 (Tanghetti 2004: 58). In Los Angeles and San Gabriel during the 1830s and 1840s, approximately 86 percent of *gente de razón* births were legitimate (Chávez-Gárcia 2004: 160). Like Francisca Benicia Carrillo, who delivered her first child one year after she wed Mariano Guadalupe Vallejo, most *gente de razón* women gave birth to their first child at least nine months after they married.

It is one thing to know that high rates of legitimate births characterized Mexican society. It is quite another to assume that Mexican Californians refrained from sex before marriage. Gender, questions of honor, and social status shaped people's responses to their sexual urges. These factors also informed their personal decisions regarding illicit sex.

Consider further the story of Mariano Guadalupe Vallejo. A 19-year-old cavalry cadet in March 1827, Vallejo admitted to the inquiring Friar Ramón Abella that he had fathered the recently baptized infant Josef Ramón Avila. With this admission, Vallejo acknowledged his sexually intimate relationship with the child's mother, a single Monterey woman named Anamaría Avila (BR no.3480).[1] Within a month, Anamaría's younger sister, María Rosalía, also single, gave birth to a girl. Rumors at first, followed by Friar Abella's investigation, and finally an admission of paternity by the young Vallejo, revealed that he was also the father of this child. Vallejo purportedly sired another child in 1831 with yet another single Monterey woman, María Antonia Zuñiga. And in 1832, Juana Lopez, a San Diego woman, gave birth to another of Vallejo's daughters a mere six months after Vallejo wed Francisca Benicia Carrillo (BR no. 3482, no. 3731). In other words, before his betrothal and also during his protracted courtship to Francisca, Vallejo did not deprive himself of sexually intimate relations with women. Perhaps Hubert Howe Bancroft knew of these trysts with the Avila sisters, María Zuñiga, and Juana Lopez when he noted with a measure of aplomb that Vallejo was not "strict in his relations with women" (Bancroft 1970, vol. V.: 759).

How did Mexican Californians view premarital sexual liaisons? Did the young Vallejo or his sexual partners lose face in a society where the Spanish concept of honor justified social hierarchy and mediated the rules of courtship, sexual behavior, and marriage? Historian Ann Twinam, who has elegantly captured the nuances of honor and its relationship to gender and social status in colonial Spanish America, rightfully cautions against thinking of "honor" as immutable across time and space. She demonstrates that gender and sex inflected differences between male and female honor. A woman's honor pivoted around her virginity; a man could be sexually promiscuous without compromising his honor. Biology had a hand in this cultural double standard. Because men do not become pregnant, they do not bear the outward physical signs of their sexual activity (Twinam 1999: 32, 33, 91). Vallejo lost nothing because of his sexual exploits. He did not jeopardize his betrothal to Francisca Carrillo, nor did his sexual conduct impede his eventual social ascent to a position of considerable political and economic prominence. At the age of 28, he became *comandante general* of Alta California, a position granted him by his nephew and Governor of California, Juan Bautista Alvarado. As grantee of the sizable Rancho Petaluma in Sonoma, Vallejo amassed a considerable fortune that financed a luxurious life of fine furnishings, a private library, and private education for his legitimate children (Bancroft 1970, vol. 5: 757; Padilla 1993: 86).

Vallejo's sexual partners did not fare as well. In the marriage market, where men and women sought mates of comparable or higher social rank, honor served as a measure of social status and respectability. When questioned by Friar Abella in 1827 as to his intentions with the Avila women, Vallejo responded he "could marry neither of the two" (BR no. 3482). Most likely their meager socioeconomic status rendered them easy targets for Vallejo's sexual advances, which in turn designated them unsuitable marriage prospects in his eyes. The Avila women lived with their widowed mother, whose deceased husband left the family with no means of support. In 1836 they still resided in Monterey in a house headed by their widowed mother, María Antonia Linares (Padrón General 1836). Neither of the two Avila sisters married. In Mexican California, single women who bore children out of wedlock had little success in securing marriage partners. They also compromised their honor, but more for not having married the father of their children than for engaging in sexual relations before marriage.

As Twinam revealed for colonial Spanish America, so too in Mexican California some couples initiated sexual relations before exchanging marriage vows. For a number of Mexican Californians, albeit a minority, the promise to marry gave license to commence sexual relations. Indeed, men might promise marriage to persuade their partners to have sex with them. Conversely, sexual intimacy preceded a promise of marriage. A woman might engage in sexual intimacies in order to extract a promise of marriage. Perhaps the Avila women pursued this strategy with the young Vallejo, albeit with no success. Mission baptismal registers reveal that some children were conceived before their parents sanctified their conjugal union in church. Couples who engaged in premarital sexual relations represented a wide spectrum of society. Mariano Vallejo's own sister and mother of one-time Governor of California Juan Bautista Alvarado was pregnant with Bonifacio Madariaga's child before she married him in May 1831. Twice widowed, Maria Isidora Vallejo became sexually intimate with Madariaga before they wed. A mere four months later, they were back at the chapel to baptize their infant daughter (BR no. 3755; Northrop 1999, vol. I: 350). So long as a woman married the father of her child or children, she could safeguard her honor.

Nonetheless, the question of legitimacy held great import in Mexican California. Indeed, Catholic clerics preferred that couples limit their sexual encounters to their marriage bed. But the Catholic Church and colonial Spanish civil law, which persisted through the Mexican period, considered fully legitimate children conceived or born before their parents married. Regardless of the timing of conception, children born to two unmarried individuals with no impediments to marriage were automatically legitimated once their parents wed (Twinam 1989: 125). Thus Doña Josefa Vallejo and Don Bonifacio Madariaga's child did not bear the stain of illegitimacy because of her parents' premarital carnal relations. As legitimate, she was entitled to parental support. Legitimate children enjoyed other benefits. Only legitimate sons could hold public office. And regardless of sex, legitimate children inherited equal shares of their parents' property. They also inherited the patriline. Such were the benefits available to Mariano Vallejo's 16 legitimate children – those born to he and his wife, Francisca Benicia Carrillo (Northrop 1999, vol. II: 308–10).

With one exception, the children Vallejo fathered with the women he did not marry left few traces in the historical record, a strong indication of their social marginality. Even though Vallejo recognized them as his biological issue, he disavowed them socially by not conferring on them his surname. Outside the bounds of Vallejo's legitimate family, these children did not benefit from his elite socioeconomic position. And while they were not labeled "illegitimate" or "bastards," their designation as *hijos naturales* (natural children) at the time of baptism signaled them as children born out of wedlock. Socially more significant, these children bore their mothers' surnames. In patrilineal Mexican society, where birth status was one of several attributes of social status, this resonated loudly. *Hijos naturales* stood outside the legitimate bounds of family patrilines. They were not entitled to equal shares of their fathers' wealth and, if men, they were barred from holding public office (Twinam 1999).

While it is unclear exactly what, if any, relationship Vallejo had with most of his "natural children," evidence reveals he had special affection for one. Like his other natural children, his daughter born just six months after he married Francisca Carrillo did not bear his surname. And yet, he may have had a hand in naming her Prudenciana after his older sister, María

Prudencia. As an adult, Prudenciana Lopez visited her father in Sonoma at least once and had a longstanding epistolary relationship with him (Long 1983). The ties that bound were not always born of legitimately sanctioned unions.

When Mariano Vallejo and Francisca Carrillo married, they united two *gente de razón* families of comparable social status into a larger family network. Their 16 children marked the bounds of their legitimate family. Like Mariano and Francisca, the majority of *gente de razón* couples created legitimate families in this manner. Families identified by the patriline – such as the Vallejos, the Peraltas, the Carrillos, the Picos, the Sepulvedas – were the most visible constituents of California Mexican society. But Mexican society did not reproduce itself solely within the confines of legitimately sanctioned couples. Mariano Vallejo and other socially prominent men, such as his nephew Juan Bautista Alvarado, engendered *hijos naturales* when they transgressed social boundaries for illicit sex with *gente de razón* women of lesser social status (Miller 1998: 32). Although a minority, families composed of unmarried women and their *hijos naturales* occupied a lower position in California's social hierarchy. Licit and illicit sex amongst the *gente de razón* had a hand in reinforcing hierarchies of social difference and simultaneously creating personal links across boundaries defined by social status.

Sex across ethnic boundaries also played a part in recreating Mexican California society. Once again, the story of Mariano Vallejo's intimate life provides additional clues to how licit and illicit sexual unions created the texture of California's social fabric, foregrounding some individuals in the social tapestry while marginalizing others. Sometime around 1830, a neo-phyte woman gave birth to a boy named José Mariano. Genealogist Marie Northrop identified this child as one of Vallejo's natural sons (Northrop 1999, vol. II: 310). This small evidentiary scrap reveals that at least once Vallejo overstepped the ethnic divide between himself and an *india neófita* to satisfy his sexual appetite. In Mexican California some *gente de razón* men looked to Indian women solely for casual sexual relations. Elite men, such as Vallejo, viewed Indian women as they did *gente de razón* women of lesser social status: that is, as adequate sexual mates but not suitable marriage partners.

The breakdown of mission communities with secularization beginning in the early 1830s pushed Indian peoples into pueblos such as Monterey and Los Angeles in search of work. Some Indian women turned to prosti-tution, selling their bodies to *gente de razón* men in order to feed them-selves. They also worked as domestics in *gente de razón* households. Disadvantaged economically, some Indian women acquiesced to sexual advances by male household members lest they lose their meager source of income (González 2005: 92–100; Hackel 2005: 410–14). Perhaps circumstances such as these explain Vallejo's intimate relations with the neophyte woman who bore his son. And as scholars have amply demonstrated, illicit sex with Indian women also took the form of rape (Castañeda 1998; Hurtado 1998; Wood 1998; Bouvier 2001).

However, to view interethnic sexual relations solely as casual or rape is to miss seeing the other ways that *gente de razón* and *indios* forged kinship networks across ethnic boundaries. *Gente de razón* men from the lower rungs of society established informal long-term relationships with Indian women. As David Weber found for the northern frontier of colonial New Spain, so in Mexican California some people of meager circumstances saw little reason to legitimate their conjugal unions (Weber 1992: 331; Tanghetti 2004). Rather, they lived in *barraganía* or concubinage, a tradition with deep roots in Spanish folk custom. While the incidence of such arrangements awaits future research, anecdotal evidence and baptismal registers reveal that informal unions such as these knit *gente de razón* and *indios* into family networks (Chávez-García 2004: 160). But Indians and *gente de razón* also legitimated their conjugal relationships. In Los Angeles alone between 1821 and 1848, marriages between *indios* and *gente de razón* represented 10 percent of marriages recorded at the San Gabriel Mission and the Plaza church (González 2005: 92).

One of the most obvious social consequences of illicit and licit sexual unions between California's *gente de razón* and Indians was the reproduction in Mexican California of a mestizo population. Less recognized is that some of the *gente de razón* were themselves the children of indigenous California women (Tanghetti 2004). As Kent Lightfoot asserts, "The line between *gente de razon* and *indio* was not fixed and unyielding but fuzzy, amorphous, and situational, as some native people reclassified themselves as de razon through marriage, education, occupation . . . residence, dress, speech, or skin color" (Lightfoot 2005: 68). Legitimate children, especially of *gente de razón* men and Indian women, enjoyed the same benefits as did the legitimate children of *de razón* couples. Having a California Indian mother did not necessarily bar mixed-race individuals from staking their place in Mexican society as *vecinos* or *ciudadanos*. For example, in Monterey, Manuel Butron, the son of a Spanish colonial soldier and a neophyte from Mission San Carlos Borromeo obtained two separate land grants in the late 1820s and early 1830s. Like other grantees, Butron ran cattle on his land and likely participated in the hide-and-tallow trade. He married a *gente de razón* woman with whom he had a number of children (Bancroft 1970, vol. II: 738). As *gente de razón* men had done in the colonial era, so in the Mexican period they married, cohabited, and had informal casual sexual relations with Indian women. These intimate unions undercut the seemingly stark polarity between peoples labeled *de razón* and *indio*. Their children, both legitimate and *naturales*, signaled the longstanding tradition of mestizaje characteristic of Mexican society.

However, Indian women and *gente de razón* men were not the only ones in Mexican California crossing ethnic boundaries to forge intimate personal relations. Beginning in 1821, when the newly independent Mexico opened her borders to international trade, foreign men, mostly from the United States but also from the British Isles and other parts of Europe, arrived in California. Fur trappers traveling overland in search of beaver entered from the east, but the majority sailed on merchant ships engaged in California's hide-and-tallow trade. Single foreign men representing a diverse occupational spectrum integrated themselves into Mexican families and society when they married or cohabited with *gente de razón* or Indian women.

The arrival of foreign men in California coincided with the acceleration of social stratification based on material wealth. With an eye toward stimulating economic growth, the Mexican Congress secularized the missions in 1834 and made available to individuals former mission land. A major shift in wealth followed as Mexican governors confirmed approximately 700 land grants between 1834 and 1846. Whereas the missions had been the primary beneficiaries of the hide-and-tallow trade, now profits accrued to rancheros, but not equally. Factors such as the size of one's herd, the quality of pasturage, and the extent of involvement in international trade contributed to disparities in wealth amongst the grantees (Weber 1982: 210; Hackel 1998: 132). While pastoralism dominated California's economy, rancheros represented a small fraction of the population. In Monterey, for example, as late as 1845, grantees totaled a mere 3.5 percent of the population (Bancroft 1970, vol. IV: 650). And contrary to popular perceptions of rancheros as baronial lords, most were modest landholders who worked their properties alongside family members and a few servants (Walton 2001). California's nascent elite represented an even smaller percentage of the population. In addition to possessing vast landholdings measuring upwards of 20,000 to 30,000 acres, elite families such as the Vallejos, the de la Guerras, the Picos, and the Sepulvedas achieved social prominence through their ties to the burgeoning market economy, public office holding, and strategic marriages (ibid.). Along with grantees of modest landholdings, merchants, artisans, soldiers, and municipal employees occupied the middle rung of California society. At the lower end, landless *gente de razon*, Indians, and foreign men labored in the pueblos and outlying ranchos.

The familiar narrative of marriage between foreigners and *hijas del país* (daughters of the country), as *de razón* women were called, highlights those of high-ranking trading firm merchants with daughters of elite ranchero families (Monroy 1990; Almaguer 1994: 59; Castañeda 1998: 242; Hurtado 1999: 21–44). The iconic marriage of Massachusetts-born merchant Alfred Robinson to Ana María de la Guerra of the prominent Santa Barbara family serves as the most well-known example, and the marriages of two of Mariano Vallejo's sisters to foreigners also illustrate the pattern.

Unfortunately, this focus on elite families has contributed to the misperception that foreign men married Californio women predominately to obtain land or solely for pecuniary interests.

Marriages between foreigners and Californio women were not solely an elite phenomenon. In Monterey between 1821 and 1845, 15 percent of *de razón* women married foreign men. Class and status considerations mattered greatly for both foreign men and *de razón* women. The same status concerns that informed Californio women when they wed *de razón* men were in play in their marriages to foreign men. Californio women from a wide social spectrum integrated socially diverse foreigners through marriage into their families. Indeed, in Monterey alone between 1821 and 1845, more foreign men married into non-landed families than those who married into ranchero families. Typically, these men were carpenters, sailors, or other manual tradesmen (Tanghetti 2004: 96.). As my research reveals, socially ascendant Californio families were not about to let their daughters marry foreign men they considered social inferiors.

Carefully scrutinized by parents, some foreign men wishing to marry daughters of the country had a long walk to the marriage altar. As historian Albert Hurtado has stated, foreign men "did not jump into marriages" with *de razón* women. Perhaps, as he claims, this resulted from the "circumspection on the part of the prospective husbands" (Hurtado 1999: 37). But the delay had less to do with men deliberating long in deciding to marry a Californiana and more with the onerous time-consuming premarital investigations. For one, the Catholic Church had sole jurisdiction over the marriage ceremony. Foreign men underwent similar ecclesiastical marriage investigations required of their *gente de razón* counterparts. In addition, if they were not Catholic, they had to submit to lengthy doctrinal education to prepare for baptism. Unless converted, they stood no chance of formally marrying a Mexican woman. In 1846, longtime resident of California William Robert Garner testified, "[B]efore a person professing any other faith can join in wedlock with a native of California, he must join the Catholic faith; and not only join that faith, but give some satisfactory proof to the Priest that he believes in all the tenets of the Roman Catholic Church" (Craig 1970: 167). Garner wrote from personal experience. Evidently he satisfied his clerical interrogator before tying the knot in 1831 with María Antonia Butron (Northrop 1999, vol. I: 94).

Foreign men faced yet additional impediments in their bids to gain the hand of an *hija del país*. As historian Andrés Reséndez has argued, the Catholic Church served as a gatekeeper, strictly regulating marriages between foreigners and daughters of the country in an effort to scrutinize prospective citizens. Foreign men believed that marriage to a daughter of the country enhanced their prospects for naturalization. They also knew that Mexican citizenship removed cumbersome regulations imposed on foreigners desiring to engage in commerce or obtain land. Thus, as arbiter of religious conviction and judge of character for would-be citizens, the Church required foreign men to obtain two dispensations: a *dispensa de extranjería* (a dispensation for foreigners) and a *dispensa de vagos* – a dispensation for vagrancy (Reséndez 2005: 124–35). Waiting for approval from far-away diocesan officials further delayed foreigners' march to the altar.

Once united in marriage to California women, foreigners gained entry into family networks and thus into local society and culture. Many went native, a process that began during their ritual incorporation into the Catholic faith. At the time of baptism, they acquired new identities when mission clerics hispanicized their first names. The sandy-haired, blue-eyed shipmaster John Roger Cooper became Juan Bautista before he wed Encarnación Vallejo, one of Mariano's younger sisters (Bancroft 1970, vol. II: 765; Northrop 1999, vol. I: 351). Foreigners also acquired a fondness for local cuisine. Another member of the Vallejo family through marriage, Jacob Leese, evinced his preference for Californio foods in a letter to a friend: "All I can say to you is that a long life in Califa a living on Carne Frijoles Papas . . . is much more pleasanter than a short life on what you call Pumpkin Pies Plumb Pudding &c &c" (Hague & Langum 1990: 213). Locals addressed resident foreigners using the honorific "don." And foreign men donned the "costume of the country," a sartorial expression of their cultural integration (Dana, Jr. 2001: 79).

While most foreign men and *de razón* women married in the Church before consummating their relationships, some lived in concubinage. Clues buried in baptismal records reveal that foreign men and *de razón* women united informally in conjugal relations of varying lengths of time. Though living together illicitly, they took their children to the baptismal font where mission clerics christened and designated them *hijos naturales.* Usually people of modest means entered into these informal liaisons. The English sailor James Stokes and María Josefa Soto, widow of a presidial soldier, exemplify this living arrangement. While they eventually wed in 1844 after the births of their three children, their story illustrates how social status shaped the trajectory of their connubial relationship (Northrop 1999, vol. II: 39; BR no. 4536, 4445, 4446).

At the end of the Mexican era, California society was ethnically diverse and socially stratified. Californios, who numbered approximately 7,500 in 1846, and an almost equal number of resident foreigners – Americans and some Europeans – lived amidst a sizable Indian population that totaled well over 100,000 (Castillo 1978: 106; Weber 1982: 206; Hackel 1998: 136). A small elite comprised a handful of Californios and a few foreigners wielded economic and political power derived from a combination of land ownership, political office, and commercial ties to a growing market economy. Though hispanicized Indians working on cattle ranchos and in pueblos were the bulk of the manual labor force, they worked alongside poorer Californios and foreign laborers (Walton 2001: 72). Also ethnically diverse, the middling sector consisted of modest landowners, artisans, and shopkeepers.

Personal decisions of the most intimate nature, specifically those concerning the selection of marriage and sexual partners, reflected and reinforced Mexican California's stratified social structure. For the most part, Californians sought marriage partners of comparable social status. Mariano Guadalupe Vallejo, for one, chose to marry a woman from the Carrillo family, a family whose social prominence equaled his own. But for casual sex, Vallejo chose women he deemed socially inferior – *de razón* women of modest means and Indians. Through his marriage to Francisca Benicia he established legitimate kinship ties that sustained elite family networks. His fathering of "natural" children with various women created personal ties across social and ethnic boundaries. Like Vallejo, Californians of modest means married within their social position. Others opted for concubinage, most often choosing partners of the same ethnicity, but also establishing inter-ethnic conjugal unions. This was Mexican society on the eve of conquest – socially stratified, ethnically diverse and yet bound through legitimate and informal family networks born of licit and illicit sexual unions between Californios, Indians, and *Ingleses*.

Early on July 7, 1846, US naval commander John D. Sloat and a few marines rowed ashore to take command of Monterey. Within a few hours an additional 250 American seamen had followed; an American flag hoisted over the customhouse, the official annexation of Mexican California by the United States had begun. As if the presence of foreign troops was not enough, a thundering 21-gun salute fired from warships anchored in the bay gave Monterey's populace ample evidence they were at war (Harlow 1982).

Like the fur trappers, merchants, and traders before them, navy and infantrymen arriving in California during the war took notice of the sights before them. After long sea voyages sometimes lasting upwards of 180 days, soldiers delighted in scenic Monterey. William Tecumseh Sherman, who would gain fame and infamy in the future Civil War, recalled his impressions of California's capital when he was billeted there in 1847. "Every thing on shore looked bright and beautiful," he wrote, "the hills covered with grass and flowers, . . . and the low adobe houses, with red-tiled roofs and whitened walls, contrasted well with the dark pine-trees behind, making a decidedly good impression upon us who had come so far to spy out the land." The people of Monterey, according to Sherman, numbered approximately 1,000 and consisted of a "mixed set of Americans, native Mexicans, and Indians" (Sherman 1990: 44, 45).

War and its aftermath forced proximity between Americans, Mexicans, and Indians. While the war irrevocably changed the circumstances of their encounters, Americans, Mexicans, and Indians continued forging intimate connections with one another in and out of marriage (Hurtado 1998; Casas 2007; Chávez-García 2004; Tanghetti 2004). Seven of Mariano Vallejo's nine surviving children married newcomers (Northrop, vol. II: 308–10). Like merchants, traders, and trappers before, soldiers, forty-niners and subsequent travelers to California encountered a variety of people. No doubt perceiving many of these people as distinct from themselves and from each other, the newly arrived could not help but overlook the intimate family and sexual relations across ethnic, racial, and national boundaries that formed American California society.

NOTE

1   Baptismal registers from San Carlos Borromeo Mission proved a rich source for revealing intimate personal connections. Hereafter the abbreviation BR refers to baptismal register and the number refers to the particular entry in the register. Microfilm copies of mission sacramental registers can be obtained at the Family History Centers of the Genealogical Society of the Church of Jesus Christ of the Latter-Day Saints. Researchers can also electronically access California's missions' birth, marriage, and burial records through the "Early California Population Project" database at the Huntington Library, San Marino, California.

REFERENCES

Almaguer, Tomás. 1994. *Racial Fault Lines: The Historical Origins of White Supremacy in California*. Berkeley: University of California Press.

Arrom, Sylvia Marina. 1978. "Marriage Patterns in Mexico City, 1811," *Journal of Family History* 3: 4.

Bancroft, Hubert Howe. 1970. *History of California*. Santa Barbara: Wallace Hebberd.

Bean, Lowell J. 1992. "Indians of California: Diverse and Complex Peoples," *California History* 71: 3.

Bean, Lowell J. 1974. "Social Organization in Native California." In Lowell J. Bean and T. F. King, eds., *Antap: California Indian Political and Economic Organization*. Menlo Park: Ballena Press.

Bouvier, Virginia Marie. 2001. *Women and the Conquest of California, 1542–1810: Codes of Silence*. Tucson: University of Arizona Press.

Casas, María Raquél. 2007. *Married to a Daughter of the Land: Spanish-Mexican Women and Interethnic Marriage in California, 1820–1880*. Reno: University of Nevada Press.

Castañeda, Antonia. 1998. "Engendering the History of Alta California, 1769–1848: Gender, Sexuality, and the Family." In Ramón A. Gutiérrez and Richard

J. Orsi, eds., *Contested Eden: California Before the Gold Rush*. Berkeley: University of California Press.

Castillo, Edward D. 1978. "The Impact of Euro-American Exploration and Settlement." In *Handbook of North American Indians*, vol. 8, *California*. Washington, DC: Smithsonian Institution.

Chávez-García, Miroslava. 2004. *Negotiating Conquest: Gender and Power in California, 1770–1880*. Arizona: University of Arizona Press.

Clinton, Catherine. 1982. *The Plantation Mistress: Woman's World in the Old South*. New York: Pantheon Books.

Craig, Donald Monro, ed. 1970. *Letters from California: From Our Special Correspondent*. Berkeley: University of California Press.

Dana, Jr., Richard Henry. 2001. *Two Years Before the Mast: A Personal Narrative of Life at Sea*. New York: The Modern Library.

Duhaut-Cilly, Auguste. 1997. *A Voyage to California, the Sandwich Islands, and Around the World in the Years 1826–1829*, translated and edited by August Frugé and Neal Harlow. Berkeley: University of California Press.

Emparan, Madie Brown. 1968. *The Vallejos of California*. San Francisco: Gleeson Library Associates, University of San Francisco.

Faragher, John Mack. 1986. *Sugar Creek: Life on the Illinois Prairie*. New Haven, CT: Yale University Press.

González, Michael J. 2005. *This Small City Will Be a Mexican Paradise: Exploring the Origins of Mexican Culture in Los Angeles, 1821–1846*. Albuquerque: University of New Mexico Press.

Gutíerrez, Ramón A. 1991. *When Jesus Came, the Corn Mothers Went Away: Marriage, Sexuality, and Power in New Mexico, 1500–1846*. Stanford, CA: Stanford University Press.

Gutíerrez, Ramón A. and Richard J. Orsi. 1998. *Contested Eden: California Before the Gold Rush*. Berkeley: University of California Press.

Haas, Lisbeth. 1995. *Conquests and Historical Identities in California, 1769–1936*. Berkeley: University of California Press.

Haas, Lisbeth. 1998. "War in California, 1846–1848." In Ramón A. Gutiérrez and Richard J. Orsi, eds., *Contested Eden: California Before the Gold Rush*. Berkeley: University of California Press.

Hackel, Steven W. 1998. "Land, Labor, and Production: The Colonial Economy of Spanish and Mexican California." In Ramón A. Gutiérrez and Richard J. Orsi, eds., *Contested Eden: California Before the Gold Rush*. Berkeley: University of California Press.

Hackel, Steven W. 2005. *Children of Coyote, Missionaries of Saint Francis: Indian–Spanish Relations in Colonial California, 1769–1850*. Chapel Hill: University of North Carolina Press for the Ohmohundro Institute of Early American History and Culture.

Hague, Harlan and David J. Langum. 1990. *Thomas O. Larkin: A Life of Patriotism and Profit in Old California*. Norman: University of Oklahoma Press.

Harlow, Neal. 1982. *California Conquered: War and Peace on the Pacific, 1846–1850*. Berkeley: University of California Press.

Hurtado, Albert L. 1998. *Indian Survival on the California Frontier*. New Haven, CT: Yale University Press.

Hurtado, Albert L. 1999. *Intimate Frontiers: Sex, Gender, and Culture in Old California*. Albuquerque: University of New Mexico Press.

Lightfoot, Kent G. 2005. *Indians, Missionaries, and Merchants: The Legacy of Colonial Encounters on the California Frontiers*. Berkeley: University of California Press.

Lockhart, Katharine Meyer. 1986. "A Demographic Profile of an Alta California Pueblo: San Jose de Guadalupe, 1777–1850." PhD dissertation, University of Colorado.

Long, Helen P. 1983. "Prudenciana Adrift in Two Worlds." *Brand Book. San Diego Corral of the Westerners*. No. 7.

Mason, William Marvin. 1998. *The Census of 1790: A Demographic History of Colonial California*. Menlo Park, CA: Ballena Press.

Miller, Robert Ryal. 1998. *Juan Alvarado, Governor of California, 1836–1842*. Norman: University of Oklahoma Press.

Monroy, Douglas. 1990. *Thrown Among Strangers: The Making of Mexican Culture in Frontier California*. Berkeley: University of California Press.

Northrop, Marie E. 1999. Reprint. *Spanish-Mexican Families of Early California, 1769–1850*, vols. I & II. Burbank: Southern California Genealogical Society.

Nunis, Jr., Doyce B. 1998. "Alta California's Trojan Horse: Foreign Immigration." In Ramón A. Gutíerrez and Richard J. Orsi, eds., *Contested Eden: California Before the Gold Rush*. Berkeley: University of California Press.

Osio, Antonio María. 1996. *The History of Alta California: A Memoir of Mexican California*, translated by Rose Marie Beebe and Robert M. Senkewicz. Madison: The University of Wisconsin Press.

Padilla, Genaro M. 1993. *My History, Not Yours: The Formation of Mexican American Autobiography*. Madison: University of Wisconsin Press.

Padrón General. 1836. *Padrón General que manifiesta el número de havitantes que existen en la municipalidad de Monterrey*. Manuscript. The Bancroft Library, University of California, Berkeley.

Pubols, Louise H. 2000. "The De la Guerra Family: Patriarchy and the Political Economy of California, 1800–1850." PhD dissertation, University of Wisconsin.

Reséndez, Andrés. 2005. *Changing National Identities at the Frontier: Texas and New Mexico, 1800–1850*. Cambridge: Cambridge University Press.

Rosenus, Alan. 1995. *General M. G. Vallejo and the Advent of the Americans*. Albuquerque: University of New Mexico Press.

Sánchez, Rosaura. 1995. *Telling Identities: The Californio Testimonios*. Minneapolis: University of Minnesota Press.

Sandos, James A. 2004. *Converting California: Indians and Franciscans in the Missions*. New Haven, CT: Yale University Press.

Sherman, William Tecumseh. 1990. *Sherman: Memoirs of General W. T. Sherman*. New York: The Library of America.

Tanghetti, Rosamaría. 2004. "Intimate Unions: Conquest and Marriage in Alta California, 1769–1890." PhD dissertation, University of California, Davis.

Taylor, Alan. 2001. *American Colonies.* New York: Viking Press.

Twinam, Ann. 1989. "Honor, Sexuality, and Illegitimacy in Colonial Spanish America." In Asunción Lavrin, ed., *Sexuality and Marriage in Colonial Latin America.* Lincoln: University of Nebraska Press.

Twinam, Ann. 1999. *Public Lives, Private Secrets: Gender, Honor, Sexuality, and Illegitimacy in Colonial Spanish America.* Stanford, CA: Stanford University Press.

Walton, John. 2001. *Storied Land: Community and Memory in Monterey.* Berkeley: University of California Press.

Weber, David J. 1982. *The Mexican Frontier, 1821–1846: The American Southwest under Mexico.* Albuquerque: University of New Mexico Press.

Weber, David J. 1992. *The Spanish Frontier in North America.* New Haven, CT: Yale University Press.

Wood, Stephanie. 1998. "Sexual Violation in the Conquest of the Americas." In Merril D. Smith, ed., *Sex and Sexuality in Early America.* New York: New York University Press.

FURTHER READING

Casas, María Raquel. 2007. *Married to a Daughter of the Land: Spanish-Mexican Women and Interethnic Marriage in California, 1820–1880.* Reno: University of Nevada Press.

Chávez-García, Miroslava. 2004. *Negotiating Conquest: Gender and Power in California, 1770–1880.* Arizona: University of Arizona Press.

Hackel, Steven W. 2005. *Children of Coyote, Missionaries of Saint Francis: Indian-Spanish Relations in Colonial California, 1769–1850.* Chapel Hill: University of North Carolina Press for the Ohmohundro Institute of Early American History and Culture.

Nash, Gary B. 1999. "The Hidden History of Mestizo America." In Martha Hodes, ed., *Sex, Love, Race: Crossing Boundaries in North American History.* New York: New York University Press.

Stern, Steve J. 1995. *The Secret History of Gender: Women, Men, and Power in Late Colonial Mexico.* Chapel Hill: The University of North Carolina Press.

Twinam, Ann. 1989. "Honor, Sexuality, and Illegitimacy in Colonial Spanish America." In Asuncíon Lavrin, ed., *Sexuality & Marriage in Colonial Latin America.* Lincoln: University of Nebraska Press.

Chapter Eight

RACE AND IMMIGRATION IN THE NINETEENTH CENTURY

Omar Valerio-Jiménez

Race and immigration have been inexorably linked in the history of California, especially during its tumultuous nineteenth century. As jurisdiction over California shifted from Spain, to Mexico, and ultimately, to the United States, racial classifications became simpler but more rigid, while immigration policies grew more exclusionary. This trend was partially fueled by California's racial and ethnic diversity, which increased in the nineteenth century due to large-scale immigration. Before the first immigrants arrived in the late eighteenth century, the region had already been one of the world's most linguistically diverse and home to over one hundred distinct indigenous communities. The eighteenth-century colonists entered California not as an immigrant underclass, but as conquerors. Instead of adapting to the established society that they were entering, these immigrants radically altered the indigenous communities in the process of creating a new society.

Spanish colonists used force to impose their ideological and cultural beliefs on California's Indians. Indigenous nations suffered not only a loss of their land, but were also subject to the ravages of Spanish-introduced diseases and the imposition of a government, religious, and labor structure by Spanish missionaries, civilians, and the military. The Spanish viewed Indians as "savages" who lacked "civilization" and would have to discard their Indian culture to become "civilized." This view was manifested in the ways that the Spanish divided people into two categories: *gente de razón* (people of reason) to refer to people who had converted to Catholicism and adopted Spanish culture (including Christianized Indians), and *gente sin razón* (people without reason) to refer to non-converted Indians. Like the territorial conquest of California, the *conquista espiritual* (spiritual conquest) also depended on the use of force by Spanish missionaries, who physically punished mission Indians, and by soldiers, who brought captured Indians to the missions and launched campaigns to subdue indigenous rebellions to colonial rule. The Spanish also viewed Indians as "children" who needed to be instructed not only in religious beliefs, but also in cultural and economic views (Monroy 1990). The missions, therefore, were centers of religious instruction as well as cultural and labor centers where Indians learned the Spanish language, customs, and ways of working. The missionaries gave instruction on cultivating European crops, tending live-stock, and various skilled crafts. In addition to forcing Indians to discard native religions, the missionaries also hoped to transform indigenous sexual practices such as polygamy and divorce (Bouvier 2001). In exchange for providing Indians with Christianity, the colonists reasoned, the Indians should willingly labor for the colonists. When Indians resisted their enforced labor, Spanish soldiers and civilians organized raids for Indian captives. The dearth of women among the first colonists meant that the Indians were also seen as potential sexual partners.

Unfortunately, the process of racial intermixture was often violent and involuntary. In the years following the founding of the mission and presidio at Monterey, missionary Junípero Serra complained that various soldiers had begun sexually abusing Indian women and impeding the conversion efforts (Bouvier 2001). The rape of women of a conquered group had been part of a pattern followed by soldiers in previous conquests in Europe and the Americas, so religious and civilian officials had reason to be concerned. In the context of California, the rape of Indian women symbolized their specific domination by the soldiers and the more general subjugation of the entire native population. Native women were vulnerable to sexual attacks because the Spanish soldiers believed them to be inferior and the spoils of conquest (Castañeda 1993). The actions of the soldiers led to Indian reprisals, escapes from the missions, and resistance to religious con-version. In addition, the sexual attacks spread venereal diseases among the Indians, which in turn led to a decline in the native population (Chávez-García 2004). The soldiers' behavior also discouraged the missionaries, who complained to the military officers and, at times, asked to be trans-ferred away from California. In order to avoid continued outrages, colonial authorities began encouraging soldiers to marry Indian women by offering incentives of land, livestock, and transportation costs. Officials believed that the marriages between Spanish soldiers and indigenous women would promote stable families, strengthen kinship ties, and increase the popula-tion of *gente de razón*. The colonial government was more successful in boosting the colonists' numbers with two other experiments. In the late eighteenth century, the government sent convicts and their families to California. Despite the men's criminal backgrounds, officials hoped that married couples would prove more stable. In 1800, officials also sent a group of orphans from Mexico City in another effort to increase the number of colonists (Castañeda 1990). The government's difficulty in attracting colonists demonstrated that California continued to be seen as an unappealing destination, where only impoverished people seeking upward mobility would seek to move.

Many of the supposed "Spanish" colonists who settled in California were in fact racially mixed. Only a few priests and high-ranking military officers were originally from Spain. The majority of the colonists hailed from poor northern provinces such as Baja California, Sonora, and Sinaloa (Chávez-García 2004). The colonists' decision to migrate to California was motivated by a desire to increase their social position by taking advantage of the colonial government's various incentives, especially the grants of land and livestock. By acquiring wealth, some colonists could pay to obtain a *gracias a sacar* (literally, thanks to be taken out) decree that officially changed their birth status to reflect a "white" lineage and *limpieza de sangre* (purity of blood) (Haas 1995). After three centuries of mestizaje (racial intermixture), most of New Spain's population (including the first Californios) had African, Indian, and Spanish ancestry. The process of mestizaje continued in California as the mestizo and mulatto colonists intermarried, while others sought indigenous spouses. Although the Spanish colonial government had developed a complex system of racial categorization, by the eighteenth century officials were hard pressed to enforce these racial categories, especially in Mexico's Far North (Haas 1995). In addition, the assignation of a category was quite subjective, as repeatedly illustrated by baptismal registers in which priests assigned different racial categories to siblings even though their parents remained the same. Throughout Mexico's northern frontier, people transcended racial categories as their class status shifted. The maxim that money whitens held true in California as the nouveaux riches were easily reclassified as *españoles* (Spaniards), the most elite category. On the eve of Mexican Independence in 1821, the *gente de razón* population of California hovered around 3,200 people.

Frustrated by failed efforts to increase the number of colonists in Mexico's northern territories, Spanish officials turned to immigrants as a solution. Royal officials established a colonization program (continued by Mexico after its independence) that offered land and tax exemptions to foreign immigrants who agreed to settle in Texas. While few European immigrants arrived, Anglo Americans flooded into Texas and soon Mexican officials began to worry about their loyalty. Faced with growing uncertainty over Texas, Mexican officials became wary of extending the colonization plan to California. A few Anglo American traders and trappers did make their way to California, but they found that the most desirable land was unavailable as it belonged to the missions. Prior to 1840, only about 400 Americanos had made their way to California. Several of these men, like Abel Stearns and John Forster, married into Californio families, became Catholics, and acculturated to Mexican society. The merchants' kinship ties helped their businesses succeed, and enabled them to acquire large landholdings. In turn, the Californio families with ties to the

English-speaking merchants obtained access to capital and business connections (Monroy 1990).

The availability of land changed with the secularization of the missions between 1834 and 1836. Among the foreigners who arrived after secularization were John Marsh and John Sutter, who played important roles in attracting more foreigners. In addition to being early California boosters, both men shared a fugitive past (Marsh in New Mexico and Sutter in Switzerland) and a desire to remake their lives in the West. Posing as a medical doctor, Marsh grew wealthy by dispensing "medical treatments" in exchange for cattle. He was instrumental in attracting Anglo American migrants through the numerous letters he wrote to eager would-be settlers in the Midwest. Sutter was a Swiss immigrant whose fort in Sacramento became a magnet for Anglo Americans, including "illegal aliens" who moved to California without securing permission from the Mexican government. Sutter assisted overland migrants by providing them with supplies, giving them jobs upon their arrival, and illegally distributing land to the newcomers. During the 1840s, many more foreigners arrived, attracted by the inexpensive land offered by Californio and Anglo American rancheros who had obtained land after secularization (Weber 1982).

The influx of a large number of foreigners placed Californios at odds with Mexican government officials. The national government became increasingly suspicious of the *arrivistes* after 1840 because many entered the state illegally, refused to learn Spanish, and did not acculturate to Mexican society. Even local officials noticed the difference, as did Governor Juan B. Alvarado, who noted, "Would that the foreigners that came to settle in Alta California after 1841 had been of the same quality as those who preceded them!" (Monroy 1990: 163). Along with other Californios, Alvarado had welcomed the first Anglo American and European immigrants who intermarried and acculturated to Mexican society, but disliked the new arrivals who arrived with families, remained apart from Californios, and expressed nativist sentiments. Worried that the flood of foreigners would lead to another separatist revolt like that in Texas, Mexican officials unsuccessfully ordered local officials to expel foreigners who lacked permission to settle and tried to discourage Americans by publishing newspaper notices denying the existence of cheap land.

In contrast to the national government's view, Californios held contradictory views of foreign immigrants who streamed into the Sacramento and San Joaquín valleys. Californios welcomed the immigrants because the newcomers brought much-needed skills and strengthened the economy, but they also feared being outnumbered by immigrants who increasingly refused to acculturate to Mexican society. After years of neglect, Californios had also grown to distrust the national government. They lacked a strong sense of nationalism but felt greater loyalty to their local region. These conflicting views meant that the Californios felt a closer affinity with the 1,300 foreigners who lived in the state by 1846 than with national government officials. On the eve of the US – Mexican War, Mexico had failed not only to control the flow of foreigners into the state, but also to gain the loyalty of the established Californios. Mexico's immigration policy had been successful in attracting foreign colonists to its Far North, but would prove disastrous in maintaining its control over the region. As David Weber has aptly observed, Mexico's experience in its Far North changed the famous dictum, "to govern is to populate," on its head. By numerically overwhelming Mexican colonists in Texas and California, Anglo Americans had provided a counterexample, suggesting that to "populate is to govern" (Weber 1982). Unfortunately, these new immigrants would establish a government that employed racial classifications more effectively to exclude non-whites from civic participation.

The arrival of a large number of Anglo Americans changed the established racial hierarchy. Unlike Spanish colonists who had adopted a "frontier of inclusion," the newcomers followed a "frontier of exclusion" policy towards Indians that did not integrate within Anglo American society (Hine & Faragher 2000). The newcomers viewed the Indians less as potential workers, trading partners, or spouses, than as obstacles to westward expansion. Anglo Americans believed that California's American Indian population was uncivilized because, among other reasons, they subsisted from hunting and gathering instead of agriculture. Rather than incorporating Indians, Americanos preferred to remove indigenous nations from their lands to make way for the newcomers' settlements. The majority of Anglo Americans also held negative views of Mexicans, who were characterized as lazy, uncouth, and filthy. Typical of these views were those expressed by Richard Henry Dana in *Two Years before the Mast* (1840). Dana, a Harvard graduate who arrived in California by ship, held the Californios in contempt while recognizing the value of their landholdings. Characterizing the Californios as "idle, thriftless people," Dana judged them to be "proud, and extravagant, and very much given to gaming." His account of California was widely read, and shaped the views of westward-moving Americans. Dana's writing helped popularize the view that Mexican men were inept and lazy, while Mexican women were exotic and loose. These negative opinions were further influenced by prevailing racial attitudes in the mid-nineteenth century regarding Mexicans' mixed racial ancestry. Americanos believed Mexicans to be a "mongrel" people due to their mixed African, Indian, and Spanish racial heritage (Horsman 1981).

The large influx of Anglo Americans was part of a larger ongoing process of American westward expansion and would become critical for the second conquest of California. Influenced by the prevailing ideas at mid-century, the newcomers justified the nation's expansion with a strong opinion about the superiority of American institutions, and a racist belief in the inferiority of the people living in the coveted territory. Their trust in the nation's "manifest destiny" included a conviction that God supported the nation's expansion across the continent and the spread of American culture and institutions. The most fervent supporters of manifest destiny viewed the acquisition of the entire Mexican nation as an ultimate goal. The "all of Mexico" movement encountered stiff opposition from those who believed that the United States could not incorporate so many "mongrel" people. Nativist opponents argued against annexing all of Mexico because they did not want the United States to add more Catholics after the large influx of Irish immigrants at mid-century. The debate also touched on the expansion of slavery, which northerners suspected was the ultimate goal of southern expansionists. Despite disagreements about how much territory to annex, most Americans believed that Mexicans could not take part in democratic institutions due to their innate inferiority. During the war, Congress continued debating how much Mexican territory to acquire. Senator Lewis Cass of Michigan minced few words when he argued, "We do not want the people of Mexico, either as citizens or subjects. All we want is a portion of their territory . . ." (Horsman 1981: 241). Ultimately, a compromise was reached to incorporate Mexico's less densely settled northern territories, including California, where expansionists believed Mexicans would either disappear or eventually identify with American institutions. The war ended with the Treaty of Guadalupe Hidalgo, which guaranteed Mexicans living in the ceded territories full citizenship rights including the respect of their property, religion, and freedom of assembly. Unfortunately, the discovery of gold at Sutter's Fort within a few months of the treaty's signing dispelled hopes that the Californios would easily exercise these rights.

Economic competition in the mines would provoke racial antagonisms as non-white immigrants arrived in California. The violence and racial antipathy unleashed during the Gold Rush had national implications, according to Kevin Starr, because they reflected the characteristics of "a nation with strong racist and ethnic prejudices in its heart" (Starr & Orsi 2000: 7). The possibility of striking it rich in the gold mines acted as a magnet that pulled numerous migrants from other parts of the United States and immigrants from various regions of the world. During the Gold Rush, over 100,000 people arrived, including immigrants from Chile, China, France, Hawaii, and Mexico. The mostly male migration disrupted the Anglo Americans' conceptions of proper gender roles as men were forced by necessity to perform domestic duties. This moment of gender confusion allowed for some inter-ethnic cooperation, as some Anglo-American men came to rely on French, Chinese, and African-American men to cook, wash, and nurse the sick (Johnson 2000). Many of these immigrants arrived with mining skills learned in their native country, such as Mexicans and Chileans who employed their skills with placer mining to gain some initial success in the gold mines. The distinct languages, clothing, and religion of the international group of miners that gathered in the state made each group acutely aware of racial and ethnic distinctions. Unfortunately, the ethnic diversity of the diggings proved too explosive for Anglo Americans imbued with mid-century racial ideologies. Resentful that Mexicans and Chileans had staked out some of the best mining claims, Anglo Americans soon outnumbered the Latinos and Asians and began organizing to drive out the immigrants, whom they viewed as "foreigners." According to Sucheng Chan, "ethnic consciousness quickly became transformed first into nativism and then into racism" (Starr & Orsi 2000: 58).

In addition to the physical assaults and intimidation, the Americans also appealed to California's legislature, which passed the Foreign Miners' Tax in 1850. This law required non-citizens to pay $20 per month for the "privilege" of mining. Although some Mexicans were US citizens, they obtained little protection from local or state officials. The law technically applied to all immigrants, but officials enforced it selectively. The legislature repealed the law in 1851, but by then it had accomplished the goal of driving many French and Latino miners away from the mines. The state passed a second Foreign Miners' Tax in 1852 that imposed a $3 per month tax, but this was primarily enforced against the Chinese. The long-term significance of the Foreign Miners' Tax was to provide legal sanction for Anglo Americans' nativist violence and to "institutionalize a pattern of race relations" that would plague the state throughout its history (Starr & Orsi 2000).

The population boom in California proved disastrous for the state's indigenous population, and led to the passage of legislation that used race to deny citizenship rights to California's Indians. Diseases, introduced by the arrival of numerous immigrants, led to a precipitous decline in the Indian population, but starvation and violence also had a considerable impact (see the essay in this volume by William Bauer, Jr.). In addition to the violence, Indians were forced to confront legal disadvantages. The state's constitution denied them full citizenship rights, and subsequent laws reinforced their disadvantaged position by prohibiting Indians from serving as witnesses in court, preventing them from attending public schools, and making it illegal for them to obtain firearms. Perhaps the most blatant discriminatory state law at mid-century was one that allowed for Indian children to be indentured by whites. This 1850 law virtually legalized Indian slavery since employers were allowed to hold Indian children in servitude until they turned 18 years of age. The legislature modified the law in 1860 to lengthen the terms of indenture for children and to allow employers to indenture Indian adults. Indenture laws gave rise to the trafficking in Indian children as Anglo Americans and Mexicans began raiding indigenous villages in order to kidnap children to sell into servitude. The 1850s also witnessed attempts by federal officials to negotiate treaties with Indians that would force them onto reservations. The state eventually created a few reservations, but these were an abysmal failure (Hurtado 1988).

Unlike California's Indians, Mexicans had more legal protections that allowed some to avoid being racialized as "non-white." The citizenship rights guaranteed to Mexicans and their "white" legal status under the state constitution helped Californios avoid some of the discrimination experienced by Indian, African, and Asian residents. Because they spoke a romance language and practiced Christianity, some scholars have argued that Mexicans were culturally closer to Anglo Americans than Asians and Indians (Almaguer 1994). Nevertheless, Mexicans' experience varied because their class status determined whether Anglo Americans would accept them as white. Californios confronted significant obstacles when they attempted to exercise their property rights. In Northern California, Mexicans quickly became a minority population as Anglo Americans flooded into the state during the Gold Rush. The newcomers brought different ideas of land tenure and property divisions than those held by Californios. Under the Spanish and Mexican land systems, the property boundaries were not as precisely demarcated as they were in Anglo American communities. These differences, along with the common practice among Americanos of squatting on unused land, created great problems for Mexican landowners. The tension was exacerbated by Anglo Americans' mistaken characterization of Mexicans as "foreigners" within California, and the newcomers' belief that Californio landowners were not properly using their land. Some Americanos also believed that the Californios' lands should be made public as a result of the war of conquest.

In the process of verifying Spanish and Mexican land titles before federal commissioners and in US courts, Californios confronted a myriad of technical and spurious challenges, including a new legal system and a different language. Some of the biggest challenges resulted from squatters and land speculators who filed claims on land belonging to Californios that delayed title confirmations, and lengthened the court proceedings – landowners spent 17 years on average securing their titles (Haas 1995). Californios lost land to expensive legal fees, and to unethical lawyers who tricked them into signing legal documents that saddled the owners with additional debts. Afraid of the lengthy appeals, some owners sold their land at bargain prices. Others abandoned portions of their land as a result of vigilante violence. For landowners who managed to secure their titles, taxes became another obstacle because the state's tax laws disproportionately targeted owners of land over owners of different types of wealth (i.e., gold). Some rancheros managed to keep their property within the family after their daughters married Anglo Americans or European immigrants, who could defend the family's property because they understood the legal system and spoke English. Another challenge confronting Californio landowners came from their lack of capital diversification. When the market in cattle decreased after the Gold Rush many rancheros, who had most of their wealth invested in land and cattle, were forced to sell their land in order to pay loans and taxes (Monroy 1990).

While the Californio elite lost vast landholdings, less privileged Californios faced increasing criminalization and violence. In the aftermath of the US – Mexican War and the Gold Rush, racial tensions remained high throughout the state. This atmosphere fueled an increase in crime in Los Angeles. While every ethnic group was represented among the criminals, journalists helped convince Anglo Americans that impoverished Mexicans were to blame for most crimes. Some writers characterized the disorder as a "race war," and soon vigilantes, like the gang of Anglo Texans known as El Monte boys, began lynching Mexicans suspected of crimes. The racial violence also gave rise to the appearance of several groups of bandits. Some, like Joaquín Murrieta in Northern California, rebelled after enduring vigilante violence. Others, like Juan Flores and Tiburcio Vásquez, rebelled in response to the criminalization and subordination of the Mexican community. These bandits targeted Anglo Americans by stealing their cattle and killing vigilantes who remained unpunished by legal officers. The bandits also targeted Chinese miners, whom Anglo Americans feminized by characterizing them as "defenseless" and the white men as their defenders (Johnson 2000).

As European immigrants arrived in California, they found common cause with Anglo American workers in their opposition to non-white workers. Most European immigrants came from Ireland, Germany, and England, with a smaller number originating in France and Italy. The state's 1870 census enumerated over 116,000 European-born residents, including 54,421 Irish, 29,699 Germans, 19,202 English, 8,063 French, and 4,660 Italians. Perhaps because they shared a common ancestry and culture with northwestern European immigrants, Anglo Americans came to accept Irish, German, and English immigrants more easily and to regard them as "honorary Americans" (Starr & Orsi 2000: 48–9). In California, Anglo Americans came to view these northwestern European immigrants as "white" because of shared experiences and alliances against racially marked "non-whites." Many Anglo Americans arriving in California at mid-nineteenth century agreed with the free labor ideology that valued individualism, competitive markets, expanding capitalism, and, above all, the value of free labor. The goal of free labor advocates was a middle-class lifestyle where they could be self-employed and economically independent. In California, Anglo Americans sought to prevent the existence of any labor system that threatened free "white" labor (Almaguer 1994). Because African Americans did not become a significant percentage of the labor force during the nineteenth century, white workers were more threatened by Chinese workers who eventually made up 25 percent of the labor force. According to Saxton, European immigrant workers (mostly Irish and Germans) united around the idea that they were not Chinese. Thus, European immigrant workers claimed the privileges of whiteness as they joined white Americans in portraying the Chinese as an indispensable enemy (Saxton 1990).

African Americans in California confronted not only racial tensions but also legislation that upheld white supremacy. White Californians, influenced by free labor ideology, successfully prevented slavery from gaining legal acceptance when the state entered the Union as a free state. Their antipathy extended beyond slavery to free African Americans, as demonstrated by various unsuccessful attempts to pass laws that would have prevented the immigration of free African Americans into the state (Almaguer 1994). Nevertheless, some African Americans arrived as slaves accompanying white southerners during the Gold Rush, while others arrived as free people searching for riches in the same mines. State officials generally ignored slave owners' use of slaves despite California's prohibition of slavery. However, free African Americans noticed the contradiction and organized to assist slaves' efforts to sue for their freedom. African American and Anglo American abolitionists gathered funds to publicize the slaves' plight and to pay for their legal fees. Their strategy worked as several slaves, including Bridget Mason and Archy Lee, successfully sued and obtained their freedom. Mason became a prominent nurse, real-estate investor, and philanthropist while Lee left the state for British Columbia accompanied by hundreds of others, frustrated by the state's attempts to pass anti-immigration laws aimed at African Americans. Other slaves earned enough money in the mines or other endeavors to purchase their freedom and that of their families (Johnson 2000).

California passed several laws meant to keep African Americans subordinate, including denying them the right to vote, serve on juries, testify in court, and marry whites; the state even passed a fugitive slave law to help slave owners retain control of escaped slaves (Lapp 1977). In response to their continual subordination, African Americans organized a series of statewide conventions to press for political and legal rights. The denial of rights affected an increasing number of people as the state's African American population, which was approximately 4,000 in 1860, hovered around one percent throughout the second half of the nineteenth century. African Americans also pressed for access to education and for the desegregation of public schools. While few African Americans became successful entrepreneurs like Biddy Mason, most labored in the food and service industries because of restrictive hiring practices.

Chinese immigrants also confronted various discriminatory laws targeting their participation in the workplace and civil society. Originally from southern China, the mostly male immigrants were pushed out by war, a bad economy, and political strife. They arrived in such large numbers during the Gold Rush that their population had swelled to 35,000 by 1860. Chinese immigrants began confronting vigilante harassment and legal restrictions soon after arriving in the mines. According to Alexander Saxton, much of the anti-Chinese legislation and violence was modeled after similar actions that white Californians had directed at African Americans (Saxton 1971). Some Chinese immigrants left the diggings to work as cooks, laundrymen, and servants. Although the Foreign Miners' Tax weighed disproportionately on them (they paid over 95 percent of the total $5 million collected), Chinese laborers remained in the mines after others left even though the gold had become more difficult to extract. Transformed into wage workers for mining companies, they made up half the mining labor force by 1870. Chinese immigrants also began working in railroad construction, taking lower pay for the most dangerous jobs that white laborers shunned (Saxton 1971). They also migrated into urban areas, formed benevolent associations, and established ethnic enclaves called Chinatowns.

Like African Americans and Indians, Chinese immigrants faced restrictive legislation because they were racially marked as "non-whites." State laws prevented them from becoming US citizens, forced them into segregated schools, and barred them from testifying in court against whites. The ruling in the case of *People v. Hall* (1854) officially relegated the state's Chinese population to the same second-class status held by African Americans and Indians. Overturning an earlier murder conviction, the California Supreme Court ruled that Chinese residents could not testify against whites (Starr & Orsi 2000). Their situation worsened during the 1870s when the state faced an economic depression and widespread unemployment. The worsening economy provided the pretext for the Workingmen's Party of California (WPC) to blame Chinese workers for lowering wages. Denis Kearney, an Irish immigrant living in San Francisco, led the WPC and ended many of his speeches with chants of "the Chinese must go!" Not surprisingly, several WPC rallies resulted in riots and arrests. The WPC managed to win numerous local and state elections before imploding in the 1880s. Riots in Los Angeles also targeted Chinese immigrants in the 1870s as white and Latino residents destroyed buildings and killed immigrants living in the city's Chinatown. While the laborers bore the brunt of these attacks, Chinese benevolent associations and merchants chafed under legal restrictions, which they challenged in court. Their lawsuits targeting

anti-Chinese legislation succeeded in overturning their exclusion from
public schools (in response the state created segregated Chinese schools)
and discriminatory laws against business owners. Nevertheless, exclusionist
politicians followed labor unions' earlier agitation by pressing for anti-
Chinese legislation, including the federal Chinese Exclusion Act of 1882,
which severely restricted immigration from China and prevented the naturalization of Chinese immigrants (Gyory 1998).

Racial exclusionary legislation had the desired effect of severely restricting the immigration of racialized "others," while at the same time welcoming European immigrants and Anglo American migrants to California. Not
surprisingly, the vast majority of migrants during the second part of the
nineteenth century had European ancestry. Boosters and real-estate developers partially contributed to the state's tremendous growth in the last
third of the nineteenth century, while inexpensive transportation and the
temperate climate of Southern California lured migrants from other parts
of the nation. Urban jobs and rural land pulled European Americans to
the state in such large numbers that first- or second-generation immigrants
made up over half of the population in 1900. In San Francisco, over 70
percent of the population consisted of first- and second-generation European immigrants. As in the rest of the nation, the state's immigrants hailed
mostly from Germany, Ireland, Italy, and Britain; a smaller number came
from Norway, Sweden, and Denmark.

California's economy changed the typical settlement patterns that these
immigrants followed in other parts of the country. In addition to working
as farmers and urban industrial workers, European immigrants found work
as sailors, packinghouse workers, winemakers, and merchants. Like other
non-white immigrants, European immigrants formed ethnic enclaves where
they could continue to speak their native languages and practice their traditional religions. However, unlike Chinese immigrants who were barred
from living in certain neighborhoods, European immigrants voluntarily
chose to live in ethnic enclaves (Issel & Cherny 1986). At the end of the
nineteenth century, the ethnic diversity of the state would continue to
increase as Japanese immigrants began arriving. Like others racialized as
"non-white," the Japanese would encounter few employment opportunities in a racially stratified labor market. When the Japanese obtained a
measure of success as small farmers, the state's white agriculturalists
mobilized to push through the next round of racially discriminatory
legislation.

Racial categories and immigration in California changed dramatically
over the course of the nineteenth century. During this period, the state's
racial and ethnic diversity challenged the white – black racial binary through
which much of US history is customarily interpreted. The century began
with Spain struggling to remain in control of Alta California, offering

numerous incentives to spur immigration, and classifying residents into some 54 *castas* (racial categories). Economic opportunities spurred large-scale immigration over the next 100 years, and increased the racial and ethnic diversity of the state. By the end of the century, California was firmly under United States rule, attempting to stem the flow of "non-white" immigrants, and increasingly relying on a process of racial construction that marked immigrants as "white" or "non-white." Immigration had radically changed the demographics of the state, leaving "white" residents as the overwhelming majority of California's population by the turn of the twentieth century.

References

Almaguer, T. 1994. *Racial Fault Lines: The Historical Origins of White Supremacy in California*. Berkeley: University of California Press.

Bouvier, V. M. 2001. *Women and the Conquest of California, 1542–1840: Codes of Silence*. Tucson: University of Arizona Press.

Camarillo, A. 1979. *Chicanos in a Changing Society: From Mexican Pueblos to American Barrios in Santa Barbara and Southern California, 1848–1930*. Cambridge, MA: Harvard University Press.

Castañeda, A. 1990. "Presidarias y Pobladoras: Spanish-Mexican Women in Frontier Monterey, Alta California, 1770–1821." PhD dissertation, Stanford University.

Castañeda, Antonia I. 1993. "Sexual Violence in the Politics and Policies of Conquest: Amerindian Women an the Spanish Conquest of Alta California." In Adela de la Torre and Beatriz Pesquera, eds., *Building with Our Hands: New Directions in Chicana Studies*. Berkeley: University of California Press, pp. 15–33.

Chávez-García, M. 2004. *Negotiating Conquest: Gender and Power in California, 1770s to 1880s*. Tucson: University of Arizona Press.

Gutiérrez, R. A. and Orsi, R. J. 1998. *Contested Eden: California before the Gold Rush*. Berkeley: University of California Press.

Gyory, A. 1998. *Closing the Gate: Race, Politics, and the Chinese Exclusion Act*. Chapel Hill: University of North Carolina Press.

Haas, L. 1995. *Conquests and Historical Identities in California, 1769–1936*. Berkeley: University of California Press.

Hine, R. V. and Faragher, J. M. 2000. *The American West: A New Interpretive History*. New Haven, CT: Yale University Press.

Horsman, R. 1981. *Race and Manifest Destiny: The Origins of American Racial Anglo-Saxonism*. Cambridge, MA: Harvard University Press.

Hurtado, A. 1988. *Indian Survival on the California Frontier*. New Haven, CT: Yale University Press.

Issel, W. and Cherny, R. 1986. *San Francisco, 1865–1932: Politics, Power, and Urban Development*. Berkeley: University of California Press.

Johnson, S. L. 2000. *Roaring Camp: The Social World of the California Gold Rush*. New York: W. W. Norton.

Lapp, R. 1977. *Blacks in Gold Rush California*. New Haven, CT: Yale University Press.

Monroy, D. 1990. *Thrown Among Strangers: The Making of Mexican Culture in Frontier California*. Berkeley: University of California Press.

Pitt, L. 1971. *The Decline of the Californios: A Social History of the Spanish-Speaking Californians, 1846–1890*. Berkeley: University of California Press.

Saxton, A. 1971. *The Indispensable Enemy: Labor and the Anti-Chinese Movement in California*. Berkeley: University of California Press.

Saxton, A. 1990. *The Rise and Fall of the White Republic: Class Politics and Mass Culture in Nineteenth-Century America*. New York: Verso.

Starr, K. and Orsi, R. J. 2000. *Rooted in Barbarous Soil: People, Culture, and Community in Gold Rush California*. Berkeley: University of California Press.

Weber, D. 1982. *The Mexican Frontier, 1821–1846: The American Southwest under Mexico*. Albuquerque: University of New Mexico Press.

FURTHER READING

Deverell, W. 2004. *Whitewashed Adobe: The Rise of Los Angeles and the Remaking of Its Mexican Past*. Berkeley: University of California Press.

Gutiérrez, D. G. 1995. *Walls and Mirrors: Mexican Americans, Mexican Immigrants, and the Politics of Ethnicity*. Berkeley: University of California Press.

Haney-López, I. F. 2006. *White by Law: The Legal Construction of Race*. New York: New York University Press.

Hurtado, A. L. 1999. *Intimate Frontiers: Sex, Gender, and Culture in Old California*. Albuquerque: University of New Mexico Press.

Jacobson, M. F. 1999. *Whiteness of a Different Color: European Immigrants and the Alchemy of Race*. Cambridge, MA: Harvard University Press.

Lee, E. 2003. *At America's Gates: Chinese Immigration During the Exclusion Era, 1882–1943*. Chapel Hill: University of North Carolina Press.

McKanna, C. V. 2002. *Race and Homicide in Nineteenth-Century California*. Reno: University of Nevada Press.

Molina, N. 2006. *Fit to Be Citizens? Public Health and Race in Los Angeles, 1879–1939*. Berkeley: University of California Press.

Pitti, Stephen J. 2003. *The Devil in Silicon Valley: Northern California, Race, and Mexican Americans*. Princeton, NJ: Princeton University Press.

Ueda, R., ed. 2006. *A Companion to American Immigration*. Malden, MA: Blackwell Publishing.

Part III

Conquest and Statehood

Chapter Nine

THE 1850s

William Deverell

California turned 150 in 2000. Scarcely anyone seemed to notice. A variety of commemorative events came and went: a lecture here and there, a few panel discussions, a parade or two. Despite the best of intentions and concerted effort on the part of a few cultural organizations, the milestone garnered far less attention than might otherwise have been expected.[1] It had been much the same with the previous 1998 and 1999 sesquicentennials marking the discovery of gold and subsequent beginning of the Gold Rush. Any hopes for an anniversary with a bang faded in the face of barely a whimper.

It had not always been so. This recent near-silence stands in marked contrast to the respective centennial celebrations 50 years earlier, each of which seem to have been viewed as a great public success, and each of which garnered crowds and buzz, if not outright bang. As an official State of California website put it succinctly, the most recent anniversaries, "burdened with an almost unpronounceable name," had been granted "inadequate public and private funding," and were "less ambitious than those a half century earlier."[2]

Explaining the lack of public interest and response to the state's 150th birthday is not so easy. There might be any number of reasons for it. It is probably true that 150 years is a less compelling, less recognizable milestone than 100 or 200 years. And "sesquicentennial" is indeed a mouthful. At a deeper level, it may be that Californians do not really care to think back to 1850 or the 1850s generally. The state's long history of immigration and tradition of ever-present new arrivals may render the historical events of the mid-nineteenth century largely inaccessible to entire cross-sections of California's population at any given time. A population in which the percentage of those born somewhere else steadily hovers around 50 percent simply may not have great purchase on public memory of an undoubtedly bygone era. Marking an event like the sesquicentennial would seem to require at least mere slivers of 1850s public memory. It may be that Californians do not remember enough to be attracted to commemoration.

Other answers suggest themselves. Some of this distance between now and then may be deliberate. It may be dissonance expressed precisely as absence. Any number – large numbers – of Californians might reasonably be expected to be wary of commemorating historical moments or entire eras no longer seen as unerringly positive in the celebratory light that "happy birthday" suggests. In other words, "inadequate funding" *may* help explain why the state's 150th birthday party fell flat (and it would be instructive to compare the generous public funding of the events of 1948, 1949, and 1950 with the paltry public expenditures on those events 50 years later). But lack of funds is probably not the full story.

Before delving further into this, I want to make a simple, declarative point. And that is to insist upon the sheer *significance* of the 1850s in California. The decade is a turning point in the state's (and certainly the nation's) history. I believe that historians are generally, by temperament and tradition, far too tied to a decade-by-decade approach to historical transitions and historical coherence. We speak and write in terms too facile of "the 1960s," or "the 1920s," as if decades are automatically synonymous with a periodic, all-too-brief *zeitgeist* or that *everything* changes from a year ending in "9" to one ending in "0" Yet as regards the topic at hand, the decade of the 1850s *was* of critical – even revolutionary – importance to California, and California to the nation; and too few Californians, too few students of history, too few commemorative-events attendees or no-shows, know it.

Even though they often begin their textbook or lecture recitations of California history with assumptions tied to decade-by-decade change, historians are implicated in this lack of public engagement with the sesquicentennial anniversary of California statehood and the ensuing decade. We'd do well to acknowledge some shortcomings in this vein. By this I mean that California historians have shortchanged their students and readership by not grappling with 1850, or the entire 1850s, as aggressively or forthrightly as we might. This might be said of the entire nineteenth century, as I believe that historians have carried their California research too quickly into the twentieth century when so many nineteenth-century questions continue to merit scholarly ideas and labors. California in the 1850s demands more scholarly attention.

The tide is changing, but it is changing too slowly. This brief essay is a survey of some of the historical literature addressing that decade. It is, simultaneously, a light scold designed to urge scholars, and especially younger scholars, to consider the possibilities, promise, and even obligations of historical scholarship focused upon this remarkable decade in California's past.

Traditional historical surveys of antebellum California, especially those dating from the middle decades of the twentieth century, tend to isolate the state from the adjacent turmoil of national issues. In doing so, earlier recitations of the history of the decade perform a kind of crude scholarly surgery; the state is unto itself historically, moving through various stages of economic or political maturity virtually unconnected (except by vaguely determined migration networks) to national, much less global, issues, trends, or influences. It is as if scholarly sleight of hand is at work or a kind of hindsight determinism, as if California's later prominence is already assured by the 1850s – that the state could, already at the very dawn of statehood, be discussed in relation only to itself. That might be true in some respects today – though even now it is problematic to examine California in any kind of historical vacuum – but it seems clearly out of balance for the 1850s. Hindsight is a dangerous impulse in historical scrutiny. California's eventual gargantuan influence is far off in the 1850s, and scholars would be well advised to contemplate instead the sheer fragility of California society in the immediate aftermath of the Mexican War of 1846–8.

Nor is it at all advisable to snip 1850s California loose from its wider moorings. Even traditional views of the Gold Rush – far more an event or conglomeration of events of the 1850s than the 1840s – spend little time and too few pages discussing or analyzing the national (much less international) content or context of the drama and its many consequences. This of course does not make much historical sense. For one, and perhaps most compelling reason, such accounts divorce antebellum California from the state's intricate relationship to the *bellum* that was the Civil War. To excise 1850s California from the coming conflagration is an act of willful historical blindness; California and the "slave or free?" fate of the state occupied center stage in many a national debate borne of sectional antagonisms at the dawn of the decade. We would do well to remember the simple contradiction of that era, that California was at once very, very far away from and simultaneously intricately interwoven into the events, lives, and disagreements of Americans to the east. And in the most obvious fashion, those thousands of Gold Rush miners and adventurers – men, women, and children – weren't simply sent off to California and forgotten. On the contrary, the shadows they left behind continued to color life in the cities, small towns, and farms they left behind. California *was* far away in the 1850s, but its very remoteness helped to insure that the place, and the loved ones who found their way there, were on the lips and in the hearts and thoughts of those who stayed behind. That remoteness would lessen very quickly, with the arrival of the telegraph, more sophisticated ocean-going transportation, and, most significantly, the transcontinental railroad, but we would do well to remember the sheer isolation of the place before these developments. A new study by the historian Aims McGuinness, *Path of Empire: Panama and the California Gold Rush*, addresses this theme in

intriguing ways, cleverly positing 1850s Panama (and its isolation) as inter-
mediary between California and the eastern seaboard and, as well, as the
literal interstice between the Atlantic and Pacific (2007).

Coincident with its intertwining in the history of a place like Panama,
California was also deeply tied to North America's Great Basin, especially
through the cultural tether of religion. Historians have been far too slow
to recognize that many a Mormon adventurer to California in the Gold
Rush era thought him/herself at the end of a Mormon emigrant ambition
that would use the Great Basin as the staging ground for settler and faith
implantations farther west. This was very much the case through the mid-
1850s, not least because Mormons helped so much in developing overland
trail routes, at least up until the Mormon leadership's anxious 1857 call
for Saints to return to Utah in time to square off, largely in stalemate, with
the United States Army in the quixotic "Mormon War" of that year. As
the historian Kenneth Owens recently noted in his important treatment of
Mormons in the California Gold Rush, the role of the Latter-day Saints in
that event has been unaccountably "overlooked, deliberately ignored, misunderstood, or forgotten" by Mormon and non-Mormon historians alike
(2005). For the former, what Owens calls a "Zioncentric" point of view
dominated official histories; the latter tended, and yet tend, to see Mormons
as mere curiosities in the gold fields, almost as if they'd gotten wildly lost
on their way to the Great Basin.

Outward views from 1850s California were not, of course, limited to
continental visions. As a few recent works have begun to make abundantly
clear, 1850s California existed at the eastern edge of a vast, complex, and
already well-established network of trade, transport, and traffic stretching
across the Pacific. This volume's co-editor, David Igler, has addressed this
issue in these pages (see his discussion of antebellum California and the
Pacific in Chapter Six), as well as in other venues (Igler 2004). What Igler's
work, as well as that of a number of younger scholars toiling away at dissertation projects, suggests is that our relatively recent awareness of the
eastward reverberations of the Gold Rush and the 1850s ought to be
accompanied by recognition of the westward vibrations of California's
rising significance. There is at this writing a nascent Pacific Studies sub-field
of world history, and California of the 1850s is likely to play a prominent
role in that sub-field's findings and conceptual coherence.

Like what essayist Shana Bernstein calls "the long 1950s" (see Chapter
Twenty-One in this volume), 1850s California is perhaps best viewed not
within the usual and arbitrary chronological boundaries made of a decade.
While the Compromise of 1850 does offer a neat – and undoubtedly significant – beginning-of-a-decade convenience, it would be unwise to
unhitch that portentous moment from either the Gold Rush or the turmoil
of the Mexican–American War. It is instead best to address the connections

between the late 1840s and the entire decade of the 1850s, on both California and national terms. In other words, there is merit to such a notion as the "long 1850s."

A "California all by itself" school of historical writing is, admittedly, a bit of a caricature or straw man. It is not fair to paint all earlier scholarship on mid-nineteenth-century California with a single brush. As early as the 1880s, the contemplative, if jaundiced, Californian Josiah Royce wrote of the early years of statehood against a larger national canvas in *California: A Study of American Character* (1886). His sub-title is marvelously illustrative of Royce's idea that California history (he concerned himself with the period from roughly 1845 to 1855) was anything but solely local in meaning, significance, or consequence. The local and the national were inextricably linked, Royce insisted, and Californians' haphazard and quixotic "search for moral ideals" could not but help illuminate and forecast national character, if troublingly:

> This is the period of excitement, of trial, and of rapid transformation. Everything that has since happened in California, or that ever will happen there, so long as men dwell on the land, must be deeply affected by the forces of local life and society that then took their origin. And, for the understanding of our American national character in some of its most significant qualities, this life of surprises and of searching moral ordeals has a still too little appreciated value. (Royce 1886: 1)

That California and the circumstances of its statehood nativity were, to its disappointed native son, evidence of moral declension in the national character and anything but cause for celebratory gusto only serves to make his interpretation all the more remarkable. Where Royce's contemporary Lord Bryce imagined late nineteenth-century California already as a triumphal nation-state in the making (recall his 1888 declaration that "California, more than any other part of the Union, is a country by itself"), Royce was disheartened by the ways in which the infant state could so well represent an entire nation's moral and political declension (for further thoughts on Royce, see Donald Waldie's essay in Chapter Two of this book).

Josiah Royce stands as an early – and accordingly path-breaking – thinker about 1850s California as a barometer of what he imagined to be a form of national decay. And while we might argue that Royce stands alone in this regard, there are other, much later, keystone texts which served to draw California and the California experience into national contexts for good or ill. Here we must especially acknowledge Henry Nash Smith's *Virgin Land* (1950). This remarkably influential study – claimed quite rightly as the founding text of the American Studies discipline – sought to reposition far western society, and especially eastern perspectives and imaginations aimed upon it, as central to cultural trends and cultural imagination in the early national period.[3] Scholars and students of the American West and California still read Smith profitably. This is not so much because of any explicit treatment of the state: "California" does not even appear in the book's index. The profit comes by way of Smith's broad-minded analysis of the role played by vernacular, literary, and governmental sources in parsing the far West for a young nation hungry for the cultural ideals it found embodied in western landscapes and western circumstances. No book that mentions California so infrequently has ever been as influential in the ways in which California has been understood by scholars. Smith published *Virgin Land* a century after the Gold Rush. But, at the same time, in examining the cultural impact of texts produced before 1850, he predicted the nation's embrace of it.

Lesser-known older works deserve mention alongside Smith's canonical study. A far less influential book such as David Pletcher's *The Diplomacy of Annexation: Texas, Oregon, and the Mexican War* is, in a sense, incorrectly titled, as the author's careful attention to international diplomacy in the mid-nineteenth century (he does in fact address issues germane to 1850s California), is an exceptionally thorough, if often dense, recitation of the thick worlds of international diplomacy operating in and out of wartime situations during the 1840s and 1850s. It remains required reading. So, too, with David Potter's stirring *The Impending Crisis* (1976), which helps to place the role of the far West in the mounting conflict between North and South; Potter's careful reconstruction of the delicate (and in the end fruitless) diplomatic maneuverings of the Compromise of 1850, which of course included provisions for California to enter the Union as a free state, is masterful.

As noted above, Henry Nash Smith tackled the entire West. As Frederick Jackson Turner had done for the literal frontier which existed between what he would have called civilization and barbarism, Smith did for the frontier imagination. Both scholars wondered what their respective subjects meant to American culture. Smith did not explicitly address California, but he has an intellectual heir who did. The historian Kevin Starr's first book of his multi-volume (and as yet incomplete) reckoning of California history is an especially important book on the 1850s. Starr's *Americans and the California Dream* focused heavily on the decade of the 1850s, and it rendered that decade into the foundation for the chapters – and multiple volumes – which came after. Starr's 1973 account is what we might call high American Studies; his sources and his historical informants tended to be elite and privileged, whereas the absolute heart of *Virgin Land* lies in the pages of cheap nineteenth-century dime novels. Starr's point of departure – what did Americans, and then Californians themselves, make of California upon encountering it? – drew national threads both into and out of the far West in important and lasting ways.

Leonard Pitt's now nearly 50-year-old monograph, *The Decline of the Californios*, remains nearly as important today as it was when first published. The volume's concerted effort to tell and analyze the 1850s struggles of the native California Mexican-descent population, on the ground and through social history, has been extremely influential through two full generations of successive scholarship. Pitt launched many a dissertation ship upon the waters of scholarly inquiry, and not a few scholars, including myself, are deeply in his debt for it. Albert Camarillo's very important 1970s study *Chicanos in a Changing Society* is a case in point. Camarillo's deftly researched analysis of the Southern California Mexican and Mexican American peoples of the latter nineteenth and early twentieth century is a companion to Pitt's earlier study, delving deeply into the social history of various ethnic Mexican communities. Both works remain in print today simply because they were done so well in their first iterations as doctoral theses.

Following bold hints laid out by Josiah Royce way back in the 1880s, Pitt was among the first of more recent historians to insist that we grapple with the realities (and legacies) of the deep ethnic and racial violence of the 1850s. In a sense, Pitt cleared away the boys-will-be-boys nonsense of many an early Gold Rush study and ushered his readers to a California still dark and bloody following the Mexican–American War. Manifest Destiny did not go away with the end of the Mexican War. A very good place to look for – and to find – it, is 1850s California. Through both domestic spasms of anti-Mexican violence within the state and treasonous paramilitary operations launched against Mexico and other nations, 1850s California revealed itself as a state and society not quite certain that the diplomatic cessation of wartime hostilities needed to be honored.

Why historians interested in race and ethnicity do not gravitate more to the nineteenth century is a bit of a mystery, though I will acknowledge the magnetic appeal (and obvious importance) of analyzing California in the twentieth century. In the California historical setting, it seems as if the post-World War II period garners most of the attention. This isn't wrong. But it is unbalanced. For every fine study of the 1950s, we need one of the 1850s.

Think, as Pitt and Camarillo both had us do, of the case of Southern California and Los Angeles. There the specter of enduring war threatens to capsize the tiny pueblo's future. Would the region emerge from the 1850s intact? We must remember that although California is far more tied to the coming and raging of the Civil War than earlier commentators expected or assumed, it is the 1850s that presents the great societal rupture on the ground out west. Regime change, the dawn of the American period, the onrushing miners and adventurers, the orgies of violence, licit and illicit land transfer: such is the stuff from which revolutions are made. If the Civil War was a revolution, it was of the 1860s. If California had a revolution, it wasn't expressed in the piracy of the late 1840s Bear Flag allegiants. California's revolution is in the tumult of the 1850s. How that upheaval then gave way to, and dissipated in, the 1860s and 1870s becomes the question historians must grapple with. That part of the answer has everything to do with violence, murder, and legal or illegal coercion seems patently obvious, though not to the point of rendering further study at all superfluous.

My own work on such themes in the 1850s and what I refer to as "the unending Mexican War" has been deeply influenced by Pitt, as has that of historical sociologist Tomás Almaguer, whose episodic analysis of California white supremacy, and the various cudgels utilized in support of its maintenance, ought still to be consulted by scholars (Deverell 2004; Almaguer 1994).

Three additional scholars deserve special mention as regards this theme of 1850s racial violence. Albert Hurtado's *Indian Survival on the California Frontier* (1988) is a "must read." It renders the 1850s appropriately grim in terms of the genocidal collapse of the state's native population (the population declined by 80 percent in the decade); William Bauer, Jr. further discusses the period from statehood to the coming of the Civil War in Chapter Eleven of this book, pointing out that in 1865, only 30,000 indigenous people remained in California. David Wyatt's imaginative *Five Fires* analyzes the metaphorical burning of California, not through actual fires per se, but through the fiery insults of racial violence and opposition (1997). Lastly, and most significantly, Alexander Saxton's *The Indispensable Enemy* (1971) is simply indispensable. In the midst of anticipating the entire sub-field of whiteness studies, Saxton lays bare the state's 1850s antagonisms aimed at racial others. On the one hand, the book is all about white California's hatred of the Chinese, a phenomenon borne of the 1850s. It is also and more deeply an exploration of the wider-scale racial hangovers of the entirety of California history. Taken together, all three texts carry us so much further than those which, in Douglas Sackman's insightful phrasing from Chapter Ten of this volume, render the 1850s as so many "footnoted versions of Bret Harte stories."[4]

Even though their analyses carry well into the late nineteenth century, Pitt and Saxton deserve special credit for reinterpreting the California Gold Rush. Both peered past the "Eureka!" moments of the period to find instead a different sort of exuberance spawned of racial violence. And the influence of both studies has been significant in this regard. To be sure, the California Gold Rush remains a cottage industry within the larger circles of California and western American history. Diaries and letter collections continue to be published, some more interesting than others, some more important than others. Some older texts remain keystones of the era, with Holliday's *The World Rushed In* (1981) holding the high ground in this regard. Holliday knew how to tell a story, and in the Swain family he discovered a level of literacy, expression, and soul-searching unusual in the historical record. Younger scholars of California would do well to read Holliday, just as they would profit from recognizing the years (and years) of care that went into researching and writing the book.

The benchmark for Gold Rush scholarship and the single best monograph on the topic is Malcolm J. Rohrbough's *Days of Gold* (1997). This terrific study, which the author modestly claims is but an "introduction" to the topic, examines not only the day-to-day social history "in the diggings," but is equally concerned with the ways in which the Gold Rush was experienced by those who *did not* make the journey to California (1997: 1). The author's patient exploration of the lives and longings of those who stayed home – the wives, children, parents, and other loved ones – helps to make his book a far more well-rounded, and national, examination than is usually the case with Gold Rush studies (see also Waldie's discussion of Rohrbough in Chapter Two of this volume). The event was, he thoughtfully asserts, "a shared national experience," the single most important national moment between the Louisiana Purchase and secession (ibid.: 2). Centering the Gold Rush between these moments not only ties it to events of obvious national significance, it reperiodizes the antebellum period. Brian Roberts, in his *American Alchemy*, another fine study of the Gold Rush, does much the same, arguing that the moment coincided and dovetailed with the rise of an American middle class and that it was a quintessential, even defining moment, of middle-class American expressions, values, and experience (2000).

As regards the Gold Rush, the historian Susan Johnson deserves to be singled out here as well; her *Roaring Camp* (2000) takes readers into the complicated social realms of miners and others in California's so-called "southern" mines. Her often lyrical reconstruction of the overlapping worlds of racial and gendered identity in the diggings demonstrates indeed that "Gold Rush California was an unusual time and place," but also that its very eccentricity is an invitation to learn a great deal about 1850s America more generally.[5]

Leonard Richards' recent book, *The California Gold Rush and the Coming of the Civil War* (2007), offers a refreshing refiguring of the Gold Rush in the coming of fratricide and national catastrophe. What Richards reminds us of is that even in the midst of the coming of the Civil War and, in fact, precisely because of those tensions, Americans thought about California, and they did so intensely. And while he does not employ the concept, his book really is all about the "long 1850s" in California, stretching back before 1850 and forward to the outbreak of the war itself. Americans thought about 1850s California because of the Gold Rush, of course, insofar as that event seemed to promise something mid-nineteenth-century people could scarcely imagine: life free of farming drudgery, for a time or for ever. But they thought about California because California meant for them the far West; it epitomized those new territories brought into the Union by way of war, and California and the West were the big question marks over the fate of national unity. In this ever-hotter debate, California was the key locale. The West: slave or free? Tied to North or South? Would there be peace or war?

Environmental historians, heed a call. The landscape and sea coast of 1850s California beckons to be more closely examined by scholars wishing to analyze environmental change in the midst of regime transition. David Igler helped us sketch out some of these changes in case-study fashion in his *Industrial Cowboys* monograph (2001), escorting readers to the mid-nineteenth century land and cattle barony of Miller & Lux in the San Joaquin Valley (both men arrived in Northern California at the very beginning of the 1850s and formed their partnership in 1858). Steven Stoll has done fine work on the rise of agricultural science throughout the state beginning at the far edge of the 1850s (1998). Andrew Isenberg's *Mining California: An Ecological History* reminds readers of the longstanding environmental consequences of the Gold Rush era (2006). The Gold Rush hastened what Henry George termed California's "rapid, monstrous maturity," of that there is little doubt, but it also left in its considerable wake widespread deforestation, watershed degradation, and despoiled farmlands. Douglas Sackman's piece in this volume, which takes up similar issues related to environmental and political conquests in the nineteenth century, suggests a number of pathways enterprising scholars might take in tackling such issues anew.

What remains for historians to tackle in 1850s California? Where to begin? It is yet surprising that we have few studies that ambitiously grapple with the sheer significance of regime change, circa the post-Mexican War. The Mexican period's rancho economy teetered, then fell, the trammeled victim of legal, extralegal, environmental, and economic forces. California scholars have been slow to address the magnitude of such change in their publications (or even in their theses).

In a similar vein, we have too few, far too few, studies of 1850s California industry outside of, or running parallel to, the Gold Rush. Gold lured thousands upon thousands of people to California, from the world over, as is well known. But the headiest days of gold hunting were short-lived: best to stand in snow-fed Sierra stream in 1848 or early 1849, when the gold was more plentiful and easier to grab. So what happened in the 1850s? Where did all those people go? Having seen the elephant, some went home. But others – most of whom are lost to us, at least for now – stayed, found their way into farming, ranching, city life, jobs (see Vaught 2007). There is much to know about these people, and social historians of the West could clearly make significant contributions by helping fill gaps in our collective knowledge. Every bit as important, though, is the aggregated or broader-brushed analysis of the California political economy in the immediate aftermath of the Gold Rush heyday. Peter Decker's classic *Fortunes and Failures*, a longitudinal study of white-collar mobility (up and down the economic ladder, as the title indicates) beginning in the Gold Rush setting, provides an apt model for further studies of similar reach and themes.

Governance, with a small "g," remains an understudied topic in California history generally. David Johnson's fine and richly detailed comparative analysis of the statehood birth and early adolescence of Oregon, Nevada, and California remains historiographically lonely; we need many more such studies of the formation of California governance structures, at the local and state level, during the regime-change decade of the 1850s (1992). And while land-use practices and land-transfer issues, especially in light of the land claims court and marketplace cases of the 1850s, have received some recent attention, much more work remains to be done on this fundamental arena of the state's changed political economy of the 1850s (Clay & Troesken 2005).

It used to be that part of the problem related to a relative paucity of work on 1850s California had to do with sources. The problem was at once too many and too few sources. There have long been small mountains of Gold Rush diaries and letters available to scholars; we are fortunate that the event provoked an outpouring of literary production the likes of which has never been replicated in America, save for the Civil War experience scarcely a decade later.[6] But the sheer volume of the letters can threaten to skew interpretations and even the significance of the Gold Rush in directions defined by race, class, gender, and literacy, to name but a few parameters. Scholars have returned to these sources to mine them of other insights, of course, finding hidden stories and meanings imbedded within the words, memories, and passages penned. Yet sources sensitive to, for example, issues of race and ethnicity within the Gold Rush remain more difficult to come by, though they are probably out there for intrepid scholars to unearth. The recognition that Gold Rush or other 1850s material lies quietly in far-flung archives and collections is an encouraging development which is gaining momentum. That 1850s Californians wrote letters to elsewhere, and that it is elsewhere that those letters remained, is not exactly a revelation, but it is nonetheless an important research perspective. Holliday encountered his Gold Rush companion William Swain in the Beinecke Library at Yale; Rohrbough used the New York Historical Society to great advantage. What treasures await scholars in other archives in other places, other nations?

It is important to point out that recent developments in the digital environment have revolutionized perspectives on what is available and what it is accessible. This is an obvious generational transition in what was and what now is: the range of sources that scholars now have at their fingertips, through web-based and other digital environments, is plainly stunning. The revolution has not yet overturned what is known, but it certainly could, and young scholars ought to approach their work with exactly that kind of revisionist ambition. On the topic of California in the 1850s, the Online Archive of California (http://www.oac.cdlib.org/) is already singularly impressive, and we can expect it to grow in scope and reach. That archive's holdings, a warehousing of collections in numerous libraries and research institutions, are textually and visually rich. And they serve as a reminder that 1850s California is the first decade of photographic California. The visual record of the 1850s is a rich resource, and scholars would do well to embrace visual sources with equal parts enthusiasm and scholarly detachment.[7]

Calisphere (http://www.calisphere.universityofcalifornia.edu/), designed as a digitized primary source repository especially with the needs of the K-12 educational community in mind, is also noteworthy. Historians trained as researchers in the era before such tools were available *must* familiarize themselves with these opportunities, if only to impart information to students. Old-fashioned research methods will never fall from grace: scholars need the web and they need to roll up their sleeves in dusty archives.

The 1850s beckon: it is a decade of seismic importance in the shaping of California. With renewed commitment to scholarly obligations to explain how the past became the present, and to uncover human stories within that past, we historians might in some small ways convince broader constituencies of the significance not only of anniversary celebrations of the California past but of that past all by itself.

NOTES

1 "Rediscovering California at 150," a cascade of public humanities programs sponsored by the California Council for the Humanities, was the most concerted effort to mark the anniversary through broad programmatic outreach.

2 See the website LearnCalifornia.org, esp. at http://www.learncalifornia.org/doc.asp?id=2457.

3 Smith was the first doctoral graduate of Harvard's American Civilization program.

4 Starr (1973), especially Chapter 2's discussion of "Beyond Eldorado," is insightful here as well regarding the "spell" of Harte's "massive fiction-history" (see p. 49).

5 Susan Johnson, " 'Domestic' Life in the Diggings: The Southern Mines in the California Gold Rush," in Vicki L. Ruiz and Ellen C. DuBois, eds., *Unequal Sisters: A Multicultural Reader in U.S. Women's History*, 3rd edn. (Routledge), quoted at p. 106.

6 While it is beyond the scope of this essay, it would be wonderful if we had more scholarly analysis of Gold Rush letters alongside the Civil War letters of

the same individual. Surely many a twenty-something in the 1850s ended up in Union or Confederate uniform a decade later. What might deliberate comparison of their letters reveal about nationalism, sectionalism, the far West, etc.?

7   From the archive's website in the fall of 2007: "The OAC brings together historical materials from a variety of California institutions, including museums, historical societies, and archives. Over 120,000 images; 50,000 pages of documents, letters, and oral histories; and 8,000 guides to collections are available."

References

Almaguer, Tomás. 1994. *Racial Fault Lines: The Historical Origins of White Supremacy in California*. Berkeley: University of California Press.

Camarillo, Albert. 1979. *Chicanos in a Changing Society: From Mexican Pueblos to American Barrios in Santa Barbara and Southern California, 1848–1930*. Cambridge, MA: Harvard University Press.

Clay, Karen and Troesken, Werner. 2005. "Ranchos and the Politics of Land Claims." In William Deverell and Greg Hise, eds., *Land of Sunshine: An Environmental History of Metropolitan Los Angeles*. Pittsburgh: University of Pittsburgh Press, pp. 52–66.

Decker, Peter. 1978. *Fortunes and Failures: White-Collar Mobility in Nineteenth-Century San Francisco*. Cambridge, MA: Harvard University Press.

Deverell, William. 2004. *Whitewashed Adobe: The Rise of Los Angeles and the Remaking of Its Mexican Past*. Berkeley: University of California Press.

Holliday, J. S. 1981. *The World Rushed In: The California Gold Rush Experience*. New York: Simon & Schuster.

Hurtado, Albert. 1988. *Indian Survival on the California Frontier*. New Haven, CT: Yale University Press.

Igler, David. 2001. *Industrial Cowboys: Miller & Lux and the Transformation of the Far West, 1850–1920*. Berkeley: University of California Press.

Igler, David. 2004. "Diseased Goods: Global Exchanges in the Eastern Pacific Basin, 1770–1850," *American Historical Review* 109 (June): 693–719.

Isenberg, Andrew. 2006. *Mining California: An Ecological History*. New York: Hill & Wang.

Johnson, David. 1992. *Founding the Far West: California, Oregon, and Nevada, 1840–1890*. Berkeley: University of California Press.

Johnson, Susan. 2000. *Roaring Camp*. New York: W. W. Norton.

McGuinness, Aims. 2007. *Path of Empire: Panama and the California Gold Rush*. Ithaca, NY: Cornell University Press.

Morrison, Michael. 1999. *Slavery and the American West: The Eclipse of Manifest Destiny*. Chapel Hill: University of North Carolina Press.

Owens, Kenneth. 2005. *Gold Rush Saints: California Mormons and the Great Rush for Riches*. Norman: University of Oklahoma.

Pitt, Leonard. 1966. *The Decline of the Californios: A Social History of the Spanish-Speaking Californians, 1846–1890*. Berkeley: University of California Press.

Pletcher, David. 1973. *The Diplomacy of Annexation: Texas, Oregon, and the Mexican War*. Columbia, MO: University of Missouri Press.

Potter, David. 1976. *The Impending Crisis*. New York: Harper & Row.

Richards, Leonard. 2007. *The California Gold Rush and the Coming of the Civil War*. New York: Alfred A. Knopf.

Roberts, Brian. 2000. *American Alchemy: The California Gold Rush and Middle-Class Culture*. Chapel Hill: University of North Carolina Press.

Rohrbough, Malcolm. 1997. *Days of Gold: The California Gold Rush and the American Nation*. Berkeley: University of California Press.

Royce, Josiah. 1886. *California: A Study of American Character: From the Conquest in 1846 to the Second Vigilance Committee in San Francisco*. Boston, MA: Houghton Mifflin.

Sackman, Douglas C. 2007. *Orange Empire: California and the Fruits of Eden*. Berkeley: University of California Press.

Saxton, Alexander. 1971. *The Indispensable Enemy*. Berkeley: University of California Press.

Smith, Henry Nash. 1950. *Virgin Land: The American West as Symbol and Myth*. Cambridge, MA: Harvard University Press.

Starr, Kevin. 1973. *Americans and the California Dream, 1850–1915*. New York: Oxford University Press.

Stoll, Steven. 1998. *The Fruits of Natural Advantage: Making the Industrial Countryside in California*. Berkeley: University of California Press.

Vaught, David. 2007. *After the Gold Rush: Tarnished Dreams in the Sacramento Valley*. Baltimore, MD: Johns Hopkins University Press.

Wyatt, David. 1997. *Five Fires: Race, Catastrophe, and the Shaping of California*. Reading, MA: Addison-Wesley.

FURTHER READING

Blodgett, Peter. 1999. *Land of Golden Dreams: California in the Gold Rush Decade, 1848–1858*. San Marino, CA: Huntington Library.

Brechin, Gray. 1999. *Imperial San Francisco: Urban Power, Earthly Ruin*. Berkeley: University of California Press.

Chen, Yong. 2000. *Chinese San Francisco, 1850–1943: A Trans-Pacific Community*. Stanford, CA: Stanford University Press.

Deverell, William. 1994. *Railroad Crossing: Californians and the Railroad, 1850–1910*. Berkeley: University of California Press.

Ellison, Joseph. 1929. *California and the Nation, 1850–1869*. Berkeley: University of California Press.

Kowalewski, Michael. 1997. *Gold Rush: A Literary Exploration*. Berkeley: Heyday Books.

Pincetl, Stephanie. 1999. *Transforming California: A Political History of Land Use and Development*. Baltimore, MD: Johns Hopkins University Press.

Robinson, W. W. 1948. *Land in California*. Berkeley: University of California Press.

Chapter Ten

NATURE AND CONQUEST: AFTER THE DELUGE OF '49

Douglas Cazaux Sackman

The Man Who Shot Liberty Valence (1962), John Ford's searching Western, is set in Shinbone – a dusty border town on the verge of a sweeping transformation from a wild territory into a cultivated and ordered American state. The new Shinbone will have a railroad connection to the East and a dam for irrigation water. The environmental transformation of the territory is just the backdrop for the movie's front story, which concerns how Ransom Stoddard (played by Jimmy Stewart) became a town and national hero while wild Tom Doniphon (John Wayne) became a has-been. Ransom got credit for killing the notorious outlaw Liberty Valence when in fact Tom had dispatched him. After telling the true story many years later to the editor of the *Shinbone Star*, the newspaperman ultimately tears up his notes, explaining, "This is the West, sir. When the legend becomes a fact, print the legend."

The history of nature and conquest in California is ultimately the saga of legend becoming fact – ideas and projections getting worked into the land, and becoming hard material reality. This essay explores the conquest of nature in California, seeking in particular to trace the roles of ideas, economics, technologies, and organisms in creating environmental change, if not domination. It considers the period from the Mexican War in the 1840s to the time when a fully articulated agro-industrial regime was in place by the 1880s. While the military conquest of California by the United States was a significant moment in this story, it was the Gold Rush that unleashed a number of forces – demographic, economic, legal, and environmental – which combined to liquidate the pre-1848 landscape that had been cultivated and maintained jointly but in conflict by Mexicans and Native Californians. Out of the mud, tailings, and effluence of the American conquest a new landscape coalesced, reflecting and perpetuating the power of a new set of actors, interests, and legends.

The Gilded Pan

Historians have long perpetuated a legend about James K. Polk, writing that he had used geographic coordinates and a threat of war as a campaign slogan in 1844. In fact, it was only after Polk was elected that "Fifty-four Forty or Fight" became a rallying cry for expansionists. In the nation's self-styled Empire City, the editor of the New York *Globe* inscribed 54° 40″ on his gold cane and 5,000 buildings were tagged with these numbers by some graffiti artists of Manifest Destiny. When voters went to the polls, they pulled the lever for Polk and expansion, even if his imperial vision hadn't yet been carved into that gem of cartographic sloganeering (Miles 1957).

Polk's election signaled to all other nations that Americans were coming to the continent's west coast, and they would not be turned away. He offered cash and debt relief to Mexico in exchange for New Mexico and California. Mexico refused, so he dispatched troops to the contested borderlands between Mexico and Texas, and, when the inevitable skirmish occurred, Polk had his proximate justification for war (Wilentz 2005). However, the skirmish and even the war with Mexico should be seen as a flash in the pan; instead of focusing on it, we should examine the pan itself – Manifest Destiny – and what it was designed to scoop up and sort out. The notion that America had a divine right to become a transcontinental Empire of Liberty went back to the founding fathers (Kagan 2006). But it was not until 1845 that John O'Sullivan coined a name for this exceptional rhetorical device, proclaiming that it was "our manifest destiny to overspread the continent allotted by Providence for the free development of our yearly multiplying millions" (O'Sullivan 1845: 5).

O'Sullivan emboldened expansionists of the 1840s, enabling them to see how scooping up the western chunk of the continent could be justified. He argued that California was destined to break free of what he saw as Mexican tyranny and torpidity, which was limiting the region's "natural growth." "The Anglo-Saxon foot is already on its borders," O'Sullivan announced; an irrepressible army of ordinary white Americans "has begun to pour down upon it, armed with the plough and the rifle, and marking its trail with schools and colleges, courts and representative halls, mills and meeting-houses." Here was a vision of peaceful, divinely scripted conquest – a matter not of aggrandizement nor conquest but of progress created by Americans unfurling the banner of democracy and civilization. Americans had every right "to the possession of the homes conquered from the wilderness . . ." (O'Sullivan 1845: 9).

Manifest Destiny was a device that needed wilderness to work. To people like O'Sullivan, wilderness was a country that was untouched by human beings, or at least untamed. But of course, California in 1846 was no wilderness. For several thousand years, the diverse peoples of California, numbering at least 300,000, had been living there – using fire to modify the landscape, harvesting and assuring the growth of plants used for food or baskets, naming places and telling stories about them, and generally "tending the wild" (Anderson 2005). Beginning in 1769, agents of the Spanish empire – Franciscan missionaries, leather-armored soldiers, and eager ranchers – had come into California with their own visions for the land and its peoples. They wanted to convert the Indians and bring them into the Christian realm, and part of what that meant was to start working for the Spanish to build new structures and plant new crops. They built missions, pueblos, and presidios along the coast, and began to grow wheat, grapes, hemp, and other crops. The missionaries brought in horses, hogs, and cattle, setting them loose to eat up the native grasses and forbs and generally increase and multiply (Preston 1997). Indians both accommodated and resisted the Spanish intrusion into their territory and the social and environmental changes they wished to install. Sometimes whip-wielding priests would mysteriously die in the night, the victims of Indians who took justice into their own hands. Others burned down missions and then retreated to the parts of California – the reedy and marshy Central Valley, the Sierra Nevada – where the Spanish exercised little power. They turned to acorns, deer, pine nuts, grass seeds, or salmon for sustenance, as well as the occasional cow or sheep, and braved this new world which they were forced to share with the Spanish newcomers.

Americans looked upon this landscape, knee-deep in the humus of human history, and vigorously wiped the slate clean. By the mid-nineteenth century, they had practiced the art of simply equating Indians with nature and not counting them as human beings who had transformed the earth with their labor. If they had no agriculture and built no houses, then they had no claim to the land, in American eyes; and so American eyes had become blind to the manifest works of Indians. California Indians became "diggers," subhuman beings who merely scratched the earth for grub. Americans at mid-century had to create a different kind of blind spot to erase the claims of the Californios. When Richard Henry Dana visited in the 1830s, he couldn't help but see the Californio presence. He admitted that Californios were present but argued that progress and industry were absent. Gushing over the potential of California's vast landscape, he concluded with an imperial reverie: "In the hands of an enterprising people, what a country this could be" (Dana 1964 [1840]: 181).

In the course of Manifest Destiny's operations, Mexicans were increasingly conceived of as a separate race from Americans, who conceived of themselves racially as Anglo-Saxons (Horsman 1981). The intersection of race, nationalism, and expansion is a large topic, but the way that "racial nationalism" became intertwined with imperialism in the 1840s is crucial to understanding the fate of peoples and places in California. Racial nationalism (Gerstle 2000) – the belief that the United States was the divinely allotted domain where whites could live up to their potential, which they thought was greater than that of any other race – created the blind spots that allowed the O'Sullivans to contemplate wresting an entire continent from other peoples and do so with a "a clear conscience." Racial nationalists identified the United States with whites, who they connected with civilization and progress; all other races were identified with wilderness and stagnation at best, degeneration or ineluctable savagery at worst (Horsman 1981; Almaguer 1994). If you believed in the legend of Manifest Destiny, then no one could possibly have the right to stand in the way, for white America's right of way came from on high.

The racial nationalists viewed the inhabitants of California – whether they were Californio or Indian – as wild people living on wild land. The so-called wilderness was seen as the raw material of nation building – a material no one had put to good use and to which no nation but the United States had a proper claim. But if America was to usurp California, it would have the responsibility to make improvements in the land. Both before and after the Mexican War, expansionists and California boosters promised to make wonderful improvements once they took the land into their hands. Mariano Guadalupe Vallejo reportedly told Abraham Lincoln that he considered Yankees to be "a wonderful people, wonderful. Wherever they go they make improvements. If they were to emigrate in large numbers to hell itself, they would somehow manage to change the climate" (Woolley 1913: 133). Yankees had envisioned doing nothing less: defeating Mexico would be but a step in a larger conquest – a conquest over nature itself. And that victory, Americans proclaimed, would be manifested in a triumvirate of improvement – of people, of plants, and of the land itself (Sackman 2005). The dream of imperial expansion into California – the legend of Manifest Destiny – gained force and power by the lure of gold.

The Elephant

Americans who ventured to California in 1849 often described the experience as having "seen the elephant." In circuses, the enormous pachyderms were the must-see attraction. California as a whole was like the nation's circus: an exotic place of adventure full of fanciful creatures and opportunities. Unfortunately, historians have long paid most of their attention to the adventure of these "forty-niners," producing footnoted versions of Bret Harte stories (Starr 1973: 49) rather than a broader analysis of the significance of the Gold Rush.

Susan Johnson, in setting out to write an inclusive account, recognized that she had to "think as complexly and critically about the conquest of history as we have begun to think about the history of conquest." She had to "dismantle" the mythologized history of gold and conquest in California to clear space for new narratives and perspectives (Johnson 2001: 11). Her book joined a group of new studies that have begun to put together a larger, more coherent and probing portrait (Rohrbough 1997; Brechin 1999; Starr & Orsi 2000; Isenberg 2005). Still, the new set of studies is divided between those that focus more on the environmental and economic dimensions of the Gold Rush and those that focus on its social dimensions. Historians have been like the proverbial blind men describing the elephant: each of us touch a part of the Gold Rush but our extrapolations end up being more chimerical than real.

To comprehensively take stock of the elephant is to see that the Gold Rush liquefied the California landscape – where landscape is understood not as the non-human environment but as the natural world modified and organized into a pattern by human beings who derive their identity and power from it (Jackson 1984; Mitchell 1996). The impact of the Gold Rush was inextricably both social and environmental, dissolving the previous relationships among people, place, and power and allowing for the formation of a new set of relationships.

The diverse groups of Native Californians bore the most brutal brunt of this social and environmental transformation. Population numbers can begin to tell the story of the great unsettling of the Native California landscape. By the eve of the Gold Rush, the Native population had already been cut at least in half to some 150,000. But 12 years after gold was discovered in their land, only one Indian survived for every five that had been alive to hear the first shouts of "Eureka" (Cook 1976; Hurtado 1988). Part of this demographic collapse was caused by the influx of tiny organisms Euro-Americans brought with them as they scoured the hills for gold – pathogens causing diseases in Indians who had no immunity to them. The encounter between Indians and whites after the Gold Rush was a microcosm of what Alfred Crosby calls the "Columbian exchange": an entire complex of plants and animals – large, small, and microscopic – migrated from continent to continent after Columbus and later ocean adventurers opened up communications among Europe, the Americas, Africa, and eventually Asia. Corn, potatoes, and tomatoes – along with a river of gold – went to Europe, and transformed land and societies there; cattle, wheat, sheep, and smallpox came to the Americas, and ate their way into the social and environmental landscape, advancing what Crosby calls "ecological imperialism" (1986). In California, the process was already well under way as a result of the Spanish *entrada*, but as forty-niners pushed more deeply into every part of the state, the plants and animals whites brought with them exploded on impact. Disease spread and the plants and animals that supported Indian economies lost ground to voracious invaders such as hogs, sheep, cattle, and plow-pushing, wheat-planting hominids. Indians outnumbered newcomers ten to one at the beginning of the Gold

Rush; in 1860, there were 12 newcomers for every Indian left alive, and those (dirty) dozens were out looking for land and opportunity in every corner of the state.

Death came to California Indians not just from the impersonal and invisible vectors of disease. White Americans, supported by their governments, used firepower to mow down Indians whom they thought stood impertinently in the way of Manifest Destiny. In the early months of the Gold Rush, some whites hired Indians to work in the diggings. And some Indians panned gold for themselves, but it was a risky business: one white merchant along the waterway the newcomers called the American River believed that "no Christian man is bound to give full value to those infernal red-skins. They are onsoffisticated vagabones and have no more business with money than a mule or a wolf" (Sandos 2000: 90). Indians were dehumanized and exploited, becoming beasts of burden to be used like mules or wild pests to be exterminated like wolves.

The Americans, who unsettled the land with their crops and cattle, continued to encroach on the lands and livelihood of California's Indians. Their own subsistence patterns left in shreds, the Indians took to hunting cattle, horses, and mules. They took flour and beans from cowboys' mountain cabins. The *Red Bluff Independent* editorialized: "It is becoming evident that extermination of the red devils will have to be resorted to . . ." (Sackman, forthcoming). Bounties were paid to self-styled Indian hunters. In 1855, a white man could ride into Shasta City with the severed head of any Indian; he would be paid $5 per head. Indian hunting militias pursuing what one called a "clean-up" of the countryside submitted their expenses to the state government, which paid out over one million dollars in 1851 and 1852. California subsequently appealed to the federal government to cover the expenses of genocide, and for the most part it did (Rawls 1984: 185–6).

Some Indians were confined to woefully inadequate reservations; others were conscripted as workers for whites. In 1850, the state legislature passed the perversely titled Act for the Government and Protection of Indians, which essentially allowed whites to take Indians as indentured laborers and set off a flurry of kidnapping raids into Indian communities. Look at the Gold Rush from the perspective of California Indians, and the linkage between nature and conquest shows up in high relief. Tens of thousands of Indians were driven off their prior claims, killed outright, or pushed into roles of servitude, forced to work for others to turn the land that once provided their sustenance into a new machine that would produce wealth and comfort for the newcomers. It is equally remarkable that, as William Bauer shows elsewhere in this volume, some Indians found a way to survive through it all, both physically and culturally (Hurtado 1988). Today, descendents from this time of upheaval are working to restore the landscape they once enjoyed and renew their sustaining relationship to nature in California (Anderson 2005).

The perspective of Chinese Argonauts, who called California *Gam Saan* (Gold Mountain), reveals another way that new social relations were created in the conquest of nature. Would-be Chinese miners faced not only the challenges of extracting gold from those mountains but also had to scale the cultural cliffs of nativism and racism. Many Chinese lost their lives to nativist white newcomers who thought the gold had been placed in those mountains for their benefit alone (Chan 2000). The Chinese, undaunted, made use of those parts of nature whites overlooked or discarded as weeds or waste (see also Robert Chao Romero's discussion in Chapter Thirteen of this volume). A Chinese entrepreneur got rich by gathering unwanted mustard from the plots of whites, and then turning it into the condiment known as Chinese gold (Limerick 1992). Others paid white miners for their tailings, eager to go through the mining leftovers for ore that had been missed by white sluices.

As nativism and a law barring Chinese from testifying against whites aided and abetted the violence that claimed scores of Chinese lives, the Chinese made a case that they were entitled to a place in the diggings. The consul general in San Francisco, Huang Zunxian, tried to configure Chinese immigrants as part of the story of Manifest Destiny, saying that, "When the Chinese first crossed the ocean, they were the same as pioneers . . . Dressed in tatters, they cleared the mountain forests . . . wilderness and waste [was] turned into towns and villages" (Limerick 1992: 1032). Whites would have none of it. A Foreign Miners' Tax was used as a means of fleecing Chinese miners and as an excuse for intimidating or even killing them. Germans and Englishmen usually did not have to pay the tax. The universalism and democratic promise imbedded in the rhetoric of Manifest Destiny was thus sliced along racial lines. Indeed, the process of determining access to the wealth and power that could be derived from nature was intimately bound up with racial formation. As Sucheng Chan explains, in the rush for gold Yankee nativism morphed into racism, and racism served as a means not only of discrimination against groups such as Chinese, African Americans, or Californios, but also as a means of creating another group – "white Americans" – and solidifying their privileged access to land and resources (2000).

Industrial capitalism was an equally strong force shaping access to the natural wealth of the California landscape. In the early years of the Gold Rush, gold mining was a labor-intensive activity that required little capital and simple tools – pans, pickaxes, sluices and the like. But by the end of the 1850s, placer mining was superseded by a new technology: high-pressure water cannons used to wash away whole hillsides, sending the resultant sludge through sluices that captured gold but let soil and gravel, along with toxic mercury used to bind the gold, flow out and clog and contaminate environments downstream – flooding farmers' fields and killing salmon trying futilely to swim upstream to spawning grounds. The hydraulic cannon symbolizes corporate California's power to utterly transform landscapes in order to make money. As Andrew Isenberg has noted, the *tools* owned by the independent placer miners were replaced by *machines* owned by corporate investors in urban centers (2005: 24). San Francisco, as Gray Brechin reveals, became the economic seat of the empire controlling the vast infrastructure of hydraulic mining – including some 5,700 miles of canals, flumes, ditches, and an arsenal of iron-forged machines created in San Francisco foundries (1999).

Hydraulic cannons eroded hillsides at astounding rates, but they eroded dreams as well: mining to get rich was no longer a real prospect for individuals of modest means, even if they enjoyed the privileged access previously allotted to whites. Corporations would now control access, and individuals would punch the clock for wages rather than panning them out of the streambeds. The new industrial California economy, fueled by complex technologies designed to extract wealth from nature, depended upon and widened the social fissures of class as well as race. C. S. Lewis once wrote: "What we call Man's power over Nature turns out to be a power exercised by some men over other men with Nature as its instrument" (Worster 1985: 50). The conquest of nature through hydraulic mining is a vivid illustration of this point: it was almost as if some witch was bent on creating a sterile and permanent winter landscape in which all wealth and power would flow to her while everyone else would live in deferential servitude.

Forests and Fields

"If mining was the heart of California's emerging industrial economy and cities its nerve centers," Isenberg argues, "then lumber made up the sinews that knit the system together" (2005: 76). Transplanted Yankees such as Andrew Pope and William Talbot set up lumber corporations in San Francisco (Cox 1974; Bunting 1997), and began to direct the cutting down of California's forests in order to supply wood for building up a new infrastructure, an artificial nature erected on top of the geography that nature had originally provided, and that Indians and then Californios had modified. Wood was used to build houses in cities like San Francisco and Sacramento; to build railroad tracks and trestles; to build bridges and wharves; and to build the framing that allowed mining companies to plump ever deeper into the earth in search of ore. One-third of California's forests were gone by 1870 (Isenberg 2005: 77). Failed miners and farmers went to work for wages in the forests and perilous mills, together with workers from Hawaii, China, and elsewhere. Between 1850 and 1900, over 600,000 of the estimated 2 million acres of old-growth coastal redwood forests had been cut down, shipped out, milled, and then consumed in the process of expanding the industrial economy (Isenberg 2005). The destruction of forests in the mountains and on the coast thus provided the building materials necessary to pursue the larger project of recreating nature all across the state – conquering it.

Cowboys have been inextricably tied to the California landscape, economically and ecologically as well as mythologically. Hollywood crafted the cowboy into a national icon of freedom, independence, and masculinity – the lone rider out on the range. Seldom was seen the actual work of cowboys in managing cattle; the movies do much to reveal that cowboys were wage earners whose way of life was inextricably connected to urban, industrializing America. After American conquest, Californio ranchers and vaqueros were gradually elbowed out of the cattle business. Requirements to prove their claims to land granted to them under the Spanish or Mexican regimes were cumbersome and legal fees and taxes mounted. Californios no longer controlled politics and law in the state, but they could not control the environment either. When "ecological catastrophe" hit – flooding and severe drought that caused astounding cattle die-offs in the 1860s – most of the Californio ranchers were ruined (Isenberg 2005: 103–30). Henry Miller and Charles Lux rode into the void and created an industrial system of cattle ranching. As David Igler explains, they "utilized institutional and natural resources to construct a ranching empire, and by rationalizing labor and nature, they flourished as industrial cowboys" (2001: 18).

Industrial ranching accelerated ecological change as a result of the expansion of domesticated livestock throughout the state. Indigenous, perennial bunchgrasses were replaced by European, invasive annual grasses. Hills that once were green year-round turned golden brown in the summer. Elk saw their habitat shrink into nothing; bears headed for the hills and then were hunted down. As Igler concludes, "the entire landscape underwent a process of change that replaced complex ecological communities with domesticated animals, constructed waterways, and irrigated fields" (2001: 34).

Miller and Lux were the most successful of the ranching entrepreneurs, and they built a complex, vertically integrated corporation linking the landscapes of production in California to the landscapes of consumption – meat markets around San Francisco and beyond. This system was built on the ownership of land, of course; Miller and Lux were quite industrious in finding ways to acquire vast tracts of it. Early on, the company acquired much of its land by purchasing holdings of Californios who went belly up.

By the 1870s, Miller and Lux were skillfully manipulating homesteading laws designed to give over land in the public domain to private citizens. These laws had been designed to foster the kind of opportunity for westward-moving Americans envisioned in the rhetoric of Manifest Destiny. But the destiny of much of this land was not homesteading families but land monopolies. By 1874, Miller and Lux owned at least a half million acres (Igler 2001: 61).

The "firm employed migrant, low-wage workers and divided them along racial and ethnic lines" (Igler 2001: 123). Californio vaqueros were the main source of actual cowboys in the 1860s, but the firm later employed immigrant Italians and Chinese for different tasks – some worked directly with cattle, many others labored to create and manage the irrigation systems that were needed to retrofit the California landscape to support cattle and agriculture, and still others worked in the company's slaughterhouses. All of these laborers worked for minimal wages and the lion's shares of the profits went to Miller and Lux. Even the Californio cowboys lost their special status as skilled laborers, "becoming migrant wage laborers on land that, in some cases, their families had once owned" (ibid.: 59).

Farming also industrialized in the decades after the Gold Rush, further accentuating the connection between intensively managed landscapes and intensively managed laborers. The big story in agriculture in the 1860s and 1870s was the bonanza wheat farms, some of which comprised thousands of acres in California's Central Valley. Out-of-work miners became farmers – if they had enough capital; if not, they became migrant harvesters. But the experience of these farm hands was far from idyllic: as Richard Street noted, "Surrounded by machine gears, pulleys, dust, steam, fire, smoke, heat, and noise, they are essentially factory laborers in the countryside" (Street 2004: ix). Some workers resented the mechanization of farm labor, seeing it as a threat; a few even set fire to a barn in order to sabotage one of the new combine machines (ibid.: 177). Nonetheless, mechanization went forward and record harvests were gathered in the 1860s and 1870s. To carry away the 1872 crop, you would have needed a train stretching from San Francisco to the outskirts of Los Angeles (ibid.: 183).

Wheat began to be seen metaphorically as gold, another form of money. On June 26, 1880, *The Pacific Rural Press* reported that "the prospect for a large crop of grain is good, and the farmers feel very jubilant about this fact, for they now think that an opportunity has arrived for them to coin money." As William Cronon has shown, a system had developed in Chicago by the 1870s that could take the variety of crops produced by wheat farmers, who were growing different strains in various climates, and transform it into something "abstract, homogenous, *liquid*." Wheat could be severed from nature. This, in turn, made possible the future's market, which "redefined the *meaning* of grain within an intricate web of market fictions, abstracting and simplifying it to facilitate its movement not as a physical object but as a commodity" (Cronon 1991: 145).

Industrial machines, routinized labor, and a managerial view of plants themselves were all part of the new form of agriculture in California that deeply commodified nature. Frank Norris, whose revealing novel *The Octopus*, set among the bonanza wheat farms that celebrated the vitality of nature and raised questions about the impact of the railroad on the countryside, fulminated against the idea that nature could be reduced to a "classification of science . . . an aggregate of botany, zoology, geology and the like [instead of] a thing intimate and familiar and rejuvenating" (Norris 1903: 42). But that is exactly what wheat farmers were doing. Farm journals presented images of wheat – diagrams that showed "the structure of the wheat kernel as it is brought to view by the microscope" – as an object to be penetrated, known, and controlled. By learning to examine the anatomy of the grain, farmers were learning to atomize nature. Nature was not an organic whole, but something that could be broken apart and reconstructed in order to maximize growth and profits.

At the California State Agricultural Society's annual meeting in 1880, H. R. Larue celebrated the 100 million tons of wheat that had been harvested. Advances in machinery and scientific agriculture had made it possible for "a single farm of fifty thousand acres [to be] cultivated by the employment of less than three hundred men" (California State 1881: 10). But Frank Pixley took Larue to task for seeing "in great fifty-thousand-acre farms, worked by machinery, evidence of the progress of the age." Pixley expressed the views of many agrarian critics of California's stupendous wheat operations by charging that, "large farming is not farming at all. It is mining for wheat." Such a "manufacturing business," in which "clods are fed into the mill," would destroy homes and families and make "the State a wilderness [turning the] beautiful valleys of our State [into] treeless, verdureless plains" (ibid.: 229). The wheat barons did rob the soils of their fertility, mining "the dirt for its last dollar" (Stoll 1998: 29). In *The Octopus*, one character criticizes industrial wheat farmers as betrayers of the promise of Manifest Destiny: people who seized good land and turned it into a wilderness. "They had no love for their land," she observes. "They were not attached to the soil. They worked their ranches as a quarter of century before they worked their mines . . . To get all there was out of the land, to squeeze it dry, to exhaust it, seemed their policy . . . 'After us the deluge'" (Norris 1986 [1901]: 298).

To these critics, there was something wrong with a purely extractive relationship to nature in California – whether it be through mining or intensively commodified wheat farming. Pixley's solution was to promote smaller-scale fruit farming. A community of horticulturists – farmers who grew fruit – would create a beautiful cultural landscape, he thought.

Horticulture would encourage a more progressive, rooted, and higher culture, and bring the landscape up to its full potential.

Fruit growing boomed in Southern California in the 1880s, and became the dominant agricultural sector by the 1890s. But the rise of fruit growing did not return California to some agrarian past of close-knit community. Instead, it represented another phase of commodification and industrial expansion, one in which national and international markets and marketing became part of the farmer's work; the soil and plants were intensively and scientifically managed in new ways; an elaborate system of water works re-engineered the flow of rivers across the entire Southwest to support the growth; foreign workers were imported on a large scale and racialized; and the climate itself was turned into a commodity (Daniel 1982; Pisani 1984; Worster 1985; Hundley 1992; Stoll 1998; deBuys & Myers 1999; McWilliams 2000; Street 2004; Sackman 2005; Nash 2006).

As *Sunset* magazine put it, Southern California had no gold but "eastern prospectors discovered an inexhaustible supply of twenty-two karat climate" (Sackman 2005: 29). Ironically, the landscape that had become suddenly inhospitable to Native Californians with the influx of European Americans was now promoted as a salubrious, restorative landscape in order to draw more and more newcomers to the state – or at least to Southern California. Guidebooks told would-be orange growers that fantasies could materialize in California, that the state was simply supernatural. "When the land within the Orange Belt of Southern California is planted with skill and cultivated with care," one pamphlet rhapsodized in 1890, "the dreams of the Orient will become realities of the Occident, and the fables of Mythology be made the facts of History" (Sackman 2005: 29).

The conquest of water was necessary to bring such dreams to fruition. Irrigation boosters like William Smythe had believed that "the Conquest of Arid America" would amount to a great boon to democracy, and that legend propelled the damming and canalling of the waterways of the entire southwest. But those waters ultimately flowed upward, toward money: as a result of this technological conquest, a small "power elite" would gain control over "a large, anonymous, dependent population" (Worster 1985: 261). In the fruit industry, that population included workers from all over the globe that were needed to keep the water flowing and the harvests going. All of the fruit was picked and packed by low-wage workers, men and women who came to the state in search of a piece of the California dream: the one they found was considerably smaller, and much less sweet, than the one the growers enjoyed (McWilliams 2000; Sackman 2005).

Sunkist, an organization of growers formed in 1893 that operated like a modern corporation, brilliantly used dreams and mythology to sell its product. Its success was scripted, like any product of Hollywood. Oranges were advertised to Americans across the country as pure products of a resplendent nature, portable pieces of the California dream one could imbibe anywhere. Sunkist's marketing department had the Midas touch. The fantasy storyline had hard material effects, creating an elaborate infrastructure of facts on the ground. An economy and culture based on fruit ultimately did little to harmonize the relationship between people and nature and growers and laborers. In fact, nature was managed in a more intensive pattern, laborers were systematically disempowered, and nature's bounty was commodified all the way down to the genes. Value was added to nature through advertising: now consumers were sold the legend that California's fruits would make them happy and healthy – and a little glamorous to boot. Sunkist and other farming companies used advertising to conquer American culture as a means of making their purported conquest of nature more profitable (Stoll 1998; Walker 2004; Sackman 2005).

Grizzly Facts and Railroad Ties

One afternoon in the spring of 1868, everything was almost set for the publication of the *Overland Monthly*, a new California magazine "devoted to the development of the country." But something was not quite right about the drawing of a Grizzly that was to go on the cover. As Mark Twain observed, it was "a bear that *meant* nothing in particular, signified nothing." So Bret Harte sketched in railroad tracks running beneath its feet. The bear full of sound and fury now signified something; Twain was more than satisfied with "the ancient symbol of California savagery snarling at the approaching type of high and progressive Civilization, the first Overland locomotive!" (Deverell 1994: 9). While symbolizing a battle between "local primitive barbarism" and "civilization and progress," the drawing was also a very accurate depiction of the position of the grizzlies in the face of the European and American conquests of California. "Look at him well," Harte prophetically instructed, "for he is passing away. Fifty years and he will be as extinct as the dodo . . ." (Harte 1868).

The grizzlies were passing away – despite the fact that the original American rebels who sought to overthrow the Mexican regime put the bear on their flag and it was later put on the official state flag. Californios and then Americans staged brutal fights between bulls and grizzlies for entertainment, dramatizing the conflict between old world and new world biota. The bears were killed outright and much of their habitat was destroyed as valley lands became pasture for cattle or went under the plow. By the 1920s, the last grizzlies had been dispatched: they had no more presence on the California landscape that had been transformed to support a new set of animals and their human sponsors (Storer & Tevis 1996). Their demise symbolizes that much broader set of environmental changes that undermined Indian communities, decimated native plant and animal life, and "denuded entire landscapes" (Anderson 2005: 120).

The railroad, as both a symbol of progress and change as well as a technological and economic force, brought about deep changes in the social
and cultural landscape. Frank Norris described it as "the leviathan, with
tentacles of steel clutching into the soil, the soulless Force, the iron-hearted
Power, the monster, the Colossus, the Octopus" (Norris 1986 [1901]:
50). "What will the railroad bring us?" Henry George asked in the *Overland Monthly* on the eve of the completion of the transcontinental railroad
in 1869. Along with many others, George believed that the railroad would
usher in "an era of steady, rapid and substantial growth," opening "up
millions of acres of the best fruit and grain lands in the world" (George
1868: 300). But George thought the railroad would concentrate wealth
in fewer hands; squalor and misery would spread; wages would plummet;
the rich would get richer, the poor, poorer (ibid.: 301–2).

The railroad galvanized California's economic and ecological connections to the rest of the nation. It changed the look and feel of the California
landscape itself, annihilating space and time (Cronon 1991; Deverell 1994;
Solnit 2004; Orsi 2005). It accelerated the industrial conquest of nature
that liquefied old landscapes and freighted into place new ones. As George
recognized, altered social relations were part and parcel of the transformations the railroad and industrial capitalism brought to California. But
boosters of the railroad – just as boosters of American conquest, and then
corporate mining, ranching, and horticulture – hailed each erosion of an
old landscape and its replacement with a new one as a great leap forward
for humanity, a victory in the battle for freedom. Old landscapes were
viewed as repressive and obsolete; the new were portrayed as progressive,
democratic, and the fulfillment of Manifest Destiny – a reinvented nature
that would produce plenty for all.

But Manifest Destiny actually revealed itself to be a script for the domination over nature that produced not democracy and equality, but racial
division and class hierarchy. Every time nature seemed to be conquered in
California for the benefit of all, the new landscape actually bequeathed to
a select few privileged access that made them wealthier and often healthier.
Others were conscripted to toil in this miraculous garden from which they
themselves were progressively alienated.

REFERENCES

Almaguer, T. 1994. *Racial Fault Lines: The Historical Origins of White Supremacy
in California*. Berkeley: University of California Press.
Anderson, M. K. 2005. *Tending the Wild: Native American Knowledge and
the Management of California's Natural Resources*. Berkeley: University of
California Press.

Anderson, M. K., Barbour, M., and Whitworth, V. 1997. "A World of Balance and Plenty: Land, Plants, Animals, and Humans in a Pre-European California." In R. Gutiérrez, and R. Orsi, eds., *Contested Eden: California Before the Gold Rush.* Berkeley: University of California Press, pp. 12–47.

Brechin, G. 1999. *Imperial San Francisco: Urban Power, Earthly Ruin.* Berkeley: University of California Press.

Bunting, R. 1997. *The Pacific Raincoast: Environment and Culture in an American Eden, 1778–1900.* Lawrence: University Press of Kansas.

California State Agricultural Society. 1881. *Transactions of the California State Agricultural Society, 1880.* Sacramento, CA: State Printing Office.

Chan, S. 2000. "A People of Exceptional Character: Ethnic Diversity, Nativism, and Racism in the California Gold Rush." In K. Starr and R. Orsi, eds., *Rooted in Barbarous Soil: People, Culture, and Community in Gold Rush California.* Berkeley: University of California Press, pp. 44–85.

Cook, S. 1976. *The Conflict Between the California Indian and White Civilization.* Berkeley: University of California Press.

Cox, T. 1974. *Mills and Markets: A History of the Pacific Coast Lumber Industry to 1900.* Seattle: University of Washington Press.

Cronon, W. 1991. *Nature's Metropolis: Chicago and the Great West.* New York: W. W. Norton.

Crosby, A. 1986. *Ecological Imperialism: The Biological Expansion of Europe, 900–1900.* New York: Cambridge University Press.

Dana, R. 1964 (1840). *Two Years Before the Mast.* New York: Modern Library, 1964.

Daniel, C. 1982. *Bitter Harvest: A History of California Farmworkers, 1870–1941.* Berkeley: University of California Press.

deBuys, W. and Myers, J. 1999. *Salt Dreams: Land and Water in Low-Down California.* Albuquerque: University of New Mexico Press.

Deverell, W. 1994. *Railroad Crossing: Californians and the Railroad, 1850–1910.* Berkeley: University of California Press.

George, H. 1868. "What the Railroad Will Bring Us," *Overland Monthly* 1 (4): 297–306.

Gerstle, G. 2000. *American Crucible: Race and Nation in the Twentieth Century.* Princeton, NJ: Princeton University Press.

Harte, B. 1868. "Etc.," *Overland Monthly* 1 (1): 99–100.

Horsman, R. 1981. *Race and Manifest Destiny: The Origins of American Racial Anglo-Saxonism.* Cambridge, MA: Harvard University Press.

Hundley, Norris, Jr. 1992. *The Great Thirst: Californians and Water, 1770s–1990s.* Berkeley and Los Angeles: University of California Press.

Hurtado, A. 1988. *Indian Survival on the California Frontier.* New Haven, CT: Yale University Press.

Igler, D. 2001. *Industrial Cowboys: Miller & Lux and the Transformation of the Far West.* Berkeley: University of California Press.

Isenberg, A. 2005. *Mining California: An Ecological History.* New York: Hill & Wang.

Jackson, J. B. 1984. *Discovering the Vernacular Landscape.* New Haven, CT: Yale University Press.

Johnson, S. 2001. *Roaring Camp: The Social World of the California Gold Rush*. New York: W. W. Norton.

Kagan, R. 2006. *Dangerous Nation*. New York: Alfred A. Knopf.

Limerick, P. 1992. "Disorientation and Reorientation: The American Landscape Discovered from the West," *The Journal of American History* 79 (3): 1021–49.

McWilliams, C. 2000 (1939). *Factories in the Field: The Story of Migratory Farm Labor in California*. Berkeley: University of California Press.

Miles, E. 1957. "Fifty-four Forty or Fight" – An American Political Legend," *The Mississippi Historical Review* 44 (2): 291–309.

Mitchell, D. 1996. *The Lie of the Land: Migrant Workers and the California Landscape*. Minneapolis: University of Minnesota Press.

Nash, L. 2006. *Inescapable Ecologies: A History of Environment, Disease, and Knowledge*. Berkeley: University of California Press.

Norris, F., 1903 (1964). "The 'Nature' Revival in Literature." In D. Pizer, ed., *The Literary Criticism of Frank Norris*. Austin: University of Texas Press.

Norris, F. 1986 (1901). *The Octopus: A Story of California*. New York: Penguin.

Orsi, R. 2005. *Sunset Limited: The Southern Pacific Railroad and the Development of the American West, 1850–1930*. Berkeley: University of California Press.

O'Sullivan, J. 1845. "Annexation," *United States Magazine and Democratic Review* 17 (1): 5–10.

Pisani, D. 1984. *From the Family Farm to Agribusiness: The Irrigation Crusade in California and the West, 1850–1931*. Berkeley: University of California Press.

Preston, W. 1997. "Serpent in the Garden: Environmental Change in Colonial California." In R. Gutiérrez and R. Orsi, eds., *Contested Eden: California Before the Gold Rush*. Berkeley: University of California Press, pp. 260–98.

Rawls, J. 1984. *Indians of California: The Changing Image*. Norman, OK: University of Oklahoma Press.

Rohrbough, M. 1997. *Days of Gold: The California Gold Rush and the American Nation*. Berkeley: University of California Press.

Sackman, D. 2005. *Orange Empire: California and the Fruits of Eden*. Berkeley: University of California Press.

Sackman, D. Forthcoming. *Wild Men: Kroeber, Ishi, and the Wilderness at the Heart of Modern America*. New York: Oxford University Press.

Sandos, J. 2000. "'Because he is a liar and a thief': Conquering the Residents of 'Old' California, 1850–1880." In K. Starr and R. Orsi, eds., *Rooted in Barbarous Soil: People, Culture, and Community in Gold Rush California*. Berkeley: University of California Press, pp. 86–112.

Solnit, R. 2004. *River of Shadows: Eadweard Muybridge and the Technological Wild West*. New York: Penguin.

Starr, K. 1973. *Americans and the California Dream, 1850–1915*. New York: Oxford University Press.

Starr, K. and Orsi, R., eds. 2000. *Rooted in Barbarous Soil: People, Culture, and Community in Gold Rush California*. Berkeley: University of California Press.

Stoll, S. 1998. *The Fruits of Natural Advantage: Making the Industrial Countryside in California*. Berkeley: University of California Press.

Storer, T and Tevis, Jr., L. 1996 (1955). *California Grizzly*. Berkeley: University of California Press.

Street, R. 2004. *Beasts of the Field: A Narrative History of California Farmworkers, 1769–1913*. Stanford, CA: Stanford University Press.

Walker, R. 2004. *The Conquest of Bread: 150 Years of Agribusiness in California*. New York: The Free Press.

Wilentz, S. 2005. *The Rise of American Democracy: Jefferson to Lincoln*. New York: W. W. Norton.

Woolley, L. 1913. *California 1849–1913 or The Rambling Sketches and Experiences of Sixty-four Years' Residence in that State*. Oakland, CA: De Witt & Snelling. Available from: http://memory.loc.gov/ammem/cbhtml/cbhome.html [cited June 7, 2007].

Worster, D. 1985. *Rivers of Empire: Water, Aridity, and the Growth of the American West*. New York: Pantheon.

Chapter Eleven

NATIVE CALIFORNIANS IN THE NINETEENTH CENTURY

William Bauer, Jr.

In the 1930s, Lucy Young, a Lassik woman living in Northern California, recalled the story her grandfather told about the coming of whites to Northern California: "My grandpa, before white people came, had a dream. . . . My grandpa say; 'White Rabbit' – he mean white people – 'gonta devour our grass, our seed, our living. We won't have nothing more, this world'" (Murphey 1941: 350). Young's story summarized the traumatic events that California Indians experienced in the nineteenth century. Beginning with Mexican Independence and accelerating with the advent of the California Gold Rush, California Indians witnessed their populations decline precipitously and resource bases shrink, and encountered a government intent on transforming their ways of life. Despite these intrusions and the ravages of their world, California Indians adapted to changing circumstances and laid the groundwork for their survival in the twentieth century.

This essay explores the experiences of California Indians in the nineteenth century. It will consider the history of California Indians from 1821 (Mexican Independence) to 1900. I do this for three reasons. First, the Spanish era (1769–1821), with a focus on Junípero Serra and the emergence of the California mission system, has been ably covered by Steven Hackel's essay in this volume. Second, after 1821, California Indians lived with two governments influenced by nineteenth-century liberalism. Mexicans and Americans wanted to free the individual and economic resources from state control, which determined their relationship with California Indians (Hackel 1998). Finally, for the sake of length I have ignored the Spanish mission system, except for population figures.

This essay begins by examining the changing depictions and interpretations of California Indians and their history. Nineteenth-century observers considered Indians inferior and racially degraded. Early twentieth-century scholars replicated these ideas in their scholarship. In the last 30 years, ethnohistorians and indigenous scholars have offered correctives to these interpretations. The essay will then trace Indian demographic and population history from 1769 to 1900. While the pre-contact California Indian population is open to debate, the most reliable sources find that by 1900, only 22,000 Indians lived in the state. In addition to the disastrous effects of Indians moving to sites of colonial domination (missions, ranchos, and reservations), disease, state militias, and reduced resource bases contributed to the rapid population decline. Next, the essay will examine the scope of federal and state Indian policy. Mexican and American government officials adhered to the tenets of nineteenth-century liberalism and strived to move California Indian labor and economic resources into the market economy. Mexican officials attempted to protect its frontier as well as ensure a compliant Indian labor force. American officials, alternatively, also created unfree labor conditions and moved Indian lands and resources into the market economy.

Despite the tragic population decline and the attempts at state and federal control, California Indians protected their cultures and survived as separate and distinct peoples. Historian Albert Hurtado writes: "The same numbers that illustrate the destruction of native populations also show where and how some Indians survived in a land that was starkly different than the one their grandparents had known" (Hurtado 1988: 1). California Indians entered the market economy and worked for Mexican and American ranchers and farmers. Indian labor put food on their tables and clothes on their backs while making the state one of the world's most productive agricultural areas. California Indians also turned to religious revitalization movements that challenged hegemonic attitudes of white Americans. Finally, California Indians resisted the worst manifestations of Mexican and American colonialism through large-scale revolts, local attacks on employers, and clashes with the United States military. Although California Indians faced terrible circumstances in the nineteenth century, their collective and individual acts ensured that they survived into the next century and ultimately the next millennium.

California Indians in the Historical Record

For most of the twentieth century, California Indian scholarship reflected the biases and misperceptions of the authors as well as the sources that scholars used. As historian James Rawls demonstrated, Euro-American interpretations of California Indians changed throughout the nineteenth century, usually to suit Euro-American interests. During the Spanish period, Franciscans depicted California Indians as children, in order to raise support for their efforts to convert Indians. After Mexican Independence, American and Mexican observers considered California Indians a useful class of docile laborers. These descriptions aided American and Mexican businessmen who participated in the global hide and tallow trade and wanted to attract capital to California. Finally, after the Gold Rush, Americans considered Indians as impediments to Manifest Destiny and westward expansion. They believed that California Indians were racially inferior, not only to whites, but to other Indians as well, and used these arguments to justify a policy of extermination (Rawls 1984; Almaguer 1994).

Twentieth-century scholars echoed these depictions. Historian William Ellison wrote that California Indians were the "least developed of all the Indians in America" (Ellison 1922: 38). In the 1940s, scholar Sherburne Cook relied on racial arguments to explain the trajectory of California Indian history: "The weaker established race gave way with little opposition to the stronger invading race" (Cook 1943a: 1). For these writers, California Indians were more degraded than other Indians in North America and lacked racial traits that could have resisted westward expansion. In the early twentieth century, anthropologists, led by University of California professor Alfred Kroeber and his students, descended upon California reservations to record the pre-contact culture of California Indians. Reflecting Kroeber's training in Boasian anthropology, with an emphasis on documenting cultural differences, the anthropologists collected Indian linguistic information, cultural practices, and ways of social organization (Heizer 1978). Yet, they reaffirmed extant and older ideas about California Indians. First, they argued that California Indians were inferior to white Americans. Kroeber wrote: "[writing a history of California Indian–white contact] requires a thorough knowledge of the local history as well as the institutions of the superior race" (Kroeber 1925: vi). Second, anthropologists believed that they were documenting and preserving vanishing cultures. They argued that contact with Spanish, Mexican, and American cultures inevitably tainted California Indians, who were rapidly disappearing.

Since the 1970s, scholars have made better use of ethnohistorical research methods in an effort to rectify some of these aforementioned misconceptions. Rather than viewing California Indians as racially degraded and victims of white aggression, scholars have examined cultural encounters from a California Indian perspective. They have emphasized themes of resistance and cultural persistence as well as offering insights into the activities of California Indian leaders, land tenure, and labor (Phillips 1975; Shipek 1987; Hurtado 1988). Significantly, the last two decades have seen the emergence of indigenous California scholars. They have documented the survival of California Indian nations in the nineteenth and twentieth centuries, such as the Tolowa and Modoc, and produced sharp criticisms of the mission system and the Gold Rush era. In addition to the ethnohistorians, these scholars have helped document the continuing vitality of California Indians as well as their ability to reconstruct their identities, economies, and social life in the wake of catastrophic experiences

(Norton 1979; Costo & Costo 1987; Nelson 1988; Reed 1999; Bales 2001; Bauer 2006).

California Indian Populations under Duress

For nearly 100 years, California academics have debated the tragic history of California Indian populations. The number of Indians in California before contact, as well as the reasons for their precipitous decline, have been hotly contested research topics. These are no simple or apolitical acts. During the past 50 years, scholars have debated the size of indigenous populations in North America and discussions about the Native population of California were central to that discussion. California boasted one of the highest population densities of Native peoples north of Mexico, and the population decline was so rapid that it provided an important laboratory to study pre- and post-contact Indian population patterns. These debates address the devastating impact that contact with Europe had on North American Indian populations (Hurtado 1989).

In 1905, anthropologist C. Hart Merriam made the first academic estimate of pre-contact California Indian populations. He calculated that there were 260,000 Indians within the state's boundaries before Spanish settlement (Merriam 1905). Twenty years later, anthropologist Alfred Kroeber suggested that Merriam's extrapolations overstated the population density of non-mission areas in California, and downwardly revised Merriam's number to 133,000 California Indians (Kroeber 1925). In the 1940s, physiologist Sherburne Cook entered the fray. For the next 30 years, he upwardly revised California Indian population figures, finally resting on 331,000 California Indians before contact. Cook suggested that previous scholars had underestimated the impact of diseases on Native population decline (Cook 1978). The most recent figure belongs to Russell Thornton. He surveyed the extant literature and averaged the state and regional figures. Thornton concluded that there were 230,400 California Indians on the eve of contact (Thornton 1980). For the most part, California scholars adhere to Cook's figures for pre-contact California populations (Hurtado 1989). Regardless of the predicted population numbers, this debate describes the horrifying impact of European contact in California. If one uses Kroeber's arguments (the lowest), California Indian populations declined by more than 85 percent. If we accept Cook's figures, then California Indian populations declined by a startling 94 percent during the nineteenth century. These are truly staggering figures.

Beginning with sustained contact in the late eighteenth century, California Indian populations began a rapid decline, from which they only began to rebound in the twentieth century. During the Spanish era

(1769–1821), moving to the newly created Franciscan missions most directly affected Indian populations. The general insalubrious living conditions at the missions created situations of high mortality and low fertility. Once Indians relocated to the missions, they lived in dormitories, which often lacked proper sanitary conditions. Mission diets were also deficient and substandard, although California Indians augmented mission food sources with hunting and harvesting. The poor diet and living conditions were a breeding ground for diseases, such as diphtheria, dysentery, measles, influenza, and tuberculosis. In addition to these maladies, sexually transmitted diseases, such as syphilis and gonorrhea, contributed to the high mortality and low fertility rates. Historian James Sandos has recently argued that Indian "sucking doctors" may have inadvertently passed these diseases to unwitting victims through their healing practices (Sandos 2004). By far, Indian women and children suffered disproportionately in the missions. At Mission San Carlos, for instance, the mortality rate fluctuated between 80 and 216 deaths per 1,000 people, but the early childhood (ages 1–4) mortality rate was 427 deaths per 1,000 children (Hackel 2005: 101, 106). The bulk of these factors were limited to Indians living along the California coast. Cook estimated that in 1830 there were only 245,000 Indians living within California's boundaries (Cook 1978).

The downward trajectory of Indian populations continued after Mexican Independence. Mexican explorers, American trappers, and ex-mission Indians carried deadly microbes into the interior of California. In 1833, cholera swept through California's Central Valley, killing perhaps as many as 5,000 Indians from the upper Sacramento Valley to Kings River. Four years later, smallpox spread from the Russian Fort Ross to Mount Shasta, primarily affecting Pomos and Wappos. It is estimated that this epidemic carried away 2,000 California Indians. Mexican and American interior incursions also contributed to the further decline of Indian populations. Mexican officials sent military expeditions into the state's interior to punish horse raiders and acquire Indian workers. In 1834, General Mariano Guadalupe Vallejo attacked a Wappo village, killing 200 and taking another 300 captive (Castillo 1978: 106). These expeditions, in addition to killing and abducting Indian people, destroyed homes and food stores, thus making survival more precarious. In less than 30 years, disease and military expeditions had reduced the Indian population in California to approximately 125,000–150,000 people, less than half of Cook's estimate for pre-contact Indian populations (Cook 1978). The worst, however, was to come.

The drastic population decline that accompanied American westward expansion occurred in two phases. Between 1848 (the discovery of gold in California) and the Civil War era, ecological changes, homicide, and the activities of state militias accounted for the bulk of the population decline in the state. The arrival of large groups of Americans changed the landscape of California Indians. The residue from hydraulic mining destroyed salmon habitats while domesticated livestock consumed grasses and acorns. The new economy reduced the amount of traditional food available to Indians. California Indians attempted to mitigate food shortages by killing American livestock. This brought the wrath and retribution of Americans down on California Indians. Between 1850 and 1865, state militias hunted down Indians and destroyed entire villages. The activities of these organizations, coupled with homicides, killed countless California Indians. By the beginning of the American Civil War, only 30,000 Indians remained within state boundaries (Cook 1978; Hurtado 1988).

The population decline continued throughout the late nineteenth century. Reservations, like the Spanish missions, were terribly unhealthy places for Indians to live. Chronic diseases, such as dysentery, tuberculosis, and measles, winnowed Indian populations. Reservation Indians also had low fertility and high child mortality rates because of these unhealthy living conditions. Considering this, many California Indians preferred to live on the ranches and farms of whites rather than on reservations. This choice was not always helpful because Indian workers lived in gender-segregated and male-only households. In other words, there were few opportunities for some Indians to procreate (Hurtado 1988). Cook estimated that only 22,000 California Indians survived the successive waves of European and American settlement (Cook 1978). Still, there have been few studies of reservation mortality, especially in the post-Civil War era, which are desperately needed.

One of the important debates that emerged from the century-long academic discussion about California Indian populations was whether or not the population decline could be attributed to genocide. While Cook lamented the trajectory of California Indian populations, his scientific approach elided the controversy. In the 1970s and 1980s, historians Jack Norton (Hupa-Cherokee) (1979) and Lynwood Carranco and Estle Beard (1981) included the word "genocide" in the title of their books. Writing in the wake of the American Indian Civil Rights movement, these authors lambasted the federal and state government's treatment of Indians as well as the heinous actions of state militias and "hunting parties." About the same time, scholars turned their attention to the California missions. Writing in response to the possible sainthood of Father Junípero Serra, the founder of the Franciscan mission system in California, historians Rupert Costo (Cahuilla) and Jeanette Henry Costo (Eastern Cherokee) published a scathing book, which condemned the missions as little more than forced labor camps that undermined indigenous subsistence patterns and precipitated the drastic population decline (Costo & Costo 1987; Sandos 1988). The last couple of years have brought a resurgence of genocide studies in

California. Newer works have placed the experiences of Northern California Indians in a transnational context and have used the United Nations
definition of genocide (prepared in the aftermath of World War II) in
their analysis (Madley 2004; Sousa 2004). While previous scholars have
approached genocide from a comparative approach (Coffer 1977) and have
utilized the UN's definition (Norton in Costo & Costo 1987), these new
works have spawned new debates on the controversial subject. Additionally,
they continue to place emphasis on what non-Indians did to Indians, rather
than on how California Indians fought for their survival and how to inter-
pret the history of population decline.

Extermination or Domestication:
State and Federal Indian Policies

After Mexican Independence, Mexican, and later American, officials confronted the task of administering the state's Indian population. Historians
have debated whether or not this was a watershed moment in the state's
history. Did Americans inherit a tradition of working with Indians from
the Spanish and Mexican regimes or did Americans create a new and more
devastating policy in California? (Magliari 2004: 358, n.17). It appears that
there was some continuity between Mexican and American political systems.
Beginning in the 1830s and continuing into the twentieth century, Mexican
and American officials sought to restrain and control Indian peoples while
simultaneously moving Indian labor and resources into an expanding capitalist marketplace. For both, the Spanish mission served as a template. The
missionaries had brought Indians under their paternalistic care, put Indians
to work, and introduced them to Catholicism. Yet, there were significant
differences between the two nation-states.

The mission system grated on liberal Mexican officials. In the 1830s,
Mexican officials began the process of dismantling the Spanish mission
system. In an effort to free land and individuals from state control, Mexican
officials initiated a program of secularization, which liberated Indian workers
from the missions' influence and placed mission land in the open market.
In theory, secularization promised to reallocate economic resources into
the hands of Indians. Mission land, property, and livestock would be distributed to Indian families and any excess would be put up for sale and
distribution to the *gente de razón* ("people of reason," a term attributed
to Spanish citizens) population. In practice, secularization allowed wealthy
or soon-to-be-wealthy Mexican landowners to acquire land and economic
resources. Mexico granted vast estates of land to military leaders, such as
Mariano Guadalupe Vallejo, or other government favorites in order to
settle the northern parts of the state. Rancheros, or Mexican landholders,

then acquired Indian land and livestock, usually through indebtedness. Rancheros permitted Indians to graze livestock on their property, but charged a rent that Indians could not work off in one year. Slowly, but surely, mission land and livestock moved into the hands of Mexican citizens (Silliman 2004).

Mexican officials, additionally, worried about the increasing international presence in Alta California (see David Igler's essay in this volume). Beginning in the 1820s, American fur traders, such as Jedediah Smith and Ewing Young, opened California to American interests. In addition to an abundance of furs, Smith and other Americans recognized the copious amount of horses in California and potential profits to be made since there was a high demand for horses in New Mexico. A flourishing legal and clandestine trade in California horses occurred between 1821 and 1848. Trade caravans from New Mexico traveled between Santa Fe and California, exchanging blankets and other items for horses. Additionally, western Indians raided Mexican ranchos, stole horses and ferried them to New Mexico. Ex-mission Indians from the interior of California secreted into Mexican settlements and absconded with horses. Moreover, Walkara, a Ute leader from the Great Basin, traveled to California, stole horses, and then took them to New Mexico. On their return trips, the Utes stole Paiute women and children and sold them into captivity in New Mexico (Broadbent 1974; Blackhawk 2006: 133–44).

In addition to the threat posed by American fur traders and Indian horse thieves, Russian settlement on Mexico's northern frontier created problems. In 1812, Russians founded Fort Ross, on the Northern California coast. Russian officials envisioned the fort as acting as a farm to provide food and supplies for Russian sea otter traders that worked the Pacific Coast from Monterey to Alaska. By the late 1830s, Russians had established four more farms in Northern California. Initially, relations between the Russians and neighboring Pomos were quite amicable, as Pomos provided their labor in return for merchandise. As the Russians expanded their endeavors, however, they resorted to force and compulsion. Russians sent armed expeditions into California, captured men, women, and children, and then forced them to work on their farms (Lightfoot 2004; Street 2004). The presence of another international party concerned Mexicans.

In response to the threats that Indians, Americans, and Russians posed on their frontier, Mexican officials made two decisions. First, much like in Texas, they permitted non-Mexican citizens to settle in the interior of California. John Sutter and John Bidwell received land grants in order to blunt the horse-raiding activities of California Indians as well as Vallejo's power. Second, Mexican officials authorized Vallejo, Sutter, and others to punish horse raiders. These men used this opportunity to capture Indians and force them to work on farms and ranches. Sutter formed an Indian military unit, outfitted them with discarded Russian uniforms, and sent them out to punish Indian horse raiders. Although Sutter punished horse thieves, there is some evidence that he was affiliated with Indians who stole horses from Californios (Hurtado 2006: 76–7). Between 1835 and 1845, Vallejo and the Southern Patwin leader Sem-Yeto, also known as Chief Solano, conducted several campaigns against nearby Indian groups, punishing horse raiders and securing laborers for Rancho Petaluma (Silliman 2004).

As the actions of Sutter and Vallejo suggest, Californios made every effort to secure Indian labor. California had a small Mexican population in the 1830s and 1840s, and rancheros turned to Indians to provide the bulk of the workforce. In the pueblo of Los Angeles town officials could arrest Indians on the suspicion or charge of public intoxication and put them to work on public works projects. Additionally, Indians in Los Angeles had to have a pass or written documentation proving they were employed. Finally, Los Angeles had the nefarious practice of allowing local ranchers to pay off the bond of incarcerated Indians. These Indians, picked up on charges of loitering, intoxication, or other misdemeanors, then worked off their bond on the rancher's property. Then, if there was any money forthcoming, the rancher paid the Indian worker the difference in alcohol, thus repeating the cycle of arrest, bail, and forced labor (Phillips 1980; Street 2004).

After the Mexican–American War, which secured the American Southwest and California for the United States, the United States brought new impulses to Indian relations that maintained the status quo. Many Americans followed the "Spanish example," and secured California Indians as laborers. Others, however, initiated a distinctly American policy, which wanted to separate and possibly eradicate the state's Indian population. Indeed, state militias and reservations accelerated the declining population numbers.

In 1850, one of the first laws passed by the new state government was the "Act for the Government and Protection of the Indians." The law granted control over local Indian affairs to the Justice of the Peace, who heard all complaints made against Indians. The law outlined specific Indian crimes, such as burning the prairie, buying alcohol, and stealing livestock. Horse or cattle theft, for instance, was punishable by up to 25 lashes. Moreover, Indians needed a pass to be in a town or the Justice of the Peace could arrest them on charges of vagrancy and loitering. Finally, this law explicated a process of indenturing Indians. Parents or relatives of an Indian minor could hand over Indian children to white ranchers for a period of indenture. Ranchers could hold Indian males until the age of 18 and Indian women until the age of 15. The rancher had to clothe, feed, and humanely treat the Indian workers. This provision was amended 10 years later to allow Indian men to be held until the age of 25 or 30 (depending on the age at which they were first indentured) and women until the age of 21 or 25 (Magliari 2004).

The Act has remained one of the most controversial, if not most criticized, state laws that pertain to Indians. In the 1920s, lawyer Chauncey Shafter Goodrich condemned the act: "[the] emphasis, it is fair to say, was on government rather than protection" (Goodrich 1926: 92). In the 1980s, historian James Rawls made a more vociferous criticism: "In practice, the law 'made slaves' of the California Indians" (Rawls 1984: 93). Most recently, historian Michael Magliari writes: "the 1850 Indian Act comprised nothing less than an American codification of the labor system inherited from Mexico and the California rancheros" (Magliari 2004: 358). In addition, it is important to note that the law gave tacit approval for ethnic cleansing, if not genocide. Mountain men publicly announced that they had killed Indian adults and then sold their children into indentured servitude.

Other decisions by the state government also sanctioned the brutal murder of California Indians. Beginning with statehood, state governors authorized locals to organize militias to attack Indians. In 1850, William Rogers, a sheriff from El Dorado County, organized a militia to punish Indians for killing livestock. For nearly three weeks, the Rogers party operated along the Cosumnes River and killed 18 Miwoks. At the end of their expedition, they provided the state government with a bill for more than $101,000 (Hurtado 1988). In Northern California, these militias operated with impunity. In the fall of 1859, a group called the Eel River or Jarboe's Rangers, named after their commanding officer Walter Jarboe, operated in the vicinity of the Round Valley Reservation with the purpose of defending white property and livestock from Indian attacks. By the time the unit was disbanded in January 1860, the Rangers reportedly killed 300 Indians and took 500 prisoners, which they claim they turned over to the reservations in the area. More chilling, though, were the comments of H. H. Buckles, a resident of nearby Ukiah: "Captain Jarboe told me that his company has killed more Indians than any other expedition that ever had been ordered out of the state" (Carranco & Beard 1981: 95). Jarboe then sent a bill to the California state legislature for $11,143.43, of which the state of California paid $9,347.39 on August 12, 1860. For whites, these expeditions were quite lucrative. By 1854, the cost of state militias had increased to nearly one million dollars, a sum that the federal government paid. These hunting parties pushed California Indians further into mountain fortresses, limited their options for food, and thus increased Indian efforts to kill livestock.

Meanwhile, federal officials made efforts to include California Indians under the umbrella of the Office of Indian Affairs (OIA). Shortly after statehood, the United States Senate authorized three men to travel to California for the purposes of meeting with Indians. The initial act did not authorize the three men to make treaties with California Indians and did not recognize California Indian land rights. A second act authorized the three men to sign treaties of friendship and peace with California Indians. The three men entrusted with these confusing and contradictory orders were George Barbour, Redick McKee, and Oliver Wozencraft. Beginning in March 1851, the men signed a total of 18 treaties with California Indian tribes, which reserved seven and a half million acres for Indian reservations within the state's boundaries. Californians were quite angry about the treaties, arguing that they provided too much potentially valuable mining and agricultural land for Indians. When the US Senate received these treaties, considerable debate ensued. Missouri Senator Thomas H. Benton, father-in-law to John C. Fremont, argued that California Indians did not have land rights because they did not present such claims to the California land claims board. Second, many senators argued that the men did not have the authority to make treaties with California Indians. Finally, the three men made exorbitant and corrupt agreements with California merchants to provision the reservations. Redick McKee, who negotiated treaties with Northern California Indians, made a deal with his *son* to provide beef cattle for Pomos in the Ukiah Valley. In the end, the United States Senate unanimously rejected the 18 California Indian treaties (Kelsey 1975; Raphael 1993).

Although the United States Senate rejected the treaties, they stopped short of removing Indians from the state, an option that many Senators and Californians supported. Rather, in 1852, the Senate appointed former Los Angeles mayor Edward F. Beale as Superintendent of Indian Affairs in California. Drawing on ideas already in circulation in California, Beale suggested a series of military posts in California. Indians would be removed to these temporary institutions and, ideally, provide enough labor to make them self-sufficient. During his tenure as Superintendent of Indian Affairs (1852–4), Beale established several reservations and farms in California, including the Tejon Reservation and the Fresno Indian Farm. His successor, Thomas J. Henley (1854–9), expanded Beale's work, creating five new farms and reservations: Nome Lackee, Mendocino, Klamath, Nome Cult Farm (later renamed the Round Valley Reservation), and the Tule River Farm. Aside from the Hoopa Valley Reservation, then, no reservation was established in California by treaty. They entered federal trust status through executive order (Wilson 1995; Phillips 1997, 2004).

The early days of the California reservation system were a failure. For one thing, both superintendents were corrupt and used the offices for self-advancement. After being removed from their positions, Beale and Henley retired to ranches located on the borders of Indian farms that they had established during their administrations. Moreover, Henley used Indian labor and OIA resources to establish his ranch. Second, California reservations were grossly underfunded. In 1854, Congress authorized nearly half a million dollars for California Indians. By 1874, that amount had declined to approximately $100,000. Thus, the amount of money expended for California Indians was not only too low, but declined over time (Sievers 1977). Finally, reservations did little to protect California Indians from state militias and other vigilante activities. These nefarious organizations operated in the vicinity of reservations, with little federal intervention. By the end of the Civil War, government officials considered the reservation system too economically cumbersome to continue and reduced the number of reservations in the state. By 1869, only three remained: Hoopa Valley, Round Valley, and Tule River. Most Indians, then, abandoned the reservations and lived in their own communities for the remainder of the nineteenth century (Hurtado 1988).

Those Indians who remained on the reservations were subjected to the vacillations of federal Indian policy. As the transcontinental railroad and the telegraph knit the nation, it became easier for OIA officials to communicate with California reservation agents and impose federal edicts on the state's Indian population. Between 1865 and 1900, Indian agents on the state's three reservations instituted the two primary policy initiatives: the Peace Policy (1868–76) and the Dawes Act (1887), also known as allotment.

The Peace Policy was initiated during the Ulysses S. Grant administration. In an effort to offer a more humane – especially in the wake of the massacres at Sand Creek in Colorado and Washita in Indian Territory (present-day Oklahoma) – and honest policy for Indians, the Office of Indian Affairs contracted with churches to choose reservation agents. The Methodist Church placed agents on California's reservations, who brought the government's mission and promise of assimilation to the reservations. Methodist agents attempted to transform Indian life by inculcating a Protestant work ethic among Indians, persuading them to dress in American clothes, cut their hair and put their children into schools, and converting Indians to Christianity (Benson 1991). On the Hoopa Valley Reservation, agent J. L. Broaddus used draconian methods to make assimilation mandatory, including arresting and imprisoning Hupas who defied his orders (Nelson 1988).

During the Grant administration, the Office of Indian Affairs also increased the number of reservations in Southern California. Until the 1860s, the federal government hewed to a "policy of neglect" for Southern California Indians (Hyer 2001: 77). In January 1870, President Grant established the Pala and San Pasqual Reservations through executive order. Government officials hoped that these reservations would protect

Cahuillas, Luiseños, and Cupeños and introduce them to the government's assimilation program. However, many Southern California Indians and non-Indians opposed the reservations. Southern California whites, as they had during the 1850s treaty debate, argued that the land was too good for Indians. Additionally, some Luiseños and Cupeños did not want to leave their homelands or support a government-appointed leader named Manuelito Chota. Considering the opposition, Grant terminated the reservations in 1871. Four years later, after meeting with Manuel Olegario, whom Luiseños and Cupeños had elected as a leader in 1870, Grant created nine Southern California reservations (Hyer 2001).

Much like those in Northern California, Southern California reservations became home to the government's efforts to "civilize" and transform Indian life in California. Government officials established schools for Southern California Indian children and promoted the English language and American clothing. Still, some so-called "friends of the Indian" were quite upset with reservation conditions for Indians in Southern California and the rest of the United States. In the early 1880s, Helen Hunt Jackson led a crusade for American Indians, specifically those in Southern California, in her two books *A Century of Dishonor: A Sketch of the United States Government's Dealings with the Indian Tribes* (1881) and her novel *Ramona* (1884). In 1883, Jackson conducted a survey of Southern California Indian conditions, discovering that whites had exploited and usurped Indian land and committed several injustices against Indians. Jackson's work reflected a general dissatisfaction with federal Indian policy in the early 1880s (Mathes 1997; Hyer 2001).

In response to the discontent with reservations and the direction of Indian policy, government officials and reform groups redirected federal Indian policy. They embarked on a campaign to individualize and detribalize American Indians. The policy of allotment, enacted in the Dawes Severalty Act of 1887, was the answer to these efforts. Allotment called for the President of the United States to select reservations for land surveys, allow Indians to select and take up individual land allotments (usually a quarter section or 160 acres), and then any remaining land would be turned over to the public domain for future sale to non-Indians. American Indians could not hold land communally and agents hoped to convince Indians to adopt the lifestyle of the independent yeoman farmer. Across the country, allotment rendered disastrous results, eventually reducing the American Indian land base in the country by 70 percent.

Perhaps surprisingly, many California Indians supported allotment. Hoopa Valley and Round Valley liked the idea of possessing their individual landholdings. The results of allotment contrasted with the hopeful aspirations of California Indians. While the Dawes Act called for Indians to receive a quarter section (160 acres) of land, California allotment agents deemed arable reservation land insufficient for this amount. Most California Indians received allotments of less than 10 acres. The average allotment on the Hoopa Valley Reservation was 6.5 acres while those on the Pala Reservation were 8 acres. These land plots were simply insufficient for California Indians to become yeoman farmers and robbed many California Indians of important resources. The federal government sold lands left over after allotment to white farmers (Lewis 1994; Hyer 2001).

The interaction between California Indians and the federal government has been open to some debate. Early scholars argued that the implementation of federal Indian policy in California was innovative and set the standard for other policy endeavors in the rest of the country (Ellison 1922). Others suggest that federal Indian policy was a more benign and humane solution or response to Indian affairs than what the state proposed – considering that the state sanctioned forced labor and ethnic cleansing (Raphael 1993). While these are important considerations, it is also worth noting that most scholars have focused on the rejected treaties and the origins of the state's reservation system, with good reason. However, we have a poor understanding of subsequent policies, especially the Peace Policy and the Allotment eras.

Indian Survival in the Nineteenth Century

Although California Indian populations dwindled and state officials exerted considerable control over Indian economic resources during the nineteenth century, California Indians were not a passive people, bending to the will of Mexican and American demands. Instead, California Indians fought for their survival in the rapidly changing state. While many California Indians lacked a choice in the matter, they found opportunities for economic, social, and cultural protection in the labor market. Rather than having their culture and ways of life eroded by interaction with the market economy, California Indians actually used the market economy to strengthen their cultures and ways of life. Additionally, California Indians looked to religious revitalization movements to express their dissatisfaction with current circumstances and hope for a better tomorrow. Finally, many California Indians resorted to violence to resist the worst manifestations of Mexican and American colonial control.

During the nineteenth century, one of the most important avenues for Indian survival in California was through participation in the wage labor market. Yet, many scholars have roundly criticized Indian participation in the workforce. Sherburne Cook concluded: "From the point of view of population changes the race was doomed to severe depletion, if not extinction, in free competition with the whites simply because it could not sufficiently, rapidly and successfully adapt itself to the labor system basic to white economy" (Cook 1943a: 101). George Harwood Phillips agreed, concluding that Mexican and American labor systems rested on Indian social instability. By entering the Mexican and American economy, Indians suffered social disintegration and collapse (Phillips 1980). Several historians, though, have revised these interpretations and recent work has demonstrated that California Indian workers entered the workforce to secure economic benefits, but also to participate in social and cultural practices forbidden on reservations (Hurtado 1988; Carrico & Shipek 1994; Silliman 2004).

During the Mexican period, California Indians found opportunities to utilize the labor market for their advantage. Certainly, many Indians came to Vallejo's rancho to work not of their own free will. However, others chose to work for Vallejo. The demand for Indian workers on Vallejo's rancho peaked during the late summer *matanza*, or round-up. Indians assisted in gathering the cattle, killing the animals, skinning the carcasses, and rendering the fat into tallow. Many of these Indians did not live permanently at Rancho Petaluma, but arrived when labor demands were high. Vallejo, then, required a stationary core of workers as well as a "reserve labor force," which floated to and from the rancho. Vallejo paid these itinerant workers in goods and food, which augmented traditional economic activities. Indians wove work at Vallejo's rancho into their seasonal economic activities. The food and clothing replaced items that livestock and Mexican settlement had destroyed (Silliman 2004).

California Indians, too, participated in the initial days of the California Gold Rush. In the summer of 1848, white observers estimated that more than half of the miners in the California diggings were Indians. They worked in gangs directed by white overseers as well as independent miners. Thus, labor arrangements varied from unfree to free experiences. Those who labored in gangs principally handed over their nuggets in exchange for clothing and merchandise. Independent miners exchanged their findings for beads, blankets, and other merchandise. Initially, unscrupulous traders paid Indian miners by weight: Indians traded an ounce of gold for an ounce of merchandise. Over time, Indian miners became astute traders and constantly haggled over the price of their goods. However, by 1850, the influx of white miners with no appreciation or contact with the Hispanic labor system pushed California Indians out of the mining districts (Rawls 1976).

Between the beginning of the Gold Rush and the end of the American Civil War, Indians continued to work. They found the wages and merchandise earned through labor a valuable resource during difficult economic times. Mining destroyed Native habitats, thus making subsistence precarious. Wages augmented these declining resources; moreover, employers protected Indian workers from militias and vigilantes. Still, labor was a precarious avenue for survival. While California Indians earned food and merchandise for their labor, the tendency of men to leave villages to work left women and children vulnerable. Mountain men and other marauders raided villages, abducted children and women, and sold them into indenture. Indian women who found jobs as cooks and domestic workers faced threats of sexual abuse and physical assault (Hurtado 1990). By the beginning of the Civil War, widespread mechanization and the tendency to hire white workers who had been displaced from the mines pushed Indians out of central California's agricultural workforce (Hurtado 1988; Magliari 2004; Street 2004).

Elsewhere, however, Indians remained a viable part of the workforce for the remainder of the nineteenth century. From San Diego to Yreka, California Indians worked in the state's growing agricultural industries. Indians worked in apricot orchards and hop fields and as vaqueros, shepherds, and sheep shearers. Meanwhile, Indian women performed domestic labor in the homes of whites. The workplace became an arena in which California Indians could invest and create new meanings. Worksites offered opportunities for socialization with other Indians, where they gambled and entertained themselves. Some Pomos used their wages to purchase land in Mendocino County. After receiving their money for picking hops, the Pomos pooled their wages and bought land and lumber for houses. Mendocino County Pomos adroitly entered the wage labor market and pooled their resources in order to provide security and hope for the future (Carrico & Shipek 1994; Sennett 1994; Bauer 2006).

While California Indians adjusted to and innovatively charted their own path in the turbulent California economy, they also made efforts to manage their shrinking populations. Indeed, California Indians viewed the Ghost Dance as an opportunity for demographic revitalization. Originating near Nevada's Walker River Reservation, the Ghost Dance spread into California in 1870. The original message called for eternal life for Indians and the elimination of whites. As the Ghost Dance spread into California, Indians augmented the message with statements that the Ghost Dance would bring about the return of wild game and family members who had passed away. The Ghost Dance also assumed new meanings and names in California, including the Earth Lodge, the Bole Maru, and the Big Head Religions. California Indians flocked to these related, but distinct, religious messages because of their promise to restore flagging population numbers as well as invert economic hierarchies in California (DuBois 1939; Miller 1976; Thornton 1986; Bauer 2006).

Finally, California Indians actively resisted exploitation and colonization, ultimately resorting to violence when conditions worsened beyond human tolerance. In 1851, Cupeño leader Antonio Garra attempted to create a

pan-Indian alliance of Southern California Indians to resist American settlement. Garra and other Southern California Indians disliked the system of
taxation implemented after California statehood and the hordes of people
coming to the state in the wake of the Gold Rush. Garra tried to enlist the
support of Cahuillas, Luiseños, Ipais, and Quechans, but could not forge
a large alliance. Garra attacked and burned Juan José Warner's ranch in
Southern California, but did little damage other than that. Ultimately, his
failure to enlist the aid of other California Indians undermined the uprising
(Phillips 1975). When American statehood threatened to undermine and
alter pre-existing relationships between Indians and whites, some turned
to violence to ameliorate their situation.

After the Gold Rush, California Indians continued to resort to violence,
even though many contemporaries and scholars considered them quies-
cent. In 1847, Andrew Kelsey and a business associate named Stone began
to raise cattle near Clear Lake, in Northern California, and hired Pomos
as vaqueros. According to Indian oral history, Kelsey and Stone mistreated
Pomo workers. The white men poorly provisioned the Pomos (William
Benson reported that Pomos earned four cups of wheat a day), whipped
workers, killed women, and took other women as concubines. In 1849,
Pomos plotted to kill Kelsey and Stone, but Pomo accounts differed on
what led to the event. Benson reported that lack of food was the primary
cause, while Augustín, a foreman for Stone and Kelsey, suggested that the
Pomos decided to act when the two white men decided to send some of
the Pomos to Sutter's Fort (Radin 1932: 268–9; Hurtado 1988: 104–6).
The Pomos confiscated or sabotaged Stone and Kelsey's weapons, and then
subsequently shot Stone with an arrow and stabbed Kelsey in the back.
Unlike the use of violence in Southern California, this episode reveals the
connection between Indian violence and California workplaces. Labor
conditions worsened throughout the 1840s and 1850s, and Indians resorted
to violence when these conditions became unbearable.

Perhaps the most famous incident of Indian–white violence in
nineteenth-century California occurred in the Lava Beds of northeastern
California. There, Modocs held off the United States Army for nearly six
months before surrendering. It is an oft-told story, replete with violence,
deception, and sensational characters, such as Captain Jack and Hooker
Jim. In the 1860s, the Modocs had agreed to move to the Klamath Reservation in Oregon. Finding living circumstances there not to their liking,
the Modocs returned to California and settled and worked near Yreka. Still,
government officials wanted to move the Modocs to a reservation. If not
the Klamath Reservation, some government officials floated the idea of a
Modoc reservation on the Lost River. Many Modocs, however, retreated
to a place called the Stronghold, in northeastern California's Lava Beds,

and fended off the United States Army. The pivotal event in the war occurred on the eve of Easter, 1873, when Captain Jack, after a night of being berated by fellow Modocs, shot and killed United States General E. R. S. Canby. This galvanized the US army to capture all the Modocs. With the aid of Warm Springs scouts, the army found Captain Jack's hiding place on June 1, 1873. A military court sentenced Captain Jack and three other Modocs to death and two Modocs to Alcatraz. On October 3, 1873, the United States hung Jack and three others. The remaining Modocs were removed to Indian Territory. Since the Modoc War shared geographic and temporal similarities with Apache, Lakota, and Nez Perce conflicts, scholars have usually examined this war in the context of other Indian wars in the American West and a "final desperate resistance to the impact of white man's culture on the ancient Indian folkways" (Murray 1959: 4; Ream 2000). To do so, however, ignores the reasons why the Modocs fought the United States. They resisted the implementation of federal Indian policy in California and were determined to stay in their homelands. After all, Captain Jack and other Modocs wanted to have a reservation in their homeland on the Lost River (Bales 2001). Rather than it being emblematic of Indian wars in the West, the Modoc War was a struggle on the part of California Indians to modify and adapt to a federal Indian policy that never really considered their wants and desires. These struggles continued in the twentieth century.

The nineteenth century was a trying one for California Indians, one fraught with violence, destruction, and the loss of control of some facets of Indian life. Nevertheless, California Indians survived. Before Lucy Young's grandfather passed away, he told her: "Long time you gonta live, my child. You live long time in this world." Many years later, Young reflected on her grandfather's statements: "Well I live long enough, I guess. 'Bout ninety-five next summer, if I living til then" (Murphey 1941: 350). Born in the 1840s, Lucy Young indeed witnessed dramatic and traumatic changes in California Indian life. The numbers of California Indians nearly withered to nothing. State and federal governments sought to forcibly bring Indians into the workforce, sanctioned the extermination of Native populations, and sought to eradicate Indian culture. Yet, it was Young's survival that was truly remarkable. She and other California Indians survived ethnic cleansing and policy endeavors by remaking the market economy to suit their interests, participating in religious revitalization movements, and turning violence back on Mexicans and Americans. They quite literally laid the foundation for the demographic revival in the twentieth century by giving birth to future generations of California Indians and turning the tables on the heinous actions of the California Gold Rush.

REFERENCES

Almaguer, Tomas. 1994. *Racial Fault Lines: The Historical Origins of White Supremacy in California*. Berkeley: University of California Press.

Bales, Rebecca. 2001. " 'You Will Be Bravest of All': The Modoc Nation to 1909." PhD dissertation, Arizona State University.

Bauer, William. 2006. " 'We Were All Migrant Workers Here': Round Valley Indian Labor in Northern California," *Western Historical Quarterly* 37 (Spring): 43–64.

Benson, Todd. 1991. "The Consequences of Reservation Life: Native Californians on the Round Valley Reservation, 1871–1884," *Pacific Historical Review* 40 (May): 221–44.

Blackhawk, Ned. 2006. *Violence Over the Land: Indians and Empires in the Early American West*. Cambridge, MA: Harvard University Press.

Broadbent, Sylvia. 1974. "Conflict at Monterey: Indian Horse Raiding, 1820–1850," *Journal of California Anthropology* 1 (Spring): 86–101.

Carranco, Lynwood and Beard, Estle. 1981. *Genocide and Vendetta: The Round Valley Wars of Northern California*. Norman: University of Oklahoma Press.

Carrico, Richard L. and Shipek, Florence C. 1994. "Indian Labor in San Diego County, California, 1850–1900." In Alice Littlefield and Martha Knack, eds., *Native Americans and Wage Labor: Ethnohistorical Perspectives*. Norman: University of Oklahoma Press, pp. 198–217.

Castillo, Edward. 1978. "The Impact of Euro-American Exploration and Settlement." In Robert Heizer, ed., *Handbook of North American Indians: California*, vol. 8. Washington, DC: Smithsonian Institution, pp. 99–127.

Coffer, William. 1977. "Genocide of the California Indians, with a Comparative Study of Other Minorities," *Indian Historian* 10 (Spring): 8–15.

Cook, Sherburne. 1943a. "The Conflict Between the California Indian and White Civilization: I," *Ibero-Americana* 21: 1–176.

Cook, Sherburne. 1943b. "The Conflict Between the California Indian and White Civilization: II," *Ibero-Americana* 22: 1–55.

Cook, Sherburne. 1943c. "The Conflict Between the California Indian and White Civilization: III," *Ibero-Americana* 23: 1–115.

Cook, Sherburne. 1976. *The Population of the California Indians, 1769–1970*. Berkeley: University of California Press.

Cook, Sherburne. 1978. "Historical Demography." In Robert Heizer, ed., *Handbook of North American Indians: California*, vol. 8. Washington, DC: Smithsonian Institution, pp. 91–8.

Costo, Rupert and Costo, Jeannette Henry. 1987. *The Missions of California: A Legacy of Genocide*. San Francisco: Indian Historian Press.

Dillon, Richard H. 1973. *Burnt-Out Fires*. Englewood Cliffs, NJ: Prentice-Hall, Inc.

DuBois, Cora. 1939. "The 1870 Ghost Dance," *Anthropological Records* 3 (1): 1–151.

Ellison, William. 1922. "The Federal Indian Policy in California, 1846–1860," *Mississippi Valley Historical Review* 9 (June): 37–67.

Goodrich, Chauncey Shafter. 1926. "The Legal Status of the California Indian," *California Law Review* 14 (January): 83–100.

Findlay, John. 1992. "An Elusive Institution: The Birth of Indian Reservations in Gold Rush California." In George Pierre Castile and Robert L. Bee, eds., *State and Reservation: New Perspectives on Federal Indian Policy*. Tucson: University of Arizona Press, pp. 13–37.

Hackel, Steven W. 1998. "Land, Labor, and Production: The Colonial Economy of Spanish and Mexican California." In Ramón A. Gutiérrez and Richard J. Orsi, eds., *Contested Eden: California Before the Gold Rush*. Berkeley: University of California Press, pp. 111–46.

Hackel, Steven W. 2005. *Children of Coyote, Missionaries of Saint Francis: Indian–Spanish Relations in Colonial California*. Chapel Hill: University of North Carolina Press.

Heizer, Robert. 1978. "History of Research." In R. Heizer, ed., *Handbook of North American Indians: California*, vol. 8. Washington, DC: Smithsonian Institution, pp. 6–15.

Hurtado, Albert. 1988. *Indian Survival on the California Frontier*. New Haven, CT: Yale University Press.

Hurtado, Albert. 1989. "California Indian Demography, Sherburne F. Cook, and the Revision of American History," *Pacific Historical Review* 58 (August): 323–43.

Hurtado, Albert. 1990. "California Indians and the Workaday West: Labor, Assimilation and Survival," *California History* 69 (Spring): 2–11.

Hurtado, Albert. 2006. *John Sutter: A Life on the North American Frontier*. Norman: University of Oklahoma Press.

Hyer, Joel R. 2001. *"We Are Not Savages": Native Americans in Southern California and the Pala Reservation, 1840–1920*. East Lansing: Michigan State University Press.

Jackson, Robert H. and Castillo, Edward. 1995. *Indians, Franciscans, and Spanish Colonization: The Impact of the Mission System on California Indians*. Albuquerque: University of New Mexico Press.

Kelsey, Harry. 1975. "The California Indian Treaty Myth," *Southern California Quarterly* 55 (Fall): 225–38.

Kroeber, Alfred. 1925. *Handbook of the Indians of California*. Washington, DC: Government Printing Office.

Lewis, David Rich. 1994. *Neither Wolf Nor Dog: American Indians, Environment, and Agrarian Change*. New York: Oxford University Press.

Lightfoot, Kent. 2004. *Indians, Missionaries, and Merchants: The Legacy of Colonial Encounters on the California Frontiers*. Berkeley: University of California Press.

Madley, Benjamin. 2004. "Patterns of Frontier Genocide, 1803–1910: The Aboriginal Tasmanians, the Yuki of California and the Herero of Namibia," *Journal of Genocide Research* 6 (June): 167–92.

Magliari, Michael. 2004. "Free Soil, Unfree Labor: Cave Johnson Couts and the Binding of Indian Workers in California, 1850–1867," *Pacific Historical Review* 73 (August): 349–89.

Mathes, Valerie Sherer. 1997. *Helen Hunt Jackson and Her Indian Reform Legacy*. Norman: University of Oklahoma Press.

Merriam, C. Hart. 1905. "The Indian Population of California," *American Anthropologist* 7 (October): 594–606.

Miller, Virginia. 1976. "The 1870 Ghost Dance and the Methodists: An Unexpected Turn of Events in Round Valley," *Journal of California Anthropology* 3 (2): 66–74.

Miller, Virginia. 1989. "The Changing Role of the Chief on a California Indian Reservation," *American Indian Quarterly* 13 (Fall): 447–54.

Murphey, Edith V. A. 1941. "Out of the Past: A True Indian Story Told by Lucy Young, of Round Valley Indian Reservation," *California Historical Society Quarterly* 20 (December): 349–64.

Murray, Keith A. 1959. *The Modocs and Their War*. Norman: University of Oklahoma.

Nelson, Jr., Byron. 1988. *Our Home Forever: The Hupa Indians of Northern California*. Salt Lake City: Howe Brothers.

Norton, Jack. 1979. *When Our Worlds Cried: Genocide in Northwestern California*. San Francisco: The Indian Historian Press.

Palmberg, Walter H. 1982. *Copper Paladin: A Modoc Tragedy. A Story of the Two Principal Role-players of the Modoc Indian War of 1872–73*. Bryn Mawr, PA: Dorrance.

Phillips, George Harwood. 1975. *Chiefs and Challengers: Indian Resistance and Cooperation in Southern California*. Berkeley: University of California Press.

Phillips, George Harwood. 1980. "Indians in Los Angeles, 1781–1875: Economic Integration, Social Disintegration," *Pacific Historical Review* 49 (August): 427–51.

Phillips, George Harwood. 1993. *Indians and Intruders in Central California, 1769–1848*. Norman: University of Oklahoma Press.

Phillips, George Harwood. 1997. *Indians and Indian Agents: The Origins of the Reservation System in California, 1849–1852*. Norman: University of Oklahoma Press.

Phillips, George Harwood. 2004. *"Bringing Them Under Subjection": California's Tejón Indian Reservation and Beyond, 1852–1864*. Lincoln: University of Nebraska Press.

Radin, Max. 1932. "The Stone and Kelsey 'Massacre' on the Shores of Clear Lake in 1849: The Indian Viewpoint," *California Historical Society Quarterly* 11 (3): 266–73.

Raphael, Ray. 1993. *Little White Father: Redick McKee on the California Frontier*. Arcata: Humboldt County Historical Society.

Rawls, James. 1976. "Gold Diggers: Indian Miners in the California Gold Rush," *California Historical Society Quarterly* 55 (Spring): 28–45.

Rawls, James. 1984. *Indians of California: The Changing Image*. Norman: University of Oklahoma Press.

Ream, Merrill L. 2000. "The Modoc Indian War," *Journal of the West* 39 (January): 35–48.

Reed, Annette Louise. 1999. "*Neeyu Nn'ee min' Nngheeyilh Naach'aaghitlhni: Lhla't'i' Deeni Tr'vmdan' Natlhsri* – Rooted in the Land of Our Ancestors, We Are Strong: A Tolowa History." PhD dissertation, University of California, Berkeley.

Salvatore, Ricardo. 1991. "Modes of Labor Control in Cattle-Ranching Economies: California, Southern Brazil, and Argentina, 1820–1860," *Journal of Economic History* 51 (June): 441–51.

Sandos, James. 1988. "Junípero Serra's Canonization and the Historical Record," *American Historical Review* 93 (December): 1253–69.

Sandos, James. 2004. *Converting California: Indians and Franciscans in the Missions.* New Haven, CT: Yale University Press.

Sennett, Beth. 1994. "Wage Labor: Survival for the Death Valley Timbasha." In Alice Littlefield and Martha Knack, eds., *Native Americans and Wage Labor: Ethnohistorical Perspectives.* Norman: University of Oklahoma Press, pp. 218–44.

Shipek, Florence Connolly. 1987. *Pushed into the Rocks: Southern California Indian Land Tenure, 1769–1986.* Lincoln: University of Nebraska Press.

Sievers, Michael. 1977. "Funding the California Indian Superintendency: A Case Study of Congressional Appropriations," *Southern California Quarterly* 59 (Spring): 49–69.

Silliman, Stephen. 2004. *Lost Laborers in Colonial California: Native Americans and the Archaeology of Rancho Petaluma.* Tucson: University of Arizona Press.

Sousa, Ashley Riley. 2004. "'They Will Be Hunted Down Like Wild Beasts and Destroyed!': A Comparative Study of Genocide in California and Tasmania," *Journal of Genocide Research* 6 (June): 193–209.

Staniford, Edward. 1971. "The California Indians: A Critique of Their Treatment by Historians," *Ethnohistory* 18 (Spring): 119–25.

Street, Richard Steven. 2004. *Beasts of the Field: A Narrative of the California Farmworkers, 1769–1913.* Palo Alto: Stanford University Press.

Thornton, Russell. 1980. "Recent Estimates of the Prehistoric California Indian Population," *Current Anthropology* 21 (October): 702–4.

Thornton, Russell. 1986. *We Shall Live Again: The 1870 and 1890 Ghost Dance Movements as Demographic Revitalization.* New York: Cambridge University Press.

Wilson, B. D. 1995. *The Indians of Southern California in 1852.* Introduction by John Walton Caughey. Introduction to Bison Books edition by Albert L. Hurtado. Lincoln: University of Nebraska Press.

FURTHER READING

American Indian Culture and Research Journal, New Perspectives on California Indian Research. (No. 2, 1988).

American Indian Quarterly, Special Issue: The California Indians (Autumn 1989).

California History, Special Issue: Indians of California (Fall 1992).

Kroeber, Karl and Kroeber, Clifton. 2003. *Ishi in Three Centuries.* Berkeley: University of California Press.

Margolin, Malcolm. 1993. *The Way We Lived: California Indian Stories, Songs and Reminiscences.* Berkeley: Heyday Books.

Starn, Orin. 2004. *Ishi's Brain: In Search of America's Last "Wild" Indian.* New York: W. W. Norton.

Chapter Twelve

TRANSFORMATIONS IN LATE NINETEENTH-CENTURY RURAL CALIFORNIA

David Vaught

"Bread the world must have," exclaimed Elijah W. Brown in 1885, extolling the virtues of wheat farming – not in the Dakotas, Kansas, or northern Texas, but in California (*Dixon Tribune*, January 3, 1885). Historians have examined in considerable detail the development of the "wheat belt" on the western edge of the Midwest in the 1880s, but for much of that decade, no state produced more wheat than California. Nearly all of the state's famous valleys – Sacramento, San Joaquin, Napa, Sonoma, Santa Clara (now "Silicon"), Salinas, San Fernando – were planted in wall-to-wall wheat from the late 1860s to the early 1890s. Using the latest technology, California growers cultivated the state's virgin soils to produce bumper harvests of 60 to 80 bushels per acre – four to five times the norm for Midwestern farms. Unlike the bonanza farmers of the Great Plains, California growers exported most of their crop to foreign markets (primarily England) – as much as three-fourths of every harvest (Smith 1969).

But just as California was earning a reputation as the "granary of the world," production ground to a halt (Rothstein 1987: 2). In the early 1880s, farmers elsewhere in the United States and thousands of miles away in Europe, Asia, South America, and Australia – many using techniques and machines imported from California – planted wheat of their own. Overproduction, along with four years of severe depression in the mid-1890s, glutted world markets and sent prices plummeting. By 1910, California imported most of its wheat from the Midwest, and fruit emerged as the state's major crop. Though Brown could not have known what lay ahead in 1885, California's farm economy was about to experience "one of the most rapid and complete transformations ever witnessed in American agricultural history" (Rhode 1995: 773).

While Brown depended primarily on wheat for his livelihood, there was more to his life than reapers and combines. After migrating from Missouri in 1855, he settled on 320 acres on Putah Creek, 15 miles west of Sacramento, and tried his hand at a little bit of everything: wheat, cattle, the hardware business, and newspaper reporting. He left his most lasting mark as a columnist for weeklies in the towns of Davisville and Dixon, both established by the California Pacific Railroad in 1868, nine miles apart, with populations of about 500 each. Brown left no subject of local interest unturned, from county politics, to crop conditions, to community gossip, to baseball (Larkey 1969). Indeed, baseball consumed Brown and his readers for much of the 1880s and 1890s. When the Davisville Oletas played the Dixon Etnas, which they did on most Sunday evenings every summer, hundreds of fans crowded around the diamond, "highly desirous of witnessing the contest" (*Dixon Tribune*, June 4, 1887). That desire stemmed not only from the excitement of the game but from the extensive, high-stakes gambling both on and off the field.

The passion for baseball in these two small rural towns was by no means unusual. The game was introduced to rural California during the Gold Rush, gradually gained a foothold over the next two decades, and then caught fire in the 1880s, right as agriculture began to change so dramatically. Nor was the timing a coincidence. Farmers' "devotion to the game" (*Dixon Tribune*, October 24, 1885) reveals that baseball – heretofore regarded by historians as a largely urban phenomenon – had become deeply rooted in the region's rural culture and that California's agricultural transformation involved much more than planting new crops. Baseball's skyrocketing popularity in the late nineteenth century both influenced and reflected important changes in farmers' social and cultural behavior.

California historians have shown little interest in farmers' social and cultural behavior. Much of what we know about rural life in the Golden State during this period comes from contemporary critics, most notably land reformer Henry George (1871) and muckraking novelist Frank Norris (1901). That approach has focused scholarly attention – Carey McWilliams (1939), Cletus Daniel (1981), and Richard Steven Street (2004), in particular – on the largest "bonanza" farms. Invariably, such accounts spotlight Hugh Glenn, who amassed an empire of 66,000 acres in the Sacramento Valley, employed 1,000 laborers, invested $300,000 in machinery and draft animals, and produced a million bushels of wheat a year by 1880. Many things about late nineteenth-century California seem larger than life, but Glenn was hardly representative of all wheat farmers. Small ranches and huge estates developed side by side up and down the state's fertile valleys (Fite 1966). Those who operated on a much smaller scale – such as Brown – rarely shared the same problems, concerns, and values as the so-called "wheat kings." Every wheat farmer was not like every other wheat farmer in regard to their production methods, labor needs, marketing strategies, community relations, and, more generally, how they saw their world.

Putah Creek offers a case in point. The Browns were one of 130 farm families who, by 1860, built this community (known simply as "Putah Creek" before Davisville and Dixon were established). Community itself is a concept at odds with the conventional wisdom that has emphasized "land barons" and "farm factories." Nonetheless, it is key to understanding what historian Rodman Paul has called "one of the most extraordinary of all agrarian episodes" – California's bonanza wheat era (Paul 1973: 22). We know next to nothing about the era's participants – their ethnicity, gender identities, class loyalties, religion, family networks, or community relations. Rural social historians have made clear that contemporary Midwestern farmers in essence had one foot in an agrarian past and the other in the modern economic order. Were California farmers – most of them from the Midwest – so different? If mechanization did not undermine the traditional values of rural Midwesterners, as John Mack Faragher (1986), Mary Neth (1995), and Hal Barron (1997) have argued, did the gang plow and the combine transform California farmers? Community in Putah Creek was every bit as important and complex as in Faragher's *Sugar Creek*. Farm people in California, no less than their counterparts elsewhere, need to be analyzed on their own terms – by what they said and did, what they believed in, what they aspired to, and how their behavior shaped their lives and their enterprise.

While not, to be sure, a traditional topic in the literature on rural California, baseball provides a rich starting point to humanize what has long been thought of only as an "industry." We would do well to adhere to the words of historian Jacques Barzun, which ring just as true today as when he penned them in 1954: "Whoever wants to know the heart and mind of America had better learn baseball, and do it by watching . . . small town teams" (Barzun 1954: 159). Barzun sensed that the essence of the game – its widespread popularity and cultural meaning – has always been fundamentally local. The Davisville–Dixon rivalry, therefore, needs to be understood in its rural context, not as a byproduct of the developing urban/professional game. The history of the game in the region was interwoven with the history of the region itself and its agricultural transformation.

That history began in the wake of the Gold Rush. A number of rural communities in Northern California proliferated in the 1850s – not in the standard American fashion of settlers moving westward along a broad front, cultivating the land homestead by homestead, but communities nonetheless. Putah Creek, named for the river that ran west to east out of the coast mountains across the lower Sacramento Valley, was one such community. Most of the transplanted Midwesterners who settled it over the course of the decade came not to farm but to seek riches in gold. Those unfortunate to arrive after 1851, however, found that surface deposits had been depleted by the 100,000 forty-niners who had arrived there ahead of them. Often too ashamed to return home, they turned to agriculture and rural life with the same intensity of expectation that brought them to California in the first place. Admitting failure a second time was simply not an option (Rohrbough 1997; Vaught 2003).

Farming along Putah Creek, though often extraordinarily productive, proved immensely challenging. Using gang plows, McCormick reapers, treadmill threshers and other cutting-edge machinery, farmers produced huge harvests of wheat – most of which helped feed the escalating populations of San Francisco and Sacramento. "The lands of Putah," proclaimed one wide-eyed newspaper reporter, revealed "the magnificent results of agriculture under the bold and energetic patronage of its farmers" (*Sacramento Daily Union*, October 8, 1852). Yet, not a single one of them made a profit in the 1850s. High production costs at the beginning of the decade and falling prices at the end, the result of the boom and bust of the Gold Rush, never gave farmers much of a chance (Gerber 1992). Greed and arrogance did not help either. Had they paid even the slightest interest to the human and natural history of the region – in particular how Indians and Mexicans before them had coped with floods and droughts – they might have limited their mistakes and excesses. Nor should the sheer power of seduction be underestimated. The abundance of natural advantages, new technology, gigantic yields, and instant fame – all on the heels of the disillusionment of the Gold Rush – drove these farmers to pursue market opportunities even though the odds were stacked against them. Their eagerness to keep pumping money into their farms was all the more astounding given the fact the title to the land itself was in question. Three Mexican land grants engulfed the region, which meant that the claimants, under the provisions of the Treaty of Guadalupe Hidalgo and the California Land Act of 1851, had to defend their property rights before federal authorities. Until the mass of litigation was resolved – a process that took two decades with one of the grants – no one truly owned the land (Vaught 2007a).

In their haste to succeed in California, farmers committed themselves not only to material pursuits but to community life as well. Neither the legal chaos caused by the land grants, nor the seductions of farming in the Sacramento Valley, nor the unfulfilled dreams of the Gold Rush dampened the community sentiments that they brought with them from the Midwest. In just a few years, residents shared a specific sense of place, similar patterns of everyday life, common obligations, and a number of public rituals and institutions that pulled men, and eventually women, together as a social unit. They gave names to bends in the creek, crossings, roads, bridges, and other elements of the landscape; gathered together for holidays, weddings, births, funerals, and other community activities; formed strong religious ties; and, obligated by tradition and necessity, participated in all facets of township and county government (Vaught 2007a).

Putah Creek farmers also shared a favorite pastime – horseracing. Those with southern roots were responsible for importing fast trotters and building racetracks, but virtually everyone cheered their favorite horses and reveled in the attention that winners, particularly at the state fair in Sacramento, gave their community. The most celebrated trotting stallion from Putah Creek was "Rattler," who won more races, took more premiums, and earned more in stud fees that any horse in Northern California in the late 1850s and early 1860s. When Rattler died in 1863, the *Sacramento Daily Union* (SDU) ran his obituary as its feature news story. "The death of this fine animal," the paper bemoaned, "will be regretted by turf men throughout the state" (*SDU*, April 13, 1863). The tradition of fine horsemanship, which began among the gentry in colonial Virginia before spreading northward and across class boundaries by the early nineteenth century, took root in the Sacramento Valley almost immediately and lasted well into the twentieth century. Indeed, horseracing symbolized how quickly rural life in California matured in the decade after the Gold Rush (Breen 1977; Vaught 2003).

Baseball, though not nearly as popular as horseracing at this point, also made its way to the Sacramento Valley in the 1850s. Legend has it that Alexander Cartwright, whose reputation for "inventing" the game is second only to Abner Doubleday's, brought baseball with him from New York by literally carrying a bat, ball, and a copy of the rules of his beloved Knickerbocker Base Ball Club overland to the gold country of California. While most serious accounts question whether such a feat can be attributed to Cartwright alone, Californians did in fact play the game that the so-called "father of modern baseball" helped create in 1845. Among the 20 rules that the Knickerbockers codified that year were the diamond-shaped infield, the inclusion of foul lines, and the insistence that players on the field had to throw to a base to get a runner out rather than hit ("soak" or "plunk") him with the ball (Nelson 2004). Less well known is the fact that rural Californians took up the sport as eagerly as urban Californians. Farmers and farmhands, wearing no uniforms but overalls and black shirts, played informal games on Putah Creek ranches as early as 1857 – "baseball in the olden time," as Brown remembered it (*Dixon Tribune*, June 28, 1895). Three years later, farmers from throughout the Sacramento Valley flocked to the state fair not only to view crop and cattle exhibits, inspect new farm machinery, and go to the racetrack, but to watch several teams play a one-day tournament with the "state title," a silver bat, and $350 in prize money on the line. Baseball's seed had been planted (Spalding 1992).

Early in the next decade, however, farmers had neither the time nor the desire for such activities. They found themselves preoccupied with two of the worst natural disasters in the state's history. In the winter of 1861–2, a flood of enormous, almost biblical, proportions hit the Sacramento Valley, when a series of warm, tropical rains melted several feet of snow in the Sierra Nevada. Rampaging rivers poured out of their channels, filling much of the valley and spreading devastation for weeks on end. Sacramento was buried deep in mud, farms and ranches were destroyed, and hundreds of people were swept away to their deaths. Most of the land along Putah Creek was completely under water. "There is nothing to indicate the locality of the ranches but a windmill," observed one stunned resident (*Sacramento Daily Union*, December 14, 1861). In what must have seemed like a cruel hoax, the "flood of the century" was followed immediately by a severe and prolonged drought. For almost three years, the rains failed. Tens of thousands of cattle perished, and crop loss was so severe that Californians imported wheat from Chile to make their bread. The back-to-back disasters postponed the state fair, and baseball fields and racetracks lay vacant throughout the region while farmers struggled mightily to recover (Kelley 1989).

Those who persisted through the end of the decade – about 35 percent in Putah Creek – were rewarded. With much of the confusion over land titles resolved, and with the return of more stable weather, farmers resumed wheat cultivation with a vengeance. Their timing could not have been better. By coincidence, California produced three straight bumper crops after the drought broke in 1865, at the same time that Great Britain and other European nations suffered dangerously deficient harvests. Enterprising grain merchants in San Francisco and Liverpool, including the legendary Isaac Friedlander, exploited the opportunity to the fullest, as did farmers in Putah Creek. Production skyrocketed between 1866 and 1869, with most of the crop feeding a single market – industrial England, the world's greatest wheat importer. Farm incomes more than tripled and land values doubled. This dramatic turn of events – the start of California's bonanza wheat era – confirmed all the more the prevailing belief among farmers that demand would inevitably outpace production. Developments over the next three decades would expose that as folly, but for the time being, farmers had finally struck gold (Rothstein 1987; Magliari 1991).

The prosperity of the wheat boom helped revive rural sports in the late 1860s. Horseracing became something of an obsession in the Sacramento Valley, with racetracks being built on the outskirts of seemingly every town. Several Putah Creek farmers began training their own trotters and pacers, and raced them throughout the year. Baseball also resumed play, but on a much more spontaneous basis. The game required little equipment or preparation. The two essentials, a bat and a ball, were often homemade – the ball from a twine-wrapped core covered with a piece of leather, the bat from a sawed-off wagon tongue. And makeshift diamonds could be set up in cow pastures or grain fields – any place where a team of horses could scrape an infield. The game was played without fans or fanfare; it was still just something that rural men and boys enjoyed between peak periods of the production cycle (Seymour 1990; Vaught 2007a).

Then, in September of 1869, baseball received an unexpected boost from a distant source. Four months after the completion of the first trans-continental railroad line, the Cincinnati Red Stockings barnstormed their way through California. On a long road trip that season – through the East, Midwest, and California – the nation's first all-professional team won 81 straight games, including five in San Francisco and another in Sacramento. With newspapers covering seemingly every movement of the players on and off the field, their brief tour ignited locals' passion for the game. Reporters marveled at the superior skills of pitching, fielding, and batting demonstrated by the Cincinnati nine; their impressive physiques and dapper uniforms; and the gala banquets held in their honor at the cities' finest restaurants. Hundreds of fans crowded the Sacramento depot to bid the Red Stockings farewell, and in smaller towns along the way, including Dixon and Davisville, rural onlookers gathered in droves to catch a glimpse of "the gallant men in stockings red" as their train passed through. With their flair for promotion and playing prowess, the Red Stockings whetted Northern Californians' appetite for baseball, including thousands who never actually saw them play (Nelson 2004).

This surge in popularity transformed the game in cities across the state, but rural baseball remained virtually unchanged. In San Francisco, Oakland, Sacramento, and Stockton, heated rivalries developed among dozens of teams participating in "match play" tournaments and, by the end of the 1870s, in the state's first two professional leagues. The players were well paid and the teams drew large and enthusiastic crowds at their expansive new ballparks (Spalding 1992). The essential elements of the modern game – the rules, fundamentals of each position, rudimentary equipment, and even the language – gradually evolved and, by mid-decade, were firmly in place. Farmers still enjoyed the game, but even those in Putah Creek, in close proximity to Sacramento, did not adopt the basic conventions of the urban game. They still played barehanded, in the clothes on their backs, with the layout of the field and number of players dictated by local condi-tions, and with no apparent enthusiasm for more organized play (Vaught 2007b). With the newer rules and state-of-the-art equipment, city teams generally played relatively low-scoring games of two hours or so in length, but the typical rural game often came to an end only with the onset of darkness. "Two square yards of blackboard were needed to record those scores of 80 to 90," Brown recalled (*Dixon Tribune*, June 28, 1895).

While farmers continued to play "baseball in the olden time," big changes in their lives, the magnitude of which they had only begun to realize, lay ahead. They were about to take part in the next great agrarian episode in California: the transition from wheat to specialty crops. Production itself posed few problems. Five times between 1872 and 1884, in fact, no state grew more wheat than California. While producing to their hearts' content, however, farmers continued to turn a blind eye to the harsh realities of supply and demand – not only the simple economics of overproduction, but the fact that farmers from around the world were beating them at their own game (Rhode 1995). As prices fell precipitously year after year, farmers along Putah Creek and elsewhere began to ask the question none of them wanted to hear: "Does it pay to raise wheat, our bread and butter for so long" (*Dixon Tribune*, January 3, 1885).

Their answer split along generational lines. "Old-timers" argued, as early as 1880, that the market had bottomed out and that wheat would surely "reign king in our district" again (*Dixon Tribune*, November 14, 1891). For their sons, however, the question was more complicated. They feared that the bottom had in fact dropped out of the market. Wheat's decline, moreover, came just as they were beginning to emerge from their fathers' shadows. They were determined, as one put it, to look forward with "fresh energy and clear vision" (*Yolo Weekly Mail*, January 1, 1892). For years, their fathers had tended small orchards and vineyards to supplement their grain incomes. The new generation did not abandon wheat in the 1880s, but turned increasingly to fruits and nuts both as cash crops and to cultivate their own identities. To an even greater degree than their fathers, they would spend their lives struggling to resolve the great paradox of agriculture in the modern economic world: farmers' very identity – their inner drive to produce, produce, produce – invariably gluts the market, brings low prices, and spreads misery and frustration (Vaught 2007a).

There is no doubt, however, that the transition from wheat to fruit eventually took place. As late as 1889, California was still the nation's second-leading wheat-producing state, with almost three million acres harvested and exports totaling 840,000 tons. By 1909, wheat acreage fell to less than 400,000 acres, with the state becoming a net importer. Over the same period, California emerged as one of the world's principal producers of deciduous and citrus fruits, grapes, vegetables, and nuts (Rhode 1995). The shift from wheat to specialty crops in Davisville and Dixon, as elsewhere in the state's rural regions, was slow, uneven, contingent, and fraught with anxiety and conflict from the beginning. Sons inherited their fathers' dreams of striking it rich in California and pursued them with equal, perhaps even greater, passion. With boldness, hard work, and a little luck (not necessarily in that order), they still believed that they could succeed materially and, just as importantly, bring stability and prosperity to their community. They did indeed transform agriculture along Putah Creek, but they also maintained strong cultural ties to the Gold Rush generation – more so than they cared to admit (Vaught 2007a).

This, then, was the context in which baseball's popularity rose to unprecedented heights. Farmers' newfound passion for the game coincided with a period of far-reaching economic, social, and generational change in rural California. "Our players are mostly farmers' sons," Brown recognized in 1885 (*Dixon Tribune*, June 6, 1885). Of 69 farmers (identified in box scores), who played for the Davisville Oletas and the Dixon Etnas in the 1880s, at least 44 (68 percent) were sons of Gold Rush generation settlers. These young men often became key players in the transition from wheat to almonds, the specialty crop of choice in the region. When, for example, the 15 charter members of the Davisville Almond Growers' Association met in 1897 to form California's first nut cooperative, 11 of them were sons of pioneer wheat farmers, and 8 of the 11 had played for either the Oletas or the Etnas in the 1880s (Vaught 2007b).

Anxious to be distracted from their arduous daily routines and the uncertainties of the times, these young men found baseball to be the perfect antidote. They might have pursued horseracing, which was still very popular, but most found playing and watching baseball more satisfying. The two sports had much in common. The racetrack helped develop rural people's fascination with swift motion and sudden action, which the ball field, located in the middle of the track in both Dixon and Davisville, cultivated to the utmost. But baseball's new rules, adopted by the Oletas and the Etnas early in the decade, imposed a more precise, detailed order on its participants than did horseracing. On defense, players trotted out together to the same positions every inning and tried their best to hone their specific, individual skills for the good of the team; and on offense, they tried to hit the ball within the foul lines and away from the fielders, run the bases without being tagged out, and parlay their individual efforts into runs, the game's most meaningful measure of achievement. They performed these actions automatically, without pause for concern, because the game itself dictated it (Barth 1980; Story 2001). For young men mystified by the operations of the grain market and wary of the future, but like their fathers unable to admit failure or even the possibility of failure, baseball offered excitement, respite, stability, diversion, mutuality, and gratification – all in powerful, albeit short-term, doses.

Other factors also contributed to the "epidemic of baseball," to use Brown's apt phrase, that hit Davisville and Dixon in the 1880s (*Dixon Tribune*, March 15, 1895). Fathers did not want play to interrupt work. During the harvest of 1885, for example, an enraged father, shotgun in hand, stormed the Davisville diamond in the fourth inning and marched his son back to the farm – an action that no doubt reinforced the link between baseball and rebellion in the young man's mind. Members of the Oletas and Etnas also spoke of the game's "manly" qualities – its aggressive, competitive aspects – as did so many young Americans, both rural and urban, of this generation (Goldstein 1989). And baseball may even have helped tame two interrelated ethnocultural conflicts in the two towns. Since the early 1870s, a disgruntled minority, led by leaders of the Davisville Presbyterian Church, had decried the region's lack of respect for the Sabbath and temperance. Baseball on Sundays served only to fuel the fire, at first. But gradually, even the most militant reformers accepted and even welcomed the idea. "Some of the more thoughtful among the temperance advocates," explained Brown, "prefer to have the crowds at the ballgame rather than the alehouse" (*Dixon Tribune*, April 10, 1886). By the end of the 1880s, the saloonkeepers were the ones grumbling over the game's popularity.

The "epidemic of baseball" spread across racial lines as well, in one particularly illuminating instance. Two of the most valuable players on the Dixon Etnas in the mid-1880s, brothers José and Isidro Peña, had roots in the area much deeper than any of their teammates'. Their grandfather, Juan Felipe Peña, migrated to California in 1841 and two years later became co-owner of Rancho Los Putos, one of the three Mexican land grants in the area. Although the US Supreme Court confirmed Rancho Los Putos in 1857, the grantees remained mired in legal turmoil with squatters, speculators, and lawyers. By the early 1860s, only a small portion of the 44,000-acre grant remained in the Peña family. The overwhelmingly Anglo community of Dixon treated José and Isidro as social outcasts as they grew up – that is, until both brothers demonstrated that they could hit. The "Peña boys" became fixtures in the Etnas' lineup, José at second base and Isidro in centerfield, and led the team to numerous victories. Though Isidro died in a farm accident in 1894, José took advantage of his prowess on the ball field to become a successful cattleman. Descendants of the Peña family still reside in the area today – not entirely because of baseball, of course, but the game did help them carve out their place in the community (*Dixon Tribune*, April 11, 1885; Larkey 1969; Young 1971). Even baseball could not penetrate the rigid racial barriers between white farmers and Asian immigrants, who increasingly dominated the agricultural work force in the region. Later in the twentieth century, however, Chinese and Japanese residents in Northern California would form their own teams and become equally devoted to the game, albeit on segregated diamonds (Regalado 1992).

Perhaps the strongest symptom of the "baseball epidemic" was the widespread gambling that permeated the life of these two towns. This was not a new phenomenon. Farmers, by the very nature of their enterprise, were gamblers, "staking their all upon the season," as Brown put it (*Dixon Tribune*, February 12, 1887). Every year, they rolled the dice on the weather, the yield of their crop, and just when to sell it to get the best price. Most Putah Creek farmers came to the Golden State on a gamble. They also bet on billiards, dice games, pigeon shooting, the outcome of elections, whether or not someone would survive an illness – on just about anything. And gambling was the mother's milk of horseracing. So smitten was one Davisville farmer that he borrowed $100 to make a bet and then refused to pay it back when his horse lost the race. When his lender took him to court, the bettor insisted that anyone with any sense of honor would have given him another chance to pick a winner, and a jury of his peers agreed with him (Vaught 2007b).

Gambling deepened almost everyone's fascination with baseball as well. The modern game, with its ordered, rational rules, provided not only an antidote to the uncertainties of modern life, but an opportunity to bet on the uncertainties of modern life. Wagers could now be placed not only on the final score, but on whether or not the next batter would get a hit, the next pitch would be a strike, or the next fly ball would be caught (prompting bettors, on occasion, to fire their guns to disconcert the fielder and make him muff the ball). The players themselves were not averse to competing for substantial, winner-take-all purses, paying "revolvers" or "ringers" from nearby teams to "beef up" their lineups for important games; or even taking bribes to throw games. Gambling was as much a part of baseball as hitting, pitching, and running, and it was every bit as "epidemic" along Putah Creek (Seymour 1990; Vaught 2007b).

The measure of success was plain in baseball, and in the end that, as much as any one factor, attracted farmers to the game. More so than the various tavern sports and even horseracing, baseball tantalized them with the illusion that they could reverse their fortunes by simply courting Lady Luck or, when teams tried to fix games, by manipulating her. There was something inherently liberating about this notion. Win or lose, the outcome of the game (not to mention the games within the game) was clearly defined, in sharp contrast to the difference between success and failure on their farms. Baseball and gambling had a cultural meaning to players and fans beyond the chance to make money. It allowed them to entertain the same impulse that had failed them during the Gold Rush, the gamble of the century (Lears 2003). That impulse, along with the tradition of baseball games on Sunday evenings, persisted well into the twentieth century in Davisville and Dixon. Even as teams changed their names, wore uniforms, and played in more organized leagues, and even as "our National game of ball," as Brown called it, became more firmly entrenched, farmers continued to experience the game first and foremost as a local and rural pastime (*Dixon Tribune*, July 6, 1889).

The uncertainties of the times notwithstanding, Davisville and Dixon farmers (and most others across the state) eschewed the most sweeping farmer movement of the late nineteenth century – Populism. Traveling lecturers from the Farmers' Alliance tried to precipitate a mass protest in the Sacramento Valley, as they did in the American South and Midwest, but the few meetings held in Davisville and Dixon "excited but little interest" (*Dixon Tribune*, March 28, 1891). The fact that farmers identified so strongly with the "natural advantages of soil and climate" of their particular regions may have deterred mass organization; and their more favorable relationship with the Southern Pacific Railroad left them without a unifying target of protest (Magliari 1989). But farmers elsewhere joined the Farmers' Alliance and People's Party for reasons deeper than economics alone. For many, social isolation, a beaten self-image, and little means of self-expression made Alliance communities that much more appealing. Populism engendered within millions of farmers a "sense of somebodiness" (Goodwyn 1978: xxiv). Two generations of Davisville and Dixon farmers, however, did not find that sense lacking.

Farmers along Putah Creek tended to respond culturally, rather than politically, to the myriad of problems that accompanied the transformation of California agriculture. When they played baseball or rooted for their local team, farmers displayed some of the central elements of the state's rural culture – competitiveness, materialism, individualism, and mutuality. Baseball offered not only an outlet for the tensions of rural life, but a means of translating a core set of values, which they inherited from their fathers, into action. Each game was a great social drama, full of excitement, suspense, and opportunity, but void of paradox. Players and spectators could express themselves freely – take risks, even poorly calculated ones – with little regard to long-term consequences. Their very identity – that inner drive to produce, produce, produce – found expression and gratification on the ball field rather than the misery and frustration they so often experienced in their wheat fields. There was nothing magical about the game. Baseball came along at the right time in the right place to satisfy farmers' insatiable appetite for achievement in a world of change and chance. It may have been a source of rural nostalgia for city people, but it was the sport of choice for farmers and a powerful cultural agent.

REFERENCES

Barron, Hal S. 1997. *Mixed Harvest: The Second Great Transformation in the Rural North, 1870–1930.* Chapel Hill: University of North Carolina Press.

Barth, Gunther. 1980. *City People: The Rise of Modern City Culture in Nineteenth-Century America.* Oxford: Oxford University Press.

Barzun, Jacques. 1954. *God's Country and Mine: A Declaration of Love Spiced with a Few Harsh Words.* Boston, MA: Little, Brown.

Block, David. 2005. *Baseball Before We Knew It: A Search for the Roots of the Game.* Lincoln: University of Nebraska Press.

Breen, T. H. 1977. "Horses and Gentlemen: The Cultural Significance of Gambling among the Gentry of Virginia," *William and Mary Quarterly* 34 (April): 239–57.

Daniel, Cletus E. 1981. *Bitter Harvest: A History of California Farmworkers, 1870–1941*. Berkeley: University of California Press.

Faragher, John Mack. 1986. *Sugar Creek: Life on the Illinois Prairie*. New Haven, CT: Yale University Press.

Fite, Gilbert C. 1966. *The Farmers' Frontier, 1865–1900*. New York: Holt, Rinehart & Winston.

George, Henry. 1871. *Our Land and Land Policy, National and State*. San Francisco, CA: White & Bauer.

Gerber, Jim. 1992. "The Origin of California's Export Surplus in Cereals," *Agricultural History* 67 (Fall): 40–57.

Goldstein, Warren. 1989. *Playing for Keeps: A History of Early Baseball*. Ithaca, NY: Cornell University Press.

Goodwyn, Lawrence. 1978. *The Populist Moment: A Short History of the Agrarian Revolt in America*. Oxford: Oxford University Press.

Kelley, Robert. 1989. *Battling the Inland Sea: American Political Culture, Public Policy, and the Sacramento Valley, 1850–1986*. Berkeley: University of California Press.

Larkey, Joann Leach. 1969. *Davisville '68. The History and Heritage of the City of Davis, Yolo County, California*. Davis: Davis Historical and Landmarks Commission, 1969.

Lears, Jackson. 2003. *Something for Nothing: Luck in America*. New York: Viking.

Magliari, Michael. 1989. "Populism, Steamboats, and the Octopus: Transportation Rates and Monopoly in California's Wheat Regions, 1890–1896," *Pacific Historical Review* 58 (November): 449–69.

Magliari, Michael Frederick. 1991. "California Populism, A Case Study: The Farmers' Alliance and People's Party in San Luis Obispo County, 1885–1903." PhD dissertation, University of California, Davis.

McGowan, Joseph A. 1961. *History of the Sacramento Valley*. 3 vols. New York: Lewis Historical Publishing.

McWilliams, Carey. 1939. *Factories in the Field: The Story of Migratory Labor in California*. Boston, MA: Little, Brown.

Nelson, Kevin. 2004. *The Golden Game: The Story of California Baseball*. San Francisco: California Historical Society Press.

Neth, Mary. 1995. *Preserving the Family Farm: Women, Community, and the Foundations of Agribusiness in the Midwest, 1900–1940*. Baltimore, MD: Johns Hopkins University Press.

Norris, Frank. 1901. *The Octopus*. New York: Doubleday.

Orsi, Richard J. 1975. "*The Octopus* Reconsidered: The Southern Pacific and Agricultural Modernization in California, 1865–1915," *California Historical Quarterly* 54 (Fall): 196–220.

Paul, Rodman W. 1958a. "The Great California Grain War: The Grangers Challenge the Wheat King," *Pacific Historical Review* 27 (November): 331–49.

Paul, Rodman W. 1958b. "The Wheat Trade between California and the United Kingdom," *Mississippi Valley Historical Review* 45 (December): 391–412.

Paul, Rodman W. 1973. "The Beginnings of Agriculture in California: Innovation vs. Continuity," *California Historical Quarterly* 52 (Spring): 16–27.

Pisani, Donald J. 1984. *From the Family Farm to Agribusiness: The Irrigation Crusade in California and the West, 1850–1891.* Berkeley: University of California Press.

Regalado, Samuel O. 1992. "Sport and Community in California's Japanese American 'Yamato Colony,'" *Journal of Sport History* 19 (Summer): 130–43.

Rhode, Paul 1995. "Learning, Capital Accumulation, and the Transformation of California Agriculture," *Journal of Economic History* 55 (December): 773–800.

Rohrbough, Malcolm J. 1997. *Days of Gold: The California Gold Rush and the American Nation.* Berkeley: University of California Press.

Rothstein, Morton. 1987. *The California Wheat Kings.* Davis: University of California, Davis.

Sacramento Daily Union. Quoted within text.

Seymour, Harold. 1990. *Baseball: The People's Game.* Oxford: Oxford University Press.

Smith, Kenneth A. 1969. "California: The Wheat Decades." PhD dissertation, University of Southern California.

Spalding, John E. 1992. *Always on Sunday: The California Baseball League, 1886–1915.* Manhattan, KS: Ag Press.

Starr, Kevin. 1973. *Americans and the California Dream, 1850–1915.* New York: Oxford University Press.

Story, Ronald. 2001. "The Country of the Young: The Meaning of Baseball and Early American Culture." In John E. Dreifort, ed., *Baseball History From Outside the Lines: A Reader.* Lincoln: University of Nebraska Press.

Street, Richard Steven. 2004. *Beasts of the Field: A Narrative History of California Farm Workers.* Stanford, CA: Stanford University Press.

Vaught David. 2003. "After the Gold Rush: Replicating the Rural Midwest in the Sacramento Valley," *Western Historical Quarterly* 34 (Winter): 447–67.

Vaught, David. 2007a. *After the Gold Rush: Tainted Dreams in the Sacramento Valley.* Baltimore, MD: Johns Hopkins University Press.

Vaught, David. 2007b. "'Our Players are Mostly Farmers': Baseball in Rural California, 1850–1890." In Donald G. Kyle and Robert B. Fairbanks, eds., *Baseball in America and America in Baseball.* 41st Annual Walter Prescott Webb Memorial Lecture Series. College Station: Texas A&M University Press. My thanks to the editors for permission to reprint parts of this essay here.

Yolo Weekly Mail. Quoted within text.

Young, Wood 1971. *Vaca–Peña Los Putos Rancho and the Peña Adobe.* Vallejo, CA: Wheeler Printing and Publishing.

FURTHER READING

Brands, H. W. 2002. *The Age of Gold: The California Gold Rush and the New American Dream.* New York: Doubleday.

Davies, Richard O. 2007. *Sports in American Life: A History.* Malden, MA: Blackwell Publishing, Inc.

Gates, Paul Wallace. 1991. *Land and Law in California: Essays on Land Policy.* Ames: Iowa State University Press.

Paul, Rodman. 1988. *The Far West and the Great Plains in Transition, 1859–1900.* New York: Harper & Row.

Prescott, Gerald L. 1977/78. "Farm Gentry vs. the Grangers: Conflict in Rural America," *California Historical Quarterly* 56 (Winter): 328–45.

Tygiel, Jules. 2000. *Past Time: Baseball as History.* Oxford: Oxford University Press.

Vaught, David. 2000. "State of the Art – Rural History, or Why is There No Rural History of California," *Agricultural History* 74 (Fall): 759–74.

Chapter Thirteen

Transnational Commercial Orbits

Robert Chao Romero

Lee Kwong Lun emigrated to Cuba from his native Guangdong province in southern China during the second half of the nineteenth century. Following a brief sojourn in Cuba, where he developed proficiency in Spanish and acquired the skill of cigar making, Lee moved to San Francisco where he settled as a merchant and transitioned into life as husband and father. During the first decade of the twentieth century, following preparation of the documentation necessary to maintain and secure United States residency privileges for himself and his family under the merchant clause of the Chinese Exclusion Act, Lee gathered his wife and children together and migrated south of the border to Sonora, Mexico. In Sonora, Lee secured his economic livelihood as a merchant, serving as an economic middleman between Chinese merchants in Mexico and San Francisco's "Gold Mountain" wholesale suppliers. Utilizing his Spanish skills acquired in Cuba, his English proficiency developed in San Francisco, and his native Chinese language skills, Lee served as a transnational commercial broker and merchant, writing letters to California suppliers who delivered goods to Mexico by train for sale in Chinese shops. Following a decade-long tenure in Sonora, the Lee family returned to the United States where Lee Kwong continued his commercial activities as a merchant in Tucson, Arizona.[1]

The multinational travels of Lee Kwong Lun mark an important trans-Pacific Chinese commercial orbit of the late nineteenth and early twentieth centuries. This transnational exchange involving China, Latin America, Canada, and the Caribbean was shaped and traveled by enterprising Chinese merchants and capitalists who pursued commercial opportunities in human smuggling, labor contracting, wholesale merchandising, and small-scale trade. The path and contours of this transnational orbit were, moreover, fundamentally shaped by changes in United States and Mexican national immigration policy; most notably, by the US Chinese Exclusion Act of 1882 which barred the legal immigration of Chinese laborers to the United States. As is particularly relevant to this essay collection, California played a key role in this economic orbit, and was home to important business interests who developed and controlled its major commercial activities. Although this transnational orbit was shaped primarily by economic considerations, one unintended consequence that it produced was the development of distinctive "Asian-Latino" communities in Mexico and Latin America. This essay examines Chinese trans-Pacific migration patterns during the late nineteenth and early twentieth centuries and traces the historical development of this Chinese transnational commercial orbit during these years.

The Chinese Exclusion Act of 1882

Although the exact date on which Lee Kwong Lun immigrated to the United States from Cuba is not clear from the historical record, it is likely that he came to San Francisco sometime before 1882, the year of the passage of the Chinese Exclusion Act. This invidious federal legislation barred the immigration of Chinese laborers to the United States for a period of 10 years. Although the Chinese Exclusion Act made certain limited exceptions for merchants, students, and teachers, this legislation nonetheless effectively closed the door on most legal Chinese immigration (Hing 1993: 24; Gyory 1998: 1). The Chinese Exclusion Act of 1882, moreover, was the first federal legislation to specifically target an immigrant group for exclusion on the basis of race or nationality. In the Scott Act of 1888, the Geary Act of 1892, and in federal legislation of 1904, Congress extended these prohibitions and further tightened the reigns against Chinese immigration. The Scott Act banned not only the entrance of Chinese emigrant laborers, but also the re-entry of immigrant laborers with valid return certificates. The Geary Act of 1892 renewed the prohibition on Chinese immigration for 10 more years and required the official registration of all Chinese laborers. In 1904, Congress permanently barred Chinese immigration through the indefinite extension of the Chinese exclusion laws (ibid.). Because of these many restrictions imposed by the United States federal government upon Chinese immigration, it is likely that Lee Kwong Lun made his journey to the United States from Cuba sometime before their inception in 1882. Based upon the available information on his life, it does not appear that he acquired the privileged merchant status in Cuba that would have entitled him to legal entry under the Chinese Exclusion Act, and so it is likely that he entered the United States as a laborer sometime before 1882.

Chinese Immigration to California

Lee Kwong Lun's immigration to California corresponded with the larger migration of more than 335,000 Chinese to the United States between the years of 1848 and 1882. As discussed in William Deverell's essay earlier in this volume, Chinese immigrants were first attracted to the United States in large numbers by the California Gold Rush of the late 1840s and early 1850s; their increasing presence exacerbated the tendencies of white Californians to respond to the Chinese with discrimination and racial violence. In the year 1852 alone, 20,000 Chinese entered the United States through the port of San Francisco in search of instant wealth. Along with ore adventurers, a small but significant number of Cantonese merchants also arrived during this first wave of Chinese immigration to California. Entrepreneurial-minded merchants like Lee Kwong made substantial fortunes through the provision of food and other supplies to Anglo and Chinese miners, as well as by serving as passage brokers and labor contractors for Cantonese immigrants wishing to try their luck on "Gold Mountain." Bringing their own financial capital from Guangdong, many invested in restaurants and stores which catered to both Chinese and Anglo clientele. As part of the "credit-ticket system," merchant passage brokers advanced funds to cover immigration expenses for laborers who agreed to repay these passage loans over a designated period of time at a monthly interest rate of somewhere between 4 percent and 8 percent. In addition, as part of this arrangement and as security for the loan, immigrant laborers also consented to sell their services to designated labor contractors in the United States (Walker 1976: 25–8; Mei 1979: 475; Chan 1991: 27–8).

The year 1867 initiated the second big wave of Chinese immigration to California, precipitated in part by the recruitment of Cantonese immigrants as laborers for the construction of the transcontinental railroad by the Central Pacific Railroad Company. Approximately 40,000 Chinese entered the United States between the years of 1867 and 1870 as part of this second movement of Cantonese immigrants to California. In 1877, the size of the Chinese community of California was estimated to be 148,000 (Mei 1979: 486; Chan 1991: 28).

Most Chinese in California emigrated from 10 districts of Cantonese South China: Xinning/Toisan, Xinhui, Kaiping, Enping, Xiangshan/Chungshan, Chixi, Baoan/Sun-on Panyu, Nanhai, and Shunde. Siyi, the term given for the conglomeration of the Xinning, Xinhui, Kaiping, and Enping districts, generated the greatest number of American-bound Chinese immigrants. In addition, although most Cantonese merchants of the early wave of Chinese migration originated from the vicinity of the port city of Canton, most emigrant laborers came from more outlying counties of the Guangdong province (Mei 1979: 476).

Although the two large waves of Cantonese migration to California were precipitated largely by the Sacramento Gold Rush and the recruitment of migrants for construction of the transcontinental railroad, Chinese immigrants soon filled a wide range of laboring activities. Cantonese immigrants were ubiquitous in the state's menial service sector, serving in various positions such as domestics, launderers, agricultural laborers, miners, and manufacturing plant workers. In the 1870s and early 1880s, Chinese comprised one-twelfth of the total population of California and made up one-quarter to one-fifth of the total number of the state's laborers. Because of their amenability to low wages and their reputation for being industrious and dependable, Chinese immigrants were initially praised and welcomed by government authorities (Saxton 1971: 7, 258; Hing 1993: 20–1).

Notwithstanding the official welcoming of Cantonese immigrant laborers, sinophobic sentiment surfaced almost from the time of the earliest arrival of Chinese nationals in the 1940s. Anti-Chinese activists successfully lobbied for an invidious tax targeting Cantonese miners in 1852, and during the early 1850s anti-Chinese xenophobia expressed itself in the forms of "anti-coolie" clubs, bigoted newspaper editorials, and boycotts of Chinese commercial products. The 1860s and 1870s witnessed a rise in anti-Chinese sentiment especially amongst white workers, and during these years the Chinese immigrant community became the focus of both a wide-scale political campaign spearheaded by the Democratic Party and a labor organization movement led by skilled trade union officials. Caucasian laborers viewed Chinese workers as unfair competition, because of their willingness to work for low wages based upon their status as indentured laborers. Moreover, according to historian Alexander Saxton, the Democratic Party and skilled craft union organizers manipulated popular anti-Chinese sentiment during these years for their selfish advantage. Crippled by its political defeat over the issue of slavery as a consequence of the outcome of the Civil War, the Democratic Party successfully resuscitated itself during the 1860s in California through the harnessing of popular anti-Chinese sentiment. Appealing to supporters of the xenophobic movement, the Democratic Party led the rally against Chinese immigrants by offering a full slate of sinophobic candidates in the 1867 state elections. In part based upon their political stance against Chinese immigration, the Democrats swept the 1867 elections, securing the gubernatorial post, a large Assembly majority, and two out of three congressional seats (Saxton 1971; Hing 1993).

Like the Democratic Party, trade union officials during the late nineteenth and early twentieth centuries also manipulated popular anti-Chinese sentiment for their own purposes. Isolated from the craft union strongholds of the East Coast, California trade union organizers reached out to unskilled workers in order to strengthen their West Coast power base. To this end, craft union officials appealed to unskilled laborers by manipulating sinophobic rhetoric as a means of attracting support. By the second decade of the twentieth century, San Francisco was hailed as a trade union bastion, in part due to the manipulation of anti-Chinese sentiment by trade union organizers.

One consequence of the scapegoating of Chinese immigrants by labor unions and the Democratic Party was the nationalization of the Chinese question and the promulgation of various types of discriminatory legislation, such as the Chinese Exclusion Act of 1882 and the Scott and Geary Acts. As previously discussed, such xenophobic legislation targeted both the resident Chinese community and potential Chinese immigrants, and had the effect of barring virtually all legal emigration from China to the United States (Saxton 1971; Hing 1993).

Unintended Consequences

One unintended consequence of the closure of the United States to Chinese immigration was the diversion of Chinese migration streams to Mexico and other parts of Latin America. In response to legal prohibitions against them in the United States, Chinese immigrants journeyed to Mexico for two main purposes: First, in order to be smuggled illegally into the United States; and, second, in search of jobs and various employment opportunities in the developing Mexican economy (Romero 2003 51). Though it is not widely known, the Chinese were the first "illegal aliens" from Mexico. The Chinese created the first organized system of immigrant smuggling from Mexico even before native Mexicans themselves (Lee 2003; Romero 2004/2005). The Chinese Six Companies, a transnational immigrant fraternal organization based out of San Francisco, was reportedly the chief sponsor of the illicit traffic of Chinese immigrants.

The Chinese Six Companies was founded in California during the mid-nineteenth century in response to the legal and racial discrimination experienced by the Chinese immigrant community of San Francisco. Membership of the Chinese Six Companies was originally comprised of representatives of the five major Cantonese district-of-origin associations of San Francisco, and the main purpose of the organization was to provide legal and political representation for the Chinese immigrant community. Over time, the Chinese Six Companies branched out and comprised an international commercial network with members involved in various forms of transnational import–export commerce (Romero 2004/2005).

As part of their efforts to circumvent the Chinese Exclusion Act of 1882 and its later legislative expressions, the Chinese Six Companies created a vast, transnational smuggling business involving representatives in China, Mexico, Cuba, and many cities in the United States, including San Francisco, San Diego, El Paso, Tucson, New York, Boston, and New Orleans. In the late nineteenth century, Havana, Cuba was reportedly the headquarters for the Chinese immigrant smuggling business established by the Six Companies. The smuggling business was coordinated from Havana because the city was home to a key official of the Six Companies who possessed strategic connections to important transportation companies. Chin Pinoy directed the smuggling trade from his offices in Havana and served as both Eastern Chief of the Chinese Six Companies and "Chinese agent" for the Pacific Railroad Company, the Morgan steamship line, and the Ward Steamship Company. Chinese agents were responsible for the supervision of Chinese passengers traveling to and through the United States, and Chin utilized his important connections to facilitate the illegal entry of Chinese into the United States. Chin and the Chinese Six Companies developed a variety of schemes and techniques to smuggle Chinese immigrants into the United States (Romero 2004/2005).

One popular technique resembled the contemporary smuggling practice of using a "coyote," or guide, to transport undocumented immigrants surreptitiously across the international border. According to this procedure, immigrants made smuggling arrangements through Six Company representatives in the United States and China. Prospective migrants traveled to Chinese port cities such as Hong Kong where they received instruction in English and American culture and were subsequently shipped to Mexico by steamship. Upon arrival in Mexican port cities such as Mazatlan, Manzanillo, and Guaymas, they were met by Six Company representatives, received vocational training and cultural instruction, and were eventually transported by train to Mexican border cities in the Southwest. Mexican "coyotes" delivered these immigrants across the international line to Six Company agents who assigned them fictive identities of United States citizens and placed them in jobs. Chinese immigrants adopted entire falsified biographies which proved their legal right to be in the country. When such immigrants were called to court by immigration officials on charges of illegally entering the United States, the Chinese Six Companies arranged for the testimony of false but convincing witnesses who corroborated the immigrants' fabricated identities. This technique was especially effective after the destruction of San Francisco municipal birth records in the earthquake and fire of 1906. The absence of official documentation made it difficult for immigration officials to disprove the fictive identities of Chinese immigrants. Commenting upon the popularity of this method, one Immigration Service official wrote "that if all of those who claimed to have been born in San Francisco had actually been born there, each Chinese woman then in the United States would have had to produced something like 150 children"(Romero 2004/2005: 4–5).

A second smuggling technique developed by the Chinese Six Companies involved the "substitution" of Chinese immigrants stopped temporarily in United States ports while en route to China or Latin America. Although

Chinese laborers were barred from immigrating to the United States after 1882, they were allowed to land by steamship at United States sea ports and travel to Mexico by train. Upon arrival in the United States, customs officials required Chinese laborers to produce a train ticket that verified their passage to Mexico. In addition, US immigration policy required that the transportation company or "some responsible person on behalf of the laborer" post a penal bond of at least $200 in order to guarantee the safe arrival of Chinese passengers at Mexican ports. These penal bonds were refunded to the sponsoring person or agency upon the timely arrival of Chinese immigrants at Mexican ports. In addition to this privilege which allowed Chinese laborers to travel "in transit" to Mexico through United States territory, a second legal loophole permitted Chinese residents of Mexico to travel by train to US sea ports such as New York City and San Francisco in order to catch commercial steamships bound for China.

Chinese smugglers exploited the "in transit" privilege through an innovative technique known as "substitution." Chinese in-transit passengers frequently spent several days of "lay over" in US port cities while awaiting the arrival of steamships that would take them to China or trains that were to transport them to Mexico. During these brief stops, Chinese immigrants were sometimes allowed to vacation in port cities under the supervision of "Chinese agents," such as Chin Pinoy, who were hired by transportation companies to ensure that undocumented lay-over passengers did not escape unlawfully into the United States. According to the "substitution" technique, Chinese agents made deals with Chinese legal residents of the United States to be "substituted" in the place of lay-over passengers. Following the swapping of identities, Chinese laborers would slip away illegally into the United States and blend themselves into the local Chinese community. In turn, "substitutes" would receive a generous payment fee and a free trip to Mexico, Cuba, or even China. Because of their documented legal status, moreover, substitutes could return to the United States whenever they wished. Because this was such a lucrative business arrangement, some even developed a niche as "professional" substitutes (Romero 2004/2005).

In summary, the passage of the Chinese Exclusion Act of 1882 resulted in the creation of a highly sophisticated transnational smuggling business organized and directed by the Chinese Six Companies of San Francisco. In circumvention of this exclusionary legislation, the Six Companies established a transnational smuggling network involving representatives in China, Mexico, Cuba, California, and various cities throughout the United States. It is estimated that as many as 1,000–2,000 Chinese illegally entered the United States annually between 1876 and 1911 (Lee 2003). This global smuggling network established by the Six Companies formed the basis for the Chinese transnational commercial orbit in the Americas during the late nineteenth and early twentieth centuries.

Chinese Immigration and Settlement in Mexico, 1882–1940

In response to the legal prohibitions of the Chinese Exclusion Act of 1882, Chinese immigrants traveled to Mexico not only to be smuggled into the United States, but also in search of economic opportunities within the developing Mexican economy. Ironically, the Chinese exclusionary movement in the United States coincided with the recruitment of Chinese immigrant laborers by the Mexican government. In accordance with the economic modernization plan of Mexican President Porfirio Diaz, Mexico first sought to attract European immigrants to colonize the frontier farming and mining regions of northern Mexico, fill labor shortages, and facilitate the westernization of Mexican society. Following its failure to attract sufficient numbers of European immigrants, the Mexican government turned to the recruitment of Chinese laborers as a means of satisfying the heightened labor demands of agriculture and mining in northern Mexico. In 1899, following extensive diplomatic negotiations, Mexico and China signed a Treaty of Amity, Commerce, and Navigation which accorded China "most favored nation" status and which, in theory, granted Chinese immigrants in Mexico all the rights and privileges owed subjects of a "most favored nation." Most significantly, the treaty opened wide the floodgates of Chinese migration to Mexico by permitting "free and voluntary" movement between the two countries.

As part of its efforts to recruit Chinese immigrant laborers, the Mexican government turned to Chinese merchants of San Francisco. Mexican officials collaborated with Chinese "mafia" tong leaders of San Francisco to develop a plan for the systematic recruitment of Chinese contract laborers. As part of their deal, Chinese merchants of California promised to solicit Chinese emigrant laborers under contract at Chinese port cities like Hong Kong and Shanghai. Tong agents covered immigration costs for emigrant laborers in exchange for repayment at steep rates of interest. In addition, as part of this arrangement between Chinese merchants and Ramon Corral, Corral and other influential Mexican officials were paid a monetary sum for each Chinese contract laborer who reached Mexican shores. In many ways, this scheme resembled the "credit ticket system" practiced in California just a few decades before, and it is possible that some Chinese merchants may have served as passage brokers and labor contractors in the recruitment of Chinese laborers in both California and Mexico (Romero 2003).

Upon arrival at Mexican ports like Mazatlan, Manzanillo, and Salina Cruz, contracted Chinese laborers were met by agents of the Chinese tongs. These agents, moreover, instructed recent arrivals in basic Spanish and the fundamentals of Mexican culture. Contract laborers were then distributed in jobs throughout various cities, towns, and haciendas. In addition, established Chinese merchants from California sometimes extended credit to recent immigrants to help them start up basic street vending businesses. Based upon the historical record, it appears that this procedure for the recruitment of Chinese contract laborers functioned as part of the same commercial network created for the smuggling of immigrant Chinese into the United States via Mexico. Both contract labor recruitment and immigrant smuggling seem to have operated within the same transnational commercial orbit, and likely involved many of the same key financial business interests and players. In both cases, influential Chinese merchants of San Francisco played central roles in the development and ultimate success of these commercial ventures (Romero 2003).

Although Chinese immigrants were first recruited to Mexico to fill labor shortages in the Mexican economy, many Chinese made the transition to employment in the commercial sector as small-scale merchants within a short period of time. By 1926, Mexico's nearly 25,000 Chinese immigrants came to comprise the second largest foreign ethnic community in the entire nation. By 1930, more than 36 percent of the total Chinese population was employed in the field of commerce. In this regard, Chinese settlement patterns in Mexico differed greatly from those in California. Although merchants formed an important and influential segment of the Chinese community in California, Chinese movement to the United States was by and large still considered a labor migration. In Mexico, however, Chinese immigrants came to be perceived as a community of merchants who operated in the Mexican economy as proprietors of grocery and dry goods stores. Chinese shops were ubiquitous and dotted the northern Mexican landscape in Sonora, Chihuahua, and Baja California. Much like "7–11" convenience stores in the United States today, Chinese grocery and dry goods stores were found on virtually every street corner in places like Sonora. By the 1920s Chinese merchants came to monopolize small-scale trade in all of northern Mexico. Their great success engendered organized anti-Chinese protests and campaigns replete with lootings, boycotts, massacres, and sinophobic legislation that banned Chinese–Mexican intermarriage and ordered the segregation of Chinese into racially restricted neighborhoods.[2] The anti-Chinese campaigns culminated in 1931 with the expulsion of virtually the entire Chinese population from the state of Sonora (Romero 2003).

Like Lee Kwong Lun, the earliest Chinese merchants of Mexico were businessmen who journeyed to Mexico from California in search of economic opportunities within the developing Mexican economy of the late nineteenth century. As early as 1889, United States consular reports record the presence of a significant community of Chinese laborers sent to work in a Baja California mining venture organized by Chinese investors from San Francisco (Romero 2003: 63). Lee Kwong himself relocated his family from San Francisco to Sonora in search of commercial opportunities, and secured his economic livelihood in Mexico by serving as an economic middleman between Chinese merchants in Mexico and San Francisco's "Gold Mountain" wholesale suppliers.

Although some of the Chinese merchant population of Mexico came from established commercial backgrounds in California, the vast majority did not. Most members of the Chinese merchant community of Mexico immigrated directly from China with small amounts of personal capital. These aspiring merchants started up small businesses in Mexico with savings earned as laborers in haciendas or as employees in shops and restaurants owned by kinsmen and fellow compatriots. As previously mentioned, some recent immigrants were also extended credit by established merchants from California in order to begin their small businesses.

Although these were common ways for generating start-up capital, one of the most important means by which Chinese entrepreneurs gained access to business capital was through the pooling of transnational capital from small, individual investors. The Yat Sang Company, a Calexico-based business that conducted transnational commercial sales on both sides of the international line, exemplifies this strategy. Specializing in wholesale and resale trade in American and Mexican groceries and general merchandise, the Yat Sang Company consisted of 12 partners. Although the daily affairs of the firm were supervised and conducted by six partners residing in Calexico, California, the remaining silent partners lived in disparate locations in Los Angeles, Oakland, and Canton, China. Each of the partners, both silent and active, contributed $1,000 towards the early capitalization of the business for an impressive capital base of $12,000 in 1923. The Yat Sang Company, was, moreover, conspicuously marked by kinship connections between its investors. Eight of the 12 partners shared a surname with at least one other investor. As shown by this example, Chinese borderland merchants were able to begin new commercial enterprises by drawing from a multiplicity of transnational familial sources. Although the financial resources of any individual Chinese immigrant might be insufficient to start a business, this strategy enabled Chinese entrepreneurs to become partners in well-capitalized commercial ventures (Romero 2003).

The Mexicali-based firm of Pablo Chee & Company further demonstrates this strategy of pooled commercial investment and also highlights the transnational nature of Chinese commercial investment. The Pablo Chee firm was a well-capitalized, high-powered commercial partnership which owned and managed a Mexican hotel, saloon, and grocery store. In 1924, the Pablo Chee firm consisted of five partners. Although Pablo Chee managed the Mexicali firm and was its principal investor, he himself was a US resident of Calexico, California. The assistant manager of the firm, Chee Chung Huey, and the grocery department manager, Quan Yuet, resided in Mexicali, Mexico. The two silent partners, Chung Wee Cho and Chung Puey, lived in San Francisco and Oakland, California. Although the firm was based in Mexico, Pablo Chee, the main partner and primary investor, lived in Calexico, California. Based upon a special border-crossing permit issued by the United States Immigration and Naturalization Service, Chee crossed regularly into Mexico to manage his business affairs. Moreover, although the firm's two other managers resided in Mexicali, Mexico, the two silent investors lived hundreds of miles away in the Bay Area of San Francisco. As with the Yat Sang Company, most of the firm's members appear to be connected by ostensible ties of kinship based upon the commonality of family names. Marked by ties of kinship and a multinational capital base, the Pablo Chee Company clearly indicates the operation of a Chinese transnational commercial orbit of the early twentieth century that encompassed northern and eastern California and the borderlands of Baja California, Mexico (Romero 2003).

In addition to this practice of transnational capital investment based upon family ties, another aspect of the transnational Chinese commercial orbit involved the provision of wholesale supplies and goods for sale in Mexican shops. Chinese grocery and dry goods merchants in Mexico purchased much of their store inventory from Chinese and Anglo wholesale suppliers of the United States. For example, Lee Kwong Lun served as an economic middleman between Chinese store owners in Sonora, Mexico and California wholesale suppliers. Taking orders from Chinese retailers, Lee Kwong wrote letters to San Francisco wholesalers who delivered goods to Mexico by train for sale in Chinese shops. As another example, the Pablo Chee Company also purchased supplies for its hotel and bar from various transnational vendors. The firm bought whiskey and alcohol from Canada and Mexico and other items from Calexico, Los Angeles, and San Francisco. The Yat Sang Company also purchased goods from United States wholesale suppliers, and even engaged in the wholesale trade itself by selling large quantities of its own merchandise to Chinese merchants in Mexico. At the height of its wholesale business activities, the Yat Sang Company averaged $5,000 per month in sales in Mexicali (Romero 2003).

Chinese merchants purchased supplies for their Mexican businesses not only through commercial middlemen like Lee Kwong, but also by crossing regularly into the United States and ordering directly from wholesale suppliers. Special border-crossing permits issued by the Immigration and Naturalization Service (INS) granted certain Chinese borderland merchants the right to enter the United States in order to purchase supplies for their Mexican stores. In order to qualify for such commercial permits, Chinese merchants went through an elaborate application process which required them to prove that they were bona fide merchants. As part of this procedure, INS agents visited the business establishments of prospective applicants and conducted extensive oral histories as a means of determining the legitimacy of alleged merchant status. Those who survived this rigorous screening process were granted the right to cross into the United States on a routine basis in order to purchase supplies for their shops. Significant numbers of Chinese borderland merchants purchased wholesale goods for their businesses in this manner (Romero 2003).

Conclusion

California played a key role in the historical development of an elaborate transnational Chinese commercial orbit during the late nineteenth and early twentieth centuries. This transnational economic orbit encompassed China, California, Mexico, and the Caribbean, and was shaped and controlled by enterprising Chinese merchants and capitalists who pursued commercial opportunities in human smuggling, labor contracting, wholesale merchandising, and small-scale trade. The development of this commercial orbit was directly shaped, moreover, by the vicissitudes of United States and Mexican immigration policy toward the Chinese. With the doors to legal immigration to the United States closed to them in the years following the passage of the Chinese Exclusion Act of 1882, thousands of Chinese emigrants traveled to Mexico to be smuggled into the United States or to search for economic opportunities in the developing Mexican economy. In response to the exclusion of Chinese immigrant laborers from the United States, the Chinese Six Companies of San Francisco organized an extensive transnational smuggling network involving California, China, Mexico, Cuba, and various cities throughout the southwestern and southeastern United States. This international smuggling network formed the basis for a broader Chinese transnational commercial orbit which thrived well into the twentieth century.

In addition to immigrant smuggling, one important activity of this commercial orbit involved the recruitment of contract laborers for the mines and haciendas of northern Mexico. Ironically, the passage of the Chinese Exclusion laws in the United States coincided with efforts of the Mexican government to recruit Chinese immigrants as laborers for its developing economy. An organized system of contract labor was developed by Mexican business interests in direct collaboration with prominent Chinese merchants of San Francisco.

Although initially recruited as contract laborers, many Chinese immigrants in Mexico transitioned into employment as merchants involved in the grocery and dry goods trade. Over a short period of time, Chinese immigrant merchants developed a monopoly on small-scale trade in northern Mexico, and their great success prompted an organized anti-Chinese movement in Mexico whose stated central aim was the elimination of the Chinese immigrant merchant. Chinese merchants thrived in large measure because of their ability to mobilize large amounts of transnational capital from family and friends residing in China, Mexico, and California. This gave them a critical commercial advantage vis-à-vis native Mexican merchants, who were likely limited in their ability to launch new business activities based upon the extent of their personal savings and resources. This strategy of pooled commercial investment from various transnational sources was one important reason for Chinese mercantile success, and it also represents one further example of the functioning of the larger Chinese transnational commercial orbit of the early twentieth century.

There is a great need for further research examining the important transnational socioeconomic and political connections which tied together Chinese diasporic communities during the late nineteenth and early twentieth centuries. While excellent studies exist which highlight and discuss the rich transnational ties between overseas Chinese communities and China, much less is known about the historical interactions between and amongst Chinese immigrants living in places like California, Mexico, Cuba, Peru, Canada, Australia, and Southeast Asia. [3] Much more research is needed to illuminate the transnational socioeconomic and political linkages shared by Chinese diasporic communities during these years in the forms of transnational border networks, transnational business investments, transnational human smuggling networks, transpacific families, and transnational political organizing.

There is also a need for further scholarship examining Asian immigration to Latin America and the experience of "Asian Latinos" in the United States. Although wide-scale Chinese migration to Mexico began in the late nineteenth century as part of the transnational commercial orbit examined in this essay, Asian migration to Latin America dates back to the sixteenth century as part of the Spanish Manila Galleon trade. Moreover, more than a million Asians of Chinese, Taiwanese, Korean, and Japanese ancestry currently reside in Latin America. Many Asian secondary migrants from Latin America have also immigrated to the United States in recent years. According to the 2000 United States national census, more than 300,000 individuals self-identify as "Asian Latino." This sociological category embraces two classes of individuals: Asian secondary migrants from Latin America currently living in the United States and individuals of cross-cultural Asian and Latino parentage. Although a growing body of scholarship is developing concerning the Japanese population of Brazil, little has been written about the experience of other Asian immigrant groups in other countries of Latin America.[4] Moreover, a very limited body of scholarship exists concerning the large population of "Asian Latinos" in the United States.[5]

A new literature is necessary which examines these overlooked populations of Asians in Latin America and "Asian Latinos" of the United States. Such a research agenda would blend the fields of Latin American Studies, Asian American Studies, and Chicano/Latino Studies, and might be termed "Asian-Latino Studies," or (more playfully), "Chino-Chicano Studies." In addition to studying the sociological and historical experiences of "Asian Latinos," this new field of study would highlight the often overlooked Asian contributions to Latin American and Chicano/Latino culture and identity, and examine historic and contemporary relations between these two ethnic groups in the United States, Mexico, Central America, South America, and the Caribbean.

NOTES

1 Mike Tom, interview with author, August 24, 2001, San Bruno, California.
2 For a detailed examination of Chinese–Mexican intermarriage in early twentieth-century Mexico, see Romero, "*El destierro de los chinos*: Popular Perspectives of Chinese–Mexican Interracial Marriage As Reflected in Comedy, Cartoons, Poetry, and Musical Recordings of the UCLA Frontera Collection."
3 See, for example, Chan, *Chinese American Transnationalism: The Flow of People, Resources, and Ideas Between China and America during the Chinese Exclusion Era*; Chen, *Chinese San Francisco, 1850–1943: A Transpacific Community*; Hsu, *Dreaming of Gold, Dreaming of Home: Transnationalism and Migration Between the United States and South China, 1882–1943*; and Liu, *The Transnational History of a Chinese Family: Immigrant Letters, Family Business, and Reverse Migration*. Adam McKeown's work represents one notable example of a study examining the transnational socioeconomic connections between Chinese diasporic communities. See McKeown, *Chinese Migrant Networks and Cultural Change: Peru, Chicago, Hawaii, 1900–1936*. For examination of the transnational socioeconomic and political ties between the Chinese communities of Mexico and the United States, see Romero, "The Dragon in Big Lusong: Chinese Immigration and Settlement in Mexico, 1882–1940."
4 Recent studies of the Japanese of Brazil include Lesser, *Searching for Home Abroad: Japanese Brazilians and Transnationalism* and Masterson, *The Japanese in Latin America*.
5 Notable exceptions include Guevarra, "Burritos and Bagoong: Mexipinos and Multiethnic Identity in San Diego, California," and "Clueless"; Delgado, "In the Age of Exclusion: Race, Region, and Chinese Identity in the Making of the Arizona–Sonora Borderlands, 1863–1943"; Ropp, "Secondary Migration and the Politics of Identity for Asian Latinos in Los Angeles"; and Park & Park, "A New American Dilemma?: Asian Americans and Latinos in Race Theorizing."

REFERENCES

Chan, Sucheng. 1991. *Asian Americans: An Interpretive History.* Boston, MA: Twayne Publishers.

Chan, Sucheng. 2005. *Chinese American Transnationalism: The Flow of People, Resources, and Ideas Between China and America during the Chinese Exclusion Era.* Philadelphia, PA: Temple University Press.

Chan, Sucheng, ed. 2006. *China and America during the Chinese Exclusion Era.* Philadelphia, PA: Temple University Press.

Gyory, Andrew. 1998. *Closing the Gate: Race, Politics, and the Chinese Exclusion Act.* Chapel Hill: University of North Carolina Press.

Hing, Bill O. 1993. *Making and Remaking Asian America Through Immigration Policy, 1850–1990.* Stanford, CA: Stanford University Press.

Lee, Erika. 2003. *At America's Gates: Chinese Immigration During the Exclusion Era, 1882–1940.* Chapel Hill: University of North Carolina Press.

Mei, June. 1979. "Socioeconomic Origins of Emigration: Guandong to California, 1850–1882," *Modern China* 13 (4): 463–500.

Romero, Robert Chao. 2003. "The Dragon in Big Lusong: Chinese Immigration and Settlement in Mexico, 1882–1940." PhD dissertation, UCLA.

Romero, Robert Chao. 2004/2005. "Transnational Chinese Immigrant Smuggling to the United States via Mexico and Cuba, 1882–1916," *Amerasia Journal* 30: 3.

Saxton, Alexander. 1971. *The Indispensable Enemy.* Berkeley: University of California Press.

Walker, Townsend. 1976. "Gold Mountain Guests: Chinese Migration to the United States, 1848–1882." PhD dissertation, Stanford University.

FURTHER READING

Chen, Yong. 2000. *Chinese San Francisco, 1850–1943: A Transpacific Community.* Stanford, CA: Stanford University Press.

Delgado, Grace. 2000. "In the Age of Exclusion: Race, Region, and Chinese Identity in the Making of the Arizona–Sonora Borderlands, 1863–1943." PhD dissertation, UCLA.

Guevarra, Rudy. 2003. "Burritos and Bagoong: Mexipinos and Multiethnic Identity in San Diego, California," and "Clueless." In Marc Coronado, Rudy P. Guevarra, Jeffrey Moniz, and Laura Furlan Szanto, eds., *Crossing Lines: Race and Mixed Race Across the Geohistorical Divide.* Santa Barbara: Multiethnic Student Outreach, University of California, Santa Barbara.

Hsu, Madeline. 2000. *Dreaming of Gold, Dreaming of Home: Transnationalism and Migration Between the United States and South China, 1882–1943.* Stanford, CA: Stanford University Press.

Hu-DeHart, Evelyn. 1980. "Immigrants to a Developing Society: The Chinese in Northern Mexico, 1875–1932," *Journal of Arizona History* (Autumn): 275–312.

Lee, Erika. 2002. "Enforcing the Borders: Chinese Exclusion along the US Borders with Canada and Mexico, 1882–1924," *Journal of American History* 89 (1) (January).

Lesser, Jeffrey, ed. 2003. *Searching for Home Abroad: Japanese Brazilians and Transnationalism*. Durham, NC: Duke University Press.

Liu, Haiming. 2005. *The Transnational History of a Chinese Family: Immigrant Letters, Family Business, and Reverse Migration*. New Brunswick: Rutgers University Press.

Masterson, Daniel. 2003. *The Japanese in Latin America*. Champaign: Illinois University Press.

McKeown, Adam. 2001. *Chinese Migrant Networks and Cultural Change: Peru, Chicago, Hawaii, 1900–1936*. Chicago: University of Chicago Press.

Park, Edward J. W. and Park, John S. W. 1999. "A New American Dilemma?: Asian Americans and Latinos in Race Theorizing," *Journal of Asian American Studies* 2 (3): 289–309.

Renique, Gerardo. 2003. "Race, Region, and Nation: Sonora's Anti-Chinese Racism and Mexico's Postrevolutionary Nationalism, 1920s–1930s." In Nancy Appelbaum, et al., eds., *Race and Nation in Modern Latin America*. Chapel Hill: University of North Carolina Press.

Romero, Robert. 2007. "*El destierro de los chinos*: Popular Perspectives of Chinese–Mexican Interracial Marriage as Reflected in Comedy, Cartoons, Poetry, and Musical Recordings of the UCLA Frontera Collection." *Aztlan: A Journal of Chicano Studies* (Spring).

Ropp, Steven Masami. 2000. "Secondary Migration and the Politics of Identity for Asian Latinos in Los Angeles," *Journal of Asian American Studies* (June): 219–29.

Yu, Henry. 2004. "Los Angeles and American Studies in a Pacific World of Migrations," *American Quarterly* 56 (3): 531–43.

Chapter Fourteen

RECONSIDERING CONSERVATION

Benjamin Heber Johnson

California's culture and landscape reflect the power and successes of conservation. Golden State residents are among the nation's most enthusiastic outdoor recreationists. The Sierra Club, the nation's oldest environmental organization, remains headquartered in San Francisco more than a century after its founding by John Muir and other Northern Californians. Yosemite National Park, run by California as a state park from 1864 to 1872, epitomizes wild nature to the three and a half million visitors it draws annually from across the world. The more materialist side of conservation is also inscribed on the landscape, with national forests still providing the watershed protection and timber production that their founders expected. It is little wonder, then, that in 2005 California Governor Arnold Schwarzenegger chose an image of Sierra Club founder John Muir admiring the Yosemite Valley to adorn the state's quarter.

Much of California's conservation landscape was created during the Progressive Era roughly from the 1890s to 1920, when large portions of the American public came to believe that the power of the government could be used to address problems created by industrialization. Conservation – the search for a material balance and psychic renewal with a nature believed to be imperiled and at risk of exhaustion by the new power of industrial society – was a critical part of Progressivism. Conservationists enjoyed numerous successes in this period, bringing millions of acres of forest and mountain under the control of public lands bureaucracies in this period, in California as the rest of the nation. Over the last 50 years, environmental and political historians have devoted great attention to the sportsmen, outdoor enthusiasts, natural scientists and others wary of the unsustainable consumption of resources who spearheaded these efforts.

A deeper look at the California landscape and how it was remade during the Progressive Era suggests the need for a broader understanding of conservation and its role in California history. Many who called themselves "conservationists" were also active in cities, where they agitated for the creation of parks. They welcomed the creation of streetcar and early automobile suburbs as places where Americans could find some respite from commercial life in the nature in their own yards and gardens. Moreover, conservation measures, whether urban or rural, came out of a wider cultural search for some kind of re-engagement with nature. Some Progressives drew no strict line between the human and natural worlds. Much of the domestic architecture of the early twentieth century, for example, was explicitly designed to evoke the wider non-human world in order to offer an antidote to the supposed psychological harms of life in industrial cities. The environmental impulse in American culture is much deeper than scholars have given credit. Long before the word "environmentalist" was coined, influential Californians from a wide range of social groups thought that the search for a balanced, healthy relationship with nature was one of the most important tasks facing them and their state.

If conservationists, in California as elsewhere, found that they had to pay attention to many kinds of places in their efforts to rectify what they saw as an alienated and exploitative relationship with nature, then they also came to realize that what they thought about nature had importance consequences for human beings as well. If the government was going to set aside large tracts of land as parks and timber preserves, then what would become of the Indians who, in many cases, still lived there? If a beautiful mountain valley could store water for a nearby city's drinking and industrial needs, should it be made into a reservoir or kept as a nature preserve? If the middle class could find respite in its bungalows and gardens, what retreat was there for the urban poor? Nature and humans, landscapes and labor, all turned out to be inseparable. And so when we look back on California conservation in the Progressive Era, we can see not only a reform impulse that was more influential and broadly based than many scholars have recognized but also one as controversial and disputed in its own day as more recent environmental debates.

Conservation and Rural California

By the late nineteenth century, a critical mass of Americans had come to believe that human beings could profoundly alter the natural world in ways decidedly not in their interest. As early as 1864, George Perkins Marsh had warned that the United States risked repeating the decline of the mighty empires of the classical Mediterranean world by cutting down its forests and grazing its grasslands to the nub. By 1900, John Muir had become the nation's best-known nature writer through the force of his lyrical depictions of how "thousands of tired, nerve-shaken, over-civilized" urbanites could find renewal in "jumping from rock to rock, feeling the life of them, learning the songs of them, painting in whole-souled exercise, and rejoicing in deep, long-drawn breaths of pure wilderness" (Sachs 2006: 314).

Conservationists were as focused on the human material dependence on nature as on the kind of spiritual vision offered by Muir. Southern Californians had particular reason to understand this dependence. Their home was in an arid region most of whose annual rainfall usually fell in a few winter months, when it came at all. Although scarcity of water was the usual problem, abundance could be its own curse, with the occasional, even surprisingly frequent, deluge pouring down from the mountains to wash away buildings and crops in Los Angeles, as happened in 1862, 1867–8, 1881, 1884, 1886, 1889, 1890, and 1891 (Orsi 2004: 2). Fire was the counterpart to water, with the smoke from burning chaparral a regular feature of life, then as now. Los Angeles profited by marketing the same temperate climate that made Southern California so well suited for citriculture, but this very dependence on a reliably fickle and violent nature made conservation a pressing concern. As real-estate developer and conservationist Abbott Kinney warned Los Angeles in 1900, "[t]he desert is at our door today. It is pushing up against the mountain barrier that divides us. It is creeping up on the passes, north and east and conquering a corner now here, now there . . . the deserts even now come into our lovely valleys for a few days with their fire and furnace breath to look at the rich booty they may some day hold" (Kinney 1900: 80).

The wider course of national politics allowed Californians to act decisively on such warnings. By the dawn of the twentieth century, the federal government, which had previously done everything in its power to transfer lands into private hands as quickly as possible, had committed itself to the permanent management of much of the nation's territory. In 1891, believing that much of the West was environmentally unsuitable for agriculture, Congress authorized the creation of Forest Reserves, which would be precluded from homestead entries. Some 34 million acres were encompassed in such reserves by 1897, including the half-million-acre San Gabriel Forest Reserve (the second reserve created, following only the forests around Yellowstone National Park) and the 800,000-acre San Bernadino Reserve. All of the reserves were transformed into National Forests in 1907, to be managed by the US Forest Service, then directed by Gifford Pinchot, one of the leading conservationists in the nation.

Many California leaders welcomed the creation of the national public lands system. The Golden State established its own forest commission in 1885, before there was a single professionally trained forester in the entire nation (Clar 1959: 95, 99). Prominent Californians lobbied for federal ownership and management of critical watersheds and timber tracts. Indeed, many of the managers of California's National Forests were selected from the ranks of regional business and conservation associations, who also

provided key political support for continued state and federal appropriations for the new conservation bureaucracies. "[N]owhere in the United
States," Gifford Pinchot appreciatively told the Los Angeles City Club in
1909, "has the Forest Service received such hearty co-operation as in
Southern California."[1] Fifty years later, scholar Raymond Clar went even
further, arguing that, "[t]he interest and effort exerted to improve and
protect the water flow [in this region] . . . has probably been unsurpassed
in any area of similar geographic dimensions elsewhere in the world" (Clar
1959: 269).

In a certain sense, conservationists felt that they were always on the
defensive, struggling valiantly to protect humanity's accomplishments
against an ever-threatening nature and the splendors of nature against a
humanity armed with ever more technological power. There were always
fires to put out. Timber harvesting and stock grazing perpetually threatened tree cover and water flow. Penny-pinching officials and political corruption, enabled by public ignorance and apathy, undermined conservation
bureaucracies, as when California abolished its Forestry Commission in the
1890s. Monopolistic businesses were everywhere the great enemy of the
common good, in environmental affairs as in other realms. The eroded
hillsides and endless stumps left behind by mining and timber companies
bore mute testimony to the ability of such corporations to destroy the
splendors of the natural world and disregard the needs of future generations for water, timber, and power. On the other side of the coin, great
cities could find themselves prostrate before the power of nature, as San
Francisco learned in its great 1906 earthquake and Los Angeles saw in
1914 when a particularly destructive flood ruined fields, inundated neighborhoods, and dumped tons of silt in the city's new harbor. These obstacles
were particularly daunting in places whose climate and topography left
them so vulnerable – where, as Abbott Kinney put it, "we are too near the
edge of conditions favorable to forest growth to take any chances on allowing important forests to be destroyed" (Kinney 1900: 28).

On the other hand, conservationists had reason to be optimistic – naïvely
so, it would turn out – about their ability to control and even transform
nature. Fires might be commonplace, but proper staffing of forests, public
education efforts, and the resources to mobilize fire-fighting crews could
bring them to an end. The modern economy was powerful enough to
resurrect San Francisco in short order. Engineers could prevent damaging
floods by straightening (and cementing) the Los Angeles River, building
levees, and catching run-off in mountain reservoirs. Parts of the earth that
seemed inhospitable for productive activity could be made to yield a
fortune. The first generation of professionally trained American silvicultur-
alists would turn mountain forests full of dead and decaying trees into
productive stands of timber. Where lack of rainfall precluded agriculture,

the government would bring water from rivers hundreds of miles away, over mountains if needed, to make the desert bloom. The city government of Los Angeles did exactly this, securing its future by constructing a 220-mile aqueduct from the Owens Valley in the first decade of the twentieth century (Reisner 1986).

Conservationists sought not only protection for the state's agricultural prosperity and a guarantee of its future growth, but also a refuge in nature from the world of commerce, work, and artificiality. John Muir was by far the most prominent of this group, but many others contributed to California's deep currents of romantic conservation. Pasadena author Charles Francis Saunders was drawn to the virtues of what he thought of as the region's primeval nature. The "real California," he wrote in 1913, consisted not of cities and orchards, but rather the "immensity of almost unexplored mountain, desert, cañon, and flowery plain." The human landscape around him was "an artificial wonderland of palms and roses and orange groves," but the thought that it might one day vanish was not so much tragic as awesome, for he loved the "wild, majestic solitude" of the nearby mountains and deserts. In these places, humans could find an immediacy of experience and spirituality absent from workaday life. As Saunders wrote of desert nights, "the veil between this world and the spiritual seems thinner than elsewhere, and one in some measure comprehends why prophets of all time have found inspiration and strength in desert regions" (Saunders 1913, preface: 6).

Muir, Saunders, and other writers such as Mary Austin tapped into deep wells of romantic appreciation for nature. In the late nineteenth and early twentieth centuries, Californians founded important organizations devoted to protecting scenic places and iconic species from destruction: the Sierra Club in 1892, the Sempervirens Club (an organization devoted to the protection of redwoods) 10 years later, and the Save-the-Redwoods League in 1918. The leadership of these organizations included some of the state's wealthiest and most powerful men, such as Stanford University President David Starr Jordan, who helped to found the Sierra Club, and scientific eugenicists John Merriam and Henry Osborn, who founded the Save-the-Redwoods League along with Madison Grant. But romantic conservation also spoke to wider sectors of the state's urban middle classes. Mountain lodges constructed by California outing and hunting clubs proliferated in the 1880s, joined by private entrepreneurs offering hiking and pack trips to nature enthusiasts. "All summer long," wrote Charles Saunders of the San Gabriel mountains, "parties both little and of both sexes, their blankets and camp kits slung upon their backs, come gaily up from the cities of the coast and the plain, from the schools and counting houses and shops, living Arcadian days and weeks in shady cañons by never-failing waters, and sleeping beneath the sky" (Saunders 1913: 50).

By the twentieth century, conservation had achieved such prominence in California that its advocates could find themselves victims of their own successes, as when John Muir complained that nature enthusiasts had denuded one of his favorite Southern California canyons of ferns and moss. They could also turn on one another, as when the city of San Francisco's political establishment went after Yosemite National Park's Hetch Hetchy Valley as a site for a municipal reservoir for power and water. The Hetch Hetchy debate, a classic event in the history of American environmental politics, split the Sierra Club and Progressive circles more generally, with those determined to preserve a place of great natural beauty and the sanctity of the park system as a whole eventually defeated by those who believed the municipal reservoir would provide freedom from predatory private power and water companies. Both sides could – and did – claim the mantle of conservation (Righter 2005).

Social History Meets Conservation

The success of conservationists in shaping rural California for both material and spiritual purposes fits quite comfortably within longstanding scholarly treatments of conservation. The "essence" of conservation, wrote Samuel P. Hays nearly five decades ago, "was rational planning to promote efficient development and use of all natural resources" (Hays 1959: 2). Hays's account – still the only book-length synthetic treatment of Progressive conservation – gave primacy of place to development-minded elites like Gifford Pinchot and Abbott Kinney, taking their assumptions and goals as the heart of conservation. At the same time, Hays acknowledged that the intensity of natural resource policy debates led these elites to appeal to others who thought of conservation "as an attempt to save resources from use rather than to use them wisely." In the process, he argued, "[a]n exclusively hardheaded economic proposition . . . became tinged with the enthusiasm of a religious crusade to save America from its materialistic enemies" (ibid.: 141). This "crusade" was the subject of Roderick Nash's account of wilderness preservation, which traced the intellectual history of the appreciation for wild places (Nash 1967). Although his cast of characters was different than Hays's and his time period much longer, Nash also attributed environmentalist sensibility to a small, powerful, and well-educated elite, whose ideas eventually trickled down to the masses.

The ideology and accomplishments of California's conservationists fit equally well with more recent revisionist accounts of conservation. Louis Warren, Mark Spence, Karl Jacoby, Alexandra Stern, and others have powerfully revisited the terrain covered by Hays, Nash, and later descriptions of the campaigns to create and preserve specific parks and other areas from consumptive economic development. This body of work argues that leading conservationists – both the utilitarians like Pinchot and the romantics like Muir – viewed rural people with deep hostility, believing their backwardness and wastefulness to number among the most formidable obstacles to the exercise of state control necessary to implement conservation. Alexandra Stern takes this argument one step further, drawing attention to what she describes as the "deep affinities between conservationist arguments about species survival and early twentieth century fears of 'race suicide'" (Stern 2005: 25). In these revisionist accounts, wilderness preservation – the valuing of a supposedly primeval nature unaltered by human action – is not the antagonist of materialist conservation, as it seemed to be in the Hetch Hetchy debate, but rather its twin. "The dream of an unworked natural landscape," William Cronon writes, "is very much the fantasy of people who have never themselves had to work the land to make a living" (Cronon 1996: 16). Although there were certainly clashes between these sides of conservation over the appropriate use of particular places, such as Hetch Hetchy, both reflected the cultural logic of industrial capitalism. Conservationist ideas had enormous ramifications not just for nature, but also for human beings, these recent works show: conservation regulations, including wilderness preservation, altered the ecology of rural America and forced many of its inhabitants away from subsistence and into wage labor and greater dependence on economic elites and the large state and private bureaucracies that they controlled. In this emerging view, conservation remains a critical part of California and US history – indeed, perhaps a more important one than in the earlier, celebratory accounts – but not entirely for the better.

This new body of work is not without its problems. Surely most Americans living today owe a great debt to conservationists, particularly for preserving wilderness from economic development (Hays 1996). Leading figures of the environmentalist pantheon were more complicated than the revisionist portrayal of them often acknowledges. Aaron Sachs, for example, shows that earlier in his life John Muir was much more interested in aboriginal peoples in the Americas, critiquing the impact of Western colonialism and demonstrating respect for native environmental knowledge and adaptation (Sachs 2006: 317, 324). Donald Worster acknowledges a similar narrowing of Muir's vision and a growing comfort with the inequalities of industrial America later in his life, but emphasizes the egalitarianism and social engagement of his earlier writings and experiences (Worster 2005). Alexandra Stern's assertion that "the apparition of eugenics sits restlessly at the heart of American environmentalism" (Stern 2005: 148) is yet-unproven extrapolation from the substantive connections between eugenicism, white supremacy, and some leading redwoods preservationists.

Nevertheless, important aspects of California conservation fit comfortably into this new paradigm of conservation. California's elite conservationists celebrated what they saw as the triumph of enlightenment over ignorance, progress over backwardness. "Communal rights in forests, that is, the right of individuals in a community to individually use the forest for personal benefit," argued Abbott Kinney in 1900, "is fatal to the forests." He noted with approval the efforts of conservation-minded officials in Europe and the United States to curtail such rights (Kinney 1900: 57), and wanted to extend this kind of intervention into the reproductive realm, to ensure that immigrant "breeding" did not result in the "extinction of the old American stock" (Kinney 1893: vi). John Muir never went so far, though by the twentieth century he was dismissing rural people as "[m]ere destroyers . . . tree-killers, wool and mutton men, spreading death and confusion in the fairest groves and gardens ever planted." Indians were particularly contemptible – "dirt," "deadly," and "lazy" – and their removal meant that "[a]rrows, bullets, scalping-knives need no longer be feared" (Muir 1901: 363, 15; Spence 1999). The Yosemite Indians learned exactly what these kinds of attitudes meant in practice. After Park Service regulations made their traditional subsistence practices impossible to continue, they managed to earn cash working as guides, drivers, and maids in the valley that bore their name, resisting efforts at their complete removal made through the 1920s. Increasingly restrictive Park Service measures allowed only active employees to remain in the valley, and the last Yosemite still residing there, Jay Johnson, retired and left in late 1996 (Spence 1999: 122, 131).

Urban Conservation

Historians have opened up a new (if not always so flattering) view of conservation by asking what it meant for social relations in Progressive-Era America, especially in the countryside. If they were to shift their attention from the mountains and forests that so preoccupied the leading conservationists in California and the nation, however, and toward debates about nature and public space within cities, they would find strains of conservation that do not fit into our received understandings of conservation's ideology and social basis. Urban environmental politics also thrived in this period, in California as elsewhere. It has been studied by urban historians, but neglected by environmental historians and rarely connected to the wider political and ideological currents of conservation. Urban environmental reformers generally shared their elite, rural-oriented counterparts' distrust of monopoly and their faith that the power of government could effectively check the dangerous excesses of industrial capitalism. Access to nature, they believed, could be provided even to the urban masses in the form of extensive park systems, whose design could invoke and emulate the aesthetics of an untouched nature. The sheer breadth of the social ranks from which these reformers were drawn suggests the need to recognize conservation as a much wider social movement than has been acknowledged in older and more recent scholarship alike. Moreover, a significant contingent of these urban conservationists held more deeply critical views of industrial society than historians have acknowledged. Conservation, like Progressivism as a whole, had its radical aspects.

Urban reformers in San Francisco and Los Angeles invoked familiar conservationist themes to argue for the creation of city parks. Los Angeles Progressive Dana Bartlett sounded much like John Muir when he extolled the virtues of "entering the silences of the mountains" in order to "there hear the small voice that cannot be heard in the noise and rush of modern commercialism." But instead of simply criticizing urban life, he hoped that with an ambitious park system Angelenos would be able to hear something of this voice in their daily lives as well (Bartlett 1907: 17, 34, 37). The architects of San Francisco's park system around the turn of the century made similar arguments, emphasizing, in the words of geographer Terence Young, that "[u]rban disorders did not arise because society was evil *by nature* but because its members were *out of touch with nature*, a source of goodness" (Young 2003: 2). Conservationists' particular fondness for wild nature left its mark on these urban park advocates. Whereas an earlier generation of landscape architects and designers featured geometric shapes, straight lines, and standardized plantings, many Progressives found those design elements to be stifling and unnatural. Instead, they argued, parks should be designed with the messiness and unpredictability of nature itself. Griffith J. Griffith, the donor of Los Angeles's Griffith Park, made this argument in 1910 when he praised other cities for "proceeding not on artificial, but natural lines; the object sought being not formal promenades, but spacious areas in which the public can lose itself, forgetting for the moment the restrictions of city life and reveling in the largeness of nature" (Griffith 1910: 13).

Although some leading conservationists in California and elsewhere saw the city and nature as sharply removed, a number of important elite conservationists supported both rural and urban conservation. William Kent, the San Francisco Congressman who created Muir Woods and tried to create a national park around Mt. Tamalpais, had been active in public parks policy in Chicago before moving to the Golden State, and once in Congress supported classic rural conservation measures such as national parks, wildlife preserves, grazing reform, and public ownership of water power. He angered Muir by backing San Francisco's successful effort to dam Hetch Hetchy, but showed his continued support for romantic conservation by helping to found the Save-the-Redwoods League in 1918 (Hyde 1994). Charles Silent of Los Angeles worked with Abbott Kinney and others in advocating the establishment of National Forests in the city's hinterland, and later in life served as City Park Commissioner in the early 1910s, warning of the city's "almost criminal neglect" of parks.[2] Pennsylvania's Horace McFarland, a leading advocate of the City Beautiful movement, worked tirelessly against the damming of Hetch Hetchy even as he advocated principles of urban design that would "endeavor to give us . . . in our urban habitations conditions . . . approximating those of the beautiful wild into which our forefathers came a few generations ago" (Wilson 1989: 78).

While intellectuals, political leaders, scientists, engineers, and business elites articulated conservation principles and managed conservation agencies, the number and kind of people involved in conservation politics was enormously broad. Thousands upon thousands of people, almost all of whose names are lost to us, flocked to city parks, demanded more parks, formed "improvement associations" to create new parks, and complained bitterly when existing parks were trampled by too much foot traffic, flooded with sewage, or neglected. They spoke eloquently of their favorite places in these parks, argued about what kind of trees should and should not be planted in them, and looked eagerly for the return of favorite birds (Gibson 1977: 52; Johnson 2006: 18). They packed into city council meetings, demanding the regulation of gas works that coated their clothes, homes, and businesses in soot and cinder (Johnson 2005). Conservation, as some works have acknowledged but few have pursued, was a mass movement (Price 2000; Rimby 2005).

Placing urban environmental politics into accounts of conservation, moreover, compels us to recognize that conservation could also be much more radical than is accounted for in either older accounts or the more recent studies set in the countryside. For Samuel Hays, as for later generations of environmental history, conservation was ultimately congruent with the corporate order coming to dominate the American economy and politics. "The conservation movement," Hays asserted, "did not involve a reaction against large-scale corporate business, but, in fact, shared its views in a mutual revulsion against unrestrained competition and undirected economic development" (Hays 1959: 266). Although that characterization may describe the ideology of the older John Muir, Abbott Kinney, and Congressional Progressives such as William Kent, it overlooks the ways in which others used romantic and materialist aspects of conservation as part of a wider critique of corporate capitalism and wage labor. Dana Bartlett, for example, belonged squarely in the long tradition of American middle-class radicalism, arguing that the highly stratified accumulation of wealth made possible by the industrial revolution "wrought havoc with the earlier ideals of liberty and equality," and that if not checked by progressive reform, the rich would reign in "a new feudalism of capital" (Bartlett 1911: 498–9). He lauded "the great army of labor fighting for industrial freedom," and warned that "the oligarchy of capital is arraying itself against labor organized in self-defense" (Bartlett 1907: 187). Labor radicals also found themselves attracted to conservation. Job Harriman, nearly elected Los Angeles mayor in 1911 on the Socialist ticket, used nature as a critique of industrial society, regularly contrasting the West's natural abundance and beauty with the harsh lot of those who labored in its fields and factories (Harriman 1913: 54–6). The Los Angeles socialist newspaper, *The Western Comrade*, urged its readers to find an escape from the world of work and artificiality in remote nature, where, "[i]n mountain fastness and shaded nooks, by brookside or seaside, in song of bird or care-free life of animals, Mother Nature spreads her bounty of life, light, and beauty" ("Nature's Banquet Table," p. 25). Even wilderness appreciation of the sort celebrated by John Muir appeared in the paper's pages, though leavened with a call for the need to redeem the world of urban toil (Wentworth 1913: 41).

Conservation by Other Means

The impulse behind conservation – the search for a material balance and psychic renewal with a nature believed to be imperiled and at risk of exhaustion – was expressed in private as well as public life. Architects, real-estate developers, women's clubs, and others helped to infuse private homes and their grounds or lots with many of the same values that wilderness and urban parks systems were designed to protect. With the properly skilled negotiations between humans and nature, these places, the provinces of individual and family life, could also ameliorate the social harms of industrial life and restore authenticity and physical vigor to daily existence. Given the environmental destruction that suburbia and urban sprawl would bring after World War II, it is understandable that the close connection between certain types of real-estate development and home designs with conservation politics has been obscured. But in fact conservation owed much of its mass appeal to this wider cultural rediscovery of nature, a topic examined in some detail by cultural and architectural historians, but generally segregated from scholarly treatments of the environmental politics and conservation leaders that were so familiar with it (Schmitt 1969; Shi 1985; Stilgoe 1988). Conservation was as much a private pursuit as a public policy debate.

It was no coincidence that the bungalow took America, and particularly Southern California, by storm in this period. An English adaptation of village houses on the Indian subcontinent, the bungalow in North America came to refer to a "comfortable-looking, one or one-and-one-half story dwelling usually preceded by a spacious front porch . . . [that] dispensed with the formal separation of public spaces seen earlier in the Victorian house" (Goss & Trapp 1995: 6). Its informality, frequent use of sleeping porches, and emphasis on light and ventilation were designed to blur the once heavily policed line between outdoors and inside. The first American bungalow appears to have been constructed on Cape Cod in 1880, and as late as 1900 "[o]f less than a dozen bungalows known to have been designed in North America . . . all apparently functioned as 'summer cottages,' in the mountains, the country or by the sea, and practically all in the North Atlantic states" (King 1995: 130). The bungalow became extremely popular in the first decade of the twentieth century, proliferating into several different regional styles. Although in some ways it became simply another dwelling, so ubiquitous that by the 1920s cultural critics associated it with Babbitry and middle-class blandness, the bungalow retained much of its original connection with a retreat to the wholesome simplicity of outdoor living. Gustav Stickley, editor of *The Craftsman*, the mouthpiece of the American Arts and Crafts movement, praised the way in which its typically low profile ensured "that the countryside is no longer *affronted* with lean, narrow, two-storey houses," appreciated how its wooden shingles "came to look like autumn leaves," and argued that proper design and detailing could "tie the building to its surroundings and give it the seeming of a growth rather than a creation." He considered the bungalow an excellent domestic counterpart to "the new wilderness areas being used by vacationers" (quoted in King 1995: 134–5).

Nowhere did the bungalow shape the suburban landscape more than in California, particularly Southern California. They had so impressed themselves upon the Southern California landscape by 1914 that Mary Austin concluded that "[i]n this group of low hills and shallow valleys between the Sierra Madre and the sea, the most conspicuous human achievement has been a new form of domestic architecture." "This is the thing that strikes the attention of the traveler," she continued. "These little, thin-walled dwellings, all of desert-tinted native woods and stones, are as indigenous to the soils as if they had grown up out of it, as charming in line and the perfection of utility as some of those wild growths which show a delicate air fluorescence above ground, but under it have deep, man-shaped resistant roots." For Austin, the omnipresent homes suggested that Anglos had become at home in this region, for "[w]ith their low and flat-pitched roofs, they present a certain likeness to the aboriginal dwellings which the Franciscans found scattered like wasps nests among the chapparal along the river – which is only another way of saying that the spirit of the land shapes the art that is produced there" (quoted in King 1995: 145.)

Other house designs prominent in California besides the bungalow
reflected a similar effort to bring nature into daily living. "Here homes are
built with reference to the climate," boasted Dana Bartlett of Los Angeles
in 1911, "with large porches used as living-rooms, with open-air bedrooms, with patios filled with blossoms and rare plants – the joy of every
season" (Bartlett 1911: 18). Several of the city's best, if not yet best-known
architects, such as modernists R. M. Schindler and Richard Neutra, emphasized taking maximum advantage of sunlight, fresh air, and scenic views in
their modernist home designs. Schindler's 1912 "Manifesto," which proclaimed that

> The man of the future does not try to
> escape the elements.
> He will rule them.

bore a remarkable similarity to Gifford Pinchot's declaration that "[t]he
first duty of the human race is to control the earth it lives upon." A decade
later, Schindler said of his celebrated Kings Road House that "[o]ur
rooms . . . will descend close to the ground and the garden will become an
integral part of the house," comparing the elements of his design to "the
basic requirements of a camper's shelter: a protected back, an open front,
a fireplace and a roof" (Gebhard 1971: 192, 48). Irving Gill, almost all of
whose enormously influential buildings were located in Southern California, described his work in similar terms: "[W]e should build our house
simple, plain and substantial as a boulder," he wrote in *The Craftsman* in
1915 in one of his few published essays, "then leave the ornamentation of
it to Nature, who will tone it with lichens, chisel it with storms, make it
gracious and friendly with vines and flower shadows as she does the stone
in the meadow" (quoted in Hines 2000: 11).

Leading conservationists found themselves drawn to the strongly environmental cast to real-estate development and home design in Los Angeles
in this period. John Muir enjoyed a long and formative intellectual relationship with Jeanne Carr, whose Pasadena home grounds were a showplace
for the beauty that homeowners could create. Charles Francis Saunders
extensively praised the bungalow alongside the more wild places close to
his heart. "The ample windows fill the house with light," he noted, "and
there is the perfume of the violets or roses, or both, in the air . . . Opened
doorways and windows admit the breeze with manifold fragrances from
hedge and garden" (Saunders 1913: 238–9). Others took conservation and
real-estate development to mean almost the same thing. Abbott Kinney
and his circle, for example, practiced what historian Ian Tyrrell calls "environmental renovation" in their real-estate and conservation projects
alike, when they sought to make productive, well-wooded, orderly, almost

gardenlike landscapes out of the San Gabriel Mountains, Pasadena, Santa Monica, and elsewhere (Tyrrell 1999: 13, 66–7).

Conclusion

A century after Progressive conservation changed the landscape of California and the United States, historians continue to debate its legacies. The questions that they ask of conservation have changed over the decades, with the rest of the discipline's focus on power and hierarchy assuming a more prominent place, and the cast of actors expanding well beyond leading conservationists. The latter portions of this essay have argued that historians of conservation should continue to broaden their work by exploring the connections between conservation and urban reform, park politics, and domestic architecture. Conceived of in this breadth, different varieties of conservation attracted a wide basis of support and political involvement, in part because they were connected to wider cultural changes. We cannot understand the landscape of modern California without grappling with the conservation movement and its legacies for nature and humans.

NOTES

1 "Pinchot Warns Us against Predatory Interests," 1909: 6.
2 Charles Silent, *A History of California and an Extended History of Los Angeles and Environs: Biographical,* vol. II. Los Angeles: Historic Record Company, 1915, pp. 456–7.

REFERENCES

Bartlett, Dana. 1907. *The Better City: A Sociological Study of a Modern City.* Los Angeles: The Neuner Company Press.
Bartlett, Dana. 1911. *The Better Country.* Boston, MA: C. M. Clark.
Bartlett, Dana. 1923. *The Bush Aflame.* Los Angeles: Grafton.
Clar, C. Raymond. 1959. *California Government and Forestry.* Sacramento: Division of Forestry, Department of Natural Resources, State of California.
Cronon, William. 1996. "The Trouble With Wilderness; Or, Getting Back to the Wrong Nature," *Environmental History* 1 (1).
Gebhard, David. 1971. *Schindler.* New York: Viking.
Gibson, Mary Katherine. 1977. "The Changing Conception of the Urban Park in America: The City of Los Angeles as a Case Study." MA thesis, University of California at Los Angeles, Department of Architecture and Urban Planning.
Goss, Peter, and Trapp, Kenneth R., eds. 1995. *The Bungalow Lifestyle and the Arts and Crafts Movement in the Intermountain West.* Salt Lake City: University of Utah Press.

Griffith, Griffth J. 1910. *Parks, Boulevards and Playgrounds.* Los Angeles: Prison Reform League.

Harriman, Job. 1913. "Making Dreams Come True," *Western Comrade* 1 (2) (May): 54–6.

Hays, Samuel P. 1959. *Conservation and the Gospel of Efficiency.* Cambridge, MA: Harvard University Press.

Hays, Samuel P. 1996. "Comment: The Trouble With Bill Cronon's Wilderness," *Environmental History* 1 (1): 29–32.

Hines, Thomas. 2000. *Irving Gill and the Architecture of Reform.* New York: The Monacelli Press.

Hyde, Anne. 1994. "William Kent: The Puzzle of Progressive Conservationists." In William Deverell and Tom Sitton, eds., *California Progressivism Revisited.* Berkeley: University of California Press, pp. 34–52.

Jacoby, Karl. 2001. *Crimes Against Nature: Squatters, Poachers, Thieves, and the Hidden History of American Conservation.* Berkeley: University of California Press.

Johnson, Benjamin. 2006. "Rethinking Conservation: City, Suburb, and Countryside in Progressive-Era Los Angeles." Autry Western History Workshop.

Johnson, Daniel. 2005. "Pollution and Public Policy at the Turn of the Century." In William Deverell and Greg Hise, eds., *Land of Sunshine: An Environmental History of Metropolitan Los Angeles.* Pittsburgh: University of Pittsburgh Press, pp. 78–93.

King, Anthony. 1995[1984]. *The Bungalow: The Product of A Global Culture.* New York: Oxford University Press.

Kinney, Abbott. 1893. *The Conquest of Death.* New York: (n.p.).

Kinney, Abbott. 1900. *Forest and Water.* Los Angeles: Post Publishing Company.

Muir, John. 1901. *Our National Parks.* New York: Houghton Mifflin.

Nash, Roderick. 1967. *Wilderness and the American Mind.* New Haven, CT: Yale University Press.

Orsi, Jared. 2004. *Hazardous Metropolis: Flooding and Urban Ecology in Los Angeles.* Berkeley: University of California Press, 2004.

Price, Jennifer. 2000. *Flight Maps: Adventures with Nature in Modern America.* New York: Basic Books.

Reisner, Marc. 1986. *Cadillac Desert: The American West and Its Disappearing Water.* New York: Penguin.

Righter, Robert. 2005. *The Battle Over Hetch-Hetchy: America's Most Controversial Dam and the Birth of Modern Environmentalism.* New York: Oxford.

Rimby, Susan. 2005. "'Better Housekeeping Out of Doors': Myra Lloyd Dock, The State Federation of Pennsylvania Women, and Progressive Era Conservation," *Journal of Women's History* 17 (3): 9–34.

Sachs, Aaron. 2006. *The Humboldt Current: Nineteenth-Century Exploration and the Roots of American Environmentalism.* New York: Viking.

Saunders, Charles Francis. 1913. *Under the Sky in California.* New York: McBride, Nast.

Schmitt, Peter J. 1969. *Back to Nature: The Arcadian Myth in Urban America.* Baltimore, MD: Johns Hopkins University Press.

Shi, David. 1985. *The Simple Life: Plain Living and High Thinking in American Culture.* New York: Oxford University Press.

Silent, Charles. 1915. *A History of California and an Extended History of Los Angeles and Environs: Biographical,* vol. II. Los Angeles: Historic Record Company, 1915.

Spence, Mark David. 1999. *Dispossessing the Wilderness: Indian Removal and the Making of the National Parks.* New York: Oxford University Press.

Stern, Alexandra Minna. 2005. *Eugenic Nation: Faults and Frontiers of Better Breeding in Modern America.* Berkeley: University of California Press.

Stilgoe, John. 1988. *Borderland: Origins of the American Suburb, 1820–1939.* New Haven, CT: Yale University Press.

Tyrrel, Ian. 1999. *True Gardens of the Gods: Californian and Australian Environmental Reform, 1860–1930.* Berkeley: University of California Press.

Wentworth, Eleanor. 1913. "The Heart of the City," *The Western Comrade* 1 (2) (May): 41.

Western Comrade. 1913. "Nature's Banquet Table," *Western Comrade* 1: 1 (April).

Wilson, William. 1989. *The City Beautiful Movement.* Baltimore, MD: Johns Hopkins University Press.

Worster, Donald. 2005. "John Muir and the Modern Passion for Nature," *Environmental History* 10 (1): 8–19.

Young, Terence. 2003. *Building San Francisco's Parks, 1850–1930.* Baltimore, MD: Johns Hopkins University Press.

FURTHER READING

Banham, Reyner. 2000[1971]. *Los Angeles: The Architecture of Four Ecologies.* Berkeley: University of California Press.

Culver, Lawrence. 2004. "The Island, the Oasis, and the City: Santa Catalina, Palm Springs, Los Angeles, and Southern California's Shaping of American Life and Leisure." PhD dissertation, University of California at Los Angeles.

Davis, Mike. 1998. *Ecology of Fear: Los Angeles and the Imagination of Disaster.* New York: Metropolitan Books.

Gisel, Bonnie Johanna. 2001. *Kindred and Related Spirits: The Letters of John Muir and Jeanne C. Carr.* Salt Lake City: University of Utah Press.

Minteer, Ben and Manning, Robert. 2003. *Reconstructing Conservation: Finding Common Ground.* Washington, DC: Island Press.

Solnit, Rebecca. 2003. *River of Shadows: Eadweard Muybridge and the Technological Wild West.* New York: Viking.

Chapter Fifteen

RELIGION IN THE EARLY TWENTIETH CENTURY

Darren Dochuk

In the midst of the Depression, 16 white southern migrants decided it was time to "plant" a Southern Baptist church in a quiet residential area of their new Southern California home, Bell Gardens. Local residents, city authorities, and other churchgoers proved less than appreciative of First Baptist Bell Gardens' efforts to engulf the neighborhood with gospel singing and fire-and-brimstone preaching, and they soon circulated a petition demanding the removal of the congregation. Though fueled by a variety of motives, the petition succeeded in sending a resounding message to First Baptist members: learn to abide by the rules of civic propriety or leave. First Baptist congregants reacted to this affront by securing a new church location on Florence Avenue, one of Bell Gardens' more traveled roadways. The congregants gathered their tools, pooled their money for supplies, and began constructing a meeting-house on Florence Avenue where they could hold services.

While relocation to Florence Avenue in 1937 signified a fresh beginning for First Baptist congregants, it did not, to their dismay, bring an end to their troubles. In their enthusiasm to obtain church property First Baptist members failed to apply for a land-use permit from city hall. City officials ordered construction stopped, with the threat of repercussions should the congregation ignore this injunction. First Baptist's handymen redoubled their efforts to finish building their church. Driven by a sense of sacred mission more authoritative and binding than any zoning law or legal decree, church members simply "bowed their necks, paid no attention to the nettling, and kept on driving nails and sawing lumber" (Looney 1954: 366). City officials quietly shuffled off in search of more winnable battles, having learned that the rules of civic propriety were easily trumped by southern evangelical zeal and fortitude.

In its very simplicity, the tale of First Baptist Bell Gardens captures the broader essence of faith in California during the first half of the twentieth century. Embedded in this parable of spiritual resolve overcoming worldly restraints are three foundational characteristics of organized religion in this formative period: its sojourning spirit, predilection for politics at the local level, and eagerness to calibrate customs according to the ever-changing marketplace of ideas. As overarching themes in the unfolding history of California, each of these propensities speak to the certainty with which sacred imperatives shaped manifold dimensions of life in mid-century California. They also remind us that religion was neither an ephemeral nor tangential influence relegated to the social, political, and cultural margins but rather a substantive and determinative force operating at the very center of California society.

As organizing principles in current scholarship, each of these characteristics underscores the degree to which sacred subjects enliven the retelling of California history. For religious scholars interested in the inner workings of faith, early twentieth-century California has offered a windfall of fresh source material and new lines of questioning. Here, in a frontier land once dismissed as inherently secular, these scholars have uncovered a vigorous religious ethos whose intensity and diversity outpaced any other on the North American continent. Indeed, why and how California religion exhibited such religious vibrancy amidst such adverse conditions, and toward what end, are queries now being asked of the nation as a whole as scholars try to make sense of America's confounding proliferation of faith in a secular, supposedly postmodern era (Ernst 2001). For historians working in other fields, early twentieth-century California religion has provided ample opportunity to incorporate dimensions of faith in their accounts of the social and cultural movements, racial and ethnic identities, and intellectual and political trends that first defined California then reshaped the nation. These efforts have resulted in a more subtle and complex retelling of the past that is attentive to religion's persistent influence in American life.

The Sojourning Spirit in California Religion

Fundamental to this narrative is a sojourning spirit animated by the migration of thousands of people and hundreds of faith communities into the state's spacious hinterlands and sprawling cities. First Baptist Bell Gardens' fervent congregants were not at all exceptional in their earnestness to plant seeds of faith in California's soil. Throughout the early twentieth century similarly devout religious folk followed different paths to California hoping to transform it into something transcendent. For some this meant carrying on a task begun by forebears. During the last decades of the nineteenth century California had come to represent a metaphysical as much as a geographical frontier. Amidst the clamor of San Francisco's burgeoning city life, white Anglo and ethnic Protestant groups from east of the

Mississippi looked to establish new centers of power from which mission agencies abroad and religious enterprises at home could be managed. Episcopalians, Congregationalists, and Methodists led the way. But no less impressive in their efforts to create denominational outposts of this kind were German Lutheran, Dutch Reformed, and Scottish Presbyterian pioneers (Ernst & Anderson 1993). On farms in the Central Valley, meanwhile, "outsiders" like the Mennonites created their own centers of activity in hope of redeeming the world they occupied but chose not to engage fully (Froese 2003). In the southern reaches of the state Protestant and Catholic groups joined a plethora of other upstart religious communities like Mormonism, Adventism, and Spiritualism, whose claims to land were as much about self-preservation as spiritual propagation (Frankiel 1988; Engh 1992).

Whether or not religious migrants entered the twentieth century already informed by earlier precedents, all who encountered California's spiritual landscape in this era recognized clearly that they were engaging something new. Indeed, if the nineteenth century marked California's beginning as the West's incubator of inherited orthodoxies, the early twentieth represented its flourishing as the nation's "laboratory of the spirit" (Davis 2006: 8). The sheer magnitude of migration in this new era helped engender this shift. Between 1900 and 1920 California's population more than doubled, from 1.5 to 3.5 million; exponential growth continued to 1940 when, on the eve of World War II and the onset of yet another wave of mass migration, 6.9 million people called California home. As Michael Quinn underscores, religious pluralism flourished because of these new circumstances. While some Asian migrants conveyed new varieties of Shintoism and Taoism, Greek Orthodox, Mexican Catholic, and Jewish pilgrims similarly encountered California as an opportunity for spiritual fulfillment and institutional growth (Quinn 1992).

This remapping of migration patterns accelerated California's transformation from colony to epicenter of national religious trends. The state as a whole grew progressively deserving of this label, but, as historians have emphasized, it was Los Angeles that proved more vital to California's expanding reputation as the world's spiritual meeting place. The cumulative effect of its favorable climate, entrepreneurial spirit, and Hollywood magnetism helped Los Angeles's population increase fivefold between 1900 and 1920 and grow to a total of 2.5 million by 1940, all the while ensuring the city's status as the most religiously heterogeneous community on the continent. This was a far cry from 1900 when it was ranked among the most homogenous (Engh 2001: 202). Los Angeles sustained its vibrant international flavor by allowing residents considerable room to practice and propagate their faith commitments. As historians David Yoo and Brian Hayashi have richly portrayed, second-generation Japanese immigrants were among the most creative at carving out lively, self-contained but broadly impacting communities in Southern California during the interwar period. Whether Shinto, Buddhist, or Protestant in form, religion often provided the axis around which these communities grew (Hayashi 1995; Yoo 1999). The rate of transcontinental migration during this same period, meanwhile, increased to unprecedented levels, bringing to Southern California every religious group at work elsewhere in North America. Protestants, Catholics, and Jews from the East Coast contributed heavily to this social ferment by expanding already plentiful institutions in Los Angeles and fortifying their cultural presence in this cosmopolitan center (Vorspan & Gartner 1970; Alexander 1993; Ernst & Anderson 1993; Engh 2001: 202).

Los Angeles's incubation of counter-cultural Protestantism lent the most energy to this religious awakening. Like their co-denominationalists in San Francisco who wielded considerable power, mainline Protestant men and women in Los Angeles assumed that their destiny in the new era was a similar claim to Christian empire on California's southern coast. Those on the margins of evangelical Protestantism, however, ultimately proved most prophetic and determined in their spiritual yearnings (Edmondson 1969; Singleton 1979). During the first half of the twentieth century, Los Angeles was indeed a magnet for zealous evangelicals seeking alternative forms of association, worship, and witness. While a few poor black and white pilgrims gathered in small storefront churches on Azusa Street in 1906, where a series of "full gospel" revival meetings sparked the modern Pentecostal movement, other religious entrepreneurs similarly overcame limited means to build important, lasting institutions (Synan 1997). Fifty years later Los Angeles's plain folk religious fervor, first witnessed on Azusa Street, was still manifest in several home-grown products like the Church of the Nazarene, Church of the Open Door, and International Church of the Foursquare, all of which accentuated Southern California's continued standing as radical revivalism's hothouse (Etulain 1991). Succeeding waves of Christian and non-Christian, white and non-white, lower- and middle-class religious folk thus guaranteed that the sacred would, amidst the tumult of social change in the early twentieth century, assume a commanding presence on California's landscape.

The Politicization of California Religion

Contemporary pundits seem bewildered by the prevailing influence of faith in American politics. How, they ask, did America arrive at such a point where the longstanding ideal of church–state separation no longer regulates patterns of civic engagement? Why does the old-time religion continue to hold sway over modern political processes? Historians are often left to do the explaining, and they increasingly point to California's past for answers to queries of this sort. Consider the consequences, they note, of a truly pluralistic society unbounded by longstanding conventions, decrees, and hierarchies. Consider also, they add, that while the separation of church and state remained a constitutional imperative for most Americans in the early twentieth century, clear distinction between faith and politics was never a maxim embraced wholeheartedly by Californians living in the previous century. Quite the opposite: while the state's free-flowing movement of peoples and faiths created an environment ripe for exchange, it also stimulated competition in the civic sphere among different faith communities and between those professing spiritual and secular priorities. No wonder, then, that in this volatile and capricious environment – one remarkably similar to the current national landscape – assumptions about the proper place of religion in the public square varied greatly, leading ultimately to a "culture war" with profound, lasting effects (Hunter 1992).

Grassroots battles over neighborhood space are where religious combatants in this culture war often fired salvos in their quests for political power. One of the most recent and exciting advances in California historiography has been the study of Los Angeles urban development and its revolutionary impact on land use policy, community formation, and political culture. Here, residents not only enjoyed exceptional freedoms in claiming land for their own purposes but also encountered intense opposition as they sought to defend these interests against others similarly invested in neighborhood space (Fogelson 1993). By extending this line of inquiry, historians now see that within this environment the politics of religion easily played out like a turf war between citizens who harbored different notions of faith's proper location – physical and otherwise – in their respective communities. Whereas Becky Nicolaides's sophisticated social history of California's blue-collar suburbs offers rich, textured analysis of this condition, First Baptist Bell Gardens' provides ready illustration of its effect (Nicolaides 2002). Difficulties associated with this congregation's land procurement were tied not only to contested zoning restrictions but also to broken rapport with so-called "Northern Baptist" leaders, exacerbated during the 1930s by the influx of southern migrants. With deep roots in the nation's Bible Belt, these migrants brought with them a religious imperative for intense evangelism and active engagement in the civic sphere, both of which seemed to Northern Baptists as directly challenging their local authority. Northern Baptist leaders such as W. Earle Smith and George H. Armacost, President of the University of Redlands, responded in kind by asserting their jurisdiction over Southern California Baptists, not only through ecclesiastical recourse but also by way of coordinated political backlash (Dochuk 2005).

Although church-centered, fights of this sort were never confined solely to the pews. And as historian James Gregory makes clear, neither were these skirmishes limited to Los Angeles's blue-collar neighborhoods. Battles of this sort in fact played out in communities across the Central Valley and other sections of the state (Gregory 1989).

Confrontation is only part of the story. The politics of religion also encouraged united action among people of different faiths. During the 1920s, for example, conservative Protestants were among the most active in building cross-denominational alliances to counter what they perceived as illicit activities in their communities. At times they employed extralegal means to act out their discontent. As elsewhere in the nation, the Ku Klux Klan found in California's fundamentalist Protestant churches the impetus to mold a movement to wield power through threats of violence. Anaheim's prominent First Christian Church, for instance, might have refrained from the most explicit forms of such violence, but its willingness to advance a Klan-based agenda nevertheless placed it within an expansive network of congregations that used religion to endorse overtly racist political agendas (Cocoltochos 1979). More common among those in the pulpit and pew at churches like First Christian, however, was an eagerness to work within the political system by organizing petitions and ballot initiatives in support of favored social measures or candidates. In the process of coordinating these political crusades, many Protestants suspended their judgment of other religious groups by befriending anyone concerned with California's moral condition. Even strident Reverend Bob Shuler, the longtime pastor of Trinity Methodist Church, California's largest Southern Methodist congregation, sought cooperation among likeminded allies as fervently as he jousted with his enemies. Shuler frequently attacked "liberal adversaries" like Hollywood, the Federal Communications Commission (FCC), labor unions, and communism. When embroiled in these public confrontations Shuler counted on the moral and financial support of other conservatives, including those less fundamentalist than he. Fostering unity, not fomenting hostility, was therefore an expression of even the most inflexible of activists in this day (Still 1988).

At the same time that conservatives drew energy from their coordinated crusades on behalf of "traditional values," religious folk stirred by new liberal alternatives in the 1920s carried out community action on their own terms. Guided by luminaries like Rabbi Edgar Magnin and Methodist G. Bromley Oxnam but energized by the "street meetings" of people from various cultural backgrounds, political initiatives undertaken to eradicate poverty, racial discrimination, and bigotry proved religion's potential to expand as much as enforce existing social boundaries in California society. As Mark Wild has recently shown, Oxnam's efforts were especially remarkable in this regard. Working from his home base, the multi-ethnic Church of All Nations located in inner-city Los Angeles, Oxnam labored to improve the plight of the poor by constructing an elaborate array of social services and advocacy from pen and pulpit. By assuming the role of mediator between white and non-white Angelenos, Oxnam came to represent the more inclusive cosmopolitan vision of liberal Christianity. That vision would shape both California's and the nation's religious ethos through the extended influence of the Federal Council of Churches (Miller 1990; Wild 2005).

As much as white progressive liberal leaders forged important connections across racial lines, faith-based civic engagement of the kind Oxnam encouraged found its most lively expression in the pews of non-white churches. Here the story of African American church life in California serves as a telling example. Early in the twentieth century, following a first wave of sustained migration from the South, black Protestants worked diligently to build up fledgling churches founded years earlier. By the 1920s many of these congregations were seeing exponential growth and in turn encouraging the extension of church power in predominantly black neighborhoods. Typical for the extent of its influence was Second Baptist in Los Angeles. Through its ministry, recent arrivals from the South gleaned the economic and social resources necessary to begin life anew on the West Coast. Second-generation black Angelenos, meanwhile, marshaled this ministry for "spiritual guidance, *and* civic analyses, political discussions, and social welfare talks and lectures" (Flamming 2005: 116). Out of this milieu stepped Reverend T. L. Griffith, who assumed the pastorate of Second Baptist in 1921, and increased its political standing in the city. By 1926, as a result of tireless work by the dynamic seminarian and World War I veteran, Second Baptist occupied an impressive building located in Los Angeles's Central Avenue business district, the heart of the burgeoning African American community and the epicenter of its engagement with civic politics.

Whether conservative or liberal in theological leaning, white or black in racial identification, faith commitments at the local level clearly shaped California's political destiny in the 1930s. Operating on California's political left during this time was a popular front of civil rights activists that enlisted the state's most vocal proponents of progressive Christianity in the crusade for racial equality and economic restructuring on a national scale. Many of California's white liberal Protestants and Jews advocated this cause, but none surpassed black Protestants in vigor and authority. As historian Douglas Flamming makes clear, left-wing political institutions as diverse as the Congress of Industrial Organizations (CIO) and Upton Sinclair's End Poverty in California (EPIC) consistently drew strength from the spirit of black Christianity (Flamming 2005). EPIC, along with related campaigns on behalf of economic redistribution and reform, also counted on leadership from the most prominent members of Los Angeles's black community. Few possessed the clout of Charlotta Bass, editor of California's most important African American newspaper *The Eagle*, who gathered strength and support for her politics from involvement with Second Baptist Church. In addition to working for change within the black community, Bass and her allies also solidified important political ties with other ethnic minorities, including those of Asian descent (Kurashige 2000).

Far less radical but even more prominent in California politics during the Depression were white clergymen to the political right who supported the state's many populist movements. These ranged in form from the sensational Ham and Eggs organization to the relatively staid Townsend Plan. The latter proved most successful at marrying theology to political ideology in designs for economic reform. With its particular appeal to people steeped in the Protestant work ethic of the American heartland, the Townsend antidote for economic strain was essentially a conservative social gospel that maintained the autonomy of the individual through its "pay as you go" approach and encouraged a basic Christian humanitarianism towards others. Although founder Francis Townsend surrounded himself with politicians and economists, much of his legitimacy in the eyes of followers came through his association with local religious leaders. A significant portion of California's Townsend Clubs held their meetings in churches and a cohort of ministers could be seen on stage with Townsend at most rallies. On the grassroots level the largest percentage of those eager to speak on behalf of Townsend at local clubs were preachers, missionaries, and evangelists, the majority of them affiliated with evangelical religious institutions (Dochuk 2005).

For many Californians living during the Depression, then, faith clearly informed politics. Research on this relationship must surely increase, as well as on the interchanges of faith that cemented both progressive liberal and conservative populist networks across the nation. By examining these linkages historians will better delineate the full range of motives that united like-minded Californians behind so many political crusades in the early twentieth century. It is by exploring the extent to which religion is embedded in these political campaigns that scholars will also better delineate the ways California's culture wars, fueled by this spectrum of causes prior to 1940, shaped national politics after this pivotal point.

California Religion and the Marketplace of Ideas

Much impetus for religion's public presence in early twentieth-century California thus stemmed from its inherent propensity for politics, but a third distinctive feature of this region's sacred landscape – its calibration to the marketplace of ideas – suggests that for most religious actors the quest for power was exercised more through effective salesmanship than political savvy. Indeed, no other feature of early twentieth-century California religion stands out more than its tendency to transform faith commitments into commodities and faith communities into marketplace competitors. Once again, First Baptist Bell Gardens' experience was typical for its time. Led by Rev. C. L. Guttery, a shrewd preacher from Arkansas, First Baptist congregants endorsed a marketing plan that matched their leader's relentlessness. Door-to-door canvassing, Sunday School callouts, and radio advertisements were just a few of the ways in which this church asserted itself in Bell Gardens. All of these endeavors, in sum, reflected First Baptist's view of religion as a bottom-line proposition whereby souls were to be won for Christ through any means and at any cost. Though manifested in different ways, this same entrepreneurialism in the practice of faith characterized California religion in the early twentieth century (Ernst 1987; Etulain 1991).

The first way in which California religion harmonized with market principles was by enabling and celebrating charismatic leadership. Throughout American history, frontier faiths have often stretched the limits of religious orthodoxy in order to win converts, and nudging them in this direction typically have been individuals able to exercise inordinate authority. During the early twentieth century, California represented the nation's last religious borderland; here movements designated elsewhere as dangerously sectarian operated free of constraints, and clerics of all ideological and ethnic backgrounds emerged eager to gather their multitudes. Reactionary, racially combative religion sometimes flourished as a result. During the interwar years, many white Californians, for example, wholeheartedly endorsed the teachings of British Israelism, an international movement for Anglo-Protestant purity that found a home on the West Coast because of the efforts of clerical demagogues like J. A. Lovell. Black Californians, meanwhile, had their own racially conscious spiritual leaders from whom to glean truth. No one held the imagination of his supporters more in this regard than George Baker, Jr., better known as Father Divine, whose two-million-member religious organization, The Universal Peace Mission, found much of its support in California (Peters 1973).

Less antagonistic and less noticeable were the host of spiritual guides who found a home in California overseeing the practice of various Eastern European and Asian faith traditions. Among them were many followers of Greek, Russian, and Ukrainian Orthodoxy, Byzantine Catholicism, the B'ahai Faith, Shintoism, Confucianism, Taoism, and Islam, all of which gained a tentative but significant foothold in California during the early twentieth century. Although institutionalized earlier through the founding of the Zenshuji Soto Mission in 1922, California's Zen Buddhism benefited greatly from Nyogen Senzaki's leadership, which in the early 1930s played out within a small group of disciples gathered at his modest home in Los Angeles. For the next quarter-century Senzaki helped his religious community gain strength, through both the difficult times of Japanese internment in the early 1940s and new encounters with prosperity in the 1950s. His legacy of leadership, moreover, proved critical to the blossoming of California Buddhism in the 1960s (Ellwood & Miller 1976; Fields 1986). Equally impressive was the initiative of Sardar Basakha Singh and Bhai Jawala Singh, immigrants from the Punjab region of India who arrived in California via Angel Island, then built a Sikh Gurdwara in Stockton, the first of its kind in the United States. Like Zen Buddhists in Los Angeles, Sikhs in Stockton looked for steady leadership as the foundation of strong community and found it in a line of Granthi Sing Jis that included Baba Vasakha Singh and Baba Jawala Singh (La Brack 1988).

As much as it thrived on the margins, charismatic leadership was not simply the purview of California's religious minorities. Mainstream Christians and non-Christians alike drew energy from popular individuals who stood out for their unmatched charm. Within California's vibrant Judaism, whose rich, diverse composition of Orthodox and Reformed, Ashkenazi and Sephardic peoples made it the most dynamic in the country, no one matched the allure of Rabbi Edgar Fogel Magnin (Stern 1980; Moore 1994). By the 1920s and for decades to come, Magnin was touted as the "Rabbi to the Stars" for his connections to Hollywood's movie moguls, yet it was as a conscientious spiritual mentor and gracious civic leader that the head of Wilshire Boulevard Temple in Los Angeles truly left a mark on his home state (Engh 2001: 208). Not to be overshadowed by their Jewish counterparts were California's Catholic luminaries. By the late 1940s Southern California Catholics were led by Archbishop J. Francis A. McIntyre, a powerful local and national voice for religious and political conservatism (Weber 1997). As dominant as he would become after World War II, McIntyre was hardly unique for his firm command over parishioners, for earlier in the century popular priests like Bishop John J. Cantwell had already demonstrated this same potential. Less explicit but no less impressive in this regard was the leadership offered California Catholics by women like Mother Maria Luisa Josefa de la Pena, first mother superior of the Carmelite Sisters of the Sacred Heart, who set standards of private devotion among her female followers and public service within her Los Angeles constituency (Alexander 1993: 67–70).

California religion's marriage to the media is the second means through which it harmonized with market principles. For many of California's most charismatic clerics, residence in the entertainment capital of the world necessitated flamboyant showmanship. No one was more adept at this than Aimee Semple McPherson, one of California's most intriguing and studied

religious figures. After arriving in Los Angeles in 1918, McPherson established Angelus Temple as a modern, permanent "revival tent" in the Echo
Park district of the city. For the next three decades, Sister Aimee captivated
her weekly audiences by translating her Pentecostal doctrine of salvation,
sanctification, and second blessing into simple messages of hope and for-
giveness. As historians Matthew Sutton and Edith Blumhofer describe in
vivid fashion, helping her in this process were her "illustrated sermons"
in which she appeared on stage in elaborate costumes to act out parables
of faith. McPherson's biographers argue that it was in these dramatic
moments that California bore witness to a new era in American religious
culture in which the medium became the message (Blumhofer 1993;
Sutton 2007).

As impressive as such theatrical displays were for McPherson's own
ministry, more important generally for California religion's embrace of
media was the radio. Several external factors made the state's airwaves
pulsate with religious programming, including ready access to powerful,
unregulated radio stations just across the Mexican border. Ultimately,
though, it was left up to religious leaders to ensure that this medium
became a staple of religious life in California. Jose David Orozco accentuated the potential of radio for consolidating Catholic religious community;
during the 1920s and 1930s he commanded a radio audience of over
40,000. Besides using his regular devotional programming to help raise
spiritual awareness, institutionalize Catholic practice, and stir up ethnic
pride, Orozco also contributed to the organization of societies designed
for cross-cultural exchange between California and Mexico. Evidence of
Orozco's contributions were on regular display in the streets of East Los
Angeles during the Depression, when thousands of Mexican American
Catholics gathered for processions in honor of Mexico's national patron,
the Virgin of Guadalupe, and in celebration of the feast of Corpus Christi
(Engh 2001).

Even broader in his reach was Charles Fuller, the evangelist who became
famous for his radio ministry, the "Old Fashioned Revival Hour." Besides
attracting capacity crowds at the Municipal Auditorium in Long Beach for
weekly broadcasts, the Old Fashioned Revival Hour was heard on over 600
stations around the western hemisphere. With radio as his method and
family wealth as his means, Fuller parlayed his success into other religious
enterprises, most notably Fuller Seminary in Pasadena, which in turn
helped recondition American evangelicalism by making it more progressive
in its theological and social vision and more certain of its political and cultural mission (Goff 2001). Historians rightly claim that because of Fuller's
efforts California evangelicalism emerged from its pre-World War II home
on the margins as a pace setter for American evangelicalism in the postwar
cultural mainstream.

Conclusion

What Jose David Orozco's and Charles Fuller's stories illustrate for Catholicism and evangelicalism hold true for California religion generally. By surviving – indeed thriving within – the conditions of change in early twentieth-century California, religion emerged as an exceptionally dynamic, supple entity fully equipped to shape patterns of development across the entire nation. It is for this reason that historians now point to California's encounter with the sacred at the dawn of the twentieth century as anticipatory of America's spiritual encounter at century's end. Scholars of modern America have recently begun to reassess postmodernity's impact on faith. Whereas they once concluded that cultural pluralism, political fragmentation, and technological advancement would limit religion, developments since the 1970s have proved this prediction wrong. Evidence abounds that faith today holds sway over the public realm; to explain this curious phenomenon scholars have looked to California, America's first postmodern landscape, for answers. Here individuals and institutions first confronted the new realities of a pluralistic society that encouraged syncretism and exchange, a "balkanized" political domain that demanded active involvement in the public sphere, and a fiercely competitive marketplace of ideas that urged full acceptance of technological innovation. In short, what scholars wonder about present American society they now see explained more fully in California's illustrious past: that forces of change associated with postmodernity in fact stimulate not suppress the sacred (Wuthnow 1990; Smith 1998; Roof 2001).

Beyond the context of early twentieth-century California history, meanwhile, lies yet more potential for fresh historical scholarship. Indeed, even as historians continue delving deeper into religion's comprehensive workings prior to World War II, they should also consider its continued effect after this critical juncture. Scholars have already hinted at the promise of this endeavor, in part by suggesting that it was not until after 1950 that California religion flourished as a model for the rest of the nation to follow (Engh 2001). Considering the evidence already turned up, they may be right. Recent studies of post-World War II African American and Latino, Jewish and Catholic, Asian and Middle Eastern, suburban evangelical and urban mainline, orthodox and New Age, cultic and occultist religious communities at work in every corner of the state suggest that California's investment in the sacred and influence on the nation only intensified with time. It is now up to historians to judge the accuracy of this claim, both in the context of these recent findings and in light of new scholarship that continues to add texture and depth to the literature on pre-World War II California religion.

Scholars would do well to measure the stories of continuity and flux seen in localized tales of sacred communities like First Baptist Bell Gardens, whose more recent past confirms the sustained vitality of faith in postwar California. In the decades following its run-in with local authorities, First Baptist adopted an even more ambitious agenda of expansion. By the early 1950s, First Baptist claimed an average attendance of nearly 450, a number that forced the church to undertake numerous expansion projects. In what would become a benchmark to which all other congregations would aspire, First Baptist entered the 1960s having already planted seven satellite churches, making it responsible for the enlistment of three thousand people in Southern Baptist Sunday Schools. By the late 1970s, after further adjustment to California's demographic change, political ferment, and competitive marketplace of religion, First Baptist members could be found helping their denomination establish other congregations in new neighborhoods scattered throughout Southern California. Among those on the receiving end of this support was Saddleback Community Church, today one of the nation's premier evangelical megachurches and most commonly used illustrations of American religion's uncommon vitality in the new millennium.

REFERENCES

Alexander, K. 1993. *Californian Catholicism*. Santa Barbara, CA: Fithian Press.

Blumhofer, E. W. 1993. *Aimee Semple McPherson: Everybody's Sister*. Grand Rapids, MI: William B. Eerdmans.

Cocoltchos, C. N. 1979. "The Invisible Government and the Viable Community: The Ku Klux Klan in Orange County, California, During the 1920s." PhD dissertation, University of California, Los Angeles.

Davis, E. 2006. *The Visionary State: A Journey Through California's Spiritual Landscape*. San Francisco: Chronicle Books.

Dochuk, D. 2005. "From Bible Belt to Sunbelt: Plain Folk Religion, Grassroots Politics, and the Southernization of Southern California, 1939–1969." PhD dissertation, University of Notre Dame.

Edmondson, W. D. 1969. "Fundamentalist Sects of Los Angeles, 1900–1930." PhD dissertation, Claremont Graduate School.

Ellwood, R. S., Jr. and Miller, D. E. 1976. "Eastern Religions and New Spiritual Movements." In F. J. Weber, ed., *The Religious Heritage of Southern California*. Los Angeles: Interreligious Council of Southern California.

Engh, M. E., S. J. 1992. *Frontier Faiths: Church, Temple, and Synagogue in Los Angeles, 1846–1888*. Albuquerque: University of New Mexico Press.

Engh, M. E., S. J. 2001. "Practically Every Religion Being Represented." In T. Sitton and W. Deverell, eds., *Metropolis in the Making: Los Angeles in the 1920s*. Berkeley and Los Angeles: University of California Press, pp. 201–19.

Ernst, E. G. 1987. "American Religious History from a Pacific Coast Perspective." In C. Guarneri and D. Alvarez, eds., *Religion and Society in the American West: Historical Essays*. Lanham, MD: University Press of America.

Ernst, E. G. 2001. "The Emergence of California in American Religious Histori-ography," *Religion and American Culture: A Journal of Interpretation* 11 (Winter): 31–52.

Ernst, E. and Anderson, D. 1993. *Pilgrim Progression: The Protestant Experience in California*. Santa Barbara, CA: Fithian Press.

Etulain, R. W. 1991. "Regionalizing Religion: Evangelicals in the American West, 1940–1990." In R. M. Cooke and R. W. Etulain, eds., *Religion and Culture: Historical Essays in Honor of Robert C. Woodward*. Albuquerque: Far West Books, pp. 78–103.

Fields, R. 1986. *How the Swans Came to the Lake: A Narrative History of Buddhism in America*. Boston, MA: Shambhala.

Flamming, D. 2005. *Bound for Freedom: Black Los Angeles in Jim Crow America*. Berkeley and Los Angeles: University of California Press.

Fogelson, R. M. 1993 <1967>. *The Fragmented Metropolis: Los Angeles 1850–1930*. Berkeley: University of California Press.

Frankiel, S. S. 1988. *California's Spiritual Frontiers: Religious Alternatives to Anglo-Protestantism, 1850–1910*. Berkeley: University of California Press.

Froese, B. 2003. "Faith in the Sun: A History of Migration, Urbanization, Pacifism and Education in the California Mennonite Experience, 1905–1965." PhD dis-sertation, Graduate Theological Union.

Goff, Philip. 2001. "Fighting Like the Devil in the City of Angels: The Rise of Fundamentalist Charles E. Fuller." In T. Sitton and W. Deverell, eds., *Metropolis in the Making: Los Angeles in the 1920s*. Berkeley and Los Angeles: University of California Press, pp. 220–51.

Gregory, J. N. 1989. *American Exodus: The Dust Bowl Migration and Okie Culture in California*. New York: Oxford University Press.

Hayashi, B. M. 1995. *For the Sake of Our Japanese Brethren: Assimilation, Nation-alism, and Protestantism among the Japanese of Los Angeles, 1895–1942*. Stan-ford, CA: Stanford University Press.

Hunter, J. D. 1992. *Culture Wars: The Struggle to Define America*. New York: Basic Books.

Kurashige, S. T. 2000. "Transforming Los Angeles: Black and Japanese American Struggles for Racial Equality in the Twentieth Century." PhD dissertation, University of California, Los Angeles.

La Brack, B. 1988. *The Sikhs of Northern California, 1904–1975*. New York: AMS Press.

Looney, F. 1954, *History of California Southern Baptists*. Fresno, CA: The South-ern Baptist General Convention of California.

Maffly-Kipp, L. 1994. *Religion and Society in Frontier California*. New Haven, CT: Yale University Press.

Miller, D. E. 1997. *Reinventing American Protestantism: Christianity in the New Millennium*. Berkeley: University of California Press.

Miller, R. M. 1990. *Bishop G. Bromley Oxnam: Palladin of Liberal Protestantism*. Nashville, TN: Abingdon Press.

Moore, D. D. 1994. *To the Golden Cities: Pursuing the American Jewish Dream in Miami and Los Angeles*. New York: Free Press.

Nicolaides, B. 2002. *My Blue Heaven; Life and Politics in the Working-Class Suburbs of Los Angeles, 1920–1965*. Chicago: University of Chicago Press.

Peters, W. B. 1973. "The Varieties of Religious Experience in Los Angeles, 1920–1950." PhD dissertation, University of California, Santa Barbara.

Quinn, M. D. 1992. "Religion in the American West." In W. Cronon, G. Miles, and J. Gitlin, eds., *Under and Open Sky: Rethinking America's Western Past*. New York: W. W. Norton, pp. 145–64.

Roof, W. C. 2001. *Spiritual Marketplace: Baby Boomers and the Remaking of American Religion*. Princeton, NJ: Princeton University Press.

Singleton, G. H. 1979. *Religion in the City of Angels: American Protestant Culture and Urbanization, Los Angeles, 1850–1930*. Ann Arbor: UMI Research Press.

Smith, C. 1998. *American Evangelicalism: Embattled and Thriving*. Chicago: University of Chicago Press.

Stern, S. 1980. *The Sephardic Jewish Community in Los Angeles*. New York: Arno.

Still, M. S. 1988. "'Fighting Bob' Shuler: Fundamentalist and Reformer." PhD dissertation, Claremont Graduate School.

Sutton, M. A. 2007. *Aimee Semple McPherson and the Resurrection of Christian America*. Cambridge, MA: Harvard University Press.

Synan, V. 1997. *The Holiness-Pentecostal Tradition: Charismatic Movements in the Twentieth Century*. Grand Rapids, MI: William B. Eerdmans.

Takaki, R. 1989. *Strangers from a Different Shore: A History of Asian Americans*. New York: Little, Brown.

Vorspan, D. and Gartner, L. P. 1970. *History of the Jews of Los Angeles*. San Marino, CA: Huntington Library.

Weber, F. J. 1997. *His Eminence of Los Angeles; James Francis Cardinal McIntyre*. Mission Hills, CA: Saint Francis Historical Society.

Wild, M. H. 2005. *Street Meeting: Multiethnic Neighborhoods in Early Twentieth-Century Los Angeles*. Berkeley and Los Angeles: University of California Press.

Wuthnow, R. 1990. *The Restructuring of American Religion*. Princeton, NJ: Princeton University Press.

Yoo, D. K. 1999. *Growing Up Nisei: Race, Generation, and Culture among Japanese Americans of California, 1924–49*. Champaign, IL: University of Illinois Press.

Further Reading

Burns, J. M. 1987. "The Mexican American Catholic Community in California, 1850–1980." In C. Guarneri and D. Alverez, eds., *Religion and Society in the American West: Historical Essays*. Lanham, MD: University Press of America.

Ellwood, R. S. 1979. *Alternative Altars: Unconventional and Eastern Spirituality in America*. Chicago: University of Chicago Press.

Ellwood, R. S. 1994. *The Sixties Spiritual Awakening: American Religion Moving from Modern to Postmodern*. New Brunswick, NJ: Rutgers University Press.

Glock, C. Y. and Bellah, R. N., eds. 1976. *The New Religious Consciousness.* Berkeley: University of California Press.

Marsden, G. M. 1987. *Reforming Fundamentalism: Fuller Seminary and the New Evangelicalism.* Grand Rapids, MI: Eerdmans.

Warner, R. S. 1988. *New Wine in Old Wineskins: Evangelicals and Liberals in a Small-Town Church.* Berkeley: University of California Press.

Chapter Sixteen

IMMIGRATION, RACE, AND THE PROGRESSIVES

Lon Kurashige

The rise of Progressive reformers, who helped to topple the Southern Pacific Railroad's longstanding influence in California politics and transformed Sacramento into a celebrated site of democratic innovation, stands as an iconic episode in the state's early twentieth-century history. The initial studies of California Progressives were sympathetic to these reformers, seeing their clean government initiatives and activist state as salvation from the Southern Pacific's monopoly politics (Mowry 1951). Later works, however, became increasingly critical of the Progressives. Historians today are less interested in studying their accomplishments and triumphs than in learning lessons from their limitations and failures with respect to land monopoly, organized labor, environmental policies, moral reform, and women's rights (Deverell & Sitton 1994). But no criticism of the Progressives has received greater emphasis than the reformers' racism and related nativism directed against Asian (and later Mexican) immigrants. This essay attempts to shed new light on themes of race and immigration in Progressive Era California by examining the discourse of one of its most articulate and influential leaders.

The study of racism and immigration in Progressive California began with a critical account of the state's land monopolies and suppression of agricultural labor (McWilliams 1939). This left-wing analysis, however, stirred up more political than scholarly debate in its day. For example, the first major history of California Progressives did little more than acknowledge that their policies stopped at the color line (Mowry 1951). Yet a younger generation of historians coming of age during the Civil Rights era incorporated McWilliams's racial critique in monographs attacking the optimistic picture painted by Mowry and other consensus- (rather than conflict-) oriented historians. Writings in the 1960s by such scholars as Spencer Olin, Jr. and Roger Daniels saw the Progressives' racism not merely as an exception to their otherwise reformist credentials but as a major (if not fatal) flaw of their movement. Ostensibly committed to the expansion of democracy, the state's reformers, in Olin's words, were "blinded by racial prejudice" and "unfounded fears of Oriental inundation" (Olin 1968: 90). In studying the debate over Japanese immigration, Daniels concludes that "one of the most glaring and too often unremarked deficiencies of the [P] rogressive was his utter disregard for civil liberties" (Daniels 1962: 107).

This revisionist scholarship established the wellspring from which has flowed a healthy stream of subsequent studies that emphasize the significance of race in Progressive Era California. The literature since the 1960s has gone in two directions. One route addresses the internal history and agency of various non-white minority groups (Chan 1986; Ichioka 1988; Sanchez 1993; Gutierrez 1995; Flamming 2005; Azuma 2005). A more recent path expands analysis of the victimizers beyond the usual political subjects (Palumbo-Liu 1999; Shah 2001; Yu 2001; Lee 2003; Lye 2005; Stern 2005; Molina 2006). Both strands are grounded in the rise of social and then cultural history, both of which diminished scholarly interest in politics proper as the bedrock of California racism. Instead the spotlight shined on a widening circle of often-overlooked agents of racial formation: intellectuals, literati, cultural performers, immigration and public health officials, and especially racialized minorities. Consequently, recent studies have been more interested in the fringes rather than the core of political power. There are, of course, many benefits to social and cultural approaches, but one problem is that in expanding our understanding of racism in early twentieth-century California, they have not questioned the earlier revisionist criticism of the state's Progressive reformers.

This essay brings Progressive leaders back to the center of analysis by reconsidering the racial discourse of Chester Rowell, a journalist, publicist, and organizer of the reformist political movement that attacked the political power of the Southern Pacific. Daniels has singled out Rowell as the "archetypal" racist within the pantheon of California Progressives, an attribute derived from Rowell's ardent and influential insistence on the exclusion of Asian immigration to the United States (Daniels 1966). Yet, as I will argue, his views were more cosmopolitan than they have been understood by scholars and need to be analyzed within the specific racial and political logic of three successive historical contexts: (1) a post-Reconstruction era in which he recoiled at "race problems" in both Washington, DC and California; (2) a post-World War I period during which he saw white supremacy as an albatross getting in the way of world peace; and (3) the age of World War II, when he called for the end of racial segregation as both a wartime and postwar necessity. The following case study will address Rowell's racial thinking in each of these periods and then conclude with brief suggestions regarding the next steps for rethinking the study of race and Progressivism in California history.[1]

Lessons from Reconstruction

Chester Rowell would have been raised in the South if his father had accepted the post offered to him as the Reconstruction governor of Texas. But as it turned out, the Rowell family remained in Bloomington, Illinois – a decidedly Republican and anti-slavery township in which Abraham Lincoln had close friends and solid political backing. Jonathan Rowell – lawyer, state attorney, and Civil War veteran – won election to the United States House of Representatives in 1883 and moved to Washington. After college, Chester joined his father on Capitol Hill, serving as the clerk of the House Elections Committee that the senior Rowell chaired. This was a crucial committee in the post-Reconstruction Congress that investigated and decided upon fraudulent elections. While electoral chicanery occurred throughout the nation, it was especially common in the South, where white Democrats clawed their way back to power by disfranchising African American voters. Chester Rowell watched the Jim Crow era unfold before his eyes. He was outraged by the way Southern Democrats would do anything – including murder – to get back into office, while Republicans in Congress looked the other way. The whole episode left him, and a generation of idealistic Northerners, powerfully disillusioned at the prospect of color-blind democracy.

The failure of Reconstruction taught Rowell lessons that influenced a life-long skepticism about interracial experimentation. While recognizing that there were exceptional individuals like Frederick Douglass, E. K. Bruce, John M. Langston, and, his favorite, Booker T. Washington, Rowell believed that the vast majority of African Americans, due both to heredity and environment, were not ready for democracy. Yet he steadfastly refused to accept the commonly held verdict that the failure of Reconstruction was due to black incompetence and corruption. Rowell had seen for himself in Washington that white Southern Democrats, with the consent of white Northern Republicans, bore the ultimate responsibility for the epidemic of corruption and violence that suffocated the hope of interracial democracy. As clerk of the House Elections Committee, he had learned first-hand what a landmark sociological study would conclude half a decade later: racial dilemmas in America were largely a problem created by white America (Myrdal 1944).

When Rowell moved to Fresno, California in 1898, it was as if a time machine had transported him back to the early days of American slavery. Business interests in the Golden State were continuing to import non-white servile laborers who threatened to become a permanent racial caste. It did not matter that out West the non-white labor came from Asia and Mexico instead of Africa. For Rowell, the issue was racial difference. Labor migrations were not a problem if they originated in Europe; history had shown that even "inferior" classes of European immigrants would eventually inter-marry with native whites. Rowell had seen for himself that the same was not true for even the most cultured and educated African Americans. While cosmopolitan, reform-minded Northerners like himself could accept inter-racial marriages, he had no confidence that the masses of white Americans could do the same. Southern race relations taught him that even the idea of black men having sex with white women would provoke the lynch mob. As a result, he believed that the only way to maintain order in a racially mixed society was to separate the races by imposing a clear color line. Thus we begin to see the complexity of Rowell's opinions and positions. It was to prevent the spreading of Jim Crow from the South to California that caused him to sound an early alarm to exclude the Japanese from immigrat-ing to the United States.

Rowell's hometown of Fresno gave him another reason for concern. He moved to California's Central Valley at the request of his uncle and name-sake Dr. Chester Rowell, who, as a physician, publicist, and mayor, was leading efforts to clean up that frontier town. Nephew Chester became editor of his uncle's newspaper, the *Fresno Republican*, and took up the cause of moral reform. While bemoaning the city's sex and liquor trade, Rowell dedicated the most editorial space to attacking its gambling indus-try. Chinatown drew his particular ire because its gambling dens combined the two evils of moral decay and racial caste. This was apparent to him when the police resorted to using a battering ram to enter a "private for-tress" in Chinatown. "Every Chinatown raid," he maintained, "is a fresh reminder of the inconsistent character of our policy or lack of policy toward the local Chinese question. As long as we have Chinese we must have an Oriental reservation in which it is impossible to impose American ways or enforce all American laws."[2]

Rowell's initial call to exclude Asian immigrants derived from both the bitter memory of Reconstruction and the promise of Progressive municipal reform. His was a decidedly middle-class and reformist strain of nativism that was distinct from the more prevalent California variety of working-men's protest. In the 1870s and 1880s San Francisco labor unions con-tributed to a successful movement to exclude Chinese immigration, and by the turn of the century these same forces were gearing up to halt the recent influx of Japanese immigrants. Rowell's rationale for Japanese exclu-sion added a Progressive dimension to the state's traditional anti-Asian hostility. The combination of workers and middle-class reformers was a rare and formidable coalition.

But there were two serious obstacles along the road to Japanese exclu-sion. The more general was the entrenched faith that Americans had in their country's ability to assimilate the world's peoples. True, Rowell showed that this faith often did not extend beyond European groups. Yet

the war in Cuba and the Philippines, and the subsequent American colonialism in the Pacific and Caribbean, had been justified in large part by
assimilationist notions of uplifting backward and savage peoples. The early,
sanguine days of American imperialism and world mission, thus, worked
against the doomsday racial scenarios pitched by Rowell and other proponents of Japanese exclusion. Next, the more specific barrier that the exclusionist confronted was the rise of Japan as a world power. While Washington
had dictated the terms of immigration exclusion to the Chinese without
fear of military reprisal, it could not resort to such bullying tactics against
the modern nation of Japan. Nothing confirmed this more than Japan's
stunning defeat of the great Russian navy in 1905.

The Russo-Japanese War proved a turning point for Rowell that distinguished him from the main currents of the anti-Japanese movement and
set him on a course leading away from its inherent racism. Japan's victory
stirred up jingoist fears that inflamed California's anti-Asian passions, and
for the first time brought national attention to the "Japanese menace."
Rowell, however, had an altogether different response to the war: it left
him with a tremendous respect for the Japanese and remarkable confidence
in the prospect of United States–Japan friendship. As publicist, Progressive
Party leader, and chair of the planning commission for California's Panama–
Pacific Exposition in 1915, Rowell was already sensitive to Japan's demand
for racial respect, as well as its fragile national ego. In fact, as befitted his
penchant to deflate America's own national and racial hubris, he lambasted
the leadership of California's anti-Japanese movement for compromising
goodwill across the Pacific. In print he called the leaders of the state's
Asiatic Exclusion League "unscrupulous demagogues who do not have nor
deserve the confidence of the public," while in a private letter he ridiculed
them as "crooks and criminals" who were "worse than useless."[3] The
importance he placed on healthy United States–Japan relations also made
him unafraid to chastise one of the richest men in California, William
Randolph Hearst, for using his extensive publishing industry to spread
rumors about Japan's alleged war plans against America.

Rowell's optimism regarding international relations balanced his pessimism about domestic race relations, giving his nativism an internationalist
bent that set him apart from (and against) the main thrust of California
exclusionists. In short, he sought to exclude Japanese immigrants in a way
that acknowledged, rather than insulted, Japan's great civilization. What
he wanted was a revision of the Gentlemen's Agreement of 1907–8 in
which officials in Washington and Tokyo agreed to restrict the immigration
of Japanese laborers to the United States. Rowell believed that another
round of diplomacy to restrict family reunification and other classes of
immigrants would be much less insulting than the unilateral Congressional
exclusion that was preferred by most anti-Japanese groups. Thus he walked

a fine line by agreeing with Hearst and other "demagogues" about the necessity for exclusion, but disagreeing with them as to why and how this was to be achieved. Rowell's differences with the basic tenor of the anti-Japanese movement would grow as World War I doomed Progressive reform.

Another Civil War and Racial Challenge

Rowell attached a powerful racial significance to World War I, seeing the destruction of Europe as impetus for the rise of a new age in which international affairs would center on the Pacific Rim. The general outline for this vision was apparent in Lothrop Stoddard's well-known book *The Rising Tide of Color* (1920). A Harvard-educated editor and international affairs scholar, Stoddard cast World War I as a civil war among white nations, whose mutual antagonism had benefited the rising powers of Asia. While Rowell was not a white supremacist, racial alarmist, or hard-core eugenicist like Stoddard, this book enabled him to connect immigration issues in California to a global framework for understanding contemporary race relations. In this way the Great War marked another milestone for Rowell, after which peaceful US–Japan relations would increasingly become the baseline for his racial analysis.

Rowell's internationalism was apparent in his absence from the anti-Japanese campaign that surrounded California's 1920 election. While both candidates for United States Senate played the race card and voters agreed to strengthen restrictions on Japanese landholding, Rowell did not take sides in the debate. To be sure, he remained steadfast in his opposition to unrestricted Japanese immigration, but he also lent his name to the masthead of a pro-Japanese organization run by Sidney Gulick, an author, missionary, and leading opponent of Japanese exclusion who promoted interracial brotherhood across the Pacific. As exclusionist sentiment increased in the late 1910s and early 1920s, Gulick proposed a pragmatic solution to severely limit (but not totally exclude) Japanese immigrants, while guaranteeing fair treatment to those Asians already in the United States. Rowell agreed with this plan in that it sought to redress the humiliations that the Japanese government felt regarding America's response to their immigrants. In due course, Rowell supported neither the total ban on Japanese immigration that Congress passed in 1924 over the strong objections of both the United States and Japanese diplomatic corps nor the discrimination aimed at those Japanese already in the United States.

Another factor that softened Rowell's pessimism about California's interracial experiment was the Americanization of the second generation of Japanese immigrants. While he had thought that Asians were

unassimilable in American society, the stellar performance of Asian Americans in Hawaiian public schools changed his mind. After visiting the islands
a number of times, he came to see Hawaii as a successful racial laboratory
that showcased the intelligence and assimilability of Asian Americans,
whom he saw as superior to many classes of southern and eastern Europeans. It is not surprising, then, that the Institute of Pacific Relations (IPR),
the greatest non-governmental gathering of Pacific Rim peoples between
the world wars, originated in Hawaii, and that Rowell was a founding
member. In 1925 he sailed to Honolulu to attend its first conference,
meeting with leading figures from every major country in or bordering the
Pacific Ocean. This historic gathering discussed the international fallout
from the United States' exclusion of Japanese immigrants. After becoming
the IPR's official publicist in 1929, Rowell waxed nostalgic about the
"experiment of understanding" that emerged at this first conference. Peace
across the Pacific, Rowell contended, was rooted in personal connections
and goodwill established among the IPR members.

The Honolulu meeting, as well as subsequent ones in California, Japan,
and Canada, transformed Rowell into an authority on East Asia affairs. As
an IPR representative, he came to see white supremacy as the single most
destructive force in contemporary world affairs. Rowell made his case
through four core points. First, technology had enabled the rise of East
Asian nations to world leadership, starting with, but by no means exclusively linked to, the military and economic power of Japan. Second, whether
the West appreciated it or not, the globalization of the Pacific was an
incontrovertible fact of life that had flattened nineteenth-century colonial
hierarchies, while encouraging former colonial victims to demand material,
political, and psychological equality with their former masters. Third, if
Westerners did not recognize these changes in the world and cast off outdated notions of white supremacy, they would miss out on tremendous
business opportunities and, more importantly, incite a race war between
the world's white and non-white peoples. Finally, the best way to prevent
such a crisis was to develop mutual respect in the new Pacific world by
getting different peoples to know each other personally under safe and
reasonable circumstances.

Rowell backed up his high praise for Asian peoples by becoming involved
in efforts to amend the 1924 Immigration Act by granting a token quota
of Japanese immigrants to the United States. This campaign was driven by
a San Francisco businessman and founder of the city's Japan Society,
Wallace Alexander, and also had great support from the tireless Sidney
Gulick. Here again Rowell was on Gulick's side, much to the chagrin of
the continuing (though seriously thinned) advocates of the anti-Japanese
movement. Despite strong support from business, diplomatic, missionary,

and peace communities, the attempt to estab   nmigration quota
faltered and ultimately failed with the growing   ional discord over
the Japanese conquest and colonialism in China (2001).

One World in War and Peace

The destruction of Pearl Harbor in December 1941 combined war hysteria, jingoism, revenge, and racism into the greatest wave of anti-Japanese animosity ever to hit the West Coast. The same racialized arguments and fears about Japanese perfidy and unassimilability that had animated earlier campaigns for immigration exclusion re-emerged as rationales for relocating and interning the Japanese along the Pacific Coast. The reaction to Pearl Harbor was so drastic that many longtime supporters of Japanese Americans, such as the American Civil Liberties Union and the Communist Party, as well as otherwise reasonable observers like columnist Walter Lippman, succumbed to the hysteria and favored internment.

But not Chester Rowell. Because the internment question turned on racial traits and potentialities, and not miscegenation, he was able to take the Japanese American side without reservation. After all, he had argued repeatedly that Japanese immigrants (and especially their children) were superior to most immigrant groups from Europe; they also were more than capable of adopting American culture, and therefore posed no threat as long as their numbers remained small. To praise the Japanese before the war was one thing, but it is a testament to Rowell that he remained steadfast after Pearl Harbor. As editor of the *San Francisco Chronicle* (a job he started in 1932) he wrote at least eight columns between Pearl Harbor and the decision on internment, arguing that race should not be a factor in any policy to protect the West Coast. As he was prone to do, Rowell took aim at opportunistic demagogues and economic interests for exciting the masses on the Japanese question. He also blamed the United States Navy for the failure at Pearl Harbor, giving no credence to the popular rumors of Japanese American deception in Hawaii. After President Franklin Roosevelt issued the internment order Rowell continued to attack anti-Japanese racism in his columns. He went a step further as a founding member of the Committee on National Security and Fair Play, an organization committed to protecting the constitutional rights of Japanese Americans. His position on internment reveals how far his thinking about race had progressed since the beginning of the twentieth century when he sounded the initial alarm against the "menace" of Japanese immigration.

Rowell's transformation also was evident in his response to other minority groups during World War II. He supported the movement to grant

China a token immigration quota that effectively repealed the humiliation of Chinese exclusion. But the main index of Rowell's evolving racial views in the 1940s was his concern about African American civil rights. As part of his post-Reconstruction disillusionment in interracial democracy, Rowell was committed to the technical training of African Americans that Booker T. Washington emphasized as a gradual way to improve race relations in the South. Rowell's embrace of this gradualist approach, which accepted the fact of racial segregation, ended during World War II when he called for the dramatic termination of Jim Crow segregation.

To understand Rowell's shift on black civil rights we need to appreciate the racial dimensions of World War II. During the war, Japan relied upon the colonial injuries that Lothrop Stoddard discussed to incite the masses of Asia and the Pacific to join the Japanese imperial forces in throwing out their white masters. Meanwhile, Germany sought to unite Europe through the creation of an even purer form of white (Aryan) supremacy. These Axis powers, with their different conceptions of race, forced Americans to distinguish themselves from either of their racial schemes. Rowell thought that the answer to both Japan's "Asia for the Asiatic" propaganda and Germany's Aryan nation rhetoric was a concerted program of anti-racism. America needed to assure the world – especially its Asian allies and the US's own racial minority soldiers and citizens – that it opposed all forms and practices of white supremacy: colonialism, Japanese American internment, Chinese exclusion, and anti-black race riots at home.

America's victory in World War II assured Rowell that removing barriers of racial caste was the only way for the nation and the world to create lasting peace. Consistent with his support for the League of Nations 25 years earlier, Rowell placed great hope in the United Nations and told Americans that they needed to abandon racial discrimination in order to prove themselves legitimate leaders of a world in which all peoples now had equal rights. He also added that increasingly powerful Asian and African nations would demand no less than the end of white supremacy in all its guises.

But postwar racial equality did not mean that anyone should have the freedom to immigrate to the United States. Here Rowell remained firmly rooted in the past. While Americans needed to show respect and consideration for Chinese and Japanese peoples overseas and at home, they should not open the floodgates to Asian immigration. He made an exception for immigrants from Mexico since they were essential for farming and returned home when they were not needed. In this way, Rowell was able to draw a line between his opposition to unrestricted immigration and support for unrestricted civil and human rights. Despite the many changes in racial discourse throughout his life, his nativism remained nourished by a consistent repugnance for white supremacy.

Progressive Meanings of Race

Chester Rowell's evolving racial views question the characterization of him as an archetype of California racism. It is true that he vigorously and consistently opposed non-white immigration and at times saw blacks and Mexicans as racially inferior to whites and Asians. But stopping at these points is misleading, as it fails to reveal his firm rejection of racial hierarchy (races were either equal or could be with education and improved conditions), or the fact that he largely blamed entrenched white racism for America's inability to embrace interracial democracy in the American South or along the West Coast. Also, classifying Rowell based only on his views that most offend us today fails to grasp the intriguing shifts in his thinking. His racial thinking changed based on historical circumstances: from the interracial pessimism rooted in post-Reconstruction disillusionment and Progressive reform; to the interracial optimism bound up in movements for peaceful international relations; and, finally, to a guarded faith in a Reconstruction-like interracial democracy that was prompted by the exigencies of World War II and postcolonialism. Well before his death in 1946, Rowell's calls for desegregation as well as civil and human rights revealed that this "archetypal racist" became an original and truly progressive thinker.

While Rowell's is a unique and fascinating story of racial transformation, it would be a mistake to assume that it was sui generis. A highly educated and well-read thinker, Rowell kept in step with the liberalization in racial theory that was circulated in the social sciences. The scholarship on this intellectual and cultural discourse traditionally has championed the challenge it posed to scientific racism, and portrayed leading lights such as anthropologist Franz Boas and sociologist Robert Park as the first modern racial thinkers (Gossett 1963; Matthews 1977). A more recent and alternative view, however, criticizes the limitations of liberal race theory, casting its story as mainly a repackaging of white supremacy through cultural rather than biological rationales (Palumbo-Liu 1999; Yu 2001; Lye 2005). Rowell's story can be interpreted through either lens of this debate, as a triumph in liberal cosmopolitanism or as a continuation of ideas justifying Asian immigration exclusion (the above case study, however, adheres more closely to the first perspective). But the basic point should not be overlooked: Rowell reveals that racial liberalization (whatever one makes of it) could occur among California Progressives at the vanguard of seemingly racist movements to exclude non-white immigrants. This surprising finding prompts one to consider how many other Californians have been misunderstood as irredeemable racists. What do their stories suggest about patterns of racist and nativist thinking?

In a related but more specific way, Rowell's case alerts one to rethink the assumption that there was a straight line of causation from movements to exclude Japanese immigration to the wartime internment of Japanese Americans. Rowell shows how a person could support the former but not the latter. And he was not the only one to question internment, having worked in earlier campaigns to curb anti-Japanese racism with many of the same educators, business organizations, philanthropists, scholars, and religious groups who supported Japanese Americans once again during their most dire time of need. It is curious that while many non-professional historians have mentioned that Rowell was a decidedly anti-racist friend to Japanese Americans, the professional scholarship almost always paints an unflattering portrait of him (Hosokawa 1982; Nakano 1990). What explains the Jekyll and Hyde portrayal of Rowell in the historiography? And what do his two faces say about the relationship between the exclusion of Japanese immigrants and internment?

Rowell's case also encourages one to reconsider the connections between western and southern race relations. It has been long known that nativism in the nineteenth and early twentieth centuries had its deepest roots in these two parts of the United States, and that westerners and southerners in Congress usually provided the main support for immigration restriction (Higham 1955). But there has been no in-depth study comparing race relations in the two sections. Rowell's story suggests that it might be fruitful to examine the impact of Reconstruction (and its demise) on California racial thinking. Rowell transferred his disillusionment with racial experimentation in the South to a decided pessimism regarding the possibility of white tolerance for Asian assimilation on the West Coast. A recent book on the connection between southern racism against blacks and anti-Chinese racism reveals an earlier linkage between Reconstruction and Asian exclusion. The author found that while Radical Republicans were willing to fight for the civil rights of Chinese immigrants in the 1870s, during the heyday of interracial democracy in the South, they gave up the cause and even supported Chinese exclusion once Reconstruction had failed (Aarim-Heriot 2003).

On the other hand, those, like Rowell, who were at one time willing to experiment with interracial democracy, may have been more prone to do it again in different ways. Rowell never lost his respect for African American leaders, and he carried on the ability to appreciate great men and women of all civilizations. Similarly, Robert Park, the famous Chicago sociologist who engaged in path-breaking studies of race relations in California and Hawaii, had ties to the South, having worked for many years as Booker T. Washington's press secretary. The intimate connections that Rowell and Park had with southern race relations distinguished them from typical California racists and can help explain how they both came to advocate interpersonal relations as the best method for learning anti-racism.

What Rowell and Park (and Stoddard as well) also shared was an acceptance and embrace of what we know today as globalization. These were intellectuals who knew full well that they were living in an extraordinary era when technologies like the steamship and telegraph were flattening the world and bringing new groups of peoples into intimate contact at an incredible pace. Park also was an IPR founding member and delighted (as did Rowell) in international travel, especially in the fast-developing regions of East Asia. To both of them, the future of the world lay in increasing contact with Japan, China, and countries that bordered the Pacific Rim. How, then, can California race relations be understood as a piece of the larger development of this sort of imagined and real Pacific World? (On this question, we might consult David Igler's essay in this volume.)

Finally, that World War II ended Rowell's disillusionment with Reconstruction, and the entrenchment of segregation in the South that went along with it, raises questions about the relationship between international relations and America's postwar civil rights revolution. Over the past decade, historians of the Civil Rights Movement have documented a direct connection between United States diplomacy and the collapse of racial segregation (Von Eschen 1997; Dudziak 2000; Borstelmann 2001). Their studies reveal that United States officials supported African American struggles for civil rights in part to counter Cold War propaganda portraying America as a racist, colonial power. This literature, however, overlooks the significance of Asian Americans and the Pacific Rim for the nation's civil rights revolution, despite the fact that diplomatic concerns also led Presidents and other prominent Americans to oppose anti-Asian racism. This was especially true in the debate regarding Japanese immigration, as Washington consistently sought to avoid potential military conflict with the rising power of Japan. In addition, the exigencies of America's World War II alliances with China, India, and the Philippines led to the repeal of exclusion against these nations. How, then, did relations between the United States and various Asian nations seed the flowering of racial tolerance in postwar America?

In short, scholars need to rethink the relationship between Progressivism and the development of racial discourse in the first half of twentieth-century California. Focusing on the racism and the hypocrisy of California reformers is one way of characterizing this relationship. But the argument here suggests that there is a far greater range of possibilities for understanding the significance of California Progressives for past and present race relations in the Golden State, in the nation, and in the world.

NOTES

1 The next three sections of this essay are a selected summary of Rowell's extensive published and unpublished writings, and personal correspondence. The only biography of Rowell covers a broad range of his thinking up to 1913:

Miles Chapman Everett, "Chester Harvey Rowell, Pragmatic Humanist and California Progressive" (PhD dissertation, University of California Berkeley, 1966).
2   Rowell, "Chinatown Raids," *Fresno Morning Republican*, October 8, 1899.
3   Rowell, "Oriental Labor," *Fresno Morning Republican*, September 3, 1910; Rowell to Montaville Flowers, April 27, 1915, Box 2, Chester H. Rowell Papers, 1887–1946, BANC MSS C-B 401 (Bancroft Library, University of California, Berkeley).

REFERENCES

Aarim-Heriot, Najia. 2003. *Chinese Immigrants, African Americans, and Racial Anxiety in the United States, 1848–1882.* Urbana: University of Illinois Press.
Azuma, Eiichiro. 2005. *Between Two Empires: Race, History, and Transnationalism in Japanese America.* New York: Oxford University Press.
Borstelmann, Thomas. 2001. *The Cold War and the Color Line: American Race Relations in the Global Arena.* Cambridge, MA: Harvard University Press.
Chan, Sucheng. 1986. *This Bittersweet Soil.* Berkeley: University of California Press.
Daniels Roger. 1962. *The Politics of Prejudice: The Anti-Japanese Movement in California and the Struggle for Japanese Exclusion.* Berkeley: University of California Press.
Daniels, Roger. 1966. "Westerners from the East: Oriental Immigrants Reappraised," *The Pacific Historical Review* 35 (4) (November): 373–83.
Deverell, William, and Sitton, Tom, eds. 1994. *California Progressives Revisited.* Berkeley: University of California Press.
Dudziak, Mary, L. 2000. *Cold War, Civil Rights: Race and the Image of American Democracy.* Princeton, NJ: Princeton University Press.
Flamming, Douglas. 2005. *Bound for Freedom: Black Los Angeles in Jim Crow America.* Berkeley: University of California Press.
Gossett, Thomas, F. 1963. *Race: The History of an Idea in America.* New York: Oxford University Press.
Gutierrez, David G. 1995. *Walls and Mirrors: Mexican Americans, Mexican Immigrants, and the Politics of Ethnicity.* Berkeley: University of California Press.
Higham, John. 1955. *Strangers in the Land: Patterns of American Nativism, 1860–1925.* New Brunswick, NJ: Rutgers University Press.
Hosokawa, Bill. 1982. *JACL: In Quest of Justice.* New York: William Morrow.
Ichioka, Yuji. 1988. *The Issei: The World of the First Generation Japanese Immigrants, 1885–1924.* New York: The Free Press.
Izumi, Hirobe. 2001. *Japanese Pride, American Prejudice: Modifying the Exclusion Clause of the 1924 Immigration Act.* Stanford, CA: Stanford University Press.
Lee, Erika, 2003. *At America's Gates: Chinese Immigration during the Exclusion Era, 1882–1943.* Chapel Hill: University of North Carolina Press.
Lye, Colleen. 2005. *America's Asia: Racial Form and American Literature, 1893–1945.* Princeton, NJ: Princeton University Press.

Matthews, Fred, H. 1977. *Quest For an American Sociology: Robert E. Park and the Chicago School*. Montreal: McGill-Queen's University Press.

McWilliams Carey. 1939. *Factories in the Fields: The Story of Migration Farm Labor in California*. Boston, MA: Little, Brown.

Molina, Natalia. 2006. *Fit to be Citizens? Public Health and Race in Los Angeles, 1879–1939*. Berkeley: University of California Press.

Mowry, George E. 1951. *The California Progressives*. Berkeley: University of California Press.

Myrdal, Gunnar. 1944. *An American Dilemma: The Negro Problem and Modern Democracy*. New York: Harper & Brothers.

Nakano, Mei, Takaya. 1990. *Japanese American Women: Three Generations, 1890–1990*. Berkeley, CA: Mina Press.

Olin, Spencer C., Jr. 1968. *California's Prodigal Sons: Hiram Johnson and the Progressives, 1911–1917*. Berkeley: University of California Press.

Palumbo-Liu, David. 1999. *Asian/American: Historical Crossings of Racial Frontier*. Stanford, CA: Stanford University Press.

Sanchez, George J. 1993. *Becoming Mexican American: Ethnicity, Culture, and Identity in Chicano Los Angeles, 1900–1945*. New York: Oxford University Press.

Shah, Nayan. 2001. *Contagious Divides: Epidemics and Race in San Francisco Chinatown*. Berkeley: University of California Press.

Stern, Alexandra Minna. 2005 *Eugenic Nation: Faults and Frontiers of Better Breeding in Modern America*. Berkeley: University of California Press.

Stoddard, Lothrop. 1920. *The Rising Tide of Color*. New York: Charles Scribner's Sons.

Von Eschen, Penny, M. 1997. *Race Against Empire: Black Americans and Anti-colonialism, 1937–1957*. Ithaca, NY: Cornell University Press.

Yu, Henry. 2001. *Thinking Orientals: Migration, Contact, and Exoticism in Modern America*. New York: Oxford University Press.

FURTHER READING

Almaguer, Tomas. 1994. *Racial Fault Lines: The Historical Origins of White Supremacy in California*. Berkeley: University of California Press.

Deverell, William. 2004. *Whitewashed Adobe: The Rise of Los Angeles and the Remaking of Its Mexican Past*. Berkeley: University of California Press.

Hayashi, Brian Masaru. 2004. *Democratizing the Enemy: The Japanese American Internment*. Princeton, NJ: Princeton University Press.

Stern, Alexandra Minna. 2005. *Eugenic Nation: Faults and Frontiers of Better Breeding in Modern America*. Berkeley: University of California Press.

Takaki, Ronald. 1989. *Strangers From a Different Shore: A History of Asian Americans*. Boston, MA: Little, Brown.

Chapter Seventeen

NEW DEAL, NO DEAL: THE 1930s

Rick Wartzman

In one sense, Californians did not get around to embracing the defining moment of the 1930s – President Franklin Roosevelt's promise to create "a new deal for the American people" – until it was nearly 1940 and the decade had almost run its course. It was at this belated moment that Democrat Culbert Olson, a courtly-looking attorney from Los Angeles, ascended to the governor's office. He pledged to fashion a state government "devoted to the services of human needs" and squarely "in sympathy with the principles and policies of the New Deal."[1]

Olson's swearing in, in January 1939, was no small occasion. He was the first Democrat of the twentieth century to win the governorship in California. Through the teens and 1920s and well into the 1930s, the Republicans had maintained such a strong grip that California was essentially a one-party state. So feeble were the Democrats, they did not even bother to field a general-election candidate for governor in 1918. Before these latest results had been tallied, only one Democratic US Senator had been sent to Washington since 1919, and just a single Democrat could be counted among California's 11-member House delegation.

This is not to suggest that FDR left no imprint along the Pacific. He carried the state in 1932 (with 58.4 percent of the vote) and again in 1936 (with 67 percent), and his alphabet soup of recovery and relief agencies – the Works Progress Administration (WPA), Civilian Conservation Corps (CCC), Farm Security Administration (FSA), Agricultural Adjustment Administration (AAA) and more – touched the lives of many Californians. Physical manifestations of the New Deal can still be found all over the state in the form of schools, hospitals, auditoriums, airports, reservoirs, parks, playgrounds, trails and much more.[2]

Even with all that, however, California stood largely disengaged from Roosevelt's grand experiment. Under the two Republican governors who preceded Olson – the invariably clueless James "Sunny Jim" Rolph and the uninspired and uninspiring Frank Merriam – "California's role in this reform period was primarily passive," historian Robert Burke has observed, "more so perhaps than that of any other major state" (1953: 230). For their part, officials within the state's Democratic Party had little affinity for the New Deal, and those politicians who identified most closely with FDR through the mid-1930s were widely viewed as "discredited hacks" (McWilliams 1978: 68).

For many Californians, it was almost as if the New Deal didn't go far enough. Masses of people, especially in Southern California, gravitated instead to far more outlandish schemes: the quasi-religious remedies of the Utopian Society, for example, and such starry-eyed pension proposals as the Townsend Plan and Ham and Eggs (McWilliams 1978; Starr 1996).

California's detachment from the more measured agenda of the White House was, in many respects, unsurprising. As Roosevelt himself noted in late 1938, the state was facing "the most complicated social problems years ahead of the rest of the country."[3] These circumstances attracted zealots on the left and hard-liners on the right – unabashed communists and socialists on one side, police forces and vigilantes doing their best imitations of fascists on the other. Forget the New Deal, which tried to stake some middle ground in American politics and society. In California, those occupying ideological extremes would see to it that there'd be no deal. Both camps were unbending.

And yet it would be a huge mistake to assume that because of this dynamic, the spirit of the 1930s somehow passed California by. Indeed, it is no coincidence that the decade's two most enduring icons – John Steinbeck's Tom Joad and Dorothea Lange's Migrant Mother – emerged from the Golden State (Loftis 1998). Roosevelt's New Deal apparatus may have had little attachment to Sacramento, but on the ground, among the people, California embodied the passions and privation of the era more than any other place in the nation.

Much of the canon on California in the 1930s chronicles specific events – for instance, the bloody cotton strike of 1933 (Daniel 1982; Weber 1996) or Upton Sinclair's remarkable run for governor in 1934 (Mitchell 1992) or the influx of migrants from the Dust Bowl over the course of the decade (Stein 1973; Gregory 1989). And some of these works (Stein, Weber, and Daniel chief among them) explore at considerable depth the impact of New Deal programs on the state. But they tend to do so in a limited way – focusing, for example, on federal agricultural policy. What is largely missing (even in broader volumes such as Starr 1996) is a fuller, more rounded picture of the complex relationship between California and the New Deal. This relatively brief essay does not intend to fill that gap. But it may provide a basis to begin thinking about how to do so.

Looking back today, it is easy to understand why all of the fiery writing and speechifying during the 1930s about insurrection in America never amounted to anything. The country was simply too conservative, and believed far too much in the existing system, to come anywhere close to mounting a Russian-style revolt. "We weren't greatly agitated in terms of society," one down-and-out San Franciscan would later recall. "Ours was a bewilderment, not an anger . . . We weren't talking revolution. We were talking jobs" (Terkel 1986: 31). Franklin Roosevelt's real genius, meanwhile, was to commandeer the liberals' most soothing rhetoric while shoring up the foundations of capitalism (Lipset & Marks 2001: 208–9).

But in the middle of those hungry years, without the benefit of hindsight, it could truly feel sometimes as if the established order was about to fall apart, as if the social fabric was about to fray. "We take the stand that we as workers have nothing in common with the employers," asserted Harry Bridges, the head of the longshoremen's union in San Francisco. "We are in a class struggle" (Denning 2000: 16–17). Bridges was intent on making a "march inland" and organizing labor from the docks of the city to the farm fields of the Central Valley – a prospect that alarmed California's powers that be and served as a pretext for cracking down against "radicalism" all across the state (Daniel 1982: 276; Denning 2000: 17).

Lest anyone discount how intense the hostility could get, consider the following 1934 newspaper dispatch from the San Joaquin County town of Lodi:

> Lodi's mammoth bullpen, constructed especially for Communists, neared completion today as a crew of carpenters erected posts and strung barbed wire. Located east of the Supermold plant and adjoining the Southern Pacific right-of-way, the pen measures 200 feet by 400 feet. A board fence 10 feet high, on which a barbed wire "overhang" is mounted, will serve to keep the agitators confined. The wire is of the "thorn barb" type used during the war. It is doubly heavy and galvanized. Watchmen with sawed-off shotguns will patrol the stockade when the agitators are herded to prevent them from tunneling out or setting fire to the framework.[4]

That California was so sharply divided was not out of character. The state had a long history of fractiousness dating back to the 1870s, when members of the Workingmen's Party (a scion of Karl Marx's International Workingmen's Association) tussled in San Francisco with armed militia and citizens wielding pickaxe handles (Starr 1996). Some 35 years later, the Industrial Workers of the World was busy stirring things up from San Diego to rural Wheatland (Renshaw 1999).[5] It was more than a militant tradition, though, that came into play as the 1930s rolled on. The epic migration of refugees from the Dust Bowl and elsewhere, which began in earnest in the middle of the decade, made the "antagonisms even more acute," as Arthur Schlesinger Jr. has noted (2003: 109).

Compared with other parts of the country, the Great Depression had descended rather slowly upon California. Thanks to a diversified economy

– by 1930, the state's interests ranged from oil to agriculture to shipping to manufacturing to entertainment to tourism – the direct hit had been relatively modest. But California felt the reverberations of a nation gone bust like nowhere else: More than 300,000 people from Oklahoma, Texas, Arkansas, and Missouri poured into the state, wooed westward by the potential of a brighter future. Metropolitan Los Angeles received a good many of these folks, but their impact was most severe in California's heartland (Cross & Cross 1937: 46).

To be sure, not all of the Okies and Arkies were poor, and plenty defied their hayseed stereotype. Historian James Gregory has pointed out that many of the migrants hailed from urban areas in the Southwest, and one in six had been business owners or white-collar employees (1989: 15). But the vast majority of these newcomers were destitute, with nearly 80 percent of migrant farm hands in California earning no more than $400 in 1935, according to one state study.[6] That was less than a than a third of what a family of four needed to cover the basics. "It is thus obvious," said economist Emily Huntington, "that vast numbers of agricultural workers in California must be ill-fed, ill-clothed, poorly housed, and almost completely lacking in many other things considered necessary for a civilized life."[7]

Despite that degree of misery, California's migrants drew scant attention from the New Dealers in Washington. There's no question that a variety of Roosevelt administration activities – including those of the Federal Transient Service, Rexford Tugwell's Resettlement Administration and, later, the FSA – had a bearing on the problem. But these agencies "did not speak directly" to what was taking place in California, Walter J. Stein has concluded. "Not until 1939 did . . . the Great Plains refugees in California receive serious interest from Congress or the president, and then only after the publication of *The Grapes of Wrath* had made the condition of the Okies a blatant fact of American life" (1973: 140).

In the meantime, the stress put on California's public coffers was immense. For a time, some big growers were delighted by the surplus of labor flooding the state; it made it easier to tamp down wages. But by the later years of the 1930s, just about everyone realized that the costs of the never-ending influx greatly outweighed the benefits. In 1936, the Los Angeles police went so far as to send 136 of its finest to California's borders with Arizona and Oregon to discourage the indigent from entering the state – a maneuver that became known as the "bum blockade" (Stein 1973: 73–5; Gregory 1989: 80). Others took to the airwaves to try to dissuade people from continuing to trek to the continent's edge. "There are no jobs in California," Thomas McManus, secretary of the California Citizens' Association, a Kern County-based group, told Oklahoma City radio listeners in 1939. Kern's population would soar nearly 64 percent from 1935 to 1940 – more than any other county's – overwhelming many public services and swelling relief rolls. "Do not go to California in spite of any-thing you have heard," McManus cautioned. "To do so will only bring hardship on yourself and your family."[8]

But by then, it was too late. The migrants had arrived, adding another volatile ingredient to a pot that had already boiled over again and again and again.

Of all the wild times in 1930s California, none could eclipse the year-and-a-half stretch in which the state's left and right came to blows – physically and philosophically – across a broad expanse: from small-town cotton patch to big-city embarcadero to capital courtroom.

The craziness began in the fall of 1933 in the lower part of the San Joaquin Valley, home to some of the state's biggest cotton barons. Many of the industry's most prominent figures, such as Colonel J. G. Boswell and Wofford B. Camp, had come to California from the Deep South, and they brought with them secrets for coaxing enormous quantities of white gold from the soil, as well as a homegrown paternalism that they used to keep workers in check (Weber 1996; Arax & Wartzman 2003).

This year, though, those getting set to harvest some 200,000 acres were in no mood to be submissive. Whipped up by organizers from the Cannery and Agricultural Workers Industrial Union (CAWIU), they rejected as inadequate the growers' offer of 60 cents for every 100 pounds of fiber picked, insisting instead on $1. From there, things escalated quickly. When the growers wouldn't budge, 12,000 workers walked off the job – and the farmers promptly ordered their laborers out of their cabins, tossing their meager possessions after them. With nowhere to go, the workers (mostly Mexicans, with some Filipinos, blacks and Okies in the mix) built their own makeshift settlements, the largest one in Kings County, on the outskirts of Corcoran (Daniel 1982; Taylor 1983; Weber 1996; Arax & Wartzman 2003).

Ella Winter – who edited the far-left *Pacific Weekly* with her husband, muckraker and Russophile Lincoln Steffens – visited Camp Corcoran one night to lend her support and was taken aback by the dire conditions there (1963: 197). "We wandered about," she'd recount, "peering as well as we could into lightless tents, at piles of cans, rusty stoves, broken-down Fords that served as bed and roof. Children lay asleep, huddled on the muddy ground." At one point, "a frowsy woman came out with a bundle, a tiny wizened baby whose face was almost black." The infant was dead, evidently from malnutrition. The union tried to funnel milk, meat, and vegetables into the camp, but local sheriff's deputies, allied with the farmers, seized the provisions and kept them from reaching the strikers (Arax & Wartzman 2003: 151).

Tensions rose until, on October 10, a pack of workers gathered outside a small brick union hall in Pixley, about 20 miles from Corcoran, listening to Pat Chambers, one of the CAWIU leaders. Chambers was a card-carrying Communist, but he and his comrade running the strike, a 21-year-old wisp of a woman named Caroline Decker, had made sure to keep their Marxist doctrine closeted; the way to win over the cotton pickers, they knew, was to keep the focus on their paltry pay. "This is no time for a backward step," Chambers told the throng in Pixley. "We will match the farmers with their own violence. Let them start something – and we will finish it." It all sounded good. But waiting across the road was a mob of 40 growers clutching pistols and rifles. Suddenly, shots rang out. Delfino D'Avilia, a Mexican consular representative allied with the strikers, was hit and died on the spot. As the workers scattered, one of them, Dolores Hernandez, was also felled by the fusillade. That same afternoon, in the Kern County community of Arvin, another striker, Pedro Subia, was gunned down after a five-hour confrontation between 250 pickets and 30 growers (Daniel 1982; Weber 1996; Starr 1996; Arax & Wartzman 2003).

Dead bodies – "Blood on the Cotton," as Langston Hughes dubbed the drama that he penned about the episode – were not exactly what Roosevelt's New Dealers had imagined when they were dreaming up their paradigm for labor relations in America. Under the guidance of the National Recovery Administration (NRA), the White House had hoped to foster "cooperation between industry, labor and government as one great team," in the words of NRA chief Hugh Johnson. In fact, Johnson explained, this partnership would run so smoothly once business executives and union officials accepted that they needed to put the national interest above their own selfish interests, there'd be no reason for the work force "to strike under the Roosevelt plan." Previously, he said, "in the old days of exploitation you had to form aggressive units literally to fight for the life of labor. You had to be sometimes militant . . . That is no longer necessary" (Daniel 1982: 170–1).

There were a couple of problems with turning the New Dealers' vision into reality, at least in California. First, agricultural workers had effectively been excluded from the labor protections of the National Industrial Recovery Act of 1933, hardly making them equal partners with the state's giant farm owners (farm workers would be conspicuously left out of the National Labor Relations Act of 1935 as well). Second, the fortunes of California's cotton pickers – as well as those toiling in peas, lettuce, cherries, berries, apricots, peaches, pears, beets, tomatoes, hops, grapes, cantaloupes and prunes, all of whom struck for higher wages in 1933 – were so bleak that Johnson's portrayal of exploitation as a thing of the past seemed like utter fantasy. It's no wonder that the CAWIU labeled Roosevelt's labor platform a "delusion" (Daniel 1982: 177).

Now, with three slain, the feds could do little but acknowledge the depth of the enmity between California's right and left, and try to impose some kind of peace. George Creel, director of the NRA's Western district and a devout New Dealer, stepped in and advocated a pay rate of 75 cents (a Solomonic split between the 60 cents offered by the growers and the dollar sought by the union), with no recognition for the CAWIU. Neither side loved the pact, but the only real choice was to sign: If they refused, Creel vowed to block the growers from valuable New Deal farm programs and to kick the strikers off welfare – their primary means of survival as the walkout had worn on. The 24-day strike was the most successful in the history of agricultural labor, increasing wages by about $1 million in all. But it would soon exact a steep price, especially for Pat Chambers, Caroline Decker, and others active in the CAWIU.

In the interim, the New Dealers found themselves watching another ugly situation unfold between business and labor in California, this time on the San Francisco waterfront. The International Longshoremen's Association (ILA) – determined to win higher wages, better working conditions, and a union-controlled hiring hall – had been contemplating a strike since December 1933. George Creel, barely rested from the contretemps in the cotton fields, intervened and persuaded President Roosevelt to appoint a special fact-finding commission that he hoped would prod the ILA and the shipping companies to hammer out an accord. And for a short while during the spring of 1934, it looked as if an agreement might be inked. But both sides dug in, and by mid-May the dispute had spread up and down the coast, leaving 35,000 maritime workers idle. Further pleas from Washington for reconciliation were to no avail.

The union's steadfastness was in large measure the result of the convictions of one man: Harry Bridges, who rose up to lead the ILA's most militant arm, Local 38–79, out of San Francisco's Albion Hall. It was Bridges – a scrappy, 34-year-old Australian with a long face and black hair brushed into a pompadour – who was most adamant about retaining solidarity among all the ports of the Pacific coast, from San Diego to Seattle. But Bridge's mulishness was not only an affront to the shippers; it also did not sit well with the ILA's top leadership, which feared that Bridges and his cronies were Soviet agents trying to do more than secure gains for the longshoremen.

Such concerns were overblown. But, if nothing else, the communist newspaper, the *Western Worker*, enthusiastically supported Bridges; a communist group ran a strike kitchen; other party affiliates sent pickets to man the lines and put up bail for arrested strikers; and West Coast communist leader Sam Darcy helped the strikers formulate strategy. Bridges himself always denied that he had joined the Communist Party, though he openly voiced his admiration for Marxism, and evidence turned up years later in Soviet archives would suggest that he probably was a member, albeit an independent-minded one whose actions were never dictated by Moscow or its agents in the United States (Selvin 1996: 63; Starr 1996: 95).[9]

Either way, the ILA's bosses were bent on distancing themselves from him: they bypassed his strike committee and forged their own settlement with the shippers in late May. It was a non-starter. The rank and file, loyal to Bridges, voted down the proposal to a chorus of hisses and boos (Starr 1996: 95). In mid-June the ILA brass tried to make another end-run around Bridges and negotiated another agreement with the San Francisco Industrial Association. Again the workers balked, sending the shippers and city authorities into a panic. "We have reached crisis threatening destruction of property and serious loss of life," an employers' representative warned President Roosevelt on June 18 (Starr 1996: 101).

If the message sounded breathless, it wound up being awfully prescient. On July 5, after a couple of days of skirmishing between police and pickets, thousands of strikers lined the streets, facing off against some 800 uniformed officers. "Not since the eviction of the Bonus Army from Washington in 1932 had an American city fielded so many police squadrons against such a large segment of its citizenry," Kevin Starr has written (1996: 105). The "Bloody Thursday" fracas that ensued – rocks, bricks, and fists against fire hoses, tear-gas grenades, and bullets – left scores injured and two workers dead. Their martyrdom, highlighted as their funeral cortege wended its way through the city to the strains of Beethoven, helped Bridges take things to the next level: a general strike, involving dozens of different unions that ground San Francisco to a virtual standstill (Larrowe 1972: 74–9; Nelson 1990: 128).

The city now teetered on the brink of a total breakdown. Nearly 5,000 National Guardsmen, some perched on trucks with fixed machine guns, swarmed San Francisco. Red hysteria reigned, as the prospect of more violence – far worse violence – loomed. Hugh Johnson, the NRA executive director, had no compunction about urging Bay Area residents "to wipe out this subversive element as you clean off a chalk mark on a blackboard with a wet sponge" (Starr 1996: 116).

Finally, on July 18, four days into the general strike and over the strenuous objections of Harry Bridges, the committee engineering the stoppage agreed to submit to arbitration. The contract subsequently drawn up gave the ILA much of what its members had been after, including hiring halls presided over by a union dispatcher. And by the end of the month, after 83 days, the longshoremen returned to work. The war was over.

Long after the labor strife of the 1930s had become a distant memory, Harry Bridges would think back on what he had done, and why it had been so effective. "You see," he said, "a strike is a small revolution . . . because you take over an industry or a plant owned by the capitalists and temporarily you seize it. Temporarily you take it away."[10] In the crucible of a tumultuous decade, however, it was not merely a temporary taking that many were afraid of.

On July 20, 1934, just as the conflict in San Francisco was simmering down, police raided Communist Party headquarters in Sacramento. More than 200 pamphlets, books, newspapers, magazines, and other documents were seized, many of which were later introduced in the trial of 17 activists charged with "criminal syndicalism" – or, more plainly, with conspiring to forcibly topple America's form of government and industrial ownership. The cache of material discovered onsite was unquestionably provocative, perfect to play in front of a jury that was already jittery because of what had occurred in the Central Valley and San Francisco (Starr 2005: 208).

Here's the tiniest taste of what they heard, straight from People's Exhibit No. 3, a tract called "Why Communism?":[11]

> We Communists say there is one way to abolish the capitalist state and that is to smash it by force. To make Communism possible, the workers must take hold of the state machinery of capitalism and destroy it.

The defendants countered with their own excerpts from the text, which were meant to showcase the Communist Party's commitment to non-violence. They argued, too, that the Criminal Syndicalism Act was unconstitutional. And they contended, above all, that they were being singled out not for any genuinely subversive behavior but for their union organizing in California's farm belt the previous year. "We are being framed because of our interest to the working class," said Jack Crane, who along with Pat Chambers and Caroline Decker was among those being prosecuted. "We are a thorn in the side of the capitalists."[12]

Crane's appraisal was not far off. Aiding the government in its case was the Associated Farmers, an alliance that had been born of the strikes of 1933 with a lone goal: to stop such a worker rebellion from ever happening again. Funded by many of the state's biggest businesses – agricultural and industrial alike – the group remained a significant political power for the remainder of the decade, ensuring the passage of anti-picketing ordinances and pushing to guarantee that if laborers did go out on strike, they would not be eligible for public relief (an aim summed up by the harshly straightforward phrase "No work – No eat") (Arax & Wartzman 2003: 168). But Associated Farmers members did more than just flex their muscles politically (Stein 1973: 257); they took up guns and bats and tire chains – a record of brutality that *The Nation* magazine would characterize as "organized terrorism in agriculture."[13]

For now, though, Associated Farmers operatives were concentrating on the task before them: digging up dirt to help convict those on trial in Sacramento (Daniel 1982: 253; Starr 1996: 170; Loftis 1998: 92). The case – which would last into the spring of 1935, becoming one of the longest-running criminal proceedings in United States history – was quite a spectacle. Some of the defendants represented themselves, lapsing into long sermons on Marxist theory and parrying against a lead prosecutor who could barely pronounce some of the terminology in the documents that had been confiscated. Adding to the atmosphere, a National Guard colonel was placed in charge of the local police, and hundreds of businessmen were deputized to help keep law and order (Starr 1996: 170). At one stage, accusations were slung that Reds had kidnapped the star witness for the state, even though the whole thing reeked of a setup. And as the jury deliberated, it was revealed that someone had drilled two holes in the ceiling to eavesdrop.

In the end, eight defendants were found guilty, including Chambers and Decker, spelling the demise of the CAWIU. Prosecutor Neil McAllister hailed the outcome as "a step backwards for Communism . . . and a step forward for Americanism and all that America stands for."[14] The convicted were sent to San Quentin and the women's prison in Tehachapi, where they would languish for several years, until a state appeals court reversed the verdict (Watkins 1999: 419).

For all its circus-like qualities, the Sacramento trial did lay bare something tremendously important. Behind the clash of bodies in Pixley and Arvin and San Francisco (and, later in the 1930s, in Salinas and Marysville and many other locales) raged a clash of ideas. And it was not just those who upheld the sanctity of capitalism versus the Communists. That is far too narrow a way to look it. The crowd encouraging change was much, much bigger than that and included Socialists, Democrats, artists, intellectuals, CIO union members and myriad others who, all together, constituted a broad-based Popular Front (Diggins 1992: 174; Lipset & Marks 2001: 74–5). In many instances, these were people who "thought of themselves as generic 'communists,' using the term with a small *c*," as scholar Michael Denning has described it (2000: xviii). To those on the right, of course, this was a distinction without a difference. It all seemed terribly menacing to the status quo.

Scary from their vantage, for example, was John Steinbeck, who described the backdrop to his masterpiece, *The Grapes of Wrath*, this way: "This is a rough book because a revolution is going on" (DeMott 1989: 154). For Steinbeck – and so many more – it was hard to conceive that capitalism would not soon just die, having withered so much already. "There is little question in my mind that the principle of private ownership of means of production is not long with us," Steinbeck said in the late 1930s. "This is not in terms of what I think is right or wrong or good or bad, but in terms of what is inevitable."[15] Equally unsettling was Carey McWilliams, whose book *Factories in the Field* (the non-fiction counterpart to *The Grapes of Wrath*) called for "the substitution of collective agriculture for the present monopolistically owned and controlled system" (McWilliams 1939:

324–5). Both Steinbeck and McWilliams, who would be put in charge of migrant farm-worker policy in the Olson administration, were repeatedly branded Communists with a big C, which neither was (Benson 1984: 294; Richardson 2005: 79–81).

Upton Sinclair was not a big-C Communist, either. He was a longtime Socialist who became a registered Democrat in September 1933, setting in motion a candidacy for governor that arguably did more to frighten California's establishment than anything else that transpired during the 1930s. Uppie, as he was known, was nothing if not bold. Author of *The Jungle* and other muckraking volumes; champion of assorted gastronomic curiosities such as the "squirrel diet" (whole wheat, nuts, raw salads, olives, and fresh fruit); later Pulitzer Prize winner; friend of Charlie Chaplain, Albert Einstein, and Mark Twain, he set forth his program to cure California's ills in a pamphlet titled *I, Governor of California And How I Ended Poverty: A True Story of the Future*. "This is the beginning of a Crusade," he proclaimed right on the cover. "A Two-Year Plan to make over a State. To capture the Democratic primaries and use an old party for a new job."

Specifically, Sinclair proposed putting private factories under government oversight and then allowing laborers to own what they had manufactured. Farmers, he envisioned, would bring their crops to the city where they'd be "made available to the factory workers in exchange for the products of *their* labor." Trade in this "production-for-use" (as opposed to production-for-profit) system would be conducted using special California-issued scrip, all administered by a new state entity called the California Authority for Money. To shrink the state's budget deficit, Sinclair had his eye on a fat target: "We are going to have to tax the great corporations of our state" (Watkins 1999: 248–51; Arthur 2006: 254–9; Newton 2006: 78).

Sinclair called his plan EPIC – for End Poverty in California – and few professional people took it very seriously at first. Then something funny happened: Sinclair's pamphlet became a sensation and he won the Democratic primary, besting New Dealer George Creel (the man endorsed by the party machine) and a handful of others (Creel 1947: 280–8).

Other states, especially in the West and Midwest, saw a fair number of far-left politicians make strides during the 1930s – members of the Commonwealth Federation in Washington and Oregon, the Nonpartisan League in North Dakota, the Farmer-Labor Party in Minnesota, and the Progressive Party in Wisconsin (Lipset & Marks 2001: 72–3). Yet it was Sinclair, more than any other, who put Franklin Roosevelt in a ticklish position. If the president backed the Democratic candidate, he could be accused of countenancing radicalism; if he distanced himself from Uppie, he might be deemed spineless. A *Washington Post* columnist, reflecting on FDR's quandary, composed this ditty (Mitchell 1992: xiii):

This is the question that's
Thinning my hair
What'll I do about
Upton Sinclair

Eventually, after a face-to-face meeting in which Sinclair came away mistakenly believing that Roosevelt would give the production-for-use formula his presidential imprimatur, FDR abandoned him (Mitchell 1992: 471; Watkins 1999: 250; Schlesinger 2003: 120; Arthur 2006: 277). That left Sinclair to fend for himself against what was perhaps the nastiest and most sophisticated smear campaign ever seen to that point (and a harbinger of the rough-and-tumble politics of today). Pilloried by William Randolph Hearst's *San Francisco Examiner*, Harry Chandler's *Los Angeles Times*, evangelist Aimee Semple McPherson, the Hollywood studios and many more, Sinclair lost the general election to Frank Merriam, 1.1 million votes to 880,000.

Uppie swiftly moved on to write a new book: *I, Candidate for Governor: And How I Got Licked*. But he had made a heck of an impression. His primary victory, said Jerry Voorhis, who would later become a California congressman, was "the nearest thing to a mass movement toward Socialism that I have heard of in America" (Lipset & Marks 2001: 209–10). Once again, Sinclair had demonstrated that California was a territory unto itself – a strange laboratory operating outside the margins of the New Deal, a place situated on the fringe of America, not just geographically but socially and politically as well.

Culbert Olson had won a state Senate seat in 1934, riding Upton Sinclair's coattails. And, once in office, he grabbed the reins of the Legislature's liberal bloc. Over the next few years, Olson almost rammed through a production-for-use bill that bore more than a passing resemblance to EPIC. By 1938, however, he tried to carve a little space between himself and old Uppie. "I was a Democrat for more than 35 years before Mr. Sinclair came into the Democratic Party," he said, "and I remain a Democrat since he left that party" (Burke 1953: 19). At the same time, Olson began touting a new role model: FDR. "The people of California emphatically declared in our recent election that this state shall go forward," he said in his inaugural address, "not only in support of the New Deal measures of the national government under President Roosevelt, but also with state measures having the same objectives."[16]

It was an odd time to be invoking the president in this manner. The New Deal was no longer expanding, following setbacks at the Supreme Court and growing resistance on Capitol Hill. What's more, the White House's attention was turning increasingly to the war in Europe. It was as if California had finally showed up at the party, and the guests were all putting on their coats to leave (McWilliams 1978: 80).

Olson, as it happened, was also a lousy governor. He showed courage and conviction during his earliest days in office, pardoning labor leader and liberal hero Tom Mooney, who had been railroaded into prison 23 years earlier on trumped-up charges of planting a bomb that killed 10 at a San Francisco parade (Burke 1953: 48–58; Klein 1999: 124–6; Newton 2006: 101). But the new administration was quickly plagued by a series of bad luck and worse decisions. Olson lost a string of tax and budget fights with the Legislature and never regained his balance (Burke 1953: 230–3). "If you want to know what hell is really like," he wound up telling his successor, Earl Warren, "just wait until you have been governor for four years" (Newton 2006: 165).

Not that the 1930s would fade away quietly in California. Three of the most extraordinary books of the period – *Factories in the Field; American Exodus* by photographer Dorothea Lange and her husband, economist Paul Taylor; and, most notably, *The Grapes of Wrath* – were published in 1939. The agricultural union that had swept in behind the CAWIU (the United Cannery, Agricultural, Packing and Allied Workers of America) was active in the late 1930s. And many of the themes that had prevailed during the decade, including Red-baiting, would carry over into the 1940s and beyond.

Still, there was an unmistakable sense as Olson took office that a chapter was closing. Also in 1939, Sen. Robert M. La Follette Jr. brought his investigation into violations of free speech and the rights of labor to California. He probed groups such as the San Francisco Industrial Association and the Merchants and Manufacturers Association in Los Angeles, which used spies and other hardball tactics to keep LA "a white spot" – that is, an open-shop city where labor could never find a real foothold (McWilliams 1946: 291). The bulk of La Follette's inquiry, though, was directed at the Associated Farmers and its unremitting union busting.

Once more, the hearings exposed just how deep a rift there was between the left and right in 1930s California. "I have felt from the outset that the La Follette investigation was the Gestapo for the Communist Party, and nothing you can say will convince me of the contrary," thundered Hank Strobel, Associated Farmers secretary.[17] And to think: By the early 1940s, everybody – left, right, and in between – would be off fighting the real Nazis, half a world away.

NOTES

1   As quoted by various newspapers throughout the state. See, for instance, "Olson Pledges Self Help Plan," *Fresno Bee*, November 9, 1938.
2   See the New Deal Legacy Project from the California Historical Society: http://www.californiahistoricalsociety.org/exhibits/new_deal/index.html

3 Letter from Franklin Roosevelt to George Creel, October 31, 1938.

4 *Lodi Sentinel*, August 11, 1934. Cited by the La Follette Civil Liberties Committee. US Senate, Subcommittee of the Committee on Education and Labor. *Hearings Pursuant to S. Res. 266, Violations of Free Speech and Rights of Labor.* Parts 1–75. 74th–76th Congrs., 1936–1940.

5 According to some accounts, it was the ardently anti-union publisher of the *Los Angeles Times*, Gen. Harrison Gray Otis, who gave the IWW its nickname: the Wobblies. For more on this, see the IWW's website: http://www.iww.org/culture/official/wobbly

6 From a 1937 report by the California Department of Employment. Cited by the La Follette Civil Liberties Committee.

7 From Huntington's testimony before the La Follette Civil Liberties Committee.

8 Transcript located in the Wofford B. Camp papers. Special Collections, Robert Muldrow Cooper Library, Clemson University.

9 Information also gleaned from "Harry Bridges and the Communist Party: New Evidence, Old Questions; Old Evidence, New Questions," by Robert W. Cherny. Prepared for the annual meeting of the Organization of American Historians, April 4, 1998.

10 Harry Bridges oral history. Oral History Collection, International Longshore and Warehouse Union, July 27, 2004.

11 From *The People of the State of California vs. Pat Chambers, et al.* Criminal No. 1533. California State Archives, Sacramento.

12 Ibid.

13 Herbert Klein and Carey McWilliams, "Cold Terror in California," *The Nation*, July 24, 1935.

14 *Sacramento Bee*, April 1, 1935.

15 Undated Q&A with Steinbeck, circa 1939. Joseph Henry Jackson papers. Bancroft Library, UC Berkeley.

16 The address is available on the State Library's Governors of California website: http://www.californiagovernors.ca.gov/h/documents/inaugural_29.html

17 Comments in the Paul Schuster Taylor papers. Bancroft Library, UC Berkeley.

References

Arax, M. and Wartzman, R. 2003. *The King of California: J. G. Boswell and the Making of a Secret American Empire*. New York: Public Affairs.

Arthur, A. 2006. *Radical Innocent: Upton Sinclair*. New York: Random House.

Benson, J. J. 1984. *The True Adventures of John Steinbeck, Writer*. New York: Viking.

Burke, R. E. 1953. *Olson's New Deal for California*. Berkeley: University of California Press.

Creel, G. 1947. *Rebel at Large: Recollections of Fifty Crowded Years*. New York: G. P. Putnam's Sons.

Cross, W. T. and Cross, D. E. 1937. *Newcomers and Nomads in California*. Stanford, CA: Stanford University Press.

Daniel, C. E. 1982. *Bitter Harvest: A History of California Farmworkers*, 1st California paperback ed. Berkeley: University of California Press.

DeMott, R., ed. 1989. *Working Days: The Journals of the Grapes of Wrath*. New York: Viking.

Denning, M. 2000. *The Cultural Front*, 2nd paperback ed. London: Verso.

Diggins, J. P. 1992. *The Rise and Fall of the American Left*. New York: W. W. Norton.

Gregory, J. N. 1989. *American Exodus: The Dust Bowl Migration and Okie Culture in California*. New York: Oxford University Press.

Klein, J. 1999. *Woody Guthrie: A Life*. New York: Delta.

Lange, D. and Taylor, P. S. 1975. *An American Exodus: A Record of Human Erosion*. New York: Arno Press.

Larrowe, C. P. 1972. *Harry Bridges: The Rise and Fall of Radical Labor in the U.S.* Westport, CN: Lawrence Hill.

Lipset, S. M. and Marks, G. 2001. *It Didn't Happen Here: Why Socialism Failed in the United States*, paperback ed. New York: W.W. Norton.

Loftis, A. 1998. *Witnesses to the Struggle: Imaging the 1930s California Labor Movement*. Reno: University of Nevada Press.

McWilliams, C. 1939. *Factories in the Field*. Boston, MA: Little, Brown.

McWilliams, C. 1946. *Southern California Country*. New York: Duell, Sloan & Pearce.

McWilliams C. 1978. *The Education of Carey McWilliams*. New York: Simon & Schuster.

Mitchell, G. 1992. *The Campaign of the Century: Upton Sinclair's Race for Governor of California and the Birth of Media Politics*. New York: Random House.

Nelson, B. 1990. *Workers on the Waterfront: Seamen, Longshoremen and Unionism in the 1930s*. Urbana: University of Illinois Press.

Newton, J. 2006. *Justice for All: Earl Warren and the Nation He Made*. New York: Riverhead Books.

Renshaw, P. 1999. *The Wobblies: The Story of the IWW and Syndicalism in the United States*. Chicago: Ivan R. Dee.

Richardson, P. 2005. *American Prophet: The Life & Work of Carey McWilliams*. Ann Arbor: University of Michigan Press.

Schlesinger, A. M. Jr. 2003. *The Age of Roosevelt: The Politics of Upheaval*, 1st Mariner Books; New York: Mariner Books.

Selvin, D. F. 1996. *A Terrible Danger: The 1934 Waterfront and General Strikes in San Francisco*. Detroit: Wayne State University Press.

Starr, K. 1996. *Endangered Dreams: The Great Depression in California*. New York: Oxford University Press.

Starr, K. 2005. *California: A History*. New York: Modern Library.

Stein, W. J. 1973. *California and the Dust Bowl Migration*. Westport, CN: Greenwood Press.

Taylor, P. S. 1983. *On the Ground in the Thirties*. Salt Lake City: Gibbs M. Smith.

Terkel, S. 1986. *Hard Times: An Oral History of the Great Depression*, paperback ed. New York: The New Press.

Watkins, T. H. 1999. *The Hungry Years: A Narrative History of the Great Depression in America.* New York: Henry Holt.

Weber, D. 1996. *Dark Sweat, White Gold: California Farm Workers, Cotton, and the New Deal.* Berkeley: University of California Press.

Winter, E. 1963. *And Not to Yield.* New York: Harcourt, Brace & World.

FURTHER READING

Chambers, C. A. 1952. *California Farm Organizations.* Berkeley: University of California Press.

Dyson, L. K. 1982. *Red Harvest: The Communist Party and American Farmers.* Lincoln: University of Nebraska Press.

Guthrie, W. 1943. *Bound for Glory.* New York: E. P. Dutton.

Haslam, G. W. 1999. *Workin' Man Blues: Country Music in California.* Berkeley: University of California Press.

Jamieson, S. 1976. *Labor Unionism in American Agriculture.* New York: Arno Press.

Kennedy, D. M., 1999. *Freedom from Fear: The American People in Depression and War, 1929–1945.* New York: Oxford University Press.

Kirkendall, R. S. 1966. *Social Scientists and Farm Politics in the Age of Roosevelt.* Columbia, MO: University of Missouri Press.

Lowitt, R. and Beasley, M., eds. 1981. *One Third of a Nation: Lorena Hickok Reports on the Great Depression.* Urbana: University of Illinois Press.

Luck, M. G. and Cummings, A. B. 1945. *Standards of Relief in California, 1940.* Berkeley: University of California Press.

Meltzer, M. 1978. *Dorothea Lange: A Photographer's Life.* New York: Farrar, Straus & Giroux.

Morgan D. 1992. *Rising in the West: The True Story of an "Okie" Family from the Great Depression Through the Reagan Years.* New York: Alfred A. Knopf.

Peeler, D .P. 1987. *Hope Among Us Yet: Social Criticism and Social Solace in Depression America.* Athens: University of Georgia Press.

Pells, R. H. 1973. *Radical Visions and American Dreams: Culture and Social Thought in the Depression Years.* New York: Harper & Row.

Rose, D. 1987. *Dustbowl Okie Exodus.* Big Timber, MT: Seven Buffaloes Press.

Steinbeck, J. 1936. *In Dubious Battle.* New York: Covici, Friede.

Steinbeck, J. 1939. *The Grapes of Wrath.* New York: Viking.

Stryker, R. E. and Wood, N. 1973. *In this Proud Land: America 1935–1943 as Seen in the FSA Photographs.* Boston: New York Graphic Society Ltd.

Part IV

MODERN CALIFORNIA

Chapter Eighteen

World War II

Arthur Verge

The rapid mobilization of California's military-industrial complex during World War II is one of the most remarkable events in California history. Working relationships forged between federal and state officials during the Depression years helped California to become the wartime leader in obtaining contracts to build an endless stream of aircraft and ships. California would emerge from the war as the West's "Arsenal of Democracy." The state, though, would also endure the trials of open racial bigotry, overcrowding, a sharp increase in crime, and substantial damage to its environment.

Despite the hostile actions of the Axis powers from the mid-1930s forward, the American people remained thoroughly opposed to military intervention in the approaching worldwide conflict. The America First Movement, fervently supported by numerous Hollywood celebrities and California newspaper magnate William Randolph Hearst, was particularly adamant about keeping the United States out of the war. So strong was anti-war sentiment that President Franklin Roosevelt continually assured the American electorate in his 1940 bid for re-election that he would keep "American boys from dying on foreign shores."

In the two decades following the end of World War I, isolationist sentiment kept the levels of US military preparedness (especially for a war of worldwide scale) low. As late as the fall of 1939, the United States Army fell to thirty-ninth place amongst the world's armies (Harris et al. 1984:17). The nation's military aviation was in equally poor shape; most American fighter planes were too outdated for modern combat. Fearing that the nation's weakness as a military power could invite attack, Americans supported a build-up of the country's defenses even as they held on to their isolationist views. Prior to the attack on Pearl Harbor, Congress authorized substantial funding increases for weapons and military facilities.

This build-up matched California ambitions. Historian Roger Lotchin has shown that since the early twentieth century, California cities worked to forge a mutually beneficial relationship between themselves and the

American military. In exchange for defense monies, which translated into local employment, cities such as San Diego, Long Beach, and San Francisco allowed the military to own large tracts of land and use of their valuable ports. As part of the nation's defense build-up on the verge of war, California officials encouraged New Dealers-turned-military-planners to take advantage of the public works they had built. With plentiful water supplies now flowing into the Central Valley, San Francisco, and Los Angeles, state officials pointed out that California was ready to meet the needs of defense manufacturers. Those officials emphasized the state's large open spaces, affordable land, exceptional weather, and supportive business climate as assets for the military build-up.

The state's struggling aircraft industry was among the first to receive Congress's newly apportioned defense dollars. The Depression had bankrupted most of the state's aircraft companies. Donald Douglas, whose company survived the shake-out, stayed in business despite going without a plane contract for months at a time in the early 1930s. Douglas kept several key engineers on the payroll by employing them as gardeners at his Douglas Aircraft plant in Santa Monica. Events in Europe and the Far East in 1938 began the turnaround for the aircraft industry. In that year, foreign contracts to build fighters, bombers, and military transport planes poured in from England, Canada, and France. By 1930, Douglas employed over 7,500 workers (Verge 1993: 87).

Henry Kaiser, who was known as a "New Deal Darling" for his ability to obtain Depression-era public works contracts to build dams and roads, used his federal connections to obtain defense monies to build ships. He did this despite the fact that he had never so much as built a rowboat. Yet Kaiser's proven ability to organize and manage made him an instant leader in helping California secure monies that would have otherwise gone to established shipyards on the East Coast.

As California's defense industries began to hum, rising tensions in the Pacific forced Roosevelt to send the American Pacific Fleet from its California homeports to Pearl Harbor. The forward naval defense was intended to dissuade the Japanese militarists from attacking the Philippines and other American possessions in the Pacific. That strategy failed. The attack at Pearl Harbor on December 7, 1941 proved particularly devastating to California. America's battleship row that had been previously home-ported in Long Beach was nearly destroyed. News of its near destruction quickly swept the adjoining communities of San Pedro and Wilmington where many of the sailors had families. The events at Pearl Harbor ended any thinking that the American people could stay out of the war. Support for pacifism, isolationism, and the American First Movement quickly evaporated.

"It all happened so fast," is a common refrain from those who recall the early days of wartime California. Newspaper headlines detailing Japanese victories in the Pacific evoked public fears of imminent raids over California. Continuing Allied losses throughout Europe and North Africa further made the state's populace realize that a world war was real and American defeat entirely possible. Californians responded immediately: young men overwhelmed military recruiting stations, while those not eligible for combat volunteered for civil defense work. So rapid was the change, and so universal the demand for bodies to serve in the military or work in defense plants, that it was difficult to believe that the country had been in the midst of the Great Depression just two years before. Bread lines of the recent past now gave way to long lines of new workers entering shipyards and factories.

As the nation mourned the loss of American lives at Pearl Harbor, California was beset by fears of Japanese invasion. Fueling the anxiety were detailed newspaper maps that emphasized that the Hawaiian Islands were only 2,550 miles away from California. Many believed that with the Pacific Fleet so badly damaged, the Pacific Coast would be the next Japanese target.

Japanese militarists did try to disrupt shipping along the coast. Using seven of their new 15 I-class submarines, the Japanese navy commenced a series of attacks that began shortly after Pearl Harbor. Although the submarine operations failed to stop American shipping, they did succeed in sinking several ships. One sub, the I-17, launched the first attack on American soil since the War of 1812. Although the I-17's shells did little damage to its intended target – an oil depot just north of Santa Barbara – it did arouse an already frightened citizenry (Starr 2002: 34–64). When a weather balloon broke from its mooring over Los Angeles, anti-aircraft spotters mistook it for a Japanese attack plane and began firing at it. Other anti-aircraft batteries quickly joined in. Of "The Battle of Los Angeles," the humorist Buck Henry recalled, "We imagined parachutes dropping. We imagined the hills of Hollywood on fire. We imagined hand-to-hand combat on the streets of Rodeo Drive" (*Los Angeles Times*, September 1, 1992).

In 1941, California was home to over 75 percent of the nation's Japanese American population. Resentment against their presence and that of other Asian Americans had been longstanding. Rumors quickly spread that the Japanese American populace was working in collaboration with the enemy. Calls quickly went forth for their removal from the Pacific Coast.

Leading the effort were such historically anti-Japanese groups as the Native Sons and the California Joint Immigration Committee. Influential politicians and military leaders soon joined in. Among those was California Attorney General Earl Warren, who stated that it was just a matter of time before people of Japanese descent living in California carried out attacks of sabotage. Los Angeles Mayor Fletcher Bowron, who had been known for his racial tolerance, went on radio to warn listeners that, "each of our little Japanese friends will know his part in the event of any possible attempted invasion or air raid." General John L. De Witt of the Western Defense Command bluntly stated: "The Japanese race is an enemy race." Stoking the embers of fear and anger, he added, "along the vital Pacific Coast over 112,000 potential enemies, of Japanese extraction, are at large today" (Verge 1993: 40–2).

Responding to political pressures, President Franklin Roosevelt issued Presidential Order 9066 in February of 1942, which authorized the removal of all Japanese (*Issei*) and Japanese Americans (*Nisei*) from the West Coast. Over 100,000 individuals were removed from the coastal West and interned in camps spread through the nation's interior. The subsequent forced internment of these Japanese Americans in particular would go down as the worst mass violation of civil liberties in American history.

Ironically, California's security actually suffered as a result of the relocation effort. Thousands of loyal Americans who had toiled to make the state the nation's leading producer of agriculture were now gone; also removed were the several thousand involved in the state's fishing industry, business entrepreneurs, and workers. On reflection, it could be understood why Hawaii, the location of the attack, took the opposite approach. The Japanese American community there was viewed as loyal to the United States and needed for the war effort. There was no internment operation enacted on the Hawaiian Islands.

To win the war, the United States embarked on the largest military production effort in human history. Central to its success was the conversion of civilian production to defense. To encourage the beating of plowshares into tanks, guns, ships, and planes, the American government guaranteed defense manufacturers a profit on every item produced. Helping to speed the conversion effort was the federal government's War Defense Plant Corporation (DPC). The DPC paid for expansion of manufacturing facilities deemed crucial to the war effort. Through DPC financing, over 5,000 factories in Los Angeles County alone were converted into war plants (Nash 1985).

Federal defense dollars utterly transformed California. Of the $360 billion spent by the federal government during the years 1940–6, California received $35 billion. This amount accounted for a staggering 45 percent of the personal income for those living in the state during the war (Lotchin 2000: 93–119). Federal defense investment also flowed into the state to develop troop training centers and to expand existing military installations. The Marine Corps enlarged its operations in San Diego and at Camp Pendleton to the north. While the US Army continued to run its Ninth Corps operations from the historic Presidio in San Francisco, it greatly expanded both Fort Ord on the Monterey Peninsula and Camp Roberts near Paso Robles. The Army also built air corps training centers at Santa Ana and at Mather Field in Sacramento. In January of 1942 Major General George S. Patton established the Desert Training Center in a large area east of Los Angeles. Over 16,000 square miles in size, it became the largest military training installation in the world. Over a million combat troops were trained there during the war. The United States Navy, in turn, expanded its historic base at Mare Island while also enlarging its presence at the ports of San Diego and Long Beach.

In the wake of Pearl Harbor, millions of Americans uprooted themselves to join the military or to find work in the nation's defense centers. Whereas every region in the United States lost population in the war effort, the population of the Pacific Coast states grew by 40 percent between 1940 and 1947. California gained the most migrants of all states, an estimated 1.4 million persons between 1940 and 1944 (Johnson 1993).

Speed was the driving force in getting the state's war industries up and running. Henry Kaiser, who had played a key role in constructing the Hoover, Shasta, and Grand Coulee dams, hired over 5,000 thousand of his dam builders to help him erect a shipyard at Richmond, California. Kaiser's vision began on an inauspicious note. The first bulldozer to begin work quickly disappeared into the site's boggy marshland. Undeterred, Kaiser's workers hammered thousands of pilings into the marshland, building what became the world's most productive shipyard. Kaiser's Richmond shipyard would produce a staggering 747 ships during the war (Foster 1989: 71).

In the very volatile and competitive aircraft manufacturing business, the CEOs of Southern California's aircraft companies agreed to put any rivalries aside in order to speed the vital production of combat aircraft. They formed the Aircraft War Production Council (AWPC) for the sharing of patents, facilities, and even personnel to meet production deadlines. One trade secret that revolutionized the rapidity and quality of aircraft produced was Douglas Aircraft's flush riveting technique. Quickly adopted by fellow aircraft manufacturers, the technique enabled them to meet and often exceed production quotas. Between 1942 and 1943, America's aircraft production doubled. In 1943, Southern California manufacturers turned out a new warplane every seven minutes (Verge 1993: 98).

The war also created a temporary social revolution. Middle-class women once relegated to the household now found themselves in demand for war work. Juanita Loveless remembers arriving in wartime Los Angeles with just the clothes on her back and a few dollars in her pocket. She quickly found work at a gas station. As cars pulled in for gas, drivers would try to lure her away for better-paying war work. She recalls, "My head was going crazy . . . You were just bombarded" (Verge 1993: 90). Adding to her confusion were newspaper and radio ads asking women to come for interviews at various defense plants with the promise of good pay and unlimited overtime. In stark contrast to the Great Depression, the abundance of employment opportunities ironically led to high worker turnover rates. In the first six months of 1943, aircraft plants in the Pacific Coast region hired 150,000 workers but lost 138,000. While some people blamed such a high turnover rate on women workers' inability to handle factory work, the truth was that both men and women left one factory for another if offered of better pay and hours.

To help stem the tide of women leaving their factory floors, Southern California aircraft manufacturers redesigned their assembly lines to include back-saving chain hoists, conveyor belts, and lighter-weight tools. In 1942, Congress responded to the need for women workers by passing the Lanham Act, which authorized federal funding for childcare at defense plants. Unfortunately, the desperately needed service was limited to daytime hours, forcing many women to miss out on the higher-paying swing shift (Johnson 1993: 125–7). Women constituted between 40 percent and 50 percent of the airplane industry's labor force, while women made up over 20 percent of the shipyard workers in Vallejo, California (Lotchin 2003: 77). While more than a few men resented their presence, women defense workers became the poster symbol of the nation's wartime spirit of "We Can Do It."

Women of color faced varying degrees of gender and racial discrimination, but war industry work in California offered opportunities that could not be found elsewhere. One of those who came to California was Sybil Lewis, an African American woman, who left her birthplace in Sapula, Oklahoma. A young adult at the time, she moved from a segregated town whose only promise was a lifetime of impoverishment. In California, Lewis worked as a riveter, arc welder, and finally as a bus driver in San Diego. Although she did encounter brushes with racial prejudice, it was rarely of the overt nature that she had experienced in Sapula. She recalled one striking difference: "I remember in transit school that they taught us that in a lot of states the colored people had to ride in the back of the bus and that in California they could ride wherever they wanted" (Harris et al. 1984: 118–21). War work for many women proved to be a consciousness-raising experience. Adele Erenberg recalled: "For me defense work was the beginning of my emancipation as a woman. For the first time in my life I found that I could do something with my hands beside bake a pie" (ibid.: 128). Working in the war plants also gave women war workers a sense of accomplishment and the feeling that they had played an important role in helping the Allies obtain final victory over the Axis powers.

In the early days of the war, California took on the appearance of a state on the defensive. Barrage balloons strung with metal cables were placed in the skies near shipyards and aircraft plants to snag possible incoming fighter planes while construction crews on the ground frantically built fortified anti-aircraft batteries. Along the shoreline, men and women on horseback patrolled the state's lengthy coastline looking for invaders and saboteurs. Hollywood set designers worked feverishly to disguise Southern California's large aircraft plants. From the air, the Douglas Aircraft plant in Santa Monica took on the appearance of a rural farm. As anti-submarine nets were refortified and others added to ports and inlets by day, the entire state went dark by night. Amusement park piers, golf driving ranges, and downtown businesses all went black as Californians attempted to maneuver around darkened office buildings and unlighted streets. The effort rarely worked perfectly. Some business owners, in a rush to get out of darkened downtowns, neglected to turn off all of the lights in their businesses. The problem was so bad one night that an air warden complained, "The city's lights of San Francisco were so bright, that you could see the glow in Tokyo."

To help get the nation fully behind the war effort, Hollywood went to work producing morale-boosting music and movies. Box office stars such as Jimmy Stewart, Clark Gable, and Tyrone Power put their careers on hold and joined the military. Those unable to enlist, due to age or infirmity, volunteered to help in other ways. Bob Hope and Bing Crosby took to the road with United Service Organizations tours. On the home front, celebrities gave freely of their time, entertaining troops at California military bases or at the famous Hollywood canteen. Starlets such as Betty Grable, Rita Hayworth, and Marlene Dietrich were special favorites of young servicemen.

The Port of San Francisco became the key embarkation point for troops headed to the Pacific theaters. Over a million and a half military personnel passed under the Golden Gate Bridge for destinations unknown. An eyewitness to the wartime city in 1943, historian Kevin Starr eloquently captured the painful dinner good-byes of husbands and wives, boyfriends and girlfriends, parents and sons. Starr describes the parents of a young Army officer sharing dinner in a San Francisco hotel: "when the conversation came completely to a halt as the three stared into their food, caught for a moment in the sheer anxiety over what might lie ahead" (Starr 2002: 84). At the city's scenic "Top of the Mark" bar ensconced above the Mark Hopkins Hotel on Nob Hill, the Marine Corps gave its men headed to battle two free drink tickets. The soldiers were instructed to take in the bar's stunning views of city and bay. They were then told, "Gentlemen – that's what you're fighting for."

World War II was everyone's war. Young boys and girls gave up cherished metal and plastic toys for scrap drives. Fashion-conscious women went without silk stockings because of the need for silk in parachutes. Housewives faithfully collected bacon grease and turned it over to the neighborhood butcher so that it could eventually be used in the manufacture of explosives. Men and women alike volunteered for civil defense duties, serving as air raid and blackout wardens as well as emergency medical volunteers.

Unlike wars that would follow, World War II was not a war one could ignore by simply turning off the television set or by not reading the newspaper. The war permeated everyday life. Roadside billboards encouraged Americans to do their part; posters inside stores and bars warned visitors not to divulge any sensitive information ("Loose lips sink ships"); and newsboys on street corners refrained from calling out news of the latest battlefield engagements. Doing one's part in the war meant working long hours, buying bonds, obeying rationing restrictions, and putting first the needs of America's fighting men and women. Roger Lotchin tells the poignant story of war workers taking a much-needed respite by enjoying a dance together. One man in attendance remembered how the dance hall suddenly began emptying out. The crowd had learned that a hospital ship laden with wounded Marines was entering nearby San Diego Harbor. While some of the dancers hurried out to donate much-needed blood, doctors and nurses immediately made their way to a hospital where, the man recalled, they would often work for days at a time without rest (Lotchin 2003: 19).

The sacrifices of the soldiers overseas made the trials of life on the home front pale by comparison. Still, life on the home front was difficult. Gas and tire rationing greatly affected transportation, forcing almost everyone throughout California's increasingly crowded cities to use already overcrowded public transport. Certain foods and consumer goods were in short supply. A common wartime refrain was: "Use it up, wear it out, make it do or do without." Those who still complained were met with angry stares or the words, "Don't you know there's a war going on?" One of the most difficult and pressing problems throughout California's cities was the stunning rate of population growth. The daily arrival of thousands of new residents pressed municipal services to the point of near collapse. The population of San Diego doubled between 1942 and 1945, while the San Francisco Bay Area grew by nearly 40 percent between 1940 and 1947. Although the city of Los Angeles experienced a slower rate of wartime population growth, the city's problems mimicked those found throughout California's urban areas (Johnson 1993: 7–8). Chief among them was the shortage of housing. With building materials limited by the needs of the war effort, new arrivals were often forced into inadequate housing. Rented rooms, garages, aging trailers, even vacated stores served as shelter. Some workers even took swing shifts so that they could sleep in their vehicles during warmer daylight hours.

The California wartime housing crisis did get the attention of the federal government. Knowing that the health and safety of war workers was crucial to the war effort, federal housing authorities stepped in to provide assistance. Many of the federally financed housing projects proved to be failures. Designed to provide temporary wartime shelter, the dwellings were plagued by shoddy workmanship. In Oakland's East Bay, for example, several burned down due to the flimsy materials used in their construction.

Municipal authorities also had to contend with overburdened city streets and mounting crime rates. Plagued by the loss of experienced officers to the war effort, police departments had to rely on aging officers and military police to contend with issues of juvenile delinquency, theft, robbery, gambling, prostitution, alcohol abuse, and increasing traffic congestion. Municipal officials also had to deal with the resentment of longtime city dwellers at those who had come in search of war work. A common complaint of these residents was that they felt like outsiders in their own hometowns. Local newspapers played up the problems of crime and congestion with headlines depicting the decline of conditions. The problems were so bad in the Oakland area that a 1943 grand jury was convened to investigate Alameda County's dramatic rise in crime (Johnson 1993).

Overcrowding also raised public health concerns. Many new arrivals had not been schooled in proper sanitation techniques. Added into the mix were the large numbers of young military personnel whose presence raised fears of sexually transmitted disease outbreaks. Faced with a drastic shortage of adequate healthcare facilities, public health officials did the best they could to prevent outbreaks of communicable diseases. It was every medical official's fear that a fast-moving epidemic could seriously hinder the war effort.

Inner-city congestion also heightened racial tensions. In Los Angeles the presence of large numbers of servicemen came into open conflict with young Mexican American males clad in Zoot suits. Although no one was killed in the wide-scale fighting that took place in downtown Los Angeles in June of 1943, the American military was forced to put parts of the city off-limits to service personnel for several weeks (Nash 1985; and see Kevin Leonard's essay in this volume). A race riot involving white sailors and African Americans also broke out in downtown Oakland in May of 1944. City officials denied that the fighting, in which one person was killed and four others wounded, was race related. They instead pointed to the fight's origins: it had broken out aboard a crowded streetcar, and officials determined that the resulting melee was due to the combined lack of enough police and streetcars (Johnson 1993).

Adding to the woes of civic officials were environmental concerns. Sewer treatment facilities were so overburdened by the war effort that public officials in the San Francisco, Oakland, and Los Angeles areas allowed excess sewage to flow untreated into their neighboring bays. Dr. Elmer Belt, president of the California State Board of Health, closed several popular

Los Angeles beaches due to contamination. Air quality, too, became a war-related issue. As early as the summer of 1940, civic workers in Los Angeles complained of breathing difficulties and eye irritation. Plagued by an inversion layer that trapped air pollutants, much of whose origin could be traced to war-related industrial pollution, the city's populace took to calling the brown air "smog" – a combination of smoke and fog.

Despite the multitude of problems that Californians dealt with during the war years, an undeniable excitement and sense of accomplishment filled the air. Everyone felt that they were part of something much bigger than themselves. Every day at the plant and every hour spent training a new military recruit raised the possibility of wartime victory. In addition, the war initiated social changes that would have otherwise taken decades more to accomplish. Women war workers developed skills and confidence that would spur their fight for women's rights. African Americans, whose participation proved vital to the wartime cause, raised the crucial question, "If we are fighting for freedom for others overseas, why can't we give those same freedoms to those of us at home?" Latinos, too, supported the war effort, and likewise paid with their blood on battlefields across the globe. Their demand to be considered part of the American national fabric was certainly beyond fair and just.

California emerged out of World War II a world leader in technology, innovation, and war material production. The state's civilian populace prospered as never before. Unemployment, which had hovered over 12 percent in 1940, fell to less than 1 percent during the height of the war. The state's annual gross income jumped from $5 billion in 1941 to over $13 billion by 1945 (Lotchin 2000: 95). Equally important in understanding what World War II meant to California was what the state meant to people who visited or visualized it from afar. For hundreds of thousands of troops who trained there or who shipped out from one of the state's ports of embarkation, California held a seemingly magical spell over them. At the war's conclusion the state's population again swelled as returning troops decided to make California their new home. As the *Los Angeles Times* editorialized on December 18, 1945, "[t]he story of the west's great industrial future has spread over the nation and like the story of the discovery of gold, it is luring hopeful men whose dreams are spun of golden opportunity."

REFERENCES

Foster, Mark. 1989. *Henry J. Kaiser: Builder of the American West*. Austin: University of Texas.
Harris, Mark Jonathan, Mitchell, Franklin, and Schechter, Steven. 1984. *The Homefront: America during World War 2*. New York: Putnam.

Johnson, Marilynn S. 1993. *The Second Gold Rush: Oakland and the East Bay in World War II*. Berkeley: University of California Press.

Lotchin, Roger W. 1992. *Fortress California. 1910–1961: From Warfare to Welfare*. New York: Oxford University Press.

Lotchin, Roger W. 2000. *The Way We Really Were: The Golden State in the Second Great War*. Urbana: University of Illinois Press.

Lotchin, Roger W. 2003. *The Bad City in the Good War: San Francisco, Los Angeles, Oakland, and San Diego*. Bloomington: University of Indiana Press.

Mazon, Mauricio. 1984. *The Psychology of Symbolic Annihilation: The Zoot-Suit Riots*. Austin: University of Texas Press.

Nash, Gerald D. 1985. *The American West Transformed: The Impact of the Second World War*. Bloomington: University of Indiana Press.

Starr, Kevin. 2002. *Embattled Dreams: California in War and Peace*. New York: Oxford University Press.

Verge, Arthur C. 1993. *Paradise Transformed: Los Angeles during the Second World War*. Dubuque, IA: Kendall Hunt.

Webber, Bert. 1984. *Silent Siege: Japanese Attacks against North America in World War II*. Fairfield, WA: Ye Galleon Press.

FURTHER READING

Blum, John Morton. 1976. *V was for Victory: Politics and Culture during World War II*. New York: Harcourt, Brace, Jovanovich.

Brienes, Marvin. 1976. "Smog Comes to Los Angeles," *Southern California Quarterly* 58 (4): 515–32.

Friedrich, Otto. 1986. *City of Nets: A Portrait of Hollywood in the 1940s*. New York: Harper & Row.

Leonard, Kevin Allen. 2006. *The Battle for Los Angeles: Racial Ideology and World War II*. Albuquerque, NM: University of Arizona Press.

Perrett, Geoffrey. 1973. *Days of Sadness, Years of Triumph: The American People, 1939–1945*. Madison: University of Wisconsin Press.

Chapter Nineteen

BETWEEN LIBERATION AND OPPRESSION: GAY POLITICS AND IDENTITY

Daniel Hurewitz

When William Mann began interviewing people about the place of gay men and lesbians in early Hollywood, he heard the same comments again and again: the classic studio era constituted both "the best and the worst of times" for gay men and women (Mann 2001: 2). Within certain confines their sexuality was "an open secret" that conferred on them great freedom and even power; if that secret broke out to the wider public, however, their professional lives were over. As costume designer Miles White told Mann, "On the one hand, they didn't care, and you had extraordinary freedom, but on the other, of *course* they did, and you weren't free at all" (ibid.: xi).

Not only is it intriguing to learn that early Hollywood could be so gay friendly but, in a sense, what we're coming to discover about the history of gay and lesbian life in California embodies just that paradox. California has been both the best and the worst place for gay men and women. Few places rivaled the wide-open sexual freedoms that Gold Rush California offered to nineteenth-century Americans and no city had a better reputation for sexual tolerance than San Francisco did by the late twentieth century. Again and again, Californians have driven forward the unfolding national story of gay and lesbian liberation: the first gay rights organization, the first lesbian rights group, the first gay newspaper, the first gay church, the first gay synagogue, the first openly gay elected official, the first legal same-sex marriages – all came out of California. Many of the landmark moments in the gay past emerged out West.

And yet that same historical narrative has also often enough veered toward oppression. California was among the first states to send homosexuals to criminal psychiatric wards. Harvey Milk, the first openly gay elected official who served as a city supervisor in San Francisco, was assassinated in 1978, less than a year after taking office. During the first wave of the AIDS epidemic, not only was it a former California governor who guided the country largely to ignore the deaths of thousands of gay men, but some of the most venomous political responses to the epidemic in the country appeared as ballot initiatives for statewide consideration. And those first legal gay marriages, authorized by Gavin Newsom, the mayor of San Francisco, who in 2004 pushed the city clerk's office to marry as many same-sex couples as possible before the opposition could intervene? They were declared null and void by the state Supreme Court, quickly turning back that page of gay history.

These contradictory developments, toward liberation and oppression both, have contributed dramatically to a profound set of transformations in the meaning attributed to homosexual activity in American social, cultural, and political life over the last 150 years. There is, of course, much work to do to bring to light the hidden history of same-sex intimacy in California. The history of sexuality, let alone gay history, is still a relatively young field: John D'Emilio's *Sexual Politics, Sexual Communities*, considered by many to be the first scholarly volume of gay history, only appeared in 1983, just 25 years ago. And yet the field has grown rapidly and, particularly in the last decade, a host of studies have been completed that begin to map out an increasingly rich history of the lives of gay men and women in California.

Much that we know focuses on the state's two major urban areas, Los Angeles and San Francisco, where historians have been interested in documenting and understanding the origins and development of gay communities and notions of sexual identity. The histories of the two cities are far from identical and can hardly be assumed to stand in for the little-known histories of rural California and its smaller towns (projects that decidedly merit attention). Yet to a growing degree, historians concur about the major developments in California's gay past. What follows is an overview of that history, marking out how a society that had little or no notion of sexual identity in the early nineteenth century slowly embraced a belief in sexuality as a defining personal characteristic that carried political weight.

A Focus on Gender: California before the 1930s

Nan Boyd entitled her 2003 study of San Francisco *Wide Open Town* and the title suggests something of the story that has been emerging about late nineteenth- and early twentieth-century California in general and San Francisco in particular. While a law criminalizing sodomy was incorporated into the new state's penal code in 1850, the law was rarely enforced in those early decades. Instead, there was a kind of social freedom afoot in the state that, among other things, allowed homoerotic possibilities to flourish. Certainly that was true out among the Gold Rush miners. In their largely male society, as Susan Johnson has noted, there existed a strong "undercurrent of pleasure taken in the constant company of men;" the men of the mines "sometimes had bright eyes for each other," and they paired up together without meeting with disapprobation, with one man sometimes explicitly taking on a female role – whether for dancing, cooking, or sex (Johnson 2000: 169–70). San Francisco, which exploded in size in the wake of the mining craze, long retained the lawless flavor of a boom-town "where anything goes" (Boyd 2003: 2). Even as city leaders invested energy in creating a governable society, the rules of social decorum were not consistently enforced (Sears 2005); although there were regular anti-vice crackdowns, the city and its environs maintained a kind of live-and-let-live ethos that could be forgiving of gendered and sexual misconduct. The city's Barbary Coast and Tenderloin districts featured thriving sex tourism areas through the first decades of the twentieth century. There, out-of-towners could find more than the usual fare in prostitution: at the Dash saloon in 1908, for instance, "female impersonators entertained customers, and homosexual sex could be purchased in booths for a dollar" (Boyd 2003: 25). And the Dash was not unique.

As historians have investigated this early, seemingly licentious period, many of their questions have focused on the meaning that people attributed to homosexual activity. One thing that is striking for both San Francisco and Los Angeles is how little evidence there is to point toward a notion of homosexual *identity* or what we might call "gayness." While some scientists and doctors in the late nineteenth century began to speak about "homosexuals" as a type of person, historians are generally convinced that most Americans at the time did not consider whom they had sex with as a defining feature of their identities. They were much more concerned with whether or not people conformed to the gender norms and acted like real men or women. Among the working classes, for instance, many men had sex with other men, but, because they continued to live and comport themselves in a masculine way, they did not consider themselves unusual.

There was a small percentage of men and women with homosexual desires, however, who did consider themselves fundamentally different. But they interpreted their desires as merely a small part of a larger difference: they viewed themselves as misgendered, or as gender inverts. They were, they felt, men trapped in women's bodies and vice versa. Their homosexual interests were part of their larger "mistaken" gender identity.

Such individuals occupy a central place in our understanding of California's early gay past: indeed, to the degree that historians can point to a significant number of people possessing a particular identity based on their sexual desires, it is these men and women who understood – and lived – those desires through a broader framework of gender inversion who loom largest. California's historical record is dotted with tales of people like

Eugene de Forest, a well-regarded LA drama instructor, who, in the throes of a 1915 marriage engagement to a woman, was forced to explain to the court that she was "in nature a man" (Faderman & Timmons 2006: 24). And many are the men in the early twentieth-century record whose expressions of homosexual desire involved dressing or behaving as women were supposed to. In 1923, when photographer Edward Weston wandered into an LA diner where civilian men went to meet sailors, he portrayed the cruising men as a particular "type of effeminate male," twitching with "impatient desire."[1] Many of the early individuals we label as having some kind of gay identity in fact understood themselves first and foremost as gender inverts.

While historians debate when exactly sexual identity emerged as a category separate from gender identity, the primary emphasis on gender seems to have held for most Californians until the 1930s. Plainly, during the vaudeville years of the late nineteenth and early twentieth centuries, Americans in general remained so captivated by issues of gender conformity that performers who impersonated the opposite sex on stage – and broke the gender rules – "numbered among the most popular and highly paid stars" (Toll 1976: 237). No one in their ranks rose higher than Julian Eltinge, who toured the world with his female impersonation shows and was wooed by the movie studios to settle in Los Angeles in 1917 and launch a film career (Hurewitz 2007).

But early in the 1930s, the enthusiasm for such performers began to change as a "pansy craze" swept the cosmopolitan set around the country (Chauncey 1994; Hurewitz 2007). Urban Americans began to delight not simply in impersonations, but particularly female impersonators who tinged their performances with homosexual innuendo. Speakeasies and nightclubs up and down the California coast now offered "fairies" and "pansies" galore. The clubs where they performed were hardly underground hideaways. In the fall of 1932, for instance, *Variety* praised the impersonators at La Boheme in Hollywood, describing the star, Leon La Verde, as "the last word in the impersonation art." According to the paper, "Boy has box-office qualities that could be cashed in with a New York revue. He does a mean rumba, and as nifty a snake hips as has been seen anywhere. Has grace in his walk, knows how to use his hands and gesturate, and is plenty of 'hot cha' when it comes to appearance."[2]

The pansy craze did not last. The homosexual desires hinted at in the nightclub acts became the subject of growing attention. The gender play of the pansy performances now appeared to be merely a cover for homosexual desires. This interpretation grew out of a mid-1930s cultural shift toward viewing sexuality as a central feature of identity. In this shift, "the homosexual" began to be widely understood as a distinct type of person, marking the start of what might be called the "era of sexual identity" in

American life, the period thus far that has received the most historical investigation.

Politics and Sexual Identity: 1930s–1980s

This change in American culture was part of a growing fascination with the interior life of emotions and feelings. But the first implication of this change for gay history was that government officials began to treat homosexual activity as a distinct threat to the general public. Across Southern California, bars were raided; impersonator shows were banned; and homosexually active men (in particular) were spied upon, entrapped, and sent to prison and criminal hospitals (Hurewitz 2007). In Hollywood, the Hays code went into effect, eliminating any portrayal of pansies and homosexuality on screen – although, as Vito Russo (1981), Richard Barrios (2003), and others have pointed out, there were still some hidden, winking portraits.

The blackout was not absolute. The Bay Area seemed to escape some of the heat of these crackdowns: during the 1940s, for instance, Finocchio's, the premier San Francisco nightclub featuring men performing as women, "filled to capacity with four different shows, six nights a week, attracting locals, tourists, and such celebrities as Bob Hope, Frank Sinatra, Bette Davis, and Tallulah Bankhead" (Boyd 2003: 55). Yet California fundamentally became immersed in a political culture that treated gender inversion and homosexual behavior as dangerous and demanding containment (Hurewitz 2007). By 1939, the state required psychiatric examinations of anyone convicted of a sex crime with the possibility of an indefinite hospitalization until "cured." And by 1950, California had increased the punishment for sodomy to 20 years in prison (Herman 2006: 109–10, 146).

Despite these draconian developments, what historians have focused on much more is how the broad cultural change that generated these sanctions also provoked a dramatic shift in how homosexually active men and women began to see themselves. To a degree, that shift was an outgrowth of World War II (D'Emilio 1983; Bérubé 1990). The massive mobilization of millions of young American men and women through California for their military service led to an enormous increase in both the number and visibility of people seeking same-sex intimacy. Uprooted from their small towns, the men and women who were so inclined found themselves forced into same-sex barracks and quarters and sent for long or short stays to the state's major cities. Suddenly, the number of bars and clubs that catered to their social desires began to increase (Hurewitz 2007). Burt Miller, 21 and stationed outside Los Angeles during the war, later told historian Allan Bérubé that one night after dinner he wandered through the Biltmore

Hotel bar, just off the city's main downtown square. "About 75 percent of the men were in uniform – and I asked myself, 'Can what I think is going on here *be* going on?' I stopped to find out, and sure enough it was! I was in that bar every night" (Bérubé 1990: 114). Many discharged service people decided to remain in Los Angeles or San Francisco and the steady increase in visibility continued (Boyd 2003; Faderman & Timmons 2006). One San Francisco paper even ran a banner headline in 1949: "Homos Invade S.F.," and declared that "San Francisco is rapidly becoming the central gathering point of lesbians and homosexuals in California" (Stryker & Van Buskirk 1996: 141).

As more and more homosexually active men and women began to congregate, they took note of new ideas about racial groups in California society (Hurewitz 2007). The war, of course, marked a watershed in racial anxiety and awareness for California: across the state, thousands of Japanese and Japanese Americans were forced out of their homes; hundreds of Southern California Mexicans and Mexican Americans were attacked in riots and police raids; and tens of thousands of African Americans flooded into the state to partake of the economic possibilities. Influenced in part by local leftists, Californians for the first time began to think about all of these groups as being comparable to one another. As Los Angeles journalist and attorney Carey McWilliams wrote to returning veterans in 1946: "Great changes have taken place in race relations in America since the beginning of the war . . . Since the war, the various aspects of the race problem, seldom correlated in the past, have been drawn together so that all phases of the matter, involving Negroes, Mexicans, Orientals, Indians, Filipinos, etc. have come to be regarded as a single national problem."[3] A notion of minority identities began to take root.

For the first time, homosexually active men and women in the state began to view themselves – and their growing visibility – as comparable to the African Americans or Mexicans in their cities: they saw themselves as distinct types who also constituted an oppressed social minority. And with that view, they began to organize a movement that would address their oppression and cultivate a sense of community (D'Emilio 1983; Hurewitz 2007). Although tentative steps in this direction had been taken before and failed, in the 1950s California gave birth to the major organizations in what would become the national gay rights movement. In 1950, the Mattachine Society formed in Los Angeles and quickly sprouted chapters up and down the coast and soon across the country. Conceived by a group of left-leaning men (mostly), Mattachine set out to cultivate a sense of homosexual identity through intimate discussion groups; they also wanted to challenge the laws which regularly landed Mattachine members in jails and prisons. In 1953, the Mattachine headquarters shifted up to San Francisco, but much of the radical energy of the Los Angeles activists was channeled into ONE, a new LA group that spun off from Mattachine while working on publishing a newsletter. Soon enough a group of middle-class women in the Bay Area launched the Daughters of Bilitis (DOB) in 1955 to address the specific needs of lesbians in American society (D'Emilio 1983; Gallo 2006; Loftin 2006; Hurewitz 2007).

These three groups became the bedrock of the self-proclaimed "homophile movement" – a movement that not only helped homosexually active men and women to see themselves as a unified minority, but also sought to overturn the laws and cultural codes that oppressed homosexuals. It was the first American gay rights and gay pride movement. In part, early Mattachine meetings were fueled with personal declarations such as, "'I just did not believe that this could happen.' 'This is the most wonderful thing in my life.' 'I can suddenly feel proud.'"[4]

Additionally, as Martin Meeker and Craig Loftin have recently argued, these early homophile groups served to foster a kind of national homosexual community (Meeker 2005; Loftin 2006). With a key goal for all of these groups to educate the public – gay and otherwise – about homosexuality, they devoted considerable energy to publishing newsletters, doing outreach, and opening up avenues of dialogue. Particularly significant were the publications of *ONE Magazine* in Los Angeles and the *Mattachine Review* and the Daughters of Bilitis's *Ladder* in San Francisco. These journals, emanating from California, served as hubs in a network of communication that spanned the country. Through them, people near and far slowly began to learn about homosexuality, the possibility of a homosexual community, and the challenges faced due to the law, medicine, and religious tenets. A man from Williamsburg, Virginia, for example, wrote to the editors of *ONE* in 1956:

> ONE is more than a magazine to me. It's a vehicle through which communion is made with thousands of brothers whose outlook, ideals, problems, etc. are my own. It is one of several important links with the world of our minority without which I would feel very parochial, not to say isolated. (Loftin 2006: 63)

Significantly, the project of public relations was not simply one of contacting isolated homosexuals; rather it also involved an effort at convincing people that as homosexuals they were part of a distinct oppressed minority group. That argument, largely accepted by the end of the twentieth century, needed making over and over again in the middle of it. As Jim Kepner, one of the major writers for *ONE Magazine* explained,

> When you continue to preach something it's because you're aware that your listeners haven't heard it yet, and that it hasn't sunk in. And you believe that

it's a message that needs to get through. We were talking about the gay community because the majority of gays were infuriated at the mention of the term. The majority of the gays considered the very wording "gay community" to be communistic.[5]

At the same time, the California homophile groups broke new ground in insisting on a political identity and set of demands for homosexuals. In 1952, the Los Angeles Mattachine sent out questionnaires to local political candidates asking their views of laws criminalizing homosexual behavior. After having their magazine seized by the postal service as obscene in 1954, ONE fought all the way to the United States Supreme Court – and, in 1958, won the right to circulate information about homosexuality through the mail. And, in 1960, DOB hosted a national conference in San Francisco for lesbian activists from around the country, bringing together this growing political community for the first time (D'Emilio 1983; Boyd 2003; Gallo 2006; Loftin 2006; Hurewitz 2007).

This analysis of the importance of the homophile organizations has been critiqued by some historians who have argued that the growing number of gay bars across the 1940s, 1950s, and 1960s outweighed these early traditional-style political groups in their significance. Bars, they have suggested, provided a forum in which community solidarity developed more dramatically and a commitment to the daily political activism of visibility was born. Boyd argued that San Francisco's bars and taverns proved a vital source for "less organized (but numerically stronger) pockets of queer association and camaraderie" than did homophile politics (Boyd 2003: 10). In San Francisco in 1951, the owner of the Black Cat bar successfully challenged the constitutionality of state laws criminalizing the social gathering of homosexuals. And by 1962, gay bar owners in that city had formed an alliance to help protect their income and their clientele (Boyd 2003). Clearly, political energy was being amassed.

But that energy was not being amassed for the same purposes as the homophiles were addressing. As Boyd has pointed out, bar activism focused much more on communal rights, such as the right to gather, whereas the homophiles emphasized individual civil rights (Boyd 2003: 162). At the same time, the homophiles tended to be more middle class and more anxious about social status than bar patrons were. While there was overlap between them, the debate about the significance of their different kinds of political action points to how varied the experiences were of different kinds of homosexuals. Historians need to keep digging at that variety to understand the diversity of homosexual lives.

One thing is certain, though: the more the homophile journals circulated, the more they attracted readers to the events in Los Angeles and San Francisco that they described. One woman wrote to the editors of the

Ladder that while she thought the magazine "a good effort and very interesting," she would have preferred to be "in San Francisco for the various social events and discussions" (Meeker 2006: 90). And, as the wider media began to write about homosexuality, the country's largest cities were repeatedly identified as bastions of sexual activity, with San Francisco regularly appearing as the most idyllic and welcoming. Indeed, in 1964, when *Life* magazine offered an unprecedented exposé on "Homosexuality in America," it identified San Francisco as the nation's "gay capital." As Meeker explained, the designation "had the effect of advertising the city to many isolated homosexuals nationwide; and in many cases the advertisement was alluring enough to encourage a number to move about the country and to San Francisco in particular" (ibid.: 178). So began what Kath Weston has deemed, "the great gay migration," as so many young men and women headed to the country's major cities, and especially to San Francisco (Weston 1995).

Gay Liberation

Curiously, in spite of how many of those migrants headed west, the story of gay life in the late 1960s and 1970s – and the birth of the more radical gay liberation political movement – has been framed in the historical record as largely an East Coast phenomenon. The centerpiece of that tale is the Stonewall riots of 1969, when bar patrons in New York's Greenwich Village fought back against the NYPD as they shut down yet another gay bar. Their resistance over the course of a few days, portrayed as the first time bar patrons had resisted police oppression, sparked multiple protests and gave birth to a handful of new organizations like the Gay Liberation Front and the Gay Activists Alliance. These groups represented a new, younger, and more radical movement than the homophiles were and they spread around the country. Urging people to "come out," these daring activists challenged politicians with sit-ins and pickets, confronted straight bar patrons with kiss-ins, provoked and promoted the passage of gay rights bills in tens of cities around the country, and forced the repeal of many states' sodomy laws, including California's (Clendinen & Nagourney 1999).

It is fair to say that this new kind of activism gained notoriety and momentum on the East Coast. At the same time, San Francisco and Los Angeles saw similar kinds of resistance – among bar patrons and others – several years before Stonewall. Why those confrontations did *not* provoke the kind of national activism that Stonewall did is a worthwhile question. Why did the activist energy of New York City seem or feel more important than what was occurring on the West Coast? In Los Angeles, when 1967

dawned with violent New Year's Eve raids on two Silver Lake bars, picketers took to the streets with signs like "Blue Fascists Must Go!" and
marched down Hollywood Boulevard (Faderman & Timmons 2006). Still
more impressive, by the late 1960s, gay bar owners in San Francisco had
not only united to strategize against police harassment, but homophile
leaders had met with city and police officials to create an open dialogue
about the needs of gay people. As Boyd suggested, the issues raised by the
Stonewall riots in New York had largely already been resolved in San Francisco (Boyd 2003: 10). Yet it seems that, as far as the rest of the country
was concerned, what happened in San Francisco or Los Angeles stayed
there as well. Hopefully, as more researchers dig their teeth into the histories of California's gay liberation and gay pride movements – a much-
needed undertaking – we will come to understand more fully what was
distinct about these developments out West.

Nonetheless, it is already apparent that part of the spirit of the new
activism in California focused on place claiming. The gay libbers set out
to create a public gay culture, particularly for men, with gay community
centers, bars, and restaurants that catered to gay clientele, and the free and
open expression of same-sex affection and desire. In multiple urban areas,
visible gay commercial life coincided with growing gay residential life and
gay liberation as a political movement evolved into a social and cultural
milieu emphasizing gay pride (Kenney 2001). No place came to exemplify
this development more than San Francisco's Castro neighborhood. As
Stryker & Van Buskirk (1996) tell the story, the Castro changed over the
course of the 1960s and 1970s from being a quiet working-class neighborhood to one that increasingly took on a gay identity. In fact, the Castro
became the nation's pre-eminent gay enclave or "ghetto."

The creation of publicly visible gay neighborhoods underscored the
complex forces in play as gay liberation took social and cultural root, and
historians have focused on three interconnected issues. First, as many
scholars have argued, although these enclaves contributed to an idea of a
unified gay community, deep divisions partitioned the expanding post-
Stonewall world. On the one hand, as Eric Wat and Yolanda Retter have
pointed out, the public face of gay ghettos in the 1970s was young, white,
and male. In Los Angeles, the sexism and racism of those young
men repeatedly divided gay liberation groups and left many women and
people of color feeling shunned from the so-called gay community and
forming separate subcultures (Retter 1999; Wat 2002; Faderman &
Timmons 2006).

On the other hand, as Gayle Rubin has demonstrated, separate subcultures also formed around sexual activities and styles. In fact, in the 1970s,
one San Francisco local described three distinct, if not equally well-known,
gay neighborhoods in that city: the "Valley of the Kings" below Market

Street where the leather crowd congregated; the "Valley of the Queens" along Polk Street where an older, less emphatically masculine crowd gathered; and the Castro, where new young arrivals filled the "Valley of the Dolls" (Rubin 1998: 258). And a similar analysis could be made comparing the residents of Los Angeles's West Hollywood and Silver Lake districts, and several less obvious parts of the city. Even at the level of sexuality, then, "gay" was not a single homogeneous category. Gay life as lived did not narrowly occupy single neighborhoods any more than a single simple identity (Kenney 2001). While Elizabeth Armstrong has argued that San Franciscans in fact embraced this diversity as the unifying feature of their gay community, many other scholars have emphasized how the variety of gay and lesbian lives provoked tensions and divisions across the 1970s and 1980s (Retter 1999; Armstrong 2002; Wat 2002; Faderman & Timmons 2006).

Secondly, beyond these divisions, as gay enclaves grew, a new gay economy emerged as well, and it quickly came to involve more than bar tabs and cover charges. The new gay economy included clothing stores, restaurants, hair salons, gyms, and more. "Gay" began to evolve into a consumer identity and places like West Hollywood, according to critics, came "to symbolize all that is problematic about the construction of sexual identity in a postliberation era: a focus on capital accumulation, conspicuous consumption, and appearance, rather than on civil rights" (Kenney 2001: 35; Gluckman & Reed 1997).

Finally, though, in addition to economic growth, the claiming of gay space also yielded gay political power. In San Francisco, because of a charter revision that provided district representation on the city Board of Supervisors, the growth of the Castro as a gay district in the 1970s led almost inexorably to the 1977 election of the nation's first openly gay official: Harvey Milk. Before his assassination, Milk played a crucial role in passing a gay rights ordinance for the city and defeating a statewide proposition, authored by state senator John Briggs, which would have banned gay men and women from teaching in the public schools (Shilts 1982). Importantly, the threat of the Briggs initiative also broadened the constituency of the gay liberation movement up and down the coast. As Jeanne Cordova, a lesbian activist in Los Angeles, commented, before Briggs, "the movement had been radicals, queens fairies, and dykes – the fringes ... [But] the atmosphere changed from being kind of radical and influenced by black civil rights and the left, to being very middle class. Now we were having luncheons at the Beverly Hilton [in Beverly Hills] to defeat Briggs."[6] David Mixner, then an advisor to Los Angeles mayor Tom Bradley, and others began to organize fundraisers featuring the likes of Burt Lancaster, Joan Baez, John Travolta, and Lily Tomlin and he succeeded in convincing the former governor, Ronald Reagan, to speak out against the initiative as well.

These coalitions represented a new level of activism and organization in the state, and through the campaign, mainstream gay political activism gained cachet around the state (Clendinen & Nagourney 1999; Faderman & Timmons 2006).

The tying of gay political power to space claiming appeared most dramatically when, not quite a decade after the defeat of Briggs, the gay population of West Hollywood banded together with the local senior citizens and Russian immigrants to incorporate as a city within Los Angeles County. While the Castro, in some ways, represented a new kind of ethnic enclave, like a Chinatown or a Little Italy, West Hollywood – known as "Boystown" – represented a more novel and significant development. As Moira Kenney explained, "what sets West Hollywood apart from similar enclaves is the political independence of the neighborhood that makes the gay political governance synonymous with a gay activist presence" (Kenney 2001: 36). The city government does not simply respond to the demands of gay constituents – they *are* the government and shape the multiple policies and practices of the city. For a gay city to emerge within a major metropolis in the late twentieth century may well have required the unusual political geography of Los Angeles, a city and region pieced together from multiple smaller cities. Given that context, gay men and women succeeded in claiming much greater political power.

AIDS and the Push beyond Identity

Of course, none of that political power protected gay men from the onslaught of AIDS. Even 25 years after the first cases became publicly known, it remains difficult to conceptualize AIDS as something other than a tragedy of epic proportions. It decimated the gay liberation generation and still seems too present and too ominous to historicize effectively. We know, of course, how the epidemic forced gay communities to construct massive social service organizations to compensate for the neglect of the public health system, though public funds eventually arrived. Some argue that the disease recharged the angry edge of activist energy of gays and lesbians, spawning ACT UP (the AIDS Coalition to Unleash Power) and drawing gay men and lesbians back together in a joint cause. And from the perspective of politics and the gay rights movement, it is striking as well how AIDS forced gay men to demand attention from the government after decades of asking that the government stop scrutinizing their lives.

Perhaps, though, one particular question that the California AIDS experience asks us to examine is the place of anti-gay politics in the rise of the new right. Certainly by the time former governor Ronald Reagan became president in 1981 and gay men began dying of HIV infection, it became

clear that his earlier opposition to the Briggs initiative drew on his libertar-
ian attitudes, not a belief in gay civil liberties. His administration's outrageous neglect of dying gay men was outdone only by the far right in
California which repeatedly proposed ending anonymous HIV-testing programs, forcing all possible carriers (and prison inmates) to be tested,
and, most dramatically, quarantining the infected in relocation camps
(Faderman & Timmons 2006). Because so much of the history of
twentieth-century American conservatism is rooted in the Southwest and
California, we need to wrestle more fully with the role of homosexuality
and homophobia as catalysts for that movement. Their response to AIDS
poses that question in stark terms.

Finally, over the last decade, as AIDS has become more of a chronic
illness than a fatal diagnosis, many intellectuals have also suggested that
we are living in a world in which the mid-twentieth-century notions of
sexual identity no longer apply. The notion that we have arrived at a post-
gay world is, in part, a product of Queer Nation, an activist group that
spun off from ACT UP at the start of the 1990s. As part of their sexual
liberation agenda, Queer Nation not only tried to strip "queer" of its
pejorative connotations, but also tried to fashion "queer" as an identity
that was not exclusively homosexual, and that included men, women, and
those who were transgender. "Queer" was meant to be broader and funkier
than "gay" and to begin to eclipse it. The organization itself quickly disappeared, but the idea of "queerness" lingered.

Queer has quite plainly become a dominant framework in academic
circles for describing scholarly projects and courses. But contemporary
observers also point to various sites in American society where they see
gayness disappearing. Some journalists, for instance, have suggested that for
today's high school students the eclipse of a narrow gay-vs.-straight notion
of sexual identity is well under way and that they choose to understand their
sex lives outside of those labels (Morris 2006). Similarly, a recent Associated
Press article suggested that some of the early gay ghettos, like the Castro,
are losing their gay identity. The account suggested that more and more
gay men and women are either opting to live as a more integrated presence
in the city or not to head to the big city at all (Leff 2007).

What is curious about these accounts of the declining significance of
sexual identity labels is that, simultaneously, "gay" and "lesbian" as terms
of identity undeniably continue to carry great cultural power. Certainly,
transsexual and transgender individuals have been embraced as part of the
queer family in a way that they were not in earlier decades. Nonetheless,
it does not seem that the old identity paradigms have simply disappeared.
In fact, of late, gay appears to be everywhere.

That definitely seems to be the case in the Hollywood slice of American
popular culture. In truth, if there remains an area of special intrigue in the

gay history of California, it rests in the untold tales of Hollywood, the secrets behind both the American aristocracy of movie stars and the hidden gay meaning in the cultural myths that Hollywood films and programs portrayed. Inspired by Vito Russo's groundbreaking *The Celluloid Closet* from 1981, numerous writers have tried to tease out those secret stories, whether by uncovering the forgotten homoerotics of Laurel and Hardy or the double life of Cary Grant (Ehrenstein 1998; Mann 2001; Barrios 2003; Faderman & Timmons 2006).

But in recent years, real gay people and gay characters have become fairly ubiquitous in Hollywood. In spring 2006, for instance, NBC's *Will and Grace* – a sitcom featuring two gay men among the four lead characters – went off the air after eight seasons and multiple years as a Top 10-rated program: the show was enormously popular. In the midst of the sitcom's final season, Hollywood also released *Brokeback Mountain*, a romance between two cowboys that proved to be an unprecedented gay blockbuster and critical success. And the following spring, Hollywood invited lesbian comedian Ellen DeGeneres to host the Academy Awards – the movie industry's most important night – before a television audience of some 40 million viewers. What is so striking about DeGeneres's appearance is that 10 years earlier she had come out, both as the central character on her own sitcom and in reality. That move, in 1997, landed her briefly on the cover of *Time* magazine, but also signaled the end of her program and, seemingly, the end of her career. In the intervening decade, however, Hollywood embraced gay characters and stars so eagerly that DeGeneres could return to the spotlight, host the Oscars, and declare, to eager applause, "If it weren't for blacks, Jews, and gays, there would be no Oscars." Clearly, something akin to the 1930s pansy craze has been sweeping Hollywood.

Yet that pop-cultural embrace has occurred at the same time as American political life has been up in arms about the rights of gay citizens. Ever since the US Supreme Court declared sodomy laws unconstitutional in 2003, gay rights have been the subject of heated political battle. Not long after the court's decision, Mayor Newson began marrying same-sex couples in San Francisco, President George W. Bush called for a constitutional amendment to ban gay marriage, and multiple states debated inscribing such bans into their local laws. And in California, not surprisingly, the state, on the one hand, began to provide same-sex couples nearly identical rights and privileges as their straight counterparts; on the other hand, the governor, Arnold Schwarzenegger, vetoed legislation fully allowing gay couples to marry. The pendulum between liberation and oppression again has been swinging widely, and gay rights, both challenged and acknowledged, have become a central American political question.

How to explain the different treatment gay people receive in politics versus popular culture seems a vital question, one meriting serious scrutiny.

But short of that, what is already clear about the twenty-first century is that it has begun with a period of contest, with conflicting notions both about sexual identity and sexual politics. If "queer" is eclipsing "gay" as a way to understand sexuality, it is a slow-moving eclipse: gay continues to dominate much of the cultural terrain. And the issue of how the state should treat those people – whether viewed as gay, queer, or otherwise – remains unresolved.

But what is also clear is that these conflicts and open questions have a long history. Given what we have been learning about that history, the fact that the political project of gay liberation sits unfinished seems less surprising than how much has been accomplished in a mere half-century despite fairly steady opposition. And if the movement from "gay" to "queer" remains rather incomplete, it is also likely quite similar to the twentieth-century process by which sexual identity slowly eclipsed gender as a framework for understanding sexual desires. The more we come to understand that history, the better equipped we will be to address these most recent developments.

Notes

1   Edward Weston, *The Daybooks of Edward Weston*, ed. Nancy Newhall. New York: Aperture, 1961, 1973, vol. 1, p. 10.
2   "Night Club Reviews: La Boheme," *Variety*, October 4, 1932, p. 52.
3   Carey McWilliams, "What We Did about Racial Minorities," in *While You Were Gone: A Report on Wartime Life in the United States*, ed. Jack Goodman (New York: Simon & Schuster, 1946), pp. 89, 99, as quoted in Kevin Allen Leonard, "Years of Hope, Days of Fear: The Impact of World War II on Race Relations in Los Angeles," PhD dissertation, University of California, Davis, 1992, p. 12.
4   James Kepner, interviewed by John D'Emilio, Los Angeles, September 27, 1976, tape 00395, International Gay Information Center, Manuscripts and Rare Books Room, New York Public Library (hereafter IGIC).
5   Kepner, interviewed by D'Emilio, tape 00434, IGIC.
6   Jeanne Cordova, interview with author. Los Angeles, April 1999.

References

Armstrong, E. 2002. *Forging Gay Identities: Organizing Sexuality in San Francisco, 1950–1994*. Chicago: University of Chicago Press.
Barrios, R. 2003. *Screened Out: Playing Gay in Hollywood from Edison to Stonewall*. New York: Routledge.
Bérubé, A. 1990. *Coming Out Under Fire: The History of Gay Men and Women in World War Two*. New York: Free Press.
Boyd, N. 2003. *Wide Open Town: A History of Queer San Francisco to 1965*. Berkeley: University of California Press.

Chauncey, G. 1994. *Gay New York: Gender, Urban Culture, and the Making of the Gay Male World, 1890–1940*. New York: Basic Books.

Clendinen, D. and Nagourney, A. 1999. *Out for Good: The Struggle to Build a Gay Rights Movement in America*. New York: Simon & Schuster.

D'Emilio, J. 1983. *Sexual Politics, Sexual Communities: The Making of a Homosexual Minority in the United States, 1940–1970*. Chicago: University of Chicago Press.

Ehrenstein, D. 1998. *Open Secret: (Gay Hollywood 1928–1998)*. New York: William Morrow.

Faderman, L. and Timmons, S. 2006. *Gay L.A.: A History of Sexual Outlaws, Power Politics, and Lipstick Lesbians*. New York: Basic Books.

Gallo, M. 2006. *Different Daughters: A History of the Daughters of Bilitis and the Birth of the Lesbian Rights Movement*. New York: Carroll & Graf.

Gluckman, A. and Reed, B., eds. 1997. *Homo Economics: Capitalism, Community and Lesbian and Gay Life*. New York: Routledge.

Herman, P. 2006. "American Homophobia: 'The Homosexual Menace' in Twentieth-Century American Culture." PhD. dissertation, Stanford University.

Hurewitz, D. 2007. *Bohemian Los Angeles and the Making of Modern Politics*. Berkeley, CA: University of California Press.

Johnson, S. 2000. *Roaring Camp: The Social World of the California Gold Rush*. New York: W. W. Norton.

Kenney, M. 2001. *Mapping Gay L.A.: The Intersection of Place and Politics*. Philadelphia: Temple University Press.

Leff, L. 2007. "Gay Neighborhoods Like NY's Chelsea May Be Victims of Own Success," AP Wire Service, March 9, 2007.

Loftin, C. 2006. "Passionate Anxieties: McCarthyism and Homosexual Identities in the United States, 1945–1965." PhD dissertation, University of Southern California, Los Angeles.

Mann, W. 2001. *Behind the Screen: How Gays and Lesbians Shaped Hollywood, 1910–1969*. New York: Viking.

Meeker, M. 2005. *Contacts Desired: Gay and Lesbian Communications and Community, 1940s–1970s*. Chicago: University of Chicago Press.

Morris, A. 2006. "The Cuddle Puddle of Stuyvesant High School," New York, February 6, 2006.

Retter, Y. 1999. "On the Side of Angels: Lesbian Activism in Los Angeles, 1970–1990." PhD dissertation, University of New Mexico, Albuquerque.

Rubin, G. 1998. "The Miracle Mile: South of Market and Gay Male Leather, 1962–1977." In J. Brooks, C. Carlsson, and N. Peters, eds., *Reclaiming San Francisco: History, Poliitcs, Culture*. San Francisco: City Light Books.

Russo, V. 1981. *The Celluloid Closet: Homosexuality in the Movies*. New York: Harper & Row.

Sears, C. 2005. " 'A Dress Not Belonging to His or Her Sex': Cross-Dressing Law in San Francisco, 1860–1900. PhD dissertation, University of California, Santa Cruz.

Shilts, R. 1982. *The Mayor of Castro Street: The Life and Times of Harvey Milk*. New York: St. Martin's.

Stryker, S. and Van Buskirk, J. 1996. *Gay by the Bay: A History of Queer Culture in the San Francisco Bay Area.* San Francisco: Chronicle Books.

Toll, R. 1976. *On With the Show: The First Century of Show Business in America.* New York: Oxford University Press.

Ullman, S. 1997. *Sex Seen: The Emergence of Modern Sexuality in America.* Berkeley: University of California Press.

Wat, E. 2002. *The Making of a Gay Asian Community: An Oral History of Pre-AIDS Los Angeles.* New York: Rowman & Littlefield.

Weston, K. 1995. "Get Thee to a Big City: Sexual Imaginary and the Great Gay Migration," *GLQ: A Journal of Lesbian and Gay Studies* 2: 253–77.

Further Reading

Abrams, B. L. 2000. "Hooray for Hollywood: Gender and Sexual Non-Conformity in the Classical Hollywood Era." PhD dissertation, American University, Washington DC.

Beemyn, B., ed. 1997. *Creating a Place for Ourselves: Lesbian, Gay, and Bisexual Community Histories.* New York: Routledge.

Corber, R. 1997. *Homosexuality in Cold War America: Resistance and the Crisis of Masculinity.* Durham, NC: Duke University Press.

D'Emilio J. 1989. "The Homosexual Menace: The Politics of Sexuality in Cold War America." In K. Peiss and C. Simmons, eds., *Passion & Power: Sexuality in History.* Philadelphia: Temple University Press, pp. 226–40.

Forrest, K. and Van Buskirk, J. 2007. *Love, Castro Street: Reflections of San Francisco.* Boston, MA: Alyson.

Loughery, J. 1998. *The Other Side of Silence: Men's Lives and Gay Identities: A Twentieth-Century History.* New York: Holt.

Mann, W. 1998. *Wisecracker: The Life and Times of William Haines, Hollywood's First Openly Gay Star.* New York: Viking.

Meeker, M. 2001. "Behind the Mask of Respectability: Reconsidering the Mattachine Society and Male Homophile Practice, 1950s and 1960s," *Journal of the History of Sexuality* 10 (1): 78–116.

Shilts, R. 1987. *And the Band Played On: Politics, People, and the AIDS Epidemic.* New York: St. Martin's.

Sueyoshi, A. 2002. "Race-ing Sex: The Competition for Gender and Sexual Identity in Multi-Ethnic San Francisco, 1897–1924." PhD dissertation, University of California, Los Angeles.

Timmons, S. 1990. *The Trouble with Harry Hay: Founder of the Gay Movement.* Boston, MA: Alyson.

Chapter Twenty

MAKING MULTICULTURALISM: IMMIGRATION, RACE, AND THE TWENTIETH CENTURY

Kevin Allen Leonard

In November 1920 California voters overwhelmingly approved an initiative designed to close loopholes in the Alien Land Law passed by the legislature in 1913, which denied "aliens ineligible to citizenship" the right to own land in the state. The ballot measure threatened the livelihoods of Japanese immigrant farmers, who challenged its constitutionality. In this era of growing nativism, however, few judges were sympathetic. Courts ruled that the state could not prohibit immigrant parents from serving as guardians for their minor children, but they upheld other sections of the law (Daniels 1962; Azuma 2005). The actions of California voters and courts reflected not only the state's long history of antagonism toward Asian immigrants but also a larger anti-immigrant trend in the United States that culminated in the passage by Congress of the Immigration Act of 1924. This law banned immigration from Asia and greatly restricted immigration from southern and eastern Europe.

The passage of the 1920 initiative and its subsequent approval by the courts marked the high point of the influence of white supremacy in California. Yet some who believed that economic opportunities in California should be reserved primarily for white people recognized that their victory was incomplete. They continued to call for restrictions on immigration from Mexico and for legislative actions designed to force Asian immigrants to leave the state. Most white supremacists, however, must have been satisfied with what they had achieved by 1924: residents of most Asian countries were denied entry to the United States and the right to own or lease land in California; restrictive covenants prevented African Americans, Mexicans, and Asians from moving into white neighborhoods; and in many places Mexican American children could not attend white schools.

Over the course of the next five decades, however, white supremacists' dream of a "white California" unraveled. In the 1920s the movement of immigrants from Latin America and of African Americans to California challenged white supremacy in the state. The Great Depression of the 1930s led some Mexican immigrants to leave California, and others were forced to leave by nativist officials. In the late 1930s, however, labor unions and other organizations began to challenge discrimination. World War II led some Anglo Americans to disavow white supremacy, and many discriminatory laws and practices were declared unconstitutional after the war. Mexican Americans and African Americans gained some political power after the war, but discrimination continued to prevent many people from participating fully in the state's economy and politics.

Most scholars who have studied various immigrant and racial groups in California have focused either on a single group or on relations between a single minority group and the dominant Anglo American or "white" group. This tendency does not acknowledge the fact that members of these different groups often lived together in the same neighborhoods (Wild 2005). The fact that people lived in the same neighborhoods, however, did not necessarily have a meaningful effect on their identities and actions. Historian Douglas Flamming has shown that black residents of Los Angeles believed that they had more in common with African Americans in other places than they did with the immigrants among whom they lived (Flamming 2005). Although members of different groups did sometimes interact, these groups came from different cultures and encountered different experiences in California. Each group responded to its experiences in a distinct way. This essay will reflect recent scholarship in the twentieth-century history of immigrants and racial and ethnic relations in California. It will deal mostly with the experiences of individual groups, although it will note similarities and differences among the groups and their experiences.

Asian Americans and Racial Ideology

The success of the anti-Asian movement in the 1920s deeply offended many Japanese Americans, who responded in a variety of ways to the discrimination they encountered before World War II. As historian Brian Hayashi has shown, the failure of Protestant denominations to prevent the passage of anti-Japanese legislation such as the Alien Land Law of 1920 and the Immigration Act of 1924 convinced Japanese American Protestants that they could not place their faith in their Anglo American coreligionists. Instead, they strengthened their ties with other Japanese Americans and embraced Japanese nationalism. The churches' women, for example, offered food and lodging to the crew members of Imperial Japanese Navy ships that docked in Los Angeles (Hayashi 1995). Discrimination led some US citizens of Japanese ancestry (mostly "second generation," or Nisei) to leave the United States. Many Nisei had attended Japanese language schools, and some were prepared to work in Japan. Welly Shibata, a University of Washington graduate who had worked in the produce business in California, for example, jumped at the chance to work as a journalist in Japan. He eventually became the English-language editor of the *Osaka Mainichi* (Azuma 2005). Other Nisei decided to remain in the United States. Many worked to convince Anglo Americans that they should not discriminate against Japanese Americans. In 1934 Japanese immigrant ("first generation" or Issei) leaders proposed a "Nisei Week" festival that they hoped would strengthen ties between the Issei and the Nisei and maintain the economic vitality of the Little Tokyo district during the Depression. Historian Lon Kurashige has pointed out that some Nisei leaders responded positively to the proposal. These Nisei leaders, however, did not see the festival as a means to increase solidarity within the Japanese American community. Instead, they saw Nisei Week as a way to break down racial discrimination by exposing Anglo Americans to Japanese American culture (Kurashige 2002).

Like the Japanese Americans who sponsored Nisei Week, Chinese American leaders in San Francisco sought to reduce discrimination by bringing Anglo American tourists to Chinatown. The efforts of activists within the Chinese community and their allies in local public health agencies transformed the popular image of Chinatown. In the early twentieth century, many people pictured Chinatown as a disease-ridden slum. By the late 1930s, according to historian Nayan Shah, Chinatown was more frequently pictured as "a sanitized tourist destination for middle-class white families" (Shah 2001: 25).

Chinese Americans in San Francisco successfully challenged some forms of discrimination in the 1920s and 1930s, but discrimination persisted. Chinese immigrants often faced intense scrutiny from Anglo Americans throughout the 1930s. A number of Anglo American Californians complained to federal officials about Chinese immigrants they insisted were in the United States illegally. The complaint of the director of the Laundryowners Association of Alameda County, for example, led to an investigation of the 66 Chinese-operated laundries in Oakland. Other Anglo Americans complained that "undesirable aliens" working in groceries and butcher shops posed threats to the health of "white" people (Lee 2003).

"Inbetween People"

Mexicans were "inbetween people" in California before World War II (Roediger & Barrett 2002). Many Anglo Americans treated Mexicans as members of a distinct and inferior race (Deverell 2004). Federal officials, judges, and some local officials, however, classified Mexicans as "white."

Some Mexicans embraced this categorization and insisted that they be treated as "white" people. Others rejected this system of racial categorization and worked to end the discrimination they faced.

As historians George J. Sánchez and Natalia Molina have shown, many reformers thought of Mexican immigrants as similar to European immigrants and attempted to "whiten" them. "Home teachers" employed by school districts attempted to teach Mexican women to speak English and to cook, clean their homes, and instruct their children in the "American" way (Sánchez 1993). Public health officials also believed that Mexicans could be "Americanized" (Molina 2006). Although reformers attempted to "Americanize" Mexican immigrants, many immigrants resisted their efforts. A majority of Mexican immigrants chose not to pursue naturalization as US citizens. Many embraced the efforts of the Mexican government to strengthen Mexican nationalism among immigrants. Public celebrations of Mexican holidays such as Independence Day (September 16) and Cinco de Mayo became more common and attracted more participants in the 1920s (Alamillo 2006). Leaders in the immigrant community, with support from the Mexican government, established libraries and Mexican schools, in which Mexican children could learn the Spanish language and Mexican history and culture (Sánchez 1993).

Many Mexican immigrants sought to retain their connection to their homeland. They often discovered, however, that their children who grew up in the United States did not share their connection to Mexico. Historian Douglas Monroy has noted that young Mexican Americans watched US films and saw ways of life that differed dramatically from their ways of life. Women saw women characters in motion pictures who had much greater autonomy than they had in their parents' homes. As a result, many young women who worked outside the home attempted to assert independence from strict parental controls (Monroy 1999).

The currents of Anglo American nativism and Mexican nationalism ran together in the early 1930s, when the Great Depression led to skyrocketing unemployment and increased demands on local relief programs. Anglo nativists claimed that Mexican immigrants were taking jobs and relief money that rightfully belonged to "white" people. Some reformers who had previously treated Mexicans as "white" changed their minds. As historian Molina has argued, for example, "Los Angeles public health officials reversed their assimilation policies during the Depression and argued that Mexicans' biological inferiority precluded any possibility of rehabilitation" (Molina 2006: 117).

Some Mexicans were convinced that conditions could be no worse in Mexico than in the United States and returned to their homeland (Sánchez 1993). Not enough left to satisfy the nativists. For several weeks in early 1931, federal immigration officials, assisted by local law enforcement officers, stopped people on the streets in their effort to frighten many Mexicans into leaving the country. The most dramatic episode in this campaign occurred on February 26, when a force of federal immigration agents and Los Angeles Police Department officers surrounded the Plaza and questioned more than 400 people, 18 of whom were arrested for deportation hearings (Escobar 1999). News of this raid spread rapidly through the Mexican community. County officials in Los Angeles, San Bernardino, and San Diego counties also sought to remove Mexicans from relief rolls by paying to transport people by train to Mexico. Special trains carried around 19,000 Southern California residents to the Mexican border between 1931 and 1934 (Guerin-Gonzales 1994).

By the middle of the 1930s, repatriation pressures had subsided, and Mexican immigrants and Mexican Americans – US citizens of Mexican ancestry – began to mobilize to demand better treatment. Many Mexicans joined labor unions in order to improve their wages and working conditions (Ruiz 1987; Weber 1994). Unions did more than represent workers in labor struggles. According to historian José M. Alamillo, United Cannery, Agricultural, Packing, and Allied Workers of America (UCAPAWA) organizing efforts in Southern California "laid the political foundation for the Mexican American civil rights movement that emerged in subsequent decades" (Alamillo 2006: 141). Historian Stephen J. Pitti has shown that in San José UCAPAWA functioned as a civil rights organization that tried to convince government officials to address the conditions in the city's eastside barrios (Pitti 2003).

In addition to joining unions and demanding fair treatment as workers, Mexicans also joined political organizations and demanded civil and human rights. In 1938 UCAPAWA organizer Luisa Moreno, a Guatemalan immigrant, began organizing El Congreso de Pueblos de Habla Española, the Congress of Spanish-speaking Peoples. El Congreso, which first met in April 1939 in Los Angeles, included Mexicans from throughout the southwestern United States (García 1989). El Congreso endorsed efforts to educate all Americans about Spanish-speaking people, supported bilingual education for Mexican American children, and urged Mexican immigrants to become US citizens and exercise the right to vote. As historian David G. Gutiérrez has argued, the organization's leaders also insisted that immigrants were "as thoroughly a part of American society as the citizen population" and should therefore enjoy the rights of citizens (Gutiérrez 1995: 113).

African Americans in Interwar California

African Americans' experiences in California differed from immigrants' experiences. Unlike most immigrants from Asia and Mexico, African

Americans were citizens. Anglo Americans in California generally did not attempt to infringe upon African Americans' right to vote, but they did try to limit African Americans' political power by drawing district lines that diluted the African American vote. Like immigrants from Asia and Mexico, however, African Americans faced often-intense racial discrimination in the Golden State. Some scholars have suggested that the large numbers of Asian and Mexican immigrants in California reduced the discrimination faced by African Americans. White supremacists were more alarmed by the large numbers of immigrants than by the small number of African Americans. Historian Albert S. Broussard, for example, has argued that African Americans in San Francisco faced relatively little housing discrimination prior to 1920 (Broussard 1993). In other places, though, African Americans encountered persistent prejudice and discrimination (Flamming 2005).

Like Asian and Mexican immigrants, African Americans were not passive victims of discrimination. African Americans organized to fight discrimination as early as the nineteenth century, and a branch of the National Association for the Advancement of Colored People (NAACP) was founded in Los Angeles in 1915. Community leaders in Los Angeles established a local branch of the National Urban League in the early 1920s. Throughout the 1920s, African Americans basked in the state's prosperity, although they struggled against police brutality and other forms of discrimination. Despite discrimination, African Americans in California tended to be able to purchase homes more readily than they could in other regions. The Depression led to widespread unemployment. Many families had to take in lodgers or rely upon assistance to survive the 1930s.

World War II, Race, and Immigration

World War II dramatically transformed California. In the months following Pearl Harbor, the war seemed to fulfill the dreams of some of the state's white supremacists. Nearly 1,300 people of Japanese ancestry – most of them immigrants with business or political connections with Japan – were rounded up by the Federal Bureau of Investigation in the 48 hours following the attack. Within two months of the attack, many of the state's most powerful officials had begun to insist that people who were "racially" Japanese would naturally be inclined to support Japanese forces in the case of an invasion of California. Under pressure from military officers, President Franklin D. Roosevelt issued Executive Order 9066 on February 19, 1942. This order gave the US Army the authority to remove all people of Japanese ancestry from any areas it deemed strategically important. In the spring and summer of 1942, the Army moved most of California's 94,000

Japanese American residents into "assembly centers" operated by the Wartime Civilian Control Administration, a military agency. Japanese Americans were later moved to more permanent "relocation centers" operated by the War Relocation Authority (WRA).

Japanese Americans faced numerous challenges in the camps. The WRA offered the imprisoned people the opportunity to work, attend school, and participate in limited self-government. However, the agency insulted Japanese Americans by restricting salaries and by initially refusing to allow Issei to participate in self-government. Camp life challenged community and family customs and traditions: Nisei were put into positions of authority over their parents, and parents of both generations found it difficult to discipline their children in the very public environment of the camps. Japanese Americans and WRA officials both expressed concern about the long-term effects of incarceration on the Nisei. As a result, the WRA attempted to "resettle" as many Nisei as possible outside the camps. Although conditions in the camps left many Japanese Americans feeling powerless, WRA policies empowered some of the incarcerated people. As historian Valerie Matsumoto has shown, the WRA's policy of equal pay for men and women increased the independence of women (Matsumoto 1993).

• California white supremacists were pleased by the Japanese American internment, but they were disheartened by another wartime development. The war led to the demise of the nation's oldest restriction on immigration. The United States and China were allies in the war against Japan. Many politicians realized that continued exclusion of Chinese immigrants was an insult to an ally that could hinder cooperation in the Pacific War. Historian Karen J. Leong has shown that popular support for repeal allowed Congress to ignore the vocal opposition of American Federation of Labor unions and patriotic organizations such as the American Legion. Congress repealed the Chinese Exclusion Act in 1943 (Leong 2003). The repeal of exclusion did not result in a dramatic increase in Chinese immigration to the United States, as the Chinese were simply placed on the quota system established by the Immigration Act of 1924. Under this quota system, only 105 Chinese were allowed to enter the country each year (Lee 2003).

Wartime migration also affected racial and ethnic relations in California. The state's geographic location and its existing aircraft industry led the federal government to pour billions of dollars into its economy during the war. Federal funds paid for the expansion of existing shipyards and aircraft factories and the construction of new shipyards and factories. About two million people moved to California during the war to take advantage of the new economic opportunities. Among these new residents were more than 125,000 African Americans. The African American population of Los Angeles more than doubled during the war years, from about 64,000 to more than 133,000, and the African American population of the Bay Area increased even more dramatically. San Francisco's black population rose from less than 5,000 to nearly 32,000, and Oakland's black population swelled from about 8,000 to more than 37,000 (Broussard 1993). Before the war only 270 African Americans lived in Richmond, a city of 24,000 residents 20 miles north of Oakland on the east side of San Francisco Bay. By 1943, wartime construction projects along Richmond's waterfront had drawn more than 5,000 African Americans to a city whose population had quadrupled in three years (Moore 2000).

Job opportunities alone did not draw African Americans to California. Many African Americans who came to California from the South wanted to escape the indignities of Jim Crow. As historian Gretchen Lemke-Santangelo has shown, they perceived California as a land of social and political as well as economic opportunities. Theresa Waller, for example, expected to be treated well in California because she had worked for people in the South who were originally from California. Her employers had "treated me so nice, and talked to me like I was a person" (Lemke-Santangelo 1996: 64). Many African Americans recalled being disappointed by what they found. "They didn't have 'No Colored' signs or anything like that, but they had other ways of telling you they didn't want you," Ruth Gracon recalled (ibid.: 67).

Although employers were desperate for workers during the war, African Americans still faced persistent job discrimination. Some employers insisted that unions would not allow them to hire or promote African Americans. Some unions, most notably the International Brotherhood of Boilermakers, which held contracts with many of the state's largest shipbuilding corporations, refused to allow African Americans to become full members. Instead, the Boilermakers directed African Americans to join "Negro auxiliaries." African American shipyard workers fought for several years for full membership in the union. Their struggle culminated with a 1945 California Supreme Court decision that required the union to admit African Americans on an equal basis with Anglo American workers (Broussard 1993; Sides 2003).

The Zoot-Suit Riots

The most dramatic changes in California race relations resulted from events in Los Angeles in 1942 and 1943. As historian Edward J. Escobar has shown, the Los Angeles Police Department (LAPD) and other officials had for many years argued that Mexicans were more prone to criminal behavior than members of most other ethnic groups (Escobar 1999). The belief that Mexicans were criminals by nature led to violence in wartime Los Angeles. On the night of August 1, 1942, a young man named José Díaz was fatally injured after a fight at a party at a home in rural Los Angeles County. Díaz's death in conjunction with fights involving young Mexican Americans prompted a crackdown by city and county law enforcement officers. In the first week of August LAPD officers and Los Angeles County sheriff's deputies rounded up more than 600 young people, most of whom were Mexican Americans (ibid.). The city's daily newspapers printed long and detailed stories about the arrests and ongoing investigations into what they described as a "juvenile crime wave." As I have shown in my book, *The Battle for Los Angeles*, these articles referred to these "young gangsters" as "Mexicans." Mexican American leaders complained about these articles. The community leaders pointed out that almost all of the arrested young people were US citizens. These complaints prompted newspapers in later articles to describe these "gangsters" as "Pachucos" (Leonard 2006). (The term "pachuco" appears to have referred originally to a person from El Paso.)

Following the arrests, the Los Angeles County Grand Jury launched an investigation into gang activity among Mexican Americans. High-ranking law enforcement officers, most notably Lt. Ed. Duran Ayres, the head of the foreign relations bureau of the sheriff's department, told the Grand Jury that Mexicans were racially prone to violent criminality. A group of Los Angeles residents, many associated with the Communist Party, mobilized to challenge Ayres's statements. They formed a committee to assist the defendants in the "Sleepy Lagoon" case – the 22 young men who were tried for a variety of crimes connected to the death of José Díaz (Leonard 2006).

A number of violent confrontations between "Pachucos" and military personnel occurred in early 1943. Historian Eduardo Obregón Pagán has argued that in May of that year tensions mounted, and many military personnel felt that they needed to teach the "gangsters" a lesson (Pagán 2003). On June 3 dozens of sailors stationed at the Naval Reserve Armory in Chavez Ravine descended on a downtown neighborhood and beat all the "zoot suiters" they could find. The next night even more sailors joined in the violence. The number of military personnel and civilians hunting "zooters" increased every night until the military declared the downtown area off limits to all military personnel on June 8. Many eyewitnesses reported that the police did not intervene in the beatings of alleged "zooters." As historian Escobar has noted, most of the people arrested during the riots were Mexican Americans (Escobar 1999).

The rioting alarmed many people in California, other parts of the United States, and Mexico. A number of community leaders sent telegrams to state and federal officials asking them to take action to end the violence and to investigate the causes of the riots. Governor Earl Warren appointed a committee to investigate the riots. Walter White, the executive secretary of the NAACP, appealed to President Franklin Roosevelt to punish the people who were responsible for the riots. First Lady Eleanor Roosevelt told reporters that she thought that the riots were the result of racial discrimination (Leonard 2006).

Not all Los Angeles residents accepted Walter White's or Eleanor Roosevelt's interpretations of the riots. Many local officials defended the actions of the soldiers and sailors and denied that they had been motivated by racism. Nonetheless, the riots embarrassed many Californians. They also made some Anglo Americans acutely aware of the persistence of prejudice and discrimination in California, and some local leaders publicly disavowed the statements made by Ayres the previous year (Leonard 2006).

The riots in Los Angeles and the threat of violence elsewhere in California also prompted some Californians to attempt to work together, across a variety of cultural boundaries, to end racial prejudice and discrimination. When Governor Warren failed to act on his committee's recommendation and create an "inter-racial" committee, the Los Angeles County Board of Supervisors established the Committee for Interracial Progress (Leonard 2006). In San Francisco, a group of Anglo American liberals enticed distinguished African American minister Howard Thurman to leave his post at Howard University to found an interracial church in San Francisco. The Church for the Fellowship of All Peoples was the first "fully integrated" church in the United States, according to Thurman (Broussard 1993). The post-riot atmosphere helped to win new trials for the young men convicted of killing José Díaz. Historian Daniel Hurewitz concluded that "the success of the Sleepy Lagoon Defense Committee suggested that inter-racialism might yet guide the city once the war drew to a close, and for a little while it seemed to do just that" (Hurewitz 2007: 213).

Ironically, the war even discredited the most vocal anti-Japanese politicians and organizations. When 19-year-old Esther Takei was allowed to return to Southern California to study at Pasadena Junior College in 1944, anti-Japanese leaders who depicted her as a threat to the region's security simply looked ridiculous. Moreover, the anti-Japanese movement had insisted in 1942 that the "Army knows best." When the Army began defending the rights of Nisei soldiers and their families later in the war, the anti-Japanese leaders could no longer employ this appeal (Leonard 2006).

Race Relations after World War II

World War II, which many Americans believed was a war against Hitler's racial ideology, undermined the ideological and rhetorical foundations of white supremacy in California. This did not mean, however, that racial discrimination disappeared. The beneficiaries of racial discrimination recast their arguments, relying on the rhetoric of the Cold War. Instead of arguing that African Americans, Mexican Americans, and Asian Americans were inferior to Anglo Americans, the defenders of discrimination insisted that racial discrimination was wrong. It was equally wrong, however, they insisted, for governments to trample on the freedoms of people who, for whatever reason, might want to discriminate. These arguments were stated most explicitly by the opponents of Proposition 11 on the 1946 ballot. Proposition 11, the Fair Employment Practice Act, would have made it illegal for employers in California to discriminate on the basis of race, color, religion, or national origin. Agreeing with the argument that the proposition was "Communistic" and therefore "un-American," voters overwhelmingly rejected the measure. At the same time, however, the voters rejected an effort to incorporate the state's alien land law into its constitution (Leonard 2006).

Mexican Americans, African Americans, and Asian Americans continued to build on their successes during World War II and to demand greater equality. They achieved some remarkable successes in the years after the war. Mexican Americans in Orange County filed suit to end school segregation; in 1947 the Ninth Circuit US Court of Appeals ruled in *Mendez vs. Westminster* that such segregation was unconstitutional (García 2001). Sylvester Davis, a Los Angeles African American, and Andrea Pérez, a Mexican American, successfully challenged California's law against interracial marriage in 1948 (Orenstein 2005).

Mexican Americans experienced some success in electoral politics. As historian Matt García has noted, Mexican Americans in the San Gabriel Valley east of Los Angeles formed Unity Leagues beginning in 1946. The Unity Leagues' primary goal was to register voters and assist political campaigns. The efforts of the Unity League in Chino paid off in the 1946 election, when Andrés Morales was elected to a seat on the city council (García 2001). Cipriano Hernández won election to the school board in Corona in 1948 (Alamillo 2006). In 1949 Edward Roybal was elected to a seat on the Los Angeles City Council. In his campaign for the city council seat, Roybal received assistance from the Community Service Organization (CSO), which became the most important Mexican American political organization in California in the 1940s and 1950s (Burt 2003; see also the essay by Miriam Pawel in this volume).

Although some barriers fell as a result of wartime and postwar campaigns against discrimination, many barriers remained. Job discrimination left many African Americans unemployed. In 1950, for example, 29 percent of Richmond's "non-white" workers were unemployed, but only 13 percent of "white" workers were unemployed (Lemke-Santangelo 1996). In Los Angeles, as historian Josh Sides has shown, African Americans' employment opportunities were hindered by industry's move to the suburbs.

Manufacturers abandoned plants in the old industrial area near the center of the African American community. Many African Americans found themselves without the means to commute long distances to the new plants, and realtors refused to sell them homes in these suburban communities. Even after the US Supreme Court ruled in 1948 that courts could not enforce racially restrictive covenants, housing discrimination persisted. Many realtors refused to show African Americans homes in "white" neighborhoods. Banks also refused to lend money to African Americans attempting to buy in such neighborhoods. Some Anglo Americans responded with threats and violence to African Americans' efforts to occupy homes in their neighborhoods (Sides 2003).

 *Side note*

Employment and housing discrimination against Asian Americans declined after World War II. When Chinese immigrant Sing Sheng purchased a home in South San Francisco in 1952, some of his Anglo American neighbors objected. Sheng asked his neighbors to vote on whether or not they wanted him in their neighborhood. Although Sheng lost the referendum, the story became national news. Historian Charlotte Brooks noted that people from around the country condemned Sheng's neighbors (Brooks 2004). The California Supreme Court struck down the state's Alien Land Law in 1952. In the same year Congress passed legislation allowing Japanese immigrants to become citizens (Kurashige 2002). Many Nisei found that they were able to find white-collar jobs when they returned to California, and housing discrimination abated so that many Japanese Americans were able to move into houses in suburban areas. In 1970 historian Roger Daniels and sociologist Harry H. L. Kitano suggested that the improved treatment of Japanese Americans was related to the migration of large numbers of African Americans into California (Daniels & Kitano 1970). No scholar, however, has thoroughly explored this possibility.

"White Flight"

As the African American and Mexican American populations of California increased after the war, some discriminatory barriers collapsed. Many Anglo Americans, however, tried to maintain a society in which most privileges were reserved for "whites." For many Anglo Americans, moving to newly developing suburbs represented an effort to escape increasingly diverse cities. The developers of some suburbs, such as Lakewood near Los Angeles, specifically refused to sell homes to African Americans (Avila 2004). Anglo Americans also found opportunities for recreation from which African Americans were largely excluded. In 1955 Walt Disney opened his theme park, Disneyland, in suburban Orange County. For more than a decade, Disneyland did not employ African Americans in "people contact" positions – with one notable exception. An African American playing Aunt Jemima allowed visitors to "relive the days of the Old South" at Aunt Jemima's Kitchen (Avila 2004: 134–5). As historian Eric Avila has pointed out, Disneyland's "emphasis on the subservient position of blacks, Indians, and Mexicans corroborated a growing backlash against racial minorities in their struggle for civil rights" (Avila 2004: 144).

In addition to moving to suburbs from which African Americans were excluded, Anglo Americans attempted to remake cities in an effort to remove "blight" – a term that usually referred to the presence of impoverished African Americans and Mexican Americans – and to create spaces in which middle-class Anglo Americans would feel comfortable. Los Angeles city officials evicted the mostly Mexican American residents of Chavez Ravine, adjacent to downtown Los Angeles. The city then turned the land over to Brooklyn Dodgers owner Walter O'Malley, who built Dodger Stadium on the site. State officials, with support from many local officials, designed freeways that would erase "slum" areas (Avila 2004).

Historian Robert O. Self has recently challenged the notion that Anglo Americans simply fled central cities as African Americans arrived. Instead, Self argues, a number of policy decisions and developments attracted Anglo Americans to the suburbs. Anglo Americans in San Leandro erected barriers that prevented African Americans from moving into the city, just south of Oakland. As a result of these barriers, only Anglo Americans could reap the benefits of policies that attracted industry to San Leandro. Taxes on new factories allowed officials to maintain low taxes for homeowners, who came to think of low property taxes as a right (Self 2003). Policies in East Bay cities such as San Leandro trapped African Americans in Oakland, where property taxes rose and municipal services declined as new factories opened in other cities.

Immigration, Race, and Politics in the 1960s

Throughout the 1950s African Americans continued to move to California in large numbers. Nearly 500,000 African Americans lived in Los Angeles in 1960. Most African Americans believed that the size of their community merited greater representation in electoral politics, but city councils continued to exclude them. In the early 1960s African Americans in Los Angeles mobilized and gained representation on the city council. The council appointed Gilbert Lindsay to the ninth district seat vacated by Edward Roybal, who decided to run for the US House of Representatives in 1962. As political scientist Raphael Sonenshein has shown, a coalition of mobilized African Americans and liberal Anglo Americans, many of them Jewish, helped Tom Bradley win the tenth district seat in the spring 1963 election. In run-off elections in May 1963, Billy Mills won the eighth district seat, and Lindsay retained the seat to which he had been appointed (Sonenshein 1993).

The election of African Americans to local offices in California cities did not solve the problems faced by many African Americans. Discrimination continued to limit housing and employment opportunities, and many African Americans expressed anger at police harassment and brutality. This anger boiled over in Los Angeles in August 1965, when a confrontation between California Highway Patrol officers and African American residents of South Los Angeles led to six days of battles between African Americans and law enforcement officers, looting, and burning. By the time California National Guard troops suppressed the uprising, at least 34 people had died, and more than 1,000 were injured. Four thousand people were arrested (Horne 1995).

The uprising in Los Angeles had implications for all Californians. As historian Kurashige concluded, "in the aftermath of the Watts riots, the apparent contrast between 'successful' Japanese Americans and 'angry' African Americans would become fixed in America's racial consciousness." But, as Kurashige further noted, the unwillingness of African Americans to continue to accept discrimination and mistreatment inspired some of the Japanese Americans who participated in the Asian American movement of the later 1960s and 1970s (Kurashige 2002: 151–3). Like the 1943 riots in Los Angeles, the 1965 violence led some officials to take action to address some of the underlying causes of the unrest. After the uprising, for example, a hospital and a community college were built to serve the needs of residents of South Los Angeles (Sides 2003). The uprising damaged the political coalition that had elected Tom Bradley to the city council, but it unified a previously divided African American community. In time, Sonenshein noted, the alliance between liberal Anglo Americans and African Americans was restored and strengthened (Sonenshein 1993). This coalition was not strong enough in 1969 to allow Bradley to unseat conservative mayor Sam Yorty, but by 1973 support for this coalition had grown. In that year Bradley defeated Yorty to become the first African American mayor of a city in which only 18 percent of residents were African Americans.

Like African Americans, Mexican Americans mounted challenges to discrimination in the 1960s. Chicano movement activists drew upon the experiences of an earlier generation of Mexican Americans. Many activists were inspired by Cesar Chávez, the charismatic leader of the United Farm Workers. As historian Lorena Oropeza has pointed out, the actions of African Americans also inspired Chicano leaders. "Whereas an earlier generation of activists had emphasized their membership within the 'white race,' Chicanos took a cue from African Americans and the tumultuous politics of the 1960s. Instead of black power, Chicanos championed 'brown power' and proudly declared themselves a 'bronze people'" (Oropeza 2005: 83). In 1968 the leaders of Young Citizens for Community Action began wearing khaki military clothing and changed the organization's name to the Brown Berets. In June of that year the Brown Berets issued a "Ten Point Program" inspired by the program of the Black Panther Party (Chávez 2002).

No issue was more critical to the Chicano movement than the Vietnam War. Rosalio Muñoz, a former student body president at UCLA, refused induction in the US Army in 1969 and encouraged other Chicanos to resist the draft. Chicano activists pointed to studies that showed that Chicanos were grossly overrepresented among the dead in Vietnam. Later in 1969 Muñoz and other activists formed the Chicano Moratorium Committee, which planned and staged anti-war demonstrations. Protests in the second half of 1970 and in 1971 were marked by violent confrontation between Los Angeles law enforcement officers and demonstrators (Chávez 2002). Like the Black Panther Party, some Chicano movement leaders saw their people as a colonized nation within the United States. As Oropeza has noted, "Chicanas and Chicanos repeatedly drew parallels – political, emotional, and cultural – between the inhabitants of Aztlán and the inhabitants of Viet Nam" (Oropeza 2005: 82).

Nearly lost in the dramatic upheaval of the 1960s was an act of Congress that would dramatically reshape California society after that tumultuous decade. In 1965 Congress passed legislation reforming the Immigration Act of 1924. Supporters of the 1965 act argued that an immigration policy based on racist assumptions damaged the nation's foreign policy during the Cold War. Members of Congress did not expect the legislation to lead to a dramatic increase in immigration, but the numbers of immigrants in California began to grow significantly shortly after the law was passed. The census indicated that the number of Chinese immigrants in the state increased from about 40,000 in 1960 to more than 77,000 in 1970. In the same period the number of Filipino immigrants increased from about 44,000 to nearly 80,000. In the 1970s the number of immigrants from Asia continued to increase dramatically. In that decade, more than 50,000 Chinese immigrants, more than 70,000 Korean immigrants, and more than 150,000 Filipino immigrants came to the state. They were joined by more than 80,000 refugees from Vietnam. These trends continued during the 1980s. By 1990 more than 480,000 Filipino immigrants, 375,000 Chinese immigrants, 270,000 Vietnamese immigrants, and 200,000 Korean immigrants lived in California. In addition, more than 100,000 Iranians and 70,000 Laotians had come to the state.

Immigration from Latin America also grew during these decades. The 1960 census counted about 250,000 California residents who had been born in Mexico. The 1970 census counted more than 650,000 foreign-born residents who either spoke Spanish or who had a Spanish surname. The 1980 census indicated that more than 750,000 Mexicans came to California in the 1970s. The 1990 census counted nearly 2.5 million natives of Mexico living in California. More than 500,000 Central Americans were also living in the state in 1990. As a result of this immigration, by 1990 nearly 6.5 million of California's approximately 30 million residents – more than 20 percent – were immigrants.

By the middle of the 1970s, California's population had become much more diverse than it was 50 years earlier. Virtually all of the discriminatory legislation that had restricted the lives of Asian Americans, Mexican Americans, and African Americans had been declared unconstitutional and repealed. Unlike the voters of 1920, who had approved efforts to strengthen the Alien Land Law, the voters of the 1970s elected Mervyn Dymally, a black native of Trinidad, lieutenant governor in 1974. In the same year voters elected March Fong Eu, a Chinese American, secretary of state. The violent confrontations of the 1960s had receded in the memories of many Californians. Most of the state's residents seemed to accept the new multicultural order, but some did not. The repeal of discriminatory laws did not undo the effects of long-term discrimination.

Many Californians from a variety of ethnic and cultural backgrounds also expressed anger at the continuing immigration from Asia and Latin America. In the 1994 election nearly 60 percent of voters approved Proposition 187, which was designed to deny state-funded services such as education and healthcare to undocumented immigrants. A federal judge ruled most of the measures unconstitutional. Nonetheless, the votes on these two ballot measures, as well as the 1992 rioting in Los Angeles, indicate that the apparent acceptance of a multicultural society in the 1970s was deceptive. The changes that occurred in California during the middle decades of the twentieth century did not eliminate racial tensions or hostility toward immigrants. Instead, the presence of immigrants and a range of racial and ethnic groups continues to provoke often heated debate among many of the state's residents.

REFERENCES

Alamillo, José M. 2006. *Making Lemonade out of Lemons: Mexican American Labor and Leisure in a California Town, 1880–1960*. Urbana: University of Illinois Press.

Avila, Eric. 2004. *Popular Culture in the Age of White Flight: Fear and Fantasy in Suburban Los Angeles*. Berkeley: University of California Press.

Azuma, Eiichiro. 2005. *Between Two Empires: Race, History, and Transnationalism in Japanese America*. New York: Oxford University Press.

Balderrama, Francisco E. and Rodríguez, Raymond. 1995. *Decade of Betrayal: Mexican Repatriation in the 1930s*. Albuquerque: University of New Mexico Press.

Brooks, Charlotte. 2004. "Sing Sheng vs. Southwood: Residential Integration in Cold War California," *Pacific Historical Review* 73 (3): 463–94.

Broussard, Albert S. 1993. *Black San Francisco: The Struggle for Racial Equality in the West, 1900–1954*. Lawrence: University Press of Kansas.

Burt, Kenneth C. 2003. "The Power of a Mobilized Citizenry and Coalition Politics: The 1949 Election of Edward R. Roybal to the Los Angeles City Council," *Southern California Quarterly* 85 (4): 413–38.

Chávez, Ernesto. 2002. *"¡Mi Raza Primero!" (My People First!): Nationalism, Identity, and Insurgency in the Chicano Movement in Los Angeles, 1966–1978*. Berkeley: University of California Press.

Daniels, Roger. 1962. *The Politics of Prejudice: The Anti-Japanese Movement in California and the Struggle for Japanese Exclusion*. Berkeley: University of California Press.

Daniels, Roger and Kitano, Harry H. L. 1970. *American Racism: Exploration of the Nature of Prejudice*. Englewood Cliffs, NJ: Prentice-Hall.

Deverell, William. 2004. *Whitewashed Adobe: The Rise of Los Angeles and the Remaking of Its Mexican Past*. Berkeley: University of California Press.

Escobar, Edward J. 1999. *Race, Police, and the Making of a Political Identity: Mexican Americans and the Los Angeles Police Department, 1900–1945*. Berkeley: University of California Press.

Flamming, Douglas. 2005. *Bound for Freedom: Black Los Angeles in Jim Crow America*. Berkeley: University of California Press.

García, Mario T. 1989. *Mexican Americans: Leadership, Ideology, and Identity, 1930–1960*. New Haven, CT: Yale University Press.

García, Matt. 2001. *A World of Its Own: Race, Labor and Citrus in the Making of Greater Los Angeles, 1900–1970*. Chapel Hill: University of North Carolina Press.

Guerin-Gonzales, Camille. 1994. *Mexican Workers and American Dreams: Immigration, Repatriation, and California Farm Labor, 1900–1939*. New Brunswick, NJ: Rutgers University Press.

Gutiérrez, David G. 1995. *Walls and Mirrors: Mexican Americans, Mexican Immigrants, and the Politics of Ethnicity*. Berkeley: University of California Press.

Hayashi, Brian Masaru. 1995. *"For the Sake of Our Japanese Brethren": Assimilation, Nationalism, and Protestantism among the Japanese of Los Angeles, 1895–1942*. Stanford, CA: Stanford University Press.

Horne, Gerald. 1995. *Fire This Time: The Watts Uprising and the 1960s*. Charlottesville: University Press of Virginia.

Hurewitz, Daniel. 2007. *Bohemian Los Angeles and the Making of Modern Politics*. Berkeley: University of California Press.

Kurashige, Lon. 2002. *Japanese American Celebration and Conflict: A History of Ethnic Identity and Festival in Los Angeles, 1934–1990*. Berkeley: University of California Press.

Lee, Erika. 2003. *At America's Gates: Chinese Immigration during the Exclusion Era, 1882–1943.* Chapel Hill: University of North Carolina Press.

Lemke-Santangelo, Gretchen. 1996. *Abiding Courage: African American Migrant Women and the East Bay Community.* Chapel Hill: University of North Carolina Press.

Leonard, Kevin Allen. 2006. *The Battle for Los Angeles: Racial Ideology and World War II.* Albuquerque: University of New Mexico Press.

Leong, Karen J. 2003. "Foreign Policy, National Identity, and Citizenship: The Roosevelt White House and the Expediency of Repeal," *Journal of American Ethnic History* 22 (4): 3–30.

Matsumoto, Valerie J. 1993. *Farming the Home Place: A Japanese American Community in California, 1919–1982.* Ithaca, NY: Cornell University Press.

Molina, Natalia. 2006. *Fit to Be Citizens? Public Health and Race in Los Angeles, 1879–1939.* Berkeley: University of California Press.

Monroy, Douglas. 1999. *Rebirth: Mexican Los Angeles from the Great Migration to the Great Depression.* Berkeley: University of California Press.

Moore, Shirley Ann Wilson. 2000. *To Place Our Deeds: The African American Community in Richmond, California, 1910–1963.* Berkeley: University of California Press.

Orenstein, Dara. 2005. "Void for Vagueness: Mexicans and the Collapse of Miscegenation Law in California," *Pacific Historical Review* 74 (3): 367–407.

Oropeza, Lorena. 2005. *¡Raza Sí! ¡Guerra No! Chicano Protest and Patriotism during the Viet Nam War Era.* Berkeley: University of California Press.

Pagán, Eduardo Obregón. 2003. *Murder at the Sleepy Lagoon: Zoot Suits, Race, and Riot in Wartime Los Angeles.* Chapel Hill: University of North Carolina Press.

Pitti, Stephen J. 2003. *The Devil in Silicon Valley: Northern California, Race, and Mexican Americans.* Princeton, NJ: Princeton University Press.

Roediger, David R., with Barrett, James. 2002. "Inbetween Peoples: Race, Nationality, and the "New-Immigrant" Working Class." In D. R. Roediger, *Colored White: Transcending the Racial Past.* Berkeley: University of California Press: 138–168.

Ruiz, Vicki L. 1987. *Cannery Women, Cannery Lives: Mexican Women, Unionization, and the California Food Processing Industry, 1930–1950.* Albuquerque: University of New Mexico Press.

Sánchez, George J. 1993. *Becoming Mexican American: Ethnicity, Culture, and Identity in Chicano Los Angeles, 1900–1945.* New York: Oxford University Press.

Self, Robert O. 2003. *American Babylon: Race and the Struggle for Postwar Oakland.* Princeton, NJ: Princeton University Press.

Shah, Nayan. 2001. *Contagious Divides: Epidemics and Race in San Francisco's Chinatown.* Berkeley: University of California Press.

Sides, Josh. 2003. *L. A. City Limits: African American Los Angeles from the Great Depression to the Present.* Berkeley: University of California Press.

Sonenshein, Raphael J. 1993. *Politics in Black and White: Race and Power in Los Angeles.* Princeton, NJ: Princeton University Press.

Weber, Devra. 1994. *Dark Sweat, White Gold: California Farm Workers, Cotton, and the New Deal.* Berkeley: University of California Press.

Wild, Mark. 2005. *Street Meeting: Multiethnic Neighborhoods in Early Twentieth-Century Los Angeles.* Berkeley: University of California Press.

Yoo, David K. 2000. *Growing up Nisei: Race, Generation, and Culture among Japanese Americans of California, 1924–49.* Urbana: University of Illinois Press.

FURTHER READING

Cox, Bette Yarbrough. 1996. *Central Avenue – Its Rise and Fall, 1890–c.1955: Including the Musical Renaissance of Black Los Angeles.* Los Angeles: BEEM Publications.

Davis, Mike. 1990. *City of Quartz: Excavating the Future in Los Angeles.* New York: Verso.

España-Maram, Linda. 2006. *Creating Masculinity in Los Angeles's Little Manila: Working-Class Filipinos and Popular Culture, 1920s–1950s.* New York: Columbia University Press.

García, Mario T. 1994. *Memories of Chicano History: The Life and Narrative of Bert Corona.* Berkeley: University of California Press, 1994.

de Graaf, Lawrence B., Mulroy, Kevin, and Taylor, Quintard, eds. 2001. *Seeking El Dorado: African Americans in California.* Seattle: University of Washington Press.

Griswold del Castillo, Richard and Garcia, Richard A. 1995. *César Chávez: A Triumph of Spirit.* Norman: University of Oklahoma Press.

Leonard, Karen Isaksen. 1992. *Making Ethnic Choices: California's Punjabi Mexican Americans.* Philadelphia: Temple University Press.

Pulido, Laura. 2006. *Black, Brown, Yellow, and Left: Radical Activism in Los Angeles.* Berkeley: University of California Press.

Yung, Judy. 1995. *Unbound Feet: A Social History of Chinese Women in San Francisco.* Berkeley: University of California Press.

Chapter Twenty-one

THE LONG 1950s

Shana Bernstein

California rose to national prominence during the "long decade" of the 1950s, from the late 1940s through the 1950s. As noted in Arthur Verge's essay in this volume, California and the rest of the West emerged from World War II as an economic, population, and military center. The Pentagon's operation of some 300 military bases and installations west of the Mississippi during the Cold War hints at the ascendancy of the state and region, which came to assume a central role in the country's defense (Dias 1998: 71). Most wartime and postwar migrants from across the nation set their sights on California, where the expanding defense industry provided jobs by the tens of thousands. California had first lured many postwar arrivals during the war itself, when servicemen had arrived to be stationed at Los Angeles, Richmond, Oakland, and elsewhere. During this long decade of the 1950s, California also became a focal point of national politics and culture. Political figures like Richard Nixon and Ronald Reagan embarked on the political ascent that soon brought both to the national stage. Two other California cultural exports, Hollywood and Disneyland – one old and one new – deepened their imprint on the nation's cultural consciousness in this era.

Writings on the history of California, and the West more generally, during this era parallels the region's increasing prominence. Much of it centers the state in a national conversation and in turn reveals how viewing history through a California lens forces a rethinking of the history of the nation. This essay assesses how some of the most significant insights from recent scholarship on California during the long decade of the 1950s help us rethink national historical narratives. The discussion will focus on three specific major themes: the Cold War, the rise of liberalism, and the concomitant rise of conservatism.

Re-evaluating the Cold War

The Cold War descended on California in 1947. As the Congressional House Un-American Activities Committee (HUAC) set its sights on

Hollywood, screenwriters Dalton Trumbo, John Howard Lawson, and nine other Hollywood figures refused to answer its question, "Are you now or have you ever been a member of the Communist Party?" The recalcitrant writers quickly found themselves summarily cited, tried, imprisoned and, along with hundreds of other Hollywood writers, actors, directors, and producers, blacklisted. In the years that followed, the state incarnation of HUAC, headed by vigilant anti-communist and increasingly zealous witch-hunter Jack Tenney, intensified its own anti-communist pursuits. An epidemic of loyalty oaths and loyalty checks struck California in 1949. Los Angeles County forced its employees to take a loyalty oath, while the city of Los Angeles required employees to take an oath of denial. The Los Angeles County supervisors ordered all communist books removed from the county libraries, and the Board of Regents of the University of California made clerks, custodians, and faculty alike take a loyalty oath.

Until recently scholars have assumed that HUAC, Tenney, and other conservative Cold War forces killed off all significant activism in the far West. They characterized the 1950s as a decade of repression, consensus, and stagnation of social reform due to the country's single-minded focus on the struggle against global communism. But a closer look at California history shows that the Cold War did not stifle previous trends and derail struggles for equality. Recent work on grassroots civil rights and women's activism is instead helping to recast the long 1950s as an important "bridge" decade between the World War II era and the 1960s.

In some ways, scholars of California join historians of other regions of the nation, whose re-examinations of the first decade of the Cold War have illuminated the era's complexity. In terms of civil rights reform, a cohort of scholars including Mary Dudziak (2000), Thomas Borstelmann (2001), and Renee Romano (2000) have nuanced the previously reigning interpretation of the Cold War's domestic impact, which argued that the onset of the early Cold War derailed grassroots civil rights activism. Scholars Michael Honey (2004) and Patricia Sullivan (1996) are among those who have most prominently cast the era in this light by arguing that such reform efforts lost their meaning as they became "deradicalized." But by shifting the focus from grassroots activism to the federal government, Dudziak and others argue that the United States' new international imperatives during the Cold War facilitated certain domestic civil rights reforms. The Supreme Court's landmark 1954 decision *Brown vs. the Board of Education* only happened, Dudziak argues in *Cold War Civil Rights*, because the US government hoped to assuage foreign criticism of domestic racism and to sway global citizens toward democracy (and away from communism) by supporting limited civil rights reforms for African Americans (Dudziak 2000).

Other scholars have further complicated the notion of Cold War repression by focusing on women's activism. Earlier studies, such as that by

Elaine Tyler May (1988), argued that the Cold War stifled advances that women had made in earlier eras. In essence, May argued that the Cold War ushered in a return to the "domestic ideal" by encouraging "Rosie the Riveter" to leave the workplace and come back to the kitchen. While a return to the domestic sphere may have characterized the lives of some women, especially white, middle-class American women, multiple essays in Joanne Meyerowitz's edited collection *Not June Cleaver* (1994) and Daniel Horowitz's work on Betty Friedan (1998) expose a more nuanced narrative. The domestic ideal did not rule all early Cold War women's lives. Instead, many women continued to work due to economic necessity. Others continued to play activist roles, whether through civil rights, labor, or elsewhere (Meyerowitz 1994). And while Friedan may have become a suburban housewife during the Cold War era, we cannot miss the important continuity in her activist life across this era. In the 1940s she organized through unions and continued this activism in the 1960s, when her feminist agenda became apparent with the publication of *The Feminine Mystique* (Horowitz 1998).

This recent revisionist scholarship on national women's and civil rights reform clearly tempers previous characterizations of the Cold War as a strictly repressive influence. But recognizing aspects of California history reveals the limitations of both the revisionist and the traditional assessments of the Cold War's relationship to civil rights progress and women's activism.

In terms of grassroots civil rights efforts, both traditional and revisionist interpretations emphasize the era's discontinuities. But historical studies of California during the long 1950s uncover a significant continuity in civil rights. In California, the Cold War allowed – and in ways even facilitated – the continuation of grassroots activism. Chinese Americans in San Francisco, for instance, made substantial gains in their struggle for fair housing in the 1950s by conforming to Cold War imperatives. Specifically, they framed their goals as part of the struggle against global communism (Brooks 2004). The Cold War had a similar impact in Los Angeles. New organizations like the Mexican American community's Community Service Organization (CSO) even emerged during the harshest years of the Cold War, in part because organizers used Cold War language of fighting anticommunism (Bernstein, forthcoming). Even among left-leaning Los Angeles communities, meaningful civil rights activism continued through the early years of the Cold War. The Asociación Nacionál México-Americana (ANMA), a radical Mexican American organization, persisted through the mid-1950s, as Zaragosa Vargas illustrates in "In the Years of Darkness and Torment" (Vargas 2001). The Los Angeles Committee for the Protection of the Foreign-Born, a left-of-center immigrant assistance organization, also continued its activism through this era (Garcilazo 2001).

While other scholars do not address the Cold War explicitly, their studies nevertheless reinforce the point that meaningful social justice struggles by racial and ethnic minority groups persisted into the 1950s, in both rural and urban settings. Most work on this topic has focused on California's cities, about which there has been an explosion of literature encompassing the long 1950s. Scholars of San Francisco, for example, such as Charlotte Brooks (2004) and Scott Tang (2002) discuss Chinese-origin populations while others uncover the lasting civil rights influences of religious minority groups like Catholics and Jews (Issel 2003). Tang and Albert Broussard (1993) also illuminate the Cold War activism of the city's smaller populations of Japanese and African Americans. In San José, studies focus on struggles by the city's large Mexican-origin population, including Stephen Pitti's *Devil in Silicon Valley* (2003). In his 2003 study of Oakland and the East Bay, *American Babylon*, Robert Self delineates the persistent activism of the region's sizeable African American population.[1] In Los Angeles, studies reflect the ongoing civil rights struggles of the area's multiracial population during the 1950s (Sides 2003; Flamming 2005). Studies by Edward Escobar and Ken Burt have focused on the area's most visible minority, the Mexican-origin community (Escobar 2003; Burt 1996, 2004).

Although most work on civil rights activism during the 1950s focuses on urban areas, scholars who study suburban and rural regions reveal that struggles for social equality were far from a strictly urban phenomenon. In California's fields, communities of Filipino, Japanese, Mexican, and other populations also fought for their rights. Most prominent is work on California's Mexican-origin population. Matt Garcia's study of greater Los Angeles helps us better understand Mexican Americans' conditions and struggles in suburban areas, while Stephen Pitti's study of Ernesto Galarza exposes the emergence of rural struggles for farm workers' rights in the postwar era (Garcia 2001; Pitti 2001).

Nevertheless, studies such as these delineate the persistence of meaningful civil rights reform during the long 1950s. Of course, it is important not to overstate the case for civil rights continuity during the early Cold War. Certain coalitions and agendas did find themselves sidelined. Vargas shows that the ANMA eventually collapsed, and Garcilazo illustrates how members of the Committee for the Protection of the Foreign Born did not exert as much influence as they hoped. Rampant repression ruined lives, and "undesirable" activists faced deportation.

Studies of California also expose a continuity which speaks to revisionist assessments by Dudziak, Borstelmann, and others that the relationship between Cold War international imperatives and civil rights advances was new during the Cold War. By focusing on especially western populations – Chinese, Japanese, and Mexican-descent people in particular – such studies reveal that the federal government's interest began in significant ways before the Cold War and continued from an earlier era into the 1950s. The United States' desire to fortify the Good Neighbor Policy, and in particular to maintain positive relations with Mexico – which provided the United States with crucial wartime labor, military support, and raw materials – catalyzed federal intervention in states with glaringly poor records concerning their Mexican-origin populations. Work on the World War II era by Justin Hart and myself on California, and Thomas Guglielmo on Texas uncovers this continuity (Hart 2004; Bernstein forthcoming; Guglielmo 2006). Furthermore, lifting long-term restrictions on the largely West Coast Chinese-origin population became a federal tool during World War II for maintaining a strong wartime alliance with China. In late 1943, for instance, the United States government overturned the 1790 Naturalization Act, which denied non-whites the right to become citizens, and liberalized the 1882 Chinese Exclusion Act, thereby reversing Chinese immigration exclusion. The new law was largely symbolic, since it allowed for only a very small number of Chinese immigrants, but it nonetheless marked a significant shift in policy (Yung 1995; Takaki 2000). Such an emphasis on western Mexican and Chinese-origin populations suggests a World War II to Cold War continuity concerning the relationship between the federal government's civil rights interest and international objectives. It also underscores the significance of non-black populations to the federal government's civil rights interventions.

Like studies of California civil rights, recent work on early Cold War-era California women's activism also forces us to rethink our understanding of the Cold War's continuities and discontinuities. Historian Michelle Nickerson demonstrated that 1950s-era California women joined Republican women's clubs and fought for conservative and other causes in the public schools (2003a, 2003b, and forthcoming). Such aggressive support for emergent Cold War conservative politics on the one hand confirms interpretations by Meyerowitz, Horowitz, and others that women's "public sphere" involvement continued from an earlier era. But it also demonstrates, on the other hand, important elements of discontinuity, since the conservative bent marked a new variety of public engagement. In other words, the Cold War incubated a new, conservative variety of women's *ongoing* political activism.

New research makes clear that the case of California suggests a "bridge" decade for grassroots civil rights endeavors, for the federal government's intervention in civil rights and equality issues, and for women's continued public sphere involvement. But a key question remains. What difference did it make that this activism emerged in California? In the West more generally? Was persistent civil rights activism and emerging women's conservative political activism merely an interesting western case study which revealed regional differences? Or did this western activism have an impact on the nation, or reveal anything significant about the relationship between California and the nation as a whole?

The Rise of Liberalism and Conservatism

California women's rising postwar conservative activism hints at a larger picture of emergent political conservatism during the Cold War. The politicians supported by Nickerson's "mothers of conservatism" quickly rose to national prominence. Richard Nixon's ascendancy to the Senate during the early years of the Cold War indicates how California nurtured a nationally influential conservatism; his anti-communist platform had clearly been constructed in Southern California, hammered into place in Nixon's successful, and vicious, 1950 campaign against Helen Gahagan Douglas, whom he labeled the "Pink Lady." Ronald Reagan, too, surged to the national scene on a tide of support from conservative Cold War Californians; Reagan's successful 1966 gubernatorial bid insured him of a national platform.

Recent research has highlighted California's centrality to the rise of American conservatism after World War II. Historian Kurt Schuparra argues in *Triumph of the Right: the Rise of the California Conservative Movement, 1945–1966* (1998) that conservatism found a particularly strong base in California – especially Southern California – in part because of the region's anti-communism, a strain even more virulent than elsewhere in the country. Strong western support for Nixon, Reagan, and for Barry Goldwater's 1964 presidential campaign, Schuparra argues, reveal California-based conservatism's national influence. Midwestern migrants to the state, and especially to Southern California, in the decades following World War II nurtured an especially potent conservatism (Spooner 1992).

Previously overlooked movements have been given historical voice by recent scholarship focusing on the social roots of conservative politics. While Nickerson's mothers built an anti-communist movement through involvement in the public schools, local politics, and other civic affairs, working-class white suburbanites in Southgate, a community outside Los Angeles, based their grassroots conservative politics on ideals of white homeowner rights. Becky Nicolaides (2002) explores these blue-collar white conservatives in *My Blue Heaven: Life and Politics in the Working-Class Suburbs of Los Angeles, 1920–1965*. Along with historian Lisa McGirr, Nicolaides illustrates how political conservatism emerged in tandem with social – and spatial – developments in the Southern California region. Both scholars root much of the region's burgeoning postwar conservative politics in its simultaneous suburbanization and other social trends. *My Blue*

Heaven shows how in the postwar era such suburbs became crucial to a burgeoning conservative politics. McGirr's *Suburban Warriors: The Origins of the New American Right* (2001) focuses even more explicitly on the postwar growth of conservative suburban politics in the state. McGirr explains the emergence of the postwar conservative "revolution" through the case study of Orange County. Like Nicolaides, McGirr sees this grass-roots revolution as more than a political movement: it was a social movement which grew in large part out of these emerging suburbs and blossomed with particular vigor in the postwar West.[2] Robert Self joins this conversation about the rise of local conservative movements, though he is less explicit about the national significance of the story he tells in *American Babylon*. Oakland and the greater East Bay helped build a postwar "populist-conservative" movement which celebrated private rights and committed itself to property and homeownership, Self finds. His study reveals that grassroots conservative political developments were statewide, if more prominent, and perhaps more prevalent, in Orange County and other Southern California locales (Self 2003).

Work on metropolitan spaces in California suggests, furthermore, that we rethink understandings that have emerged in the last decade about the so-called "urban crisis" which postwar African American communities confronted. Self's work reveals the limitations of models built on an eastern framework and speaks especially to findings by Thomas Sugrue in his important study of postwar Detroit, *Origins of the Urban Crisis* (1996). Sugrue's careful historical research on one city revealed that the so-called urban crisis developed long before the 1960s, and had much earlier roots than previous studies had identified. At least in the case of Detroit, it emerged from post-World War II deindustrialization. Self's study of San Francisco's East Bay region, though, shows that such models based on the industrial "North" do not apply to all US cities, and cannot entirely explain the origins of all postwar American inner cities. The postwar West was different from Detroit. In Oakland and its environs, the so-called urban crisis resulted from complex struggles over power and access, and occurred without deindustrialization. Another California metropolitan region, Los Angeles, exposes the limits even of the term "urban crisis." As Sides (2003) has argued, the story of African Americans in postwar Los Angeles illuminates more than a tale of absolute decline, indicating that the term does not accurately describe African American conditions in all postwar US cities. The community made important gains in the era, even though the 1965 Watts riots suggest obvious (and important) similarities with black experiences in rust belt cities back east.

These regional suburban and metropolitan studies suggest that understanding developments during the long decade of the 1950s helps us reinterpret the era in two ways. First, as studies of conservatism illustrate, developments in California shaped a national political consciousness and reflect far more than an interesting, perhaps peripheral, regional variety. Second, as works by Self and Sides on the "urban crisis" indicate, we must recognize the limits of supposedly national models, which obscure the reality of western transformations. Further studies on these subjects will help us confirm such conclusions, which for now remain mostly suggestive. More comparative work on the emergence of grassroots conservative politics, and on the role of the suburbs in facilitating their emergence, will help us more clearly determine how important suburbs in California (and the West/Sunbelt region more generally) were relative to those emerging elsewhere.

Besides raising these questions about rising postwar conservatism and its relationship to metropolitan spaces, Self's study also speaks to the ways scholarship on the 1950s helps us rethink the emergence of postwar liberalism. Self argues that Oakland and the greater East Bay "incubated two of California's most important postwar political traditions: a broad liberal one that sought expansions of the social wage and racial equality . . . and an equally broad populist-conservative one . . ." (Self 2003: 7). In other words, at the same time as developments in the East Bay facilitated the rise of a conservative tradition, they also produced a liberal political stance that focused on equality and wage equity. The national prominence and influence of California Governor Earl Warren also hints at California's significance in terms of nationwide liberalism. Warren left the state to preside as Chief Justice of the Supreme Court as it shifted leftward over issues of civil rights during the 1950s, most prominently through the case of *Brown vs. the Board of Education*.

The emergence of liberal racial politics in postwar California is partly a story of how the state's residents, especially in the wake of diverse World War II migrations, confronted a complex multiracial landscape well ahead of most of their fellow Americans. The experiences of Warren and other Californians foreshadowed what eventually would become a national complex of tensions, struggles, and cooperation, which most Americans would not face until decades later. In the postwar West, early postwar battles for fair employment, equality in the workplace, and other civil rights took place in a multiracial context. The California Federation for Civic Unity, Los Angeles County Commission on Human Rights, and other civil rights organizations reflected collaboration among African Americans, Jews, white liberals, Mexican Americans, Japanese Americans, and others. Such multiracial collaboration shows the limits of the black/white framework that applied to much of the rest of the country in the era before 1960s immigration reform transformed the racial landscape into one which resembled California's. How residents of diverse racial and ethnic backgrounds navigated their relationships with each other in this era adds an important historical perspective for an entire country, which in the twenty-first century looks more like California looked during the long 1950s.

The state's racial diversity led to a multifaceted set of resident interactions. In some cases, Chinese, Japanese, Filipinos, Mexicans, and others lived side by side, socialized, and even intermarried, showing how they had come to think of themselves as an increasingly cohesive group of "non-white" people by the 1950s (Varzally, forthcoming). This identity predated coalitions between people of color during the national civil rights struggles of the 1960s and 1970s. Interracial relations in postwar California also manifested themselves in ways besides cooperation. Strategies pursued by California minority groups from the postwar era through the 1970s sometimes did lead them to cooperate for change, particularly in the decade following World War II, as Mark Brilliant shows in his forthcoming *Color Lines: Civil Rights Struggles on America's "Racial Frontier," 1945–1975*. But fractures among communities over issues such as bilingual education and immigration reveal that they just as often, or even more so, reflected fault lines among populations with disparate interests, despite a supposedly common "minority" status. These mid-century fault lines foreshadowed fissures that have emerged nationwide in the early twenty-first century between Asian, Latino, and African American populations.

Brilliant and Varzally's books represent just the tip of an iceberg of recent historical interest in relations among California's racial and ethnic minority groups. Of historians of California, those studying Los Angeles and its surrounding areas – whose main postwar diversity stemmed from its Mexican, Japanese, African American, Jewish, as well as other European immigrant populations – most often have approached their subject through a multiracial lens. Scholars Albert Camarillo, Matt Garcia, Scott Tadao Kurashige, George Sánchez, Katherine Underwood, Daniel Widener, and myself examine relations among the city's minorities as well as between them and the Anglo majority. Some emphasize fissures, while others highlight cooperation (Underwood 1997; Kurashige 2000; Garcia 2001; Widener 2003; Camarillo 2004; Sánchez 2004; Bernstein forthcoming). Why scholars of Los Angeles focus on multiracial relations more than scholars of other California regions with multiracial denizens is unclear. It may be that communities in Los Angeles interacted with each other more than communities elsewhere; or it rather may result from the nature of the questions asked by scholars of each region. The prevalence of multi-ethnic Bay Area coalitions that sprang up in the 1940s and 1950s (including the California Federation for Civic Unity and the Bay Area Council against Discrimination) suggests that scholars may find more commonalities across the state than they had previously expected.

Scholarship emphasizing the significance of both fissures and cooperation helps demonstrate how California foreshadowed relations which permeated the nation by the twenty-first century. But as with Californians' conservative political support during the 1950s, cooperation among civil rights communities during the long 1950s does more than indicate the future. It also had a lasting impact on the nation. Scholars in the fields of law, education, and history have begun to emphasize the influence of western racial liberalism upon the nation. Multiracial civil rights struggles in California influenced the shape and timing of national civil rights advances, including school desegregation, the elimination of miscegenation laws, and the abolition of restrictive covenants.

School desegregation suits filed in the postwar era on behalf of Southern California Mexican Americans, and supported by racially diverse populations, influenced national school desegregation. In 1946, Mexican American plaintiffs brought a school desegregation case, *Mendez vs. Westminster*, to court in Orange County. An African American lawyer named David C. Marcus argued the case. Multiracial civil rights organizations, including the American Jewish Congress, the Japanese American Citizens League (JACL), and the National Association for the Advancement of Colored People (NAACP), as well as the American Civil Liberties Union (ACLU), all filed amicus curiae briefs in support of the 1947 appeal of the *Mendez* case. Unlike the *Brown vs. the Board of Education* decision, the Supreme Court desegregation victory almost a decade later, *Mendez* did not rule against segregation per se. It sidestepped the issue of race by ruling that the California Constitution prohibited the segregation of Mexican-origin children, not any racial group.

But in some ways, *Mendez* set a precedent for *Brown* and served as a training ground for lawyers active in the later case. For one thing, the American Jewish Congress, the NAACP, and others who tested their strategies and abilities in *Mendez* also argued on behalf of the *Brown* plaintiffs seven years later. The JACL's Saburo Kido and the American Jewish Congress's Will Maslow helped file friends-of-the-court (amicus curiae) briefs in both cases. Los Angeles NAACP activist Loren Miller assisted in filing the amicus curiae briefs in both *Mendez* and *Brown*. Moreover, individuals like Robert Carter and Thurgood Marshall, who were among the most prominent attorneys in *Brown*, also helped with this earlier California Mexican American case and developed arguments in California which they later relied upon in *Brown* (Arriola 1995; Brilliant 2002; Valencia 2005). Evidence also indicates that even *Brown* lawyers who had not been involved in *Mendez* relied upon strategies and tactics developed in the earlier case to advance their now national case, thereby suggesting that *Mendez* seems to have been the first step toward overturning the *Plessy vs. Ferguson* doctrine of "separate but equal" (González 1990; Johnson 2004; Valencia 2005). Moreover, *Mendez* set a precedent for employing social scientists to offer "expert" testimony against segregation, a strategy which *Brown* lawyers pursued several years later. Robert Carter, Thurgood Marshall, and others arguing *Brown* even relied upon the same arguments articulated by experts who testified in *Mendez*. Carter later explained that the amicus curiae brief he and Marshall filed in the appellate court in support of the district court's *Mendez* decision was a "dry run for the future." And David Marcus, the attorney for the *Mendez* plaintiffs, provided Marshall with all the briefs and notes he had compiled during the case (González 1990; Valencía 2005).

Earl Warren's trajectory also illustrates the national impact of California's multiracial context. In 1946, the same year that California's courts ruled on *Mendez* and almost halfway through his tenure as Governor (1943–53), Warren's attorney general convinced him to see the writing on the wall: segregation's time had come to an end. Just seven years before he left the governorship to his successor – Lieutenant Governor Goodwin J. Knight – to lead the Supreme Court to its desegregation decision in *Brown*, Warren signed into California law a bill that prohibited any form of racial segregation in the state's schools.

Struggles against anti-miscegenation laws and restrictive covenants in California during the long 1950s also had national significance. During this era, California became the first state to outlaw prohibitions against racial intermarriage. The California Supreme Court's 1948 decision in the *Perez vs. Lippold* case marked the first time since Reconstruction that a state court declared state miscegenation law unconstitutional, Peggy Pascoe argues (Pascoe 1996). This law predated the Supreme Court decision on the issue of miscegenation law by two decades, as the Supreme Court did not outlaw such laws nationally until the 1967 decision *Loving vs. Virginia*. Pascoe does not connect the California case to the national case in as much detail as the scholarship on *Mendez vs. Westminster*'s impact on *Brown*, but she does reveal how some of the same issues emerging out of the California case shaped later national discussions and decisions. Moreover, she makes clear that California clearly set a precedent on this issue (Pascoe 1999).

The national impact of anti-restrictive covenant activism in postwar California also has come to light recently. California activists played key roles during the late 1940s and early 1950s in delegitimating state and national laws permitting restrictive housing covenants, which prohibited "undesirable" ethnic and racial groups from purchasing homes in certain neighborhoods. African American NAACP members from Los Angeles like Loren Miller played an especially important role in both local and national struggles. Efforts by activists like Miller helped secure the first national victory against restrictive covenants, the 1948 Supreme Court decision *Shelley vs. Kraemer*, which ruled that restrictive covenants were unenforceable. The Los Angeles NAACP alone filed more suits against restrictive covenants between 1945 and 1948 than were filed in any other part of the country, as Josh Sides shows (Sides 1999, 2003). Los Angeles NAACP members continued to fight after the inadequacy of the *Shelley vs. Kraemer* decision became clear, as whites continued to evade the restraints the court had placed on them. Miller and other Los Angeles NAACP members joined, and even led, teams lobbying the Supreme Court to close these last loopholes in restrictive covenant legislation. Such efforts resulted in the 1953 *Barrows vs. Jackson* decision, which extended the earlier *Shelley vs. Kraemer* decision to not only blacks but also to whites who sold to them (Sides 1999, 2003; de Graaf et al. 2001). Studies by scholars like Sides, Pascoe, González, Valencía, Johnson, Arriola, and Brilliant make clear that civil rights activism in postwar California eventually helped reshape national liberal policies, particularly in terms of race, while work by Nickerson, Schuparra, Nicolaides, and McGirr reveals California's impact on national conservative political trends. Such historical, legal, and educational scholarship makes clear that emerging liberalism and conservatism in postwar California reveals more than merely an interesting "local variation." It contributes to a developing recognition of the state's importance for nurturing both national racial liberalism and political conservatism during the long 1950s. These two trends in California left a dual legacy on the nation, and this recognition forces us to rethink national historical narratives. In other words, work on the long 1950s centers the state in national history and forces us to recognize how Californians shaped the face of the nation for years to come.

NOTES

1 Self's argument in *American Babylon* is more complex than one of continuity. He does argue that African American activism for greater civil (including economic) rights continued during the Cold War, especially through groups like the Brotherhood of Sleeping Car Porters, other black railroad unions, the International Longshoremen's and Warehousemen's Union and Marine Cooks and Stewards Union, which all helped nurture "through the dark days of Cold War anticommunism a social and political milieu in which antiracism and progressive ideas, debate, and struggle were the order of the day" (Self, *American Babylon*, pp. 4–6). Similarly, East Bay African Americans built a statewide alliance of liberal, labor, and black civil rights forces, which grew stronger during the 1950s. At the same time, though, Self also argues that the local labor and civil rights initiatives became weaker and ultimately failed during this time (pp. 85–6). Specifically, Self asserts that anti-communism helped "narrow[ed] the possibilities for deeper changes" (p. 78).

2 McGirr acknowledges that suburbanization and other similar social and spatial transformations occurred elsewhere around the country – she especially indicates the centrality of other Sunbelt regions besides Southern California, but argues that in the western context they were particularly influential in terms

of facilitating the emergence of conservative grassroots politics. In the West such transformations became especially important to the development of American political conservatism, as the national prominence of California conservatives like Nixon and Reagan makes clear.

References

Arriola, C. 1995. "Knocking on the Schoolhouse Door: *Mendez v. Westminster* – Equal Protection, Public Education, and Mexican Americans in the 1940s," *La Raza Law Journal* 8: 166–207.

Bernstein, S. Forthcoming. *California Dreaming in a Divided World: Building Multiracial Bridges in World War II and Cold War Los Angeles.* New York: Oxford University Press.

Borstelmann, T. 2001. *The Cold War and the Color Line: American Race Relations in the Global Arena.* Cambridge, MA: Harvard University Press.

Brilliant, M. 2002. "Color Lines: Civil Rights Struggles on America's 'Racial Frontier,' 1945–1975." PhD dissertation, Stanford University.

Brilliant, M. Forthcoming. *Color Lines: Civil Rights Struggles on America's "Racial Frontier,"1945–1975.* New York: Oxford University Press.

Brooks, C. 2004. "Sing Sheng vs. Southwood: Residential Integration in Cold War California," *Pacific Historical Review* 73 (3): 463–94.

Broussard, A. S. 1993. *Black San Francisco: The Struggle for Racial Equality in the West, 1900–1954.* Lawrence: University of Kansas Press.

Burt, K. 1996. "Latino Empowerment in Los Angeles: Postwar Dreams and Cold War Fears, 1948–1952," *Labor's Heritage* 8 (1): 6–25.

Burt, K. 2004. "The Battle for Standard Coil: The United Electrical Workers, the Community Service Organization, and the Catholic Church in Latino East Los Angeles." In W. Issel, R. W. Cherny, and K. W. Taylor, eds., *American Labor and the Cold War: Grassroots Politics and Postwar Political Culture.* Piscataway, NJ: Rutgers University Press.

Camarillo, A. 2004. "Black and Brown in Compton: Demographic Change, Suburban Decline, and Inter-Group Relations in a South Central Los Angeles Community, 1950–2000." In G. M. Fredrickson and N. Foner, eds., *Not Just Black and White: Historical and Contemporary Perspectives on Immigration, Race and Ethnicity in the United States.* New York: Russell Sage Foundation.

Dias, R. 1998. "The Great Cantonment: Cold War Cities in the American West." In K. J. Fernlund, ed., *The Cold War American West, 1945–1989.* Albuquerque: University of New Mexico Press.

Dudziak, M. 2000. *Cold War Civil Rights: Race and the Image of American Democracy.* Princeton, NJ: Princeton University Press.

Escobar, E. J. 2003. "Bloody Christmas and the Irony of Police Professionalism: The Los Angeles Police Department, Mexican Americans, and Police Reform in the 1950s," *Pacific Historical Review* 72 (2): 171–99.

Flamming, D. 2001. "Becoming Democrats: Liberal Politics and the African American Community in Los Angeles, 1930–1965." In L. B. de Graaf,

K. Mulroy, and Q. Taylor, eds., *Seeking El Dorado: African Americans in California*. Los Angeles: Autry Museum of Western Heritage, in association with the University of Washington Press.

Flamming, D. 2005. *Bound for Freedom*. Berkeley: University of California Press.

Garcia, M. 2001. *A World of Its Own: Race, Labor, and Citrus in the Making of Greater Los Angeles, 1900–1970*. Chapel Hill: University of North Carolina Press.

Garcilazo, J. M. 2001. "McCarthyism, Mexican Americans, and the Los Angeles Committee for Protection of the Foreign-Born, 1950–1954," *Western Historical Quarterly* 32 (Autumn): 273–95.

González, G. G. 1990. *Chicano Education in the Era of Segregation*. Philadelphia: Balch Institute Press.

de Graaf, L. B., Mulroy, K., and Taylor, Q., eds. 2001. *Seeking El Dorado: African Americans in California*. Los Angeles: Autry Museum of Western Heritage, in association with University of Washington Press.

Guglielmo, T. A. 2006. "Fighting for Caucasian Rights: Mexicans, Mexican Americans, and the Transnational Struggle for Civil Rights Legislation in World War II Texas," *Journal of American History* 92 (4): 1212–37.

Hart, J. 2004. "Making Democracy Safe for the World: Race, Propaganda, and the Transformation of U.S. Foreign Policy during World War II," *Pacific Historical Review* 73 (1): 49–84.

Honey, M. K. 2004. "Operation Dixie, the Red Scare, and the Defeat of Southern Labor Organizing." In R. W. Cherny, W. Issel, and K. W. Taylor, eds., *American Labor and the Cold War: Grassroots Politics and Postwar Political Culture*. New Brunswick, NJ: Rutgers University Press.

Horowitz, D. 1998. *Betty Friedan and the Making of the Feminine Mystique: The American Left, the Cold War, and Modern Feminism*. Amherst, MA: University of Massachusetts Press.

Issel, W. 2003. "Jews and Catholics against Prejudice." In A. F. Kahn and M. Dollinger, eds., *California Jews*. Lebanon, NH: University Press of New England, Brandeis University Press.

Johnson, K. R. 2004. "Hernández v. Texas: Legacies of Justice and Injustice." [Online]. Davis, California: UC Davis Law, Legal Studies Research Paper, 19 (November). Available from: http://ssrn.com/abstract=625403.

Kurashige, Scott Tadao. 2000. "Transforming Los Angeles: Black and Japanese American Struggles for Racial Equality in the Twentieth Century." PhD dissertation, University of California Los Angeles.

May, E. T. 1988. *Homeward Bound: American Families in the Cold War Era*. New York: Basic Books.

McGirr, L. 2001. *Suburban Warriors: The Origins of the New American Right*. Princeton, NJ: Princeton University Press.

Meyerowitz, J. ed. 1994. *Not June Cleaver: Women and Gender in Postwar America, 1945–1960*. Philadelphia: Temple University Press.

Moore, D. D. 1994. *To the Golden Cities: Pursuing the American Jewish Dream in Miami and L.A.* New York: Free Press.

Nickerson, M., 2003a. " 'The Power of a Morally Indignant Woman': Republican Women and the Making of California Conservatism," *Journal of the West* 42 (Summer): 35–43.

Nickerson, M. 2003b. "Women, Domesticity, and Postwar Conservatism," *OAH Magazine of History* 17 (January).

Nickerson, M. Forthcoming. *Mothers of Conservatism: Women and the Postwar Right*. New Jersey, NJ: Princeton University Press.

Nicolaides, B. 2002. *My Blue Heaven: Life and Politics in the Working-Class Suburbs of Los Angeles, 1920–1965*. Chicago: University of Chicago Press.

Pascoe, P. 1996. "Miscegenation Law, Court Cases, and Ideologies of 'Race' in Twentieth-Century America," *Journal of American History* 83 (1): 44–69.

Pascoe, P. 1999. "Race, Gender, and the Privileges of Property: On the Significance of Miscegenation Law in the U.S. West." In V. J. Matsumoto and B. Allmendinger, eds., *Over the Edge: Remapping the American West*. Berkeley: University of California Press.

Pitti, S. 2001. "Ernesto Galarza, Mexican Immigration, and Farm Labor Organizing in Postwar California." In C. M. Stock and R. D. Johnston, eds., *The Countryside in the Age of the Modern State: Political Histories of Rural America*. Ithaca, NY: Cornell University Press.

Pitti, S. J. 2003. *The Devil in Silicon Valley: Northern California, Race, and Mexican Americans*. Princeton, NJ: Princeton University Press.

Romano, R. 2000. "No Diplomatic Immunity: African Diplomats, the State Department, and Civil Rights, 1961–1964," *Journal of American History* 87 (2): 546–79.

Sánchez, G. 2004. " 'What's Good for Boyle Heights is Good for the Jews': Creating Multiracialism on the Eastside during the 1950s," *American Quarterly* special edition, Los Angeles and the Future of Urban Cultures, 56 (3): 633–61.

Schuparra, K. 1998. *Triumph of the Right: The Rise of the California Conservative Movement, 1945–1966*. Armonk, NY: M. E. Sharpe.

Self, R. 2003. *American Babylon: Race and the Struggle for Postwar Oakland*. Princeton, NJ: Princeton University Press.

Sides, Josh A. 1999. "Working Away: African American Migration and Community in Los Angeles from the Great Depression to 1954." PhD dissertation, University of California Los Angeles.

Sides, J. 2003. *L.A. City Limits: African American Los Angeles from the Great Depression to the Present*. Berkeley: University of California Press.

Spooner, Denise Suzanne. 1992. "The Political Consequences of Experiences of Community: Iowa Migrants and Republican Conservatism in Southern California, 1946–1964." PhD dissertation, University of Pennsylvania.

Sugrue, T. 1996. *The Origins of the Urban Crisis: Race and Inequality in Postwar Detroit*. Princeton, NJ: Princeton University Press.

Sullivan, P. 1996. *Days of Hope: Race and Democracy in the New Deal Era*. Chapel Hill: the University of North Carolina Press.

Takaki, R. 2000. *Double Victory: A Multicultural History of America in World War II*. New York: Little, Brown.

Tang, Scott Harvey. 2002. "Pushing at the Golden Gate: Race Relations and Racial Politics in San Francisco, 1940–1955." PhD dissertation, University of California Berkeley.

Underwood, K. 1997. "Pioneering Minority Representation: Edward Roybal and the Los Angeles City Council, 1949–1962," *Pacific Historical Review* 66 (August): 399–425.

Valencia, R. 2005. "The Mexican American Struggle for Equal Educational Opportunity in *Mendez v. Westminster*: Helping to Pave the Way for *Brown v. Board of Education*," *The Teachers College Record* 107 (3): 389–423.

Vargas, Z. 2001. "In the Years of Darkness and Torment: The Early Mexican American Struggle for Civil Rights, 1945–1963," *New Mexico Historical Review* 76 (October): 383–413.

Varzally, A. Forthcoming. *Coloring outside Ethnic Lines: The Making of a Non-White Nation in California, 1925–1955*. Berkeley: University of California Press.

Widener, D. 2003. "'Perhaps the Japanese are to be Thanked?' Asia, Asian America, and the Construction of Black California," *Positions: East Asia Cultures Critique* 11 (1): 135–81.

Wu, J. 2005. *Doctor Mom Chung of the Fair-Haired Bastards: The Life of a Wartime Celebrity*. Berkeley: University of California Press.

Yung, J. 1995. *Unbound Feet: A Social History of Chinese Women in San Francisco*. Berkeley: University of California Press.

FURTHER READING

Avila, E. 2004. *Popular Culture in the Age of White Flight: Fear and Fantasy in Suburban Los Angeles*. Berkeley: University of California Press.

Gardner, D. 1967. *The California Oath Controversy*. Berkeley: University of California Press.

Gutiérrez, D. G. 1995. *Walls and Mirrors: Mexican Americans Mexican Immigrants, and the Politics of Ethnicity*. Berkeley: University of California Press.

Hise, G. 1997. *Magnetic Los Angeles: Planning the Twentieth-Century Metropolis*. Baltimore, MD: The Johns Hopkins University Press.

Littauer, A. H. 2003. "The B-Girl Evil: Bureaucracy, Sexuality, and the Menace of Barroom Vice in Postwar California," *Journal of the History of Sexuality* 12 (2): 171–204.

Lowen, R. S. 1997. *Creating the Cold War University: The Transformation of Stanford*. Berkeley: University of California Press.

Matthews, G. 2002. *Silicon Valley, Women, and the California Dream: Gender, Class, and Opportunity in the Twentieth Century*. Stanford, CA: Stanford University Press.

Olin, S. C. 1991. "Globalization and the Politics of Locality: Orange County, California, in the Cold War Era," *The Western Historical Quarterly* 22 (2): 143–61.

O'Mara, M. P. 2004. *Cities of Knowledge: Cold War Science and the Search for the Next Silicon Valley*. Princeton, NJ: Princeton University Press.

Parson, D. 2002. "The Burke Incident: Political Belief in Los Angeles' Public Housing during the Domestic Cold War," *Southern California Quarterly* 84 (Spring): 53–74.

Rose, M. 1994. "Gender and Civic Activism in Mexican American Barrios in California: The Community Service Organization, 1947–1962." In J. Meyerowitz, ed., *Not June Cleaver: Women and Gender in Postwar America, 1945–1960.* Philadelphia: Temple University Press.

Chapter Twenty-two

APPORTIONMENT POLITICS, 1920–70

Douglas Smith

In retirement, former Chief Justice Earl Warren acknowledged that most people considered *Brown vs. Board of Education* (1954) the most important decision handed down by the Supreme Court during his tenure. The Chief Justice himself, however, disagreed. Instead, Warren unequivocally gave that designation to *Baker vs. Carr* (1962), *Reynolds vs. Sims* (1964), and a series of companion cases that established the principle of "one person, one vote" in all congressional and state legislative apportionments. Those decisions, according to Warren, ushered in a revolution that changed the face of representative democracy in the United States (Warren 2001: 306–12).

If the importance of the Court's rulings can be measured by the backlash they produced, then the reapportionment decisions of the 1960s were indeed as important as Warren suggested. In fact, the Court's rulings proved so controversial that opponents launched a campaign to call what would have been the first constitutional convention since the founding convention of the 1780s. Financed by many of the largest corporations in the United States, the effort played out in relative obscurity, overshadowed by more tumultuous events that dominated headlines in the 1960s. But by 1969, 33 states, just one short of the required two-thirds, had petitioned for a convention.

Although none of the cases that led to the Supreme Court's landmark reapportionment rulings originated in California, the state figures prominently in any discussion of apportionment politics in the twentieth century. Beginning in the 1920s, California moved away from a straight population basis in apportioning seats in the state senate. By 1960, the California senate was as malapportioned as any legislative body in the entire United States, an arrangement supported by most Californians as a check on the power of Los Angeles. Consequently, the Supreme Court's determination that all legislative bodies be apportioned on a population basis had as profound an effect on the distribution of political power in California as in any other state. For that reason, Californians played a disproportionate role and spent a vastly disproportionate amount of money on the effort to limit the Court's reapportionment rulings.

From statehood until the 1920s, both branches of the California legislature remained apportioned on a population basis. By 1920, however, rural and Northern Californians confronted a stark reality that threatened their ability to maintain control over the legislature: Southern California continued to grow at a much faster rate than the rest of the state. Los Angeles had surpassed San Francisco in total population, and two-thirds of the state's residents now resided in urban areas. As a 1965 legislative report explained, "by 1920 rural groups were determined to control at least one house of the Legislature while the continual decline of San Francisco encouraged an alliance with the other northern groups to prevent Los Angeles and southern California from gaining additional seats in relationship to population gains" (Allen 1965: 9).

The California constitution called for reapportionment after each federal decennial census. After the 1920 census, however, a deadlocked legislature failed on three successive occasions to pass any reapportionment measures. In 1926, opposing forces put the issue before the state's electorate. The All-Parties Reapportionment Commission, led by Los Angeles geologist Ralph Arnold, sponsored Proposition 20, an initiative that would have maintained a population basis in both houses and that would have empowered a Reapportionment Commission to draw new legislative boundaries if the legislature refused. On the other side, a coalition led by the California Farm Bureau Federation and the San Francisco Chamber of Commerce supported Proposition 28, a measure that proponents dubbed the "Federal Plan" because it created a legislature with an assembly based on population and a senate based on geography.

California was by no means the first state to model its legislature on some version of the federal plan. Proponents of Proposition 28 argued that 29 other states had a similar system. But no state's federal plan created disparities as excessive as California's. Opponents of Proposition 28 objected in particular to the provision of the initiative that mandated that no county could have more than one senator, and that no senator could represent more than three counties. In practical terms, that meant that Los Angeles, Alameda, and San Francisco counties – with a combined population of more than 50 percent of the state's total – would be represented by only 3 of 40 senators. In November 1926, the state's voters overwhelmingly adopted the federal plan. Only Los Angeles County opposed the initiative.

California's new method of reapportionment took effect with the 1930 elections, and remained in place until the Supreme Court intervened more than 30 years later. By 1960 the continued growth of Los Angeles and other urban regions meant that malapportionment in California was as severe as in any state in the nation; 11 percent of the state's residents were able to elect a majority of the state senate. Nearly 6.4 million residents of Los Angeles had one representative in the state senate, as did the 14,294 residents of Alpine, Mono, and Inyo counties on the eastern slope of the Sierra. A voter in the eastern Sierra, therefore, enjoyed the electoral might of 446 residents of Los Angeles. California's 38th senatorial district (Los Angeles County) was not only the most populous legislative district in the United States, but it contained five times as many residents as the next most populous district (Wellman 1962: 16; McKay 1965: 285–9; Dixon 1968: 370–1).

Unlike voters in many other malapportioned states, residents of California had at their disposal the initiative and referendum, which provided numerous opportunities to revise the state's apportionment system. But on three different occasions – 1948, 1960, and 1962 – California voters resoundingly affirmed their version of the federal plan. The battle over Proposition 13 in 1948 proved the most interesting of these attempts and, in many ways, prefigured later debates.

Financed almost entirely by the California Federation of Labor, supporters of reapportionment presented their plan simply as an attempt to "restore more representative government" to the state. Emphasizing that ongoing demographic change ensured that urban residents had become increasingly underrepresented with each passing year, backers of Proposition 13 proposed to apportion seats in the senate on a modified population basis that would allow a county to have no more than 10 senators, a clear concession to those worried about the potential power of Los Angeles. Furthermore, advocates of Proposition 13 argued that the current system discriminated against taxpayers of the 10 most populous counties, who contributed 81 percent of the sales taxes and 94 percent of the income taxes but elected only 10 of 40 representatives in the senate (Barclay 1951: 313–24).[1]

Proponents of the federal plan, on the other hand, seized upon labor's support of reapportionment, reminded voters that urbanites already controlled the assembly, and issued grim warnings about the dangers of allowing labor and big-city political bosses to control both houses of the legislature. As the state Chamber of Commerce declared, "this proposal is backed by Organized Labor, whose purpose is to gain control of our State Legislature. Don't let THEM get away with it. Keep the American form of government." Apparently the chamber felt no need, at the start of the Cold War, to explain further the danger posed by "THEM." Nor did the chamber recognize the irony in advocating a form of government as "American" which, in fact, left control of the state senate in the hands of a small minority.[2]

The 1948 initiative battle highlighted the extent to which many urban business interests supported malapportionment and rural political domination as a means of keeping taxes low, regulations to a minimum, and the labor unions politically weak. Although proponents of the federal plan persistently defended the need to protect vulnerable rural areas of the state, the campaign was funded almost entirely by urban business interests. In Los Angeles, for example, the Chamber of Commerce fought hard against the initial referendum in 1926, but had determined by the 1940s that the rural-dominated state senate better protected its interests than a more equitably apportioned legislature. Lobbying one representative from Los Angeles County was much easier, and no doubt less expensive, than trying to exert influence on the $14\frac{1}{2}$ senators the county elected after 1965. Furthermore, many urban businesses had extensive holdings in rural areas. In fact, as one observer of California politics noted at the height of the reapportionment debate of the 1960s, the farmers and businessmen were not only friends, but "often the same person." The agribusiness, railroad, oil, liquor, and racing industries especially fit this description (Boyarsky 1965: 12).

Consequently, each time California voters went to the polls to consider revising the state's federal plan, business and industrial groups, including many of those based in Los Angeles, warned that reapportionment would benefit organized labor and urban political machines. The situation led noted author Carey McWilliams to conclude, "This amazing spectacle of a people approving their own disfranchisement can only be explained by the control which the present system of representation gives to the dominant economic interests." For McWilliams, who was not naïve about the exercise of political power elsewhere, the severity of malapportionment in California bolstered his belief that the state did, in fact, constitute a great exception (McWilliams 1949: 212).

The 1948 campaign also foreshadowed the role that key Californians would play in the national reapportionment battles of the 1960s, most especially Earl Warren and the San Francisco political consulting firm of Whitaker & Baxter. As governor of California, Earl Warren expressed unqualified support for the state's federal plan, a fact that his opponents delighted in raising in the 1960s. Meanwhile, opponents of reapportionment in 1948 turned to Whitaker & Baxter to spearhead their efforts. The husband-and-wife team of Clem Whitaker and Leone Baxter made their initial mark on California politics in 1934 when they were hired to defeat Upton Sinclair's End Poverty in California (EPIC) campaign. In the late-1940s the pair made the jump to national politics when they were hired by the American Medical Association to defeat Harry Truman's plan for national health insurance. In between, they managed numerous campaigns and ballot initiatives in California, almost always on the winning side. In the late 1950s, Clem Whitaker and Leone Baxter turned over the reins of their business to Whitaker's son, Clem Jr., who borrowed heavily from the playbook created by his father and stepmother to turn back reapportionment initiatives in 1960 and 1962.[3]

Although Earl Warren stood with Whitaker & Baxter on the same side of the reapportionment debate in the late 1940s, he had moved in a starkly different direction by the 1960s. Ironically, Whitaker & Baxter had managed Warren's 1942 gubernatorial campaign. But while Whitaker & Baxter continued to manage the campaigns of those opposed to reapportionment, Earl Warren came to see the issue in starkly different terms as chief justice. Warren told one law clerk that as governor he considered California's plan a "sensible arrangement" from a political standpoint. But as chief justice, he recognized a constitutional rather than political mandate, and came to see that as governor he was "just wrong." In the 1960s, Warren's change of perspective ignited a backlash so severe that Whitaker & Baxter nearly succeeded in pushing through a call for a constitutional convention (Schwartz 1983: 504).

In the late 1940s and early 1950s, municipal officials and members of civic organizations throughout the United States began to agitate for reapportionment. No organization spent more time on reapportionment than the League of Women Voters. Chapters of the League in more than two dozen states studied the issues, highlighted the problems, and lobbied for change. State Leagues were especially active in Washington, Wisconsin, Maryland, Minnesota, Illinois, Oklahoma, and Tennessee. The clamor for reapportionment prompted President Eisenhower to appoint a Commission on Intergovernmental Relations in 1955. Not only did the commission single out the failure of state governments to provide adequate funds for slum clearance, urban renewal, low-income housing, and metropolitan transportation projects, but it also noted that this failure left urban officials no choice but to turn to the federal government for aid (Kestnbaum 1955: 227–8).

Soon thereafter, Senator John F. Kennedy began to prepare for his bid for the Presidency. Fully aware that urban voters would constitute an important share of the electorate in 1960, Kennedy condemned urban blight and decay as a clear consequence of urban underrepresentation. Borrowing language from muckraker Lincoln Steffens, Kennedy referred to malapportionment as "the shame of the states," and cited a litany of consequences: "overcrowded and hazardous schools, undermanned with underpaid teachers . . . slum housing, congested traffic, juvenile delinquency, overcrowded health and penal institutions and inadequate parking" (Kennedy 1958: 12).

As Kennedy recognized, identifying the problem was far easier than finding a solution. Defiant legislatures across the country simply refused to reapportion. Such intransigence flew in the face of state constitutional mandates to reapportion every 10 years (and in a few cases, every five years), and yet state courts repeatedly deferred to the legislatures and opted not to get involved. Meanwhile the federal courts heeded Felix Frankfurter's admonition to avoid the "political thicket" (*Colegrove vs. Green*, 328 U.S. 549 [1946]).

In 1959, the Tennessee legislature again refused to consider reapportionment, just as it had done since 1901. In response, representatives of Tennessee's largest cities filed suit in *Baker vs. Carr*. A three-judge federal court acknowledged the obvious inequality in Tennessee's apportionment scheme, but refused to accept jurisdiction. By the time *Baker vs. Carr* reached the Supreme Court of the United States, the city attorneys of Los Angeles, Dallas, Portland, Oregon, Minneapolis, and other municipalities had joined the case, clear evidence that urban residents throughout the United States shared a common complaint.[4]

In March 1962, the Supreme Court decided by a vote of 6–2 that the time had come to enter the "political thicket" and ruled that Tennessee's system of apportionment violated the Equal Protection Clause of the Fourteenth Amendment. The Court, however, declined to set a standard that states had to meet under the Equal Protection Clause, but instead limited its ruling to the question of jurisdiction. In short, *Baker* opened the doors of the federal courts to adjudicate apportionment disputes, but went no further.

In the immediate aftermath of *Baker vs. Carr*, litigants in more than three dozen states filed reapportionment suits in federal district courts. Fifteen of these disputes eventually made their way to the Supreme Court. Ultimately the justices chose to hear oral arguments in the six that originated in Alabama, Colorado, Delaware, Maryland, New York, and Virginia. The facts presented by each case differed to some degree, but all raised the question as to what standard was required by the Equal Protection Clause.[5]

Legal scholars have always emphasized the importance of *Baker vs. Carr* in constitutional terms, but the reaction to the Supreme Court's decisions of June 15, 1964 suggests that the sweeping nature of the state reapportionment decisions had a greater impact on the nation's political system. Chief Justice Earl Warren selected *Reynolds vs. Sims*, the Alabama case, to announce that the Equal Protection Clause required that all state legislative bodies be apportioned according to the principle of "one person, one vote." Warren wrote that, "the right to vote freely for the candidate of one's choice is of the essence of a democratic society, and any restrictions on that right strike at the heart of representative government. And the right of suffrage can be denied by a debasement or dilution of the weight of a citizen's vote just as effectively as by wholly prohibiting the free exercise of the franchise." Furthermore, added Warren in his most frequently quoted line, "legislators represent people not trees or acres. Legislators are elected by voters, not farms or cities or economic interests."[6]

Having established the "one person, one vote" standard in the Alabama case, the Court proceeded to overturn apportionment schemes in Maryland, Virginia, Delaware, New York, and Colorado. While eight members of the Court voted to overturn Alabama's system of apportionment (only John Marshall Harlan dissented in all of the cases), the Court's ruling in the Colorado case proved much more contentious. In 1962, not 1901 as had been the case in *Baker* and *Reynolds*, voters in every county in Colorado had passed a referendum that provided for a federal system. In addition, the voters rejected a separate ballot measure that specifically called for the apportionment of both houses on a population basis. Justices Potter Stewart and Tom Clark argued passionately in favor of Colorado's plan. The six-person majority, again led by the Chief Justice, recognized the differences between the situation in Colorado and that in Alabama, but concluded nevertheless that "an individual's constitutionally protected right to cast an equally weighted vote cannot be denied even by a vote of a majority of a State's electorate if the apportionment scheme adopted by the voters fails to measure up to the requirements of the Equal Protection Clause." Furthermore, added Warren, "A citizen's constitutional rights can hardly be infringed simply because a majority of the people chooses that it be." A week later the Court cited its decision in *Reynolds* to overturn apportionment schemes in nine additional states – Florida, Ohio, Illinois, Michigan, Idaho, Connecticut, Iowa, Oklahoma, and Washington. No region in the country was spared (Cortner 1972: 214–19, 232–6).[7]

The Court's rulings stunned observers. Solicitor General Archibald Cox had enthusiastically supported a challenge to the "invidious discrimination" that pervaded Alabama's apportionment scheme, but had never expected a ruling that unequivocally rejected a federal system at the state level. The *New York Times* remarked that the Court's rejection of the federal analogy was "the farthest reaching" decision "since *Marbury vs. Madison* established the power of judicial review in 1803." A *Times* editorial added that "when the history of the Court under Chief Justice Warren is written, these decisions may outweigh even the school integration decision of 1954 in importance" (Gormley 1997: 176–7; Cortner 1972: 235–6).

Reynolds vs. Sims produced a backlash unlike anything contemplated in the aftermath of *Baker vs. Carr*. Members of Congress introduced more than one hundred bills and resolutions aimed at overturning or modifying the Court's ruling. Senator Everett Dirksen of Illinois, the Republican minority leader, soon emerged as the leader of congressional opponents to the Court's rulings. Dirksen first supported a campaign to pass a constitutional amendment to remove apportionment disputes from the jurisdiction of the federal courts. When that proposal failed to generate much support, Dirksen offered an amendment to the Constitution that would have explicitly allowed a federal system at the state level, precisely the sort of arrangement that had existed in California since the 1920s.

Political and business leaders in California rushed to embrace Dirksen's proposals. State senator Edwin J. Regan, the powerful chairman of the Judiciary Committee, affirmed the soundness of California's system as one that worked "to the advantage of all," and emphasized that the state's electorate had repeatedly reaffirmed its support for a federal plan. In a clear attempt to define California's system as moderate and reasonable, Regan refused to attack the Supreme Court directly and, in fact, acknowledged that the Court had been forced to intervene by the abject failure of some states to reapportion either legislative body along the lines of population. But the Court went too far, he argued, in rejecting the federal analogy.[8]

Other proponents of California's system disputed assertions that the malapportioned state senate proved hostile to urban needs. One legislative staffer emphasized that, "the problems of cities have received close and sympathetic attention from the Senate." In particular, he argued that many state programs "recognized as among the best in the nation" – including those for social welfare, urban development, smog control, civil rights, and employment protections – had not only received support in the senate but had originated in that body.[9]

Given the political history of reapportionment in the state, it should have surprised no one when California's political and business leaders turned to Whitaker & Baxter to manage a response to the *Reynolds* decision. Beginning in the late summer and early fall of 1964, Whitaker & Baxter oversaw every aspect of a campaign to allow California to keep its federal plan. In March 1965, the firm announced the formation of the Citizens Committee for Balanced Legislative Representation. Chaired by James Mussatti, a former general manager of the California Chamber of Commerce, the Citizens Committee signed up members from across the state, who fanned out across the country in an effort to lobby members of Congress to pass a constitutional amendment. In an appeal to potential members and donors, Mussatti cited "the reapportionment issue as the gravest governmental crisis in the United States since the civil war."[10]

Such a campaign, of course, cost money, and Whitaker & Baxter knew just where to turn. In 1962, the firm had managed the opposition to Proposition 23, an initiative to reapportion the state senate. In that campaign, Whitaker & Baxter solicited $250,000, led by $25,000 each from Standard Oil of California and Pacific Gas & Electric. Between January and June 1965, Whitaker & Baxter raised an almost identical amount of money from a range of industrial, agricultural, manufacturing, and petroleum companies. Once again Standard of California and PG & E led the way, upping their investment to $30,000 each. As had been the case each time California voters weighed in on reapportionment, urban-based corporate interests – and not the rural residents supposedly most affected – proved most willing to open their wallets.[11]

While obtaining a majority of votes in the United States Senate, Everett Dirksen failed in 1964 and again in 1965 to muster the necessary two-thirds to send a constitutional amendment to the states for ratification. Before launching his third and final attempt, Dirksen hired Whitaker & Baxter to spearhead a national effort to provide support for his campaign. Dirksen commended California's Citizen Committee for the leading role its members had played up to that point, but announced that the time had come to disband operation in favor of a national organization.

Although Dirksen waited until January 1966 to announce the formation of the Committee for the Government of the People, he had spent months in consultation with Whitaker & Baxter, laying the groundwork and lining up financial resources for a viable campaign. Clem Whitaker, Jr., moved to Washington to guide the effort personally, meeting with Dirksen in his Senate office nightly to plot strategy. While supported generally by the American Farm Bureau Federation, the United States Chamber of Commerce, and the National Association of Manufacturers, among others, Whitaker & Baxter concentrated its efforts between September 1965 and January 1966 on procuring significant donations from major American corporations. Ultimately, hundreds of thousands of dollars, perhaps more than a million, was raised. DuPont and General Electric matched the earlier donations from Standard Oil of California and PG & E, contributing $30,000 each. Proctor & Gamble and Standard Oil of Indiana followed next with $25,000, while the Ford Motor Company and an anonymous donor added $20,000. After the official announcement of the formation of the Committee for the Government of the People, Whitaker & Baxter churned out almost daily press releases, announcing the support of various members of Congress or groups of prominent state officials.[12]

In April 1966, Everett Dirksen failed for the third and final time to push a constitutional amendment through the United States Senate. But rather than give up the campaign, Dirksen and his supporters intensified their efforts at the state level to exploit a little-known and still never-used clause in Article V of the US Constitution which allows the states to call a convention for the purpose of amending the Constitution. Whitaker & Baxter monitored the progress in every state, drafted a suggested document to ensure that all states worded their petitions in the same form, and contacted favorable individuals in states where passage remained a viable possibility. By the end of June 1967, 32 states had petitioned Congress for a convention (Yadlowsky1965).[13]

Despite the potentially historic significance of the campaign, it received relatively modest attention until May of 1969 when Iowa became the thirty-third state to petition for such a convention, just one state short of the required two-thirds. Soon thereafter, a congressional committee took notice and set out to determine how such a convention would be convened. Pundits and legal scholars debated whether a convention could be limited to the issue of apportionment or if, in fact, the entire United States Constitution would be up for discussion. In September 1969, however, Everett Dirksen died from cancer, depriving pro-convention advocates of a forceful leader. When the Wisconsin legislature declined later in the fall to provide a thirty-fourth petition, the campaign to call a convention effectively came to an end (Kyvig 1996: 370–9; 2002: 76–83).

Ultimately, time proved the ally of those who supported the Court's reapportionment decisions. By 1968, legislative action and court orders had reapportioned at least one branch of the legislature, and usually both, in 49 out of 50 states. As legal scholar Robert Dixon wrote at the time: "in the space of five years, reapportionment virtually remade the political map of America." And despite the most dire predictions, reapportionment proceeded with relative ease – perhaps not a surprise given that the decisions did affirm the individual rights of a majority of citizens (Cortner 1972: 253).

In California, a federal district court ruled in December 1964 that *Reynolds vs. Sims* left the legislature with no choice. The court ordered lawmakers to reapportion the state senate on a population basis, and to do so by July 1, 1965. The strongest proponents of California's federal plan, however, were not quite ready to concede defeat. Just weeks after the district court ruling, approximately 20 state senators met for two days to design both "battle" and "capitulation" plans. The group recognized the need to adhere to all court orders, but also expressed its determination "to exhaust all possible remedies to allow us to keep the bicameral legislative system as we have known it." The senators pledged to explore the possibility of appealing the court order, but if no such option existed, they promised to turn their energies to passing a constitutional amendment or calling a constitutional convention (Allen 1965: 46–7).

Consequently, reapportionment dominated the 1965 session of the legislature. Buoyed by what one observer referred to as "a frontier sense of optimism" for Everett Dirksen's proposals, opponents of a population-based reapportionment ensured that lawmakers failed to pass a bill by the court-imposed deadline. But when Dirksen's proposal failed for the second time in August 1965, the California Supreme Court stepped into the breach and ordered lawmakers to pass an acceptable reapportionment measure by the end of the year. Most importantly, the state court provided a series of specific mathematical guidelines that ensured districts would not deviate substantially from the average size. The court's guidelines essentially ended further resistance and the legislature quickly passed an acceptable bill. Los Angeles County gained an additional $13\frac{1}{2}$ senators, sharing one with Orange County. Political power shifted overnight to Southern California, although not necessarily with the consequences most feared by many participants (Dixon 1968: 374–8).

Had Everett Dirksen lived, he would have discovered that despite his failure to overturn the Court's "one person, one vote" standard, the subsequent transformation of political power did not pan out quite as anticipated. Throughout the 1940s and 1950s, support for reapportionment was commonly understood in terms of urban underrepresentation and rural/small-town overrepresentation. Opponents of reapportionment feared that big-city political machines would come to dominate state legislatures. But by the 1960s, the United States had become a suburban nation, a development largely ignored by the key players who litigated the reapportionment battles. Few observers at the time, in fact, were as quick to recognize the importance of the link between demographic change and reapportionment as was Karl Meyer. Writing in the *New Statesman* in the immediate aftermath of *Baker*, Meyer noted: "Time has given a fresh twist to the problem. It is not the starving urban masses who are cheated by electoral devices in the states. By and large, the chief injustice is to suburbia, where, if only half a dinner is eaten, it is for reasons of dieting" (Meyer 1962: 478).

The facts bore out Meyer's observations. As the 1960 census revealed, the vast majority of major American cities lost population between 1950 and 1960. Meanwhile, suburban populations in every major metropolitan area grew by extraordinary margins. In New York, the suburbs exploded by 75 percent, in Los Angeles by 83 percent, in Chicago by 71 percent, and in Detroit by nearly 80 percent (Boyd 1965: 294–8; Congressional Quarterly Service 1966: 38–41).[14]

The importance of such demographic change was not lost on William Boyd who, as an employee of the National Municipal League, had supported reapportionment as ardently as anyone in the nation. In the wake of the *Reynolds* decision, as opponents of reapportionment denounced the Court and warned of big-city domination, Boyd examined the results of the 1960 census. In a report entitled "Suburbia Takes Over," Boyd explained that "the suburbs and, in the long run, only the suburbs will gain in the upheaval resulting from reapportionment . . . Rather than being dominated by the big cities, as is commonly supposed, the new legislatures will see suburban representation increase the most in number . . . The suburbs," Boyd concluded, "own the future" (Boyd 1965: 294–8).

From the moment Earl Warren announced the Court's "one person, one vote" standard, political operatives, pundits, and journalists tried to figure out which party would benefit. According to *Newsweek*, Democrats appeared poised to make gains in about 20 states, especially in those where rural-based Republicans had been able to maintain control of both branches of the state legislature. Meanwhile, Republicans expected to see immediate gains in six southern states plus five more outside the South. But, as *US News & World Report* opined, "suburban populations have been found generally to be more 'conservative' and more likely to vote Republican than city populations." Not coincidentally, the Republican Party denounced the *Reynolds* decision in its 1964 platform, but before long the Republican National Committee recognized the possibility of significant gains in all regions of the country. It turned out that a lot of potential Republican votes resided in the suburbs.[15]

Ironically, reapportionment freed suburbanites from urban control just as effectively as it ended rural and small-town domination. Prior to reapportionment, urban and suburban populations were often lumped together into districts. As long as suburbanites remained outnumbered by urban residents within these districts, suburban legislators required the support of city political leaders and residents to win elections. But once apportioned their own seats in the legislature, newly elected suburban representatives found themselves in agreement with rural and small-town legislators just as often, if not more often, than with their urban neighbors. These representatives, like their constituents, had fled the core cities for a reason and felt no inclination to appropriate taxpayer funds for sewer construction, busing for urban schoolchildren, and other items on the municipal agenda (Kovach 1967: 26–32).

The political rise of the suburbs meant, of course, that cities throughout the United States never attained the help they so desperately needed. Tom Osborn, a Nashville lawyer involved in the *Baker* litigation, remarked, as urban centers broke out in violence in the mid-1960s, that the reapportionment decisions came too late to adequately address urban needs. Earl Warren concurred with Osborn's analysis, and went on to explain that the worst of the urban ills might have been avoided if urban residents had had adequate representation at the time that urban populations swelled – between World War I and World War II. In this regard, California once again found itself at the center of a national story. Quite simply, reapportionment came too late to prevent the eruption of violence in the Watts neighborhood of Los Angeles in August 1965; the very mention of Watts, of course, quickly became symbolic of America's urban crisis (Graham 1972).

In addition to a new demographic reality, the consequences of the Supreme Court's reapportionment decisions turned out differently than expected because the Court consciously chose to leave for another day the second half of what the *New York Times* referred to as the "twin evils of malapportionment and gerrymandering." Over time, of course, political operatives of both major parties have become increasingly successful at subverting the will of majorities without running foul of the Court's mandate in *Reynolds*. Nowhere have such operatives proven more effective than in California, where both parties have consistently signed off on apportionment bills that protect incumbents and ensure that congressional and legislative seats will remain safe. In the most recent elections, for example, only 3 out of 53 candidates for Congress won with less than 55 percent of the vote; only 4 out of 80 candidates for state assembly won with less than 55 percent of the vote; and only one of 20 contested state senate races was decided by less than 20 percentage points.[16]

More than 40 years ago, an analyst with the Library of Congress's Legislative Reference Service recognized the limits of the Court's reapportionment rulings and predicted prophetically that "we may be passing from the age of the grossly malapportioned district to that of the strangely gerrymandered one" (Norton 1964: 28). Thus far the Supreme Court has refused to enter the thicket of gerrymandering; to do so would require a decision as revolutionary and controversial as the reapportionment rulings of the 1960s.

NOTES

1   Full text of "Argument in Favor of Initiative Proposition No. 13 (1948)," California Ballot Propositions Database, University of California, Hastings Law Library, http://library.uchastings.edu/library/Research%20Databases/CA%20Ballot%20Measures/ca_ballot_measures_main.htm. This database includes a complete list of arguments in favor of and opposed to all propositions from 1911 to the present.

2   Full text of "Argument Against Initiative Proposition No. 13 (1948)," ibid.; "Proposition No. 13, Vote 'No,'" *California: Magazine of the Pacific* 38 (October 1948), p. 3 (quotation).

3   "Warren Stresses Legislative Role of Rural Counties," *The Sacramento Bee*, November 21, 1947, p. 13; "Warren Opposes Reapportionment," *Los Angeles Times*, October 30, 1948, p. 1; "Redistricting: A Warren View in '48," *US News & World Report* 57 (July 6, 1964), p. 34; Ross (1959); McWilliams (1951); Oral History with Clement Sherman Whitaker, Jr., pp. 99–102, State Government Oral History Program, California State Archives.

4   *Baker vs.Carr*, 369 U.S. 186 (1962).

5   In addition to the six suits that addressed malapportionment in the state legislatures, the Court also heard oral arguments in *Wesberry vs. Sanders* 376 US 1 (1964), a congressional reapportionment case from Georgia. In February 1964, the Court provided a hint as to where it was headed in the state cases when it ruled in *Wesberry* that congressional districts must be drawn according to the standard of population equality.

6   *Reynolds vs. Sims*, 377 US 555 (1964), quotations at pp. 562–3.

7   *Lucas vs. Colorado General Assembly*, 377 US 713 (1964), quotations at pp. 736–7. *New York Times* reporter Anthony Lewis, who covered the Court at the time of the reapportionment rulings, has argued persuasively that the Court would have lacked the votes for so sweeping a standard as "one person,

one vote" if not for the appointment of two new justices between the decisions in *Baker* and *Reynolds*. The six-man majority in *Lucas vs. Colorado* included Byron White and Arthur Goldberg, who were appointed in 1962 to replace Charles Whittaker and Felix Frankfurter. See Anthony Lewis oral history interview with Nicholas Katzenbach, Washington, DC, November 16, 1964, pp. 78–80, John F. Kennedy Library.

8   Draft of letter from Regan to *Saturday Evening Post*, September 22, 1964, Box 98, Whitaker & Baxter Papers, California State Archives, Sacramento. The Whitaker & Baxter Papers, which constitute the single most important archival source consulted in connection with this essay, is a massive collection that contains a wealth of material pertaining to almost every important statewide election and ballot initiative in California from the 1930s to the 1960s. The collection is difficult to navigate as it has never been fully processed and has no finding aid. Nevertheless, every student of twentieth-century California politics ought to be aware of its availability.

9   Harold Winkler, Special Research Unit Report No. 2, undated, Box 98, Whitaker & Baxter Papers.

10   Press release, March 8, 1965, Box 96, Whitaker & Baxter Papers.

11   A complete list of donations in support of and in opposition to Proposition 23 in 1962 is located in Whitaker & Baxter, "Report on No. 23," pp. 11–20, Senator Randolph Collier Papers, LP 229: 334, California State Archives. Figures from the first six months of 1965 are discussed in a letter from William F. Bramstedt, Vice President of Standard Oil of California, to Ralph B. Johnson, November 4, 1965, Box 99, folder "Contributions," Whitaker & Baxter Papers. See also McWilliams (1949: 212), for an analysis of the nearly $300,000 spent in opposition to Proposition 13 in 1948.

12   Oral History with Clem Whitaker, Jr., pp. 101–15; Whitaker & Baxter, "Report to the Advisory Committee, Committee for the Government of the People," May 6, 1966, Everett McKinley Dirksen Working Papers, folder 2289, Dirksen Congressional Center, Pekin, Illinois.

13   See also "Congress: Three-Time Loser," *Newsweek* (May 2, 1966), pp. 19–20.

14   See also "One Person, One Vote – Who Wins, Who Loses," *US News & World Report*, August 23, 1965, pp. 42–4.

15   Sweeping Decision," *Newsweek* 63 (June 29, 1964), pp. 22, 25; "After Redistricting Decision," *US News & World Report* 57 (July 6, 1964), pp. 34–6; Congressional Quarterly Service (1966: 43–4); "The 1964 Platform of Republican National Convention," July 22, 1964.

16   "The Governor's Vetoes," *The New York Times*, May 29, 1965, p. 26; *Los Angeles Times*, November 9, 2006, pp. B5 & B6.

REFERENCES

Allen, Don A. 1965. *Legislative Sourcebook: The California Legislature and Reapportionment, 1849–1965*. Sacramento: Assembly of the State of California.
Baker vs. Carr, 369 US 186 (1962).

Barclay, Thomas S. 1951. "The Reapportionment Struggle in California in 1948," *Western Political Quarterly* 4 (June 1951): 313–24.

Boyarsky, Bill. 1965. "Why They Fight Against Reapportionment." *Frontier* 16 (March): 11–13.

Boyd, William J. D. 1965. "Suburbia Takes Over," *National Civic Review* (June): 294–8.

Colegrove vs. Green, 328 US 549 (1946).

"Congress: Three-Time Loser," *Newsweek* (May 2, 1966): 19–20.

Congressional Quarterly Service. 1966. "Background Report: Representation and Apportionment." Washington, DC: Congressional Quarterly.

Cortner, Richard C. 1972. *The Apportionment Cases*. New York: W. W. Norton.

Dixon, Robert G. 1968. *Democratic Representation: Reapportionment in Law and Politics*. New York: Oxford University Press.

Gormley, Ken. 1997. *Archibald Cox: Conscience of a Nation*. Reading, MA: Addison-Wesley.

Graham, Gene. 1972. *One Man, One Vote: Baker vs. Carr and the American Levelers*. Boston, MA: Little, Brown.

Kennedy, John F. 1958. "The Shame of the States," *New York Times Magazine*, May 18: 12, 37, 38, 40.

Kestnbaum, Meyer, chairman. 1955. *The Commission on Intergovernmental Relations: A Report to the President for Transmittal to the Congress*. Washington, DC: Governmental Printing Office.

Kovach, Bill. 1967. "Some Lessons of Reapportionment," *The Reporter* 37 (September 21): 26–32.

Kyvig, David E. 1996. *Explicit and Authentic Acts: Amending the US Constitution, 1776–1995*. Lawrence: University Press of Kansas.

Kyvig, David E. 2002. "Everett Dirksen's Constitutional Crusades," *Journal of the Illinois State Historical Society* 95 (Spring): 68–85.

Lucas vs. Colorado General Assembly, 377 US 713 (1964).

McKay, Robert B. 1965. *Reapportionment: The Law and Politics of Equal Representation*. New York: Twentieth Century Fund.

McWilliams, Carey. 1949. *California: The Great Exception*. New York: A. A. Wyn.

McWilliams, Carey. 1951. "Government by Whitaker and Baxter," *The Nation* 172 (April 14): 346–8; (April 21): 366–9; (May 5): 418–21.

Meyer, Karl E. 1962. "Shame of the States," *New Statesmen* 63 (April 6): 478.

Norton, Bruce F. 1964. "Recent Supreme Court Decisions on Apportionment: Their Political Impact." Washington, DC: Library of Congress, Legislative Reference Service.

"One Person, One Vote – Who Wins, Who Loses," *US News & World Report* (August 23, 1965): 42–4.

"Proposition No. 13, Vote 'No'," *California: Magazine of the Pacific* 38 (October 1948): 3.

Reynolds vs. Sims, 377 US 533 (1964).

Ross, Irwin. 1959. "The Supersalesmen of California Politics: Whitaker and Baxter," *Harper's* 219 (July): 55–61.

Schwartz, Bernard. 1983. *Super Chief: Earl Warren and His Supreme Court – A Judicial Biography.* New York: New York University Press.

Warren, Earl. 2001. *The Memoirs of Chief Justice Earl Warren.* Lanham, MD: Madison Books. (Originally published by Doubleday in 1977.)

Wellman, Charles A. 1962. *Report of the State of California: Study Commission on Senate Apportionment.* Sacramento: Senate of the State of California.

Whitaker, Clement Sherman, Jr. (1988) "Oral History with Clement Sherman Whitaker, Jr." State Government Oral History Program, California State Archives, Sacramento.

Yadlowsky, Elizabeth. 1965. "State Petitions and Memorials to Congress." Revised and updated by Johnny Killian, February 1, 1968. Washington, DC: Library of Congress, Legislative Reference Bureau.

FURTHER READING

Baker, Gordon E. 1966. *The Reapportionment Revolution: Representation, Political Power, and the Supreme Court.* New York: Random House.

Bushnell, Eleanore, ed. 1970. *Impact of Reapportionment on the Thirteen Western States.* Salt Lake City: University of Utah Press.

Cain, Bruce E. 1984. *The Reapportionment Puzzle.* Berkeley: University of California Press.

Cox, Archibald. 1987. *The Court and the Constitution.* Boston, MA: Houghton Mifflin.

Cox, Gary W. and Jonathan N. Katz. 2002. *Elbridge Gerry's Salamander: The Electoral Consequences of the Reapportionment Revolution.* New York and Cambridge, UK: Cambridge University Press.

Cray, Ed. 1997. *Chief Justice: A Biography of Earl Warren.* New York: Simon & Schuster.

Jacobs, John. 1995. *A Rage for Justice: The Passion and Politics of Phillip Burton.* Berkeley: University of California Press.

Mitchell, Greg. 1992. *The Campaign of the Century: Upton Sinclair's Race for Governor of California and the Birth of Media Politics.* New York: Random House.

Navasky, Victor S. 1971. *Kennedy Justice.* New York: Atheneum.

Powe, Lucas A., Jr. 2000. *The Warren Court and American Politics.* Cambridge, MA: Harvard University Press.

Rarick, Ethan. 2005. *California Rising: The Life and Times of Pat Brown.* Berkeley: University of California Press.

White, G. Edward. 1982. *Earl Warren: A Public Life.* New York: Oxford University Press.

Chapter Twenty-three

UNDER THE WARM CALIFORNIA SUN: YOUTH CULTURE IN THE POSTWAR DECADES

Kirse Granat May

California's influence on popular culture has always been dynamic, tinged with nostalgia for a romanticized past as well as offering glimpses into a cutting-edge future. The Golden State is the setting for the big-screen apocalypse as well as for the beach party. Alongside nightmarish visions runs a sunnier mythology, seen most keenly in the period immediately following World War II. California emerged as a political, cultural, and demographic force, while selective images of its youth – white, suburban, middle class – became part of the national lexicon, a key part of the state's identity, and by extension, the nation's character. These iconic images profoundly influenced the baby boom generation coming of age at the height of mainstream media's power. These appealing youthful visions, ones that refracted reality and reflected cultural needs, turned a profit for magazine editors, theme park dreamers, record producers, television writers, and drive-in movie studios. More troubling California trends emerged in the late 1960s along well-worn paths of popular culture exploitation. Throughout the twists and turns of the postwar period, images of California's youth attracted audiences, finding resonance in surprising places and lasting ways.

In the late nineteenth century migrants and hopeful boosters constructed powerful mythologies of identity. Many scholarly studies demonstrate the ideological power of a manipulated past and a skewed view of California's history. This myth making is often in conflict with California's more complicated realities: the decimation of native peoples, the often nightmarish conditions of the Gold Rush, the ethnic and racial difficulties of settlement, the political infighting between north and south, virulent red scares, the plight of the Okies, and so on (Starr 1973; Gregory 1989; Deverell 2004; Hackel 2005). For millions of migrants, California was a place of new beginnings, with an accompanying lack of introspection or attention to past or current problems. From the construction of meaning for the newly arrived, the state gradually became a powerful symbol for outsiders as well. "California" was often employed more as an idea and a dream than an actual location.[1]

World War II's influx of people, industry, and dollars dwarfed all other eras. There is broad debate surrounding the extent and impact of World War II on the state's development – whether the influx of migrants and federal money fostered new paths or simply sped up existing trends (Lotchin 1992). In either case, the explosion of mass media, combined with California's phenomenal postwar growth, pushed the state front and center in the national consciousness. California was a place where many postwar suburban dreams came true, and offered a selective peek into America's rosy future. Magazine profilers trekked along with the moving vans. In 1945, *Life* magazine reported on the emerging lifestyle, calling it the "California way of life" and predicting that it "may in time radically influence the pattern of life in America as a whole" (*Life* 1945, pp. 105–16). This mythology resonated in a nation ready to leave behind war and the Depression and embrace the suburban ideal.

At the center of this picture postcard were California's children, growing up amidst promise and plenty, depicted, with few exceptions, as members of a sunny, prosperous, and promising generation. Before World War II, California's median age was the highest of all the states, four years older than the country as a whole (Vance 1987). The youthquake demographically transformed the state, necessitating the construction of schools, the expansion of the university system, and an unprecedented surge in suburban housing. Magazine pronouncements and real-estate advertising rarely reflected the conflicts and challenges that accompanied this building of a new society, finding more profits in the appeal of America's tomorrowland. There was money to be made by real-estate developers in the construction of suburbs. Equally lucrative and influential was mainstream marketing of the California suburban lifestyle. California's youth stood at the heart of these portrayals, a reflection of that sunny outlook and glorious self-promotion. For millions, California had always been a place of dreams, and in the postwar period, these dreams became the dreams of youth.

Popular culture reflected the simplicity and exclusivity of that dream, tapping into imagery that had already enchanted millions. California was present at the creation of modern popular culture, becoming the home of the film industry soon after its emergence, and a key player in television, fashion, and music by the mid-1960s. This geographic proximity intensified the Golden State's influence, and images of California youth were easily available and exploitable. Disneyland, the Mouseketeers, surfing and Gidget, the music of the Beach boys, and Beach Party movies all focused on a very specific model of California living, conjuring up suburban landscapes under sun-kissed skies. There was an easy gloss and an evasion of many ethnic, racial, and economic realities beyond the freeway exits of the suburbs or the beach, in keeping with California's earlier "whitewashed" boosterism. National and worldwide audiences absorbed this "fun in the sun" imagery, beamed particularly from Southern California, with little sense of the state's regional differences or more complicated past. Yet in many ways, the popular image did reflect a certain authenticity, as suburbanization patterns and freeways in California (as elsewhere in the nation) circumvented discussions of race and class.

Postwar social and technological changes, the advent of television, and the takeover of mass media by the youth market made popular culture more ubiquitous than ever before. The emergence of a specifically marketed youth culture meant that baby boomers around the nation shared collective experiences more than any other previous generation. Many of these communal tales originated in the Golden State, helping American youth vicariously experience a California childhood whether they lived in the state or not. The postwar explosion in leisure time as well as an increase in pocketbook power marked this generation as a breed apart. As the new youth market emerged, young baby boomers were trained to look towards California for their entertainment imaginings.

Walt Disney was among the first to see the potential of the new baby boom demographic, taking advantage of several postwar developments to become a multifaceted powerhouse in the entertainment industry. Examined from almost every angle, there exists a wide-ranging literature about Walt Disney and his societal, architectural, historical, and cultural influence on decades of popular culture (Gabler 2006). Somewhat less scrutinized is his choice of California as the location of Disneyland and the hometown of his carefully selected Mouseketeers. The iconic power of California played a large part in Disney's postwar resurgence. Disney had found success in film animation beginning in the 1930s, but his studio faced economic hardships in the 1940s and early 1950s. Disney's ambitious idea was the creation of a new type of amusement park that would appeal to baby boom families and visitors to California. Disney chose the building site based on freeway construction projections, and gambled on the emergence of a new medium to realize his dream.

Disneyland was literally created on television, financed with television dollars, and advertised to potential visitors on the small screen. The *Disneyland* program premiered in the fall of 1954, with episodes that mirrored the themed lands under construction. Several installments focused on the engineering progress of Disneyland, the park. Millions watched the drama of its creation on television, becoming part of the process while dreaming of their future vacation. In July 1955, Disneyland opened in Anaheim with a live coast-to-coast television broadcast, a playground that made real the magic of California. By the end of the 1950s, Disneyland was the biggest tourist draw in the western United States, an icon intrinsically part of California, and a destination on every child's wish list.

The same year of Disneyland's debut, Disney produced a new television show that made California kids television stars. *The Mickey Mouse Club* was specifically designed for a new type of audience, featuring kids as entertainers rather than adults to amuse children. For the Mouseketeers, Disney drew almost exclusively from certain types of California's youngsters. He uniformed his Mouseketeers and circumscribed their conduct both on and off the set, wanting ordinary and unpretentious youngsters for his program. Presented as role models and by implication examples of young California, millions sought to emulate and join the club, buying mouse-eared hats and tuning in every weekday afternoon. Annette Funicello was the most famous member of the troupe, parlaying her Disney fame into merchandise, a book series, and a movie and music career. Watching television was now a generationally defined experience, a club to join with merchandise to buy. Combined with the power of Disneyland – the television show and the theme park – *The Mickey Mouse Club* gave California a mythic power in the hearts, minds, and pocketbooks of baby boom families.

Disney created icons for a national audience intrinsically linked to images of life in California. Close by in Hollywood, producers and moviemakers quickly realized the ease and power of capitalizing on their location, creating their own icons of California youth and exploiting the beach. Early 1950s films had mirrored the concerns of an adult nation obsessed with juvenile delinquency. As the 1950s progressed and the baby boomers aged, youth-marketed films changed course, portraying more innocent stories to the drive-in crowd. Hollywood film studios employed visions of California living both to appeal to baby boom audiences and compete with the new medium of television. The troubled teens of Los Angeles featured in *Rebel without a Cause* gave way to the neighboring beach-bum surfers of Santa Monica Beach in *Gidget*.

"Gidget" was born when the daughter of a Hollywood screenwriter began surfing in Malibu, learning to ride the waves and coming home with tales of a new lifestyle and language. Frederick Kohner turned his daughter's summertime experiences into a best-selling novel in 1957, which was then optioned by Columbia Pictures. The 1959 film offered a fun and innocent coming-of-age tale, set in the mildly rebellious world of surfing, and was followed by two sequels. For millions of moviegoers, *Gidget* was their first introduction to the captivating world of surfing and the beach. In the wake of *Gidget*'s success, surfing traveled far beyond its obvious borders. National magazines highlighted the alluring features of the sport and its participants. *Gidget*'s role in popularizing surfing demonstrated the remarkable ability of mass media outlets to subsume organic cultural movements, smoothing out the rough edges and injecting them into the mainstream. Surfing's appeal even to those in the vast landlocked middle was a testament to the power of images of California living, as well as the ability of mass media to market a lifestyle. Not surprisingly, many dedicated surfers despised *Gidget*.

Surfing's growing popularity was also tied to a new musical brand. Surf music sang the sport's praises, creating a soundtrack that spanned the globe. The geographical specificity, songs about California, sung by Californians, yet appealing far beyond those boundaries, was a unique phenomenon. The songs found eager listeners far from the West Coast, boomers ready to embrace surf music and the images it conjured. The surf sound began as instrumental guitar music, imitating the sound of the waves. The Beach Boys added lyrics that glorified the heralded lifestyle of young California. Despite the Beach Boys' marginal surfing experience, the record company marketed the band as clean-cut California surfers. Songs like "Surfin' USA" gave radio listeners a tutorial in California hot spots and surfing lingo. The Beach Boys expanded their repertoire to include odes to the automobile, a celebration especially suited to the new freeways and automobile culture of California. Songs such as "409," "Little Deuce Couple," "Fun, Fun, Fun," and "I Get Around" combined car specifications with rock and roll, racing up the Billboard charts. So strong was the pull of California's magnet that groups far away from the state recorded tributes to its appeal. In 1964 the Rivieras, a boy band from Indiana, sang of a desire to join those living under the "California Sun" (Hoskyns 1996).

The appeal of surf culture soon crossed into film and turned the California beach into a drive-in star. The *Beach Party* films, beginning in 1963 and ending in 1966, combined elements of the surf sound, fashion trends, and popularized ideas about California youth. The studio American International Pictures (AIP) made movies that were self-conscious and calculated in their presentation of good, clean fun, casting former Mouseketeer Annette as their female lead, and moving Philadelphia crooner Frankie Avalon to the Golden State. Regardless of cast, the California beach was always the real star. The *Beach Party* exploitation movies and their imitators represented the apex of this certain brand of California dreaming – the last party celebrating California teens and their leisure time.

In the mid-1960s, challenges surfaced as the rougher edges of California's youth culture, those groups left out of the mass-mediated picture, began to show. Opposition emerged not from Hollywood movie lots or recording studios, but from communities pointedly left out of the cultural picture. Real world events confronted the mythology of suburbs, cars, and beaches, jarring examples of the different types of California youth culture uncelebrated and initially not easily commodified. The extreme national confusion and fear surrounding both student uprisings at Berkeley

and racial unrest in Watts reveal how powerful and pervasive earlier images
of life in California had become.

California's public education, particularly the University of California
(UC) system, was lauded as a postwar marvel, with Berkeley as its most
prestigious campus. Then as now, the Berkeley Free Speech Movement is
recognized as a key event of the 1960s, with historical debate continuing
to surround the origins, consequences, and character of the movement.
Interestingly, campus protest emerged as a national issue in 1964, the first
year that baby boomers entered college. The disconnect between images
of youth culture in the state and the actual free speech storm on campus
was summed up by *Life* magazine's December 1964 story on the crisis:
"Panty Raids? No! Tough Campus Revolt" (*Life* 1965, pp. 46A–46B).
Trouble on campus continued throughout the academic year, particularly
surprising to a nation accustomed to tales of golden youth. The deluge of
contemporary media attention was partly the result of its location – the
revolt happened on the flagship campus of America's flagship state.

Watts was another community not reflected in popular culture visions
of life in the state. Many Americans believed the idea that Los Angeles,
unlike other American cities in the north and south, was free of racial tensions. Freeways and suburbs obscured neighborhoods like Watts. The
frustration of living amidst the California dream while being cut off from
its possibilities helped create an explosive situation. Those who participated
in the August 1965 riot were marked by their youth (Sears & McConahay
1973). While youthful, these rioters did not share the class or racial identification of the heralded baby boomers. The racial rioting sent a troubled
message to Californians, as well as to the nation that looked to Los Angeles
as an example. Watts emerged as a national byword, a message out of mass
media's control and an assertion of California realities. This was not the
Southern California of Disneyland, Hollywood, or the beach. Instead, it
was an urban California created by residential segregation, unemployment,
and police discrimination (Davis 1990).

The Watts riot, together with the protests at UC Berkeley, tested earlier
images of California youth culture and the nation's ideas of what California
represented. Into these perilous times emerged a politician who promised
not only a return to California's greatness, but a crackdown on California's
youth. Those concerned about the shifting environment found a champion
in former actor Ronald Reagan. Despite his lack of political experience,
Reagan entered the 1966 governor's race, partly fueled by the hostile
response of the California electorate to challengers of the golden dream.
Reagan used "Berkeley" as a codeword for all that was threatening, tapping
into widespread fears about California youth and their political and cultural
activities. On the campaign trail, Reagan utilized his own brand of youth
imagery, outfitting white, blonde-haired "Reagan girls" with beanies and

modest uniforms to appear on stage at rallies. Their look and conduct was closely monitored by the campaign, a conscious response to the growing counterculture movement and a purposeful message to voters that matched Reagan's campaign diatribes.

Recently, historians have focused on this turning-point election of 1966 as the genesis of a rightward political turn on a national scale. Lisa McGirr (2001), Matthew Dallek (2000), and Kurt Schuparra (1998) all point to the Reagan/Brown gubernatorial race as a key to understanding postwar conservative political culture. At the heart of much of the political rhetoric were images of California's youth and problems of Californian identity. While the late 1960s offered many cultural examples of rebellious youth, it was the backlash against those movements that proved equally powerful electorally, perhaps more so. Reagan's overwhelming gubernatorial victory in 1966 represented the power of his message, and demonstrated that while alternative voices of protest inspired media headlines, reactionary rhetoric could be more powerful at the ballot box. Reagan gave the growing youth counterculture in California a reverse political power, campaigning with electoral success against both the real and imagined influences of troubled, angry youth.

The varied counterculture movement of the late 1960s was an international event, but one with a truly California flavor. Visions of California's hippies quickly entered the national consciousness, borrowing some of its flavor from the previous decade's Beatnik phenomenon. News coverage highlighted the more salacious details, editorializing picture choices and sensationalizing content. This was partly an attempt to marginalize the growing subculture as well as sell newspapers and magazines. It also served to school new adherents in the uniform and attitudes of the cause: long hair, beads, tie-dyed clothes. This give and take between the news media and the growing counterculture helped create the images that were widely imitated and largely Californian, although the vast majority of young Californians did not embrace the hippie lifestyle. The counterculture, as its name implies, stood in stark contrast to the postwar suburban materialism widely celebrated in images of California living. Yet the media borrowed one key element of these earlier portrayals, focusing almost exclusively on disaffected youth from the white middle class.

Mass media outlets in Hollywood reacted to the sea change, quickly marching in step with the counterculture's commercial possibilities. What started out as partly an authentic movement quickly became commodified – a look available for purchase and a pose to help sell a product. Hippies lent themselves to imagery, easily categorized and recognizable. Highlighting the fashions and attitude co-opted the more radical nature of the counterculture challenge. This new product traveled the clichéd path of popularized California fads. Just as surfing traveled from an exclusive sport practiced by a few to a worldwide phenomenon, the hippie image was quickly seized upon by mainstream popular culture.

Like surfing, the counterculture arrived on the national scene with its own soundtrack. San Francisco usurped the traditional cultural power of Los Angeles, becoming the new headquarters of the counterculture. In that city music born from the convergence of folk and rock and roll found its home (Unterberger 2003). The songs celebrated the new lifestyle, and the musicians themselves seemed to embody the new young California ethos. The 1967 Monterey Pop Festival was the first public venue to celebrate the new sound. The concert featured such California-based artists as the Byrds, Jefferson Airplane, the Mamas and the Papas, and Buffalo Springfield. The Beach Boys did not attend. Jimi Hendrix set his guitar on fire at the festival proclaiming, "Now we'll never have to listen to surf music again" (Wise 1994: 111). A new era of California music had begun. Radio airwaves broadcast hymns to California living, but artists were singing very different tunes than the falsetto harmonies of the Beach Boys. The Mamas and the Papas' "California Dreamin'," a hit in 1966, was a tale of homesickness and a tribute to the warmth of Los Angeles. Scott MacKenzie's 1967 hit "San Francisco (Be Sure to Wear Flowers in Your Hair)" promised peace and love to the city's newcomers.

On the heels of the Monterey Pop Festival, *Time* magazine put "The Hippies: Philosophy of a Subculture" on its July 1967 cover. The tone of the article was largely sympathetic to the ideas and goals of the counterculture. Focusing on the Haight-Ashbury district, the article indicated that a key part of its appeal was voyeuristic; "Rubberneckers are now as much a part of the Hashbury scene as are the hippies" (*Time* 1967). The Bay Area became a new kind of California magnet to those wanting to join the revolution and others just wanting to take a peek.

As the 1960s progressed, California still seemed to represent the future, but a more sobering and worrisome kind to many Americans. A resurgent concern about juvenile delinquency and the growing drug culture replaced the celebratory representations of California's youth. Hippies encapsulated mainstream America's worst fears about the baby boom. Newscast profiles sensationalized the emergent problems of the counterculture, becoming less tolerant of its negative aspects. In 1967, CBS aired a news special curiously entitled "The Hippie Temptation." Hosted by Harry Reasoner, the program featured the denizens of Haight-Ashbury and appearances by the Grateful Dead, highlighting the pervasive drug use and pleasure-seeking lifestyle of its residents. Intense media attention combined with the siren call of the music and drug scene drew youth from around the country to join the ranks. The Haight gradually became more like the nightmare of CBS news reports, plagued by public health concerns, problems of poverty and homelessness, and the repercussions of a widespread drug culture.

While news agencies expressed dismay, television fiction producers used the new California icons in an attempt to attract younger viewers. *The Mod Squad* debuted in 1968, featuring three young people recruited by the police to fight crime: a blonde hippie, an African American veteran of the Watts riot, and a rich boy from Beverly Hills. The show ran successfully for five years. Hippies made other appearances on the small screen as well, as TV networks and producers adopted some of the counterculture poses to appeal to the baby boomer audience. For many viewers, the television world was their only connection to hippie slang, dress, and lifestyle (Bodroghkozy 2001).

The faddish nature of popular culture meant the hippie heyday, both in real life and in media imagery, was short-lived. In the wake of its challenge, however, images of California youth failed to return to a monolithic presentation. Since the 1960s, Californians have faced an identity crisis. No longer simply celebrated as a baby boom paradise, the state has become in many ways a cautionary tale for the rest of the nation – a tale about the perils of suburban sprawl, multiculturalism, and immigration. Despite the complexity added to its glossy image, American youth culture is still in many ways defined by a California mindset. Throughout the rest of the twentieth century, the state continued to be the birthplace of influential and wide-ranging youth culture movements, marking some continuity with the postwar period.

The popularity of California-born or -influenced sports is one such example. Skateboarding began as an alternative to surfing, a pastime that was the next best thing to riding real waves. Nearly 50 million skateboards were sold in the 1960s, due to the new craze dubbed "Sidewalk Surfin'" by the California duo Jan and Dean (Blair 1985). Skateboarding was re-energized in the 1970s by new tricks, new wheels, and new venues to ride. Before the explosion of skate parks and sanctioned skating areas, the sport projected an extreme rebelliousness. It was a dangerous, out-of-bounds pastime, skirting vandalism and urban destruction in order to skate. Today skateboarding is a multi-million dollar industry, which, like surfing, allows one to sport the lifestyle without jumping on a board. Snowboarding emerged in a similar fashion, taking elements of surfing and skateboarding to the slopes. California again led the way: the United States Amateur Snowboarding Association held its first national championship in Snow Valley, California in 1990.

California-based clothiers uniform the world's surfers, skateboarders, and snowboarders in the lucrative trifecta of the "surf, skate, snow" market. Brands such as Quiksilver, Volcom, and DC Shoes, among others, market clothing, shoes, and accessories, interconnecting the three sports to produce styles of clothing that grow beyond the practices of the sports themselves. As the brand Quiksilver explains on its website, their product is geared towards "young-minded people" that enjoy "brands that represent a casual lifestyle driven from a boardriding heritage" (Quiksilver 2006). The image is more important than the actual ride on a board, and therefore able to travel the globe. California remains the nucleus, the place where these and other trends happen first.

The rise of the West Coast rap/hip-hop scene was the first new musical genre since the 1970s to come out of California and capture the national imagination. Like the birth of the San Francisco sound, "gangsta" rap focused attention on a new type of counterculture. New York City was the primary birthplace of hip-hop, but in the late 1980s a new California strain emerged. NWA's 1988 album, *Straight Outta Compton*, proclaimed their South Central Los Angeles neighborhood as key to their identity and a direct challenge to East Coast superiority. The album generated controversy across the political spectrum with shockingly violent and profane lyrics, providing a window into the tensions within less celebrated California communities. Interestingly, the appeal of this image grew beyond its natural borders to those not part of the urban neighborhoods celebrated by the music. The music enjoyed a curious embrace by listeners entranced by the message and style, particularly white suburbanites miles of cultural distance from neighborhoods like Compton (Quinn 2004).

Although West Coast rap cinematically glamorized debauchery, chauvinism, and violence, it did recognize California's diversity. In the real world, white California youth are a minority, and a growing Hispanic population will soon become the dominant demographic force of the region. These changes may help bring about a recapturing of the Hispanic influence and identity that was lost in the whitewashing of the twentieth century. Just as California historiography has addressed the diversity inherent in the California story, perhaps future popular culture images might more accurately reflect the true face of California's youth.

If recent television dramas that use the California setting are any example, however, popular culture may remain wedded to enduring postwar imagery of white, middle-class, leisure-minded youth for some time to come. Recent incarnations of "California youth" on the small screen are much like the 1950s and 1960s counterparts, harking back to the Gidget and Beach Boy era. Mainstream television has found easy success and syndication with these portrayals. *Baywatch*, set in the world of greater Los Angeles lifeguards, was the most universal example of this trend. It premiered in 1989, and after moving to syndication became the most popular show in the entire world, demonstrating not only the limitless appeal of attractive women in swimsuits, but also the magic of California-based stories and the enduring appeal of the beach. The 1990s hit *Beverly Hills 90210* dramatized beautiful young people with dramatic adolescent traumas, all the while exploiting the iconic power of their California location. In the fantastic world of *Buffy the Vampire Slayer*, young demon-fighters were all the more compelling as they fought the darkness in the world of Sunnydale, California. More recently, *The O.C.* (short for Orange County), dramatized the travails of the young, wealthy, and fashionable. Its success inspired MTV to launch a reality series called *Laguna Beach: The Real Orange County*. Each season of the program shadows juniors and seniors at an actual coastal California high school, dramatizing their shopping and dating adventures.

Baby boomers grew up in a world inundated with images of life in California, an idealized and exclusionary version of fun in the sun enjoyed by the white middle class.

As the 1966 governor's race demonstrated, the worldview that popular culture helps mold can have political repercussions, shaping myth and memory. This vision has real-life consequences for today's Californians, as the state tries to define itself anew. California has been tremendously transformed in the last four decades – like the nation but, as always, more so, creating a society far different than that of the immediate postwar period. California was largely a land of newcomers, forming its cultural identity in those years after World War II based largely on the dreams of white, middle-class suburbia. That identity creates dissonance with the reality of now, as immigration has altered the familiar face of California. As Peter Schrag (2006) has recently argued, this disconnect between a middle-class electorate and the realities of California's rapidly changing demographics causes real-world difficulties in providing government and social services. Voters are often unwilling to support programs or people that do not correspond with their preconceived ideas of what their fellow citizens require or what they should look like. Californians currently confront similar challenges of identity and growth that faced earlier eras. It remains to be seen how the various mythologies and histories of California will play themselves out, and to what extent popular culture will play a role.

California once again finds itself led by a creature of Hollywood, promising to restore the state's greatness. Governor Arnold Schwarzenegger appeals to positive memories of the postwar era, evoking nostalgia for the state's role as the nation's cheerleader. Despite the sunny rhetoric, in a reversal of the postwar trend, the 2000 census figures reveal that more Americans, many of them baby boomers, have left California than have moved in from other states. The population continues to climb, fueled by births and foreign immigration. A recent *New York Times* article noted that baby boomers consciously evade the reality of California, many expressing the idea that as California marches into a transformed future, as one interviewee explained, "I'm glad I'm not going to be here" (Murphy 2005). California remains the same only in the rear-view mirror, colored by nostalgia for a golden era of golden youth.

Popular culture became synonymous with youth culture after World War II, and since that time, California has been at the forefront of tastes and trends, both creating and reflecting the national mood. Today, there is less of a shared culture than was enjoyed by the baby boom generation, and in many ways a more complex imagery coming out of California. The fragmentation of popular culture and the multiplicity of entertainment options enjoyed by the increasingly segmented masses mark the present popular culture as very different from the past. In many ways, there is no longer a mainstream, just various demographics. The idea of a single domi-nant cultural ideal is no longer relevant. Yet, California's imprint can still be felt. Internationally, California still plays a major role in shaping visions of American youth. Many countries view the United States through a California lens, largely because of its power both as locus and focus of popular culture. With the explosion of media outlets, old images are imme-diately accessible along with the new. No piece of popular culture, no imagery, ever really disappears. Even as California the place evolves, Cali-fornia the product will continue to reign supreme. The Golden State remains both the geographical and psychological center of pop culture production geared towards youth, enjoying a unique place in the American dreamscape. As Brian Wilson, the leader of the Beach Boys, explained, "All good teenagers go to California when they die" (Winokur 2004: 3).

NOTE

1 The evolution of California's cultural power has been well chronicled by historian Kevin Starr's multi-volume "California Dream" series. As that title implies, the Golden State enjoys a long history of influencing the American mind.

REFERENCES

Blair, J. 1985. *The Illustrated Discography of Surf Music, 1961–1965*, rev. ed. Ann Arbor, MI: Pierian.

Bodroghkozy, A. 2001. *Groove Tube: Sixties Television and the Youth Rebellion.* Durham, NC: Duke University Press.

Dallek, M. 2000. *The Right Moment: Ronald Reagan's First Victory and the Deci-sive Turning Point in American Politics.* New York: Free Press.

Davis, Mike. 1990. *City of Quartz: Excavating the Future in Los Angeles.* New York: Verso Press.

Deverell, W. 2004. *Whitewashed Adobe: The Rise of Los Angeles and the Remaking of Its Mexican Past.* Berkeley: University of California Press.

Gabler, Neal. 2006. *Walt Disney: The Triumph of the American Imagination.* New York: Alfred A. Knopf.

Gregory, James. 1989. *American Exodus: The Dust Bowl Migration and Okie Culture in California.* New York: Oxford University Press.

Hackel, Steven W. 2005. *Children of Coyote, Missionaries of Saint Francis: Indian –Spanish Relations in Colonial California, 1769–1850*. Chapel Hill: University of North Carolina Press.

Hoskyns, B. 1996. *Waiting for the Sun: Strange Days, Weird Scenes, and the Sound of Los Angeles*. New York: St. Martin's.

Hoskyns, B. 2006. *Hotel California: The True-life Adventures of Crosby, Stills, Nash, Young, Mitchell, Taylor, Browne, Ronstadt, Geffen, the Eagles, and their Many Friends*. Hoboken, NJ: Wiley.

Life Magazine. 1945. "The California Way of Life," (October 22): 105–16.

Life Magazine. 1964. "Panty Raids? No! Tough Campus Revolt" (December 18): 46A–46B.

Lotchin, Roger. 1992. *Fortress California 1910–1961: From Warfare to Welfare*. New York: Oxford University Press.

May, K. G. 2002. *Golden State, Golden Youth: The California Image in Popular Culture, 1955–1966*. Chapel Hill: University of North Carolina Press.

McGirr, L. 2001. *Suburban Warriors: The Origins of the New American Right*. Princeton, NJ: Princeton University Press.

Murphy, D. E. 2005. "The Nation: California Looks Ahead, and Doesn't Like What It Sees," *New York Times*, May 29.

Quiksilver, 2006. [online]. Available from: http://www.quiksilverinc.com [cited October 20, 2006].

Quinn, E. 2004. *Nuthin' but a "G" Thang: The Culture and Commerce of Gangsta Rap*. New York: Columbia University Press.

Schrag, P. 2006. *California: America's High-Stakes Experiment*. Berkeley: University of California Press.

Schuparra, K. 1998. *Triumph of the Right: The Rise of the California Conservative Movement*. New York: Oxford University Press.

Sears, D. O. and McConahay, J. B. 1973. *The Politics of Violence: The New Urban Blacks and the Watts Riot*. Boston, MA: Houghton Mifflin.

Starr, K. 1973. *Americans and the California Dream, 1850–1915*. New York: Oxford University Press.

Starr, K. 2003. *Embattled Dreams: California in War and Peace, 1940–1950 (Americans and the California Dream)*. New York: Oxford University Press.

Time Magazine. 1967. "The Hippies: Philosophy of a Subculture" (July 7): 1, 57.

Unterberger, R. 2003. *Eight Miles High: Folk Rock's Flight from Haight-Ashbury to Woodstock*. London: Backbeat Books.

Vance, J. E., Jr. 1987. "Revolution in American Space since 1945, and a Canadian Contrast." In R. D. Mitchell and P. A. Groves, eds., *North America: The Historical Geography of a Changing Continent*. Lanham, MD: Rowman and Littlefield, pp. 438–59.

Winokur, J. 2004. *The War between the State: Northern California vs. Southern California*. Seattle: Sasquatch Books.

Wise, N., ed. 1994. *In Their Own Words: The Beach Boys*. London: Omnibus.

FURTHER READING

Ashby, L. 2006. *With Amusement for All: A History of American Popular Culture Since 1830*. Lexington: University Press of Kentucky.

Avila, E. 2004. *Popular Culture in the Age of White Flight: Fear and Fantasy in Suburban Los Angeles*. Berkeley: University of California Press.

Cohen, R. and Zelnik, R. E. eds. 2002. *The Free Speech Movement: Reflections on Berkeley in the 1960s*. Berkeley: University of California Press.

Deverell, W. 2004. *Whitewashed Adobe: The Rise of Los Angeles and the Remaking of Its Mexican Past*. Berkeley: University of California Press.

Doherty, T. 1988. *Teenagers and Teenpics: The Juvenilization of American Movies in the 1950s*. Boston, MA: Unwin Hyman.

Eymann, M. and Wollenberg, C. M. eds. 2004. *What's Going On? California and the Vietnam Era*. Berkeley: University of California Press.

Gregory, James. 1989. *American Exodus: The Dust Bowl Migration and Okie Culture in California*. New York: Oxford University Press.

Hayes-Bautista, D. E. 2004. *La Nuevu California: Latinos in the Golden State.* Berkeley: University of California Press.

Heikkila, E. J. and Pizarro, R. eds. 2002. *Southern California and the World*. Westport, CT: Praeger Publishers.

Horne, G. 1997. *Fire This Time: The Watts Uprising and the 1960s*. New edition. Cambridge, MA: Da Capo Press.

Hoskyns, B. 1996. *Waiting for the Sun: Strange Days, Weird Scenes, and the Sound of Los Angeles*. New York: St. Martin's.

Lotchin, Roger. 1992. *Fortress California 1910–1961: From Warfare to Welfare*. New York: Oxford University Press.

Perry, C. 2005. *The Haight–Ashbury: A History*. New York: Wenner Books.

Rorabaugh, W. J. 1990. *Berkeley at War: The 1960s*. New York: Oxford University Press.

Watts, S. 2001. *The Magic Kingdom: Walt Disney and the American Way of Life*. Columbia, MO: University of Missouri Press.

Chapter Twenty-four

AT THE CENTER OF INDIAN COUNTRY

Nicolas G. Rosenthal

By the turn of the twenty-first century, many California Indian tribes had moved back into the mainstream of the state's social, cultural, political, and economic life. Thousands of people a year journeyed to California's Indian reservations, primarily to gamble at tribally owned casinos, but also to shop at outlet malls, dine at upscale restaurants, relax at health spas, attend performances by popular entertainers, and visit tribal museums. These casino-resort complexes developed as well into large employers of non-Indians, offering jobs with benefits that were largely insulated from fluctuations in the state economy. Off the reservation, tribal members became major philanthropists, contributing millions of dollars to various causes. Table Mountain Rancheria, for instance, donated $10 million to California State University, Fresno's library building fund in 2006, the largest single cash gift in the university's history. California Indian tribes also joined the ranks of the state's major political players, investing over $150 million in election campaigns. Even Arnold Schwarzenegger, who promised a hard line against the tribes as a "special interest" during a combative gubernatorial recall campaign in 2004, quickly recognized the reality of the Indian political presence in California. Less than a year after taking office, Schwarzenegger appeared in a blanket given to him by tribal leaders and declared a new round of gaming compacts that made the state budget dependent upon tribal contributions, effectively guaranteeing an Indian monopoly on high-stakes gaming into the future.

This resurgence of Indian power in California stands in stark contrast to what we know about Native people's experiences during the first century and a half of colonization. Scholars have charted the journey of Native people from before European arrival through the Spanish, Mexican, and early American periods of California history (as attested to by other contributions in this volume), showing how American Indians became the poorest and most marginalized peoples in the state. The subsequent history of Indians in California, however, has received scant attention. In part this is because historians of Native America in general have been slow to take up the modern period. But it may also be because contemporary scholars have been too quick to accept the pronouncements made by an earlier generation of anthropologists. Indeed, when Ishi, dubbed the last of the Yana people, came out of hiding to live his final days at the University of California's Lowie Museum of Anthropology in San Francisco, it was widely understood to symbolize the passing of the state's entire indigenous population. How California's Native peoples negotiated the rest of the twentieth century has remained a mostly untold story, to say nothing of what forces led to the most recent and dramatic return of the tribes to prominence statewide.

Lately, however, scholars have begun to see the potential in, and necessity of, charting the last one hundred years of Native American history in California. Recent studies have built upon the "New Indian history," or the development of the field since the 1970s, to include California's Native peoples in wide-ranging conversations addressing, among other topics, cultural adaptation, racial formation, political activism, and subaltern resistance. Part of this project has been the recognition that, during the twentieth century, the state and especially its cities were not only the home for tribes indigenous to the area, but also major destinations that attracted Native migrants from throughout the nation. In fact, after World War II, California became the state with the largest and most diverse American Indian population. Many gaps in the scholarship remain, leaving much to be done. But future studies of Native Americans in California promise to make contributions across the profession, while shedding further light on how the state became one of the most vibrant and important centers of Indian Country in modern America.

California Tribes and Cultural Adaptations

Since the 1970s, the field of American Indian history has been defined by the "New Indian history," a movement that has involved both anthropologists and historians in stressing Indian perspectives and taking a critical view of European and American colonialism. In particular, New Indian historians emphasize cultural adaptation, or how Native peoples negotiated the social and cultural changes that came with contact and subsequent relations with Euro-Americans. These studies detail the often devastating impact that such forces had upon American Indians but also examine the myriad ways that Native peoples responded in order to survive and remain distinct. The best of this work employs careful analysis in isolating the markers of Indian social and cultural identity and exploring change over time. Language, economic activity, community organization, government relations, settlement patterns, social and religious affiliations, marriage, leadership, education, relations to land, and political ideology, among other categories, have proven fertile ground for probing the shifting ways of "being Indian" in many different settings through five centuries of North American history.

California Indians have followed the trend of cultural adaptation and much of the scholarship on the state's Native peoples is firmly grounded in the New Indian history. A rare, early history of a California Indian reservation is Lowell John Bean's "Morongo Indian Reservation: A Century of Adaptive Strategies" (1978), which provocatively argues that the "failures" of Indians to exploit the economic resources of their lands can also be understood as a successful adaptive strategy, enabling "a subordinate population to maintain its local power, autonomy, ethnic boundaries, and traditional value system" (1978: 159). Specifically, Bean focuses on the Morongo Reservation and explores seven institutions – traditional ceremonial groups, churches, the Cattlemen's Association, the Malki Fruit Cooperative, the Malki Museum, tribal health clinic, and the Morongo Fire Department – that to outsiders look disorganized and plagued by political factionalism, but remain functional and supportive to Morongo culture and society. Joel R. Hyer's *"We Are Not Savages": Native Americans in Southern California and the Pala Reservation, 1840–1920* (2001) addresses the period in the early twentieth century when Cupeño Indians were removed from their historic homes at Warner's Ranch and forced to adjust to life at the Pala Reservation. Following a number of works in American Indian history that cover the early reservation period, Hyer highlights both American colonialism and the creativity of Indian responses. For instance, when government officials introduced agricultural fairs, Native people embraced them for their own purposes, while continuing to observe the fiestas the fairs were meant to replace. David Rich Lewis, *Neither Wolf Nor Dog: American Indians, Environment, and Agrarian Change* (1994), uses the Hupa, a Northern California people, to more generally discuss American Indian economic adaptation. As one case study within a larger work, Lewis shows how the Hupa took up agriculture, livestock raising, and wage work in ways that were consistent with their traditional social, cultural, and economic activities. Gaming represents the most recent adaptation by California Indians to the market economy. My article, "The Dawn of a New Day? Notes on Indian Gaming in Southern California" (2004), charts a history of Southern California Indian efforts to develop tribal lands and resources, documents the rise of Indian casinos as the most lucrative of these efforts, describes the economic impact that gaming has had on reservations, and discusses the dramatic entry of California Indian tribes into state politics. Finally, I suggest some ways that this type of economic development has spurred cultural change. For instance, Southern California tribes have been able to invest substantially in efforts at tribal revitalization, including tribal museums, support of tribal elders, education of tribal youth, and language programs.

Lately, one factor that has helped spur research on California tribes has been the effort by many tribes to gain federal acknowledgment, or official recognition from the US government. Federal recognition has long been a requirement for access to government Indian programs and a factor in the ability to retain tribal lands, but as a precondition for operating gaming ventures it has taken on new importance. If tribes wish to gain federal status, those that historically have been overlooked or denied recognition must apply to the Branch of Acknowledgement and Research (BAR) of the Bureau of Indian Affairs (BIA). Of all the criteria for federal recognition, the most important is "cultural persistence," defined as the tribe's ability to "be identified as an American Indian entity on a substantially continuous basis since 1900" (Field 2003: 84). Tribal entities have called upon anthropologists, historians, and other researchers to assist them in writing historical narratives and assembling relevant documentation, much as they did during federal Indian Claims Commission hearings of the 1950s. Focused as these studies are upon BAR's requirement for cultural persistence, they have stressed tribal continuity in the context of the state's changing society, culture, and economy (with somewhat less nuance than works on cultural adaptation). An example is Heather Valdez Singleton, "Surviving Urbanization: The Gabrieleno, 1850–1920" (2004), which addresses the experiences of the Gabrieleno, or Tongva tribe, the group indigenous to the area that became Los Angeles. Though overlooked by the commission charged with setting aside lands for Mission Indians in the 1890s, Singleton finds that a close-knit Gabrieleno community continued to live in the town of San Gabriel, the site of a Spanish-era mission, well into the 1920s. Often passing as ethnic Mexicans to mitigate discrimination, Gabrielenos nonetheless attended tribal boarding schools (such as the Sherman Institute in the nearby town of Riverside), served as cultural informants to the same anthropologists who declared them extinct, joined the Mission Indian Federation (an Indian rights organization), and registered on the state's 1928 Census of Indians. A similar story of cultural persistence in the absence of federal recognition is Les W. Field, "Unacknowledged Tribes, Dangerous Knowledge: The Muwekma Ohlone and How Indian Identities are 'Known'" (2003). In the early twentieth century, officials determined that the Verona Band of Muwekma Ohlone Indians was not significant enough to receive land or federal status, yet Field argues that these Native people "continued to behave like a band" (2003: 88). Residing in the San Francisco Bay Area, Verona Band members served as godparents for each other's children, married within the band, attended tribal weddings, baptisms, and funerals, buried their dead in the same cemeteries, continued to speak indigenous languages, enrolled on BIA censuses, and wrote letters arguing for their rights at Indian peoples. Additional research related to the federal acknowledgment process and Indian policy in California has been published in the form of reports and government proceedings, rather than in scholarly journals and monographs (Advisory Council on California Indian Policy 1997).

Just in the last decade, a wave of scholarship has promised to push American Indian history to a new stage, beyond the New Indian history. These works build upon the insights, methods, and standards put in place by a generation of scholars, but also make larger connections and valuable contributions to conversations ranging across the historical profession (Rosenthal 2006). Studies of California Indians and cultural adaptation should and can be a part of such efforts, as shown by a recent article on the Round Valley Reservation in Northern California. In "Working for Identity: Race, Ethnicity, and the Market Economy in Northern California, 1875–1936" (2004), William J. Bauer examines how reservation residents embraced wage work, using the cash and mobility that these jobs offered to recreate tribal institutions and reclaim land in their indigenous home-lands. On non-Indian farms and ranches, for instance, Round Valley Indians were able to continue traditional cultural practices that were prohibited on the reservation, such as sweats, dancing, gambling, and shamanism. Fur-thermore, some Round Valley residents pooled the wages they earned to buy communal lands, where they settled according to traditional patterns. Bauer also goes a step further to bridge the gap between American Indian history and studies of racial formation in the United States. Looking at the segregated wage market, Bauer sees a specific, racialized status for Round Valley residents, who were all considered "Indians," despite their ethnic differences. As such they were paid more than ethnic Chinese workers, but less than white workers, with whom they competed for agricultural and ranching jobs. Moreover, the racialization that Round Valley Indians faced in the workplace was translated to the stores, schools, and other local institutions, where Native people faced discrimination. By linking a complex history of cultural adaptation to larger questions of racial formation, Bauer joins a handful of historians who have sought to make American Indian history part of wider-ranging conversations that move beyond the boundar-ies of Indian history. In doing so, Bauer has also shown that the study of California Indians can be central to this project.

Migration, Urbanization, and Activism

According to the US Census Bureau, in 2004 California was home to over 670,000 American Indians, making it the state with by far the most Native people (Oklahoma was second at almost 400,000). Yet members of tribes

indigenous to California represented only a small percentage of this population, with the vast number of Indians coming from groups with reservations and homelands outside the state. Scholars have only just begun to
explore how Native people came to California in the post-World War II
period and their experiences of settling into its increasingly diverse communities. Even this small body of work, however, makes clear the prominent role that California has assumed for Indians in modern America.

The lives of Native migrants to California were shaped by forces unique
to Indian people, even as the choice of California as a destination linked
Indians to the same historical trends affecting other Americans throughout
the twentieth century. Charles Roberts, "A Choctaw Odyssey: The Life of
Lesa Phillip Roberts" (1990), provides a fascinating, albeit uncritical biography of the author's grandmother and her family's journey to California.
By the early twentieth century, most Choctaws subsisted as farmers and
wage laborers in rural Oklahoma, where they had been settled by the government following forced removal from the southeastern United States.
After suffering through the Great Depression, many Choctaw, including
the Roberts family, traveled to California, following the allure of work
made available by World War II. Like many Americans from all over the
country, they settled in Richmond, found well-paying jobs in the bustling
shipyards, and adapted to life in an urban, multi-ethnic society. After the
war, they moved to the San Joaquin Valley, where they found agricultural
work, intermarried, and put down roots. Over the next 40 years, the
extended family continued to spread out across the country, but its center
remained in the town of Chowchilla, the home for most of its four surviving generations.

In fact, California's towns and cities were the destinations for the vast
number of American Indian migrants to the state, leading a national trend
by which the majority of Native people in the United States came to live
in urban areas after World War II. The Los Angeles metropolitan area
became the city with the largest Native American population; San Francisco
Bay Area cities ranked among the top 10; and several other cities and towns
in the state developed significant Indian communities. Studies of American
Indian urbanization in California, however, have only scratched the surface
of this significant trend. Beginning in the 1970s, anthropologists became
interested in urban American Indians, which led to a flurry of articles that
culminated with the publication of Joan Weibel-Orlando, *Indian Country
L.A.: Maintaining Ethnic Community in Complex Society* (1991). Like a
good deal of this work, Weibel-Orlando focuses on urban Indian organizations and the creation of "pan- Indian" identities and communities, providing pieces of historical narrative and some ways of thinking about urban
Indian experience in California, but adhering mostly to anthropological
questions and concerns. Another study is Susan Lobo's *Urban Voices: The*

Bay Area American Indian Community (2002), which serves as an album of essays, photographs, stories, art, and oral histories on Native people in the Bay Area over the past 70 years. While not a systematic approach to writing the twentieth-century history of American Indians in the Bay Area, it does offer various perspectives on urban Indian life, including many Native voices. My own work presents a twentieth-century history of American Indians in the Los Angeles metropolitan area, focusing on the migration of Indians to the city, their experiences with work, housing, and leisure, the formation and development of urban Indian communities, and the changing relationships between Los Angeles and Indian reservations throughout Southern California (Rosenthal 2005b). A few additional studies have addressed various aspects of Indian urbanization in the state (Blackhawk 1995; Peters 1998; Jacobs 2007).

Urbanization also contributed to the rise of American Indian activism, which stands as another defining theme of Native American experience in California. The late 1960s and 1970s saw the emergence of the "Red Power Movement," or a systematic effort by Native people to address historical patterns of inequality and discrimination. Its first major event was the occupation of Alcatraz Island in San Francisco Bay, as recounted in Troy Johnson, *The Occupation of Alcatraz Island: Indian Self-Determination and the Rise of Indian Activism* (1996). Johnson shows how a longer history of Native American activism in the Bay Area was the backdrop for the frustration developing over conditions in rapidly expanding urban American Indian communities. Moreover, following the establishment of American Indian Studies programs at some University of California and California State University campuses, a first generation of Native college students began using the classroom as a forum for strategizing about how to achieve Indian sovereignty and self-determination. Both students and community members came together in the seizure of Alcatraz in November 1969, which continued for 19 months, drawing Indian people from across the nation. Alcatraz helped inspire Native Americans to take pride in Indian identity and to demand more attention to their concerns, becoming the model for a wave of high-profile Indian protest over the next decade. That longer Red Power Movement is addressed by the edited collection, *American Indian Activism: Alcatraz to the Longest Walk* (Johnson et al. 1997), which mixes essays by academics with remembrances by observers and participants, offering various perspectives on the occupations of Alcatraz and American Indian activism in general. As a whole, these contributions shed light on how Native people came to California, the conditions they faced, and how their concerns were translated into actions that profoundly impacted Native Americans throughout the country.

Yet even prior to World War II, these forces of American Indian migration, urbanization, and activism in California were intricately linked. My article, "Representing Indians: Native American Actors on Hollywood's Frontier" (2005a), traces the history of American Indians who worked in Hollywood film studios from the 1910s through the 1930s, arguing that these jobs were highly sought as alternatives to wage work and reservation poverty, allowing many Native people access to the cosmopolitan society of early twentieth-century Los Angeles. Furthermore, American Indian actors became an important part of the city's growing Native American community, by organizing large gatherings, helping to establish and support the Los Angeles Indian Center, and performing at events such as the annual Indian Day celebration. Some Indian entertainers were troubled, however, both by the depictions of Indians that they acted out on film and by the working conditions for Native actors in Hollywood. Such dissatisfaction led them to form an Indian Actor's Association and to more generally advocate for accurate and sympathetic portrayals of Indian history and culture. By choosing to "represent" Indians, both on film and as Native American advocates, these actors joined other people of color in exploring the possibilities of using ethnic performance as an arena for struggling with the dominant society over issues such as culture, dignity, and identity. In this way, California became another important venue for Native peoples, not just because it offered opportunities for employment, but because it was central to the cultural production of ideas about American Indians. Thus, early in the twentieth century, California became vital to the development of modern Native America.

During a 2005 interview, Randy Edmonds, a Kiowa/Caddo Indian born in Oklahoma, reflected on some of the changes he had seen in California over the past 50 years, a period in which he had lived and worked for various federal programs and non-profit organizations serving American Indians in Los Angeles, Madera, and San Diego. Edmonds noted with some satisfaction that several California tribes had become "very rich" through "gaming, hotels, and other kinds of business development," which enabled them to invest in the types of reservation infrastructure, healthcare, and other improvements that had been promised yet neglected for so many years by the federal government. When asked whether these newly empowered tribes had reached out to urban Indian communities and the types of organizations he had worked for, however, Edmonds replied:

> I've tried to get the tribes to fund [the Indian Human Resource Center in San Diego]. But their feelings are now that we're not a viable organization. And so they just don't fund us. They might give us a little, maybe $1,000, $2,000, $3,000 here or there, you know, for this and that . . . but they haven't given us any big money . . . We're out of state Indians in their eyes. (Edmonds 2005)

Edmonds went on to note that even those Indians who in earlier decades received help from the Indian Human Resource Center, and later returned to their reservations, seemed to forget what the organization was doing for the intertribal community of Indians in the city. They instead preferred to use gaming profits and resources to concentrate on tribal issues. While there has been excellent work on the cultural adaptation of California tribes and the migration of Native people to the state from all over the country, these studies hardly explain the type of complex relationships indicated by Edmonds, or more generally how Native Americans in California have gotten to where they are today.

The survival and recent return to prominence of California tribes, the development of American Indian communities in cities and towns, and the complex and shifting relationships between Native people indigenous to California and Indian migrants to the state all cry out for more scholarly attention. Any number of additional topics might be explored as well. These include a longer history of American Indian activism in California, especially through the exploration of early twentieth-century organizations such as the Mission Indian Federation and California Indian Rights Association, both of which helped to lay a foundation for later struggles such as the occupation of Alcatraz. Studies of Indian boarding schools in California, such as the Sherman Institute in Riverside and St. Boniface Indian School in Banning, should be put into a comparative context with the other work that has lately been done on American Indian boarding schools across the country, then related to Progressive-era ideas about Americanization and the education of ethnic and racial groups. The development of water resources in Southern California has lately received attention from scholars, yet American Indians are largely absent from these studies, despite the importance of this issue for the vitality of reservation economies (Erie 2006). While bound together politically and by the common strategies they have adopted, tribes in Southern California and those in Central and Northern California have also had fundamentally different historical experiences over the past one hundred years, grounded largely in the contrasting patterns of European and American colonization during the nineteenth century. Scholars have yet to grapple with this issue, preferring to focus on one part of the state or the other, or to simply refer to California Indians without complicating the matter in this way. All of these studies have tremendous promise, not only for enriching our understanding of Native Americans and California in the twentieth century, but also for contributing to larger themes and discussions in the fields of California history, the history of the American West, and United States history. It is now clear, in the twenty-first century, that California is at the center of Indian Country. What remains is for scholars to continue the project of exploring how this came to be.

References

Advisory Council on California Indian Policy. 1997. *Final Reports and Recommendations to the Congress of the United States: Pursuant to Public Law 102-416.* Washington, DC: Government Printing Office.

Bauer, W. J. 2004. "Working for Identity: Race, Ethnicity, and the Market Economy in Northern California, 1875–1936." In B. Hosmer and C. O'Neill, eds., *Native Pathways: Economic Development and American Indian Culture in the Twentieth Century.* Boulder: University Press of Colorado, pp. 238–57.

Bean, L. J. 1978. "Morongo Indian Reservation: A Century of Adaptive Strategies." In S. Stanley, ed., *American Indian Economic Development.* The Hague: Mouton Publishers, pp. 159–236.

Blackhawk, N. 1995. "I Can Carry on From Here: The Relocation of American Indians to Los Angeles," *Wicazo Sa Review* 11: 16–30.

Edmonds, R. 2005. Interview with the author on October 13, 2005. San Diego. [Cassette recording in possession of author.]

Erie, S. P. 2006. *Beyond Chinatown: The Metropolitan Water District, Growth, and the Environment in Southern California.* Stanford, CA: Stanford University Press.

Field, L.W. 2003. "Unacknowledged Tribes, Dangerous Knowledge: The Muwekma Ohlone and How Indian Identities are Known," *Wicazo Sa Review* 18: 79–94.

Hyer, J. R. 2001. *"We Are Not Savages": Native Americans in Southern California and the Pala Reservation, 1840–1920.* East Lansing: Michigan State University Press.

Jacobs, M. D. 2007. "Working on the Domestic Frontier: American Indian Domestic Servants in White Women's Households in the San Francisco Bay Area, 1920–1940," *Frontiers: A Journal of Women Studies* 28.

Johnson, T. R. 1996. *The Occupation of Alcatraz Island: Indian Self-Determination and the Rise of Indian Activism.* Urbana: University of Illinois Press.

Johnson, T. R., Nagel, J., and Chamagne, D., eds. 1997. *American Indian Activism: Alcatraz to the Longest Walk.* Urbana: University of Illinois Press.

Lewis, D. R. 1994. *Neither Wolf Nor Dog: American Indians, Environment, and Agrarian Change.* New York: Oxford University Press.

Lobo, S., ed. 2002. *Urban Voices: The Bay Area American Indian Community.* Tucson: University of Arizona Press.

Peters, K. M. 1998. "Continuing Identity: Laguna Pueblo Railroaders in Richmond, California," *American Indian Culture and Research Journal* 22: 187–91.

Roberts, C. 1990. "A Choctaw Odyssey: The Life of Lesa Phillip Roberts," *American Indian Quarterly* 14: 259–76.

Rosenthal, N. G. 2004. "The Dawn of a New Day? Notes on Indian Gaming in Southern California." In B. Hosmer and C. O'Neill, eds., *Native Pathways: Economic Development and American Indian Culture in the Twentieth Century.* Boulder: University Press of Colorado, pp. 91–111.

Rosenthal, N. G. 2005a. "Representing Indians: Native American Actors on Hollywood's Frontier," *Western Historical Quarterly* 36: 329–52.

Rosenthal, N. G. 2005b. "Re-imagining Indian Country: American Indians and the Los Angeles Metropolitan Area." PhD dissertation, University of California, Los Angeles.

Rosenthal, N. G. 2006. "Beyond the New Indian History: Recent Trends in Historiography on the Native Peoples of North America," *History Compass* 4 (July): 962–74. Available from World Wide Web: http://www.blackwell-compass. com/subject/history/ <http://www.blackwell-syngery.com>10.1111/j.1478-0542.2006.00340.x

Singleton, H. V. 2004. "Surviving Urbanization: The Gabrieleno, 1850–1920," *Wicazo Sa Review* 19: 49–59.

Weibel-Orlando, J. 1991. *Indian Country LA: Maintaining Ethnic Community in Complex Society.* Urbana: University of Illinois Press.

FURTHER READING

Anderson, M. K. 2005. *Tending the Wild: Native American Knowledge and the Management of California's Natural Resources.* Berkeley: University of California Press.

Bauer, W. J. 2006. "'We Were All Migrant Workers Here': Round Valley Indian Labor in Northern California, 1850–1929," *Western Historical Quarterly* 37: 43–63.

Buckley, T. 2002. *Standing Ground: Yurok Spirituality, 1850–1990.* Berkeley: University of California Press.

Eargle, D. H. 2000. *Native California Guide.* San Francisco: Trees Company Press.

Fortunate Eagle, A. 1992. *Alcatraz! Alcatraz! The Indian Occupation of 1969–1971.* Berkeley, CA: Heyday Books.

Goldberg, C. and Champagne, D. 2002. "Ramona Redeemed? The Rise of Tribal Political Power in California," *Wicazo Sa Review* 17: 43–64.

Karr, S. M. 2000. "'Water We Believed Could Never Belong to Anyone': The San Luis Rey River and the Pala Indians of Southern California," *American Indian Quarterly* 24: 381–99.

Lane, A. I. Sr. 1995. *Return of the Buffalo: The Story Behind America's Indian Gaming Explosion.* Westport, CN: Bergin and Garvey.

Sennett, B. 1996. "Wage Labor: Survival for the Death Valley Timbisha." In A. Littlefield and M. C. Knack, eds., *Native Americans and Wage Labor: Ethnohistorical Perspectives.* Norman: University of Oklahoma Press, pp. 218–44.

Shipek, F. C. 1988. *Pushed into the Rocks: Southern California Indian Land Tenure, 1769–1986.* Lincoln: University of Nebraska Press.

Sutton, I. 2006. "Researching Indigenous Indians in Southern California: Commentary, Bibliography, and Online Resources," *American Indian Culture and Research Journal* 30: 75–127.

Thorne, T. C. 2003. *The World's Richest Indian: The Scandal over Jackson Barnett's Oil Fortune.* New York: Oxford University Press.

Weibel-Orlando, J. 1998. "And the Drumbeat still goes on . . . : Urban Indian Institutional Survival into the New Millennium," *American Indian Culture and Research Journal* 22: 135–62.

Chapter Twenty-five

SEXUAL REVOLUTIONS AND SEXUAL POLITICS

Josh Sides

If historians seek among other things to refine popular notions of the past, then the task of restoring accuracy, precision, and nuance to the history of sexuality in California is a particularly daunting task. Because that unholy collection of historically suppressed sex practices – including prostitution, homosexuality, and the performance and consumption of sexual entertainment – is such a familiar element of the state's past and present, we generally understand its proliferation in the San Francisco Bay Area and the greater Los Angeles region to be indicative of an exceptionally permissive culture of California. From the dizzying array of sexual amusements offered on San Francisco's nineteenth-century Barbary Coast, to the tawdry and well-publicized affairs of Hollywood celebrities, to the creation of the world's premier gay district in San Francisco's Castro District in the 1970s, to the rise of Los Angeles as the pornography capital of the globe, the history of sexuality in California often appears to resemble an unbroken line of extraordinary libertinism. But this is simply not the case.

In fact, after the heyday of the Barbary Coast, and particularly during and after World War II, campaigns for the suppression of prostitution, homosexuality, and sexual entertainment flourished in California, much as they did elsewhere. Bolstered ideologically by the Cold War crusade against "deviancy," and logistically by administrative changes in California state regulation of alcohol control, Californians hostile to open displays of purportedly deviant sexuality triumphed through the quarantining of prostitutes, the widespread closure of gay bars, and the restraint of sexual entertainment. Historian Nan Boyd's work, for example, amply demonstrates the extent to which San Francisco's uneasy tolerance of queer entertainment was eclipsed in the 1950s by an aggressive campaign to eradicate even its most benign vestiges (Boyd 2004); scholar Daniel Hurewitz discusses this changing world as well in his fine essay in this volume and in *Bohemian Los Angeles* (Hurewitz 2007). And the records of the Department of Alcoholic Beverage Control (ABC) in Sacramento reveal the extensive resources the agency devoted to eradicating gay bars, as well as a remarkable level of commitment among the ABC officers who regularly "played queer" and initiated homosexual liaisons in order to have documented proof of the sordid activities taking place on the premises. Nor were the "anti-vice" campaigns of the 1950s limited to eradicating homosexual deviancy. In 1953, the California State Legislature passed the so-called "B-girl statute," which empowered the Division of Liquor Control and local police agencies to arrest "B-girls" who received a "cut" of drink sales at bars where they enticed men to drink with them with the implicit promise (seldom fulfilled) of sexual favors (Littauer 2003). Meanwhile, the Los Angeles Police Department regularly raided "stag parties" in which female strippers or pornographic films were offered as entertainment.

Failing to appreciate the thorough circumscription of these expressions of sexuality in California prior to the 1960s has the troubling effect of diminishing our capacity to appreciate just how radical and revolutionary the changes in sexual behavior during the Sexual Revolution really were.[1] For the mostly young people who found the sexual mores of the 1950s stifling, the Sexual Revolution was utterly transformative. It was empowering for gays and lesbians who could walk the streets, finally free to express their affection, though never truly free from fear; it was liberating for unmarried women and men who "shacked up" before marriage, often to the wagging consternation of their older neighbors. It was ecstatic for the young men who crowded around (and even occasionally paid to enter) the thousands of strip clubs, sex shops, and massage parlors that arched like a neon constellation across metropolitan America. And it was profitable for the small armies of female and male prostitutes who – recognizing that sexual freedom needn't be free – swarmed from the hinterlands to the metropolis like so many harried salesmen. Sharing their profits in the highly sexualized metropolis were legions of pornographers, whose wares, once relegated to back rooms of only the seediest skid row stores before the Sexual Revolution, were now displayed prominently in storefront windows throughout the city, and even in the suburbs, those bastions of putative morality.

But the Sexual Revolution also generated great animosity. Most famously, it unleashed a wave of wrathful judgment and vitriolic homophobia among the religiously orthodox, particularly in California's suburbs, which would become prime recruiting grounds for the Religious Right by the 1970s. But there were many counterrevolutionaries whose animosity stemmed not necessarily from the Scriptures, but rather from a sanctified view of the traditional distinction between private and public sexuality. These folks – both Democrats and Republicans – simply resented the brazen intrusion of sex into the public sphere. In Hollywood and San Francisco – to say nothing of the dozens of other large American cities where the symbols of Sexual Revolution were on display and writ large – homeowners and parents clamored for laws to hide pornography and shut down adult theaters, to relocate prostitutes, and to limit their exposure to incidents of homosexual contact.

Since the days of Comstockery, moralists had wielded the charge of "obscenity" with tremendous effect. But beginning in the late 1950s, the United States Supreme Court consistently narrowed the legal domain of obscenity to the point where the charge was seldom effective. Just as the moralists lost their prime weapon, and therefore much of their influence, civic leaders carried the mantle of anti-obscenity in creative, and highly effective, new ways. In the 1960s and 1970s, civic leaders in San Francisco, Los Angeles, and many other cities throughout the nation created a host of zoning controls – modeled on pre-existing nuisance-abatement ordinances – which carefully avoided the suppression of free expression, while achieving the desired reduction in sexual spectacles.

While some of the California public officials who sought the elimination of public spectacles of sexuality did so for moral reasons, many more did so for the livelihood of their cities. From their perspective, the Sexual Revolution came along at an extremely inconvenient time, just as middle-class white residents were leaving cities in pursuit of the jobs now relocating to suburbs, just as urban economies fell into a protracted slump, and just as crime rates skyrocketed. Although the Sexual Revolution had very little, if anything, to do with these developments, those problems were very difficult to solve. On the other hand, crackdowns on so-called "non-victim" crimes allowed law enforcement agencies (who were naturally sensitive about public perception in the midst of an extended crime wave) to statistically demonstrate a ballooning arrest rate. In this process, the spectacles of the Sexual Revolution were conveniently wrapped into a longstanding narrative of "urban decline" in which sexuality played a far more important role than it, in fact, deserved. This narrative also guaranteed that sexual politics would be integral to metropolitan politics in California long after the 1960s.

Pornography and Adult Entertainment

In July of 1945 Los Angeles District Attorney and future California Attorney General Fred N. Howser proudly lit a pornography pyre. Following the bust of a "smut ring," the ambitious young DA mugged for cameras at a South Los Angeles dump where he burned 500,000 feet of film and over 150,000 photographs. In a ritual performed in a number of American cities during the late 1940s and 1950s, defenders of morality demonstrated their victory over the proliferation of obscenity. But these ritualistic blazes scarcely mattered to pornographers and their distributors. Buoyed by

Supreme Court victory in the famous *Roth* decision in 1957, which significantly narrowed the scope of materials fitting the legal definition of obscene, magazine distributors in the late 1950s and early 1960s began requiring newsstands to purchase "girlie magazines" in order to receive mainstream magazines. This "bundling" process brought salacious magazines into public view in ways that would have been unimaginable in an earlier era. In an early version of spamming, pornography distributors often bought mailing lists from magazine distributors, and then flooded mailboxes with pornography advertising more pornography. This phenomenon exploded in the late 1950s and by 1959, the US Postal Inspection Service estimated that about 1 million children – or 1 out of every 35 school-age kids – received such pornography. If parents were willing to accept the gradually increased spectacle of sexuality at newsstands, they were not willing to see it increase in the bastion of private life, the home. Postmaster Otto K. Olesen estimated that of the $500 million pornography grossed each year, about $300 million of that was produced in Los Angeles.[2]

The volume of pornography increased exponentially during the 1960s, but its form and venues also changed. The explosion of topless and bottomless dancing in the mid-1960s – which bore little relation to the satirical, imaginative precursor of burlesque – not only introduced a new form of erotic entertainment to cities but also expanded markets for pornography. Cigar stores and newsstands were now gradually replaced by adult bookstores, massage parlors, video arcades, movie theaters, and encounter parlors (where, according to parlor owners who called it "nude therapy," men paid to discuss their problems with a nude woman). A 1970 report by the Commission on Obscenity and Pornography found no fewer than 47 stores selling erotic material, 6 video arcades and 28 pornographic movie theaters in San Francisco, leading the President of the Board of Supervisors and future California Senator Dianne Feinstein to ruefully admit to a *New York Times* reporter that San Francisco had become "a kind of smut capital of the United States."[3] In North Hollywood – which has always sat uncomfortably between the suburban San Fernando Valley and the gaudy streets of Hollywood – there were already 15 topless or bottomless bars and four adult bookstores by 1969.

Traditionally, opponents of pornography framed their arguments in terms of the moral content of the materials. But after *Roth* and subsequent victories, the moral case against pornography was seldom a success. While religious groups continued to argue for the immorality of pornography, feminists made the more high-profile inroads with the moral argument. In the San Francisco Bay Area, anti-pornography feminists gathered around the banner of a group called Women Against Violence in Pornography and Media (WAVPM), the records of which are today housed at the Gay, Lesbian, Bi-Sexual, Transgender, Historical Society in San Francisco.

Although WAVPM initially limited its activism to eradicating pornography that depicted women being "bound, raped, tortured, or murdered for sexual stimulation," it quickly expanded its scope to include all pornography. This programmatic shift was consistent with the increasingly popular belief – most closely associated with activist, writer, and WAVPM member Andrea Dworkin – that pornography, by its very nature, inflicted violence on women by objectifying their bodies. Beginning in 1976, WAVPM staged numerous pickets in North Beach, culminating in the "Take Back the Night March" on November 18, 1978 in which over 5,000 women marched down Broadway in protest at the district's objectification of women. Symbolically and emotionally important to the participants, the marches in San Francisco's pornography district had little appreciable impact on the sale of pornography or the character of North Beach, and strip club owners smugly declared that the protest had only increased business.

Yet if the moral case against pornography failed in California, the application of zoning laws was considerably more successful. Building on the legal precedent of nuisance abatement, civic opponents mounted a critical challenge to what they called the "porn blight" by arguing for the noxious secondary effects of pornographic bookstores, adult theaters, video arcades, and massage parlors. Such establishments, they insisted, attracted pimps, prostitutes, and other criminals and therefore created a nuisance to the neighborhoods in which they were located. After the United Sates Supreme Court validated a Detroit ordinance limiting and dispersing adult business establishments in the 1976 *Young vs. American Mini Theaters* decision, representatives from cities throughout the nation scrambled to create similar ordinances. In 1978, Dianne Feinstein successfully pushed through such an ordinance in San Francisco, with considerable support from downtown business and hotel interests who feared that the spectacle of sex would deter tourism and degrade their establishments. In Hollywood, a vigorous law enforcement campaign by legendary Police Chief Edward M. Davis, coupled with new zoning rules and the installation of brighter street lighting, effectively curtailed much of the adult businesses there after the mid-1970s. It is an issue still very much in play, for where such establishments exist today, they are often the subject of protest campaigns by parents, homeowners, and pedestrians who insist that they have a fundamental right to be shielded from the most noxious symbols (or symptoms) of the Sexual Revolution.

Prostitution

The Sexual Revolution brought metropolitan California's already-thriving prostitution trade an enormous bounty. If Los Angeles and San Francisco competed for the dubious honor of "prostitution capital" of California during the 1960s, San Francisco claimed the title decisively by the mid-1970s. Under San Francisco Police Department Chief Charles Gain and the liberal Mayor George Moscone, longstanding efforts to curb prostitution were largely abandoned, creating a veritable Gold Rush for prostitutes that drew them from Los Angeles, Sacramento, and other regions of the state where enforcement was not as relaxed (Weiss 1984: 133–41). After 11 months, Moscone scuttled the plan under intense political pressure and a rising crime rate, but San Francisco's reputation guaranteed a steady supply of migrating prostitutes well into the 1980s even as "sweeps" escalated, particularly in the tourist-friendly Union Square area. An equally significant cause of the proliferation of prostitution in San Francisco during and after the 1970s was the renewal of the downtown area, which brought dozens of new, stylish hotels adjacent to the historic center of prostitution, the Tenderloin. Although the hotel industry was loath to admit it, it was an open secret that traveling businessmen and conventioneers were reliable "Johns." Referring to such convention attendees, prostitute rights activist Priscilla Alexander recognized that they "feel that a visit to a strange city is not complete without a visit to a prostitute."[4]

In one of the most remarkable developments in California prostitution, on Mother's Day, 1973, an eccentric and articulate woman named Margo St. James founded a prostitutes' rights organization called COYOTE (Call Off Your Old Tired Ethics). One of the first such organizations in the world, COYOTE demanded the decriminalization of prostitution and sought legal, educational, medical, and financial services for prostitutes. Though COYOTE's victories were few, St. James is credited with helping to overturn the city's policy of quarantining prostitutes and coercing them into medical treatment (Jenness 1993). Implemented during World War II ostensibly to control the spread of venereal disease, the policy allowed the San Francisco Police Department unprecedented, and clearly unconstitutional, power to quarantine any women suspected of carrying venereal disease. The Records of the Northern California Branch of the American Civil Liberties Union, now housed at the California Historical Society, reveal the extent to which police officers exploited the quarantine policy simply to rid the streets of socially undesirable women, some of whom were prostitutes, but others of whom were simply bar-flies, drunks, or famously promiscuous. St. James's triumph over that policy in 1975 permanently changed the nature of the prostitution arrest process and restored many of the rights prostitutes in San Francisco had not had for more than 30 years.

During the 1960s and 1970s, the history of prostitution in California – as elsewhere – was also deeply shaped by general racial tensions in cities, and by the continued second-class status of blacks in particular. Records of the Board of Supervisors in the John Anson Ford Collection at the Huntington Library reveal the Board's aggressive pursuit of black prostitutes in South Central Los Angeles and the unincorporated area of Lennox while ignoring the mostly white, "high-class," call girl trade in Hollywood. More damning, the Records of COYOTE, housed at Harvard's Radcliffe Institute, reveal the striking disparity in arrest and sentencing between black and white prostitutes. A survey conducted by COYOTE in November of 1976, for example, found that although approximately two-thirds of the women arrested for prostitution were white, two-thirds of the women serving time for prostitution at the San Francisco County Jail were black. On the other hand, the Police Department generally tolerated prostitution in the predominantly black Western Addition, while discouraging it in the whiter Union Square shopping area. This had the effect, blacks argued, of degrading all black women in the Western Addition, many of whom were subjected to solicitations from passing white motorists who assumed they were prostitutes. Organized as the Ghetto Youth Movement in 1971, Western Addition youth began a successful campaign of intimidation by taking pictures of "Johns" and conspicuously writing down license plate numbers.

Homosexual Revolution

By far the most spectacular transformation of the Sexual Revolution in California was the shocking new visibility of homosexuality. Though homophile organizations like the Mattachine Society, Daughters of Bilitis, and the Society for Individual Rights (SIR) – precursors to the modern gay rights movement, all founded in California – were assertive in their demand for equal treatment during the 1950s and early 1960s, none advocated "coming out" en masse. Theirs was generally a politics of respectability designed to foster contacts and communication among gays and lesbians, while projecting an image of professionalism and seriousness to the outside world (Meeker 2006: 37–150). For the young gays of the 1960s, however, radicalized by the movement for Black Power and by the Vietnam War, the strategies of the homophile movement seemed far too accommodating to homophobes (for further discussion, see historian Daniel Hurewitz's essay in this volume).

Almost four months before the 1969 Stonewall Riot in New York – an event which is widely regarded as the official beginning of the gay liberation movement – a group of young, radical gays began picketing the States Line Steamship Company in what must have been one of the largest and most assertive protests among homosexuals in history. The protest, led by Leo Lawrence, the editor of SIR's *Vector* magazine, sought to reverse the firing of a young gay man named Gale Whittington. Unbeknownst to Whittington, a risqué photograph of him had appeared in the *Berkeley Barb*, the radical newspaper that was widely disseminated downtown where buttoned-up businessmen perused its many listings for erotic massages. Simultaneously, Lawrence issued a call for "gay revolution" in the pages of the *Berkeley Barb* and *Vector*, much to the dismay of the leadership of SIR, which he characterized as "timid, uptight [and] conservative." "Society has made us perverts for too goddamn long," Lawrence railed:

> Tell your boss, family – everybody – that you're gay . . . After we can admit "gay is good" the revolution will come . . . All our lives we've been made butts of jokes, laughed at, made to feel guilty. Human beings shouldn't have to live like that . . . If the uptightness of the present leaders breaks the revolution, then they must go.[5]

Young gays heeded the call, and later that year activists in San Francisco, Los Angeles, and New York founded chapters of the Gay Liberation Front (GLF), the first gay rights group to call itself "gay" rather than "homosexual." With the GLF, the gay revolution had begun in earnest.

Because the gay liberation movement quickly gained momentum in California, it naturally became a choice destination for homosexuals trapped in deserts of intolerance in the United States and internationally. An epic migration of gays was underway by the late 1960s and their quickly rising numbers guaranteed – particularly in a relatively small city like San Francisco – that they would become an influential political force. There, aspiring candidates diligently courted the "gay vote" by the early 1970s and San Francisco elected its first openly gay supervisor, Harvey Milk, in 1977. In 1978 gay Californians also successfully mobilized in opposition to the Proposition 6, a bill proposed by Orange County State Senator John Briggs, which would have expelled all gay teachers from California's public schools. Milk only served for 11 months before he was assassinated, along with Mayor George Moscone, by former SFPD officer and supervisor Dan White. But Milk's legacy lived on, and San Francisco elected several other gay supervisors, though none with the popular following and widely recognized charisma of Milk. In Los Angeles, where the Mattachine Society had been founded, gay power was in the ascendance in the 1970s, but with a characteristically Los Angeles twist: rather than concentrating in one specific neighborhood like New York's Greenwich Village or San Francisco's Castro, homosexuals in Los Angeles congregated in several areas, including Silverlake, Long Beach, and, most famously, in West Hollywood. If their potential political power was somewhat diminished by virtue of the region's size, their victories in places like West Hollywood have been dramatic. When the largely gay city incorporated in 1984, it became a pioneer in providing a variety of municipally supported AIDS services.

For many gay men in the 1970s, gay liberation was not simply about gaining political rights; it was also about having uninhibited, frequent, and even anonymous sex. An extraordinarily profitable gay sex industry, consisting of bathhouses, leather bars, and sex clubs, emerged in California during the 1970s to cater to this feverish demand. Additionally, some state and local parks became famous "cruising grounds" for that segment of the gay population seeking anonymous, quasi-public, sex. The most vivid account of that moment came with the 1977 publication of John Rechy's *The Sexual Outlaw*. Since the 1963 publication of *City of Night*, a graphic tale of a male hustler that shocked reading audiences, Rechy's work had become increasingly explicit. Scrapping much in the way of literary form or even the minimal character development of *City of Night*, *The Sexual Outlaw* simply sought to chronicle Rechy's public "sexhunt." When the protagonist is not having sex, he is preparing for sex by working out with weights, pounding muscle-inducing protein beverages, and compulsively preening in the mirror. At this point in Rechy's career, he had come to see public sex and promiscuity as a "righteous form of revolution." Ultimately, the protagonist has dozens of sexual encounters with even more men (in 1977, Rechy conservatively estimated that he had had sex with more than 7,000 men).

From an epidemiological perspective, the timing of the "golden age of promiscuity," could not have been worse. The outbreak of the AIDS epidemic in 1981 forever changed the meaning of the gay revolution. While public health officials initially had no definitive proof that the virus causing AIDS was transmitted through sex, they already suspected as much by the end of 1981 and many issued calls for the closure of bathhouses and sex clubs as early as 1982. However, in San Francisco – the national epicenter of the disease in AIDS' early years – politicians were loath to alienate gay supporters by forcing the closure of bathhouses. And for their part, many homosexuals were loath to close such businesses because of the reasonable fear that the disease would be exploited to force them "back into the closet." In 1984, the San Francisco Department of Public Health finally closed the bathhouses, but by that time, most of them were closing their doors – as they were in Los Angeles – because so many patrons were dying or dead. An entire landscape of sexual entertainment in San Francisco and Los Angeles had all but disappeared by the early 1990s.

An Indecent (Research) Proposal

Few aspects of California's history are as open to innovative research, as inviting to radical reinterpretation, and as likely to produce dynamic scholarship in the future, as is the topic of sexuality. At the time of this writing, the bulk of scholarship on sexuality in California focuses on queer history. Nan Boyd, Martin Meeker, Gayle Rubin, and Susan Stryker, among others, have made remarkable strides in the recovery and analysis of the state's gay, lesbian, and transgender past. Yet there is still much to be done in this realm. Of particular interest, and still insufficiently explored, is the historic geography of gay neighborhoods. The act of colonizing neighborhoods is one of profound social and political significance, yet we know relatively little about those residents who resisted, and often fled, the arrival of gays and lesbians in conspicuous numbers to their communities. The reason we know so little about this dimension of queer history is that historians are generally liberal and tolerant folks who find the intolerance of previous generations intolerable, and we'd rather celebrate the accomplishments of persecuted groups anyhow. Of course, I generally share these sympathies, but this does not absolve us from our professional duty to clearly understand how people have dealt with thorny issues in their own time, and on their own terms. To put it more provocatively, one need not have been a raging homophobe to disapprove of the transformation of a "family neighborhood" into a "gay neighborhood." Beyond homophobia and racism, what forces have shaped the way people perceive of, and value, urban space, and what does sex have to do with it?

Another potentially fruitful – although undoubtedly challenging – line of inquiry concerns the sex lives of those who resisted the Sexual Revolution most vehemently. I think that we have casually misinterpreted the historic hostility to homosexuality, abortion rights, and "free love" among social conservatives as a hostility to sex per se. But clearly "family values," both then and now, are not asexual. Rather, such values have prescribed certain sexual practices while proscribing others. Understanding how opponents of the Sexual Revolution framed and "enacted" proper sexuality, and balanced that behavior with the tenets of their religious faiths, would be a fascinating study.

Finally, I believe that there is a critical need for an historical study that measures the costs of policing sexuality. How effective have "crackdowns" on prostitution been in reducing the practice? How much money have local governments devoted to the suppression of prostitution in California's recent history, and has that investment ever paid off? And what, historically, have campaigns against pornography and adult entertainment had to show for themselves? A study that investigated these and similar questions would be of enormous benefit to contemporary policy makers, who often seemed misguided by distorted perceptions of the past. And what greater good can come from historical inquiry than that it makes women and men make better decisions today?

NOTES

1 For the purposes of this essay, I have limited my discussion of the Sexual Revolution to those aspects which manifested themselves most conspicuously to urban dwellers, and about which residents sought expanded law enforcement and new legislation. Of course, there are other crucial aspects of the Sexual Revolution – abortion rights and the expansion of women in the workplace to name the two most important. But neither of these issues is particular to the metropolitan experience in California and they are therefore not treated here. I deal with these and other issues in greater detail in my forthcoming manuscript.

2 United States Congress, Senate Committee on the Judiciary, *Control of Obscene Material: Hearings before Subcommittee on Constitutional Amendments and Subcommittee to Investigate Juvenile Delinquency of the Committee on the Judiciary, United States Senate, Eighty-sixth Congress, First and Second Sessions* (Washington, DC: Government Printing Office, 1960), pp. 4–16, 70.

3 W. Murray (1971) "The Porn Capital of America," *New York Times* (January 3), p. SM8.

4 P. Alexander (1983) *Working on Prostitution*, a paper presented to California Now Inc., p. 5.

5 "Homo Revolt: 'Don't Hide It," *Berkeley Barb*, March 28–April 3, 1969, pp. 5, 23.

REFERENCES

Boyd, N. 2004. *Wide Open Town: A History of Queer San Francisco to 1965.* Berkeley and Los Angeles: University of California Press.

Hurewitz, Daniel. 2007. *Bohemian Los Angeles and the Making of Modern Politics.* Berkeley: University of California Press.

Jenness, Valerie. 1993. *Making it Work: The Prostitutes' Right Movement in Perspective.* New York: Aldine de Gruyter.

Littauer, A. 2003. "The B-Girl Evil: Bureaucracy, Sexuality, and the Menace of Barroom Vice in Postwar California," *Journal of the History of Sexuality* 12 (2): 171–204.

Meeker, M. 2006. *Contacts Desired: Gay and Lesbian Communication and Community, 1940s–1970s.* Chicago and London: University of Chicago Press

Rechy, John. 1963. *City of Night.* New York: Grove Press.

Rechy, John. 1977. *The Sexual Outlaw.* New York: Grove Press.

Rubin, G. 1994. "The Valley of the Kings: Leathermen in San Francisco, 1960–1990." PhD dissertation, University of Michigan.

Stryker, S. and Van Buskirk, J. 1996. *Gay by the Bay: A History of Queer Culture in the San Francisco Bay Area.* San Francisco: Chronicle Books.

Weiss, Mike. 1984. *Double Play: The San Francisco City Hall Killings.* London: Addison-Wesley.

FURTHER READING

Allyn, D. 2001. *Make Love, Not War: The Sexual Revolution: An Unfettered History.* New York: Routledge.

Armstrong, Elizabeth. 2002. *Forging Gay Identities: Organizing Sexuality in San Francisco, 1950–1994.* Chicago: University of Chicago Press.

Asbury, H. 1933. *Barbary Coast: An Informal History of the San Francisco Underworld.* Garden City, NY: Garden City Publishing.

Brook, James et al., eds. 1998. *Reclaiming San Francisco: History, Politics, and Culture.* San Francisco: City Lights Books.

Califia, P. 1994. *Public Sex: The Culture of Radical Sex.* Pittsburgh and San Francisco: Cleis Press.

Cochrane, Michelle. 2004. *When AIDS Began: San Francisco and the Making of an Epidemic.* New York: Routledge.

D'Emilio, J. 1983. *Sexual Politics, Sexual Communities: The Making of a Homosexual Minority in the United States, 1940–1970.* Chicago: University of Chicago Press.

Kenney, M. 2001. *Mapping Gay L.A: The Intersection of Place and Politics.* Philadelphia: Temple University Press.

Perry, Charles. 1984. The *Haight-Ashbury: A History.* New York: Random House.

Shepard, Benjamin. 1997. *White Nights and Ascending Shadows: An Oral History of the San Francisco AIDS Epidemic.* London: Cassell.

Shilts, R. 1982. *The Mayor of Castro Street: The Life and Times of Harvey Milk.* New York: St. Martin's Press.

Shilts, R. 1987. *And the Band Played On: Politics, People and the AIDS Epidemic.* New York: St. Martin's Press.

Chapter Twenty-six

A GENERATION OF LEADERS, BUT NOT IN THE FIELDS: THE LEGACY OF CESAR CHAVEZ

Miriam Pawel

In 1943, Juan Rivera Govea abandoned his studies at a Mexico City conservatory and signed up as a temporary worker for the Santa Fé Railroad, joining thousands of Mexicans who streamed north to provide cheap manual labor while the United States was at war. At 23, Juan had already worked a variety of jobs to support his mother and eight younger siblings. But in a cycle that would be repeated for generations, Govea jettisoned his plans to build a life in Mexico because the wages a bracero could earn in California were too enticing.

The aspiring singer and amateur photographer became, in the words stamped on his temporary visa, a "peon de via" – a railroad worker. Like all Mexican braceros (the name of the guest worker program was derived from the Spanish word for "arms"), Govea was entirely at the mercy of his employer. Unlike most braceros, he had learned to speak English and could type, skills that propelled him from cook's helper to an office job in the central California city of Bakersfield. On Sundays, Govea often accompanied a fellow bracero to visit his friends in the nearby countryside. There Juan Govea met Margaret de la Rosa, a quiet teenager who had dropped out of school after eighth grade to work in the fields, where she excelled at picking oranges. Within a few years, the two married and moved to Bakersfield. Juan was now a legal immigrant working for the railroad in the ice plant, but the chances of moving beyond the narrow physical and mental confines of the barrio seemed remote. Margaret's world was circumscribed by her shyness; sheltered since childhood and uncomfortable around strangers, she talked to few outside her family. Juan chafed at his position, angered by the daily slights and the ever-prevalent racism. He told his daughter she would be a lawyer, to fight injustice, even as he saw how she was treated in the second-class schools: just another Mexican kid of whom little or nothing was expected. School officials even changed her name. They decided Maria de Jesus was too difficult to pronounce, and she became Jessica.

In 1954, Govea heard about a fledging group, the Community Service Organization (CSO). He began attending meetings run by an organizer who talked persuasively about ways that poor Mexicans could fight for their rights: a short, soft-spoken man who pointed to dramatic electoral and legal triumphs in Los Angeles, San Jose, and Oakland. That leader was Cesar Estrada Chavez. He was still more than a decade away from international fame when he organized the Community Service Organization chapter in Bakersfield and noticed the man taking notes during meetings at Our Lady of Guadalupe church. Chavez and Govea began to talk, as Chavez did what he had learned to do in other cities: identify local leaders, build a volunteer-run organization, and show disenfranchised citizens how to exert power.

Within three years, the Bakersfield CSO had registered more than 2,000 voters, sponsored English and citizenship classes for hundreds more, and lobbied successfully with the NAACP (National Association for the Advancement of Colored People) to make Bakersfield the second city in the state to adopt a Fair Employment Practices ordinance. Juan Govea, with a combination of charm and passion for justice, soon emerged as a leader in a CSO chapter that grew to 800 members. Margaret Govea overcame her shyness, first by attending the monthly meetings, then running the social committee, serving as recording secretary and eventually chapter president. She returned to school to become a nurse and worked at a clinic for farm workers. The Goveas' oldest daughter, Jessica, grew up to be not a lawyer but an organizer, rising in the United Farm Workers (UFW) and serving on the union's executive board. Forced out in the 1980s, she took the lessons of La Causa, as the movement was called, and taught them to Dominican garment workers, Salvadoran coffee processors, and Chinese healthcare workers.

The Community Service Organization, a largely overlooked but remarkably successful experiment, was a watershed for Mexican Americans in California. As CSO grew from 1947 to 1961, its success marked the start of the civil rights movement of the West, a struggle that has been historically overshadowed by the black–white battles of the South. That CSO is often relegated to a footnote in history, its successes largely unknown, stems in part from the dearth of attention the organization has received in the scholarly literature. With a few exceptions – most notably David G. Gutierrez's work (1995 and 2004), which discusses CSO in the broader historical context of immigration, assimilation, and citizenship – CSO has been overlooked even in the field of Chicano studies. From more narrow perspectives, Jacques Levy's early biography of Chavez (1975) offers a detailed, if somewhat romanticized and uncorroborated, account of

Chavez's experiences in CSO, and Stephen Pitti (2003) details the importance of CSO in one particular region.

CSO was the catalyst for the election of Mexican American city council members and congressmen, the prosecution of police officers in brutality cases, the registration of more than 450,000 California voters and tens of thousands of US citizens. But more fundamentally, CSO was instrumental in developing leadership and empowering Mexican Americans who had thought themselves helpless to fight for such basics as street lights and more complicated demands like better schools. In the words of one of CSO's early presidents, Herman Gallegos: "More than any other benefit, the CSO was a psychological turning point for Mexican Americans . . . No longer did Mexican Americans relegate to thinking of themselves as passive victims of history. They learned how to generate and use power constructively."[1]

CSO was historically significant for another reason as well. Its most prominent alumnus, Cesar Chavez, was profoundly shaped by his experience as an organizer and later director of CSO. During the decade he worked for CSO, Chavez learned the art of organizing people one by one, the importance of offering services to members, the need to form strategic alliances with religious and labor associations – all tactics that helped him build the first successful union for farm workers. At the same time, Chavez's leadership of the UFW was shaped by his determination to avoid the disappointments that drove him out of CSO in 1962 – frustrations over his inability to control the organization, its agenda, and its members. His CSO experience influenced key decisions that ultimately hastened the tragic demise of an organization that had the potential to transform agricultural labor in the United States. The expectation in the late 1970s that there would be widespread unionization of field workers, comparable to the impact of the industrial unions, never materialized.

The saga of the Govea family illustrates the lasting influence of CSO and its power to change lives. And the family's story parallels the trajectory of Cesar Chavez and the movement he founded – its against-all-odds success and international appeal, its legacy of activism, and its ultimate failure as a labor union.

The Power of CSO: Not Just the Dog Catcher Anymore

The Community Service Organization arose out of the nexus of two events in Los Angeles in 1947: Edward Roybal's unsuccessful campaign for a city council seat, and the arrival of Fred Ross, an organizer and protégé of the Chicago-based organizer Saul Alinsky. Ross, who had been working in a migrant camp in Central California and then with workers in the citrus belt, convinced Alinksy that the Industrial Areas Foundation (IAF) should fund an effort to organize poor Mexicans in Los Angeles.

Ross met with a small group trying to rebuild after Roybal's thrashing at the polls. The talented politician's loss in a heavily Latino district pointed to the obvious yet unprecedented organizing tactic of conducting voter registration drives among Mexican Americans. Though the task would prove easier said than done, the idea sparked one of CSO's most successful long-term campaigns. Roybal's victory in the same district two years later offered a concrete example of the potential power of Mexican American voters, helping CSO in its crusade not only to register voters but also to convince Mexicans it was worth their time and effort to become US citizens.

CSO grew rapidly through a tactic pioneered by Ross. This was the "house meeting" method of organizing, a sort of Tupperware system where one supporter invited a group of friends over to listen to a pitch from Ross or another organizer. The concept would prove to be one of CSO's lasting legacies, a point stressed by Carl Tjerandsen in a book that draws on numerous site visits, interviews, and primary documents to provide the only lengthy, detailed discussion of CSO's activities and impact (1980).

By 1952, Ross was expanding CSO to San Jose. A public health nurse suggested he talk to Cesar Chavez. The Chavez family had become migrants after losing their land in Arizona during the Depression, and Cesar had worked on and off in the fields since leaving school after eighth grade. He served in the Navy and, like many returning veterans who were drawn to CSO, Chavez was angry and disillusioned at the discrimination he faced when he returned home (Levy 1975).

Chavez became Ross's star student, and excelled at the house meeting system of organizing. He soon was hired as an organizer. By 1954, CSO held its first national convention, where Roybal gave the keynote address: "We are not going to stop until we have reached that point that we are a part of the overall community and that overall community responds to our needs and wishes . . . We are no longer Mexican hyphen Americans . . . We are Americans."[2]

Later that year, Chavez began setting up the CSO chapter in Bakersfield, a sprawling city surrounded by farmland about 100 miles north of Los Angeles. Then as now, the poor Mexicans lived in slums on the east side of town, known as the Little Okie because of the previous generation of poor migrants.

Chavez followed the pattern CSO had established elsewhere, recruiting volunteers who could be trained and then sworn in as deputy registrars, which enabled them to register voters. The battle with Vera Gibson, the Kern County registrar, proved particularly troublesome; she delayed swearing in the CSO volunteers for months and then conducted background investigations that prompted an outraged letter from Ross to Chavez calling her actions "outright racial discrimination."[3]

Because Juan Govea was not a citizen, he could not serve as a deputy registrar. But he helped in the drives by knocking on doors to identify potential voters, bringing along his young daughter. Jessica was one of a group of children who learned to "bird dog" – placing chalk marks outside the houses of non-voters so the adults knew where to go.

The 1960 election marked a highpoint of CSO's power: the organization registered record numbers of Mexican American voters – 137,000 that year, bringing their total to 450,000 – and also helped make sure voters went to the polls, providing key support for John F. Kennedy. (Though CSO was officially non-partisan, its efforts generally helped Democrats.) In Bakersfield, in 22 precincts where CSO registered voters, 93 percent of those registered voted (Tjerandsen 1980: 113: 86–7).

The same year, the first Mexican American was elected to the Hanford city council. Tjerandsen recounts the comments of a CSO member exulting that Mexican Americans were no longer routinely sent to the dog catcher, by tradition the one Spanish-speaking city official:

> Imagine, every time something came up which had anything to do with the city we would have to go to the dog catcher! But not anymore! . . . All has changed since the Community Service Organization. (Tjerandsen 1980: 88)

By then, the Govea home had become an unofficial CSO headquarters. Visitors seeking help arrived almost every night at the cramped house, where four children shared one of the two bedrooms. In between translating forms and offering advice, Juan Govea labored for months to translate the California driver's manual into Spanish, so it could be used in classes.

"My values and beliefs about people and justice were formed by the example set by my parents and their associates," Jessica Govea later wrote. "I grew up seeing poor people take charge of their destiny and create positive change."[4]

She followed their example at an early age. The summer after eighth grade, when a close friend was killed by a car after walking several miles to take her younger siblings to the closest park, Jessica took a petition to all the neighbors asking for a county park in the Little Okie. (It was built four years later.) She formed a Junior CSO and presided over meetings at her house, using Roberts Rules of Order.

CSO kept her from becoming bitter, Jessica later wrote, when she encountered prejudice in high school, where she was placed in sewing and cooking classes until her father demanded she be put on an academic track.

Like her father, Jessica spoke her mind, often earning high marks on the debating team for presentation, but losing points for content. Her favorite speech was about the misery of farm workers, which she knew firsthand; she picked cotton at the age of four and often worked in the fields in summer and weekends to help out.

The plight of farm workers was very much on Chavez's mind by the time CSO was celebrating victories in 1960. The year before, he had scored his first success in the fields, working with a local union, the United Packing House Workers Association, which gave CSO a $20,000 grant to help workers in Oxnard who were being denied jobs. Growers were subverting the laws and hiring cheaper and more easily exploited braceros, instead of local workers. After an 11-month campaign, Chavez had recruited 950 CSO members, enrolled 650 people in citizenship classes, registered 300 new voters and precipitated a state investigation that forced growers to hire local workers (Tjerandsen 1980).

The textbook lesson in creative organizing is recounted by Ross in *Conquering Goliath: Cesar Chavez at the Beginning* (1989), a step-by-step recollection of how Chavez prevailed in Oxnard. What Ross did not relate, however, is what happened six months later. The Oxnard CSO board had lost interest; members were fighting with each other; in effect, all Chavez's earlier work had been undone. Chavez recalled how he felt when he returned to Oxnard: "I was so mad – I don't know at whom, at the leadership and at the people for not fighting for what I was sure was there. And I thought of all the time and energy that I had put in. If I had had the support of CSO, I would have built a union there" (Levy 1975: 143–4).

The Lessons of CSO: What Not to Do

The Oxnard experience crystallized growing frustrations for Chavez, focused on money and control. First, CSO was financially dependent on foundations and donors, so the organization had to undertake programs that its funders would support. Such precarious funding also made any long-term strategy difficult.

Second, although Chavez was director of the national CSO, he served at the pleasure of the board. "He was not part of the board and he had no vote. He had a voice, but he was their servant," Fred Ross recalled. He added: "They were always questioning whatever it was he was doing . . . That was one of the mistakes he wasn't going to allow himself to be trapped into when he went out on his own."[5]

In addition, CSO was highly decentralized – there was a national organization and board, but each local chapter had great autonomy in setting its own agenda. Finally, perhaps Chavez's biggest disappointment was with the members themselves. CSO had succeeded in empowering people: now they wanted to set their own agendas, which did not necessarily coincide with Chavez's vision. The clash resulted in a split roughly defined as poor vs. middle class. Some CSO chapters, particularly in cities and along the coast, began to be dominated by middle-class professionals, many of whom wanted to use the organization for their own advancement. Teachers, public employees, or aspiring politicians, they were reluctant to take on issues that could prove controversial. In more rural areas, the chapters tended to hew closer to their original mission, still run by low-wage workers and focused on the needs of the working poor and disenfranchised.

Over the years, in writing and in conversations, Chavez often referred bitterly to the emerging middle class and their dominance of an organization formed to empower the poor. In many areas, CSO chapters withered because their core constituency no longer felt welcome.

By 1962, after seeing his work in Oxnard unravel, Chavez made a pitch to the board at the national CSO convention, arguing the group should organize farm workers. When the idea was rejected, as he had anticipated, Chavez quit. "He concluded that only an organization free of the drag of middle-class interest could be made to serve this purpose," Tjerandsen reported after interviewing Chavez (1980: 115).

The Chavez family moved to Delano, a small farming community a half-hour north of Bakersfield, where Cesar's wife had family. Chavez began organizing the National Farm Workers Association, drawing heavily on the roots of CSO: he traveled the state, held house meetings, canvassed workers. He offered services to attract members – a death benefit, a credit union for small loans, help filling out income tax forms. He started a newspaper to publicize the association's victories. Unlike CSO, however, Chavez insisted on collecting monthly dues, to avoid a dependence on outside money. He was convinced that people needed to be financially invested in the organization for it to succeed.

He took with him from CSO not only his experience but also a cadre of supporters and key alliances. Some, like Dolores Huerta and Gilbert Padilla, left jobs at CSO and worked directly with Chavez. Others, like Chris Hartmire, director of the Migrant Ministry, formed a network of key outside supporters who helped pay staff salaries, scavenge supplies, and build support in the religious community. Fred Ross stayed in touch, and later played a key role in the UFW's strike. And around the state, Chavez relied for hospitality and contacts on such CSO stalwarts as the Goveas, who transferred their loyalty to the farm workers union. "We always supported Cesar," Margaret Govea said.[6] Chavez held organizing meetings at their home, and the Bakersfield CSO voted to help Chavez in his earliest effort, conducting a farm worker census in 1962.[7]

In 1964, Jessica graduated from high school. Knowing the speech she planned to deliver would be censored, she submitted a different script and then delivered her unsanctioned message, challenging her classmates to practice tolerance: "Do you try to understand the many cultures which have combined to make what is known as the American culture or do you call your fellow students niggers, Okies, cholos?" She concluded with a quote from President Kennedy:

> Each man is sometimes called upon to stand for what he believes to be right against the pressures and opinions of friends, fellow workers, constituents or the force of popular attitude . . . the rest of us can contribute to the vitality of our democracy by refusing to join in unreasoning attacks upon those with whom we disagree, and by respecting them for having the strength to wage such a lonely struggle.[8]

The UFW: From Heady Movement to Troubled Union

Jessica Govea dropped out of college after her first year and went to work for the UFW, where she waged her own lonely struggle. In September 1965, Mexicans in Chavez's new organization had joined Filipino workers who had walked out of the vineyards in central California, launching a grape strike that would last five years and cement the reputation of the United Farm Workers.

Govea's duties were typical: helping prepare legal papers, answering phones, doing case work for members, organizing picket lines, going to jail. At 21, she left home to help run a boycott operation in Canada, first in Toronto with her boyfriend, UFW organizer Marshall Ganz, and then on her own, in Montreal. Life was chaotic and heady, if sometimes lonely, on the front lines of a crusade that attracted an eclectic mix of people – students, housewives, nuns, and lawyers – all drawn to the cause and the man, all convinced they could do anything. She worked 16 to 20 hours a day, seven days a week, and often went to sleep hungry.

Growers, who point out that the number of actual strikers was quite small, like to say they won the strike, but lost the public relations war. By 1970, under pressure from the boycott, the major grape growers caved to the inevitability of union contracts. Chavez called each of the key boycott leaders to tell them the news in July 1970. There was triumph and warmth in his voice when he reached Jessica Govea in Montreal and read her the long list of growers who had finally agreed to negotiate contracts. He saved the union's biggest adversaries for last.

> "Are you kidding?" she said on a tape of the conversation made by Chavez. "Oh wow. This is like heaven . . . That's amazing; how did that happen?"

"I don't know, I think the boycott," Chavez responded with an understated chuckle.[9]

The union's celebration was short-lived; a strike in the vegetable and lettuce fields of Salinas soon followed, draining resources. Administering the more than 100 grape contracts proved difficult. The union was learning from scratch, and both employers and workers were often frustrated and angry. Richard Chavez (Cesar's brother and a member of the UFW board) would later call the hiring hall he oversaw a mess, blaming the problems in large measure for the loss of the contracts when they expired in 1973.[10]

Growers, eager to say they were still producing union grapes, brought in the Teamsters when the UFW contracts expired. The UFW went back on the picket line and launched a new boycott, skillfully exerting economic pressure by dramatizing the plight of farm workers. At the height of the grape boycott, a Harris poll reported that 17 million Americans said they were refusing to buy grapes.

Pressure from the boycott, thousands of picketers jamming jails across California, and the 1974 election of liberal Democrat Jerry Brown as California's new governor set the stage for a legislative solution: the first law in the country giving agricultural workers the right to organize. The landmark 1975 law establishing procedures for union elections is still the only such measure in the United States (farm workers are excluded under the National Labor Relations Act). Jessica Govea helped organize the first elections under the new law, persuading workers to mark their X in the box with the black eagle, rather than voting for the Teamsters or "No Union." At dawn on September 8, 1975, she cried as she watched hundreds of vegetable workers at Bruce Church line up to vote, many casting their first ballot ever. The UFW won.

The David versus Goliath story of the UFW in those early years has been often told and written, most eloquently by John Gregory Dunne (1967) and Peter Mattheissen (1969) and most carefully by Ronald Taylor (1975). But little has been written about the UFW in the late 1970s and 1980s, when Chavez struggled unsuccessfully to make the transition from war to peace and lost many of his most talented and dedicated staff. Frank Bardacke, a writer and activist who worked on and off in the fields, has written most extensively about the decline of the UFW in work he is expanding in a forthcoming book (Bardacke 2002). Problems in the later years are mentioned in Ferris & Sandoval (1997), but not fully explored.

Where CSO had been about developing leadership, the UFW already had a leader. The UFW was about a cause, and the leader was determined to build a financially self-sustaining organization that stayed devoted to the cause he prescribed. In the early years when the enemy was clear, the cause and the leader were inseparable. All that changed, however, with the 1975 law, which led to hundreds of successful elections, thousands of new members – who made demands of their own – and contracts that had to be administered. To win elections, negotiate contracts, and oversee the union medical and pension plans required competent, decentralized leadership and staff. A movement morphed into large, complex bureaucracies that needed to be run efficiently. And no one person, no matter how brilliant, could single-handedly hold it together.

The issue of paying staff members came to symbolize the conflicting visions and illustrated the rift that tore apart the union, just as it appeared to be on the verge of lasting success. Chavez consistently expressed a strong antipathy toward paying staff, for financial but above all philosophical reasons. As early as 1973, he predicted the board would try to change the volunteer system, with disastrous consequences. "If they had been with me organizing from the beginning they would understand how valuable it is," he said in November 1973, arguing that the union was able to successfully make its case because of the ethos of sacrifice. They will start to pay salaries, he said: "And then, when we need the public support, we're not going to get it."[11]

Internal calls for changing the volunteer system intensified after 1975, as the union's rapid expansion underscored the need for competent staff who would stay in their jobs. And salaries were necessary if farm workers were going to help run the union, some UFW leaders argued, since workers could now earn decent wages under union contracts.

When the UFW lawyers – who were already receiving small salaries – asked for raises in the spring of 1978, Chavez turned the request into a rallying cry for the volunteer system. The lawyers became poster children for arrogant, greedy Anglos who were not committed to the cause. Chavez forced a board vote on whether to maintain the status quo and narrowly prevailed on a 5–4 split, after threatening to quit. Jessica Govea and Marshall Ganz were on the losing side, and briefly considered leaving the union. Such strong opposition must have shaken Chavez; certainly, the divide brought back memories of CSO. In a note to Jerry Cohen, who resigned as chief counsel in the wake of the vote, Migrant Ministry director and Chavez confidante Chris Hartmire said he believed Chavez was thinking about making a transition from the UFW to lead a new, broader movement on behalf of poor people. "He has told me several times that he is in the exact spot he was in with CSO," Hartmire wrote.[12]

Chavez's brilliance at mobilizing public support was in stark contrast to his shortcomings running a large organization. In the late 1970s, he convened conference after conference to study everything from word processing departments to budgets. He recruited management consultants, used encounter group techniques, and closely monitored spending, often railing about telephone bills and car repairs. He developed an alliance with Synanon, a drug treatment program that had morphed into a cult, and its leader Charles Dederich, who was accused of placing a rattlesnake in an enemy's mailbox. Part of the attraction of Synanon was that everything worked – it was a clean, efficient operation. Chavez could never achieve that degree of control over even his physical surroundings, much less the complex machinery of a young, fast-growing union for transient farm workers.

As Chavez struggled to exert strong, central leadership and control an unwieldy behemoth – medical clinics in Mexicali, lettuce workers in the Imperial Valley, grape pickers in Coachella – he began accusing once-trusted aides of disloyalty. He warned that traitors were out to destroy the union, and conducted numerous public purges of staff. Between 1977 and 1981, many key staff members were forced out. The leader and the cause had diverged, and the conflicting visions of the union could not coexist. Jessica Govea was elected to the executive board in 1977, just as the future looked both promising, in terms of the union's potential, and threatening, in terms of Chavez's struggling leadership. In 1977, she did the work she later said made her most proud – establishing a union-run health clinic across the border, in Mexicali, for the families of the many workers who crossed over to work in the fields of the Imperial Valley. She set up a council with workers from the major companies, documented their needs, calculated costs, and negotiated with doctors and pharmacies in Mexico.

In January 1979, when vegetable workers launched a massive strike, Govea helped Ganz coordinate the strike and administer the benefits, working closely with many of the farm worker leaders who had established the Mexicali clinic. By March, the widening rift on the UFW board had become so crippling that Chavez called a special meeting to discuss the problems. His exchange with Govea was nothing like the one seven years earlier, according to a tape of the meeting:

"Whose faction am I in, Cesar?" she challenged him.

"Well, Jessica, I think you're in Marshall's faction," Chavez said in an emotionless monotone. "I'm not sure. Let's face it, that's what's happening in this union. That's what's happening."[13]

The strike emboldened the leadership in the fields, setting up an inevitable confrontation with Chavez. After seven months, Chavez wanted to end the strike and send workers out on another boycott instead. They essentially refused, telling him respectfully that it was their strike, and they believed they would win. The fact that they did win, and negotiated the best contracts the union had seen, heightened the tension. Those contracts also established paid union representatives; many of the strike leaders thus became the first farm workers paid salaries to work for the union.

Despite the increasing conflicts, Jessica Govea stayed and worked on the union's medical plan. By 1981, she felt she had to leave. On June 5, 1981 she submitted her resignation. She never received an acknowledgment from Chavez, the leader who had known her since she was seven years old and had eulogized her father just a few years earlier.

A Generation of Leaders, but Not in the Fields

During the last decade of Chavez's life, the union's strength steadily declined. Republican administrations threw up roadblocks, growers found loopholes to get out of contracts, and the UFW lost some major lawsuits. The exodus of talented staff accelerated, and the union was progressively less able to devise creative paths around obstacles. The staff who remained were absolute loyalists, including many members of the extended Chavez family. Chavez often spoke about grooming the sons and daughters of movement leaders, including his own.

In late 1981, Chavez quashed an effort by leaders in the vegetable fields to run candidates for the union's executive board. Viewing the workers' campaign as a traitorous move, Chavez drummed out the leaders that Govea and Ganz had developed, trained, and encouraged. They sued; he countersued. A generation that could have been the future leadership of the union became pariahs instead.

Ganz, who had resigned at the same time as Govea, was blamed for masterminding the plot with the worker-leaders, and conspiring to take over the union. The fallout was so ugly that, years later, Margaret Govea was forced to cross a union picket line to attend a fundraiser when her daughter-in-law campaigned for a judgeship.

After Chavez died in 1993, his son-in-law, Arturo Rodriguez, became president of the union. Cesar's son Paul was already a key player, running an affiliated non-profit organization, the National Farm Workers Service Center. Together, the two preside today over a network of interlocked non-profit organizations that exploit the UFW name and trademark eagle to raise millions of dollars in public and private money – money that does little to help farm workers. In the fields, a new generation of immigrants, most of them in the United States illegally, know little if anything about the UFW and are likely to associate the name Cesar Chavez only with a famous Mexican boxer who shares the name (*Los Angeles Times*, 2006).

In 1993, Jessica Govea was diagnosed with breast cancer; she believed it came from the pesticides in the fields where she worked as a child. For the next 12 years, she worked, taught, and wrote about organizing – at

Cornell and Rutgers Universities, and with various unions and advocacy groups.

She died on January 23, 2005. Her memorial service in California a few months later turned into a reunion of UFW alumni who had not seen each other for decades. They form the union's lasting legacy: a generation of organizers and activists who had taken their talents elsewhere – helping society, but not farm workers.

"We all know that Jessica was one hell of an organizer," Eliseo Medina said at the service, "because even when she's not here, she's still bringing us together." Medina, a farm worker who rose in the UFW, left in 1978 and went on to become one of the most successful organizers in the country, tied the successes of decades ago to unfulfilled promises of the twenty-first century. Describing Jessica Govea's role in the boycott, Medina said:

> We won. We won. And when we did that we captured the imagination and the hearts of millions and millions and millions of people throughout this world. But we also raised the hopes of millions of workers around this country, who saw what farm workers had done and said, "Maybe I, too, can do the same thing. And if I fight, I can help change my life, and create a better life for myself and my children."

As he spoke, the UFW had no contracts in grapes, where the strike began four decades earlier, and fewer than 5,000 members, many working under substandard contracts. The compound that is the union's headquarters has been transformed at public expense into an elaborate shrine to Cesar Chavez; the center and the grounds around his grave are available to rent for weddings and parties (*Los Angeles Times*, 2006).

In Bakersfield, Margaret Govea and two friends kept a small CSO office going long after the statewide organization had largely fallen apart. Until the late 1990s, each spent one day a week in the office. Since the office closed, Govea still fields frequent calls for advice and assistance and is active in doing the work she has done for so many years.

In the spring of 2007, she was approached by Paul Chavez, who proposed naming a new housing project in Bakersfield after her daughter and husband, who died in 1976. In recent years, the Service Center has expanded rapidly, building and operating government-subsidized housing in California, Texas, Arizona, and New Mexico. Though many projects are located in farm worker communities, they are not designed for farm workers, who cannot afford the rents. Most of the work is done by non-union labor.

Paul Chavez has named several of the projects after leaders who worked with his father in the early years, including Fred Ross. After a family meeting, Margaret Govea agreed. On March 9, 2007, a 150-unit complex in Bakersfield was christened Govea Gardens.

NOTES

1 Herman Gallegos, January 20, 2007 email exchange with author.
2 Edward Roybal collection, Charles E. Young Research Library, University of California, Los Angeles.
3 Fred Ross letter to Cesar Chavez, April 6, 1955, Walter P. Reuther Library, Wayne State University, Detroit.
4 Jessica Govea, November 30, 1988 application. Personal papers of Jessica Govea.
5 Jacques E. Levy Research Collection on Cesar Chavez, Yale Collection of Western Americana, Beinecke Rare Book and Manuscript Library, New Haven.
6 Margaret Govea interview, March 2, 2007 with author.
7 Minutes of Bakersfield CSO meetings, personal papers of Margaret Govea.
8 Jessica Govea graduation speech, personal papers of Jessica Govea.
9 Levy collection.
10 Ibid.
11 Ibid.
12 Chris Hartmire letter to Jerry Cohen, July 17, 1978, personal papers of Jerry Cohen.
13 Tape of National Executive Board meeting, March 11, 1979. Walter P. Reuther Library, Wayne State University, Detroit.

REFERENCES

Bardacke, Frank. 2002. "Cesar Chavez: The Serpent and the Dove." In Clark Davis and David Igler, eds., *The Human Tradition in California*. Latham, MD: Scholarly Resources Inc.

Dunne, John Gregory. 1967. *Delano – The Story of the California Grape Strike*. New York: Farrar, Straus & Giroux.

Ferris, Susan and Sandoval, Ricardo. 1997. *The Fight in the Fields: Cesar Chavez and the Farmworkers Movement*. New York: Harcourt Brace.

Gutiérrez, David G. 1995. *Walls and Mirrors: Mexican Americans, Mexican Immigrants, and the Politics of Ethnicity*. Berkeley and Los Angeles: University of California Press.

Gutiérrez, David G., ed. 2004. *The Columbia History of Latinos in the United States Since 1960*. New York: Columbia University Press.

Levy, Jacques. 1975. *Cesar Chavez: Autobiography of La Causa*. New York: W. W. Norton.

Matthiessen, Peter. 1969. *Sal Si Puedes (Escape If You Can) Cesar Chavez and the New American Revolution*. Berkeley and Los Angeles: University of California Press.

Pawel, Miriam. 2006. "UFW: A Broken Contract," *The Los Angeles Times*, January 8–January 11.

Pawel, Miriam. 2006. "For UFW, Contracts are Give and Take," *The Los Angeles Times*, March 20.

Pitti, Stephen J. 2003. *The Devil in Silicon Valley: Northern California, Race and Mexican Americans.* Princeton, NJ: Princeton University Press.

Ross, Fred. 1989. *Conquering Goliath: Cesar Chavez at the Beginning.* Keene, CA: El Taller Grafico Press.

Taylor, Ronald B. 1975. *Chavez and the Farm Workers.* Boston, MA: Beacon Press.

Tjerandsen, Carl. 1980. *Education for Citizenship: A Foundation's Experience.* Santa Cruz, CA: Emil Schwarzhaupt Foundation, Inc.

COLLECTIONS

Edward Roybal Papers, Department of Special Collections, Charles E. Young Library, University of California, Los Angeles.

Fred Ross Papers, Special Collections, Cecil Green Library, Stanford University, Palo Alto, CA.

Jacques E. Levy Research Collection on Cesar Chavez, Yale Collection of Western Americana, Beinecke Rare Book and Manuscript Library, New Haven, CT.

FURTHER READING

Bernstein, Shana Beth. 2003. "Building Bridges at Home in a Time of Global Conflict: Interracial Cooperation and the Fight for Civil Rights in Los Angeles, 1933–1954." PhD dissertation, Stanford University.

Chapter Twenty-seven

HOLLYWOOD CHANGES ITS SCRIPT

John Horn

The Los Angeles intersection of Hollywood and Highland boulevards can be seen quite fittingly as both the geographical and metaphorical center of the motion picture business.

Within a few paces of the junction stand two of the nation's most storied theaters, the El Capitan (now a meticulously restored movie palace, it was built in 1926 and originally presented live plays starring, among others, Clark Gable, Buster Keaton, and Joan Fontaine) and Grauman's Chinese Theatre, which opened in 1927 with Cecil B. De Mille's *The King of Kings* and whose entry carries the handprints of most of Hollywood's biggest stars, including Clint Eastwood, Elizabeth Taylor, and Jimmy Stewart. The first Academy Awards were presented in 1929 at the Hollywood Roosevelt Hotel, just west of the El Capitan (Lord 2003).

In a nearly equal radius of several miles from the intersection are the homes of all the major movie studios – 20th Century Fox and Sony to the southwest, Universal, Disney, and Warner Bros. to the northeast (Paramount is just a few miles away, the only studio in the neighborhood). Any number of sound stages and office complexes for movie production and editing can be found by walking a few blocks in any direction. In the summer of 2007, the actor Will Smith was filming a superhero movie right in the middle of the street where Hollywood and Highland converge.

Though Hollywood exists not as an incorporated city but instead as a figurative landmark, the Hollywood and Highland intersection is also the hub for the thousands of tourists who come to California every day looking for a glimpse of the movie business. Crowded tour buses depart from neighboring streets throughout the day, out-of-town visitors pile into area T-shirt and souvenir stores, and street performers wearing superhero costumes pose for pictures in front of the Chinese Theatre.

Nearly a century earlier, it was from this very neighborhood that Hollywood emerged as not only the birthplace of the nation's modern movie business but also as the focal point of California and, by extension, the nation's popular culture. After establishing their creative and technological roots in New York and the East, filmmakers headed to California for two basic reasons: to escape the monopolistic chokehold of Thomas Edison's Motion Picture Patents Company and to take advantage of the state's diverse locations and fair weather, the latter of which would attract millions more new residents through the years (Gabler 1988). "It was one of the few things that happened to Southern California spontaneously," writes Remi Nadeau. "No booster program drew this industry – except the general campaign that advertised the climate. Not even the imaginative boosters could foresee the magical growth of Hollywood" (Nadeau 1960: 204).

Arriving in the early 1900s, Hollywood's earliest settlers established the movie business as a beacon to immigrants. The earliest show business titans included any number of mostly working-class immigrants: the Hungarian-born Adolph Zukor and William Fox, Poland's Samuel Goldwyn, Germany's Carl Laemmle, Canada's Mack Sennett, and Russia's Lewis Selznick and Louis B. Mayer (Katz 1990). Hollywood, in other words, was entertainment's Ellis Island. And, with the arrival of sound – turning silent movies into "talkies" – the town's new occupants built and centralized the business in very short order.

"By 1920, Hollywood was no longer just a place but a way of doing business," writes Steven Ross, noting that in 1921 the film business, even in its embryonic stages, employed 250,000 in Los Angeles:

> The large number of modest-sized, geographically scattered producers, distributors, and exhibitors that dominated the prewar era were steadily supplanted by an increasingly oligarchic, vertically integrated studio system based in Los Angeles and New York and financed by some of the largest banks and corporations in the nation. When we talk about a "Hollywood" production, we usually mean a film that is made by a big studio, costs millions of dollars, features famous movie stars and expensive sets, and is distributed to theaters throughout the world . . . In short, Hollywood means big business – nearly $1 billion of business in 1921. (Ross 1997: 118)

As Kevin Starr recounts, Hollywood's ascension mirrored (and, no doubt, helped to guide) the state's rise. Before 1930, Starr writes,

> Southern California had emerged into the sunlight as both an imagined and a fully materialized American place. It had been a rapid rise, resembling the construction of a set at a motion picture studio; indeed, the set for the film *Intolerance* (1916) between Sunset and Hollywood boulevards might very well stand as a paradigm for the interconnection of the nascent film industry and the rising region. Intended to depict the essence of the city of Babylon at the height of its power, the three-hundred-foot-high set . . . functioned, like the expositions recently concluded in San Francisco and San Diego, as a dream city referencing the past and suggesting the future. (Starr 2005: 183)

That future included the movie business growing into a global artistic and business phenomenon. By 1947, the six major movie studios' share of North American movie theater ticket sales surpassed $1 billion, which put movies third in line behind grocery stores and automotive sales as the nation's largest retail businesses. By the early twenty-first century, *a single* blockbuster – *Spider-Man, Finding Nemo,* or *Pirates of the Caribbean* – could generate profits in excess of $1 billion per film (Epstein 2005).

Hollywood and Highland is also the shorthand address for an outdoor shopping mall that houses the Kodak Theatre. The mall itself is gaudy, adorned with giant elephants that recall a movie set from decades earlier. But it is what happens every year inside the Kodak Theatre that offers a more fitting comparison with Hollywood's past, because the Kodak is the home to the Academy Awards.

When *Crash* captured the "best picture" prize in the 2006 Academy Awards, the ensemble drama accomplished more than causing surprise to countless show business awards prognosticators, most of whom had confidently forecast that *Brokeback Mountain* would collect Hollywood's top Oscar. On a more meaningful level, the *Crash* triumph cemented the decades-long ascendancy of independently financed and distributed cinema, and hinted at the dramatic shifts occurring inside the film business at the start of the twenty-first century.

Through Hollywood's earliest years and into its relatively recent past, the Academy Awards have played out as an insular, company town party: filmmakers, actors, studio executives, and talent agents congratulated themselves on their own home cooking. Movies that were conceived, financed, produced, marketed, and distributed by one of the industry's major studios invariably dominated both the Oscar nominations and wins. The closest any interloper could hope to come to the Oscars was by grabbing a seat in the grandstands above the ceremony's requisite red carpet. But in very short order, the very people who had been on the outside looking in ended up sitting at Hollywood's head table.

While the six major studios – Disney, 20th Century Fox, Paramount, Universal, Warner Bros. and Columbia (later known as Sony) – through much of Hollywood's history had controlled the development, production, and distribution of almost every feature film, their stranglehold loosened dramatically in the 1980s with the rise of movies financed without major studio money (Biskind 2004). By 1986, none of the five best picture nominees – *Platoon, A Room with a View, The Mission, Hannah and Her Sisters,* and *Children of a Lesser God* – was born at a studio (Levy 2001). These movies all originated in the world of independent cinema: movies that were developed, produced, and often distributed without any help from the big studios.

It wasn't simply that the studios were abandoning artistically ambitious dramas – the kinds of movies that tend to dominate awards such as the Oscars – in favor of more unoriginal commercial fare like remakes, sequels, and comic book adaptations, although that programming shift was certainly underway. It was also that a new kind of movie producer had come to town, and was starting to supplant Hollywood itself as the source of quality movies.

While the studios tried to keep their increasingly sprawling conglomerate parents happy with a slate of films that would theoretically deliver predictable quarterly profits, these new financiers were gambling on projects that offered narrative daring instead of *Spider-Man* safety – movies, in other words, like *Crash*, a story about Los Angeles race relations whose financing was cobbled together by Bob Yari, a real-estate speculator turned independent film producer. As soon as the outside investors such as Yari started filling Hollywood's creative vacuum, the studios came to realize something else: these external deep pockets also could underwrite the mainstream fare that dominates a studio's output. The same year *Crash* won the "best picture" statue, five of Warner Bros.' summer movies – *Poseidon*, *Lady in the Water*, *Superman Returns*, *The Ant Bully*, and *Beerfest* – were not solely financed by the studio's parent, Time Warner Inc., but rather were backed by hundreds of millions of dollars of private equity from two non-Hollywood hedge funds.[1]

The studios, to put it another way, were no longer operating as soup-to-nuts content creators. They had become the show business equal of a package delivery outfit, pocketing a fee – often, about 15 percent of a film's ticket sales – for shipping someone else's wares. Companies such as Sony, Paramount, and 20th Century Fox were still bringing movies into theaters and usually organizing the marketing campaigns, but the films they were distributing represented an increasingly smaller percentage of their own creative and financial capital. Hollywood was turning into more of a distribution enterprise, less of a creative business. As movies became more of a commodity, it became increasingly important to be aligned with films that stood out in the marketplace. The simplest solution was to focus a larger and larger share of attention (and, naturally, money) on movies with built-in sales hooks: sequels, remakes, and adaptations of pop culture bestsellers, from novels to superhero comic books.

What certainly could be seen as an artistic regression was, in the bottom-line eyes of Wall Street analysts, mutual fund managers, and chief financial officers, a step in the right direction. Moviemaking has been and likely always will be an unpredictable endeavor. It is impossible to guess at audience tastes and, because most narrative movies require at least two years to make, a forward-looking guess of movie-going predilections at the moment a film commenced production could be hopelessly moot by the time that same movie arrived in theaters. The box office record books are filled with movies – the three *The Lord of the Rings* movies being an excellent recent example – that were initially rejected by any number of studios as being commercially unworthy.

As the consolidation of the movie studios accelerated through the 1990s, the studios were left searching for answers: they wanted (and, actually, needed) bigger rewards, but not commensurate risks. But how could a business with $30 billion in annual revenues take as much of the audience's fickleness out of the equation as possible? The answer was to manage chance, and that is what transformed the business.

At one point, Hollywood's studios were either their own corporations or parts of only slightly larger entertainment companies. By the end of the twentieth century, those stand-alone businesses had, thanks to a series of mergers and acquisitions, been absorbed by sprawling international conglomerates, as the recent history of Universal Pictures dramatized. Universal, the studio that made *Frankenstein*, *Jaws*, and *American Graffiti*, was in 1962 part of MCA Inc., whose few businesses eventually would include television production and theme parks (Katz 1990). In 1990, MCA was sold to the Japanese electronics manufacturer Matsushita Electric Industrial Co. for $6.6 billion, which sold it five years later to Canada's beverage concern Seagram Co. for $5.7 billion. Seagram was in turn purchased by the French utility company Vivendi for $34 billion in 2000, and America's General Electric Co. (GE) bought 80 percent of Vivendi's entertainment assets in 2003 in a deal valued at $45 billion.

In the vast wardrobe of General Electric, which had in 2006 some 300,000 employees and businesses as diverse as jet engines, kitchen appliances, and consumer credit, Universal Pictures was little more than pocket lint. With revenues in 2006 of more than $163 billion, GE said its combined NBC Universal division (which includes not only the television network NBC, but also several cable channels) accounted for just 10 percent of the conglomerate's revenues, and about 11 percent of its profits.[2]

But the conglomerate nonetheless counted on its movie division to contribute steady and predictable quarterly income. The creation of artistic content, of course, is not exactly like appliance manufacturing. The success of both, however, can be shaped by outside forces such as consumer confidence or competition. Research and development within manufacturing follows a predictable path, but the route is more difficult to understand in Hollywood. Any given screenplay might be rewritten by half a dozen writers, all at a cost of several hundred thousand dollars, over several years. But if the right actor or director does not commit to the screenplay, the entire project can be dispatched into the trash, a process the studios euphemistically call "turnaround." As Universal executives would privately complain, General Electric's accountants did not understand that kind of waste, even if it sometimes led to profitable films. Wouldn't it be better, the town's new accountants and studio managers wondered, if someone else's money paid for the development (and abandonment) of so many screenplays?

As the new century began, other studios found themselves in similar predicaments – they were still working in a creative enterprise, but in the shadow of immense conglomerate parents. As part of the merger boom that brought Universal into General Electric, the Walt Disney Co. had merged with ABC; Time Warner, the parent of Warner Bros., joined up with America Online; 20th Century Fox was a part of News Corporation; and Columbia Pictures had become part of Japan's Sony Corporation. Even one of Hollywood's smaller, more entrepreneurial movie studios, DreamWorks, was folded into Paramount Pictures when Viacom Inc. bought the formerly stand-alone movie company for $1.6 billion in 2005.

Faced with relentless pressure to deliver consistent profits, the studios turned toward their production slates, and overhauled them. In would come sequels, remakes, and pop-culture adaptations; out would be character-driven dramas aimed at sophisticated patrons. Some studio executives would tell producers and screenwriters they did not want to hear the word "drama" mentioned in their offices – the "D-word," as it was called in industry parlance, suggested an impossible financial gamble. Michael London, the producer of the critically acclaimed (and, ultimately, profitable) drama *Sideways*, recalled that when he looked for a studio to underwrite his movie, one potential funder dismissed him by saying, "We've already done our one movie about people."[3]

From a ticket-selling perspective, the studio's evasion of movies like *Sideways* and *Crash* was an irrefutable success. Of the top 10 highest-grossing movies of all time through the end of 2006, only three – *Titanic*, the original *Star Wars*, and *E.T.: The Extra-Terrestrial* – could be considered purely original works. The rest were either sequels (*Pirates of the Caribbean: Dead Man's Chest*), adaptations of previously published material (*Spider-Man*), or both (*The Lord of the Rings: The Return of the King*, *Spider-Man 2*). The three *Pirates of the Caribbean* movies were based upon (and heavily promoted within) a theme park ride. As well as those movies did in domestic theaters, they generated commensurate, if not superior, returns overseas and on home video. While the final *Lord of the Rings* movie sold more than $377 million in tickets in American and Canadian theaters, it grossed nearly $800 million more outside of North America.

If the studios had found, for at least a moment, a winning financial formula, critics and cineastes had to wait a long time for something as rewarding from an artistic perspective. Yet that discerning segment of the audience was no longer a top studio priority. Even in the early years of the twenty-first century, the studios would routinely hold advance screenings of all of their films so that reviewers could publish their appraisals in a timely fashion. A handful of films – usually low-budget slasher movies – would be released without the benefit of these press previews, under the theory that the core audience for horror films would not be influenced by a newspaper review. Any other kind of film released without advanced screenings, it was usually proven out, was usually so irredeemably terrible that it needed to be released under the cover of critical darkness. To not preview a movie, consequently, was to send the unmistakable message that the movie was a dud.

Then the studios began to ask – a dud in whose eyes? As they were now much more focused on winning market share than Academy Awards, did they even need film critics and the people who rely upon their opinions? The answer came in early 2007, when Sony released the $120-million comic book adaptation *Ghost Rider* without advance screenings for the news media. By the time the critics eventually weighed in, *Ghost Rider* had grossed an enormous $52 million in its first four days of release – making it both one of the most expensive, and certainly one of the most financially successful, releases of a movie released without reviews.[4]

Ghost Rider also called attention to the new influx of private equity into Hollywood. While the film business has long relied on other people's money, the early 2000s marked the arrival of a new kind of show business backer – the hedge fund. With more than $1 trillion under management, these loosely regulated funds were drawn to Hollywood by the undeniably tempting (but frequently fleeting) combination of fame and fortune. Like dozens of other films released in 2007, *Ghost Rider* was partially financed by Relativity Media, a privately held financing company whose investors included hedge funds. Other prominent hedge fund-supported financing arms included Virtual Studios (which helped finance *The Good German* and *Blood Diamond*) and Legendary Pictures (whose investments included *Superman Returns* and *300*).

But the real hedge went to the studios. In selling off as much as half of the production budgets of their movies to these investors, the studios were able to spread their capital much further without a proportionate reduction in potential profits. The game was rigged in the studios' favor. For a hypothetical film costing $100 million, a hedge fund would contribute half its budget, or $50 million. But as soon as the movie was released, the studios would first collect a distribution fee of roughly 15 percent; the remaining revenues would be split between the studio and the hedge fund. So even though the hedge fund was assuming 50 percent of the risk, it was only receiving 42.5 percent of the reward. (If that hypothetical $100 million film grossed $100 million, the studio would pocket $15 million in distribution fees. The remaining $85 million would be divided in half, with both the studio and the hedge fund netting $42.5 million.)

Hollywood needed that money because the cost of making and marketing the most expensive films was soaring. The biggest summer movies – *Spider-Man 3*, *Pirates of the Caribbean: Dead Man's Chest* – were budgeted at more than $250 million apiece, and were backed by advertising budgets of more than $100 million. The surge in costs was related to a combination of factors, but primarily movie-star salaries (which surpassed $25 million in 2007) and increasingly elaborate visual effects that were often created by hundreds of computer technicians. A group of only three such movies, in other words, could carry a total combined production and marketing price tag of $1 billion. To make room for those kinds of unprecedented expenditures, the studios not only required the assistance of outside investors but also needed to cut out movies considered less likely to turn a profit – the very dramas that win Academy Awards.

As the millennium turned, the studios pursued even more aggressively movies with as much pre-sold awareness as possible. In one four-week period of 2007, Sony, Disney, and DreamWorks respectively released the third installments in their *Spider-Man*, *Pirates of the Caribbean*, and *Shrek* franchises. That same year, Paramount released a movie, *Transformers*, based on a children's action toy; Fox unveiled *28 Weeks Later*, a sequel to its horror movie *28 Days Later*, sequels to *Fantastic Four*, *Die Hard*, and *Alien vs. Predator*, and a film version of the television series *The Simpsons*. New Line Cinema, meanwhile, offered up *Hairspray*, a movie based on a musical which itself was based on a movie, a third *Rush Hour* movie, and a film version of the book *The Golden Compass*. Universal delivered the sequels *The Bourne Ultimatum* and *Bean II*; and Warner Bros., the most resolute disciple of the familiarity-breeds-ticket-sales form, introduced the comic book adaptation *300*, the remake *Teenage Mutant Ninja Turtles*, the sequel *Ocean's 13*, the book adaptation *Nancy Drew*, the sequel *Harry Potter and the Order of the Phoenix*, and the remake *The Invasion*. It's hard to imagine how some of cinema's most innovative artists – Orson Welles, Preston Sturges, Buster Keaton – would have ever made an original work in such an environment.

Fortunately for the fans of quality, handmade movies, as the studios and their hedge funds pursued bigger and bigger potential blockbusters, a new source of equity filled the creative vacuum. These were high net-worth individuals who made their money in businesses as varied as real estate (*Crash*'s Bob Yari), the internet venture eBay (*Good Night, and Good Luck*'s Jeff Skoll), or mortgages (*Little Miss Sunshine*'s Marc Turtletaub).[5] Because these millionaires were spending considerably less on their movies (often no more than $20 million) than the studios, they didn't need to turn out global smashes. Because these financiers were more interested in making quality movies than windfalls, some of Hollywood's best actors and directors began collaborating with them. George Clooney, for one, could do nothing but high-profile studio sequels if that is what he chose to do. But since Skoll was willing to back Clooney's *Good Night, and Good Luck*, the actor-director was able to make a movie he personally cared about.

The qualitative gulf between independently financed dramas and the studio slates was bound to grow even wider, unless some disruptive technology entered the picture. While many predicted the internet and electronic communication tools would change the way audiences see movies – shifting the venue from the movie theater to a personal computer or hand-held device – they also held the potential promise to improve the artistic merits of future movies. That's because they accelerated the spread of word of mouth; some moviegoers would send email messages to their friends during a movie, while many others would ring up their acquaintances on a mobile phone as soon as the film let out.

If the studios were able to fool audiences with carefully crafted (and often disingenuous) advertising campaigns into buying a ticket for a film's opening night, the audience itself was able to communicate a more accurate assessment of a movie's real merits by the time that opening night was over. No matter how slick the coming attractions preview or enticing the poster, bad movies would collapse in a matter of hours, not days or weeks, as had been the case in the late 1990s. The studios, consequently, were thus obligated to start trying to make movies as accomplished as their marketing materials. And that, at least, was one very hopeful sign.

NOTES

1 The funds operate as Legendary Pictures and Virtual Studios. See John Horn, "Investors hope to cruise but sometimes sink; Equity funds and other emergent sources help to finance costly films. But as *Poseidon* shows, downsides can go deep," *The Los Angeles Times*, May 16, 2006; and Claudia Eller, "Picture This: Warner Bros. Having a Rare Down Year; Underperformers such as *Poseidon* have given the studio and investors a sinking feeling," *The Los Angeles Times*, August 18, 2006.

2 For detailed information, see http://www.sec.gov/Archives/edgar/data/40 545/000004054507000006/ex99.htm.

3 Patrick Goldstein, "This Year, the Safe Bets Are Off," *The Los Angeles Times*, January 26, 2005, p. A1.

4 Nicole Sperling, "*Ghost* ablaze with $52 mil; 'Terabithia adds to bounty," *The Hollywood Reporter*, February 21, 2007.

5 Rachel Abramowitz, "Big-money dreamers: These multimillionaires are Hollywood outsiders hoping to be insiders. Are they here for the long haul?" *Los Angeles Times*, April 13, 2003.

REFERENCES

Biskind, Peter. 2004. *Down and Dirty Pictures*. New York: Simon & Schuster.

Epstein, Edward Jay. 2005. *The Big Picture: The New Logic of Money and Power in Hollywood*. New York: Random House.

Gabler, Neal. 1988. *An Empire of their Own: How the Jews Invented Hollywood*. New York: Crown Publishers.

Katz, Ephraim. 1990. *The Film Encyclopedia*. New York: Harper Perennial.

Levy, Emanuel. 2001. *Oscar Fever: The History and Politics of the Academy Awards*. New York: Continuum.

Lord, Rosemary. 2003. *Hollywood Then and Now*. San Diego: Thunder Bay Press.

Nadeau, Remi. 1960. *Los Angeles from Mission to Modern City*. New York: Longmans, Green.

Ross, Steven. 1997. *Working-Class Hollywood: Silent Film and the Shaping of Class in America*. Princeton, NJ. Princeton University Press.

Starr, Kevin. 2005. *California: A History*. New York: The Modern Library.

FURTHER READING

Bach, Steven. 1985. *Final Cut: Art, Money, and Ego in the Making of "Heaven's Gate."* New York: W.W. Morrow.

Biskind, Peter. 1998. *Easy Riders, Raging Bulls: How the Sex-Drugs-and-Rock 'n' Roll Generation Saved Hollywood*. New York: Simon & Schuster.

Dunne, John Gregory. 1969. *The Studio*. New York: Straus & Giroux.

Friedrich, Otto. 1986. *City of Nets: A Portrait of Hollywood in the 1940s*. New York: Harper & Row.

Lumet, Sidney. 1996. *Making Movies*. New York: Vintage.

Ross, Lillian. 2002. *Picture*. Cambridge, MA: Da Capo.

Salamon, Julie. 2002. *The Devil's Candy: The Anatomy of a Hollywood Fiasco*. Cambridge, MA: Da Capo.

Part V

California Prospects in the Twenty-first Century

Chapter Twenty-eight

IMMIGRATION AND RACE IN THE TWENTY-FIRST CENTURY

Bill Ong Hing

Walk through any downtown metropolitan area or college campus in California, take a look around, listen, and you get a very good picture of immigrant and racial California in the twenty-first century. In 1970, 80 percent of the state was white, but within 30 years, California became the first big state to have a "minority majority," joining the ranks of Hawaii and New Mexico. Expect more of the same, because flows of newcomers from Asia and Latin America will continue throughout the century – whatever immigration reforms come about – and the face of California will be ever more diverse. The flows will continue to be significant, although globalization will lead to some equilibrium in terms of migration patterns.

Your walk through California cities or campuses gives you a sense of the state's diversity, but as you peer beneath the surface of that diversity, you realize that the diversity does not come without some tension. Resentment between different racial groups exists and, even worse, hate crimes are on the rise. Anti-immigrant sentiment, directed principally at Latinos, has reached a fever pitch, epitomized by border vigilantes and support for more border fencing. As Proposition 209 has slashed the enrollment of African Americans and Latinos in public universities, resentment over the large enrollment of Asian American students (most of whom are foreign born) has surfaced as well. Students self-segregate into their own social ethnic enclaves at ethnically diverse middle and high schools.

Yet your look at the state will reveal positively exciting things about race as well: greater diversity in business, government, and social leadership, bringing new ideas and perspectives about our society; neighborhoods brought to life with newcomer families, excited about being here and becoming contributing members of society; the ability to learn about new cultures and to take part in their practices and cuisine; the amazing talents of diverse young adults who thrive on learning and challenging us to do better.

Immigration and racial changes in twenty-first-century California will be exciting, but those changes also will bring challenges, for which we should prepare. Demographic changes, diversity, and racial tension are not too difficult to foresee. The challenges presented by these changes will be substantial. How California addresses those challenges is hard to predict, but our responses will shape the kind of society we become. The California society of the future can thrive and be stronger if we take those challenges and see the wonderful opportunities they present.

Mexican Migration

Let's face it. Most of the debate over immigration policy is about Mexican immigration. Proposition 187 may have been tossed out by the courts, but great attention has been paid to vigilantes "defending" the borders and Congress appropriating millions for more fencing to block undocumented migration. Many Americans also are troubled by the entry of so many non-English speakers who challenge "our" culture, irrespective of immigration status. But Mexican migration, driven by employment opportunities or family reunification, will not be curtailed by immigration laws or fences. If the Mexican flow decreases in the twenty-first century, the cause will be substantial economic or social adjustments that have been made in Mexico, not laws.

Immigration laws will not be amended to reduce lawful immigration from Mexico. The days of racial-specific immigration restrictions have long passed, and modern constitutional law interpretation would not sustain something like the Chinese exclusion laws of old. In recent years, more than 40,000 migrants from Mexico lawfully immigrate to the United States annually, and almost half (49 percent) select California as their residence. The proportion that chooses California may decline as Mexican immigrants are attracted to other parts of the country. The same is true of most immigrants; in 1990, 44.5 percent of legal immigrants intended to live in California but by 2000, the proportion was 25.6 percent. But the numbers coming to California will remain significant.

Current strategies to reduce undocumented migration will continue to fail. Efforts to resolve the so-called undocumented alien problem with reforms in 1986 and border strategies of the 1990s have been disasters. Although three million undocumented aliens (the vast majority from Mexico) were able to benefit from legalization (amnesty) provisions of the Immigration Control and Reform Act of 1986 (ICRA) and laws were instituted making it unlawful for employers to hire undocumented workers, the undocumented population continues to grow. The main legalization provision required prior residence of almost five years, so a large segment of the undocumented population was not eligible. Employer sanctions have also been ineffective in stemming the flow because economic and social factors are simply too strong to dissuade Mexican migrants from crossing the border. For the same reasons, the institution of a "control through deterrence" strategy by building up Border Patrol presence and fencing at places along the border – Operation Gatekeeper – has not decreased attempts at surreptitious entries. Instead, deaths through heat stroke or hypothermia (depending on the time of year) have increased as border crossers hike through more dangerous areas along the border. Today, demographers estimate that half a million undocumented immigrants continue to enter the country annually.

The failed resolution of the undocumented alien problem through ICRA and Operation Gatekeeper provides a lesson on how the problem will be addressed today and in the future. The social and economic reasons that motivate Mexicans to cross the border will not soon dissipate, and the US business need for workers from Mexico is being recognized. President George W. Bush's push for a large guestworker program has growing bipartisan support, and at some point in the foreseeable future, either that plan or other avenues of entry for substantial numbers of low-wage workers from Mexico would be expanded.

The North American Free Trade Agreement (NAFTA) is a likely avenue for the lawful migration of greater numbers of Mexican workers and their families to occur. In 1994, NAFTA was touted as a vehicle that would reduce undocumented Mexican migration to the United States. The idea was that since economic development in Mexico was a goal of NAFTA, development would create jobs in Mexico, and Mexicans would stay home. In fact, NAFTA did not work as a method of reducing undocumented migration. Even though NAFTA coincided with a new border enforcement regime, illicit border crossing continued to rise.

The low-wage labor sector is not the only migration from Mexico that has been accelerated since the country initiated new economic reforms. Mexico adopted major economic reforms in 1986, when President Carlos Salinas and a new ruling elite successfully pushed the country's entry into the General Agreement on Tariffs and Trade (GATT). Soon after that, Salinas approached the United States about establishing a continent-wide free trade zone, and those efforts eventually culminated in NAFTA. Over the past 20 years, trade between Mexico and the United States has increased by more than eight times. Just since NAFTA was signed in 1994, trade and investment among Mexico, the United States, and Canada has tripled, and Mexico became the largest supplier of goods and services to the United States, edging out Japan. Business visas for Mexicans have tripled (now about 438,000 annually), while the number of intra-company transferees (for executives and key managers) and investors also has grown dramatically. The number of Mexican tourists has increased by six times (to over 3.6 million each year), while the number of foreign students doubled.

Wage differentials also help explain undocumented migration from Mexico. Recent migration is a manifestation of historic restructuring of the Mexican economy. After 10 years of NAFTA, real wages in Mexico were lower and income inequality grew, even though productivity was up. It turns out that many, if not most, Mexicans who come to the United States looking for work were not unemployed in Mexico. That means that efforts to improve economic conditions in Mexico have to look beyond employment to wages, job quality, and perceptions of opportunity. So their migration is not so much about escaping abject poverty, but to improve their economic situation in the new NAFTA economy.

Of course the problem with this picture is that while the economic arrangements facilitated the movement of goods and services as the integration under NAFTA provisions was unfolding, nothing new was provided to facilitate the movement of labor beyond existing immigration law categories. That means that the need and recruitment of low-wage workers from Mexico that has resulted from increased economic integration has had no lawful channel to use. The interpersonal connections formed between Mexicans and Americans in the course of daily business transactions create a social infrastructure of friendship and kinship that encourages migration and facilitates further movement. North American economic integration and development in Mexico actually has promoted labor migration. Failing to provide for labor migration in NAFTA was, at best, an oversight and certainly, in retrospect, a mistake. Providing for large-scale labor migration through an amendment to NAFTA certainly is one way that Mexican migration may be facilitated in the future.

Thus, the future will bring more and more Mexican workers and families to the United States through legal channels, but the overall numbers will not be unlimited. A significant portion of those migrants will come to California. Providing guestworker visas or more permanent immigration visas is one way to reduce undocumented migration, as legal channels are opened up. However, the floodgates will not be opened. Most undocumented workers from Mexico want to work in the United States temporarily to finance projects back home, like building a house, purchasing land, buying consumer goods. If given the opportunity, they would work on temporary trips to the United States and retire back home to enjoy the fruits of their labor. Demographic changes also suggest some slowing of migration to the United States from Mexico over time. The Mexican birth rate is dropping, the population growth rate is lower, and fewer youngsters are approaching working age. And Mexican President Felipe Calderon is taking steps to enhance job creation in Mexico through financial incentives to businesses to reduce the numbers of those leaving to find work in the United States.

Asian Americans

California always has been the most popular destination for Asian immigrants to the United States. Today, Asian Americans make up 14 percent of California's population, and that proportion will steadily increase. Even Asian Indians, who have chosen the Northeast as their primary destination in the past, have established new and vibrant communities in Silicon Valley and pockets of Southern California like Artesia.

The diversity of California's Asian Americans is often overlooked. In addition to Chinese Americans, who are the largest subgroup of Asian Americans, and Japanese Americans, who were the largest subgroup up to the 1970 census, Asian American communities include Koreans, Indians, Thais, Filipinos, as well as refugees from Vietnam, Laos, and Cambodia, who began entering in significant numbers in 1975. Today, almost 40 percent of all Southeast Asians in the United States reside in California, including approximately half a million from Vietnam, 85,000 from Cambodia, and over 140,000 from Laos (Hmong, Iu Mien, and Lao). Asian Americans are entrepreneurs and high-tech engineers in Silicon Valley, but many, particularly Southeast Asians, are poor, receive public assistance, and live in public housing.

Asian immigrants and Southeast Asian refugees will continue to be attracted to California. Each year, 20,000 to 40,000 newcomers arrive from each of the following countries: the Philippines, South Korea, and India. Chinese from Taiwan, Hong Kong, and the People's Republic of China also total around 40,000 annually. A few thousand Southeast Asians enter the United States each year. While more and more are living in other parts of the country, California remains a primary destination for newcomers from Asia.

The steady, immigrant-driven, growth of Asian American communities has not occurred without controversy. As large numbers of Chinese immigrants moved into Monterey Park, some long-term residents pushed through a local ordinance (later rescinded) that prohibited Chinese-only business signs. Since the 1980s, in order to curtail "chain migration," certain members of Congress and immigrant restrictionists have advocated eliminating the sibling immigrant category – a category heavily used by Chinese, Korean, Indian, and Filipino immigrants. Most recently, concern has been raised about the dominance of Asians in certain educational settings. For example, some white parents in Silicon Valley say they are pulling their children out of some of the local public high schools because they have too many Asian students and "are too academically driven and too narrowly invested in subjects such as math and science at the expense of liberal arts and extracurriculars like sports and other personal interests"

(Hwang 2005). And the fact that the undergraduate enrollment at UC Berkeley is 41 percent Asian American is viewed as coming "at the expense of historically underrepresented blacks and Hispanics" (Egan 2007).

However, the flow of Asian immigrants to California will continue. Ethnic enclaves of Filipinos, Indians, Cambodians, Vietnamese, Chinese, Koreans, and Thais will be commonplace. Over time, through assimilation and intermarriage, aspects of these enclaves will dissipate, but a steady flow of newcomers will keep them vibrant for some time.[1]

Of course the California immigrant story is not simply about Latinos and Asians. Armenia and Middle Eastern émigrés have contributed to the diversity of California for decades. Pockets of Russian newcomers can be found in all parts of the state. Post 9/11 events reminded us of Arabs and Muslims from all over the world who come to California. And, more likely than not, as the United States braces for an influx of Iraqi refugees at some point in the near future, California will host many of those who arrive.

The Challenges

Given the opportunities and challenges that immigration and diversity will bring to California in the twenty-first century, the importance of how the challenges and opportunities are addressed cannot be understated. How we respond, in fact, will help to determine the type of society in which we will live. Let's consider two distinct opportunities – immigrant integration and the pro-immigrant marches of spring 2006 – in order to understand the importance of what could happen.

Immigrant integration

Reports that the July 7, 2005 London subway suicide bombings were perpetrated by Muslim terrorists who were born and brought up in respectable suburbs of northern England came as a surprise to many observers. Three were born in Great Britain, went to British schools, raised children there, worked in local shops, and were part of the community. Sometime, somehow, they were inculcated with a message of hate, revenge, and contempt. In recalling that the 9/11 hijackers who attacked the United States were foreigners rather than home grown, the United States received stellar marks for being welcoming to people of different backgrounds. British Parliament member Boris Johnson praised the United States for giving its immigrants an equal stake in society, and Fareed Zakaria of *Newsweek* agreed that American Muslims did not turn on the United States because they are well integrated into America. Although I believe Johnson and

Zakaria give the United States too much credit, their premise makes sense. Integrating minority groups can only be beneficial to our society – culturally, economically, and now as a matter of national security.

Every day, Californians are reminded that the United States is a land of immigrants. For most of us, we need only walk outside our front door and travel to work to notice the diverse ethnic backgrounds, languages, cultures, customs, and foods that make up California. The immigration system, refugee policies, family ties, economic opportunities, and political tensions abroad have all come together to fuel the diversity that is California. The question raised is whether we can integrate the new Americans in a manner that respects their culture in a pluralistic manner.

Unfortunately, cultural pluralism is under siege in many quarters of California society. The rise in hate violence directed at law-abiding Arab Americans, Pakistani Americans, American Muslims, and those of Sikh descent following 9/11 demonstrates that things can go terribly wrong in some neighborhoods. Misguided individuals act in an emboldened manner against Americans who do not fit a particular, European-descent image.

Consider these examples of hate that took place within two weeks of 9/11. In San Francisco, vandals threw a bag of blood on the doorstep of an immigration center that serves Arabs and the city's large Asian population. They also threw a large plastic bag labeled "pig's blood" at the front door of Minority Assistance Services in the primarily Latino Mission District. An Indian American walking in the South of Market area of San Francisco was beaten and stabbed by a gang of individuals yelling anti-black and anti-Arab epithets. In Los Angeles, a Pakistani man parked his car at the Glendale Galleria Mall and returned to find it scratched across the right side with the words "Nuke 'em" written all over.

For all the reasons that native-born Americans should be encouraged to participate in civic life, newcomers should be encouraged as well. Engaging Americans in working to better our communities, schools, and neighborhoods – to work for the common good – is a goal that we must constantly pursue. In the case of newcomers, an added need to encourage civic participation and integration flows from the need to address the misinformation that abounds about them, which at times leads to misunderstanding, tension, and even hate.

Integration policies "generally refer to helping immigrants understand, navigate and participate in the social, economic and political aspects of society" (Little Hoover Commission 2002: 23). These may include efforts to help newcomers understand US law and cultural practices or to assist in starting a business, finding a job, or otherwise becoming self-sufficient, while encouraging them to participate in civic organizations and community groups. When it comes to the integration of immigrants and refugees, state and local governments should help lead the way. Immigration and naturalization policy largely falls in the hands of the federal government. However, while federal policies determine how many immigrants and refugees enter the country, state and local governments are presented directly with the challenges and opportunities that newcomers present. With newcomers settling into their neighborhoods and cities, local and state entities have the most direct contact with immigrants and much to gain for developing integration policies. And governmental leadership can set the example for social and community groups to follow. Traditionally, given their location, community-based organizations (CBOs) play an important role in integration efforts. Of course, CBOs must and should continue assisting with integration efforts, but compared to CBOs, governmental entities have more resources.

The importance of state and local government leadership in promoting the civic integration of newcomers is appreciated by many governmental entities. California's bipartisan Little Hoover Commission (LHC) recognizes that the state has a responsibility to ensure that public programs, including education and training, public health and welfare, and economic development services effectively serve immigrants, enabling them to contribute to the state. Understanding the importance of investing in immigrants is critical. Many immigrants are young and others come to the United States with limited formal education. The LHC knows that "high quality education and training programs can improve [immigrants'] earning potential and enhance their self-sufficiency" (Little Hoover Commission 2002: 37–8). The LHC emphasizes the importance of this investment, because education and skills, more than any other factor, determine the earning capacity of immigrants. The LHC offers the example that Latinas who have bachelor's degrees, on average, earn 82 percent more than those with only a high school degree. Further, adult immigrants without high school educations "over their lifetime, draw more from public services than they pay in taxes at a cost of about $13,000 each, while more educated immigrants contribute about $198,000 more than they cost" (Ginorio & Huston 2001: 13). In short, the LHC believes that investment in immigrants is necessary to ensure that they are able to make lasting contributions.

To emphasize the importance of promoting civic integration, the LHC proposed the creation of a California Commission on Immigrants, charged with initiating statewide dialogues on immigration, advocating for effective programs, and monitoring progress in immigrant integration. The statewide dialogues would "promote public awareness of the contributions of immigrants and how immigration can support community goals." The Commission would advocate for improvement in public programs that promote "immigrant responsibilities to their communities and community responsibilities to immigrants," and "pay particular attention" to community-based organizations that promote integration and citizenship. Further, the Commission would "identify ways to define and measure immigrant integration and self-reliance and report progress to policy makers and the public" (Little Hoover Commission 2002: 53).

Fundamental to the LHC's position is the understanding that California's continued prosperity is dependent on the opportunities and achievements of all its residents – including its immigrants. In short, all of California benefits when immigrants are successful. Conversely, when immigrants are trapped in poverty and isolation, the state bears a higher tax burden for providing services. Thus, "California's primary goal [is] to support the ability of all residents, including immigrants, to be safe, healthy and law abiding, as well as live in safe affordable housing and be economically self-sufficient." Immigrants should participate in self-governance and feel they belong and are responsible to their community. The state also should try to influence federal policies to better align federal immigration practices with community goals. The reason is clear. "Public polices that hinder immigrants' ability to become self-reliant, responsible community members hinder the success of all Californians" (Little Hoover Commission 2002: 65).

Santa Clara County has initiated an immigrant integration program that has been quite positive. In this home to San Jose and Silicon Valley, officials have recognized the importance of newcomer integration: "Our collective need to integrate, improve, and transform the lives of all residents of Santa Clara County depends upon our ability to integrate, improve, and transform the lives of immigrants and the need to re-think planning, policies, and practices" (*Bridging Borders* 2000: 21).

> The improvement and transformation of our lives in Santa Clara County is integrally inter-wound with the improvement and transformation of the lives of immigrants in Santa Clara County. To the extent that immigrants are not provided the opportunities to integrate into existing structures, our economy, society, and culture will decline. We will slide into a Silicon Valley culture less rich in diversity, in knowledge, in growth, and in meeting human needs and potential. (*Bridging Borders* 2000: 30)

County officials know that speaking about immigrant families in a vacuum is impossible. Not only is the interrelationship with the native-born population significant, but families that are comprised of both immigrant and native-born members (mixed families) are quite common: "Mixed status households of US-born and immigrants means that when we address immigration policies and practices, we are in fact addressing issues that affect vast numbers of people in our county, many more than those who are foreign born" (ibid.: 22).

The positive effect of integration programs on newcomers is readily apparent. Sia Thompson, an immigrant from Sierra Leone, participated in Santa Clara County's Immigrant Leadership course. With a strong interest in women's rights, she was able to bond with other women participants to lay the groundwork for collaboration during the course. The course also was helpful in providing information on resources available for immigrants generally. She also developed a sense of "where to go so that our voice will be heard." But even before she participated in this course, Sia had helped to form a Pan-African women's organization – African Refugee Women Rebuilders (ARWR). She explained part of the reason for forming the organization this way:

> When the African women come here and resettle as refugees, organizations like Catholic Charities, Jewish Family Services, International Rescue Committee, they work with the women for three months . . . [W]e are filling in the gap. Even on the very basic things like the operation of vending machines, opening a savings account, where you can find the African food market – generally circumnavigating the system. We encourage the women to come in and get assistance.[2]

The Church can also help promote civic participation and integration. Another participant in the Santa Clara County Immigrant Leadership course, Juventino Flores, an immigrant from Mexico, attributes his involvement in civic affairs to his church's leadership program:

> Before I took the course, I went to church, prayed and went home. The course helps everyone take responsibility. I took the class by accident. There was one old lady who was working at the church and told me that the Diesis [sic] is offering the course, and asked if I wanted to take it. I didn't want to say yes or no – so I said maybe. Then the priest sent a letter telling me when the orientation was. [I went] and I liked it. I am fortunate. I have no regrets and [was] very happy to learn all the stuff.

The course covered a range of social, political, religious, and economic subjects. Flores reflected: "It made me want to get more involved in the community and once you are there it is hard to get out. When are you sure that you have done enough – that you have solved all the problems?" The course coupled religion with social activism. Flores continued:

> They make you strong in the faith and then you have to follow Jesus and Jesus is justice . . . It is hard to have more responsibilities, but you start growing and you take on more and more. Leadership for the community – helping the community [is] related to the faith that something better will happen, like Martin Luther King [and Dolores Huerta].

In the matter of such things as involvement with his children's school, Juventino now believes that "the parents – we – should help the kids, not just teachers alone but also the parents need to be involved. It needs to be 50/50."[3]

Of course, while an ugly side of America reared its head following 9/11 in the form of hate crimes and intolerance directed at Arab Americans, American Muslims, and Sikhs, Muslims have benefited from efforts at immigrant integration and understanding as well. In spite of the highly publicized prosecution of an alleged al Qaeda supporter there, the California Central Valley town of Lodi, California, is a good example of efforts at understanding. The town's population of 57,000 is more than a quarter Latino. Yet the community also has 2,000 Muslims, mostly from Pakistan (Bell 2001: 23). So Pakistani men playing cricket on a field across from their mosque and women wearing *hijabs* – head scarves – walking in the park are a common sight. But when the mosque was vandalized, concerned citizens, led by a Japanese American mayor, came forward to form the Breakthrough Project to combat bigotry. High school students volunteered to help clean up the mosque and police started meeting regularly with mosque leaders. In the wake of 9/11, the pastor of the local United Congregational Christian Church conducted a four-part class on Islam for members of the community to gain better understanding of their Muslim neighbors. Isolated incidents of intolerance have occurred. However, one member of the United Congregational Christian Church who attended the Islam classes hoped that everyone across America was reaching out: "I came to be supportive of our neighbors so they do not feel persecuted" (Bell 2001: 23).

A concerted effort to promote civic engagement among newcomers is in our own best interest. Large-scale efforts like those in Santa Clara County and smaller ones such as that in Lodi represent some good thinking on the subject. However, when we put our creative minds together, the potential for newer, more exciting, and innovative ways of promoting civic integration is enormous. Although state and local governments (including city service agencies and even community policing programs) should lead the way, just think of the amazing things that could be accomplished when other vital institutions become involved: schools, daycare centers, local businesses, chambers of commerce, churches, recreation clubs, neighborhood groups, senior groups, and youth groups; they bring such rich possibilities to the enterprise.

We have a choice of Americas – one narrow and one broad. One choice is closed-minded, resistant to continuing changes, and will breed tension and violence. The other is one that embraces change and encourages integration in the hopes of building a stronger, better community. The choice we make, individually, locally, and statewide, will shape the communities in which we live. Avoiding the pitfalls of division, insular living, and unknowing bias is a worthwhile goal as a society.

Political influence of the marches

For weeks in the spring of 2006, television and newspapers featured spectacular images of masses of humanity lined up for miles in marches across the United States. What was most startling about the marches was that they were overwhelmingly pro-immigrant. Hundreds of thousands of US citizens and immigrants peacefully marched in Los Angeles, San Francisco, San Jose, New York, and Chicago, with thousands also taking to the streets in other cities across the country. Such mass demonstrations advocating for the rights of immigrants are unprecedented in American history.

Energy, enthusiasm, and a deep sense of urgency filled the air. Activists proclaimed that the marches represented "the new civil rights movement" (Mangaliman 2006). The leaders of the National Immigrant Solidarity Network, for example, see themselves as the vanguard of the first civil rights movement of the twenty-first century. Emma Lozano, a community organizer from Chicago, proclaimed that "[Latina/os] need to transform [the movement] into political power so we can change these immigration laws" (Hendricks 2006). Yvette Felarca, the California coordinator of By Any Means Necessary, asserted that "[t]his is the birth of a new civil rights movement" (Marcucci & Sholin 2006).

The first round of protests targeted a punitive bill passed by the US House of Representatives in December 2005, popularly known by the name of its sponsor, Representative James Sensenbrenner. Among other things, the Sensenbrenner bill would have made the mere status of being an undocumented immigrant a felony subject to imprisonment as well as deportation from the United States. Arguably, it also would have imposed criminal sanctions on persons who provided humanitarian assistance to undocumented immigrants.[4]

The immigrant rights movement initially spread like wildfire. A second wave of marches in the spring followed the initial ones in March. Instead of merely demanding the simple rejection of punitive immigration measures, the protesters sought justice for immigrants and supported legislation allowing undocumented immigrants the opportunity to regularize their immigration status. Many activists believed that the anti-immigrant tide that had dominated the national debate since the terrorist acts of 9/11 might have turned. In the heady days following the marches, even positive immigration reform, including an amnesty for millions of undocumented immigrants, appeared possible.

By the summer of 2006, however, there were signs that the immigrant rights movement had lost steam. A series of marches on and around Labor

Day 2006 attracted far fewer people than those just a few months before. Immigration policy proved to be too volatile an issue for Congress to address constructively in an election year. The headway made by the immigrant rights movement visibly slowed. Ultimately, after much skirmishing during the summer, Congress failed to enact any comprehensive immigration reform legislation. Instead, Congress passed a law appropriating funds for extension of the fence along the United States–Mexico border.[5]

The purpose of raising the phenomenon of the spring 2006 marches is not to dwell on the substantive details of immigration reform. Rather, by considering the prospects of a new, multiracial civil rights movement seeking social justice emerging from the immigrant rights marches, one can ponder the possibility of what the future can bring for racial/ethnic coalition politics in a major immigrant state like California. Today one discerns decidedly mixed signals about the possibility of such a movement. Importantly, despite signs of promise and potential, there are many formidable hurdles to the emergence of a new, multiracial civil rights movement.

Among the first hurdles is defining the scope of the new movement. Who will participate if there is to be a new civil rights movement? Will it be a Latino civil rights movement or a broader one? Will it include African Americans? Will the movement address more than immigrant rights? And just who will be the leaders of the new movement for civil rights and social justice?

How these questions are answered – especially in a state where more and more Latinos and Asian Americans are entering politics – can have a significant effect on the future of race relations in California. For example, if leaders – and the immigrants themselves – move toward a truly broad-based civil rights movement that includes African Americans, the atmosphere in the state would be far different than if the movement went down a fragmented path. The civil rights movement in the 1960s was very much about civil rights for blacks whose enslavement and segregation has had a lasting legacy on modern America, but it also advocated for the civil rights of other minorities. Incorporating similarly broad civil rights concerns in a movement that also includes the goal of guaranteeing the rights of immigrants would build much-needed political support for change.

A truly multiracial civil rights movement will need to identify common ground. For rather obvious reasons, Latinos and Asian Americans generally are more concerned with the excesses of immigration law and enforcement than African Americans, who may, at times, demand greater enforcement of the immigration laws. To find common ground, minority groups may have to reach beyond immigrant rights. Most of all, minorities want wage and labor protections in the workplace, safe and affordable housing, equal access to education, and fair treatment by government and employers. The congruence of social and economic justice interests among African Americans, Asian Americans, and Latinos is clear. They seek full membership in American society. This is the type of high moral ground that is conducive to more lasting collaborations.

Good faith and inclusion will need to be demonstrated by each group, and racism between communities will need to be addressed. For example, through efforts of immigrant labor leaders, union negotiators have successfully bargained to ensure that a substantial percentage of employees hired in certain industries, such as janitors, are African American. At the same time, African American leaders such as Jesse Jackson, Barack Obama, and Cornel West have spoken out on behalf of immigrant rights. In fact, a number of African American leaders joined immigrant rights leaders in denouncing immigrant bashing during the demonstrations in 2006.

The National Latino Congress convened in Los Angeles in September 2006 and considered the possibility of building a national Latino political movement. Although the most burning issue was to persuade Congress to pass comprehensive immigration reform, the conference delegates also passed resolutions backing a broad range of issues that provide a basis for collaboration with other subordinated communities: voting rights reforms; universal healthcare; and environmental protection. This is a good sign that the future could bring a broad-based agenda embraced by a variety of different minority groups.

The prospect for a mass social movement supporting social change emerging from the immigrant rights movement and the mass marches of 2006 is uncertain. The 1950s and 1960s saw a mass movement that achieved much and literally transformed the racial landscape of the United States. The legal and political climate was right to facilitate the change advocated by activists, and political and judicial institutions played important roles in that change. However, the demographics of the country have changed dramatically over the last 50 years. To form a lasting civil rights movement, the issues must stretch beyond immigrant rights and must include African Americans, Asian Americans, and other minority groups.

There are barriers between the immigrant rights marches of 2006 and a modern-day multiracial civil rights movement. Black–brown tensions are one issue, with constructive dialogue necessary between and among the affected communities. Moreover, the courts and political branches are not what they were in the 1960s. Neither the current Supreme Court nor the political branches can be relied upon to protect the rights of minorities. Politicians often play the immigration card to curry nativist support and play off the tensions between African Americans and Latinos.

Although we can dream of a new civil rights movement, it is easy to be skeptical. Latinos, African Americans, and Asian Americans have too many different, and at times competing, agendas. The mass activism of the spring of 2006, however, offered a glimmer of what could happen. We saw what true grassroots organizing can do. Increasing rates of naturalization among immigrants in recent years also has resulted in increased political power for Latinos and Asian Americans. Only time will tell what the future holds. One thing is certain – nothing will just happen. Just as Thurgood Marshall spent decades planning the litigation strategy leading to *Brown vs. Board of Education*, and Martin Luther King, Jr. and César Chávez orchestrated political activism at the community level in the 1960s, new visionaries will need to plan for coalitions, cooperation, and social change.

Conclusion

The demographic changes in California, fueled by a steady flow of immigrants from all over the world, will continue unabated in the twenty-first century. These changes present challenges to race relations, but also great opportunity for continued creativity, economic activity, cultural enrichment, vibrant political leadership, and prosperity. The key to whether we can take advantage of these opportunities is whether we take positive approaches to the incorporation of newcomers and others into all facets of society – social, political, and economic.

California remains highly attractive to newcomers around the world. Coupled with the ubiquity of American culture throughout the world, the basic idea of an American empire and the California mystique appeal to would-be immigrants and refugees who seek the American dream of freedom, prosperity, and consumerism. Migrant workers, refugees, high-tech workers, multinational executives, and relatives (both from the working class and the professions) all respond. These images are responsible for luring thousands of migrants to California each year. Viewed in this manner, the debate over the profile of new immigrants is disingenuous. Since the nation and the state has attracted these immigrants, the appropriate response is a commitment to integrating the newcomers and bridging all groups in order to incorporate them into a system devoted to the political, economic, and social vitality of our community. Hopefully, that's the type of state the future will bring, setting an example for the rest of the country.

NOTES

1 Steadily increasing interracial marriage will lead to more individuals of mixed race in California. About 3 percent of California marriages are interracial, and the figure increases by about half of a percent each decade. Out-marriages range depending on certain Asian ethnic communities – from about 10 percent (Vietnamese Americans) to 30 percent (Japanese Americans). The majority of

out-marriages are actually intra-ethnic (e.g., Chinese and Japanese) versus interracial (e.g., black and Korean). In California, about one in ten births are mixed race.

2 Interview with Sia Thompson (on file with author).

3 Interview with Juventino Flores (on file with author).

4 See Border Protection, Antiterrorism, and Immigration Control Act of 2005, H.R. 4437, 109th Cong. §§ 203, 205 (2005). For a useful summary of the myriad immigration reform proposals floated in Congress during the last few years, see Bill Ong Hing, *Deporting Our Souls: Values, Morality, and Immigration Policy* (New York: Cambridge University Press, 2006), pp. 17–38.

5 Department of Homeland Security Appropriations Act, 2007, Pub. L. No. 109–295, tit. II, 120 Stat. 1355 (2006).

REFERENCES

Bell, Elizabeth. 2001. "Fear and Suspicion," *San Francisco Chronicle*, October 21.

Bridging Borders in Silicon Valley: Summit on Immigrant Needs and Contributions. Santa Clara County Office of Human Relations Citizenship and Immigrant Services Program, 2000.

Egan, Timothy. 2007. "Little Asia on the Hill," *New York Times Education Life*, January 7.

Ginorio, Angela and Huston, Michelle. 2001. *¡Si Se Puede! Yes, We Can: Latinas in School*. Washington, DC: American Association of University Women Educational Foundation.

Hendricks, Tyche. 2006. "Latino Political Clout Grows; Convention a Step Toward Creating National Movement," *San Francisco Chronicle*, September 10.

Hing, Bill Ong. 2006. *Deporting Our Souls: Values, Morality, and Immigration Policy*. New York: Cambridge University Press.

Hwang, Suein. 2005. "The New White Flight?" *Wall Street Journal*, November 19–20.

Little Hoover Commission. 2002. *We the People: Helping Newcomers Become Californians*. Sacramento: Commission on California State Government Organization and Economy.

Mangaliman, Jesse. 2006. "Immigration Rights Backers Marching On," *San Jose Mercury News*, September 2.

Marcucci, Michelle and Sholin, Ryan. 2006. "Hundreds March for Immigration Rights," *Oakland Tribune*, September 5.

FURTHER READING

Hing, Bill Ong. 2004. *Defining America Through Immigration Policy*. Philadelphia, PA: Temple University Press.

Hing, Bill Ong. 2006. *Deporting Our Souls*. New York: Cambridge University Press.

Johnson, Kevein R. 2004. *The "Huddled Masses Myth": Immigration and Civil Rights*. Philadelphia, PA: Temple University Press.

Johnson, Kevin R. 2007. *Opening the Floodgates: Why America Needs to Rethink Its Borders and Immigration Policies*. New York: NYU Press.

Simon, Julian. 1999. *The Economic Consequences of Immigration*, 2nd edn. Ann Arbor: University of Michigan Press.

Zolberg, Aristide. 2006. *A Nation by Design*. Cambridge, MA: Harvard University Press.

Chapter Twenty-nine

POLITICAL PROSPECTS IN THE TWENTY-FIRST CENTURY

Raphael J. Sonenshein

New York was the pivotal American state in the twentieth century. California is America's state in the twenty-first century. Nowhere is this clearer than in the realm of politics.

Think of what New York meant to United States politics in the twentieth century. The nation's leading melting pot, New York became a symbol of America itself. Mayors like Fiorello LaGuardia defined what a big city leader could do. Governors, from Al Smith to Franklin Roosevelt, and Nelson Rockefeller to Mario Cuomo, competed for national office. Roosevelt became the defining president of the century. In mid-century, three major league baseball teams had the greatest center fielders all in one city: Mickey Mantle for the Yankees, Willie Mays for the Giants, and Duke Snider for the Dodgers.

No wonder New Yorkers thought of the world as centered around their city and state. But in the late 1950s the Dodgers and Giants left for California and so did a lot of Americans. New York lost population. California gained. New York lost electoral votes and California picked up new ones. The immigration flood that had defined New York became a trickle, and the floodgates instead opened up on the West Coast.

National political trends began to be seen in California by the 1960s. The 1965 Watts riot inaugurated a series of urban riots and symbolized the new racial polarization that became a core feature of American national politics. The 1966 election of an anti-tax Republican governor, Ronald Reagan, two years after a Democratic national landslide, foreshadowed the long decline of the national Democratic Party for the rest of the century. "Reagan Democrats," white middle-class and working-class voters, foreshadowed the "silent majority" that Richard Nixon carved into national politics in 1968. The passage of Proposition 13 in 1978 was the first great victory of the tax revolt that still shapes American politics. Finally, the great immigration waves that transformed California's communities began in earnest to reshape its politics in the 1990s, with consequences still to play out.

Now, astride the twenty-first century, California's diverse politics are much studied. What were once ignored phenomena are now tea leaves for pundits and political scientists. The old model of partisan, well-organized politics in New York State, with party machines and powerful office holders with access to tremendous reserves of patronage, is passing. Today's national politics draws more on the reformist, non-partisan, big media politics of California. The state's complex political movements and expressions continue to evolve and to exert influence on American politics, and the state will likely maintain this power for decades to come.

California and the Politics of Reform

California is the true home of the Progressive politics that changed America a century ago. In this state bursting with migrants and immigrants, the old forms of politics had little sway. The dominance of large corporations, none so important as the railroads, engendered deep resentment of "private power" and led to statewide and local victories of the Progressive forces in the first decades of the twentieth century. Led by the philanthropic Los Angeles physician and socialist John Randolph Haynes and political giants like Hiram Johnson, the Progressives quickly emerged as politically dominant. In 1911, voters passed constitutional amendments, for example, that enshrined non-partisan elections in all cities and towns.

As in other parts of the nation, Progressive politics was not always progressive politics. Haynes's egalitarian presence notwithstanding, the Progressive movement was often marked by anti-immigrant attitudes and a suspicion of mass democracy. In the space left by the decline of political parties and the rise of ballot democracy, private interests often remained powerful. Immigrants were often poorly treated in California long after – and in some cases deriving from – Progressive political victories. Governor Hiram Johnson furthered the state's long, grim history of racial discrimination aimed at Asians and Asian Americans and, within a few short decades, the state's Japanese-descent residents were cruelly hauled off to World War II internment camps. Nor did Mexican immigrants fare especially well in the wake of Progressive reforms: the pattern continued to be one in which Mexican laborers were imported into California's agricultural fields, then deported as economic conditions changed. Depression-era California even dress-rehearsed Japanese internment with the resident ethnic Mexican population, deporting tens of thousands of Mexicans and Mexican Americans in a spasm of 1930s racial scapegoating and fear.

The Progressive juggernaut of the early twentieth century crossed party lines, but only to a point. The Republican Party was at the heart of the movement, at least in its electoral forms, and Republicans reaped the benefits for decades to come. Aided by the cross-filing system that allowed candidates to run for both party nominations, Republicans were led after 1942 by their popular, three-term governor Earl Warren, who was tapped by President Dwight Eisenhower to become Chief Justice of the Supreme Court in 1953.

As California grew, the basis for a new sort of politics began to take root. In the 1950s the population continued to rise apace, and groups that might become forces for Democratic Party strength increased in numbers. Organized labor, long at a disadvantage in California, began to flex its muscles. Jewish Democrats developed a new, liberal version of reform politics through the California Democratic Club movement. They found an ally in future Senator Alan Cranston and positioned themselves as rivals to the "regular" Democrats led by Jesse Unruh. They managed to get rid of cross-filing.

The year 1958 became a major turning point in the state's politics. Democrats shocked the state by winning the governorship behind Attorney General Edmund G. Brown, Jr. and won major gains in the state legislature. In 1960, Democrats held their national convention in Los Angeles (the event itself was a hugely symbolic indication of the rise of California and California Democrats), and Unruh played a key role in John F. Kennedy's presidential campaign.

By 1962, the state capitol was becoming firmly Democratic, with Brown popular and with Unruh, now Speaker of the Assembly, reshaping the legislature into a professional body with the passage of a 1966 ballot measure. The Brown era was a high-water mark for public investment in California's infrastructure.

But there were problems under the surface that forged cracks in the Democratic regime. Chief among these was race, which of course had never gone further away than just below the surface in California politics or culture more generally. In 1964, state voters passed Proposition 14, a measure to repeal the Rumford Fair Housing Act. The vote on Proposition 14 was shocking because it accompanied the massive re-election of Democratic President Lyndon B. Johnson.

A year later, the Watts section of Los Angeles exploded, the first in a wave of urban riots that shook the nation. The reaction to the riot reshaped local and state politics. Mayor Sam Yorty, a conservative Democrat, grabbed the law-and-order mantle, and in 1966 entered the Democrat primary for governor against Brown. He scored strongly against Brown, and weakened the incumbent for his general election race against an actor, Ronald Reagan. Riding the law-and-order theme, Reagan beat Brown by more than a million votes.

Reagan's election inaugurated a period of divided government in California, with three of the next four governors Republicans, and the Legislature mostly Democratic. Spurred by the tax revolt and Proposition

13's passage in 1978, California's public investment began a long, slow slide from its peak under Brown to its pinched and starved nature today.

The next great shift in California's political scene emerged from massive immigration beginning in the 1970s. California was one of the principal immigrant destinations after the liberalization of immigration laws in 1965, and newcomers from Latin America and Southeast Asia soon transformed the daily life of the state.

Immigration became a political issue long before it became a source of political mobilization for California Latinos. In 1994, Republican Governor Pete Wilson faced a very tough re-election campaign during an economic recession. He grabbed onto the explosive immigration issue as his lifeline, tying himself to Proposition 187, a measure to bar undocumented residents from receiving public services. The measure passed 2–1 in November 1994, ensured Wilson's re-election, and was then declared unconstitutional by the federal courts.

While Proposition 187 saved Wilson's hide, it became a catastrophe for Republicans in California, and ultimately nationwide. Before 1994, Republicans had a strong opportunity to win Latino votes and ensure a statewide majority. The battle over Proposition 187 and subsequent actions by Congressional Republicans to reduce services for legal immigrants drove more than one million new Latino voters to enter the rolls in the decade. The new Latino electorate was poorer and more Democratic than the previous Latino voters, and they powered Democrats statewide.

In 1998, Democrats swept back into power with Gray Davis winning the governorship and large majorities in the Legislature. The number of Latino elected officials jumped and began to weigh heavily in the competition to lead the state legislature. New legislation supported Democratic objectives, and the party seemed poised for a long run at the top. Then the energy crisis hit, and the state reeled from what later turned out to be shortages manufactured by energy companies allied with and protected by the Bush administration. Gray Davis's support collapsed with stunning alacrity. A historic recall election drove Davis out of office in 2003, to be replaced with another Republican actor, Arnold Schwarzenegger. While the recall was devastating to Democrats, it did not halt their dominance of the state, nor could it halt the erosion of the Republican Party.

In the presidential elections of 1992, 1996, 2000, and 2004, California remained reliably Democratic by large margins. What was once a Republican stronghold had turned into a Democratic redoubt not worth contesting. Meanwhile, California Republicans languished in minority status, controlled by their most conservative wing despite the moderate Schwarzenegger's political success.

So California government is now not only Progressive, but progressive. And yet, it is extremely difficult to implement progressive policies. Some of this has to do with the state's odd governance structure, but it also derives from limits on the will of the majority, and the centrism of the state's voters. While there is much to do and build in California, the elements are not yet in place to undertake the work of progressive change.

Government Structure and Policy Change

While the political system of California has changed dramatically, the government structure through which politics changes policy has not kept pace. The state still has an odd duck system. For instance, the governor and lieutenant governor are elected separately, and could easily be of different political parties. This anomaly, abandoned in the national Constitution after the election of Thomas Jefferson as President in 1800, creates the odd situation of a leadership team disunited by party. The large number of statewide elected officials means that the governor's cabinet is not really under the executive's control. This "plural executive" means that the executive branch can be fractured by party.

But all this pales beside the bizarre budget situation. California is one of only three states that require a two-thirds vote of both houses of the Legislature to pass the budget. This is a formula for gridlock and for unmet needs. A determined minority can hold up the budget, and prevent majority programs that involve expenditures from winning passage.

Added to these continuing governing issues are a series of voter-approved measures that were passed during the height of the tax revolt. In the wake of Proposition 13, tax opponents made it extremely difficult for the majority to impose its will in fiscal matters. City after city has found that it must gain a two-thirds majority to pass revenue measures for critical needs. Long after the tax revolt receded, it has hamstrung California's government.

Questions for California in the Twenty-first Century

How California is governed – and how well – in the twenty-first century will depend in large measure on how the state's voters and elected officials respond to a small number of complicated challenges, posed here as questions.

1. How can immigrants best be incorporated into the life of the state?

California has not had a history of being hospitable toward immigrants. In this regard it differs from New York, whose great metropolis glorified the new immigrants a century ago. No Statue of Liberty stands at Los Angeles

International Airport to greet the tired, the poor, and those yearning to breathe free. Immigrants have been a convenience in California rather than a core piece of the social fabric. They have been subject to deportation and to nativist attacks.

Today's immigrants to California are the subject of divisive political debate, with conservative voters angrily demanding all sorts of punitive actions against them. The explosiveness of this issue emerges in election after election, and is particularly volatile in Republican primaries.

Some recent demographic research speculates that immigration to California may be slowing. But we cannot easily project from today's figures to those of the future. Immigrants *may*, although it is too soon to tell, be able to consolidate greater social and economic gains in the next generation. As California becomes a more non-white state, we might assume that it will see a greater degree of integration of the children of immigrants.

Even if the gains are modest, the incorporation of immigrant communities will have major political consequences for the state. While mobilization of Latinos has strengthened the Democratic Party in California, there are still a great number of unmobilized immigrants who are not yet citizens. Major changes in citizenship may further alter the political system.

2. Can the state regain its history of public investment?

Latinos report in poll after poll that they strongly support public investment even if that means tax increases. The tax revolt may have been the last gasp of an older white conservative block declining in numbers. But because they managed to change the rules by which tax increases are approved, they continue to have disproportionate impact.

As the state becomes more progressive, there will be strong public sentiment for investment in infrastructure and education. It is likely that new ways to raise revenue will be explored, and there may even be a push to revise the strictures of the previously inviolate Proposition 13. It is a simple matter of politics. A majority can amend the Constitution to change rules that require a two-thirds vote, but it will be a titanic struggle that will bring the conservative forces back to the table in defense of their earlier victory.

If the revenue issue is resolved, California may once again lead the nation in public investment, particularly in the schools, but also in the environment, transportation, and other areas.

3. Can California avoid budget gridlock?

With all the problems the state faces, how can the state continue to allow itself to be held hostage every budget cycle? When a small minority can block the budget and hold out for unreasonable demands, the budget is late, and the voters become further alienated from ineffective government.

If the political dynamics of the electorate continue to shift, there may be support for a statewide measure to eliminate the two-thirds requirement for passing the budget. A higher mountain to climb would be eliminating or reducing the two-thirds requirement for new taxes. Another alternative is to take the annual appropriations process to the people through ballot initiatives. This highly risky approach would have the legislature pass bills, but then pay for them through voter-initiated measures.

The lack of a predictable, time-bound, majority-driven budget process will handicap California in the twenty-first century.

4. Can California avoid partisan gridlock?

While the Democrats are dominant in contemporary California, and are likely to become further entrenched through redistricting after the 2010 census, their continued reign is by no means assured. The political history of California suggests that today's top dog may well be in the doghouse not long after. Consider the precipitous drop in Gray Davis's fortunes from his election in 1998 to his ignominious recall in 2003.

One difference, though, is the fractious condition of the state Republican Party. Following trends in national politics, the California Republican Party has turned inward, granting authority to its most conservative elements. The more power the Democrats gain, the more the Republicans see themselves as "dead-enders," trying to hold back the sea of change. Rather than following the lead of their popular moderate governor Arnold Schwarzenegger and moving to the center, the party seems determined to act as a resistant block to Democratic proposals. This stance depends on the perpetuation of the majority-busting structures of California government, such as the two-thirds rule for the budget and limitations on majority votes for tax increases. If those structures are eliminated through voter action, the Republican strategy will doom the party to irrelevance.

The broader problem for Republicans is that they now stand outside the emerging consensus for public investment. Their hopes of winning Latino support are evaporating in the face of their anti-immigrant rhetoric and resistance to supporting public education with tax dollars. They will become the last gasp of resentful whites, hardly the place to be in the new century's most dynamic and diverse state.

The weakness of the state Republicans could easily lead Democrats to overreach. While there is great support for public investment and the state's electorate is generally progressive on social issues, there are limits to how far left the leading party can go. In the 1990s, confident Democrats supported driver's licenses for undocumented residents, going well past the consensus of public opinion. If taxes go too high to support public investment, there will be a reaction.

Democrats have to be wary to build strength in the growing Inland Empire. As a coastal party, Democrats are at a disadvantage with the new suburban developments that are drawing thousands of young families to Riverside and similar environs. The leadership of the Democratic Party is from the Bay Area and Southern California, and they will have to learn the language of the moderate voters, up for grabs by both parties, who live there.

5. Can California find enough water?

Water has been essential to California's growth. For much of its history, California dominated the allocation of western water resources. As the chief investor, and the largest population base by far, California could claim a big share of the water of the Colorado River and other projects.

But California now has major competition for population and for resources from growing southwestern states, such as Nevada, New Mexico, and Arizona. Las Vegas and Phoenix are growing by leaps and bounds. As the Colorado River's water is allocated in coming years, California will have to negotiate and bargain with these growing states that are arguing for a much larger share.

In any case, California's growth and shrinking water access are certain to create new regional politics of water scarcity that will affect the relationship between Northern and Southern California. For many years, the north has resented what it sees as the south's squandering of water, not to mention the aqueduct that carries water from the north to the lawns of the south.

6. Will California play a larger role in national politics?

Although one out of eight Americans lives in California, the footprint of California in national politics continues to be less than one might expect. The dominance of the East Coast in national politics is expected, in simple geographic terms because of the proximity of the seat of power to Washington, DC. But the trend-setting power of California suggests a much greater potential role.

To some degree, structural factors have limited California's reach. In both the nominating and general election phases of the presidential election, California's role has been muted. Until 2008, California held its presidential primary in June. Other than the 1968 Democratic primary that seemed on the verge of driving Robert F. Kennedy to the nomination (before his assassination on primary night), California has voted long after the nomination has been settled. In 2008, the state moved its primary to early February, leading a flock of states to follow suit.

The Electoral College both strengthens and weakens California's role in national politics. California has by far the largest number of electoral votes, at 55. These votes represent one-fifth of the total 270 needed to win the presidency. Because they are allocated on a winner-takes-all basis, there is little to gain from finishing second. Democrats have dominated the presidential race in California since 1992, and as a result the major candidates rarely appear in the Golden State. If the Electoral College were revised in all 50 states and the District of Columbia were to grant electoral votes proportionately, California would be a great prize. Attempts to enact this reform only for California are properly seen as a partisan attempt to weaken the Democrats in national politics.

7. Will California politics ever be taken seriously?

California both attracts and repels those who examine politics. It is obvious that trends are created here that resonate nationally. But there is also a widespread sense that California is a little . . . weird. This belief holds as much in political life as in the voyeuristic examinations of the lives of celebrities.

Because California's political parties have been weakly structured, and because there are numerous openings for creative political action (such as financing and running ballot initiatives, or running for a statewide office that in another state might be appointive), unusual characters and career paths have emerged in the state's politics. Knowledge of the media and how to reach the broad public are essential to reach the top in a state where politics is not a central activity of the public.

Those who make it to the top of the system in California may well have an extraordinary sense of the media version of the public pulse. Engaging the California public means accepting the less-than-involved nature of the voters. Thus, Edmund G. Brown, Jr. (Jerry), the mercurial governor elected in 1978 and re-elected for two terms, regaled the voters with his low-spending ways, eschewing the governor's mansion to sleep on a plain mattress in a modest apartment and driving in a cheap Plymouth. He parlayed his creativity into the mayoralty of Oakland, and election as attorney general. But to the rest of the nation he was Governor Moonbeam, in the memorable phrase of cartoonist Garry Trudeau.

California has now had two actors as governor: Reagan and Schwarzenegger. Their popularity also excites resentment. Both mastered the art of reaching the California voter, but their professions made them easy targets for lampooning (and for underestimating). In an age of media politics, with billionaires financing their own presidential campaigns, and with generals considering quests for the nation's highest office, California's offbeat politicians are not to be dismissed so lightly.

8. Will California continue to set the trends in national politics?

As the largest state, and the colossus of the West, California will benefit from the belated recognition in national politics that the sunbelt and the Rocky Mountain states are likely to determine which political forces dominate the nation in the twenty-first century.

What makes these regions different from the traditional East, Midwest, and South? These are states shaped by political reform movements, and the organized party politics of the past is likely to seem foreign to them. They have been deeply influenced by Latino immigration, and how states deal with the influx of Spanish-speaking residents is their fundamental issue of diversity. The ideological battles of the old days are often surmounted by pragmatic governors of either party, who fit in with the unconventional norms of the American frontier.

It is likely, then, that if California enters a new era of public investment, backed by public opinion, and by voters willing to pay for first-class services and infrastructure, this state could set the trend for the nation.

Conclusion

California has always had within it the wellsprings of America's vitality, the capacity to renew and reinvent itself in each generation. In the twenty-first century, California is on the verge of another historic turn.

Whether or not California becomes the pivot for the nation in the twenty-first century depends on whether political structures can be revised and rebuilt to empower majorities; whether immigrant communities can become part of the mainstream; whether the two major political parties can avoid either demoralization or overconfidence; and whether hard choices are made or avoided.

But of all great states, California has the most flexibility to accomplish great things. Unconstrained by the past, imbued with the frontier mentality of practicality, not awaiting permission from the powers-that-be across the continent, California is likely to chart its own path, and in so doing, mark out a path for the nation.

Further Reading

Boyarsky, Bill. 2007. *Big Daddy: Jesse Unruh and the Art of Power Politics*. Berkeley: University of California Press.

Edsall, Thomas Byrne and Edsall, Mary D. 1992. *Chain Reaction: The Impact of Race, Rights, and Taxes on American Politics*. New York: W. W. Norton.

Gerston, Larry N. and Christensen, Terry. 2004. *Recall! California's Political Earthquake*. Armonk, NY: M. E. Sharpe.

Myers, Dowell. 2007. *Immigrants and Boomers: Forging a New Social Contract for the Future of America*. New York: Russell Sage Foundation.

Newton, Jim. 2006. *Justice for All: Earl Warren and the Nation He Made*. Riverhead.

Noll, Roger G. and Cain, Bruce. 1995. *Constitutional Reform in California: Making State Government More Effective and Responsive*. Berkeley: Institute for Governmental Studies Press.

Sears, David and Citrin, Jack. 1982. *Tax Revolt: Something for Nothing in California*. Cambridge, MA: Harvard University Press.

Sonenshein, Raphael J. 1993. *Politics in Black and White: Race and Power in Los Angeles*. Princeton, NJ: Princeton University Press.

Chapter Thirty

ENVIRONMENTAL PROSPECTS IN THE TWENTY-FIRST CENTURY

Jon Christensen

Shortly after the turn of the century, I was sitting among a room full of conservationists in Santa Barbara contemplating the past, present, and future of California's environment. A series of maps were projected in the front of the room like X-rays for an audience of doctors. The maps showed suburbanization spreading like a cancer through the body of California. The brightly colored disease of development coursed out from nodes in San Francisco, Los Angeles, and Sacramento along roads stretched out like unhealthy veins. The cities, towns, and spaces in between swelled with brightness as we moved from the past to the present and then on into the future. The prognosis did not look good. By 2050 there would likely be a contiguous sprawl from north to south along all the major transportation corridors.

These maps were meant to set off alarm bells. Instead, I found myself thinking, "That's it?" I wasn't looking at the bright colors. I was seeing all the spaces in between.

Driving back home to the San Francisco Bay Area north along Highway101, I realized that much of what I could see from the road to the foothills would change. Some of it was already changing, from oak-studded grassland pasture to vineyards, from farm fields to housing tracts. But there was still a lot of open space in the hills beyond, and would be even in 2050. Would it be enough?

I thought about the grizzly bear, long gone but still on the state flag, and the California condor, which is soaring over these hills again after nearly disappearing, and the Quino checkerspot butterfly, an endangered species. Like many other species, the Quino checkerspot appears to be on the move, headed north, most likely as a result of global warming. It is vanishing from the southern edge of its range in Baja California. Maybe someday it too could try to make a home in these hills. The only problem is that much of the habitat in between here and there, at the northern end of the butterfly's current range in San Diego and Los Angeles, is filled with houses, roads, freeways, and shopping malls.

Californians have an extravagant sense of their state going to hell in a handbasket – but here that basket is a cornucopia, a paradise, always on the verge, or already lost. In 1965, Raymond Dasmann, the dean of modern California conservationists, set the tone for the late twentieth century with his book *The Destruction of California*. Around the turn of the millennium, Peter Schrag, one of the state's keenest political observers, penned a jeremiad entitled *Paradise Lost*. The subtitle added a prediction: *California's Experience, America's Future*. The future remained the same between the first edition, published in 1998, and an updated edition in 2004.

It would behoove the future to remember, however, that the end has seemed nigh for quite a long time in California. This state has long borne the burden of America's dreams, most poignantly when the flaws in the dream have been exposed out west, when the state of the future turned out not to be all that it was cracked up to be in the present. When ideas about time and space got mixed up, as they did so often in America's westward spatial expansion, the Pacific Coast was just as far as it seemed one could go into the future. California was the end of the trail for that particularly American story, where the frontier ran out of space and time. Walt Whitman observed it in the nineteenth century; John Steinbeck commented on it in the twentieth century. And at the beginning of the twenty-first century, the dean of California history, Kevin Starr, was still pursuing his multivolume project on the California dream. And as he had made clear from the beginning of his project, the dream always had its shadow side, and always will (2004).

In no small measure, that is because an essential element of the California dream has always been about restoring the dream. For this to work, the fall must have already occurred or be imminent. The dream is that California can be redeemed and redeeming. It is the promise of the dream that it may redeem the dreamers.

Reform is often about restoration. And as we think about the future of California's environment, it may be useful to remember that we still often get time and space mixed up, and that environmental reform and restoration are often measured against what likely never was, but instead, what we imagine it to have been, making it very difficult to think clearly about what is, let alone what might be. But at its best, environmental history may provide useful ideas for thinking productively about our prospects, by stripping away our romantic reconstructions of the past as yet unredeemed fall from grace, and seeking the possibilities that have been overlooked in our relationship with a still astonishing state of nature.

Climate Change

Nowhere is our present confusion about the state of the environment in California more often and exuberantly mixed up than in the urgent cacophony around climate change. While scientists have been busy calibrating and recalibrating their climate models in recent years, politicians have been busy calibrating and recalibrating their positions on climate change. And researchers in California have been studying how wildlife has adapted to climate change in the last century and thinking about how humans might adapt in the next hundred years.

In the backcountry of Yosemite National Park, biologists from the University of California Berkeley's Museum of Vertebrate Zoology have been resurveying nearly century-old transects along which biologist Joseph Grinnell and his colleagues and students captured small mammals between 1914 and 1920. In the new survey, the biologists have found that Western harvest mice, piñon mice, and Inyo shrews, once found only at lower elevations, have expanded their ranges 2,100 feet up the slopes of the Sierra Nevada. As environmental journalist Michelle Nijhuis wryly observed, "the piñon mouse is no longer really a piñon mouse," though the trees may someday follow the mice upslope (2005). Meanwhile, high-elevation species like the Alpine chipmunk and pika have retreated from the lower slopes of their ranges on the same mountains by almost as much. These small mammals are all moving uphill as a result of global warming, presumably, although none of the existing models for climate change precisely predict the data the researchers are gathering at the scale of Yosemite National Park. And ecosystems are simply too complex. Indeed, defying the trend, some small mammals have moved downhill in Yosemite, perhaps because fire suppression has changed their habitat at higher elevations. All of this new data is now being put back into the climate models, which will continue as researchers expand the resurvey to 700 sites statewide visited by Grinnell and his students in the early twentieth century.

Scientists believe this kind of tacking between history and forecasting will improve the predictive power of their models. For scientists, history provides a baseline from which to measure change. But it is not just the things that have changed; it is also change itself that needs to be understood. And this may be where history can contribute even more.

In 2004, scientists felt confident predicting that even in the best case scenario, with aggressive emissions reduction policies, global warming will bring more extreme temperatures to California, with longer, hotter summer heat waves, substantially less snow in the winter, and earlier spring runoff. Changes in the Sierra Nevada snowpack and timing of runoff, which provides most of the state's water, will force Californians to make difficult decisions between managing river flows for flood protection and storing water for drinking and irrigating crops. Agriculture currently consumes around 80 percent of the fresh water used in the state. About a third of that is pumped from underground. With reduced runoff, communities and farmers may have to use more groundwater. And there will likely be reductions in agricultural production. Up in the mountains, lower-elevation mixed evergreen forest will expand at the expense of higher-elevation conifer forests, and high-elevation alpine and sub-alpine forests will suffer the most. Some may simply disappear from the tops of mountains as their habitat vanishes. Lower down, grasslands will expand at the expense of shrub lands. Sea level will rise along the coast, contributing to beach erosion and flooding some low-lying areas. Adding insult to injury, the quality of California wines could decline because grapes will ripen earlier during hotter weather. More likely, being at least as adaptable as chipmunks, vintners will move upslope or to cooler climes.

Many of these changes, like changes in the weather, will be out of our control, but what we make of the changes will depend on how we adapt. And it is here that history can usefully enter the picture, not just as a baseline for science, but also as a key to understanding the human variable. Take the most dramatic human impact of dramatic climate change: death. During the entire decade of the 1990s, there were approximately 165 excess deaths attributed to heat-related mortality in California. The authors of the 2004 report on climate change impacts in the state predicted that the number of heat-related deaths would increase two to three times, even with tough carbon emissions restrictions, and up to five to seven times if there were little or no efforts made to curb emissions. Just two years later, state officials reported that 143 people died of heat-related causes in the single record-setting 2006 summer heat wave, more than eight times the average of the 1990s. And a year later, an Associated Press investigation of county coroners' records revealed the temperature spike may have killed as many as 466 people, more than 28 times the 1990s average.

It is important to note, however, as the authors of the 2004 report on climate change cautioned, that these deaths, like other results of climate change, have social as well as climatic causes and "actual impacts may be greater or lesser depending in part on demographic changes and societal decisions affecting preparedness, health care, and urban design" (Hayhoe 2004: 124–5). The coming decades will put our human and natural systems to the test. Make that *tests*. Make that *severe tests*. But the results will depend as much on the decisions people make as on natural events outside of our control. And there is the rub in thinking historically about the environment in the future.

Hazardous Hybrids

One place to watch this unfolding drama is along the 1,600 miles of aging levees in the Sacramento–San Joaquin River Delta in Northern California. In the aftermath of Hurricane Katrina's devastation of New Orleans in 2005, an investigative series in the *Sacramento Bee* concluded that there was "no major city in America more at risk of a catastrophic New Orleans-style flood than Sacramento" (Kollars 2005).

Hurricanes are not the worry here, however. It is earthquakes. According to a state-appointed Delta Vision Committee, the odds are two to one that a series of levees will fail in a cascading catastrophic collapse sometime in the next 25 years, most likely triggered by a major earthquake. The levee failures from Sacramento on down into the Delta could flood up to 3,000 homes and 85,000 acres of farmland that produces a large portion of the nation's fruits and vegetables. Up to 30,000 jobs could be lost. Damages could total $30 to $40 billion. On top of all of that, the quality of the Delta's fresh water would be compromised as salt water rushed in from the San Francisco Bay. It is difficult to predict the consequences for the 750 plant and animal species that live in this hydraulic landscape, a hybrid eco-system crafted by natural forces and human history. It is easier to predict that the pumps that pull water from the Delta into canals headed south to Los Angeles would have to be shut down because of the intrusion of salt water back into the Delta, cutting off the major source of fresh water for 23 million Californians, two-thirds of the state's inhabitants for weeks, months, or years.

As Jared Orsi points out in *Hazardous Metropolis*, an environmental history of flood control in Los Angeles, disorder and failure are endemic in the hybrid human and natural systems that Californians have constructed to control nature (2004). Orsi writes: "As southern Californians have sought to impose order on their waters, they have discovered that their own hydraulic systems are just as disorderly as the rest of nature's" (2004: 3). Orsi sees disorder everywhere he looks in Los Angeles: in the natural systems, in the built systems, in the political systems, and in the best hope for solutions. Orsi envisions making "flood control more ecological" (2004: 181). And he means this not just literally, but also figuratively, embracing the ecological disorder of human politics too. Ecology is about relation-ships. And although it can be a very slippery term when applied to society, the boundary between our understanding of human communities and natural communities has always been a productively porous one. And Orsi's insight could be applied to the north as well.

Over the past century, 140 levee failures have been recorded in the Delta, an average of more than one a year. Of course, levees do not fail in a regular, predictable one-a-year pattern. In 1997, during a particularly wet January storm, 30 levees broke, causing nine deaths, $2 billion in damage, and the biggest evacuation in California history. In the wake of that flood, voters approved a $995 million bond measure as part of a massive state and federal effort to improve the state's water system. For Kevin Starr this was a signal event: "For the first time in history, California voters of every background and political persuasion had authorized a comprehensive program based on adjustments and compromises between human and environmental needs" (2004: 513). A decade later, in 2006, voters approved another $6 billion bond measure to repair the state's flood-control system. The Bay Delta was still on the verge of collapse. The Sacramento smelt, a signal species, was nearing extinction. The massive and massively expensive Central Valley Improvement Project and the CalFed Bay-Delta programs of the previous decade had only masked business as usual. More water was being sucked up by pumps and sent down the long canal to Southern California, which needed the water more than ever because its own overuse of the Colorado River had been curtailed. Sometime soon, Californians are also likely to reconsider a proposal voters rejected in 1982: a peripheral canal to carry fresh water from the north around the Delta and directly into a canal headed south.

Meanwhile, state water officials are moving toward "forecast-based operations" to manage river flows. In addition to potential levee failures, they worry about the ability of Folsom Dam, upriver from Sacramento, to withstand a series of warmer winter storms sending a huge surge of runoff cascading down from the Sierra Nevada. But now, rather than simply waiting to see how much water storms dump into the state's rivers, they are melding future forecasts with historical weather and river flow data to anticipate the impact of storms in an era of increasing variability in the weather and vulnerability in our hydraulic systems. Like climate models, these models will continually be tweaked as climate and weather continue to change and we see the results. The model will never be a perfect fit or make perfect predictions. We can prepare for the unpredictable, like earthquakes, which we know will hit but we don't know when. But unlike earthquakes, we can see storms coming and we can measure the results, and adjust our thinking, as we repair for another inevitable season. This could make ecological flood management more feasible. Out of necessity, these seemingly contradictory efforts will continue for a long time to come: building, repairing, and armoring rigid systems of control; managing them more flexibly; *and* learning to live with the disorder and risk inherent in these hybrid natural and human ecosystems. And the debates that these contradictions engender will be critical in shaping the future of California's environment.

Restoring Efficiency

Yet, the dream of restoration will not die either. Within the first decade of the new millennium, water was flowing again in the Owens River after being sucked dry for decades to fill a pipeline to Los Angeles. Salmon may soon be back in the San Joaquin River for the first time in more than half a century. And the ultimate restoration fantasy could be played out most dramatically at the site of one of the greatest set pieces of American environmental history: Hetch Hetchy Valley.

The story of the damming of this smaller twin of Yosemite Valley to provide water for San Francisco – usually told as a morality tale in the context of the rift that it opened between preservationists, represented by John Muir, and conservationists, represented by Gifford Pinchot – has been unpacked and complicated by historians in recent years (Righter 2005). But some environmentalists would like to go way beyond just learning the lessons of this history. They want to undo history by tearing down the dam, or at least punching a hole in it, draining the reservoir and restoring the valley to Muir's vision of a temple more holy than ever "consecrated by the heart of man" (Righter 2005: 212). Only this time the reconsecration of Hetch Hetchy would be our doing through the undoing of its damnation.

While the theology might be complicated, Sprek Rosenkrans of Environmental Defense has said that "a few straightforward plumbing fixes" and more efficient use of water are all that's needed to make up for the lost water storage by diverting the water to other existing reservoirs below Hetch Hetchy (Stokstad 2006: 582). Restoration ecologists imagine gluing lichens to the bathtub ring that will be left on the granite walls of the valley and pulling weeds to prevent them from taking over the newly exposed "vacant lot" at the bottom of the reservoir to allow the "gardens, groves and meadows of its flowery park-like floor" described by Muir to return (Stokstad 2006: 582–3). Because granite erodes slowly, researchers estimate that only a few centimeters of sediment have been deposited behind the dam. Still, restoring Hetch Hetchy is not likely to be as easy as this metaphor of a living laboratory envisions. But it may, alas, actually be one of the simplest things that could be done. Perhaps it is too simple, however, to imagine that we can expiate the sins of the past and simply turn back time without thinking long and hard about how the enduring political legacy of this history shapes the present and the future.

Whether successful or not, this effort provides an opening to revisit a story at the heart of the history of conservation and preservation in California. Unfortunately, the political possibilities imbedded in this Progressive Era history may be irretrievable, ironically because of some of the core progressive ideas that triumphed then and are now taken for granted. The early twentieth-century debate about Hetch Hetchy was as much about democracy and public power as it was about nature (see Benjamin Johnson's essay in this volume). The debate about Hetch Hetchy still ought to have everything to do with human needs and the greatest good for the greatest number. Around 2.4 million people now drink Hetch Hetchy water. But this century's debate has yet to arouse much democratic politics. Instead the debate remains entombed in the realm of experts, where it was consigned by the progressive politics that consolidated around the first Hetch Hetchy battle.

Advocates invoke restoration of nature's cathedral still, but their argument is made largely on the grounds of efficiency. Environmental Defense has championed successful efforts to increase efficiency by making water a more marketable commodity that will more freely flow to its highest value use. Everywhere these days, efficiency and markets are touted as the answer to environmental limitations. Efforts are underway to commodify all kinds of ecosystems services. These are powerful pragmatic ideas. And in many ways they hark back to the old progressive gospel of efficiency. But the new efficiency will have costs just like the old efficiency. Already there are signs that some of the goods inadvertently created by inefficiencies in our current hydraulic systems will be some of the first targets of the new efficiency crusade. There are efforts underway, for example, to plug leaks from the All American Canal in Imperial Valley, which create wetlands and recharge groundwater for farms on the Mexican side of the line – some owned by Americans, many growing food for Californians.

Whether the dam holding back Hetch Hetchy is breached or not, there are historic changes happening throughout this "colossal, intricate" system that Kevin Starr calls "a wonder of the modern world" (2004: 505). And it will be interesting to watch just how much flexibility the historical ideas of efficiency and restoration have in this entrenched hydraulic society. Like concrete channels, these ideas give us possibilities. They also hem us in.

Ecological Health

The Central Valley is at the heart of this hydraulic wonder. And it is not a healthy modern heart. The Central Valley seems to be rushing toward a smog-choked, suburb-clogged future. In 1995, the California Agriculture Department gave the Central Valley dismal grades for economic vitality, transportation, health, and education. Drinking water in the valley was reported to be some of the worst in the country. Nevertheless, the valley got a "B" on the environment. And this mixed report card reflects just how mixed up we are about the relationship between human wellbeing and the environment. It boggles the mind that human communities could be failing, one of our primary connections – drinking water – could be abysmally bad, and yet the "environment" – that is, all that surrounds us – could get a passing grade. In one way, however, it is an interesting reversal of the modern trope of "the destruction of California" (Dasmann 1965). In this case, it is not California that is being destroyed, but Californians. The report card can be seen as a modern artifact of the separation of people and the environment. But it was not always this way, and may not be this way ever again.

In the nineteenth century, newcomers to California were not sure what to make of the environment or, more important, what the environment would make of them. They were environmentalists in the sense that they were sure the land would shape them. Linda Nash writes that these transplants saw their own bodies as "porous and vulnerable" (2006: 6). And physicians at the time, Nash writes, believed that "human bodies were the most sensitive and reliable indicators of place" (ibid.: 18). So they took careful note of correlations between disease and places. The swampy, malarial Central Valley proved a particularly "pathological space" for early Californians, with death rates from typhoid two to four times higher than in San Francisco (ibid.: 62). In the late nineteenth and early twentieth centuries, improvers strived to sanitize the landscape by clearing fields and digging irrigation canals, and used germ theory to explain disease as a vector that infected individuals independent of the environment.

By the second half of the twentieth century, however, the valley was "awash in chemicals" from agriculture, and the permeability of bodies to the environment came back with a vengeance (Nash 2006: 132). We are porous to the environment still. And human bodies are still the primary instruments by which we measure ourselves and our environment. The evidence was borne in the bodies of farm workers and manifested in mysterious cancer clusters. Nash writes: "As humans have industrialized the land, the land has, in turn, industrialized them" (2006: 210). Does that make us more natural or more unnatural now? Nash concludes: "Neither the realm of nature nor the realm of the human remains pure" (ibid.).

In most histories of science and medicine, modern germ theory triumphs over older environmental conceptions of disease. But Nash shows that the modern conception of the individual body independent of its environment is the historical artifact that needs to be explained. Alas, what she calls "the brief period of modernist amnesia" is not over (2006: 6). It too survives. Californians have come back to an ecological sense of health. But we still live in modern bodies. Bottled water, anyone?

The desire to sanitize our bodies and environment, however, is constantly undermined by disorderly ecological realities that transgress the boundaries we erect between us and the world. Contaminated groundwater doesn't stay put. Chemical traces show up in children's blood.

Nash believes that it should be possible to foster medical, scientific, and regulatory systems that make visible the dense connections between our bodies, our health, and our environment. This is an optimistic conclusion. What Nash's history makes clear are the many ways in which regulators, politicians, public health officials, and polluters play different patterns on the themes of the relationship between human health and a healthy environment to obscure connections and avoid responsibility. And we, the people, often go along, eager to think that there is something we can change about our individual habits that will save us from our environment, when what we need is a historically informed politics of ecology, for our own health, and our environment. Such a politics would understand that the boundaries between human beings and their environment are as porous as the borderlands between ideas about human and natural communities. And it would use those ideas to organize politically for healthy human and natural communities on the same scales.

Planning Politics

Instead, what we have in California is a peculiar politics of human and environmental planning that often work in the same space and time but not on the same scales. In recent years, citizens in dozens of California cities have embraced "ballot-box zoning," imposing urban growth boundaries and other limitations on elected officials, planning agencies, and themselves (Starr 2004: 495). Kevin Starr writes: "This was radical populist politics, the land-use equivalent of Proposition 13, which twenty years earlier had put a severe statewide cap on property taxes" (2004: 542). In some cases, it went well beyond land use. Ojai, for instance, passed a law limiting population growth through 2010 to 1 percent a year, which would allow around 78 people a year, including newborns, to join the exclusive, artistic community.

At first glance, it may seem like not much has changed since 1995, when William Fulton wrote a report entitled *Beyond Sprawl: New Patterns of Growth to Fit the New California* for an unlikely set of patrons – Bank of America, the California Resources Agency, the Greenbelt Alliance, and The Low Income Housing Fund. Fulton was once an advocate of what geographer Richard Walker calls the "metro-topians" – modernist planners seeking rational comprehensive regional and statewide solutions for the distribution of transportation, housing, industry, jobs, and the environment (2007: 136). But "Beyond Sprawl" represented their last gasp of surrender. No longer were they aiming high and wide for the perfect

California. Instead, they were headed for the trenches to do battle in communities around the state. The subsequent trajectory of the author shows the curious trail that at least one of them has tried to take since then to get beyond sprawl.

In Ventura County, where Fulton lives, voters approved a landmark series of anti-sprawl measures between 1995 and 2000 that went by the name of SOAR – Save Open-space and Agricultural Resources. The initiatives took power away from county and local officials by establishing greenbelts, limiting annual building permits for new home construction, and requiring ballot approval of any major subdivisions or redrawing of urban boundaries. And Fulton soon found himself turning from worrying about the costs of sprawl to worrying about the costs of limiting "the capacity of local communities to meet their planning goals and objectives" (2001). Fulton warned that Ventura County would face a housing supply crisis as SOAR limits new housing development between 2005 and 2010 and supply tightens dramatically over the following decade. By 2020, the county is likely to have permitted less than half of the new housing that planners believe will be needed. That is the year that some of the SOAR measures expire. And it will be a landmark year for considering the consequences of these planning strategies.

But the political debate has already begun. Fulton, for instance, has concluded that the politics is at least as important a limiting factor in planning as the environment. In 2004, he ran for the city council, won, and suddenly found himself inside the planning system he had spent his career analyzing, criticizing, and advising from on high as the editor of California Planning and Development Report. Only now, he had his hands tied by the legacy of "ballot-box zoning," the major tool of slow-growth advocates in California, as he embarked on the Houdini trick of trying to get out of a bind he had helped fashion in many ways as an advocate for controlled growth and better planning. And as he has championed in-fill development as a solution, he has found some of his former allies replying with a familiar refrain: not in my backyard.

SOAR is an extreme example. More often, during this same period, voters have been willing to approve massive bonds to invest in conserving nature and in shoring up the state's crumbling infrastructure – often together on the same ballot. Between 1994 and 2005, there were 54 conservation finance measures on ballots in California. Thirty-one measures were successful, raising over $7.4 billion for water, parks, wildlife habitat, and open space protection. Four statewide measures accounted for nearly $5.5 billion, with other notable measures in Oakland ($195.25 million in bonds), Placer County ($200 million to be generated by a sales tax increase), and San Francisco ($150 million to be generated by a property tax increase).

There are two pragmatic problems with this neo-progressive planning and environmental politics we have inherited from the twentieth century. On the one hand, power has been taken away from elected officials, through ballot measures limiting taxes and their ability to plan for growth. This is accountability on a short leash. And yet, on the other hand, power has been given back to government through bonds for conservation, often administered, however, by agencies and non-profit organizations that are one or two steps removed from ballot box accountability. In both cases, politicians may be happy to hand over tough decisions about planning. But taken together, both moves make it much harder for communities to change. And yet, change is what human communities do.

Conservation is now a powerful force shaping communities. The amount of land conserved in California each year through acquisitions and easements which permanently retire development rights is now nearly on par with the acreage of annual conversion of agricultural land for new residential and commercial development. When combined with growth control measures, people are determining where not to build even more than where to build. In stark contrast to the early twentieth-century conservation ideology of wise use, in the late twentieth and early twenty-first centuries conservation has curiously co-opted the preservation ideal of permanent protection. Despite mounting evidence that ecosystems are forever in flux – and will be especially in a time of dramatic climate change – conservation is now stuck with perpetuity, as an ideal, and as a practical matter enshrined in such legal instruments as easements. But politics and perpetuity do not mix well, setting up a contradiction that will likely come to a head in many places and in many ways in the years to come. Perpetuity will inevitably give way, like a shoreline pounded by rising waves of change.

Continent's End

"The tides are in our veins," Robinson Jeffers wrote in 1924. When Jeffers looked out at the Pacific Ocean from Big Sur, he saw an unchanged nature. We cannot. Even the ocean is a space with a history now, not well understood still, but with a history and, therefore, a present and a future and no longer an undifferentiated essence. Defining that history and present and future takes us beyond the boundaries of California itself. It opens up the body of the state – which has always been porous too – to the Pacific and beyond.

Of course, this too is not new. Hubert Howe Bancroft wrote a book entitled *The New Pacific* back in 1899 to cheer the westward course of empire. Bancroft wrote:

We have no longer a virgin continent to develop; pioneer work in the United States is done, and now we must take a plunge into the sea. Here we find an area, an amphitheatre of water, upon and around which American enterprise and industry, great as it is and greatly to be increased, will find occupation for the full term of the twentieth century, and for many centuries thereafter. (1899: 13)

Take away the bombast – admittedly not an easy thing to do even to this day when people wax enthusiastic about the Pacific Rim – and put this shoreline in historical context, and what one actually may find is the opposite of Bancroft's notion. Sure, we must take a plunge. But the Pacific has been washing ashore here for a long time. As David Igler and other historians have shown, California was part of a Pacific world long before it was part of the United States (2004). And it will be for a long time to come. That much is safe to predict.

It is impossible to contain many important aspects of nature, such as salmon or El Niño, within national, let alone state boundaries. As Richard White has written, the scales at which we need to understand nature "intersect and superimpose themselves one atop another," from the household to the local, from the state to the national, from the transnational to the global (1999: 985). Fish, which move from the ocean to our dinner plates, provide a particularly personal way to think about these connections, as the stocks of the fish that we eat have crashed one after another.

Arthur McEvoy's 1986 book, *The Fisherman's Problem: Ecology and the Law in the California Fisheries, 1850–1980*, remains the landmark in this history. McEvoy argues that the law, economic production, and the environment that produces fish are all interrelated and affect each other. The decline of a fishery is usually framed as a tragedy of the commons. Even McEvoy uses the metaphor. But this research actually shows that the tragedy of the commons was invoked when one group of people was struggling to wrest control of fishery resources from another group. McEvoy's deeper argument is that ecology and justice have to be weighed in the same balance, and that solutions that fail on one side of the scale are likely to fail on the other. This is a troubling insight and not just at sea.

Capital is currently fleeing commercial fishing. Direct spending at the Monterey Bay Aquarium – what visitors spend, plus the aquarium's payroll and costs – is nearly equal to all of the commercial fish landings in California now. Recreational fishing and conservation are the new rulers of the ocean off the California coast. And neither is well understood or studied historically. Conservation models developed on land are being transferred offshore – with marine protected areas, property rights in fisheries, and conservation acquisitions and easements – all based on ecosystem models that have proven problematic on land. Marine environmental history is

booming too, but mainly with historians serving as data gatherers for ecological model builders. These models, in turn, are meant to serve policy
purposes to establish historical baselines and contemporary catch limits.
The model builders, for the most part, however, are not much interested
in historicizing the role that models of fisheries have played in bringing us
to this point – and questioning the enterprise of modeling nature. They
know the map is not the territory, but the model is often taken to be a
stand-in for the ecosystem. Not only is the model already twice removed
from what it represents, because the ecosystem is itself an abstraction of
relationships, but what it represents cannot even be seen standing on the
shoreline, the vantage point from which most of us gaze out at a Pacific
still powerfully inscrutable.

Questioning History

And history is not just data. Nor is it just a way of telling stories about the
ways things sometimes were and how we got to the state we are in. History
is also a way of asking questions. Many people use history to tell compelling stories to inform and shape their version of where we should be going.
This is inevitable. And even by suggesting that history can do more, I am
doing the same. But there is a distinction that I think can make a difference. In all of the prospects that I have discussed, history can be used to
ask questions about the stories that we have inherited – not to suggest a
way forward at first, although that is an important goal down the road, but
to open up a conversation about the possibilities and problems we may
find in the past and present that could shape how we understand and
approach our prospects.

Jenny Price has written provocatively of "Thirteen Ways of Seeing Nature
in LA" (2005). And everywhere we look in California there are at least as
many ways of seeing nature, people, and history. As it happens, public
environmental histories are blossoming across the California landscape in
conjunction with planning and interpretation of restoration efforts, environmental and conservation projects, and in places like Cannery Row, in
Monterey, where social history is so richly entwined with environmental
history. John Walton (2001) writes in *Storied Land* that this scholarship
has become increasingly sophisticated as it has become more engaged. In
the century to come, a century that it is safe to predict will bring enormous
changes, environmental history will become even more important for
Californians to make historically informed decisions about the present
and future of the state.

Tropes like the "destruction of California" and "paradise lost" not only
have narrowed the compass of our possibilities for thinking about our state

of nature; in some cases, these ideas may have contributed to the demise of what they sought to save. Conservationists, for example, have taken such historical accounts to justify the protection and preservation of remnant patches of California native grasslands, wildflowers, and butterflies from any disturbance such as fire and grazing, as if time had stopped. But it was these very processes of change, often directed by human hands, that kept them alive, and may even bring them back to life.

In recent years, we have been plagued by ideas about the end of history, the end of nature, the end of the wild, and the end of environmentalism. These ideas are mercifully wrong because they would deny these powerful ideas to the future, which simply will not be denied, whatever foolhardy predictions we make. Instead of trying to deny ideas to the future, perhaps it would be better then to offer ideas and tools that might be useful to the future, a gift outright, as it were, from our history. It is only fair. We will certainly be leaving more than enough problems as well.

References

Bancroft, H. H. 1899. *The New Pacific*. New York: Bancroft.

Bank of America, California Resources Agency, Greenbelt Alliance, and The Low Income Housing Fund. 1995. *Beyond Sprawl: New Patterns of Growth to Fit the New California*.

Dasmann, R. F. 1965. *The Destruction of California*. New York: Macmillan.

Fulton, W. 2001. "The Impact of Smart Growth on Housing," *Planetizen*, 18 December. http://www.planetizen.com/node/35.

Hayhoe, K., et al. 2004. "Emissions Pathways, Climate Change, and Impacts on California," *PNAS*, 101 (34): 12422–27.

Igler, D. 2004. "Diseased Goods: Global Exchanges in the Eastern Pacific Basin, 1770–1850," *The American Historical Review* (June): 693–719.

Jeffers, R. 1924. "Continent's End," in *Tamar, and Other Poems*. New York: P. G. Boyle.

Kollars, D. 2005. "Tempting Fate: Are We Next?" *Sacramento Bee*, October 30.

McEvoy, A. F. 1986. *The Fisherman's Problem: Ecology and Law in the California Fisheries, 1850–1980*. New York: Cambridge University Press.

Nash, L. 2006. *Inescapable Ecologies: A History of Environment, Disease, and Knowledge*. Berkeley: University of California Press.

Nijhuis, M. 2005. "The Ghosts of Yosemite," *High Country News*, October 17.

Orsi, J. 2004. *Hazardous Metropolis: Flooding and Urban Ecology in Los Angeles*. Berkeley: University of California Press.

Price, J. 2005. "Thirteen Ways of Seeing Nature in LA." In W. Deverell and G. Hise, eds., *Land of Sunshine: An Environmental History of Metropolitan Los Angeles*. Pittsburgh: University of Pittsburgh Press.

Righter, R. W. 2005. *The Battle over Hetch Hetchy: America's Most Controversial Dam and the Birth of Modern Environmentalism*. New York: Oxford University Press.

Schrag, P. 2004. *Paradise Lost: California's Experience, America's Future.* Berkeley: University of California Press.

Starr, K. 2004. *Coast of Dreams: California on the Edge, 1990–2003.* New York: Alfred A. Knopf.

Stokstad, E. 2006. "Restoring Yosemite's Twin," *Science*, 314 (October 7): 582–4.

US Department of Agriculture. 1995. *Report Card for Rural California.*

Walker, R. 2007. *The Country in the City: The Greening of the San Francisco Bay Area.* Seattle: University of Washington Press.

Walton, J. 2001. *Storied Land: Community and Memory in Monterey.* Berkeley: University of California Press.

White, R. 1999. "The Nationalization of Nature," *The Journal of American History* 86 (3): 976–86.

FURTHER READING

Brechin, G. and Dawson, R. 1999. *Farewell, Promised Land: Waking from the California Dream.* Berkeley: University of California Press.

deBuys, W. and Myers, J. 1999. *Salt Dreams: Land & Water in Low-Down California.* Albuquerque: University of New Mexico Press.

Deverell, W. and Hise, G., eds. 2005. *Land of Sunshine: An Environmental History of Metropolitan Los Angeles.* Pittsburgh: University of Pittsburgh Press.

Didion, J. 2003. *Where I was From.* New York: Alfred A. Knopf.

Fulton, W. B. 1998. *California, Land and Legacy.* Englewood, CO: Westcliffe Publishers.

Gumprecht, B. 2001. *The Los Angeles River: Its Life, Death, and Possible Rebirth.* Baltimore, MD: Johns Hopkins University Press.

Hundley, Jr., N. 2001. *The Great Thirst: Californians and Water – A History.* Berkeley: University of California Press.

Kahrl, W. L. 1982. *Water and Power: The Conflict over Los Angeles' Water Supply in Owens Valley.* Berkeley: University of California Press.

Luers, A. L., et al. 2006. "Our Changing Climate: Assessing the Risks to California – A Summary Report of the California Climate Change Center," and associated detailed documents and reports available at http://www.climatechange.ca.gov/ biennial_reports/2006report/index.html. As well as other materials available at the California Climate Change Portal: http://www.climatechange.ca.gov.

Merchant, C., ed. 1998. *Green versus Gold: Sources in California's Environmental History.* Washington, DC: Island Press.

Pincetl, S. S. 2003. *Transforming California: A Political History of Land Use and Development.* Baltimore, MD: Johns Hopkins University Press.

Reisner, M. 2003. *A Dangerous Place: California's Unsettling Fate.* New York: Pantheon Books.

Index

Page numbers in *italics* denote an illustration.